THE
PENGUIN
DICTIONARY
OF
Religions

EDITED BY

John R. Hinnells

ALLEN LANE

ALLEN LANE
Penguin Books Ltd
536 King's Road
London sw 10 0UH

First published 1984
Published simultaneously by Penguin Books

British Library Cataloguing in Publication Data
The Penguin dictionary of religions.
1. Religion – Dictionaries
I. Hinnells, John R.
200'.3'21   BL31

ISBN 0 7139 1514 5

Diagrams drawn by Raymond Turvey
Maps drawn by Reginald Piggott

Set in Linotron Bembo by Longman Malaysia
Printed in Great Britain by Richard Clay (The Chaucer Press) Ltd,
Bungay, Suffolk

This book is dedicated to
Marianne, Mark and Duncan,
a much-loved family

CONTENTS

LIST OF CONTENTS
BY
SUBJECT AREA AND AUTHOR

BRN = Bibliographical reference number

INTRODUCTION

This *Dictionary* has been produced to answer the needs of a broad range of readers in many countries. There is in the twentieth century a growing 'global' awareness of 'other' religions – whether it is American and European interest in Indian religions, or the new movements in 'Primal' societies as they fuse with such international religions as Christianity. Books for the general public and the student have sought to satisfy the demand for knowledge, a demand which has arisen from a diversity of motives: the fascination of the inquiring mind; the practical needs of teachers, social workers or reporters; and the unsatisfied religious yearning of individuals. A common need for all is to understand the specialized vocabulary used by those who practise a religion and by those who write about it. This work is intended to answer that need.

The function of a dictionary is essentially to define the meaning of terms, typically done in short entries. But it was decided from the outset that in this *Dictionary* definitions should consist of longer entries, so that they would provide a flowing readable text, enjoyable as well as useful. Further, the technical terms in religions do not lend themselves to simple, short explanations. The interests of the general reader and the requirements of scholarship demand appropriately sized entries.

An international team of twenty-nine scholars, from as far apart as Japan and Europe, New Zealand and the U.S.A., has collaborated in the production of this book. They come from a variety of academic disciplines – as historians, orientalists, classicists, archaeologists, sociologists, anthropologists, linguists, art historians, philosophers, theologians – all reflecting the many aspects of the study of religions. Care has been taken both to make use of the respective specialist interests and yet to provide a reasonably consistent approach to the individual religions. Obviously, different emphases are necessary in handling subjects as different as, for example, the archaeological sources of ancient religions in Egypt and the contemporary evidence for new religious movements in the West. Nevertheless, it is important for the reader to have confidence that the *Dictionary* reflects a well-balanced approach to the subject as a whole and also to the specific religions. Authors were, therefore, provided with a matrix of thirty topics, including beliefs and practices, people and places, texts and arts, society and institutions, on which to model their material. The Editor wishes to express publicly his sincere thanks for the way all authors cooperated effectively in this important but difficult task.

A fundamental question confronting the editor of a dictionary of religions is to decide what subjects to include and in what proportions. As Penguin dictionaries on such related disciplines as sociology and philosophy exist or are in preparation, an initial decision was taken to concentrate space on the terms used in the various religions rather than on technical words used by scholars. Although the study of religion *per se* has an essential place within this *Dictionary* it has, perhaps, been given less space than some scholars might have allocated. Ancient religions – of Europe or Mesoamerica – evidently require inclusion because of their importance and interest. But the bulk of space has been allocated to 'living' religions. New religious movements, in diverse societies, as well as astrology, magic, and the occult are subjects attracting wide interest. Precisely because it is difficult to find reliable introductory material on them, these subjects merited inclusion here. Similarly, some note has been taken of what have been termed 'Secular alternatives to religion', such as Marxism and Humanism. The 'living' traditional religions of 'Primal' societies in the Pacific, Africa, and North America require incorporation not only because of their fascination but also because of their common neglect in general books on world religions. It was obviously important that proper coverage be given to the various traditions of Asia from Iran to China and Japan. But the greatest wordage has been reserved for those religions which have a large following, such as Hinduism and Judaism, and especially those which have spread over various continents, notably Islam, Buddhism, and Christianity.

The explanation of terms occupies the core of the *Dictionary*, but there are two extremely important additional sections to the book: the Bibliography and the Index section (comprising a Synoptic Index and a General Index). For the specialist moving outside his own field and for the interested reader who wishes to pursue a particular topic in greater depth or breadth than a dictionary entry can provide, the extensive Bibliography offers an invaluable guide to a wide network of information. The notation system which is used (see explanation below) permits reference either to books on quite specific details inside the entry or to general works relating to the overall theme of the piece. The intention is to enhance the value of the *Dictionary* as a scholarly aid, without detracting in any way from the broad interest of the text.

An index may at first sight appear superfluous in a dictionary. It is, however, essential here if the reader is to be given reasonable access to the many thousands of terms explained within the 1,150 entries. In an entry of 200 to 300 words on one technical term, e.g. Confucius or Yoga, a number of important words will be explained. This is inevitable inasmuch as one word commonly needs explanation in terms of, or alongside, another. The 'headword' of an entry, therefore, often functions as an umbrella term below which a variety of terms are elucidated. The General Index provides a guide to these numerous explanations.

The General Index has an additional purpose. The headwords are usually technical terms from the religions concerned and not the common English word. For example, the Sikh doctrine of God appears under **Akal Purakh**, not under 'God (Sikh doctrine of)'. There are two reasons for this. First, the alternative would have meant that such general headings as 'God' or 'Ritual' would have required up to thirty versions of them relating to the different subjects encompassed in the *Dictionary*. Second, the use of such general English terms would have entailed the imposition of a Western conceptualization on the material and could therefore have distorted non-Western concepts. Sometimes authors have considered this not a danger but an aid, especially where a range of religions is subsumed under one heading, for instance the Ancient Near East, when no one technical term from a single appropriate religion exists. Given that it is generally desirable to have technical words as headwords, it was thought necessary to guide the reader who wanted to know what a particular religion taught on a subject when he or she did not know what the appropriate technical term was. The General Index, therefore, includes English terms in order that the reader may find the idea sought. In the Sikh example, **Akal Purakh** is the headword, but this is also referenced in the General Index under 'God'. It is thus possible to look up themes in the various religions without knowing in advance all the technical terms.

Considerable thought was given to the possible inclusion of a guide to pronunciation. In view of the many variations in the pronunciation of major languages this was eventually excluded, with reluctance, as highly desirable but impracticable.

Diacritical marks, which have not been used in the main body of the text, are included in the General Index for the interested reader.

Because of the religious assumptions underlying the abbreviations 'BC' and 'AD' ('Before Christ' and 'Anno Domini', which assume acceptance of Jesus as Messiah or Lord), these are unacceptable to many religious people who belong to other religions. In this *Dictionary* the letters BCE (Before (the) Christian Era) and CE (Christian Era) are used throughout. These make no assumption about a person's religious position. For readers not familiar with this usage it may be said that AD 1983 refers to the same year as 1983 CE: the date is constant, only the nomenclature changes.

USING THE DICTIONARY

The Bibliography

Each subject area (see list on page 9 above) has a separate bibliography.
These are numbered from I to XXX. The number of the relevant bibliography is indicated in square brackets immediately after the headword in
each entry. All the bibliographies are in alphabetical order with the books
numbered in arabic figures. In the entries bibliographical references are in
square brackets. The first arabic figure indicates the number of the book,
and a subsequent roman numeral indicates a chapter in that book whereas a
subsequent arabic figure refers to a page number. For example, [10: v]
refers to chapter v of book number 10, whereas [10: 5] refers to page 5 of
that book. In the rare cases where one author refers to a book in a bibliography other than his or her own, the relevant bibliography, in roman
numerals, precedes each and every reference. An example will be found at
the end of the first paragraph of **Festivals and Rituals (Hindu)**, where the
first book reference only in those brackets is to another author's bibliography. In a limited number of cases the same book appears in more than one
author's bibliography. Such double listings have been allowed to stand,
because the text references are to different paginations in different editions.

The Bibliography lists various editions of a book (e.g. American, Asian,
or European) where these are available. As a guide to the availability of
books the Bibliography also indicates which books were in print or in
paperback while this *Dictionary* was in preparation (1981). Time-scales and
publishers' decisions necessarily make this a less-than-perfect guide, but
nevertheless it is thought that the information will be of help to the reader.

The Indexes

To find where the meaning of a technical term is explained, and what the
technical term for, and details of, a concept are in a given religion, consult
the General Index. Important terms that cannot be located in the body of
the *Dictionary* under one spelling may be traced in the General Index under
the variant spellings (for example, 'Koran, *see* Qur'an', or 'Hasidism, *see*
Chasidism'), and roughly equivalent terms may be similarly traced (for
example, 'Brotoi, *see* Thnetoi Anthropoi').

To find all the terms covered by the *Dictionary* on a specific religion,
consult the Synoptic Index.

The Maps

All important places named in the text are shown on the maps (pages 365–80) and map references are included in the General Index.

Variant Spellings

In a number of religions technical words appear in more than one language (e.g. in Zoroastrianism in both Avestan and Pahlavi, in Buddhism in Sanskrit, Pali and other languages, in Latin and Greek for some Classical Greek and Roman terms). The practice in this *Dictionary* is to use the language which the author considers most appropriate in any given context. Cross-references are given in the General Index.

Abbreviations Used in the Text

b.	born	f (ff)	following page(s)
BCE	before Christian era	*fl.*	*floruit*
c.	*circa*	pl.	plate(s)
CE	Christian era	r.	reigned, ruled
d.	died	s.v.	*sub voce, sub verbo*

Cross-references are shown by printing the appropriate headword in SMALL CAPITAL LETTERS.

ACKNOWLEDGEMENTS

My profound thanks go to the many people who have helped in the preparation of this *Dictionary*. All contributors have been extremely cooperative. Special thanks are due to the bibliographer, Miss Nora Firby, not only for the exemplary care and characteristic thoroughness with which she has edited the Bibliography, making it a major contribution to the book, but also for her considerable assistance with the General Index. I wish to record my gratitude to Peter Phillips, for his great editorial help and labours. In the planning of the *Dictionary*, invaluable advice was given by Lance Cousins and Trevor Ling, my colleagues at Manchester; Richard Gordon of the University of East Anglia; Jean Holm of Homerton College, Cambridge; Professor Geoffrey Parrinder, Emeritus Professor of the Comparative Study of Religion at London University; Professor Ninian Smart of the Universities of Lancaster and Santa Barbara; Cyril Williams of Aberystwyth University; and Peter Woodward, Inspector for Religious Education in Birmingham. It has been a genuine pleasure to work with Michael Dover, Editor at Penguin Books. He has always been both helpful and wise. Thanks are due also to the publishers for the honour as well as the stimulating challenge of being asked to think in terms of such a broad geographical and temporal canvas. Above all thanks are due in inexpressible measure to my family, Marianne, Mark and Duncan. Without their help, support, understanding and encouragement this task could not have been contemplated, much less completed. To them, this *Dictionary* is dedicated as a token of thanks, and love.

J. R. H.

· A ·

Abhidhamma [IX.B] The content of the third part of the Buddhist scriptures (TIPITAKA). *Abhidhamma* (Sanskrit *abhidharma*) probably arose as a non-sectarian movement in the 4th and 3rd centuries BCE, developing the earlier SUTTANTA approach, but with the formation of sects differing schools arose. Two distinct versions survive; others probably existed. For the North Indian *abhidharma* of the SARVASTIVADINS, *see* VAIBHASHIKA. In the south the THERAVADA preserved a canonical *abhidhamma-pitaka* attributed to the BUDDHA himself in the PALI language. The earlier works set out a description of mental processes and their interactions with the physical and the transcendent (LOKUTTARA) by giving elaborate accounts of specific events. These were seen as short-lived minds (*cittas*) related to specific sense objects and accompanied by a number of structures composed of basic mental elements (*dhammas*). These minds are viewed as constantly changing in level, object, and content in a sequential stream. The aim of this *abhidhamma* analysis is not really theoretical; it is related to insight (VIPASSANA) meditation and offers a world-view based upon process in order to facilitate insight into change (ANICCA) and no-self (ANATTA) so as to undermine mental rigidity.

By the early centuries CE the chief centre of activity had moved from India to Ceylon. An elaborate system was worked out, specifying many details which had initially been left undecided. This was summarized by BUDDHA-GHOSA (*c.* 430 CE) in his *Visuddhimagga*

and *abhidhamma* commentaries and at about the same time by Buddhadatta. A series of subcommentaries followed, notably those of Ananda (perhaps 6th century) and DHAMMAPALA, but the standard introduction was written later by Anuruddha (probably 11th century). [40] Pali commentaries on *abhidhamma* have continued to be written down to the present century, especially in Burma.

Abraham (in Islam) [XIV] Abraham or Ibrahim, called the 'Friend of God', is the most important and, with MOSES, the most frequently mentioned of the former prophets in the QUR'AN. He is regarded as the rebuilder of the Ka'ba in Mecca (HARAMAIN), after its destruction by the Flood, and as the propagator of the original pure monotheism, the 'religion of Abraham', later restored and perfected by the Prophet MUHAMMAD (*see* HANIF). [10 s. v.; 21 'Ibrāhīm'; 81 index]

Adi Granth [XXVII] The principal SIKH scripture, known by a variety of names. Originally called the *Granth Sahib*, or 'Revered Book', it became the *Guru Granth Sahib* after the line of personal GURUS terminated in 1708. It is also known as the *Adi Granth*, or 'First Book', a title which distinguishes it from the later DASAM GRANTH [4: III]. The volume was compiled in 1603–4 by Arjan, the fifth Guru. In it he included his own works and those of his four predecessors, together with a selection from earlier representatives of the SANT TRADITION such as Kabir. Three recensions exist. The printed text used today represents the third of these, a slightly expanded version of Guru Arjan's original compilation incorporating compositions by the ninth Guru. [23: 60–63, 73–9] Although a substantial collection, the scripture communicates a consistent message of spiritual liberation (SACH-KHAND) through belief in the divine Name (*nam*). There is also a general consistency in terms of language. The Gurus, like their Sant predecessors, used a simplified form of early Hindi known as *Sant Bhasha* (SIKH LANGUAGES). The entire volume was recorded in Gurmukhi, the script used for modern Punjabi. Consistency is also a feature of the volume's organization, its contents being carefully arranged according to metre, form, and author [24: 286–8]. The hymns which comprise its contents are known as *bani* or *gurbani*, 'utterances of the GURU'. Sikh doctrine recognizes only one Guru, successively incarnated in ten individuals. When the personal line ended the functions of the Guru passed to the community (the PANTH) and to the scripture (the *Granth*). The scripture thus came to be regarded as the physical embodiment of the eternal Guru and as such is treated with impressive reverence.

Advaita Vedanta [XIII.B] The best-known school of VEDANTA, one of the classical Indian DARSHANAS (salvation-philosophies). The earliest extant writer is Gaudapada (perhaps 7th century CE), but SHANKARA is the principal ancient authority. 'Advaita' means 'non-dual' and the system of Shankara is a near monism, holding that there is in the last analysis only one reality: BRAHMAN – the divine power. Knowledge of *brahman* is devoid of any multiplicity or duality; such knowledge leads to liberation (MOKSHA). It is reached by contemplation on the received teachings of the Vedanta, ritual and devotion being merely auxiliary. There is a marked convergence with MADHYA-MIKA Buddhism, which strongly influenced the early Advaita [8: 328ff]. The Advaita Vedanta is probably the most influential of all schools of Hindu thought, with a long tradition of writers and authorities. The 20th century has seen its revival in a modernized dress, with some success outside India through the work of the Ramakrishna Mission, such Vedanta-influenced writers as Aldous Huxley and Christopher Isherwood, and more recently the Maharishi Mahesh Yogi (TRANSCENDENTAL MEDITATION) [5: 1, 406–94; 14: 207–28; 15: 28–38]

Advaitin Cosmology [XIII.B] By the medieval period in India the ADVAITA VEDANTA had developed an organized 'cosmology', largely based upon combining the earlier VEDANTA tradition with the closely related SAMKHYA world-view. What was held to be an inferior or conventional understanding was distinguished from the salvific knowledge of ultimate reality (a distinction deriving from SHANKARA and ultimately from Buddhism). From the standpoint of this lower knowledge the world is hierarchic and emanationary, with gross, subtle, and causal levels. The gross body experiences the gross world in the waking state through the senses; the subtle body experiences subtle images and forms through the mind especially in the dream state (and in visionary experience); while the causal body experiences a more unified consciousness especially in dreamless sleep (and in yogic experience – YOGA). Underlying this account is an acceptance of the principle of correspondences between psychological states and the universe at large: the gross world emanates from a subtle world, the subtle from the causal; both the universe and the individual vary between a state in which the three worlds are emanated and one in which the gross and subtle are withdrawn into the unified causal realm.

BRAHMAN is in each of these realms both separately and in their totality, appearing on each level both as individual souls and as a collective soul or deity. From the conventional standpoint

brahman is the creator (ISHVARA) or
personal deity with positive attributes
(*saguna*). Motivated by LILA he creates
the cosmos through the power of MAYA
(2). Nevertheless, from the ultimate
point of view true reality is without
differentiating attributes (*nirguna*); the
appearance of separation is the result of
ignorance (*avidya*), i.e. illusion on the
individual level.

Aesir [v] The Aesir (cf. '*Ansis*' of the
Goths) [30: IX, 190–91]) are the main gods
of Norse mythology, excluding Freyr,
Njord, and other VANIR deities. ODIN,
the All-Father, THOR, LOKI, Heimdall
[6: VII, 172–6], and BALDER, together
with an unspecified number of lesser
gods, dwelt at Asgard, a stronghold
built with the help of a giant who was
afterwards cheated out of his payment
[6: I, 31]. There are references to a war
with the VANIR, ending in a truce [8: 1],
but a threat remained from the FROST-
GIANTS, and Heimdall was on constant
watch against attack, while THOR kept
his hammer ready. In the Poetic EDDA
[18: 1–13] the Aesir are described as
builders and craftsmen, playing board-
games, establishing law, meeting at
their Assembly (the 'Thing'), and creating mankind, but they are doomed to
perish at RAGNAROK. The idea of a
group of divine powers must be old,
and other words used for them are *regin*,
hopt, and *tivar*, but the picture of local
deities dwelling together in Asgard is
presumably a late development by poets
and story-tellers. In Iceland a new religious sect, the Asatruarmenn ('Believers
in the Aesir'), was officially recognized
in 1973, the aim of the founders being to
restore the ancient rituals of pre-
Christian Iceland.

Africa, Christianity in [XI.B] Roman
Christianity in northern Africa was
largely destroyed by the Islamic
invasions. The major survivors are the
Monophysite Coptic churches of Egypt
and Ethiopia (CHRISTOLOGY). Elsewhere in Africa Christianity was largely
produced by later MISSIONS. In West

Africa, apart from Portuguese ROMAN
CATHOLICISM in the 16th century,
most work was done in the 19th century, first by PROTESTANTISM, then by
Roman Catholics. The areas of activity
of the two churches generally corresponded to the religion of rival European trading and colonial powers. The
same is true of East Africa after exploration by David Livingstone (1813–73).
In southern Africa Dutch settlement
from the 17th century produced a local
Reformed (CALVINISM) Church as well
as missions. The apartheid policy
(theologically supported by the local
Reformed Church) has led to much tension with missionary churches. Local
versions of European churches of missionary origin have achieved independence since the 1950s. In East Africa
some groups of Christians have spontaneously converted to the ORTHODOX
CHURCH. There are also numerous
African Independent Churches of a
messianic, PENTECOSTALIST type
mixed with traditional African religion
(AFRICA, NEW RELIGIOUS MOVE-
MENTS). [59; 61: IX–XII; 82 vol. 5: VIII,
vol. 7: IX; 83 vol. 3: XVI, XXIII, vol. 5:
XVII].

Africa, Islam in [XIV] Islam spread
very early along the Mediterranean
shores from Egypt to Morocco, Islamization being well advanced by the 9th
century, so that the northern shores of
the continent belong essentially to the
Mediterranean basin and the heartlands
of classical Islamic civilization. These
constitute the Egyptian and Maghrebi
zones of Islamic culture distinguished
by Trimingham, the remaining two
being the Negro and the Hamitic (i.e.
Saharan–Sudanese) ones, embracing the
Sahara and areas to the south of it. The
Nilotic Sudan region is, in particular, a
meeting-place for Arab, Hamitic, and
Negro peoples. In subSaharan Africa,
Islam came only later: in the west and
centre across the desert from the
Maghrib, brought by traders and dervishes, so that SUFI ORDERS have

always been strong in Hamitic Africa
[55]; and to the East African coastlands
again by traders, but coming by sea
from South Arabia and the Persian Gulf.
In both cases, the lure was gold and
black slaves. For many centuries, the
existence of the Christian kingdoms of
Nubia and then of Ethiopia impeded
Muslim penetration of north-eastern
Africa, and it was really only with the
imposition of European colonial rule on
East and central Africa that the expansion of Islam into the interior was facilitated. Hamitic African Islam has its own
particular emphases, such as on *marabouts*, or dervishes, on holy men, and on
local pilgrimages to saints' tombs (*see*
MAHDI, SUFISM, WALI), not found in
Negro Africa. Islam here has also generally been accompanied by Arabization.
Negro African Islam, however, with its
more decentralized society groupings,
has rejected the latter, and there has
always been a process of interaction
between the old, animistic, indigenous
religions and the incoming Islam, in
which many aspects of the former, such
as ancestor-worship and respect for
medicine-men and magic-workers, persist alongside the new faith. Impatient
of delays in these transitional processes,
with their syncretism and accommo-
dations in belief and practice, there arose
in West Africa in the 18th and 19th
centuries militant, rigorist Muslim
movements, like the Fulani JIHAD of
'Uthman dan Fodio (1754–1817) [55;
68]. At present, the greatest concentrations of Muslims in the continent
are in the North African countries and
in the Sudan, Ethiopia, and Nigeria. [6:
VIII–XI; 37 vol. 2: 209–405; 71]

**Africa, New Religious Movements
in** [xx] Black Africa in its interactions
with Christianity (but not with Islam)
has produced perhaps 8,000 movements
with some 9 million members, about a
third of these being in South Africa
alone (*see* AFRICA, CHRISTIANITY IN).
Some seek to revive traditional religions
in new forms with Christian borrow-

ings; these would include the Church of
the Ancestors in Malawi, the Religion
of the Ancestors in East Africa [2: 119–
21], the Reformed Ogboni Fraternity
[2: 122] and Godianism in Nigeria, and
the Dëima cult in the Ivory Coast [12:
56]. Some model themselves on the
Jews of the BIBLE, such as the Israelites
under Enoch Mgijima in South Africa
from 1912 [12: 42–3; 16: 72–3; 19: 61–
3], the Bayudaya in Uganda since
1923, and the God's Kingdom Society
in Nigeria from 1934. Most movements, and all the larger ones, would be
regarded as independent churches since
they use the Bible and intend to be
Christian, however confusedly, and
they fall into two broad classes,
ETHIOPIAN CHURCHES and prophet-
healing or ZIONIST MOVEMENTS.
Among the more notable movements
have been the Harrist churches of the
Ivory Coast derived from prophet
HARRIS; the Nigerian ALADURA
churches; the KIMBANGUIST CHURCH
in Zaire; the African Apostolic Church
of Johane Maranke and the Apostolic
Sabbath Church of God of Johane
Masowe in Zimbabwe [4: 315–49]; the
Lumpa Church of Alice LENSHINA in
Zambia; Reuben Spartas's African
Greek ORTHODOX CHURCH in East
Africa; the Kenya movement of MARIA
LEGIO; in Malawi the PROVIDENCE
INDUSTRIAL MISSION; and in South
Africa Shembe's NAZARITE CHURCH
and the Zion Christian Church with
some 300,000 members. Rather different are KITAWALA in central Africa,
the various sections of the Bwiti cult
among the Fang in Gabon with creative
attempts at a synthesis of African and
Christian elements [2: 27, 55; 12: 56],
and those few movements regarding
their founder as a new Black Messiah
replacing JESUS CHRIST. [15: 323–37]
Altogether these developments represent a remarkable religious ferment
among African peoples [2].

African Religions [II] There are as
many African religions as peoples or

'tribes', that is, many hundreds. This *Dictionary* can only refer to a few, selected somewhat arbitrarily to illustrate different types or areas, or to an account of available literature in English. The following receive individual attention: AKAN, DOGON, FON, MENDE, and YORUBA in West Africa, and ZANDE in central Africa; DINKA, NUER, and SHILLUK among the NILOTICS; GANDA, LOVEDU, SHONA, and ZULU among BANTU.

A crucial factor in the differentiation between African religions is the deep diversity of African social and political systems. Religious belief and ritual both reflect and mould social structure and would be largely incomprehensible apart from the latter. Despite the contrasts there are also profound similarities. [General and thematic surveys: 6; 9; 12; 17] African religions do not exist in a vacuum. They have influenced each other through human contact – migration, military conquest, marriage – and through the action of religious specialists. Within one people there could be significant differences in regard to religion, caused by the sectional activity of secret societies or local shrines: religion was thus in part associational. Equally, religion frequently crossed tribal frontiers, not only by borrowings, but also by the enduring sense of a wider community. Major territorial cults (MBONA, MWARI, Luak Deng) provided pilgrimage centres for people of different tribes [13; 16], while systems of divining, secret societies, cults of affliction, and WITCHCRAFT ERADICATION often passed from people to people. So did the name of God.

African religions belonged to pre-literate societies. This has affected their character and our knowledge; however, non-literate societies can possess an extensive oral literature, and many African religions have significant texts, some of which we now possess [20; 28; 29]. Non-literate religions change at least as much as literate ones, but changes go unrecorded, hence the mistaken view that African religions are unchanging. Their historical development may be partially plotted through analysis of layers within current ritual and myth, and from the evidence of earlier written sources [11]. There is some historical documentation available in Latin and Portuguese from the 16th century on, especially in regard to the Congo and Zambezi valleys, and much more in many languages dating from the wider entry of missionaries and other Europeans into Africa in the 19th century. The greatest problem in the study of African religions is that almost without exception books are the work of outsiders: sympathetic or unsympathetic, they inevitably import alien categories, even when written by Africans.

Much discussion has centred on belief in God. Some early observers denied any such concept; subsequently many missionaries and African scholars have pointed out, even over-stressing, an underlying African monotheism interpreted in rather Christian terms [6; 7; 15; 32]. There has been some sharp reaction against this [10]. There are certainly some peoples with either no conception of a supreme God or one so limited as to be effectively otiose (Acholi, Lango, LOVEDU, Nyakyusa, Swazi, ZANDE; JOK). These are significant exceptions. The great majority of African religions recognize a single supreme creator God, witness to whom in prayers [14], proverbs, and creation myths is massive (IRUVA; KATONDA; LEZA; MODIMO; MULUNGU; NZAMBI). Nevertheless, the prayers of only a few are concentrated upon God (NUER; *see also* MWARI). More characteristic is a pattern of intermediaries – ancestors or nature gods – to which most ritual and prayer are immediately directed, although direct access to the deity remains possible, especially in emergency (ANCESTOR VENERATION; MIZIMU; ORISHA).

Attention must also be paid to DIVINE KINGSHIP and RAIN-MAKING; to rituals of initiation (CHISUNGU) and secret societies (BAGRE; MENDE; NYAU); to SPIRIT-POSSESSION, so-called fetishes or objects of impersonal power (NKISI), systems of DIVINATION (IFA), witchcraft and sorcery (NGANGA; WITCHCRAFT ERADICATION movements; ZANDE).

It is impossible to describe the overall present state of Africa's religions. Many ethnographic studies using the present tense in fact give a picture 40 years old. The advance of Christianity, Islam, and modernization have greatly altered things, destroying the coherence of many systems (*see also* AFRICA, CHRISTIANITY IN). There have also been religious revivals (YORUBA), producing a neo-traditionalism, sometimes incorporating elements from the world religions, in which divination and spirit-possession cults particularly flourish (*see also* AFRICA, NEW RELIGIOUS MOVEMENTS IN).

Afro-Americans (Caribbean and South America): New Religious Movements [xx] The descendants of African slaves in the Caribbean and South America, especially in Brazil, have created new movements ranging from revivals of the old tribal religions with varying degrees of Christian influence to independent Christian churches. Best known is VOODOO in Haiti and the Dominican Republic [15: 64–71, 295–303]. In Grenada, Trinidad, St Lucia, and Brazil Shango combines African and Catholic elements [15: 73–86, 103–6, 190–95]; likewise Santería in Cuba and the Maria Lionza cult in Venezuela [15: 86–94, 163–70, 308–9]. The Cumina and Convince cults of Jamaica focus on ancestral spirits, with little Christian content [15: 98–102]. The three groups of Bush Negroes, Saramaka, Djuka, and Boni, living in the interior of Surinam and French Guiana developed cults with some Christian borrowings. This influence produced

reforming prophets such as Wensi in 1936, and Akalali from 1972 who further reformed the Gaan Tata or Masa Jehovah cult, itself a more Christian form from the 1880s. [15: 204–11] A similar range occurs in the AFRO-BRAZILIAN CULTS of coastal Brazil. Syncretistic movements resembling a more revivalist type of Christianity include the Revivalists, a general term in Jamaica for Pocomania [12: 138; 19: 59–60], Revival Zion, etc., as well as the Shakers of St Vincent and the Shouters or Spiritual Baptists of Trinidad [15: 111–27]. In Guyana the Jordonites (from 1917) are strongly influenced by the Hebrew scriptures (BIBLE) and by Jewish religious forms, as also are the House of Israel and various 'back-to-Africa' cults of which the most notable are the RASTAFARIANS of Jamaica. Traditional African spirit-possession provides a congenial background for the great growth of Pentecostal forms of Christianity (PENTECOSTALISM; *see also* WEST INDIES, CHRISTIANITY IN THE), some Western-influenced but much of local origin [15: 45–50, 309–10]. There are also many independent churches in orthodox or EVANGELICAL traditions and all types of Jamaican Black churches have travelled with immigrants to Britain, such as the large New Testament Church of God [15: 274–80]. [12: 133–41; 17: 701; 19: 108–14]

Afro-Brazilian Cults [xx] Many varieties of these cults have developed (since about 1830), first among the descendants of African slaves in north-east Brazil and latterly more widely. There are traditional YORUBA cults; Candomblé (known as Xango, Batuque, or Pará in different areas) incorporating Catholic and West African elements; Macumba, with further Bantu African contributions and local Indian spirits and curative practices; and Umbanda, drawing on all the above together with European spiritualism and occultism to form a nation-wide religious complex sharing its adherents with folk ROMAN

CATHOLICISM. [15: 177–204, 158–63; 19: 108–14]

Afterlife (Amerindian) [III] Despite a rather widespread lack of definition regarding man's post-mortem fate, conceptions of afterlife differed greatly among Indian tribes of North America. Speculations were usually closely linked to conceptions of the SOUL as well as to a particular view of man's life in this world. Most tribes held that man possessed more than one soul (usually a 'free' soul and a 'life' or 'breath' soul), the former departing the body at death, perhaps lingering for some time near the corpse, before passing to its final disposition. [8: IX, 134–9] Among the Algonquian (ALGONQUIN), Cherokee, and IROQUOIS, for example, the soul might be required to pass a test before entering the land of the dead. A SHAMAN might serve as the soul's guide. Mortuary customs reflect varying conceptions of afterlife. In general, the dead were feared (not by the SIOUX, a notable exception), and elaborate funeral rites were intended to effect the soul's smooth transition to the other world [23: VII–VIII]. With the exception of the PUEBLO tribes, who possessed a rather detailed conception of afterlife, most notions were of a vague, shadowy existence, often an indistinct continuation of earthly life. Among the nomadic tribes of the prairies and plains, the notion of a 'happy hunting ground' was common. Generally, however, human life was viewed neither as a testing-ground nor as a preparation for eternal life, though later Christian influences may be noted.

Afterlife (Ancient Egyptian) [IV] A belief in continued existence after death was common to all levels of ancient Egyptian society and, apart from the Old Kingdom (*c.* 2600 BCE) when only the royal hereafter was clearly defined (RE') [5], rich and poor expected an individual eternity. To this end, tombs were prepared with articles of daily and religious use (FUNERARY PRACTICES),

according to the individual's wealth; many were mummified (MUMMIFICATION) and provided themselves with elaborate coffins [6]. The complex concept of the personality that included, in addition to the body, the immortal elements – the *Ba* (soul) and *Ka* (spirit) – was the foundation of the funerary beliefs and practices. The Egyptians believed that the deceased would require a preserved body and tomb (MANSION OF THE KA) environment to which the *Ka* could return to partake of sustenance (food-offerings provided by relatives, *Ka*-priests, or, later, by means of models of food, wall-paintings, and a menu inscribed on the tomb wall (HIEROGLYPHS)).

A celestial afterlife was envisaged for royalty, and the wealthy lavishly equipped their tombs for a continued existence. The cult of Osiris (OSIRIAN TRIAD), although originally associated only with royalty, underwent democratization during the Middle Kingdom (*c.* 1900 BCE). Osiris achieved widespread popularity because he offered his followers, regardless of their status, the promise of resurrection and a continued existence tilling the land in the 'Fields of Reeds'. This was dependent upon a satisfactory assessment of the individual's life by the divine tribunal at the Day of Judgement, when the deceased recited the Negative Confession, affirming his moral fitness. His heart was weighed in the balance against the feather of truth; the final verdict was recorded by Thoth. Having been declared 'justified', the deceased then passed to the Osirian underworld, but the hearts of the unworthy would be devoured by a mythological creature. [6]

Afterlife (Ancient Near Eastern) [VI] Fine funerary goods have been discovered at various ancient Near Eastern sites, such as: (1) the Royal Tombs at Ur (*c.* 2500 BCE) [26: 74–81]; (2) a burial at Ashur, *c.* reign of Tukulti-Ninurta (*c.* 1240 BCE) (both cremation and inhumation customs existed concurrently in

HITTITE society [13: 164–9]); and (3) Ugarit, where provision was made to feed the deceased buried in subterranean vaults (PHOENICIANS).

However, the mythology (ANCIENT NEAR EASTERN RELIGIONS) in literary sources indicates a general belief that only the gods were immortal, although even they might die. Man either had no hope of survival after death, or, as in SUMERIAN mythology, his spirit would descend to a dark underworld, where life would dimly reflect the joys of earthly existence [16: 153–66]. The concept of individual resurrection seems to be missing, although a number of myths recall the story of a vegetation god who dies, thus depriving the earth of his bounty, but who finally returns to life and restores abundance to the land and its inhabitants.

Afterlife (**Christian View of**) [IX.B] Traditionally, the Christian view of MAN sees his soul as surviving death. At death an interim judgement is made. This distinguishes between worthy souls destined for heaven, and the unworthy consigned to eternal punishment in hell. ROMAN CATHOLICISM teaches that most saved souls undergo a period of purification in Purgatory, but PROTESTANTISM rejects this. A few enter the immediate presence of God (beatific vision). At the end of time the Second Coming of JESUS CHRIST takes place and the New (Heavenly) JERUSALEM (the home of Christians) descends (cf. MILLENARIANISM). In a general resurrection of the dead, souls are clothed with a transfigured body. The Last Judgement settles the final destiny of the resurrected: eternal bliss in heaven or eternal torment in hell. Heaven is also the dwelling place of angels, i.e. immaterial beings who act as God's messengers and some as men's guardian angels. Catholics offer devotion to them as they do to SAINTS. The Devil (Satan) is the leader of evil angels fallen through pride. They tempt and torment Christians but are con-

signed to eternal fire at the Last Judgement. (Belief in demon-possession was once common and exorcism to remove demons is still occasionally practised (DEMONOLOGY) [107: 493–4].) These teachings have been elaborated by legend, speculation, and folklore. Modern Christian views of the afterlife emphasize that all language about it is highly symbolic, picturing the bliss of communion with God and the agony of separation from him (e.g. the 'flames' of hell). There has been widespread reaction against the notion of eternal punishment. Some think of conditional immortality (the wicked being extinguished); others of universalism (the ultimate salvation of all). 'Resurrection of the body' has also been very variously interpreted, e.g. not only the resuscitation of the physical body but also the survival of the personality in some form. [76: XVII; 116]

Afterlife (**Greek**) [XII] In earliest eschatology all *shades* (souls) went to Hades, a subterranean, gloomy, dark land of the dead. A rapidly growing belief soon challenged this: select HEROES were thought to inhabit a paradise (Elysion; or *Makaron Nesoi*, Isles of the Blest). MYSTERIA and, later, ORPHISM promised a blissful afterlife close to the gods, to anyone who underwent initiation and followed certain precepts – both ritual and later (in most circles) also ethical. From here the notion of post-mortem rewards and punishments after a general judgement spread into mainstream eschatology. Reincarnation (ETHIKE; ORPHEUS) remained a marginal belief. Celestial/astral immortality, among the stars in the sky, appeared in the 5th century BCE and grew in popularity later, with many variants. All these beliefs, and doubts about the afterlife, coexisted. The Late Hellenistic craving for assurances of immortality found satisfaction primarily in *Mysteria* and the belief in astral immortality. [1: 357–68; 2: IV, 2, VI; 5: VI; 8: 261–8; 17: 62–3, 796–8]

Agama [IX.A] The collection of *sutras*, or discourses of the BUDDHA, which are used in the Sanskrit-based tradition of BUDDHISM. There are four *agamas* and they correspond approximately to the first four *nikayas* of the Pali SUTTA-PITAKA.

In the Sanskrit corpus of scripture the four are *Dirghagama, Madhyamagama, Samyuktagama*, and *Ekottarikagama*. The contents of the two different series, Pali and Sanskrit, are similar in basic matters but are not identical. In fact, each important school of Buddhism appears to have had its own four *agamas*. According to a Chinese source seven distinct series of *agamas* were known in the 7th century CE. [37: 202].

Aggadah [XVII] Aramaic term referring to the non-legal material in rabbinical literature (RABBI), dealing mainly with theology, ethics, and folklore [50: 253]. All of the main elements of later Jewish belief are found in the Aggadah, but they are presented in the fluid form of PARABLES and stories, which have enabled Jews in very different cultural environments to interpret Aggadic teachings in a meaningful way [52: 55]. Some Jewish pietists accept Aggadic ideas as doctrinally binding, but most Jews adopt a selective approach [9 vol. 2: 354].

Agni [XIII.A] A Sanskrit word meaning 'fire' (compare Latin *ignis*) and hence the BRAHMANS' sacrificial fire, and the Hindu god of fire. The eastward expansion across India of the ancient Aryans (INDO-EUROPEANS) was regarded by them as the advance of the fire-cult of Agni, a reference possibly to the clearing of jungle by burning, a practice still followed by tribal peoples of Asia. For example, the *Shatapatha* BRAHMANA refers to the unwillingness of the Aryans to move eastwards across the Gandak river (in modern Bihar) until the fire-god Agni had been carried over. Agni was the god of the domestic hearth as well as of the Brahmans' altar, and was present in the sky in the form of light-ning; hence the idea of the divine all-pervasiveness, which generally develops at an early stage of Hindu thought [2: 237]. Agni is regarded as both benevolent and malevolent, but primarily is thought of as the messenger, carrying the sacrifice to the gods. Another of his roles is that of the dispeller of darkness [3: 187]. More sinister is his 'unholy' activity of consuming the corpse in the crematory fire [3: 193]. In short, Agni, as fire, provides the basis for 'a whole nexus of mythology' linking the human world of the family with the greater world outside [25: 26].

Ahimsa [IX.A] The principle of non-violence, or non-injury to living beings (from *han*, 'to kill', with negative prefix *a*-). Common to Buddhist and JAIN ethics, the basis of the principle is that violence produces a harmful entail (or KARMA) for the person who practises it, with consequent ill effects in terms of unfavourable future rebirth. Buddhists take the view that it is the act of killing an animal or other living being which is harmful, but not the eating of meat which someone else has killed.

Ahmadis [XIV] The movement founded in India by Mirza Ghulam Ahmad (*c.* 1839–1908), who claimed to have received divine revelations and who proclaimed himself the MESSIAH, the MAHDI, an avatar (AVATARA) of KRISHNA, and a reappearance of MUHAMMAD. Whether he claimed to be a new prophet is unclear, but orthodox Indian ISLAM regarded him and the mainstream Qadian movement of his followers as having placed themselves outside Islam. A more moderate minority, based on Lahore, has however maintained closer links with orthodoxy. The Ahmadis have carried on vigorous missionary work in Europe and Africa, and their aggressive methods in Pakistan have in recent decades caused considerable tension, and even public disorder, there. (SOUTH ASIA, ISLAM IN) [5: XIX; 10 'Aḥmadiyya movement';

14: x; 21 'Aḥmadiyya'; 46: xi; 83:
243–4]

Ahura Mazda [xxx] 'The Wise Lord'
or 'Lord Wisdom', the term used by
ZOROASTER and his followers for God.
Zoroaster did not introduce a new God,
but rather exalted one of the popular
'lords' (ahuras) to a unique position as the
wholly good, sole creator who is alone
worthy of absolute worship. Zoroaster
claimed to have visions of Mazda,
whom he spoke of as his friend and
teacher, a judge and helper of man who
is characterized by wisdom and benevolence. Mazda's first creations were the
AMESHA SPENTAS, his helpers who
reflect the divine nature and unite man
to God, and the YAZATAS (beings worthy
of worship), and finally he created the
seven creations which together make up
the whole of the Good Creation (namely
man, cattle, fire, earth, sky, water,
and plants). [6: VII, VIII; 8: II; 23: 10–14]

In the PAHLAVI literature the two
words 'Ahura Mazda' coalesce to
'Ohrmazd'. What Zoroaster implied
about God, these texts clarify. The good
creator Ohrmazd is opposed by an
independent 'devil' Ahriman (ANGRA
MAINYU). Both beings have existed
from eternity. Ohrmazd is responsible
for all that is good in the world – light,
life, health, and joy. Good is characterized by order, stability, harmony.
The destructive forces of evil are outside
Ohrmazd's control. He is not, therefore,
all-powerful (omnipotent). The world,
Zoroastrians believe, is the arena for the
battle between Ohrmazd and Ahriman
(BUNDAHISHN). It is only when good
ultimately triumphs that Ohrmazd will
become omnipotent (FRASHOKERETI)
[49: I, IV; 50: XII]. Most PARSIS nowadays deny that Angra Mainyu is a being,
declaring rather that the concept represents an evil tendency in man. Under
Christian influence they have come to
believe that Ahura Mazda is omnipotent, and so reject the traditional
teaching of a wholly good but not all-
powerful God [7: 202–4; 23: pt III].

Ajivaka [XIII.B] A member of an Indian
religion founded by GOSALA (fl. c. 500
BCE). The Ajivakas were influential during the Mauryan period (3rd–2nd centuries BCE) but largely disappeared from
North India after the 2nd century BCE,
surviving in South India on a small scale
until about the 15th century. Ajivaka
doctrines are known only from hostile
sources, but they were evidently closely
related to the JAINS and probably
played some part in the evolution of the
VAISHESHIKA. The Ajivakas were
naked ascetics, undertaking severe
austerities. A late source gives the four
cardinal points of the faith as (1) the
Lord, i.e. Gosala, (2) the categories
(padartha), (3) the modifications, and (4)
the scriptures. The Ajivakas seem to
have been the first Indian school to
develop a form of atomism, involving
seven kinds of permanent 'atoms'.
[Standard work: I]

Akal Purakh [XXVII] The Sikh doctrine
of God is succinctly stated at the beginning of the ADI GRANTH in words attributed to GURU Nanak (the Mul Mantra).
In an ultimate sense God is unknowable.
There is, however, a sufficient revelation communicated by the grace of the
Guru, the 'voice' of God mystically
uttered within. Nanak begins by declaring the unity and creating power of
God. Although God is nirankar 'without
form', his presence is visible to the enlightened believer, for God is immanent
in all creation. The creation constitutes
God's Name (nam) and he who comprehends the nam grasps the essential
means of release from transmigration
(GURMAT). God is thus pre-eminently
Satnam, the True Name. The other
Nanak term which continues to be regularly used is Akal Purakh, the Eternal
One [25: V]. Nanak laid the foundation
and as the Sikh PANTH evolved so too
did its concept of God. The belief that
justice may require resort to arms is
reflected in a corresponding extension of
the doctrine of God. For Guru Gobind
Singh (GURU) a characteristic epithet

was *Sarab Loh*, 'All-Steel', He who is incarnated in the sword. A further development resulted from the ending of the line of personal Gurus in 1708. Although the personal succession had terminated, the eternal Guru remained, embodied in the scripture and present in the corporate community. As such the eternal Guru merges with the godhead. This development is reflected in the meaning attached to the important term *Vahiguru*. Originally an ascription of praise to the Guru [22: 45–6] it became a noun designating the eternal Guru himself and eventually coalesced with *Akal Purakh*. Today God is called both *Akal Purakh* and *Vahiguru*.

Akali [XXVII] During the 18th and 19th centuries the title *Akali* (devotee of AKAL PURAKH, God) designated SIKH warriors noted for their bravery and disdain for official authority. In this sense their modern descendants are the NIHANGS. Early in the 20th century the title was assumed by radical Sikhs agitating for freedom of GURDWARAS from private control. The Akali Dal (Akali Army), formed for this purpose in 1920, still continues as a major political party in the Punjab. [19: XIII, XVIII]

Akan Religion [II] The Akan form a large group of matrilineal peoples inhabiting southern Ghana, among them the Ashanti and Fanti. While their religions are not identical, there are common features. Nyame is the name of the supreme god (possibly related to the Central African NZAMBI). The name probably relates to the sky. Nyame is by no means 'withdrawn'. In the past he has had altars, *nyamedva* (God's tree), outside many small homes. He is frequently invoked, but has little organized worship comparable with that of the many lesser gods, the Abosum, Nyame's 'children'. Greatest of these is Tano, the river deity. Beneath Nyame but above the Abosum is Asase Yaa, the earth – female and his 'wife' – whose special day is Thursday, as Saturday is Nyame's.

As important as the Abosum are the Asamanfo, ancestors (ANCESTOR VENERATION), of each clan and lineage. The symbol of Akan social and political identity is the sacred stool of each lineage, chiefship, and kingship. The stool, resting in its stool-house, is the point where living and ancestors meet. The most important religious, but also political, activities of life are the installation of a new chief, 'upon the stool of the ancestors', and the stool festivals – the Adae (every 21 days) and the new year Odwira ceremonies. Through the stool, its symbolism and rituals, sacred chiefship is placed at the heart of Akan life from village to kingdom, and all the elements of belief – Asamanfo, Abosum, and, above both, Nyame – are integrated into a unity at once social and religious. [4: VIII; 40]

Akhenaten [IV] PHARAOH Amenophis IV (*c.* 1367–1350 BCE) repudiated the state-cult of Amen-Re' (AMUN), introducing instead the exclusive 'monotheism' of the Aten (ATENISM). His name changed to Akhenaten, he moved his capital to Amarna, and disbanded the traditional priesthoods (MANSION OF THE GODS). His personal devotion is expressed in the 'Great Hymn to the Aten' (*c.* 1360 BCE) [9: 282–8], the indirect inspiration of Psalm 104. Nefertiti, his queen, shared his cult [22: VI, 79] but the counter-revolutionary king, Horemheb (1335–1308 BCE), obliterated the cult after Akhenaten's death.

Akhira [XIV] The afterlife in ISLAM, contrasted with the present life, *dunya*. After the Last Judgement, the righteous will be separated from the damned (QIYAMA). Paradise is described in physical terms in the QUR'AN and HADITH as a luxurious garden (*jannat al-firdaus*), with all sorts of sensual delights and the vision of God (ALLAH) as its culmination (earlier Persian and Judaeo-Christian concepts seem to have had an influence here). Some later theologians, however, without denying the material joys, emphasized also the spiritual bliss. On the other hand, hell (*jahannam*) is a place of fire, sometimes pictured as comprising concentric zones for differing classes of sinners and manned by the keeper Malik and the demons of hell. There was much discussion on the nature of sin and whether consignment to hell was permanent or might be for a fixed term only (DHANB) [29: 53–5; 43: 197–250]

Akhlaq [XIV] The Islamic term for ethics. ISLAM took over many of the pre-Islamic Arab virtues (JAHILIYYA) and gave them moral and religious sanction, and as the spiritualization of the faith proceeded, theologians came to emphasize individual responsibility and morality. To these indigenous strains were added the practical, opportunist morality of the Persians, especially prominent in the sphere of statecraft, and an acquaintance with Greek ethics through Galen (*fl.* 3rd century BCE), Plato (428–348 BCE), Aristotle (384–322 BCE), etc. In recent times, ISLAMIC MODERNISM has favoured activist ethics rather than the quietist ones of traditional SUFISM, as familiarity with Western moral philosophy and ethics has increased. [10 'Ethics (Muslim)'; 18; 21 'Akhlāk'; 45: XIII; 47: V]

Al-Azhar [XIV] Possibly from an epithet, 'the shining one', applied to Fatima, daughter of the prophet MUHAMMAD and wife of 'ALI. It is the name of the mosque in Cairo founded by the Fatimids in 972 as a training college for ISMA'ILI missionaries. Over the centuries it has become the most famous educational institution of the Sunni Muslim world, in the past for the training of the ULEMA, but recently, under the influence of reformers from Muhammad 'Abduh onwards (ISLAMIC MODERNISM), modern subjects such as Western languages and science have been introduced into what was essentially a theological curriculum, and women students have been admitted. Thus Al-Azhar now approximates in many ways to a modern university. (*See also* MADRASA) [21 S.V.; 38: VI]

Aladura [XX] A YORUBA term ('prayer people') for various independent prophet-healing churches spreading from Western Nigeria around West Africa and to Britain since about 1918. The main expansion came with Joseph Babalola's mass divine-healing movement in 1930, which issued under leaders like (later Sir) Isaac Akinyele in the Christ Apostolic Church. Other main sections are Oshitelu's Church of the Lord (*Aladura*), and the many Cherubim and Seraphim societies [12: 50–52], together with numerous smaller churches. [14; 19: 160–67]

Alaya-vijnana [IX.B] 'Store consciousness', the most fundamental of the eight consciousnesses of YOGACARA Buddhism. *Alaya-vijnana* is the wellspring from which all ordinary experience arises – a storehouse of tendencies accumulated over innumerable previous lives. Constantly taken from and added to in the present, it modifies itself to appear both as the world of mental experience and as the world of external things. In this light waking life is considered to differ from dream life only in degree, not in kind. Mistakenly taken as a stable core of selfhood, the store consciousness is in fact a continuously arising flux underlying apparent mental activity. Since it must be both correctly understood and transformed in nature for the mind to be liberated, the Yogacarins emphasized the necessity for deep meditation (SAMATHA), penetrating to the centre of being.

Alchemy [XVIII] The quest for a substance (the 'philosopher's stone' or 'elixir') which will transform ('transmute') base metals into gold or confer immortality on man, often accompanying or symbolizing the pursuit of spiritual perfection. Pre-scientific societies regarded gold as incorruptible, hence symbolizing or conferring changeless perfection in other spheres. Alchemy combines spirituality and chemistry, aspects which its practitioners have variously integrated, mixed, or selectively ignored. Chinese Taoist (TAO CHIAO) alchemists (5th to 9th centuries CE) sought the elixir by chemistry and contemplative techniques reputed to confer spiritual harmony and immense longevity. Western alchemy descends from 2nd-century Gnostic (GNOSTICISM) texts on metallurgy. Perhaps purely technological in intent, these none the less invited mystical interpretation: man was base metal; transmutation signified his spiritual perfection; the elixir was the means to the immortality of the soul. Laboratory procedure was an outer discipline corresponding to inner spiritual practices. [6] Alchemy spread (9th century) to the Arab world, later returning to Christendom, where it reached a high point between 1400 and 1700, stimulating scientific research (R. Boyle, 1627–91, and Sir Isaac Newton, 1643–1727, were both deeply interested) and generating a vast literature with a rich symbolism. With the secularization of science, alchemy lost much of its prestige and by the mid 19th century was almost dead in the West. Interest in the spiritual dimension was revived by the psychologist C. G. Jung (1875–1961), who argued that 'the alchemist projected . . . the process of individuation into the phenomena of chemical change' [14]. It is still practised by a dedicated few in Europe and the U.S.A. and more widely in South-East Asia, where it shades off into traditional medicine and MAGIC.

Alchemy (Chinese) [x] Alchemy in the Chinese context is almost invariably associated with the quest for immortality. The two basic forms of alchemy were: (1) the compounding of the 'External Elixir' (*Wai Tan*) of immortality from chemicals, metals, and drugs; (2) the compounding of the 'Inner Elixir' (*Nei Tan*) by controlling the vital substances or energies of seminal essence (*ching*), breath (*ch'i*), and spirit (*shen*)

within the body. *Nei Tan* alchemy employs the terms and symbols of *Wai Tan* alchemy, while actually engaging in mental and physical disciplines such as meditation and control of the breathing. The distinction between *Nei Tan* and *Wai Tan* probably dates from the 6th century CE. [47: V, 128–43; 77: III, 55–78; 100: 126–35]

The forerunners of the early alchemists were the recipe masters (*fang shih*) of north-east China in the 3rd century BCE. They are said to have incorporated the YIN–YANG and WU HSING (Five Elements) theories with their own methods of controlling the spirits and transforming their bodies, in order to achieve a quasi-physical form of immortality. According to Ssu Ma Ch'ien (140–87 BCE) in the 'Historical Records' (*Shih Chi*), the Emperors Ch'in Shih Huang Ti (d. 210 BCE) and Han Wu Ti (d. 87 BCE) encouraged the *fang shih* in their arts, in the hope of achieving immortality for themselves. One famous *fang shih*, Li Shao Chun, advised Han Wu Ti that by sacrificing to the furnace he could transmute cinnabar into gold, and then by eating from vessels made from the gold he could prolong his life. Having achieved longevity he could undertake the voyage to P'eng Lai island to meet the immortals, sacrifice to heaven and earth, and achieve immortality himself. [69: XXXIII, 12–50]

The oldest extant treatise on alchemy is the *Ts'an T'ung Ch'i* (Kinship of the Three) written by Wei Po Yang between 120 and 150 CE. It describes in cryptic terms the method of preparing the elixir of 'returned cinnabar' (*huan tan*) by heating the dragon (lead) and the tiger (mercury) in a sealed crucible. It quotes extensively from the TAO TE CHING and I Ching and employs YIN–YANG theory. The treatise also advocates meditation, and the refining and circulation of the breath (*ch'i*) through the channels of the body. All these practices and methods are described in such vague and cryptic terms as to defy easy classification into internal or external alchemical categories. [69: XXXIII, 50–75; 80]

Alexandria, Early Christianity at [XI.A] The first known Alexandrian Christian is Apollos, a Jew by birth, skilled in messianic interpretation of the Hebrew scriptures, who visited Ephesus and Corinth about 52 CE [3: XXV; 4: XXIII]. He is sometimes thought to have written the Letter to the Hebrews [6: I, 261–4]. Some decades later another Alexandrian Christian wrote the Letter of Barnabas [6: I, 288–93]. No continuous record of the church of Alexandria is available before 180 CE. In the earlier 2nd century Alexandrian Christianity was influenced by GNOSTICISM. [14: III; 20]

Algonquin [III] The term denotes a North American tribe of the Algonquian linguistic stock, originally inhabiting the Ottawa valley and adjacent areas east and west. As with other Eastern Woodland tribes, the reality of MANITOU, an all-pervasive force in nature, was affirmed. In addition, a supreme being (often portrayed as a THUNDERBIRD), with intermediate divinities (brother sun, sister moon), and earth-mother, Nolomis, source and nourisher of life, were portrayed in myth. The WINDIGO and TRICKSTER-transformer culture-Hero figured in shamanic practice (SHAMAN) as did the VISION QUEST. [8: II–V, VII]

'Ali, 'Alids [XIV] 'Ali (c. 598–660 CE) was the fourth CALIPH or 'successor' to the Prophet, and since he was MUHAMMAD's cousin and son-in-law, his partisans in the civil warfare over political and religious leadership in early ISLAM regarded his claims as especially cogent (SHI'ISM); they held that the Prophet himself had expressly designated 'Ali and his descendants the 'Alids as caliphs and IMAMS. Over the centuries, the 'Alids often sought political power through revolutionary outbreaks, with minimal success, but the consequent repressions did create a

characteristic atmosphere in SHI'ISM of emotionalism and sympathy with martyrdom (see PASSION PLAY (IN ISLAM)). The body of 'Alid descendants, eventually very numerous, were always regarded with respect by all Muslims of whatever sectarian affiliation, being called *sharifs* or *sayyids*, 'noble ones', and often accorded social and financial privileges. [17; 21 S.V.; 41]

Allah [XIV] The name for God in ISLAM (meaning uncertain: perhaps *the* God). Allah was known as the supreme, but not sole, deity in Arabia before MUHAMMAD's mission, but it was the Prophet's task to proclaim him as the one, unique God. The QUR'AN accordingly stresses God's unity (*tauhid*) and makes polytheism (*shirk*) the supreme, unforgivable sin; the trinitarian Christians are thus to be condemned (TRINITY). God is the creator of all existence (KHALQ), the controller of nature and the bestower of its fruits, the transcendent sovereign lord, and in the last days he will judge mankind (QIYAMA). Later theologians tried to define Allah's attributes, but stressed their difference from those of his creation. The fact of God's omnipotence created problems for these scholars over the degree of free will granted to mankind (FATALISM (IN ISLAM)) [82: IV]. Notable for liturgical and devotional purposes (used e.g. by the Sufis in their sessions of *dhikr*: SUFI INSTITUTIONS) are the 'Ninety-nine most beautiful names' given to Allah. [10 'God, concept of'; 21 'Allāh'; 39 'God'; 43: 553–5; 81 index s.v. 'God']

Alms-giving (Buddhist) [IX.A] *Dana* (liberality or generosity) is one of the prime Buddhist virtues. In the special form of liberality by lay people towards members of the SANGHA (offerings of food, robes, etc.) *dana* is one of the commonest ways for Buddhists to express and strengthen their commitment to the Buddhist way. The value of constant alms-giving is seen in the spirit of generosity which it encourages in the giver, and the consequent discouragement of self-centredness. Together with the observance of the moral code (SILA) and meditation (SAMADHI) it is regarded as a prime means of gaining merit in a context that prevents this from becoming selfish merit-making. For the layman in a country where the Buddhist order (*sangha*) is established, one of the ordinary recognized ways of practising alms-giving is by offering food to monks on their daily alms-round; sometimes a special ceremonial meal is arranged by a householder for monks known to him. Lay people also contribute the resources to build and maintain monasteries, and to provide monks with robes. Another way of showing generosity, especially in Burma, is by building a pagoda (STUPA) or Buddhist shrine. At the domestic level hospitality to fellow laymen is also reckoned as a form of alms-giving.

Altjiranga [XXII] The Aranda word (sometimes written *alcheringa*) conventionally used to denote the concept of sacred time in AUSTRALIAN RELIGION. It refers to the beginning of time, when primordial mythical beings ('totemic ancestors'), in human or animal form, roamed the earth and made it habitable. Their spirits remain in the land, or in rocks (*see* WONDJINA), or in sacred objects (TJURUNGA), to be periodically incarnated in human foetuses. They also left tracks on the ground for men to follow in their everlasting search for food, and they laid down the correct rituals for ensuring its continuous supply. Thus there is an eternal aspect to the *altjiranga*, like a timeless dream state; hence the common translations, 'the eternal dream-time' or 'the Dreaming'. [10: 42–50; 27: 610–15]

Alvar [XIII.A] Name of a type of ardently devotional Hindu saint of the VAISHNAVA tradition meaning, literally, 'diver', that is, into the depths of mystical experience. They are particularly associated with the Tamil region of South India. Their hymns, the collec-

tion of which is called the *Prabandham*, had by the time of RAMANUJA acquired the status of sacred scripture, whose expositors were known as *acaryas*. [14: 258f, 263; 21]

Amaterasu-Omikami [XVI] Literally 'Heavenly-highest-shining deity', popularly, the Sun Goddess, the chief KAMI in the native Japanese pantheon, a goddess created variously by the union of Izanagi and Izanami (SHINTO MYTHOLOGY), from her father's left eye or from a mirror held in his left hand [2: 1, 10–83; 17: 284–304; 32: 3–28]. Capable of spontaneous reproduction, she became the chief *kami* after the activities moved to earth, sending her grandson Ninigi no-mikoto to secure the Eight-Island Country. She was, by tradition, enshrined at ISE JINGU in the reign of Emperor Suinin (*c.* 4th century CE) and remains as a source of divine inspiration and guidance, a rather vague, ancestral spirit from whom all emperors are descended. She is not represented in the arts.

American Indians (Central and South): New Religious Movements [XX] New religious movements developed early in Indian contact with whites, and have continued ever since. Some arose deep in the Amazon area, focused on young men regarded as reincarnated CULTURE HEROES in the form of 'new Christs', and were short-lived. In contrast the Hallelujah religion among the Akawaio in the Guyana hinterland began in the mid 19th century. A succession of prophets with visionary experiences developed its emphasis upon prayer and moral discipline, with a holy village, Amokokopai (NEW JERUSALEM). The local Anglican missionaries have been cooperating with the movement since the 1960s. In Maranhão State, Brazil, a typical short-lived movement appeared among the Canela Indians in 1963, led by a prophetess promising the tribal culture hero's return to reverse their position in relation to the civilized and white peoples. The practices of folk ROMAN CATHOLICISM were adopted and whites' goods bought, but the birth of a messianic figure did not occur as expected and after a clash with a government agency the movement collapsed. In Panama a new movement appeared in 1961 among the Guaymi mountain people, where Mama Chi, after a vision of Jesus and the Virgin Mary, became woman leader of a syncretist religion that united the Guaymi and imposed a new life-style. Those organized more like independent indigenous churches prove longer-lasting and there are numbers of these in Peru such as the Israelites of the New Universal Covenant (Israelitas del Nuevo Pacto Universal) among the Aymará Indians. There are Pentecostal movements (PENTECOSTALISM) as among the Toba of the Argentine Chaco but elsewhere these tend to shade into the *mestizo* or mixed-race inhabitants and into more orthodox Christian churches. (*See also* AFRO-AMERICANS.) [12: 141–53; 17: 701].

American Indians (North) and Eskimos: New Religious Movements [xx] North American Indians have maintained the three oldest ongoing interaction movements found among any tribal peoples. At Charlestown, Rhode Island, the Narragansetts' one independent church has sustained tribal identity since it separated from the mission churches in the 1740s. In northern Mexico the Yaqui and Mayo have maintained independent churches ever since the Jesuits were suppressed in the 1760s and have taken them to new settlements in Arizona, as well as having produced a number of prophets and shorter-lived movements. The HANDSOME LAKE religion goes back to 1800. In the 20th century the NATIVE AMERICAN CHURCH developed from the new peyote cult (PEYOTISM), while the INDIAN SHAKER CHURCH began in 1881–2. Among the Apaches of New Mexico the Holy Ground religion

founded in 1921 emphasizes morality and one God, absorbs JESUS CHRIST into traditional mythology, and has a syncretistic symbolism and ritual. There are more orthodox independent Indian churches, usually derived from Christian missions; some are among urbanized Indians but most are on reservations, as among the Seminoles in Florida, the Creek and other Indian tribes in Oklahoma, and in Arizona especially among the NAVAJOS and HOPIS. Among the Plains Indians the traditional SUN DANCE has been revived in the 20th century, with some new forms and functions showing Christian influence. During the last century United States movements have passed from resistance to peaceful coexistence, from millennial to non-millennial hopes, and from nativistic to more Christian forms, despite current revivals of tribal religions in their original modes. Canadian and Alaskan movements have been more local and ephemeral, or have derived from the larger movements in the U.S.A. The independent church form has been less common, although Albert Tritt's church lasted among the Kutchin in Alaska from about 1910 into the 1930s. Since 1970 a Pan-Indian Ecumenical Conference (ECUMENICAL MOVEMENT) has met in Montana and on the Stoney Reserve in Alberta, uniting traditionalist and Christian leaders in seeking religious and cultural renewal for all Indians. ESKIMO movements go back to 1790 in Greenland, and include the Belcher Islands millennial movement that ended with police action in the early 1940s. [12: 101–32; 17: 701–2]

Amerindian Religions [III] During a period extending over 25,000 years, from the time of the earliest migrations across the Bering land bridge to the present day, the religions of the aboriginal inhabitants of North America have displayed a vast variety of forms. These have ranged from simple hunting rituals, through more elaborate calendric rites (CALENDAR ROUND) based upon settled agricultural economies, through the hunting and war-related cults of the nomadic tribes of the plains to more recent manifestations including the GHOST DANCE, PEYOTISM, syncretistic forms bearing Christian influence, the REVITALIZATION MOVEMENT, pan-Indianism, and the Red Power movement. The great diversity of belief and practice, the relative scarcity of archaeological data, the near absence of historical records, the virtual extinction of many tribes, the influence of missionary efforts, and the general pattern towards acculturation present the scholar with a near impossible task of reconstruction and generalization. Most Amerindian religions, however, affirm the existence of a supreme power (personal or impersonal), as well as the divine origin of the cosmos (COSMOLOGY; CREATION MYTHS). The ontological good of this world, the possibility of direct human contact with the supernaturals through visions (VISION QUEST) and rituals, and man's ability to acquire and direct supernatural power for his own ends are equally important. The 'sacramental' character of the physical world, the essential interrelatedness of the human, divine, animal (OWNER OF THE ANIMALS), and vegetative realms, and the composite nature of man himself (namely, a body, plus a 'free' SOUL and a 'life' soul), are central themes of Amerindian religions. Most

groups affirm the perfectibility of man in this life through behaviour in keeping with fundamental relationships, as well as the possibility of some post-mortem existence. Individual and collective rites seek to discern the significance of natural patterns (e.g. the movements of animals, celestial and seasonal variations, and the intentions of the supernaturals) in order to channel, influence, or act in accordance with the sacred realities. Amerindian religions generally stress the priority of actions over belief and, although the centrality of individual religious experience is commonly affirmed, the consequences for the community are usually underscored. [2: I, II, IV, VI; 12; 17: V–VIII]

Amesha Spentas [xxx] The 'Holy' or 'Bounteous' Immortals in ZOROASTER's teaching. Their number is traditionally seven, but modern scholars and PAHLAVI texts disagree on which Immortals are to be included in that number (*see table*). In the Pahlavi literature Ohrmazd (AHURA MAZDA) is identified with Spenta Mainyu and so becomes one of the seven Amahraspands (the Pahlavi form of Amesha Spentas). Some scholars argue that this was also Zoroaster's belief [5: VIII], but others disagree [50: 43–51]. The Amesha Spentas are thought of as heavenly beings, somewhat resembling the archangels of Christian belief. Each Immortal is thought of as a guardian of

THE AMESHA SPENTAS

Avestan form	Later form	English 'name'	Creation protected
Ahura Mazda	Ohrmazd	Wise Lord	Man
Spenta Mainyu	. . .	Holy (Creative) Spirit	Man
Vohu Manah	Bahman	Good Purpose	Cattle
Asha	Ardvahist	Righteousness	Fire
Khshathra	Shahrevar	Power, Kingdom	Sky
Armaiti	Spendarmad	Devotion	Earth
Haurvatat	Hordad	Health	Waters
Ameretat	Amurdad	Immortality	Plants

one of the seven creations which constitute the Good Creation. All the Immortals are symbolically represented through their respective creations in the central rites (YASNA). They are described in human terms; for example some are male, some female and one of them, Vohu Manah, greets the righteous soul at the CHINVAT BRIDGE to conduct it to heaven. There is also an important abstract dimension to their nature. Their 'names' are not personal ones, but denote aspects of the divine nature in which man can and should share (except Spenta Mainyu, the Holy Spirit). So, by embodying the good purpose, by living a life of righteousness and devotion, man can share in the kingdom, enjoy health and immortality. Man's religious duty can, therefore, be described as making the Immortals dwell within him. [7: 21–4; 50: 45–50]

Amida Worship [XVI] The Japanese combined AMITABHA (Infinite Light) and Amitayus (Infinite Life) into Amida, the Buddha of the Pure Land (Jodo = Chinese CHING T'U) Western Paradise (*Saiho*) (JAPANESE BUDDHAS AND BODHISATTVAS) [8: 74–87; 13: 61–3). Within TENDAI, following ENNIN's return from China in 847 CE, meditation halls were built and the chanting of *nembutsu* (a contraction of *Namu-Amida-Butsu*) started. The Fujiwara aristocrats were ardent believers, erecting large Amida temples, some for retirement purposes. The priest Genshin (Eshin Sozu) (942–1017) wrote *Ojoyoshu* (Essentials of Salvation or Birth in the Land of Purity) in 985, stressing the practice of the repetition of Amida's name, with the mind fixed on the BUDDHA IMAGE. Purely Japanese, it was the first reasoned exposition of Jodo, Pure Land doctrine.

All Amida worship was still under this-worldly Tendai until *Yuzu-nembutsu* was founded by Ryonin in 1124, the first Amida sect, based in Osaka. Genku (1130–1212) or Honen Shonin (Enko Daishi) left Mt Hiei for Kyoto and, using the *Ojoyoshu*, emphasized faith and the saving grace of Amida, initiating the concept of Pure Land as rebirth in the next existence. His teaching dates the formation of the Jodo sect from 1175 [34: 192–7]. His thesis *Senchaku Hongan Nembutsu Shu* (Collection of Passages on the Original Vow and the Nembutsu) of 1198 resulted in banishment in 1206. On returning in 1211, he built the large Chion-in, the chief temple of the sect and the parent of many offshoots.

Shinran (1173–1262) [21: 133–4] broke the customary priestly celibacy and taught *akunin shoki*, grace for the inevitable sinner, drawing a large following among farmers. His successors separated into Jodo Shinshu (True Pure Land sect), the largest group today, for which later generations built the Hongan-ji in Kyoto, headed by the Otani family, now in east and west branches. Followers of Ippen Shonin (Chishin) (1239–89) [21: 109–10], known for the *odori-nembutsu*, the dancing *nembutsu*, built the sect around his name. Amida worship now thrives in many subsects, whose members revere the founders and recite incantations, in temples which assume most of the funeral business in Japan because of the generous promises they make for the soul's eternal bliss.

Amidah [XVII] The central prayer of the Jewish LITURGY, the word meaning 'standing' since the prayer is said standing facing towards Jerusalem [52: 167]. It consists of 19 benedictions, and is also known as the *Shemoneh Esreh* ('Eighteen'), a benediction having been added in the 2nd century against heretics [20: 92; 48: 50]. The *Amidah* is recited thrice daily, and in a slightly different form on Sabbaths (SHABBAT) and festivals (CHAGIM) when an extra *Amidah*, *Musaf*, is added. [9 vol. 2: 838]

Amitabha [IX.A] A heavenly BUDDHA, whose name means 'unmeasured light', who dwells in the heavenly realm of Sukhavati, and is one of the

many cult-figures of MAHAYANA
Buddhism. Those who set their minds
on him and on thoughts of enlightenment, and cultivate the 'roots of goodness' are, it is said, reborn in Amitabha's
heaven when they die. The cult of Amitabha probably originated in the area to
the north-west of India, and in Japan
AMIDA WORSHIP developed. [37: 360–
62] (*See also* CHING T'U TSUNG.)

Amun [IV] Originally a local god of
Thebes, Amun was elevated by the
Theban princes (18th dynasty, *c*. 1550
BCE) to become the great state-god of
Egypt's empire. Associated with RE' as
Amen-Re', Amun assimilated his
powers; in the vast temple complex at
Karnak, he was worshipped with his
consort, Mut, and son, Khonsu. So
great was his influence that his priesthood (MANSION OF THE GODS) threatened the king's sovereignty, perhaps
contributing to the 'revolutionary' Aten
cult championed by Akhenaten
(ATENISM).

Anabaptists [XI.B] The nickname ('re-
baptizers') of a variety of 16th-century
sects, some pacific, some violent [142].
A common characteristic was baptism
of mature believers instead of infants, as
a mark of church membership. The
peaceful Mennonites (Menno Simons,
1496–1561) survive in America [107:
902].

Anagami [IX.A] In THERAVADA
Buddhism, a 'non-returner', that is, a
being who will not return to the earthly
round of birth and death, but will be reborn in a heavenly sphere, where he will
attain the state of an ARAHAT.

Anagarika [IX.A] The original form of
the Buddhist life. The term designates
one who has gone forth from his home
in order to search for the truth about
life. Such a person is called *an-agarika*
because he is a 'non-householder', that
is, a homeless wanderer. This practice
of leaving the regular life of a householder was fairly common in ancient
India, and is still practised. It was, and
is, regarded as very honourable. Sakya-

muni (the BUDDHA) himself left his
home and family in this way, in order
to attain supreme enlightenment, and
became Buddha (GOTAMA). The order
of *bhikkhus* (monks) which he later
founded consisted of such *anagarikas*.
Like other groups of this kind in northern India at that time, they depended on
the goodwill of householders for their
sustenance (ALMS-GIVING). Buddhist
scriptures contain accounts of the
reasons which prompt a person to become an *anagarika*, and the procedure
for doing so, such as the following: 'The
life of the household is full of obstacles.
It is the path of impurity; it is not possible to lead the higher life which is
extremely pure and clean by one living
the life of a householder. How now, if I
were to shave my hair and beard, put on
the yellow robe and walk forth from
home to homelessness.' (*Anguttara-
nikaya*, II.208)

Ananda [IX.A] GOTAMA'S personal
attendant and one of his principal disciples (*see also* BUDDHA); a first cousin
of Gotama and his exact equal in age (to
the day). When other disciples were in
doubt concerning the teaching Ananda
was frequently called on to explain, and
his skill in doing so, which became
known to Gotama, was highly praised.
He also championed the cause of the
women disciples and persuaded Gotama
to admit them to the SANGHA. After
Gotama's death he took a leading part in
reciting the received version of the master's teaching.

Ananda Marga [XXI] Founded in India
in 1955 by Shrii Shrii Anandamurti. The
movement spread in the West during
the 1970s. Spiritual practices relating to
e.g. cleanliness, diet, posture, and service are clearly laid out for devotees,
who are expected to practise YOGA or
meditation several times daily. Sexual
intercourse is permitted for procreation
purposes within marriage, but the most
fully committed members lead celibate
lives. The movement claims that it is
primarily a philosophical, social-welfare

or political organization rather than a religious movement. [40] Protests over the imprisonment in India of their leader have led to the self-immolation of some of the members.

Anatta [IX.A] According to Buddhist teaching, one of the three principal characteristics of everything in the universe. It is a necessary corollary of the doctrine of ANICCA. Since all things in the entire universe are impermanent, there is no enduring unchanging 'personality' or 'self' which is the basis of the human person, but only a temporary collocation of changing constituents, or *khandha* (Sanskrit *skandha*). [5: 36ff]

Ancestor Cult (**Chinese**) [x] The veneration of ancestors (*pai tsu*) is one of the most ancient, persistent, and influential themes in Chinese religion and traditional Chinese society. From excavations of Shang dynasty sites (1500–1000 BCE) it is known that the Shang rulers provided their dead with all the essentials for continued sustenance, and consulted their royal ancestors by means of ORACLE BONES for advice on ritual, military, agricultural, and domestic matters. [14; 17; 99] The principal deity, SHANG TI, was quite possibly a supreme royal ancestor in origin. The oracle bones and inscribed bronze ritual vessels are concerned almost exclusively with royal ancestors. By the time of the Western Chou dynasty (1027–770 BCE) the idea of the interdependence of the living and the dead was clearly established. The formal ritual and ethical requirements of the ancestor cult are described in the 'Classic of Rites' (*Li Ching*) [61; 83].

The motives and underlying ideas behind the beliefs and practices of the ancestor cult are varied and complex. Clearly the formal and ceremonial expression of grief by the relatives serves an important function. The funeral and mourning rites serve to re-establish and maintain the unity and continuity of the family. The reverence and respect paid by a devoted son to his deceased father is clearly an application of the important virtue of filial piety (*hsiao*). There is also an element of self-interest or self-preservation. The *hun* (spiritual soul) and the *p'o* (gross soul) of the dead are dependent for their survival and happiness upon the offerings of spirit money, incense, and food and drink made by their descendants. In return the *hun* soul, as a spirit (*shen*), can achieve considerable benefits for the family by means of its supernatural contacts. In the case of ordinary beings this relationship is only considered to last for between three and five generations. The souls are then succeeded by more recent ones. The *p'o* soul normally resides in the grave, but if it is not accorded the proper respect and offerings it could emerge as a malevolent ghost (*kuei*); so it is very much in the interests of the family to supply them (FUNERAL RITES). [1; 39; 43; 46; 85: XX, 155–9; 86: III, 34–55; 105: II, 28–57]

Ancestor Veneration (**African**) [II] In most although not all African religions (among the exceptions are the Masai, NUER, and Tiv) ancestors play a major role; they are generally the immediate recipients of most prayers and sacrifices. This reflects the profound importance of kinship in the ordering of society. Ancestors protect the living, but insist also upon the maintenance of custom, punishing by sickness or misfortune those who breach it. There are, nevertheless, many major differences upon which it is unwise to impose a single model of interpretation. In general ancestors are seen as elders, named and approached in much the same way as the most senior of living elders: yet they have additional mystical powers and, among many peoples, different or additional names (*see* MIZIMU). In more God-conscious societies ancestors may be approached simply as intermediaries to God, but where ritual, petition, and sacrifice are regularly directed to ancestral spirits with little or no reference to God, it seems linguistically perverse to deny that this is worship – a word itself admitting a range of meaning. Among some peoples a clear verbal distinction is certainly made between reverencing ancestors and worshipping God; thus the Gikuyu use *gothaithaya* (their word for worship) for the latter but never for the former, as the Zulu use *ukukhonza* for worshipping God. The usual Zulu word for venerating ancestors, *ukuthetha*, means literally 'speaking with'.

In some religions a wide range of male and female ancestors – perhaps the collective dead – are venerated, in others a rather narrow jural line of authority holders; in some, ancestors are seen as concerned chiefly (or only) with the supply of continued gifts to them, in others rather with the wider social behaviour of the living; in some, their individual characteristics may be remembered, in others these appear irrelevant. Ancestors normally enter into full status only after completion of various post-funerary rituals. In some West African societies (for example, Benin and the Ibo) ancestor veneration is combined with belief in their reincarnation in descendants.

It is in small agricultural societies which lack political structures beyond lineage heads (for example, Lugbara and Tallensi) that the worship of ancestors can be most clearly found. In larger kingdoms it tends to become a more varied communion with the dead, while among pastoralists it is often absent. [5: 16–21, 122–42; 21; 27; 38]

Ancestor Worship [xxviii] Devotion, going beyond veneration, to persons who have died [18: 56–7, 291–2; 21: 46–8, 61–3, 172–4]. To honour the dead and hallow their memory is common. Many peoples go further, believing that the dead (especially leaders and heroes) live on and can affect the life of later generations [1: 127–54; 8: 64–7]. Hence prayers and rites (RITUAL), often SACRIFICES, are directed to them. Some theorists have claimed to find the

ORIGIN OF RELIGION in such practices [25: 34] or in the deification of heroes (Euhemerism) [18: 18–19; 25: 6].

Ancient Egyptian Religion [IV] Geographical factors profoundly affected the development of religion in Egypt. The multitude of tribal deities in existence before the unification of Egypt (*c.* 3100 BCE) formed the basis of the pantheon which consisted of state-gods (mainly cosmic deities with some elevated local gods) and local gods (each town had its own divinity). These had temples (MANSION OF THE GODS) and received a cult, but the majority of people worshipped household gods at village shrines [6]. By the Old Kingdom (*c.* 2600 BCE), the priests had attempted to rationalize the multitude of divinities; some were grouped into 'families', the most famous being the Great and Little Enneads (nine gods) of Heliopolis and the Ogdoad (eight gods) of Hermopolis. Later, divine triads (AMUN; OSIRIAN TRIAD; SETH) were established [18: VII, 142].

The twin forces of the Nile and the sun moulded FUNERARY PRACTICES and beliefs. The annual inundation revived the parched land and vegetation – a cycle reflected in the life, death, and resurrection of Osiris, god of vegetation. Similarly, the sun died each night, renewing its birth at dawn. The Egyptian concept of human existence (life, death, rebirth – *see* AFTERLIFE) was inspired by the cyclic pattern evident in these natural phenomena. [6]

The Egyptians called their country Kemet (the 'Black Land'), referring to the black mud deposited on the river banks by the inundation; with scanty rainfall, Egypt supports a thriving community only because of the Nile's inundation. Even so, irrigation provides only limited cultivable land, and in earliest times (pre-dynastic period, *c.* 3400 BCE), the dead were buried outside this area, in the desert, where the heat and dryness of the sand naturally desiccated the corpses. This led the Egyptians to regard the artificial preservation of the body (MUMMIFICATION) as essential to the person's continued existence.

SYNCRETISM was an important feature of ancient Egyptian religion. In the pre-dynastic era, early religious development reflected political events. As communities were amalgamated, following intertribal conflicts, and larger political units were formed, so the characteristics and cult-centres of the deities of the conquered tribes were absorbed by the victors' deities [18: VII, 139]. Also, cosmic deities may have adopted the attributes and centres of older, tribal gods. Later, the deities of foreign neighbours or conquered peoples were sometimes incorporated into the Egyptian pantheon.

Ancient Europe [V] The main pre-Christian religions known to us, outside Greece and Rome, were those of the GERMANIC and CELTIC peoples. We know very little of the beliefs of the SLAVS and BALTS. Celts and Germans were in contact in Roman times [29: 1, 42–9], and again in the British Isles in the Viking age. The Celts were converted by 500 BCE, but the old religion survived up to the 11th century in Scandinavia, and ancient myths influenced Icelandic [6: 1; 30: 1] and Irish [21: X–XVII] literature. Writing was limited in pre-Christian cultures to RUNES and early inscriptions, so for our knowledge of this subject we depend upon archaeological finds, Greek and Roman writers, early missionaries, material recorded after the conversion to Christianity, inscriptions identifying deities with their Roman counterparts, names of persons, places, and gods. While these religions were never centralized, a main outline can be discerned. There is a sky-god fighting monsters with club or hammer (DAGDA; Perkunas (see BALTS); Perun (see SLAVS); THOR); a god of eloquence, magic, and the dead (LUG; ODIN); fertility deities (BRIGIT; MATRES; VANIR); a trickster figure

(Bricriu [21: VIII, 184–5]; LOKI); and female battle spirits (VALKYRIES). Little is known of the Germanic priesthood, but the DRUIDS helped to preserve Celtic traditions [14: IV]. Sacred places were in forests, on hills and islands, near lakes and springs, and at burial places [23: 1; 29: VI, 187–98]. Regular feasts were held (SAMHAIN [25: VIII, 173–5]), and sacrifices and offerings made for fertility and victory (VOTIVE OFFERINGS). There were simple temples and Celtic sanctuaries for healing [7: VI, 138–47; 22: VI, 136–40]. Divination was widely practised [3: 116–26], and there was elaborate funeral symbolism (SHIP-FUNERAL [7: V, 106–9, VI, 111–23]). Myths of creation and the world's ending (RAGNAROK), tales of exploits of the gods and journeys to supernatural realms (LAND OF YOUTH), survive in later literature.

Ancient Near Eastern Religions [VI] Mesopotamia – the 'land between the rivers' Tigris and Euphrates – was the cradle of ancient Near Eastern religions. Although it was successively occupied by new peoples, who brought their languages, ideas, and religious beliefs (ASSYRIANS; BABYLONIANS; SUMERIANS), there was a continuing civilization which passed on the earliest traditions [10; 16; 20; 23]. Central to this was the city-state [23: 13–14]; each city-state had its own deity and TEMPLE, which held a key position in the community and provided an indication of its wealth. At first loosely associated in a league (SUMERIANS), the cities eventually acknowledged a supreme overlord, and the Akkadians and Assyrians developed the concept of universal rulership, creating state pantheons to emphasize national unity. Local gods continued to exist alongside the great gods.

The Old Babylonian period was very important, for an extensive written literature now arose (GILGAMESH, EPIC OF; MARDUK) [24], in which the earlier Sumerian elements – names and characteristics of gods, myths and legends, omens (DIVINATION), and MAGIC – were preserved and eventually handed down to the Assyrians [11] and, through the HURRIANS [9], to the HITTITES, thus providing the basis of most primitive Near Eastern religions. Monuments [6; 26] and seal impressions (ART AND SYMBOLISM) [5; 23: 27–32] amplify our knowledge of these gods and their temples.

It was generally accepted that men were created solely to serve the gods and to supply their basic needs – food, drink, and shelter (TEMPLES). The Sumerians introduced the doctrine of the creative power of the divine word [16: 130–31] and this became widely accepted throughout the Near East. Similarly, most societies regarded KINGSHIP [7; 12; 19] as divine, and the king as the chief priest of the great state-god.

Comparatively little attention was given to the AFTERLIFE (PHILISTINES; PHOENICIANS), and although some elaborate grave goods have been discovered, the concept of individual immortality was disregarded in these religions.

The main textual sources of knowledge concerning religion include the extensive literature of the Old Babylonian period, when myths and epics relating the proceedings of gods and men in earliest times were mostly written down in Sumerian; the hymns and psalms addressed to gods and kings; and the incantations and prayers recited by private persons or priests to alleviate sickness and affliction (MAGIC) [24]. Hittite literature includes Babylonian 'scientific works', as well as creation and resurrection epics such as the myth of 'Slaying the Dragon Illuyankas' and of the 'Missing God' [13: 180–94]. Paucity of written evidence about other societies (ELAMITES; PHILISTINES; PHOENICIANS) limits our understanding of their beliefs.

Myths and legends relate the his-tory of the gods since the first creation and the deeds of ancient heroes (GILGAMESH, EPIC OF; SUMERIANS) [24]. They attempt to explain the world (COSMOLOGY); and they return to the recurrent themes of the victory of good over EVIL ('Slaying the Dragon' – a New Year Babylonian and Hittite myth [13: 181–2]) (FESTIVALS; MARDUK), and the disappearance and return of a vegetation god who deprives the earth of its fertility and then restores it [for the Hittite myth see 9; 13: 184–9; see also the Ugaritic myth of Aqhat, PHOENICIANS, 4: 27].

Angakok [III] A term used among the hunting and fishing peoples of the central Arctic (Tonralik, in Alaska), referring in the most general sense to someone, male or female, who has a helping spirit, thus a SHAMAN or sorcerer. Those who, by a variety of traditional shamanic techniques or initiation, make contact with *sila*, the fundamental, elemental, and all-pervasive power of the universe, gain an *angakog* or *qaumaneq*, a 'lighting' or 'enlightenment' whereby they obtain divinatory and curative powers. [22: II] Through the tuition of an elder *angakok* (plural, *angak ut*), a youth was prepared for contact with the supernatural world by fasting and physical ordeals. At length, through dream or vision, a transformation of psyche and body was experienced, often symbolized by dismemberment and reconstitution at the hands of the *tunrag* (helping spirits). The ecstatic experience thus confirmed and supplemented by instruction in techniques of curing and divination, the neophyte assumed a public role, assisted henceforth by his spirit helper. Varying degrees of intensity of the initial experience, together with the importance of the helping spirits contacted (the benevolent spirits of the deceased were regarded as of lesser rank), resulted in a hierarchy, the *angakok* having a more intimate and personal relationship with the *tunrag* than others.

Angelology (Biblical) [XI.A] In earlier books of the BIBLE the 'angel of Yahweh' appears as the messenger of GOD to human beings. There are vaguer references to other angels, attendant on Yahweh. In post-exilic times, possibly under the influence of ZOROASTRIANISM, a hierarchy of angels emerges, with seven named archangels. Some of these angels control separate nations; others have charge of natural elements like fire and water. In the New Testament such angels are specially active in the Apocalypse. [5: 166–8; 6: 1, 280–82]

Angels (in Judaism) [XVII] Despite the frequent references to angels in the BIBLE there seem to have been some rabbinical sages who doubted the desirability of ANGELOLOGY in JUDAISM [21: 109]. The MISHNAH does not mention angels, and some Talmudic rabbis seem to avoid mentioning angels in their interpretations of scripture (RABBI; TALMUD). This attitude is carried over into the Haggadah, the Passover liturgical text, which emphasizes that the deliverance of the Israelites from Egypt was 'not through an angel, and not through a messenger' but by God himself, despite biblical evidence to the contrary. That this was a minority view is clear from the many, highly personified, descriptions of angels found throughout rabbinical literature [9 vol. 2: 956]. Angels also play an important role in Jewish mysticism, the MERKABAH mystics confronting angels who guarded the entrances of the various stages of ascent to a vision of the divine throne. They also appear in Jewish folklore [15: 35].

Anglicanism [XI.B] The established (*see* STATE, CHRISTIANITY AND THE) Church of England became independent of Rome through the REFORMATION, but contains 'Catholic' and PROTESTANT elements. (The Anglo-Catholic party originated in the Oxford (Tractarian) Movement in the 1830s; the Evangelical party during the Evangelical Revival.) Church government (CHURCH ORGANIZATION) is by bishops. WORSHIP is primarily in fixed liturgies: the Book of Common Prayer (1662) and new services since 1965. Doctrine was classically expressed in the Thirty-Nine Articles (1563) (cf. CREEDS). Bishops of the world-wide 'Anglican Communion' (e.g. U.S.A. Episcopalians) have met in Lambeth (in London) conferences since 1867. [101; 104]

Angra Mainyu [XXX] The 'Hostile Spirit', one of the twin (or opposed) spirits (the other being AHURA MAZDA), considered by ZOROASTER to be the source of all evil and good respectively (Ahriman in PAHLAVI literature). In order to destroy the good, Angra Mainyu created his own spiritual forces: the demons, *daevas* (usually male in later texts) and *drugs* (later generally female). These may be represented in various forms – animal, insect, human, or as a monster (e.g. Azi Dahaka). Their 'names', however, reflect their generally abstract nature and function, e.g. Aeshma (Wrath). The characteristics of evil are violence, chaos, untruth, i.e. it is wholly negative and destructive. It is believed that Angra Mainyu has existed from eternity, wholly independent of Ahura Mazda. Evil is, therefore, a reality over which Mazda has no control, until the final victory (FRASHOKERETI). The world is essentially good; all the evils within it are the weapons by which Angra Mainyu seeks to destroy it, notably sin, disease, dirt, decay, and death (BUNDAHISHN). Evil exists in non-material or spiritual form (*menog*), like a parasite in men's bodies in the form of Wrath or Greed, or in harmful repugnant forms (*khrafstra*) such as beasts of prey or snakes. It is man's religious duty to eradicate all evil, thereby making Angra Mainyu impotent and Ahura Mazda omnipotent. So man is Ahura Mazda's fellow worker (*hamkar*) in the battle against evil. [5: VIII; 7: 19–21; 20: 54–6; 49: I–IV; 50: XII]

Anicca [IX.A] In THERAVADA Buddhist teaching the first of the three general characteristics of existence (the *ti-lak-khana*). As the first, it is the basis for the other two, DUKKHA and ANATTA. Literally 'non-permanence', it is explained as meaning that 'things never persist in the same way, but are dissolving and vanishing from moment to moment'. It is also held that without insight into the impermanence and insubstantiality of all phenomena there is no way of attaining deliverance from the round of rebirth. [5: 34]

Animal Cults (Ancient Egyptian) [IV] In prehistoric Egypt, many tribal deities had animal forms. During the earliest dynasties, anthropomorphization occurred gradually (Archaic period, *c.* 3000 BCE), but most towns continued to worship a particular animal deity [21: I, 8]. Regarded as repositories of the deity's divine powers, many animals, including cats, crocodiles, and ibises, were revered and cared for. They were mummified (MUMMIFICATION) [4; 15: 155–6] and buried in large cemeteries during the Late Period (*c.* 800 BCE) – excesses which invited the ridicule of other countries.

Animal Slaughter (Jewish) [XVII] According to traditional JUDAISM meat may only be eaten if it comes from an animal of a kosher (KASHRUT) species which has been ritually slaughtered (*shechitah*) [16: VI]. This is done by the slaughterer (*shochet*) passing a sharp, smooth knife across the neck of the animal thereby severing the windpipe, the oesophagus, and the jugular vein. The animal loses consciousness almost immediately. The slaughterer has to be highly trained and a reliable person. [52: 202]

Animism [XXVIII] (1) The belief that a SPIRIT (or spirits) is active in aspects of the environment. The term may cover *animatism* [19; 25: 67, 165], the belief that life, power, and feeling are all-pervading, even in the physical environment. Animism, more strictly defined,

has reference to belief only in personal powers [5: 62–72; 8: 49–58].
(2) The theory that the ORIGIN OF RELIGION lies in 'belief in spirits', which is the minimum definition of religion [24: 13; 25: 55–8; 28: 27–9; 29].
(3) A loose, misleading, designation for religion in any tribal culture.

Anselm [XI.C] (*c.* 1033–1109) A native of Lombardy who became a pupil of Lanfranc, succeeding the latter as prior at Bec in Normandy and later as Archbishop of Canterbury. His relations with the Norman kings were stormy since he refused to compromise the spiritual rights of the church. Intellectually he was a brilliant philosopher and theologian. His *Proslogion* and *Liber apologeticus pro insipiente* put forward the classical version of the ontological argument (ARGUMENTS FOR THE EXISTENCE OF GOD) and his *Cur deus homo?* presents a classical expression of the satisfaction theory of the Atonement. (SALVATION) [6; 26]

Anthroposophy [XVIII] An esoteric movement founded by the Austrian Rudolf Steiner (1861–1925). Strongly influenced by Goethe, whose scientific works he edited, Steiner formulated his system in quasi-scientific terms. The universe and man himself, who is reborn many times, have evolved through three states of mind and matter. The early phases ('astral' and 'etheric') were characterized by intuitive and clairvoyant modes of consciousness (PSYCHIC POWERS) and rarefied forms of matter. These still exist but are now concealed by physical matter and intellectual consciousness. They may be recovered and used purposefully by meditation and other practices. The birth of JESUS CHRIST was the central event of human history: man had evolved to a point where material existence had caused him to forget his spiritual capacities. Christ came to reverse this trend, inaugurating an era of spiritual reintegration. Anthroposophists have used Steiner's ideas as a basis for experimental work in agriculture, education, and other fields. [11]

Anti-Christ (in Islam) [XIV] Known as *al-Dajjal* ('the deceiver'), Anti-Christ plays an important role in Islamic eschatology (AKHIRA; QIYAMA) as the false MESSIAH whose appearance on earth will presage the end of the world and the Last Judgement. *Al-Dajjal* is pictured in HADITH (the idea is absent from the QUR'AN) as a one-eyed monster with the name Kafir ('unbeliever') branded on his forehead, who will appear from the East (certain sources localize this as Indonesia) and establish a reign of tyranny for 40 days or years before being vanquished by JESUS or the MAHDI in Palestine or Syria. [10 'Dajjāl'; 21 'Dadjdjāl; 39 'Al-Masīḥu'd-Dajjāl']

Anti-Cult Movement [XXI] The term 'anti-cult movement' covers numerous groups and individuals constituting a backlash to the NEW RELIGIOUS MOVEMENTS (generically referred to as 'cults') which swept across North America and Europe in the 1970s [44]. Membership of the movement consists largely of relatives of converts to the new religions, but there are also strong components of ex-cultists, 'concerned persons', and adherents of more established religious movements (particularly Evangelical Christians) who are anxious to expose theological error as well as the allegedly harmful aspects of the cults. [8; 11; 12; 16; 25; 26; 37; 46; 47; 57] Many of these allegations are similar to those historically made about religions now generally considered socially respectable (e.g. CHRISTIANITY (EARLY), JUDAISM, METHODISM, the QUAKER movement and ROMAN CATHOLICISM). Criticisms most frequently levelled at the contemporary cults include allegations of brainwashing, the splitting up of families, bizarre sexual practices, the amassing of large fortunes for leaders by exploited followers, tax evasion, and political intrigue. [3] The mass suicide

in 1978 of members of the PEOPLE'S TEMPLE has provided a particularly potent cause for anxiety for the movement.

Groups in the movement disseminate anti-cult propaganda through newsletters and the media. They can also employ various degrees of persuasion to remove persons from the cults. These range from informal counselling to illegal kidnapping and the 'deprogramming' of 'victims' [1; 15: V; 34]. In the U.S.A. there have been several attempts (some of which have been successful) to institute legal proceedings which allow cult members to be held against their expressed wishes (by, for example, conservatorship orders).

Main targets for attack have included the CHILDREN OF GOD, HARE KRISHNA, SCIENTOLOGY, TRANSCENDENTAL MEDITATION, and the UNIFICATION CHURCH, but almost all the new religions have been critically examined by the anti-cultists and deprogramming attempts have been extended to converts to Catholic, Episcopal, and BAPTIST churches.

Since the late 1970s there has been a further development, particularly in the U.S.A., in the rise of an anti-anti-cult movement. The membership of this is composed of some members of the cults themselves and of various bodies and persons concerned with civil liberties and/or religious freedom.

Anti-Semitism [XVII] Antagonism to Jews on religious, economic, or racial grounds [9 vol. 3: 87]. Prejudice against Jews was widespread in the pre-Christian era, but active persecution of Jews is inextricably bound up with Christian attitudes towards them. They were accused of being deicides, collectively responsible for the death of JESUS. They were thought to desecrate the consecrated wafer used in the EUCHARIST, and to perform the ritual murder of Christian children whose blood went into the unleavened bread eaten at Passover. This latter accusation, known as a 'blood libel', was often the excuse for Christian pogroms against Jews, ending in pillage, rape, and massacre [26: 171; 31: 402]. During the Middle Ages Jews were expelled from almost every country of Christian Europe. They were forbidden to own land or engage in the crafts but were restricted to lending money at interest or to peddling. The influence of Christianity on anti-Semitism may be seen by comparing the situation of Jews in Christian lands with that of Jews in Islamic countries. In the latter they were second-class citizens, having to pay special taxes, but they were rarely forced to convert to another faith, or to live at the mercy of mob rule. Jewish attitudes to GENTILES have been shaped by the history of anti-Semitism, culminating in the Nazi HOLOCAUST of 1939–45 [25: VII; 52: XIV].

Antioch, Early Christianity at [XI.A] There was a substantial Jewish settlement in Antioch on the Orontes from its foundation in 300 BCE. In the dispersal of Hellenistic Christians from Judaea after Stephen's death (33 CE), many came to Antioch and spread their message there, first among the Jews and then also among Greek-speaking pagans. Many of these embraced CHRISTIANITY; Antioch thus became the headquarters of the first Gentile CHURCH and the centre from which Cilicia, Cyprus, and central Asia Minor were evangelized in the following decades. [4: 129–33, 175–87]

Anukampa [IX.B] The motivation which impels a BUDDHA and his ARAHAT disciples to teach. *Anukampa*, 'sympathy', which leads them to give help to the world at large, is distinguished from *karuna*, 'compassion', which refers to the meditational practice of extending compassion to all living beings. In later Buddhism, especially the MAHAYANA, *karuna* is used for both purposes and the concept of the wider compassion (*mahakaruna*) of a Buddha is introduced. [39]

Apocalyptic [XI.A] A genre of Jewish and Christian literature, called after the Apocalypse, the New Testament Revelation to John. The word means 'unveiling', and apocalyptic literature undertakes to disclose matters inaccessible to normal knowledge, such as the mysteries of outer space or (more especially) those of the future, often in symbolic language. The heyday of apocalyptic was the period 175 BCE to 135 CE. Apocalyptic frequently takes the form of visions allegedly seen by a figure of the past, like Enoch or Ezra. (FRASHOKERETI; MESSIAH) [16: XXXII]

Apostles [XI.A] In early Christianity the designation 'apostles' (from the Greek word meaning 'to send out') was first given to the twelve DISCIPLES, whom JESUS CHRIST sent two by two throughout Galilee as an extension of his own ministry. In the first days of the JERUSALEM church they were its leaders. The designation later included others whom Jesus after his resurrection commissioned to preach in his name, such as his brother James and, pre-eminently, PAUL.

Among the original apostles Peter was outstanding. After leading the Jerusalem church for some twenty years he embarked on a wider ministry in the eastern Mediterranean which brought him ultimately to ROME, where he was martyred under the Roman Emperor Nero (54–68 CE). John, another leading apostle, was associated in later life with EPHESUS. His brother James was executed by Herod Agrippa I about 43 CE. Of the later career of most of the original apostles nothing is known. [3: 168–9, 200]

'Aqida [XIV] 'Creed', in ISLAM. The profession of faith in the unity of God and the prophethood of MUHAMMAD (SHAHADA) provides a simple basic creed for believers, and it is this alone which is used liturgically in the Muslim worship (SALAT). However, as Islam has developed, various theological schools and conflicting sects (FIRQA) have embodied their beliefs and principles in more formal documents, comparable e.g. to the Christian CREEDS. Although basically arising from within Islam itself, the wording and argumentation of some of these may have been influenced by techniques of Greek philosophical discussion (KALAM) [43: 339–71; 52: 294–370]. Both Sunni and Shi'i creeds exist (SHI'ISM; SUNNA), but there is no consensus even within these two main groups of Muslims concerning one particular, supremely valid document. [10 'Creed (Islam)'; 21 ''Akīda'; 82]

Arahat [IX.A] Alternatively *arahant* (Sanskrit *arhat* or *arhant*), from the verbal root *arh*, 'to be worthy', this term is used in THERAVADA to denote one who has achieved the goal of the Buddhist life, that is, one who has gained insight into the true nature of things. Thus, the BUDDHA was the first *arahat*, according to Theravadins. A major criticism levelled by the exponents of the MAHAYANA against the *arahat* ideal was that it was essentially a selfish goal, a striving for liberation that did not entail working for the liberation of all beings. This ideal was contrasted with that of the BODHISATTVA. [4: 93ff]

Architecture (Christian) [XI.B] Early Christian worship was in houses, later specifically adapted for the purpose. There followed the basilica, a rectangular building with a semicircular apse for the altar at one end, and sometimes a separate baptistery for baptism (since early times 'altar' in Christianity has denoted the table where the 'elements' of the EUCHARIST are placed). In the East, domed churches developed which have remained characteristic to this day; and the building itself acts as an ICON. In the West the basic rectangle persisted, divided into a nave (for the congregation) and chancel (for the priest and main altar). Church plans then grew more elaborate (especially those of cathedrals and monasteries – *see* CHURCH ORGANIZATION) to allow for multiple altars and masses. They also reflected the increased numbers and enhanced status of the priesthood – and more elaborate worship. The medieval Gothic cathedral [50; 108: III, IV] was a complex symbol of the heavenly Jerusalem, expressed in the vertical emphasis of the building. Churches were filled with images which were the 'Bible' of the illiterate laity [43; 99: VIII]. Renaissance centre-plan domed churches of the 15th century used styles influenced by classical antiquity. They have been accused of being merely 'humanist' [108: 182–4]. Their architects, however, explained them in religious NEOPLATONIC terms as symbols of God [145: I]. The COUNTER-REFORMATION compromised between the centralized domed church and the basilican rectangle. Their luxuriant, even theatrical baroque ornament and images emphasized ROMAN CATHOLIC doctrine and devotion, unlike PROTESTANTISM, in a highly emotional way [108: VI]. Protestantism drastically purged images for theological reasons. The English Dissenters and their American followers used plain buildings suited to worship based on preaching rather than on sacraments [28 vol. 2]. Churches in ANGLICANISM reflected the use of sacramental worship, fixed liturgy, and preaching. In the 19th century Anglo-Catholics pioneered a revival of Gothic. The LITURGICAL MOVEMENT encourages centralized church plans; and style is now influenced by modern architecture and materials [30: 21–41; 57]. Churches were formerly used for many social as well as religious purposes [29].

Ardas [XXVII] The 'Petition', a formal prayer recited at the conclusion of Sikh RITUALS (GURDWARA). It begins with an invocation extolling the 10 GURUS. This is followed by an intermediate section recalling past trials and triumphs of the PANTH. Finally there comes the actual prayer of petition. Although an approved Punjabi text has been published [17: 2–3] only the first eight and last two lines are unalterable. Elsewhere the wording may be varied and personal intercessions introduced. [4: 180–83; 6: 95–111; 26: x]

Arguments for the Existence of God [XI.C] In Western thought there are generally considered to be five arguments for the existence of God: (1) The *ontological* argument, classically given by ANSELM and R. Descartes (1596–1650) and recently reworked by Hartshorne (b. 1897) (PROCESS THEOLOGY). It maintains that the concept of God as perfect entails that he be regarded as existing – for Hartshorne as existing necessarily – since otherwise he would not be perfect. The argument is mainly criticized for illegitimately inferring reality from a concept. (2) The *cosmological* argument, classically given by Aquinas (*c.* 1225–74) (THOMISM). It argues from the contingent or causal nature of reality that it must have a necessary ground, a 'first cause', identified as God. Critics argue that the contingent quality of reality does not show either that it had an absolutely first originator or that the qualities of such a primal entity must be those of 'God'. (3) The *teleological* argument, classically found in W. Paley (1743–1805). It argues from supposed evidence of design or purpose in the world to its having an intelligent Creator. Critics question whether there is such evidence and, if there is, whether it indicates creation by a perfect being. The most famous critics of the above arguments are D. Hume (1711–76) and I. Kant (1724–1804). (4) The *moral* argument, offered by Kant and H. Rashdall (1858–1924). It asserts that moral obligation is only adequately understood when it is held to point to God as the source or justification of the moral sense. Critics question this interpretation of moral experience. (5) The *experiential* argument, as in A. E. Taylor (1869–1945) and John Baillie (1886–1960). It holds that God's reality is so self-evident that on reflection it cannot justifiably be doubted. Critics challenge the interpretation of the experience as being neither justified nor self-evident. [8; 11]

Arianism [XI.C] A doctrine which held that JESUS CHRIST was not of one substance with GOD but had been created by 'God the Father' as the medium of creation. Christ, although not God by nature, was held to have received the status of 'Son of God' from God on account of his perfect goodness. The name 'Arianism' comes from Arius (*c.* 250 to *c.* 336 CE), who maintained these views in ALEXANDRIA. Under the influence of Athanasius (*c.* 296–373), Arian views were condemned at the Council of Nicaea (COUNCILS OF THE CHURCH) in 325. [6; 10]

Arioi [XXII] A pre-Christian fertility cult of travelling actors and actresses in the Society Islands, similar to Hawaiian *hula* dancers. Their mythical founder was the god ORO. Even commoners could rise through the ranks of *arioi* societies to gain divine patronage and great MANA (but only for themselves, as most members with offspring were required to practise infanticide). *Arioi* initiates believed that a heaven of sensual delights awaited their spirits after death. [16; 22; 30]

Ariya-Sacca [IX.A] The 'noble truths', in THERAVADA Buddhism. They are four in number: (1) all forms of existence are subject to suffering (DUKKHA); (2) suffering and rebirth are produced by desire, or craving (*tanha*); (3) the cessation of suffering comes with the complete cessation of craving; (4) the cessation of craving is reached by means of the noble EIGHTFOLD PATH. These four 'noble truths' constitute the central teaching of the BUDDHA (GOTAMA). [4: 43–8]

Arminianism [XI.B] The Dutch theologian Jacobus Arminius (1560–1609) modified the doctrines of CALVINISM, especially predestination. His followers protested against Calvinism in the *Remonstrance* (1610) [11: 268–9]. This declaration allowed for free will in man's SALVATION and asserted that

JESUS CHRIST died for all men. They were condemned at the synod of Dort (Dordrecht, the Netherlands, 1618–19). Later Arminians in Holland and England inclined to UNITARIANISM and questioned substitutionary views of the Atonement (cf. SALVATION). But by the 18th century most METHODISTS and ANGLICANS combined orthodoxy on these points with rejection of predestination. [107: 90]

Art (in Islam) [XIV] The fundamental religious feature of Islamic art is usually held to be the ban on depicting living forms. This seems to have arisen not so much from explicit Qur'anic doctrine (the QUR'AN attacks images, but as focuses for idolatry) as from both a fear of rivalling God's creative power and a general indifference to the representational and aesthetic side of religious experience, later given a retroactive legal basis by HADITH. An influence from Byzantine iconoclasm seems improbable [33: IV, VII; 47: 252–3]. In fact, representation of living beings has nevertheless flourished in the arts of e.g. Persia, India, and Turkey, despite pious disapproval; yet the archetypal decorative motifs in Islam have been vegetal and arabesque, seen especially in religious architecture such as MOSQUES, mausoleums [56], etc., with emphasis also on calligraphy [66A] and artistic forms of the Arabic script. [7; 10 'Art, sacred (Islam)'; 24; 34; 44; 49: II; 64: IX]

Art (Jewish) [XVII] Jewish attitudes to representational art have differed down the ages, but one can trace a deeply held suspicion of the use of ICONOGRAPHY for religious purposes. The BIBLE associated the making of images with idolatry, and this attitude carried over into rabbinical and medieval JUDAISM. The 3rd-century Dura Europos SYNAGOGUE remains, with many murals of biblical scenes, indicate that some early Jewish communities were not averse to using art-forms as long as God himself was not represented [34: 1]. Synagogues in the Middle Ages tended not to have human figures for decoration, and abstract designs or animals like the lion were preferred. This is still the practice today. Jewish craftsmen devoted their creative energies to scribal arts, to illustrating manuscripts, and to fashioning ceremonial objects in silver and gold. In general Jewish culture has influenced Jews to express themselves through instrumental music (MUSIC), song, literature, and poetry rather than through representational art, which has no Jewish cultural roots. [9 vol. 3: 499; 24: 1]

Art and Symbolism (Ancient Egyptian) [IV] Art-forms in ancient Egypt were primarily developed for religious purposes, and then extended for secular use. Architectural innovations were devised for tomb and temple architecture (MANSION OF THE GODS; MANSION OF THE KA; PYRAMIDS); relief sculpture

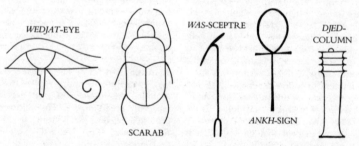

WEDJAT-EYE   SCARAB   WAS-SCEPTRE   ANKH-SIGN   DJED-COLUMN

See ART AND SYMBOLISM (ANCIENT EGYPTIAN)

and wall-painting were developed for religious decoration; and craftsmen employed in the minor arts and jewellery-making supplied items for FUNERARY PRACTICES. Although often exquisitely executed, the prime function of all religious art-forms was to provide models and representations of animate or inanimate objects which could be magically activated.

Various symbols achieved widespread popularity and magical significance in Egypt; these included the *ankh* (life), *djed* (stability), and *was* (dominion) signs; the scarab or dung-beetle (renewal of life); and the *wedjat*-eye (spiritual and physical wholeness). Amulets in these forms were made for both the living and the dead, to give protection against evil and dominion (MAGIC). Symbolism was present in many aspects of religion, including representations of RE' and Osiris (OSIRIAN TRIAD) reaffirming their cyclic rebirth (AFTERLIFE).

Art and Symbolism (Ancient Near Eastern) [VI] Monuments, reliefs, sculpture, and cylinder seals all provide additional information regarding ancient Near Eastern religions [5; 6]. Finest metalwork, shell-engraving, and mosaic-work are evident in the grave-goods from the royal cemetery at Ur [26]. Monumental stone bas-reliefs decorating HITTITE religious centres (1250–1220 BCE) indicate the debt they owed to earlier Mesopotamian sources [1: 195–214]. Seal impressions show the characteristics of many deities in the presence of their worshippers.

Animals sometimes occur as the cult symbols of deities – a bull for the Hittite weather-god [13: 134], the dragon (ANCIENT NEAR EASTERN RELIGIONS) as the symbol of EVIL [13: 181], and the serpent as an ELAMITE divinity [17: 38]. Other symbols sometimes replaced the human form: Hittite underworld deities were sometimes represented as swords and the *huwasi* stone (an inscribed or decorated stele) could replace a god's

statue [13: 149]. Gigantic animals perhaps symbolized natural cycles and semi-divine beings (half-human and half plant or animal) probably represented the land's fertility in Elam [17: 37].

Artha [XIII.A] One of the four goals of life recognized in Hindu tradition (KAMA, DHARMA, and MOKSHA being the other three) [1: 211–15]. *Artha* represents the whole range of activities associated with material gain and the protection of it [1: 236–57]; in other words, the world as dealt with by economists and politicians. Hindu tradition includes a special classical treatise dealing with this realm of life (and others dealing with *kama* and *dharma*): this is the *Artha-shastra*, the authorship of which is attributed to Kautilya, the BRAHMAN minister of Candragupta, the Indian emperor of the 4th century BCE [2: 51]. It is a feature of *Artha-shastra* that it 'concerned itself primarily with the attainment of the ends irrespective of the nature of the means employed'. [1: 237]

Arupa-Loka [IX.A] In Buddhist cosmology, the highest of the three spheres in which beings are subject to continual rebirth. Above the gross sphere of sensual pleasure (*kama-loka*), and above the world of form-only (*rupa-loka*), this highest sphere is one of 'formlessness'. Beings are reborn in this sphere as a result of the practice of concentration (SAMADHI). Within the sphere of formlessness there are four levels, based on four successive stages of attainment of concentration.

Ashkenazim [XVII] Jews from Christian Europe. In the late Middle Ages when the European and West Asian worlds were divided between Christian and Islamic countries, the Jewish people also found itself divided into two main groups. The term *Ashkenazi*, originally meaning 'German', was applied to Jews of central and eastern Europe [9 vol. 3: 719]. The main Jewish communities of the early Middle Ages were in the Franco-German Rhineland

(EUROPEAN JEWRY) whence they spread east to Poland and Russia. Hence the name *Ashkenazim*. *Ashkenazi* Jewry, cut off from SEFARDI Jewry in Islamic lands, developed its own cultural complex, customs, traditions of interpreting the TALMUD, pronunciation of Hebrew, calligraphy, MUSIC, and its own lingua franca, Yiddish – an originally German dialect with Hebrew and Slavic accretions. *Ashkenazim* and *Sefardim* do not differ in theology or basic Jewish practice [52: 211; 54]. In modern times the vast majority of Jews are of *Ashkenazi* stock, and they have dominated Jewish intellectual and cultural life.

Ashoka [IX.A] An Indian emperor of the 3rd century BCE, whose edicts, inscribed on rock faces and pillars, provide evidence of his policy of promoting *Dhamma*. This is not identical with the DHAMMA of the Buddhist canon, although there are resemblances; Ashoka's *Dhamma* appears to have consisted in the cultivation of moral virtues. There are many legends about Ashoka, notably in the Pali chronicles of Ceylon (DIPAVAMSA and MAHAVAMSA) and the corpus of legends known as *Divyavadana*, and in a Sanskrit text, the *Ashokavadana*, which is found also in a Chinese version. [17: 184–202; 35]

Ashrama [XIII.A] A stage of human life, of which there are four in the Hindu tradition: (1) that of the pupil, or *brahmacarin*; (2) the householder, or *grhastha*; (3) the forest-dweller, or *vanaprastha*; and (4) finally, when all human ties are ended with the total renunciation of the world, the stage of the *sannyasin*. Each of these ashramas has its own appropriate rule of life or DHARMA; there are thus four *ashrama-dharmas*. The four may rarely have been fully followed in reality, but the existence of the scheme emphasizes what is regarded as the ideal way of life. It has been suggested that the scheme affirms the necessity of the householder stage in order to counter the practice followed by some ascetic movements of omitting this stage and passing directly to homelessness, which thereby robs society in so far as families are not founded [2: 160; 25: 146]. Even among Hindus the four stages apply only to the 'twice-born' classes or VARNAS.

Asia and the Pacific, New Religious Movements in [XX] In Asia the Burkhan (meaning BUDDHA) millennial movement among the Altai Mountains Kalmucks from 1904 was anti-SHAMAN and anti-Christian. Some 300 new religions have appeared in Korea since about 1860, when Tonghak (Eastern Learning) began, and one, T'ongil Kyohoe, has spread widely in the rest of the world as the UNIFICATION CHURCH. The hill and forest tribes of India in interaction with Hindu and Christian influences have produced many reforming and prophet movements [6], and in Burma, Thailand, and Vietnam there have been similar reactions to Buddhism and Christianity. Indonesian movements are often messianic (MESSIAH) and apocalyptic, usually with traditional and Christian sources, but especially in Java drawing on Islamic and JAVANESE mysticism. Agama Islam Desjati (True Islamic Religion) from 1950 represents a rare anti-Arab syncretistic form. The Bungan cult in Kalimantan and Sarawak from 1947 has been a reforming Christian syncretism. In the PHILIPPINES [5] millennial revolts are endemic and include the intermittent syncretistic Colorum movements; also millennial but more nationalistic are the many Rizalist cults believing in a return of the national martyr, José Rizal; chief of these is the Watawat ng Lahi (Banner of the Race). The largest movement is the IGLESIA NI CRISTO (Church of Christ). MELANESIAN movements [20] often take the form of CARGO CULTS but there are also more political forms, such as Paliau's movement on Manus from 1946 and the Hahalis Welfare Society on Buka Island from the 1950s [19: 466–

83], and independent churches such as Sila Eto's CHRISTIAN FELLOWSHIP CHURCH in the Solomon Islands from 1959. Hawaii and the POLYNESIANS also have independent churches such as the Congregation of the Poor and the Daku Community in Fiji; the main MAORI MOVEMENTS are Ratana and Ringatu. Australian (AUSTRALIAN RELIGION) aboriginals have produced few movements apart from the peaceful Elcho Island cult from about 1958 and some Pentecostal churches (PENTECOSTAL-ISM) more recently. [12: V–VII; 17: 703–4; 19: 73–5]

Asia, Christianity in [XI.B] A few Monophysites and Nestorians (CHRIST-OLOGY) reached INDIA and CHINA in early centuries. Monophysitism once had substantial churches in western Asia, but competition with other Christians undermined them in the face of Islam; and Christianity was permanently weakened in this area. Substantial penetration of India, China, and JAPAN came with Roman Catholic (ROMAN CATHOLICISM) MISSIONS of friars and Jesuits (MONASTICISM) from the 16th century. They were decimated by persecution a century later. Fresh work in these areas came with Protestant missions and renewed Roman Catholic effort in the 19th century. These efforts were most successful in the South Seas, less secure in China, and not numerous in Japan [39]. Indigenous cultures and major religions (BUDDHISM; HINDUISM; ISLAM) have proved generally resistant to Christianity in Asia, except possibly in the Philippines and Vietnam. Nationalism has also given an adverse image to Christianity as an alien Western religion. [82 vol. 3: X–XIV, vol. 6: IV–VII; 83 vol. 3: XVIII–XXIII, vol. 5: XI–XVI]

Assyrians [VI] The classical age of Sumer (SUMERIANS) was brought to an end by the conquest of the city-states by Sargon of Agade, a northern ruler. Sargon and these Akkadian kings created the idea of a universal empire and, many years later, the Assyrians adopted the same concept [18].

Ashur, a trading city in the Ur III empire, successfully maintained independence when the Kassites took Babylonia and the north fell to the HURRIANS. Although incorporated into the loose confederation of Mitannian states, Mitanni's weakness eventually enabled Ashur to assert its independence under Ashur-uballit I (1365–1330 BCE), the first real king of 'Assyria'; and with the later emergence of Assyria, Ashur retained its prominent position.

The idea of a universal empire was embodied in the concept of a universal deity. The cult of Sin, the moon-god, played an important role throughout Assyrian history, and he had many centres – Ur in Babylonia, Harran in Mesopotamia, in Lebanon, and in Palestine. In the Neo-Assyrian period, he became royal patron (KINGSHIP), and Shamash the sun-god was also widely revered. However, the religion was overwhelmingly dominated by the national god, Ashur, who embodied the homeland and the capital city, as well as being a god of the region around Kanesh where many Assyrian merchants lived. Ashur gradually supplanted MARDUK, the Babylonian god, as national deity. Other important deities were Enlil, Adad, and Ishtar. Gods were remote from men, and this was frequently emphasized by the custom of representing them by symbols (ART AND SYMBOLISM). [10]

The Assyrians believed that events on earth reflected the recurrent groupings of the heavenly constellations. It was thought that the 10 deities representing the fixed and moving stars took turns in ruling the universe. Thus, the king of all these lands was expected to reside in a city dedicated to the ruling deity of that particular time-span, and so the kings periodically changed their royal residences to satisfy this belief. There were four capitals: Ashur, Nineveh, Khorsabad, and Nimrud.

They acknowledged and preserved BABYLONIAN culture; Ashur-ban-apli (631 BCE) assembled a corpus of cuneiform literature, including religious and omen texts. In earlier times, Assyria employed scribes trained in Babylonia and built up libraries [25: 38].

Astrology [VIII] The art of predicting the future or of interpreting events, human lives, and character from the positions of the heavenly bodies [general surveys: 2, 11; brief history: 15]. Astrology originated in the taking of astral omens for state purposes in Mesopotamia in the 2nd millennium BCE (ASTROLOGY (ANCIENT NEAR EASTERN)). From about the 5th century it developed there, and subsequently in the Greek world (especially in Egypt after Alexander's conquest), into the technical system for predicting the fates of individuals (HOROSCOPE) which survives today [astrology in the ancient world: 3; 4; 6; 10; 13]. Contrary to popular belief, pre-Greek Egypt contributed virtually nothing. The art reached its definitive form in the Roman empire by c. 100 CE. Refinements were made in the later empire, in the Middle Ages in Byzantium, Islam, and western Europe, in the Renaissance [1], and in modern times (e.g. the inclusion of the planets discovered since the 18th century). Astrology in India, though ultimately derived from Mesopotamian and Greek sources, has developed and flourished in a separate tradition [15: 223]. An entirely independent system developed in China, largely concerned with correspondences between celestial events and the condition of the empire.

Historically, astrology has had links both with scientific astronomy and with religion. Astronomical data are necessary ingredients for astrological predictions, and generally the borderline between astronomy and astrology has been somewhat blurred. Though sometimes treated with scepticism, astrology was until the 18th century usually regarded as a valid branch of a single science (for example, Ptolemy, 2nd century CE, wrote both the greatest text of Greek scientific astronomy, the *Almagest*, and a treatise on astrology, the *Tetrabiblos*). In Mesopotamia, and subsequently in the Graeco-Roman world, STAR-WORSHIP fostered the growth and influence of astrology [6; 7; 10]. Logically, however, astrology is independent of religion, and in the West with the triumph of Christianity it was accepted that the stars were no more than the indicators, not the ultimate agents, of fate. Nevertheless, astrology has always raised quasi-religious questions, notably the problem of determinism: if the future can be foretold, it is presumably determined; what place then is left for human free will? It was on that ground that astrology was in the past most vehemently attacked (modern astrologers, though, concern themselves more with human character than with future events and so sidestep the issue). Modern criticism focuses more on the scientific implausibility of astrology [5]. Although it still enjoys a certain vogue (millions, with more or less credulity, follow in the daily newspapers forecasts which are astrologically very naïve) and is practised by a relatively few dedicated adepts [apologetics: 8; 16; manuals: 12; 14], educated opinion in the West now generally holds that astrology is outside the realm of intellectual respectability and thus valueless [critiques: 5; 7]. Recently, however, there have been attempts to re-establish at least parts of it on a statistical and empirical basis [8].

Astrology (**Ancient Egyptian**) [IV] The practice of astrology was imported into Egypt from Mesopotamia, perhaps in the Persian period (c. 500 BCE). The use of hemerology – the determination of lucky and unlucky days – was derived from mythology and not from astrology. However, the Egyptians had a long-standing interest in astronomy; 'star-ceilings', with charts of the heavens, occur in tombs and temples [7]. These were tables giving the movements of the stars at night. Also, a calendar, based on the agricultural year, was devised and used – at least from earliest historical times (*c.* 3100 BCE).

Astrology (Ancient Near Eastern) [VI] Astrology [22] superseded extispicy (DIVINATION) as the favoured method for obtaining omens for political and military purposes in Mesopotamia in the 2nd millennium BCE. Individual fates could be determined by portents, warnings of the gods, or predicted by the HOROSCOPE, which was developed later. Both the Egyptians and the Greeks adopted some aspects of its study. According to the Epic of Creation [24: 60–71], each great god was assigned a position in the sky, and each star or constellation was allotted to one of these deities.

Asura [IX.A] In Indian mythology a class of non-human beings who are the enemies of the *devas* (heavenly beings), and thus represented as responsible for encouraging evil tendencies. There is controversy concerning the relation of these beings in Indian mythology with the Iranian *ahura* (AHURA MAZDA; ZOROASTRIANISM). Both traditions descend from the Indo-Iranians (INDO-EUROPEANS) but the roles of the *asuras* (Iranian *ahuras*) and *devas* (Iranian *daevas*) appear to be reversed. In the ATHARVA-VEDA *asura* is used collectively, and indicates hostile beings. In Pali Buddhist literature (THERAVADA) the most frequent references are in connection with continual war between *asuras* and *devas*. In MAHAYANA Buddhist literature they constitute one of the six forms of existence, together with denizens of hell, ghosts, animals, humans, and *devas*. Other, minor forms of evil spirits mentioned in Buddhist literature (from common Indian folklore) are *pisacas* and *yakkhas*. [19: 21–6]

Atenism [IV] The Aten (sun's disc) is mentioned long before AKHENATEN's reign, but he elevated the god to an unprecedented status (*c.* 1360 BCE). Aten-

ism was a version of the Heliopolitan doctrine (RE') [5], but the deity now became 'sole god' and a universal source of life. Atenism continued the 'monotheistic' trend already evident in AMUN's cult, but also expressed a uniquely close relationship between god and king. New, roofless temples (MANSION OF THE GODS) were built at Thebes, Amarna, and elsewhere [22: X, 122].

Atharva-Veda [XIII.A] A collection of ancient Indian hymns, chants, and spells, which was later added to the existing collection of VEDA material. The contents are different in nature from the earlier collections (*Rig-veda*, etc.), which were mainly addressed to the gods of the Aryans (INDO-EUROPEANS), whereas this consists to a larger extent of charms (of various kinds and for various purposes), exorcisms, magical spells, and incantations. Some of the material contained in the *Atharva* is, however, of cosmological nature. This is a later development of some of the speculative material about the origin of the universe which is found in the tenth and last book of the *Rig-veda*. Compared with most of the earlier Vedic material, however, there are few hymns in the *Atharva* addressed to specific gods, and the general stance is pantheistic.

These differences have been explained as being due to the extent to which the ideas and cultic practices of the immigrant Aryan pastoral tribes had been influenced by those of the more predominantly agricultural people of north-west India, whose territory they had invaded. [14: 57f; 19: 72–8; 26: 15–30]

Atheism [XXVIII] (1) Disbelief in the existence of any GODS or of God. This may take the form of: (a) dogmatic rejection of specific beliefs, e.g. of THEISM; (b) scepticism about all religious claims; or (c) agnosticism, the view that humans can never be certain in matters of so-called religious knowledge (e.g. whether God exists or not) [17: 110]. An atheist may hold belief in

God to be false, or irrational, or meaningless [6: VI; 12: 160–61; 13: 3–4; 24: 238].

(2) A form of religion which rejects the reality or ultimacy of all superhuman beings [13: 31; 17: 114–19].

Atman [XIII.A] A Sanskrit word, the earlier meaning of which in the *Rig-veda* (VEDA) is 'breath', but whose later meaning is 'soul' or 'principle of life' and 'the person or whole body considered as one and opposed to the separate members of the body' [15: 135]. Eventually, in the philosophy of the Upanishads, *atman* is equated absolutely with BRAHMAN, the impersonal absolute.

Atua [XXII] Gods and supernatural beings in POLYNESIAN RELIGION, other than the uncreated supreme being (TANGAROA or IO). Highest 'departmental' gods are TANE (light and forests), Tu (war), Rongo (cultivation), Whiro (underworld), Haumia (uncultivated food), and Tawhiri (storm). Hine, the first woman, formed from earth by Tane, becomes goddess of darkness and guardian of Po, the place of the dead. As the moon-goddess Hina she teaches crafts to women, giving her name to heroines in many legends. Pele is the great Hawaiian goddess of volcanoes. [15; 22] Lesser tribal *atua*, local gods. goddesses, and spirits regulate everyday life, punishing breaches of *tapu* (TABU) by sickness or accident. They guide devout worshippers through dreams and omens. Ghosts (*kehua*) and monsters (*taniwha*) are also *atua*, who guard their own people but can be used by sorcerers to harm others. When pleased by offerings and ritual chants (*karakia*) *atua* may communicate through a medium or prophet (*taura*), or become present in animals, images, or the TOHUNGA's carved 'god-stick'. Right relations with the *atua* result in MANA, the power which comes from kinship between gods and mortals. [6; 7; 16; 30]

Augustinianism [XI.C] A movement of Christian thought influenced by doctrines classically developed by Augus-

tine of Hippo (334–430 CE). Against the Manichaeans (MANI), he maintained that GOD was the sole creator and that evil is a lack of some good; against the Donatists he argued that it was the purposes and not the character of its adherents that made the CHURCH 'holy'. He regarded the civil authorities as serving God's providence and as good so far as they acted justly. Against PELAGIANISM he developed doctrines of the Fall, Original SIN, and Predestination, holding that by heredity man is tainted by sin and that God, acting in inexplicable wisdom and justice, has chosen ('elected' or 'predestined') only some persons to be saved, the rest being consigned to everlasting damnation. [6; 10; 12]

Auspicia [XXV] The *auspicia* (omens) were the special province of the Roman augurs (SACERDOTES) and were sent by Jupiter, as the chief state-god. The senior officials (magistrates) in charge, either in Rome or on campaign, had the right to take the *auspicia*, to consult the gods about the coming action; the augur was the expert adviser or interpreter [6: 598]. The original *auspicia* were taken from the flight of birds, interpreted in relation to the appointed TEMPLA; other techniques were accepted later. The signs were divided into those sought deliberately by the magistrate (*signa impetrativa*) and those sent unasked (*signa oblativa*), which were held to be valid only if actually observed by the magistrate [6: 594–600; 12: 10–19; 17: 55–9]. In early times all action, public or private, was supposed to be accompanied by *auspicia*, but by the late Republic (*c.* 100–31 BCE) constitutional change had separated command from the old rituals and under the empire, although augurs continued to be appointed until the 4th century CE, their importance was lost [12: 63].

Australasia, Christianity in [XI.B] Christianity in Australia originated in British and, later, European churches, conditioned by colonial experience.

Some Anglicans evidently carried church 'establishment' ideas with them, which failed in face of competition from other churches. Public money, which was often available for church buildings and schools, by the 1870s gave way to self-support. Churches gained independence from Europe at different times, from ANGLICANISM as late as 1962. ROMAN CATHOLICISM was originally strongly Irish and working-class, influenced by anti-English feeling, and involved in the founding of the Australian Labour Party. Social differences between the churches today are much reduced. Australian missionary work is chiefly in Papua New Guinea [82 vol. 5: V, vol. 7: VIII; 83 vol. 3: XIII, vol. 5: VI]. New Zealand missions came with colonization in the 19th century, predominantly Anglicanism with substantial PRESBYTERIANISM and METHODISM. The indigenous Maoris eventually became officially Christian but some joined charismatic cults [65: 260–65]. (ASIA AND THE PACIFIC, NEW RELIGIOUS MOVEMENTS IN; MELANESIAN RELIGION; PACIFIC RELIGIONS; PHILIPPINES RELIGION) [82 vol. 5: VI, vol. 7: VIII; 83 vol. 3: XIV, vol. 5: VII]

Australian Religion [XXII] The Aborigines of Australia have one of the oldest living religions, although Christian and Western incursions in recent times have been highly destructive of it. Tribal differences across the vast continent make a general description difficult, but the Aranda of central Australia have a typical system. It is based on 'totemic ancestors', supernatural beings who are *altjiranga ngambakala*, 'born of eternity' (*see* WONDJINA and DEMA DEITIES), who shaped the landscape into a habitable place filled with their various sacred animals, plants, or natural phenomena; and a concept of sacred time or eternity (ALTJIRANGA) expressed in sacred myths, rituals, and objects (TJURUNGA). Each human being is an incarnation of one of these ancestors

(the spirit having entered the foetus when the pregnant mother passed by the sacred spot where the totemic ancestor sleeps). The ancestor continues his or her slumber even though reincarnated and, indeed, in more than one child at the same time.

The person receives his totem from his particular ancestor (be it a plant, an animal, or a heavenly body such as the sun). A male kangaroo person, for example, after being initiated into his totemic clan, is empowered and obliged to perform 'increase rituals' to ensure the constant supply of kangaroo meat to his community. Women have their own secret traditions and rites, but male relatives carry out totemic rituals for them. Initiation for boys, after puberty, was by physical ordeal, such as circumcision, subincision (cutting the urethra), and removal of a tooth.

Each person is in a sense his or her own priest, but the medicine-man has special powers of divination, healing, and sorcery (e.g. the death-rite of bone-pointing, *see* TJURUNGA); his powers often come through visionary experience of the totemic ancestors and their insertion of quartz crystals in his body [11]. Everyone has two souls, one human and immortal derived from the natural parents, the other immortal and eternal which returns to the totemic ancestor at death. Although the existence of sky beings and even a sky father is widely recognized, they are considered to have no control over mankind: the totemic ancestors of the earth and the social group are the active forces working on a human being. [4; 10; 11; 21; 22; 27]

Authority (Christian) [XI.B] Christianity claims that its truth rests ultimately on a revelation from God through JESUS CHRIST, transmitted through scripture (BIBLE) and 'tradition' in the CHURCH. The early church regarded 'tradition' as Christian belief centred in the CREEDS of major church centres. For the ORTHODOX CHURCH 'tradition' is the living authority of the church's whole life and teaching, which includes scripture. ROMAN CATHOLICISM sees Christian truth as contained in scripture and 'tradition'. The Catholic church's developing understanding of both is promulgated infallibly as 'dogma' (doctrines binding on Catholics) through COUNCILS and the PAPACY [19]. The Council of Trent (1545–63) asserted that scripture and 'tradition' were to be received as of equal authority; but Vatican Council II (1962–5) appeared to minimize the distinction [1: 114–18]. PROTESTANTISM originally appealed to the Bible alone for authority, interpreted by individuals under the guidance of the HOLY SPIRIT. However, Confessions of Faith and church authority soon provided a fresh 'tradition'. Christians have often claimed that reason can by itself discover some religious truths (NATURAL THEOLOGY) as well as interpret revelation. Since the 18th century in the West reason has sometimes (e.g. DEISM) seemed to overshadow church authority if not scripture, especially for LIBERAL PROTESTANTISM. But Protestant 'Fundamentalism' takes scripture alone as an infallible guide. [31; 76: II; 89; 129]

Autocephaly [XI.C] Self-government. Fully independent ORTHODOX CHURCHES are called autocephalous. Churches which enjoy a large measure of independence but rely on their mother church, e.g. for the appointment of their most senior hierarch, are called autonomous. In principle every local church is the CHURCH, rather than part of it. Autocephaly represents the interface between this theological principle and the need for order required by the COMMUNION of the individual local churches with each other.

Avadana [IX.A] A type of Buddhist Sanskrit literature consisting in legends of past Buddhist heroes. In PALI literature the form *apadana* is used. Outside Buddhist literature the term denotes a 'heroic exploit', as applied, for instance, to RAMA.

Avalokiteshvara [IX.A] The most popular BODHISATTVA in the MAHAYANA Buddhist tradition. A compound name from Avalokita and ISHVARA, of which the meaning is ambiguous, various meanings have been suggested for Avalokiteshvara, from 'Lord of what we see', or 'Lord who sees', to 'The Lord who looks from on high' and 'Lord of compassionate sight'. (JAPANESE BUDDHAS AND BODHISATTVAS) [16.A] (*See also* KUAN (SHIH) YIN.)

Avatara [XIII.A] The *avatara* is a Hindu concept, signifying the 'descent' (*ava* = down) to earth of the deity. The concept is peculiar to the tradition associated with the worship of the major deity, VISHNU [16: 175–237]. This deity is thought of as assuming human or animal form from time to time in order to save the world from imminent destruction, or chaos, or some other great peril. The forms which he is believed to have assumed in the past are conventionally listed as nine. The first three are non-human: fish, crocodile, and boar. The fourth is a hybrid, a man-lion. The remaining five are human, that is: a dwarf; Rama-with-the-axe (Parasurama); RAMA; KRISHNA; and the BUDDHA. The *avatara*-to-come is Kalkin. The last four of the past *avataras* are probably historical or semi-historical figures. Rama-with-the-axe was, according to tradition, a Brahman who destroyed the KSHATRIYA class when there was a danger that they would dominate the world. The story probably reflects a conflict in early times between the BRAHMAN class and the Kshatriyas for social and political supremacy. The seventh *avatara*, Rama, is the hero of the epic poem the RAMAYANA [19: 133–9]. The sixth, Krishna, is the hero of many legends and stories which deal with him as divine infant, boy, youthful lover, and amorous companion of the *gopis* (milkmaids), and finally, as the divine being who appeared to Arjuna on the eve of the great battle at Kurukshetra and urged Arjuna to do his duty disinterestedly as a member of the warrior class [26: 249–325]. The inclusion of the Buddha in this list of Hindu manifestations of the deity has been explained variously: as a way of subsuming the cult of the Buddha and bringing it under Brahmanical control, and as a subtle way of discrediting the Buddha by interpreting the appearance of the Lord Vishnu in the form of the Buddha (a heretic) as a means of leading astray evil men. To this list of nine past *avataras* has been added a tenth, Kalkin, who will appear at the end of the present age, a messianic figure combining elements of Zoroastrian (FRASHOKERETI) and Hindu eschatology.

Avesta [XXX] The scriptures of ZOROASTRIANISM, traditionally believed to have been revealed in their entirety to ZOROASTER. Only 17 hymns, the *Gathas*, can, however, be attributed to him. Some parts of the Avesta, notably some ancient hymns, *Yashts*, are substantially pre-Zoroastrian in origin, whereas other portions date from approximately the time of Christ. But the contents can, as a whole, be considered pre-Christian in date because (at least by the 1st century) the language of the Avesta was a dead one, used only for recitation of prayers and not for new compositions.

The material was originally transmitted in oral form only. Writing was considered an alien art and therefore unsuitable for sacred words. The passages were memorized by priests. The first move to collect the diverse traditions was probably in Parthian times (early centuries CE), but it was a few centuries before a special, phonetically accurate, alphabet was devised which made it possible to commit the Avesta precisely to writing. The written Avesta was composed in 21 divisions (*nasks*). Copies were preserved in important FIRE temples for scholar priests but

these were, presumably, little used by most Zoroastrians because of the strength of the oral tradition [3: v]. The manuscripts were probably destroyed in the Arab (7th century), Turkish (11th), and Mongol (12th) invasions. The only portions of the Avesta now extant are the liturgical portions memorized and used regularly by priests (MAGI), but judging from ancient summaries this represents only a quarter of the original. Secondary to the Avesta were the translations from the sacred language with commentary. These were known as the *Zand*. The only surviving *Zand* is in PAHLAVI. The Avesta was partly translated into Sanskrit by early Parsi scholars, notably Neryosang Dhaval in the early 12th century.

The main liturgy is the YASNA [translation: 32]. The central section of this is known as the *Staota yesnya* and is considered by many Zoroastrians to be one of the most powerful prayers (MANTHRAS). It was probably one of the first fixed liturgies of the religion. At the heart of the *Yasna* are the 17 hymns of Zoroaster, the *Gathas* (*Yasna* 28–34, 43–51, 53). Encased within these hymns is the 'Yasna Haptanghaiti', substantially a pre-Zoroastrian liturgy adapted to the revealed religion and recited during certain offerings. Other main sections of the Avesta are the *Visperad* [translation: 32], a supplement to the *Yasna*; the *Vendidad*, or *Videvdat* (anti-demonic law) [9]; the *Yashts* (hymns) [10; 17], a number of which are summarized as litanies (*Nyaishes*) [11]. These with other prayers are collected into the *Khordeh* (or smaller) *Avesta* intended for use in private devotions.

Avidya [IX.A] (Sanskrit; literally 'non-knowledge', or lack of understanding of the nature of reality) In its Pali form, *avijja*, it indicates lack of knowledge of the four Noble Truths (ARIYA-SACCA). The inability to see the true nature of things is regarded in Buddhist tradition as the root of all evil.

Ayatullah [XIV] 'Miraculous sign from God', a title held by high dignitaries of the Shi'i religious hierarchy. SHI'ISM provides the nearest approach in ISLAM to what might be called a clergy, and among the body of scholars trained in the shrine-cities of Iraq and Persia (or Iran) (MASHHAD) there evolved in the upper echelons a group of *mujtahids* ('those who exert themselves in interpreting the faith') considered as qualified to give authoritative judgements in matters of faith and practice. Recently, the title of *Ayatullah* has been applied to outstanding leaders in this latter group, but its application seems to depend on the personality and charisma of the scholar concerned and his consequent recognition by the community at large. This process is seen clearly at work in regard to the Ayatullah Khumaini, who in the 1960s emerged as the main political opponent of the Shah of Iran, Muhammad Riza Pahlavi, and after the 1978–9 Revolution became recognized as Vilayat Faqih or supreme temporal representative in Iran of the Hidden IMAM [21 Suppl. s.v.]

Aztec Sculpture [XIX] (1400–1521 CE) Monumental stone sculpture was one of the finest achievements of Mesoamerican culture (MESOAMERICAN RELIGIONS). The master sculptors of the Aztec traditions developed the aesthetic forms of their Toltec predecessors and decorated their temples and palaces with major and minor pieces. [11: 53–67] Some of these works were mass-produced in small and large sizes to express a standardized symbolic system concerning sacred warfare, fertility, solar worship, and death. [17: 108–35] All carvings were part of a great sacred art related to the ceremonial cycles and myths of the religion. The largest number of carved objects were statues of male and female deities in nude or nearly nude appearance. Also, large numbers of animal and insect stone images were produced including serpents, feathered serpents, jaguars, frogs, turtles, and grasshoppers. Stone masks in various local styles were produced and sometimes buried at major ceremonies at the temples. Also remarkable were the year bundle stones called *xiuhmolpilli* (NEW FIRE CEREMONY), which were deposited in ritual tombs at the end of a 52-year calendar cycle. The Aztecs also produced exquisite reliefs of deities, warriors, and religious events. Most of these works display a combination of poignant realism and intricate entanglement of symbols decorating larger forms, along with technical polish. Among the most outstanding large pieces are the CALENDAR STONE, the statue of Coatlicue, the mother goddess, the mammoth *cuauhxicalli* ('eagle vessel') of King Tizoc which held human hearts, and the oval of the goddess Coyolxauhqui-Chantico, all of which appear to have been associated with the cult of the TEMPLO MAYOR in the centre of Tenochtitlan.

· B ·

Ba'al [VI] A central figure in many Ugaritic accounts (PHOENICIANS), Ba'al was widely worshipped as a warrior-god in Canaan. The son of either Dagon, the corn-god, or of El, chief Ugaritic deity, Ba'al's consort was 'Ashtoreth (Ishtar), the goddess of battle; his daughters were Mist and Dew. Ba'al destroyed his enemies, including Mot, god of dryness and death, although his brief submission to Mot brought drought to the earth. Ba'al's revival, as rain-god, brought back the land's fertility. (ANCIENT NEAR EASTERN RELIGIONS) [4: 27]

Babis [XIV] A Muslim sect arising out of Persian SHI'ISM in the early 19th century, and important as the precursor of the BAHA'IS. It arose from the atmosphere then current of messianic expectations (MAHDI) under the leadership of Mirza 'Ali Muhammad (1819-50) of Shiraz, who in 1844 proclaimed himself the Bab ('gateway') to the Hidden IMAM and the inauguration of a new prophetic cycle after the Prophet MUHAMMAD, with his own message now abrogating certain prescriptions of the Islamic law or SHARI'A. Mirza 'Ali gathered round himself a band of enthusiasts who attempted to seize power in various parts of Persia. These outbreaks were bloodily suppressed and the Bab himself executed in 1850, but the movement continued both in Persia and in other parts of the Middle East, and under a new leader Baha'ullah evolved into Baha'ism in the second half of the century. [10 S.V.; 21 S.V.; 46: XI]

Babylonians [VI] The remnants of the last SUMERIAN allegiance – the Ur III Dynasty (c. 2113 BCE) – were taken over by the Amorites. New dynasties arose at Larsa, Kish, and Babylon, where King HAMMURABI, having devoted his early years to internal affairs, now took Sumer and Akkad in his 31st year, and Mari and Eshnunna thereafter [7; 24: 482-3]. This was a turning-point: the warring city-states now became one country, and an area equal to the southern part of modern Iraq was united as 'Babylonia'. Babylon itself became a political and cultural capital.

In his Law Code, Hammurabi states that the chief gods of Sumer had exalted MARDUK, god of Babylon, as supreme deity; he ordered the king to establish justice in the kingdom (KINGSHIP). Culturally, the 1st Dynasty of Babylon (c. 1792-1595 BCE) inherited and preserved Sumerian wisdom and religious lore. Scribes copied Sumerian texts, although this language was no longer spoken, and Sumerian myths were now compiled and set down as epics (ANCIENT NEAR EASTERN RELIGIONS) [24: 37-57, 383-91]. Akkadian also flourished as a literary language [24: 60-149, 331-43]. The Epic of GILGAMESH [24: 60-71] was an important religious poem in praise of Marduk, which was recited in the course of the New Year rituals at Babylon (FESTIVALS) and told of the rebellion by the underworld gods against the great gods, and Marduk's eventual creation of the world (COSMOLOGY).

The Babylonians were famed for their astronomical observations (ASTROLOGY) [22; 24: 449-51], and their science of DIVINATION to foresee events. In addition to oracular priests there were incantation priests who used MAGIC against EVIL or to obtain good fortune. Their TEMPLES incorporated ZIGGURATS which housed the god's shrine.

New Kassite rulers (*c.* 1600–1200 BCE) replaced Babylonian kings, but they adopted Babylonian culture, incorporating their own gods into the pantheon. Later, Assyria (ASSYRIANS) adopted and modified the Babylonian heritage [11], and finally, with the advent of the Neo-Babylonian Empire (700–500 BCE), Nebuchadnezzar (*c.* 600 BCE) restored the city of Babylon and the ancient shrines.

Bagre [II] The Bagre is one of many special associations or 'secret societies' found in West Africa. It belongs to the LoDagaa people in north-west Ghana and has spread also into northern Ivory Coast and Upper Volta. Membership of such associations is optional, an additional dimension to the religious or social life which some never join. Unlike many secret societies the Bagre does not use masks, but it does possess what is probably the most lengthy and remarkable 'myth' text to be found anywhere in Africa. This is recited, and repeated by the neophytes, during the long series of ceremonies which constitute the initiation of new members (male and female) and are closely related to the agricultural cycle.

The LoDagaa are an acephalous people (i.e. without governmental institutions above the village level) whose regular religion, like that of Tallensi or Lugbara, appears to consist principally of ANCESTOR VENERATION. But the Bagre myth has little to say about ancestors, its orientation being strikingly theistic. While the myth is concerned to explain the many Bagre ceremonies, it does this in the context of a doctrine of creation, the relative remoteness of God (Naangmin), and the relationship between God, man, and 'beings of the wild' – man's mysterious brothers in the world who taught him most of his skills.

The Bagre provides one of the richest sources for African traditional theology and a warning to the student to recognize the great complexity discoverable in popular religion even in small societies. [29]

Baha'is [XIV] A faith arising out of the Islamic BABI movement in Persia. Baha'ullah (1817–92) was originally a Babi who in exile acquired the conviction that he was the prophet foretold by the Bab. His faith of Baha'ism developed subsequently from an authoritarian, post-Shi'i (SHI'ISM) sectarianism into a universalist religion of humanity, with stress on the essential unity of all faiths, education, sexual equality, monogamy, and the attainment of world peace. It claims to be a scientific, undogmatic faith. It has no formal public ritual or priesthood, and no really authoritative scriptures. Local congregations hold informal devotional sessions and function within an administrative framework. There has always been an emphasis on missionary work, so that Baha'ism has been carried to Europe, the Americas, Africa, etc., while still remaining strong in Persia (Iran) despite sporadic persecution. [10 S.V.; 11; 21 S.V.; 23; 46: XI; 59A]

Balder [V] The Icelandic story of Balder, slain by the blind god Hother with a shaft of mistletoe after other plants and substances had sworn not to harm him, is well known. It comes from a late source, the 13th-century prose EDDA [20: 80–86]. There are some cryptic references to his death in earlier poems, and to LOKI's malice in causing it and punishment by the angry gods. In Saxo's 12th-century account [24 vol. I: III, 65–76], Balder is ODIN's son by a human mother, killed by the Danish hero Hother after a battle in Jutland [6: VII, 182–9]. Balder, like Freyr, means 'lord', and could be the title of a fertility god; this would be consistent with the legend that all creation weeps for Balder when a thaw comes after frost. However, Balder has close links with Odin, who tries to rescue him from HEL, and begets another son to avenge him; and Balder's death is a precursor of RAGNAROK. Balder's wife is Nanna, and his son Forseti was said to be worshipped in Frisia. Places were named after Balder in Germany, Norway, and Denmark, and his name occurs in an early German spell [6: VII, 183], but no reliable evidence for a cult of Balder has been found [30: IV].

Balinese Religion [XXII] The religion of Bali (an island of Indonesia) is officially HINDUISM, but this is combined with indigenous practices and beliefs. The Balinese call it Agama Tirtha (Religion of Holy Water), indicating the centrality of sanctified water in their rituals. The water is blessed by a BRAHMAN priest (*pedanda*) reciting Sanskrit incantations (MANTRA). He is a devotee of SHIVA or (in a few cases) the BUDDHA. Women are not entirely excluded from this role. Another priest (*sengguhu*) has a special relationship with VISHNU and he is concerned with the underworld. The village priest (*pemangku*) officiates at temple ceremonies, receiving offerings of food and flowers for the gods. Trance is a recognized means of communication with ancestors, spirits, and deities; a special functionary (*balian*, male or female) acts as a trance-medium for divine revelation. Seasonal festivals revolve round the cultivation of rice in irrigated terraces. The Balinese temple is walled but unroofed. Ritual battles are staged there between the forces of good (led by Barong, a lion) and evil (Rangda, a witch), usually ending in a balanced compromise. Cremation, often preceded by temporary burial, is the normal funeral rite and an occasion for great festivity. [17; 26; 28]

Ball Court [XIX] An outstanding feature of the ceremonial centres of MESO-AMERICAN RELIGIONS was the ball court or Tlachtli, the scene of ritual ball games which in some traditions re-enacted the sacred drama of the sun's journey through the underworld and the struggle between the powers of light and darkness for its destiny. [2: 8–12] Played on a court shaped like an I, representing the four-quartered cosmos (CEMANAHUAC) and the night sky, with raised viewing platforms for spectators who wagered for their team, the ball-game cult was inspired by various local mythical traditions which, in part, focused on solar motion and agricultural fertility. The game was determined when a small bouncy rubber ball was hit through a carved stone disc embedded in each of the long walls. [7: 312–19] In some regions, the captains of the losing teams were decapitated on a sacrificial stone (HUMAN SACRIFICE) to revitalize cosmic processes.

Balts [V] The Balts were INDO-EUROPEANS, ancestors of the Lithuanians, Letts, and Old Prussians [11: 1]. Their conversion to Christianity in the 14th century was slow, but little is known of their beliefs. Sixteenth and seventeenth century chroniclers like Grunau are often misleading. Something, however, may be learned from folksongs and traditional symbolism [1: 631–4; 11: VIII]. A thunder-god, Perku-nas, overcame evil spirits, established order, and helped farmers. Zemepatis and his sister Zemyna were master and mistress of the earth, Kalvaitis the heavenly smith, and Laima a goddess of fate. There were many supernatural beings resembling Celtic fairy-women. Songs tell of Saule the Sun and her daughters, and Menuo, the fickle Moon. The Balts had powerful priests, and 'sacred' towns and villages. Their holy trees, particularly oaks, were destroyed by missionaries. Cremation continued until the 14th century; there were human sacrifices at funerals, and communities accepted voluntary death rather than defeat. [11: VIII, 188]

Bantu Religion [II] The large majority of peoples in central and southern Africa can be classified, on a linguistic basis (use of the *ntu* root in the word for person), as Bantu; *see the entries on*

GANDA, LOVEDU, SHONA, and ZULU
RELIGION. While Bantu religion has
many diversities, as the entries show, its
most widespread features are the
following: a great concern for ancestral
spirits, who constitute the principal
guardians of morality (so that some
would describe its predominant characteristic as 'ancestralism'), a fear of witchcraft, and a belief in one supreme God
who, while seldom fairly described as
'otiose', is hardly ever the recipient of
much public worship (*see* IRUVA, KAT-
ONDA, LEZA, MODIMO, MULUNGU,
NZAMBI). The extensive sharing of
religious beliefs and practices between
different Bantu peoples is evidenced
not only by the inter-tribal use of
such god-names as Nzambi and Leza,
but by the still wider spread of other
basic religious terms such as NGANGA
and MIZIMU.

Baptism (in Early Christianity) [XI.
A] The distinctive Christian initiation
rite of dipping in water may have been
taken over from the practice of JOHN
THE BAPTIST, Christianized by the
added words, 'in the name of JESUS
CHRIST'. It betokened the convert's
repentance and faith in Christ, and was
accompanied by the reception of the
HOLY SPIRIT. In Paul's teaching it
denotes the believer's union with Christ
in his death, burial, and resurrection,
and is the sign of incorporation into
the 'body of Christ' (the church
SACRAMENTS). [4: 280–83; 5: 48–52,
69–72; 13: 47–60]

Baptists [IX.B] Though once nick-
named 'ANABAPTISTS', Baptists trace
their origin to John Smyth (*c.* 1554–
1612) who used baptism of mature believers only as a mark of church membership. Baptists strongly emphasize the
independence of the local church,
although individual churches are linked
in associations of various kinds at
various levels. Almost from their 17th-
century beginnings there were 'General'
Baptists (ARMINIANISM) and 'Particular' ones (CALVINISM) as well as

varieties of each. The 18th-century
Evangelical Revival (cf. REVIVALISM)
made some of the Particulars enthusias-
tic missionaries. The Baptists are a loose
family of churches. Their main numerical base is in the U.S.A. (particularly
among black Christians) with an important North/South division. Periods of
religious conflict or revival often produce new groups of Baptist churches.
Although there are international bodies
(such as the Baptist World Alliance,
with its headquarters in Washington DC,
U.S.A.) and national bodies, many
Baptist churches belong to neither.
Hence there is a great diversity of belief
and practice which makes generalization
impossible. [130; 138]

Bardo [XXIX] The Buddhist doctrine of
bardo refers to the intermediate state between death and rebirth. Although the
doctrine is mentioned in ABHIDHAMMA
and TANTRA, its most famous expression has been in the NYINGMA texts
known collectively as *Liberation through
Hearing in the Bardo*, which teach that
liberation is attained by recognizing the
peaceful and wrathful deities encountered in the *bardo* as manifestations of
the luminosity and emptiness of one's
own mind. [7; 11]

Batak Religion [XXII] The Bataks are
an Indonesian tribal group of northern
Sumatra, now largely Christianized,
with a Muslim minority. Long known
internationally as anthropophagous,
they had written texts and a religion
partly influenced by India (e.g. *debata*,
'god'). The Toba Bataks believed in a
three-tiered universe: men in the middle
world; the fettered dragon Naga Padoha
in the underworld; the gods in the
upper world, notably the creator Mula
Jadi and his three sons Batara Guru,
Soripada, and Mangalabulan. Creation
involved a struggle between the upper
world and the underworld. Mula Jadi's
tree named Jambubarus had leaves inscribed with fates (e.g. poverty, wealth,
sorrow), and each soul (*tondi*) took a leaf
as its lot. *Sahala* (the power of the *tondi*)

resembled MANA; it could be increased by feeding on another person's *tondi* in ritual cannibalism. The priest (*datu*) had magic books, and practised healing and divination. [19; 26]

Bhagavadgita [XIII.A] Literally translated 'The Song of the Lord', the *Bhagavadgita* is probably the most popular book of Hindu scripture. It forms part of the great epic, the MAHABHARATA, which can be dated between the 2nd century BCE and the 2nd century CE. For most HINDUS it represents the essence of their religion with its message that there are many ways to salvation, of which, it is affirmed, all are valid, but not all are necessarily universally appropriate. The 'Song' is a long dialogue between the hero Arjuna and his chariot-driver, who is the Lord KRISHNA in human form. On the eve of the battle of Kurukshetra Arjuna has scruples about the prospect of killing his fellow men, some of whom are his kinsmen. He is told by Krishna that he must perform in a disinterested way the duty that is appropriate to his VARNA, i.e. that of the warrior. The poem may be interpreted as teaching the value of action unaccompanied by desire as one of the ways to salvation (MOKSHA), but it has received many interpretations, some of them conflicting, especially in the course of its use in the modern period by such Hindu leaders as Gandhi and B. G. Tilak. This is not surprising in that it has been characterized as a work of religious compromise. It would be difficult, in view of the teaching of this most popular and influential Hindu text, to describe Hinduism as a pacifist ideology unless its teaching is understood in an entirely allegorical sense. [B. 19]

Bhajan [XIII.A] Literally 'adoration' or 'worship'. The term is commonly used of Indian hymn-singing sessions held, usually, by VAISHNAVAS, at which there may also be some brief exposition of scripture. *Bhajans* are well-known features of Vaishnava religion in India,

especially, for example, in Madras [23: 90–172] and Gujarat [18: 102ff], where *bhajan-mandali* (hymn-singing groups) are the commonest form of village religious devotion. In recent times they have been introduced by Gujarati immigrants into their new places of abode, for example in the West.

Bhakti [XIII.A] One of the three major recognized paths to salvation in HINDUISM. It is the attitude and activity of devotion to God; hence a *bhakta* is 'a devotee'. The other recognized 'paths' to salvation are ritual activity (KARMA) and spiritual knowledge (JNANA). The emphasis on worshipful devotion, as distinct from sacrificial rituals, is found in India at least as early as the 2nd century BCE; the cult of the god Vasudeva is attested by Megasthenes, then Greek ambassador at the Indian capital. Bhakti cults seem to have grown notably in the later Buddhist period in India and after, that is from about the 8th century CE. The *bhakta* is usually devoted to a particular manifestation of deity, such as RAMA, or KRISHNA, and thus adheres to a school of devotion. These schools have their great theologians, such as RAMANUJA (d. 1137) [25: 130–33; 2: 334f], whose role has been to expound theologically the nature of the relationship between the worshipper and the personal God. Other great exponents of *bhakti* religion are its poets, for example, Namdev (b. 1470), Tuka Rama (1598–1649), whose hymns are still sung in Hindu households in Maharashtra, and Chaitanya (1485–1533), of Bengal.

Bhakti Yoga [XIII.B] 'The way of devotion' is one of three or four alternative routes of spiritual development (YOGA) widely recognized in Indian thought. The emphasis in this mode of practice is on loving devotion and self-surrender to the deity, leading to inner transformation through grace. Eventually elaborate BHAKTI theologies were developed (e.g. VAISHNAVA VEDANTA). [4: 105–8; 18: 145–7; 19: 26–8]

Bhavana [IX.B] What has become known as Buddhist meditation, *bhavana*, literally 'bringing into being', refers to the fourth truth (ARIYA-SACCA) – the bringing into being of the EIGHTFOLD PATH in its two aspects of SAMATHA (Sanskrit *shamatha*) or stillness of mind and VIPASSANA (Sanskrit *vipashyana*) or insight. Buddhist meditation practice is of two types according to which aspect is emphasized: calm meditation and insight meditation. These are ultimately harmonized and developed together in order to give rise to a higher order of mind (*see* LOKUTTARA). The precise relationship between the two approaches has been variously described, from an early date. One tendency is to view *samatha* meditation practice as preliminary to the practice of insight and as identical to Hindu DHYANA-YOGA, whereas *vipassana* would be seen as more advanced or more efficacious and uniquely Buddhist. Earlier authorities (e.g. BUDDHAGHOSA) permit the less usual possibility of omitting all but the most preliminary stages of *samatha*, but more recently a tradition has emerged or been revived (especially in Burma) which sees this as a desirable short cut and emphasizes the danger of attachment to pleasant experiences in *samatha*. The alternative tradition, which emphasizes full development of *samatha* and sees disadvantages in premature development of advanced insight, remains widespread (especially in Thailand). The two approaches may be distinguished as the Insight and Calm schools respectively, but intermediate positions are often found and the two are frequently considered as complementary or suited to different psychological temperaments.

Manuals of *bhavana* have been written at most periods in different Buddhist countries. For THERAVADA Buddhism the most important non-canonical account is that of Buddhaghosa. For the Indian MAHAYANA the most influential writings are those attributed to Asanga (*see* YOGACARA) and the work of Kamalashila (8th century CE), but most later Mahayana schools have their own manuals of instruction. [44: 11–44; 49; 52: 137–58; 55: 61–84]

Bible (**Christian**) The Bible of the CHURCH comprises two collections, which Christians call the Old Testament and the New Testament.

The collection called the Old Testament is substantially the Hebrew Bible, with its three divisions – Law, Prophets, and Writings – amounting in all to 24 documents (in the traditional Jewish reckoning) or 39 (in the conventional Christian reckoning). The Law, comprising the first five books, is frequently called the Pentateuch (from a Greek adjective meaning 'consisting of five scrolls'). There are differences of practice and doctrine among Christians about the inclusion of the Apocrypha – books not found in the Hebrew Bible but mostly (though not entirely) belonging to the SEPTUAGINT.

The New Testament comprises 27 documents, written within the century following the death of Jesus (CANON). These are five narrative works (the four GOSPELS and the Acts of the Apostles), 21 letters (13 of which bear the name of PAUL), and the APOCALYPTIC Book of Revelation. In large measure the New Testament represents the written deposit of first-generation Christian preaching and teaching, in the light of which the Old Testament has traditionally been interpreted in the church.

The unique status given to the Bible in the church is shown in several ways – notably by the established place of Bible reading in public worship, by the exposition of the Bible in public preaching, and by the appeal to the Bible as the standard for belief and conduct. This has necessitated a theology of scripture, to ascertain the nature of the authority attaching to its contents and, in particular, to lay down lines along which it should be interpreted and applied. This involves not only rules of interpretation but also the question of who is empowered to interpret it authoritatively. A further question, still debated, is how far (if at all) the authority of extra-scriptural tradition should be acknowledged alongside the authority of scripture. [1; 6] In ROMAN CATHOLICISM and ORTHODOX CHURCHES the revelation of scripture has to be understood through the tradition of the church (AUTHORITY).

Biblical Criticism [XI.A] The application to biblical documents of those critical methods which are applicable to literature in general. It includes: (1) textual criticism, the ascertaining as far as possible of the original wording and the assessment of various readings in the thousands of manuscripts of all or part of the New Testament; (2) source criticism, the investigation of literary sources lying behind the documents which have been preserved; (3) tradition criticism, the examination of the stages by which the material in our documents was transmitted orally before being written down; (4) form criticism, the study of the 'forms' or moulds in which the tradition was cast while it was being handed down; (5) historical criticism, the investigation of the historical setting of the existing documents and their sources; and (6) redaction criticism, which considers the contribution of the authors who finally received the tradition and incorporated it in the works. [1; 6: III, 238–338]

Biblical History [XI.A] For the period up to the 1st century CE biblical history is largely identical with the history of Israel, especially its religious history.

The ancestors of the Israelites (the patriarchs) migrated from Mesopotamia to Canaan (Palestine) soon after 2000 BCE. A number of them continued their migration south-west into Egypt, and with their return from Egypt c. 1250 BCE the history of Israel as a nation properly begins. Those who returned from Egypt and settled in Canaan formed a

tribal confederacy with their kinsfolk who had stayed there. About 1050 BCE their national identity was threatened by the Philistines (invaders from the Aegean); this threat led to a better-organized unity under Saul and David, the first kings of Israel. David (1010–970 BCE) subjugated the Philistines and established a modest empire for himself. The dynasty which he founded survived in its capital city, JERUSALEM, until it was crushed by the Babylonians in 587 BCE. The upper strata of the population were deported. This 'Babylonian exile' lasted until Cyrus the Persian captured Babylon (539 BCE) and allowed the exiles to return home.

The post-exilic Jewish community formed a temple-state, with the completed Hebrew law-book as its constitution. Under the Persian empire, and then under Alexander the Great (r. 336–323 BCE) (and his earlier successors), the community lived peacefully. An attempt by one of Alexander's successors, Antiochus Epiphanes (175–164 BCE), to replace the Jewish cult by the worship of a Greek deity provoked a successful uprising under Judas Maccabaeus and his family (the Hasmonaeans). They established a dynasty of priest-kings which lasted until the country was forcibly incorporated in the Roman empire (63 BCE).

The Roman empire provides the context for the century of New Testament history (ROME (EARLY CHRISTIANITY AT)). [2; 3]

Bismillah, Basmala [XIV] The words 'In the name of God, the Merciful, the Compassionate', which begin all but one of the *suras* of the QUR'AN. They are used by Muslims as a validating formula for solemn acts; as invocation of a divine blessing before many acts of daily life, such as eating; and as a frequent calligraphic motif in Islamic ART and the writing-out of talismans and amulets. [43: 556–9; 81: 60]

Black Muslims [XIV] Officially called 'the Nation of ISLAM', a semi-religious, semi-black nationalist organization among Afro-Americans, with the declared aim of raising the moral, social, and economic standing of non-whites against the dominant, white, Caucasians in the U.S.A. Developed by Elijah Muhammad (1897–1975) and his lieutenant Malcolm X (1925–65) and venerating Wallace D. Fard Muhammad (*c.* 1877–?1934) as a MAHDI, a prophet and incarnation of ALLAH, it diverges from Islam proper in denying an afterlife, in according (in effect) divine status to Fard, and in its specifically black racialism. [10 s.v.; 50]

Bodhgaya [IX.A] The place of the enlightenment (*bodhi*) of GOTAMA (BUDDHA), near Gaya, in Bihar (India); sometimes known also as Buddha-Gaya. In Buddhist tradition the Bodhi tree beneath which the event occurred (on the west bank of the Neranjana river) is regarded as the navel of the earth [21: 319]. The site is now marked by the Maha Bodhi temple, and is one of the four principal places of pilgrimage for all Buddhists.

Bodhi-Pakkhiya-Dhamma [IX.B] (Pali; Sanskrit *bodhi-pakshika-dharma*) The later name for the 37 items, in a set of seven groups of mental qualities, given in the earlier Buddhist discourses (SUTTA-PITAKA) as a mnemonic summary of the Buddhist path. The first three groups, foundations of mindfulness, right efforts, and bases of psychic power (*iddhi*), are each fourfold. After them come the five qualities of faith, strength, mindfulness, concentration, and wisdom viewed either as exercising control (*indriya*) or as unshakable powers (*bala*). The sixth group lists seven factors of awakening (*bodhi*), while the last group is the EIGHTFOLD PATH itself. In later Buddhist writings the set is interpreted in two ways. The series of groups may describe the stages of the spiritual path in sequence [e.g. 57: 232ff]. Alternatively the 37 items may list the most prominent contents of the mind occurring simultaneously in

a given moment of transcendent (LOKUTTARA) consciousness or partially in the later stages of insight (VIPASSANA) meditation. [64: 121–33, 417]

Bodhisattva [IX.A] Literally 'Enlightenment Being' (Pali *Bodhisatta*), the title indicates one who is destined to become enlightened, a future BUDDHA. According to Buddhist tradition such a being, before reaching the final birth as a human, and a Buddha, lives in the Tusita heaven (DIPANKARA). The concept has special importance in MAHAYANA Buddhism, where the ability of the Bodhisattva to help lesser beings by the strength of his own spiritual power is emphasized by way of contrast to the equally great emphasis in some of the Hinayana schools on what appears to be self-salvation. The Bodhisattva thus becomes virtually a heavenly saviour; AVALOKITESHVARA is most usually regarded in this way. The doctrine hence comes to resemble deity-worship, and in India assisted the assimilation of Buddhism, at a popular level, to the village cults (HINDUISM). Mahayana texts refer to very large numbers of Bodhisattvas. Of these, fewer than ten are of universal importance. Besides Avalokiteshvara, Manjushri and AMITABHA are widely known (*see* JAPANESE BUDDHAS AND BODHISATTVAS). An important feature of the Bodhisattva's nature, in Mahayana tradition, was the conscious decision to delay entrance into the final birth as a human about to become Buddha; this was in order to be able to continue to help other beings, a decision which shows the predominantly compassionate nature of the Bodhisattva. [5: 234ff; 37: 355ff]

In Pali Buddhism (THERAVADA) the title is used mainly to refer to Sakyamuni Buddha (GOTAMA) immediately before his enlightenment at BODHGAYA.

Böhme, Jakob (1575–1624) [XVIII] A German mystic. Born near Görlitz, Upper Lusatia, Böhme was a shoemaker and devout Lutheran (LUTHERANISM).

In 1600 he underwent a profound religious experience which showed him 'good and evil, love and wrath' in all things; this insight was followed by a revelation of the presence of God in all things. After 12 years of reflection he composed an account of his experiences and beliefs, *The Aurora*. It was denounced by the local pastor and Böhme was forbidden to write again. He obeyed until 1619, when he began a series of writings culminating in *The Great Mystery* (1623), a visionary account of the creation in terms of three divine principles which Böhme, drawing his terminology from ALCHEMY, calls salt, sulphur, and mercury (manifest in man as material body, spiritual body, and soul). Böhme's theology is complex but forcefully poetic in expression and notable for its emphasis on human freedom and inner regeneration. [23]

Bon [XXIX] The indigenous pre-Buddhist religion of Tibet. Although its relationship to Shamanism (SHAMAN) is a complex one, in the earliest form of the religion there seem to have been definite similarities. The term 'Bon' itself was probably derived from the ritual recitation (*bon*) of its practitioners. The developed form of the religion still in existence today is the result of a synthesis of the original doctrines and the Buddhism introduced in Tibet from the 7th and 8th centuries onwards. According to tradition the founder of the later 'purified' Bon was Shenrab Miwo, who hailed from the mystic land of Zhang Zhung and who in myth became an equivalent of Shakyamuni BUDDHA, being credited with the dissemination of *sutras* and *tantras* and the foundation of a monastic order. [9]

Bon is said to have existed in Tazig (Iran) in ancient times and indeed some accounts have suggested influence from ZOROASTRIANISM and in particular ZURVAN. Tibetan Buddhist scholars often identify Shenrab with Lao-Tzu, thus making Bon a derivative of Taoism

(TAO CHIAO). However, modern scholars postulate Shaivite (SHIVA) influence from Kashmir as a factor in the development of Bonpo doctrine. [24]

In its earlier forms Bon doctrine was both theistic and dualistic, suggesting that the creation of the world was brought about by coexistent good and evil principles. However, the doctrine of developed Bon is generally in accord with Buddhist non-theistic tenets. In particular it shares with the NYINGMA school the soteriological structure of nine *yanas* ('vehicles') [20]. The nine *yanas* climax in the meditation of 'the great perfection' which Bonpos claim was transmitted first by Shenrab and only later entered the Nyingma tradition.

Brahma [XIII.A] A Hindu god, the personified creator of the universe. In classical Indian thought the other two major deities, VISHNU and SHIVA, together with Brahma, form a 'trinity', the significance of which is that just as Vishnu and Shiva represent opposite forces, namely, existence and annihilation, light and darkness, concentration and dispersion, preservation and destruction, so respectively, Brahma is the balance between them, 'the possibility of existence resulting from the union of opposites' [5: 232]. But whereas BRAHMAN is an impersonal principle, and of neuter gender, Brahma is personal, and of masculine gender. Brahma is also regarded as the all-inclusive deity, and is the name for the one deity behind all the many names of gods used in Hindu popular parlance. Brahma, unlike the various deities of the Hindu pantheon, does not receive worship, although he is represented iconographically, and his name sometimes occurs in rituals.

Brahma is not a deity of the earliest Vedic period of Hindu religion (VEDA), and is perhaps the result of later developments of thought. This is possibly represented in the Sanskrit epic, the MAHABHARATA, where it is said that 'the notion of individual existence (*ahamkara*) appeared first and from it Brahma was born' [5: 233]. The 'trinity' of gods, referred to above, had developed recognizably by about the end of the 1st century BCE. It was short-lived, and the cult of Brahma, such as it was, diminished in importance, leaving Vishnu and Shiva the two principal forms of Hindu deity. SHAKTI, the female principle of deity, then came to occupy the third place. [4: 232–49; 16A: 25–55; 24A: 164–6]

Brahma-Sutra [XIII.B] The fundamental text of the systematic VEDANTA, attributed to Badarayana and probably dating from about the 1st century CE. The first two chapters aim to establish the Vedanta interpretation of the Upanishads (VEDA) and refute various rival systems, especially the SAMKHYA. The remaining two chapters are mainly concerned with the nature of the soul (ATMAN) and the divine power, destiny after death, methods of meditation, and liberation (MOKSHA). The individual statements (*sutras*) are very concise, sometimes even cryptic, and occasionally allow fairly divergent acceptable alternatives on matters of later theological importance. As a result many of the authoritative works of the different schools of Vedanta have taken the form of commentaries on the *Brahma-sutra*. [Summary: 6: 54–61; translation: 15: 227–564]

Brahman [XIII.A] In Hindu thought *brahman* (neuter gender) is the abstract, impersonal Absolute. The Absolute is said to be *nirguna* (beyond-quality), pure, eternal. When characterized with qualities, the 'qualified brahman' (*saguna brahman*) becomes the immanent cause of the universe [3: 336f]. In the Upanishads (VEDA) the realization of the equation of the soul (ATMAN) with *brahman* is the ultimate goal, the attainment of which constitutes MOKSHA, or release from empirical existence and the round of rebirth. The earliest sense of the word *brahman* (BRAHMANS) appears

to have referred to the sound of the sacred chant uttered by the Aryan priest at the time of offering the Vedic sacrifice (VEDA). The sound itself was believed to be efficacious, and thus came to represent the power of the eternal sacred Absolute.

Brahmanas [XIII.A] Ancient Hindu texts, written in Sanskrit, setting out the rationale and principles of the BRAHMANS' sacrificial system [1: 21–5]. They are later than the hymns in the VEDA and are composed in the form of commentary on them. The commentary, or exposition, often takes the form of a speculative account of the nature and meaning of the sacrifices. It has been suggested that they represent a period when sacrifice had increased in importance in view of the growth of threats to prosperity entailed in the scarcity of resources in the later Vedic period; increased sacrifice was the Brahmans' solution for this. [11: 87] The stage of development of Brahmanical religious thought represented here is one in which the Vedic gods were losing importance and an introspective preoccupation with ideas of a supreme impersonal principle were beginning to find early expression, later to be developed in the Upanishads (VEDA). This is likely to have applied only, however, to the élite company of priestly specialists, not to the common people.

Another difference between the ideas represented in the Vedic hymns and those of the *Brahmanas* concerns the characters of the gods. The *Brahmanas* provide evidence of a shift in emphasis; in the early Vedic period the gods of the Aryans (INDO-EUROPEANS) were virtually all male, but in the *Brahmanas* the effect of the intermingling of the invading Aryan culture and that of the indigenous peoples is seen in the 'first signs of the return of the mother-goddesses into power' [3: 10]. Some of the male gods of the Vedic hymns, such as Rudra and Yama (and others), in the *Brahmanas* become sinister, dark, malevolent, and associated with destructive functions [3: 51; 6: 11].

Brahmans [XIII.A] The most elevated of the four VARNAS or Hindu social classes. (Sometimes the name is anglicized to 'brahmins'.) The traditional occupations of the Brahmans are transmission of the Sanskritic sacred traditions (VEDA), and the performance of priestly sacrificial rituals. As composers of the ancient normative religious, social, and legal texts, the Brahmans had great prestige and the three lower *varnas* had to follow the Brahmans' teaching. To kill a Brahman was one of the five deadly sins (the other four being to violate a *guru*'s bed, to steal a Brahman's gold, to associate with outcastes, and to drink spirituous liquor). The king in ancient Hindu society was an absolute ruler, with the exception that he was not the master of the Brahman, and could not take his wealth. In Hindu cosmology the Brahman is said, at creation, to have emerged from BRAHMA's head.

Having dominated Hindu society for many centuries the Brahman class has in the 20th century become the target for attack by various lower-caste anti-Brahman movements. Some of the most notable of these have been in south India (in Tamil Nadu), and in Maharashtra. In modern India Brahmans are found as landowners, politicians, civil servants, teachers, and in various other professional classes, and, sometimes (more usually in rural areas), pursuing their traditional occupation as priests. In the latter case they sometimes only eke out a bare existence.

Brigit [v] The Gauls worshipped a Celtic goddess equated with Minerva, associated with arts and crafts. Her equivalent in Ireland was Brigit ('High One'), the DAGDA's daughter, expert in poetry and prophecy. She was sometimes a threefold goddess. Like Brigantia, in northern Britain, she was associated also with flocks and herds, springs and rivers [23: VIII, 358–62; 26:

III, 25]. The Christian St Brigit of Kildare took over traditions of the earlier goddess, and kept the spring feast, Imbolg (SAMHAIN), as her festival.

Britain, Christianity in [XI.B] After the fall of the Roman empire Celtic Christianity [92] and the Anglo-Saxon church developed on different lines. During the REFORMATION separate established churches developed as the Church of England [101] and Church of Scotland [17] (PRESBYTERIANISM). The ANGLICAN church was disestablished in predominantly Roman Catholic Ireland (1869) and strongly Nonconformist Wales (1920). Religious TOLERATION (1689) allowed substantial bodies of Dissenters (also known as Nonconformists and Free Churchmen) to develop [138] (BAPTISTS; CONGREGATIONALISM; METHODISM; Presbyterians; QUAKERS). These have played an important part in English life. ROMAN CATHOLICISM increased greatly from the 19th century, chiefly through Irish immigration.

Buddha [IX.A] The word Buddha is not a proper name; it denotes a state of being. In the classical language of India it means 'the enlightened' or 'the awakened', the state of having direct knowledge of the true nature of things, that is, of DHAMMA (Sanskrit *dharma*), or truth. 'He who sees the truth sees the Buddha, and he who sees the Buddha sees the truth' is a Buddhist way of expressing it.

According to Buddhist philosophy, the Buddha-nature or 'body' (*Buddha-kaya*) is of three kinds. More precisely, the *Buddha-kaya* has three levels: the *dharma-kaya*; the *sambhoga-kaya*; and the *nirmana-kaya*. It is difficult in a few words to explain the significance of these terms; it is more likely to become clear in the process of studying Buddhism. The *dharma-kaya* is the pure essence of Buddha-hood; it is sometimes called the 'self-being body' (*sva-bhava-kaya*), or the truth 'remaining within its own nature'. A Japanese scholar, D.T. Suzuki, calls it 'the absolute-aspect' of the Buddha-nature.

The *sambhoga-kaya* can be understood broadly as the 'bliss-body'. This appears to indicate the aspect of 'awakenedness', or truth, as it is perceived in the realm of celestial bliss, that is, the nonmortal realm. The term is sometimes translated as 'glorious-body', that is, Buddha-hood as it appears in glory and splendour in the non-mortal realm.

As for *nirmana-kaya*, the closest equivalent here is the English word 'assumed'. The *nirmana-kaya* is the form assumed by Buddha-hood, or the Buddha-nature, when a historical manifestation occurs, in the form of a human life. One example of this, it is said, was Sakyamuni Buddha, also known as GOTAMA (his clan name) and Siddhartha (his personal name), who lived in India in the 6th century BC. According to Buddhist thought of all schools there have been many such manifestations in the course of cosmic history, and there will be many more.

This doctrine of the three *kayas* of the Buddha-nature is, in its developed form, a product of the MAHAYANA schools of Buddhism. The representation of the historical 'Buddha' in iconic form is known as the *Buddha-rupa* and is used by all schools of Buddhism as a devotional device, and represents the Buddha in the form (*rupa*) and with the special characteristics which all Buddhas are held to possess (BUDDHA IMAGE). [8; 17; 35A]

Buddha Image [IX.B] Buddhism initially avoided representing the BUDDHA in human form, presumably to emphasize the transcendental nature of the knower of NIBBANA. Symbols were employed both for devotional purposes (especially the STUPA and the *bodhi* tree) and in narrative iconography (e.g. the royal parasol and the DHAMMA wheel), probably recalling different episodes in the life of the Buddha. The

Buddha image was created about the 2nd century CE in the Indian territories of the Kushana empire (CENTRAL ASIAN BUDDHISM). Two artistic schools arose; one more Indian, centring on Mathura, and another in Gandhara in north-west India under Hellenistic influence. The canonical description of the 32 characteristics of a great man by which a Buddha could be predicted (probably intended for visualization meditation) was taken as the basis. Hence features such as lengthened ears, a curl or mark on the forehead (the *urna*) and elongation of the crown of the head into either a topknot of hair or a protuberance (the *ushnisha* – originally a 'turbaned head'). The use of the Buddha image is not sectarian and spread rapidly. For cultic purposes it should enshrine relics, but in practice this is not necessarily the case (especially in East Asia). Both small and large images have been constructed as works of merit in very large numbers throughout the Buddhist world and an extremely rich artistic heritage has evolved. The various formalized gestures (*mudra*) tend to symbolize events in the life of the Buddha and (in the MAHAYANA) aspects of the nature of Buddha-hood. The Buddha image is sometimes known as the *Buddha-rupa*. [56; 58]

Buddhaghosa [IX.B] The most influential authority for THERAVADA Buddhism. Indian in origin, Buddhaghosa (*c.* 430 CE) went to Ceylon to study at the Theravada monastic university (Mahavihara) in Anuradhapura. Existing commentaries in the local language, Sinhala Prakrit, were translated by him into PALI, which was more widely understood. His commentaries (*atthakatha*) were accepted as an authoritative interpretation of the Pali Canon (TIPITAKA). In the *Visuddhi-magga* ('Path of Purification'), intended as a general commentary to the Canon as a whole, Buddhaghosa outlined the stages and methods of the practice of Buddhist meditation (BHAVANA), together with a detailed account of ABHIDHAMMA theory. [42: xvff]

Buddha-Sasana [IX.A] Literally the 'Buddha-teaching' or 'Buddha-doctrine', this term is used in modern Asian contexts as an equivalent for 'Buddhist religion', as in the Buddha Sasana councils and commissions set up by governments in countries such as Burma, Sri Lanka, and Thailand.

Buddhism [IX.A] The tradition of thought and practice associated with Shakyamuni, the BUDDHA, who lived in India in the 6th/5th century BCE, and is sometimes referred to by his clan name, Gautama (Sanskrit; Pali GOTAMA). His personal name was Siddhattha. The tradition tells of the experiences leading to his enlightenment at BODHGAYA, and his subsequent journeyings in northern India as one of the wandering ascetic philosophers of the day. His teaching consisted of the four Noble Truths (ARIYA-SACCA), the last of which was the affirmation of a way (*magga*) of deliverance from the endless round of birth and dying. The Buddha's way is set out as threefold: SILA (morality), SAMADHI (meditation), and *panna* (wisdom); and in a fuller form as the EIGHTFOLD PATH. The disciples he attracted formed a community (SANGHA), which had as its rule of life a collection of decisions called the Vinaya (discipline). After the Buddha's decease, or PARINIBBANA, the Sangha, at the first Council (SANGITI), rehearsed the teaching, or DHAMMA, contained in the Buddha's discourses (SUTTA-PITAKA) and the discipline (VINAYA-PITAKA). In later centuries the teaching was elaborated in various sects and schools by philosopher-monks such as NAGARJUNA, who is associated with the MADHYAMIKA school of philosophy, within the MAHAYANA (cf. THERAVADA) tradition. Also associated with this tradition was the development of the BODHISATTVA ideal. For the lay follower who, unlike the *bhikkhu*, does not become a homeless wanderer (ANAGARIKA), the Buddhist life consists in taking the three REFUGES, in the pursuit of morality (*sila*), especially generosity (ALMS-GIVING), in the keeping of special days and festivals, notably VESAKHA, in pilgrimage to Buddhist sacred places such as Bodhgaya and KUSINARA, and in social responsibilities as set out in principle in the SIGALOVADA Sutta.

The Buddha Shakyamuni is regarded as one in a long and continuing line of Buddhas, the next to come being known as MAITREYA. Buddhism has developed various regional variations, such as the SINHALESE and those of CENTRAL ASIA, CHINA, JAPAN, SOUTH-EAST ASIA, and TIBET and, most recently, WESTERN BUDDHISM.

Bundahishn [XXX] Creation in ZOROASTRIANISM. There is a PAHLAVI text of this name which deals with the origins, purpose, and nature of creation. In its present form it dates from the 10th century CE but essentially it represents a compilation of ancient teachings contained in the AVESTA. [40: 40f; translation: 1.]

AHURA MAZDA and ANGRA MAINYU (God and the 'devil') have existed independently of each other from eternity. Mazda dwells on high in light, but Angra Mainyu dwells down in darkest hell. Mazda, being omniscient (all-knowing), was aware of his adversary's existence but Angra Mainyu, being ignorant, did not have such knowledge. When he came to learn of it, then with characteristic violence he sought to destroy Mazda, and so the cosmic battle between good and evil began. Each side produced its own creations. Ahura first created the spiritual (*menog*) world (AMESHA SPENTAS; YAZATAS) and later the material (*getig*) world. In Zoroastrian belief the spiritual and material worlds are not opposites. The material is the visible, tangible expression, almost fulfilment, of the spiritual.

In traditional Zoroastrian belief the

world lasted for 3,000 years in spiritual form and then 3,000 in perfect material form before evil assaulted it. Against health Angra Mainyu created disease; against beauty, ugliness; against life, death. The archetypal man, Gayomaretan (Pahlavi Gayomard), and bull died from his attack, but as they did they emitted sperm from which grew humans and animals. Thus began what Zoroastrians know as the time of mixture (*Gumezishn*), the time when good and evil are mixed together in the world. The turning-point in the period of battle was the birth of ZOROASTER, occurring 3,000 years after Angra Mainyu's assault. He brought the revelation from God, which it is believed will inspire men to fight for the good. The 3,000 years following his death are the age in which we now live, a period when good and evil are locked in battle, but a time when good is gradually emerging triumphant. The final defeat of evil will take place at FRASHOKERETI. The world is therefore by nature perfect. All evils in it are due to Angra Mainyu. It is 'the Good Creation' of Ahura Mazda. [5: IX; 20: 56–60; 49: v, x; 50: xv].

· C ·

Calendar (in Islam) [XIV] The religiously sanctioned system of dating in ISLAM is one of purely lunar months, so that a year comprises 354 days and the months do not correspond to the seasons of the solar year. There are approximately 103 Muslim lunar years to 100 in the Gregorian solar calendar. The Muslim era is computed from the Prophet MUHAMMAD's migration or *hijra* (*hegira*) from Mecca to Medina, which took place in September 622 CE, although the year actually begins from the opening of the lunar year in which the migration took place, i.e. 16 July 622. For practical purposes, such as the collection of taxes and agricultural operations, a lunar year was unsuitable, and over the centuries various solar adaptations were made, e.g. the Ottoman Turkish (ISLAMIC DYNASTIES) fiscal year and the Persian solar year computed from the *hijra*. At present, the *hijra* year is used mainly for religious purposes. [20 'Zamān'; 26; 29: 182–4; 45: IX]

Calendar (Jewish) [XVII] The Jewish calendar consists of a year made up of 12 lunar months each of 29 or 30 days [9 vol. 5: 43]. In ancient times these months began when witnesses testified to the sighting of the new moon. From about the 4th century the calendar was calculated in advance, and eyewitness testimony disregarded. The average lunar year of 354 days is just over 11 days short of the solar year. In order for the festivals (CHAGIM), which are based on the agricultural year, to fall at their appointed times as well as on their correct lunar date the lunar year has to be brought into line with the solar year. An extra lunar month is intercalated in February–March seven times every 19 years. The religious year begins with the New Year festival, falling around September–October, when the world is thought to be judged on its activities during the past year (*see also* FASTS) [44: XIII; 52: 172].

Calendar Round (Amerindian) [III] Among the settled agriculturists of the North American south-west, calendric rites achieved their fullest development as emphasis on collective efforts to ensure fertility and social well-being gradually supplanted more individualistic forms. Thus major ceremonies of the PUEBLO tribes are intimately connected with calendric observances, notably the seasonal transitions, so critical to planting economies. Among the HOPI, for example, calendar rituals are elaborately structured. The yearly pattern of planting, growth, and harvest microcosmically recapitulates the original stages in the creation of the world: pre-dawn, dawn, and full sunrise – a pattern that is further reflected in the daily cycle (COSMOLOGY). [25: III] The principal Hopi ceremonies of Wuwuchim, Soyal, and Powamu still further reflect the basic pattern. Typically, these rituals include the following elements: preparation through isolation in the *kiva* (or underground ceremonial chamber); avoidance of food and sexuality; recitation of the creation narrative; use of prayer-sticks and tobacco (CALUMET); dry-paintings (SAND-PAINTINGS); and culminating in public dancing. The critical transitions, the summer and winter solstices and the spring and autumn equinoxes, are thus marked by the cooperative efforts of man and the supernaturals.

Calendar Stone [XIX] One of the finest pieces of MESOAMERICAN RELIGIOUS sculpture is the Calendar Stone (1500 CE), 3½ metres in diameter, weighing 24 metric tons, more accurately called the Piedra del Sol, because it is a carved image of the cosmogony depicting the five ages or 'suns' of the universe (*see figure*). [12: 37] At the periphery of a series of concentric circles are two giant fire-serpents whose pointed tails meet at the date (13 Reed) of the creation of the fifth sun. These serpents enclose a series of star symbols and solar rays which are attached to 20 day signs of the Aztec calendar. The central section [11: 60] is divided into four square panels signifying the four ages of the universe, Sun of Jaguar, Sun of Wind, Sun of Fiery Rain, and Sun of Water (CEMANAHUAC), which surround and constitute the glyph for the Aztec age, Sun of Movement. The central face is probably the sun-god Tonatiuh, whose protruding tongue is a sacrificial knife. On either side of his face are jaguar claws holding human hearts. The symbolic meaning of the image is that the Aztecs considered their age to be the Age of the Centre, which

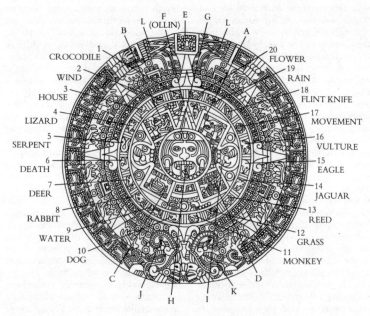

A Sun of Jaguar.
B Sun of Wind.
C Sun of Fiery Rain.
D Sun of Water.
E Sun of Reed (ritual date 13, or 1011 CE).
F *Ollin* motif (ritual date, 17 Movement)

enclosing central figures of the stone.
G Sun-god Tonatiuh.
H Sacrificial knife.
I Claws holding human hearts.
JK Fire serpents.
L Fire-serpent tails.

incorporated all universal space and time within itself.

Caliph, Caliphate [XIV] The institution of the caliphate dates from MUHAMMAD's death in 632, when caliphs ('successors') were chosen to lead the community, preserve and extend its borders (see JIHAD), ensure the canonical celebration of the cult (see SALAT) and the application of the SHARI‘A [29: VIII; 47: VII]. It continued through the lines of so-called 'Rightly guided' or 'Orthodox' (632–61 CE), Umayyad (661–750), and Abbasid (750–1517) caliphs (ISLAMIC DYNASTIES) until 1517, and the Ottoman Turkish sultans (or secular rulers) subsequently assumed, on their own initiative, the title, only abolished formally by Kemal Atatürk in 1924. The mainstream Sunni (SUNNA) community regarded the caliphate as a temporal necessity only, for there could be no divinely inspired figure after the Prophet; but the Shi'is viewed it rather as a divinely designated office or imamate (IMAM; SHI‘ISM). Hence the unity of the original caliphate, already impaired by sectarian quarrels over its exact nature (see FIRQA, KHARIJITES), was broken by the 10th century, when the Shi'i line of Fatimid caliphs arose in Egypt side by side with the official Sunni one in Baghdad. Yet its concept as a focus of loyalty for all Muslims continued until the 20th century, with a special appeal for Muslim groups away from the heartlands (PAN-ISLAMISM), and its abolition called forth the evanescent and fruitless 'caliphate movement' in the 1920s, notably in Muslim India. It is in such areas as this, also, that the idea of the early caliphate as a golden age, whose simplicity and austerity should be restored, has recently been influential (SOUTH ASIA, ISLAM IN). [8; 21 'Khalifa'; 83: II]

Calmecac [XIX] The centres for religious and political education in AZTEC times were the *calmecacs* or Row of Houses (14th to 16th centuries CE). These priestly residences were schools for the children of the nobility, but occasionally admitted a commoner child when the parents committed his life to the priesthood and the patron deity, QUETZALCOATL. [10: 204–10] *Calmecacs* were connected to the important temples in towns and cities throughout central Mesoamerica and trained the future leaders of all communities. The painting, reading, and oral telling of the pictorial traditions were essential to this training because they contained the vital knowledge concerning the cosmos, sacred hymns, astrology, the interpretations of dreams, the calendar, and the sacred histories of the ruling dynasty. [17: 322–31, 452–8] The priests (TEO-PIXQUE) who guided life in the *calmecacs* had extensive influence in society, including the direction of the ritual schedules in the temples, control of lavish sacrifices, the construction of monumental architecture, and the timely waging of war and trading expeditions.

Calumet [III] The original French designation of the 'reed pipe' found among the Miami and Illinois of North America is now generally applied to all ceremonial smoking instruments of Amerindians, and localized variations have been supplanted by pan-Indian custom. [17: VIII] Vouchsafed to mankind by the White Buffalo Woman (*ogalala* is the SIOUX variant), the pipe is a microcosmic symbol of the universe. The clay of the stone bowl represents the earth; the wooden stem represents vegetation; and the stem carvings symbolize animals and birds. The act of smoking is thus a reaffirmation of the cosmic network of relationships. [1: III]

Calvinism [XI.B] John Calvin (1509–64) established a partial theocracy (STATE) in Geneva backed by the theology of his Institutes of the Christian Religion [11: 212–14]. This inspired the Reformed Church type of PROTESTANTISM (e.g. Scottish PRESBYTERIANISM). Calvinism expressed the sovereignty of God in predestination but also in closely supervised church and civic life. Calvinistic CONGREGA-TIONALISM and Presbyterianism were influential in the American colonies and affected by REVIVALISM (e.g. Jonathan Edwards, 1703–58). Karl Barth (1886–1968) has been the most influential modern Calvinist theologian. [91; 140]

Canada, Christianity in [XI.B] Canadian Christianity reflects its colonial origins. French colonization of the 17th century brought Jesuit missions to the Indians, hostile to Gallicanism (STATE) and JANSENISM as well as PROT-ESTANTISM. Conquest by Britain (1763) brought various forms of Protestantism. The early establishment of ANGLICANISM with church lands ceased as other denominations grew. The United Church of Canada (1925) incorporated METHODISM, CONGREGA-TIONALISM, and PRESBYTERIANISM. ROMAN CATHOLICISM of a conservative type remains strong in the French provinces as part of their cultural identity. [58; 82 vol. 3: v; 83 vol. 3: x, vol. 5: II]

Canon (Christian Bible) [XI.A] The canon of the BIBLE is the list of books acknowledged by SYNAGOGUE and CHURCH as uniquely authoritative.

The three divisions of the Hebrew Bible – the Law, Prophets, and Writings – may represent three stages by which it received 'canonical' recognition. The main content of the Hebrew canon was recognized before the beginning of the Christian era, but it was re-examined and finally 'closed' by the rabbis at Jamnia between 70 and 100 CE.

The Christian canon of the Old Testament was wider than the Hebrew Bible; it included also documents found in the SEPTUAGINT and elsewhere. The main outlines of the New Testament canon were fixed during the 2nd century, largely through the controversy over Marcionism. There were disagreements over the inclusion or exclusion of some of the documents, notably Heb-

rews and Revelation. But the traditional canon of 27 books was widely agreed by 367 CE. [1: 95–113; 6: 1, 113–59, 284–308]

Cantor [XVII] The prayer leader in the synagogue, particularly on Sabbaths (SHABBAT) and festivals (CHAGIM), known in Hebrew as a *chazan* [13: 498]. The cantor is not a priest, and any layman can fulfil this role [52: 209]. In modern times, with the use of choirs in SYNAGOGUES and the development of Jewish liturgical music (MUSIC (JEWISH)), the cantor has become a full-time, paid synagogue official. Certain pieces of the liturgy have become standard parts of the cantorial repertoire. [9 vol. 7: 1542]

Cargo Cults [XX] The name given to hundreds of new movements occurring primarily but not solely in Melanesia, expecting a new order of equality with whites and human fulfilment to be achieved supernaturally, and symbolized by the arrival of a cargo of Western-type goods by ship or plane, perhaps accompanied by returning ancestors. Wharves, airstrips, and warehouses may be built, and to hasten the event new rituals and behaviour replace the traditional customs and economy. The social consequences form a problem for governments and churches, but most movements are short-lived, even though cargo thinking (that development depends on ritual and the supernatural) is deeply rooted in Melanesian cultures. Over 70 *koreri*, *mansren*, etc., movements have been recorded in Irian Jaya since the 1850s [10; 19: 199–206]. The earliest, much noticed, in Papua was the so-called 'Vailala madness' from 1919, but others include the Mambu cults from 1937, Yaliwan's Yangoru movement from 1971, and JON FRUM in Vanuatu. [12: 166–80; 19: 313–17; 20]

Caste [XIII.A] Strictly speaking this is not a religious concept, but it is closely related to Hindu religion and society. Portuguese in origin, the word 'caste' is normally used to refer to what in India is called *jati*, the social status which is one's inheritance at birth, whether high or low. *Jati* may be identified with a particular occupation; there is a *jati* of scavengers, another of weavers, of potters, ironworkers, leatherworkers, and so on. All these *jatis* are regarded as low; some of them are regarded by high-caste Hindus as ritually polluting. The list of *jatis* runs into many hundreds, and varies greatly, not only from one region of India to another but also from one village to another. Not all follow their traditional occupation. This is often the case with BRAHMANS, and with some of the lower castes; for example, palanquin-bearers will nowadays more frequently be cultivators. With caste membership go certain restrictions on social intercourse, especially in such matters as intermarriage, and interdining; in urban areas, at least, the latter is now difficult to observe strictly.

Caste therefore assumes a religious character, in that: (1) priesthood is, in orthodox terms at least, the prerogative of the Brahman caste; (2) the superiority of the Brahmans to all others is regarded as religiously sanctioned in the sacred texts of the VEDAS; (3) the theory of KARMA, i.e. the law of moral cause and effect, is regarded as providing an explanation of why some men are born high while others are born low; and (4) the distinction between 'unclean' and 'clean' castes (or castes which are ritually polluting and castes which are not) is to some extent (but only partly) a religious conception. 'Caste' sometimes refers also to the ancient theoretical scheme of VARNAS, and attempts are made to correlate *jatis* and *varnas*, but without clearly satisfactory results. In modern India it is found that the dominant *jati* (in practice) is not always that of the Brahmans (although it may be so in theory), and where some other *jati* is dominant the attitudes and values of that *jati* tend also to be dominant, rather than those of Brahmans. [4; 24: 9–11, 89–93, 103–5]

Caste (Sikh) [XXVII] In terms of status or privilege CASTE is explicitly rejected by Sikhs. Nanak denounced it, subsequent GURUS reinforced his message, and ritual observance confirms it. [6: 80–82; 26: 8–10] At baptism all must drink the same water; and in GURD-WARAS all sit together, receive the same KARAH PRASAD, and eat in the same *langar*. Caste is, however, retained within the PANTH as a social order. The Gurus were married according to caste prescription and gave their children in marriage similarly. This convention has survived virtually intact, with the result that practically every Indian Sikh belongs to a particular caste. An absolute majority are Jats, members of rural Punjab's dominant caste.

Other important castes with both Sikh and Hindu sections are the Khatri and Arora. Distinctively Sikh castes are the Ramgarhia (a composite artisan caste), Ahluwalia, Ramdasia, and Mazhabi, the latter two comprising Sikhs from outcaste origins. The Gurus were all Khatris. [23: v]

Catholic From a Greek word meaning 'general' or 'universal'. The commonest uses of it by Christians today are: (1) to describe 'orthodox' as distinct from 'heretical' Christians (HERESY; ORTHODOXY; SCHISM); (2) as the term preferred by Roman Catholics to describe themselves; (3) in contrast to PROTESTANTISM for churches such as ROMAN CATHOLICISM, the ORTHODOX CHURCH, Old Catholics (PAPACY) and ANGLICANISM, which emphasize church tradition (AUTHORITY), episcopal MINISTRY, and SACRAMENTS in continuity with the early church.

Celtic Religion [v] The Celts were established in central Europe by 500 BCE as nomadic warrior tribes. They moved eastwards into Asia Minor, where they were known as Galatians, and westwards into Gaul, Spain, and Britain [19: I, 20–28; 22: I, 15–32]. Early

Welsh and Irish literature preserves Celtic myths [21: 1]. Religious practices are described by Posidonius (c. 135–50 BCE) and other classical writers [28]. Art and archaeology also provide evidence for cults and religious symbols [19: III]. The religion had many local variations, but in the west the organized professional class of DRUIDS taught and preserved religious traditions [14: IV]. Teutates, Esis, and Taranis (Thunderer) are said by Roman writers to have received human sacrifice in Gaul [26: II, 21–3]. There was a goddess equated with Minerva (BRIGIT), and many fertility goddesses (MATRES) and goddesses of battle (VALKYRIES). Deities were frequently represented in sets of three. The chief gods remembered in Ireland were DAGDA, a primitive figure with club and cauldron, LUG, a warrior-god skilled in many crafts, and Manannan, god of the sea [26: IV, 45–6], together with many powerful goddesses with both fierce and benevolent aspects [23: V]. Two- or three-headed figures, as well as horned heads, have been found (HEAD CULT). There were small local temples, and more elaborate ones under Greek or Roman influence [17: II, 40–54], and many holy places on hills or by water (VOTIVE OFFERINGS). There were four main festivals with sacrifice at the quarters of the year (SAMHAIN), and ceremonial feasting played an important part [22: VII, 151–4]. The supernatural world was associated with the depths of earth or sea, or distant islands (LAND OF YOUTH). Birds and animals, especially boar, bull, horse, swan, and raven, were symbols of divine power [23: VII].

Cemanahuac [XIX] The Aztecs (MESO-AMERICAN RELIGIONS) conceived of the world as a land surrounded by water, Cemanahuac, with their capital, Tenochtitlan, located at the *tlalxico* or navel of the earth from which extended four quadrants, *nauhcampa*, literally four directions of the wind. In an alternative version, the earth was conceived as a giant crocodile floating in the primal waters. Each of the four quarters had specific names, colours, and influences associated with it. Though the pattern varied from culture to culture, a typical Mesoamerican version was: east/Tlacopan, 'Place of dawn', yellow, fertile, and good; north/Mictlampa, 'Region of the underworld', red, barren, and bad; west/Cihuatlampa, 'Region of women', blue-green, unfavourable, humid; south/Huitzlampa, 'Region of thorns', white; centre/Tlalxico, 'Navel', black. [2: 3–8; 12: 46–61] (*See figure.*) The waters surrounding the inhabited land were called *ilhuicatl*, the celestial water, which extended upwards in a vertical direction, merging with the sky and supporting the lowest level of heaven. This cosmological pattern of a central space with four cardinal sections surrounding it became the organizing principle for a multitude of supernatural, political, tributary, and economic conceptions in central Mesoamerican society.

The vertical cosmos was conceived of as a series of thirteen layers above and nine layers below the earth [17: 406]. Each celestial layer was inhabited by a deity, a sacred bird, and a specific cosmological influence and colour. The nine underworld layers were hazard stations for the souls of the dead, who, aided by magical charms buried with the bodies, were assisted in their quest for eternal peace at the lowest level, called Mictlan.

The Aztecs and their neighbours believed that they lived in the Fifth Sun or age of Nahui Ollin, Sun of Movement. This fifth age was preceded by four universal ages, Sun of Jaguar, Sun of Wind, Sun of Fiery Rain, and Sun of Water, each named after the cataclysmic event which destroyed it. Each age was ruled by one of the great deities who became the sun during one age: TEZCATLIPOCA, QUETZALCOATL, TLALOC, and Chalchuihuitlicue. [12: 25–46] This cosmogony appears as a pictorial image in the centre of the CALENDAR STONE.

Central Asian Buddhism [IX.B] Buddhist missions reached China during the 1st century CE. By this time monasteries appear to have been established from India into northern Afghanistan, Tadzhikistan (Soviet Central Asia), and Sinkiang (Chinese Turkestan) along the trade routes terminating near TUN-HUANG. The area was inhabited during the 1st millennium CE mostly by peoples speaking Middle Iranian languages such as Sogdian and

Khotanese Saka. Buddhism in company with other religious traditions was well-established in the area until after the coming of Islam. Local climatic conditions have preserved written materials, paintings, etc., which have contributed greatly to our knowledge of ancient Buddhism as well as of MANICHAEISM, Nestorian Christianity (CHRISTOLOGY), and East Iranian languages and culture. Both MAHAYANA and earlier Buddhist schools were present, especially the SARVASTIVADA and the MAHASANGHIKA. Most Buddhist

The Aztec five world regions

missionaries to China before 265 CE
were from central Asia, which consequently had a formative influence on
CHINESE BUDDHISM.

Cernunnos [v] Horned male heads or
figures occur frequently in Celtic art, a
tradition going back to the Northern
Bronze Age. On a Paris relief an
antlered god sitting cross-legged is
inscribed '(C)ernunnos' (Horned One),
and the name has been adopted for this
type of deity [22: VI, 162–4]. He
frequently has a neck-ornament and a
purse, and is accompanied by a
ram-headed serpent, a stag, and other
animals [22: VII, 203–4], as on the
Gundestrup cauldron (probably 1st
century BCE).

Chagim [XVII] Literally 'festivals'. The
Jewish ritual year (CALENDAR) begins
with the two-day New Year festival
(Rosh Ha-Shanah), a time of repentance
when the *shofar* or ram's horn is blown
to awaken the Jews to turn back to God.
Two weeks later (usually mid-October)
is the festival of Tabernacles (Sukkot),
when Jews live in a temporary booth or
sukkah reminding them of the time the
Israelites spent wandering in the wilderness. Tabernacles ends with a separate
festival when the annual reading of the
Pentateuch (BIBLE) is concluded with a
celebration of the Rejoicing of the
TORAH (Simchat Torah). Two months
later the minor festival of Chanukah
commemorates the religiously inspired
revolt of the Maccabees against the
Hellenistic rulers of Palestine in the 2nd
century BCE (BIBLICAL HISTORY).
Lights are lit in the Jewish home for
eight days. Ten weeks later Purim commemorates the deliverance of the Jews
as recorded in the Book of Esther. At
the beginning of spring Jews celebrate
the Passover (Pesach), when the
EXODUS from Egypt occurred. No
leavened bread is eaten; unleavened
wafers or *matzah* are eaten instead. At
the beginning of Passover a Seder meal
is held, at which four cups of wine are
drunk and the story of the Exodus re-

cited from a Haggadah text ('Haggadah'
is the Hebrew equivalent of the Aramaic
AGGADAH, and is generally used to refer
to this text). Seven weeks later Pentecost (Shavuot) commemorates the
revelation of God at Mt Sinai (MOSES).
[11: 170; 13: XI; 44: V–XXIX; 52: X–XI]

Ch'an [X] The term *ch'an* (Japanese
zen) is an abbreviation of *ch'an-na*, the
Chinese transliteration of the Sanskrit
'DHYANA' (PALI *jhana*). In Chinese
Buddhism *ch'an* was used as a general
term for meditation. The Ch'an school
(Ch'an Tsung) is summarized in various
texts as: 'A special transmission outside
the scriptures;/No depending on words
and letters;/Direct pointing to the
human mind;/Seeing into one's own
nature, and attaining Buddha-hood.'
[27: V, 67; 84: V, 176] Although this
summary is attributed to Ch'an master
Nan Ch'uan (748–834 CE), most of the
ideas were present in the teachings of
Tao Sheng (360–434 CE) [32: VII, 270–
84; 27: IV, 61–6].

Ch'an tradition regards Bodhidharma as its founder in China. He is said to
have arrived in China from India in
520 CE. After attempting to teach the
Emperor Wu the truth of EMPTINESS
(*shunya*), he spent nine years in meditation facing a wall. He emphasized the
teachings of the *Lankavatara-Sutra*
(YOGACARA). [27: III, 45–51, V, 67–87;
84: V, 163–228]

The 'special transmission', and the
Ch'an patriarchal lineage from
Bodhidharma to the fifth patriarch,
Hung Jen, was generally accepted; but
the succession of Shen Hsiu (600–
702 CE) as the sixth patriarch was publicly contested in 734 CE by Shen Hui,
who claimed that Hui Neng (638–
713 CE) had been the true sixth patriarch. He accused Shen Hsiu of
deviating from true Ch'an by endorsing
a gradual method of training. He
insisted that Hui Neng's direct approach
of sudden awakening, which rejects all
distinctions between enlightenment and
ignorance, and between ordinary beings

and BUDDHAS, was the true Ch'an teaching. Eventually Hui Neng's position became generally accepted. He was particularly associated with the Diamond Sutra (*Vajracchedika*), a verse of which had stimulated his own 'inner awakening' (Chinese *wu*; Japanese *satori*). [7: XXVI, 425–49; 9; 15: XII, 350–64; 24: XIV, 346–68; 27: V, VI; 32: IX, 386–406]

After the government persecution of Buddhism in 845 CE, Ch'an emerged as the strongest survivor. By this time five Ch'an sects had developed. Only the Lin Chi (Japanese *rinzai*) and Ts'ao Tung (Japanese *soto*) survived during the Sung dynasty (960–1126). During this period the Lin Chi masters developed the *kung an* (Japanese *koan*) as subjects for meditation and systematic training, to bring their students to awakening (*wu*; *satori*) [78]. The Ts'ao Tung sect had developed the teaching of the Five Ranks on the relationship between relative and absolute, and they stressed the value of constant attention and formal seated meditation (*tso ch'an*; Japanese *zazen*) (ZEN). [11; 27: VII, VIII; 78]

Chasidism (or **Hasidism**) [XVII] A movement founded in the late 18th century by Israel Baal Shem Tov, known as the Besht. The early centres of Chasidism were in the Ukraine and southern Poland, but within two generations it had spread throughout eastern Europe. Chasidic teachings were a popularized form of KABBALAH, emphasizing the importance of the inner service of God rather than the keeping of Jewish ritual laws [52: 107]. God can be served in everyday activities as well as through the *mitzvot* (MITZVAH). The single most important aspect of this service is *devekut*, or cleaving to God, in joy. Chasidism gave new value to the life of the ordinary Jew who could not aspire to any great understanding of Jewish lore. The PARABLE or story, conveying its message to simple and sophisticated Jews alike, was widely used as a

teaching medium. Many of these Chasidic stories have been retold by modern Jewish theologians [5; 6]. The Chasidic movement was strongly opposed by rabbinical conservatives, known as Mitnagdim, who suspected it of heterodox tendencies and put it under the ban of excommunication or *cherem*. Today Chasidic Jews are indistinguishable from their Orthodox co-religionists, except for the organization of their communities around the figure of the *tzaddik* or Chasidic leader [36: 37].

Chen Yen [X] The Tantric (TANTRA) school of Buddhism in China. The term *chen yen* (True Word) translates the Sanskrit term MANTRA. The school was introduced into China in 716 CE by Shubhakarasimha, who translated the *Mahavairocana-Sutra*, and was developed by Vajrabodhi (663–723), and by Amoghavajra (705–74). Although Amoghavajra gained the patronage of Emperor T'ai Tsung, the school was never generally popular. Tibetan Tantric Buddhism was introduced by the Yuan dynasty (1279–1368) and survived as the Tibetan Esoteric sect (Tsang Mi Tsung) (SHINGON). [15: XI, 325–37; 81: X, 135–6]

Cheyenne [III] A North American Indian tribe of the ALGONQUIN linguistic stock. Originally agriculturists of the central plains, its members later became nomadic hunters. Many of their religious rituals were associated with warfare. The annual Renewal of the Sacred Arrows (a cosmogonic ritual), founded on the Cheyenne story of creation according to which a bundle of sacred arrows symbolized the whole tribe (COSMOLOGY), was intended to ensure regeneration and prosperity. Also practised were the SUN DANCE (occasionally still danced today), the Buffalo Head Dance, and the GHOST DANCE. More recently, the Peyote Cult (PEYOTISM) has assumed prominence. [23: XIV]

Children of God [XXI] The Children of God, or, as they subsequently called themselves, the Family of Love, began as part of the JESUS MOVEMENT. It was originally founded in California in 1968 by David Berg, who later became known as Moses David, or just 'Mo'. Although the movement is based on Evangelical Christianity, it is highly critical of the established church, espousing what it calls 'godly socialism', its main theological reference being the 'Mo letters' which issue from the leader and cover a wide range of subjects from prophecies of doom to instruction on health and sexual practices. It is believed that these are 'the last days' and that capitalism and communism (being materialistic in practice or philosophy) will destroy each other. The survivors will be those who have committed themselves to a godly life. [2: 12; 11: II; 25: III] Members are typically young adults who give up their careers and possessions in order to live in 'colonies' and spend the majority of their time 'litnessing' on the streets, i.e. selling literature and seeking new recruits. The movement grew fairly rapidly in the early 1970s, spreading over North America and into parts of Europe, but the total membership at any one time is unlikely to have exceeded 6,000. The C.O.G. was one of the first NEW RELIGIOUS MOVEMENTS to receive the attention of the ANTI-CULT MOVEMENT. One of the practices of the group which has been most publicized is that of 'flirty fishing' (using sex as a conversion technique).

China, Christianity in [XI.B] Early Nestorians (7th century) (CHRISTOLOGY) and medieval Western missions to China died out in the 14th century. The Jesuit Matteo Ricci (1552–1610) began a tradition (condemned in the 18th century) of accommodating Christianity to Chinese ceremonies and religious language. A fresh start in the 19th century was facilitated by European political influence. Identification of Christianity with this influence aggravated traditional Chinese xenophobia and intellectual antipathy to Christianity, demonstrated in the Boxer rising (1900). The T'ai P'ing rebellion (1850s) included a measure of Christian SYNCRETISM [20 vol. 6: 286–8; 65: 266–75]. An important aspect of missionary policy was a Christian higher education system. The advent of a communist state (1949) soon led to the exclusion of missionaries, and necessity as well as government policy compelled churches to be self-supporting. The 'Cultural Revolution' (1966) brought persecution but current (1981) reports suggest less religious intolerance. Christianity, however, has never been more than a minority influence in China. [65: IV, IX, XVII; 70; 82 vol. 3: XIV, vol. 6: V, vol. 7: XIII; 83 vol. 3: XIX, vol. 5: XIII]

China and Central Asia, Islam in [XIV] Islam arrived on the China coast in the 8th century through the efforts of Arab–Persian traders, but the numerical strength of the indigenous Chinese Muslims today (called Hui in Chinese) is in the interior mountain and steppe areas of western and south-western China, such as Sinkiang (Eastern Turkestan), Inner Mongolia, Kansu, Yunnan, and Szechwan, where there are anciently established communities. In the last two centuries they have often been in revolt against imperial Chinese attempts at centralization. The 1936 China census counted 47 million Muslims out of a total population of 452 million; no figures are available under communist China, but the Muslim population may well have doubled. Always cut off by distance from the mainsprings of Islamic piety and scholarship, Chinese Islam, under its native religious leaders, the *ahungs*, had to coexist uneasily with Confucianism (CONFUCIUS) and thus became in many ways eclectic, at least until the 19th-century movements of Islamic revivalism in China. Since the communist Revolution, it has, like other religions, been persecuted, but the post-Mao period seems to have brought some relaxation of official disapproval [20 'China'; 40].

Muslim missionaries worked in the steppelands of Turkestan and Siberia from the 10th century onwards, an activity in which dervishes were probably prominent. Certain Central Asian SUFI ORDERS, like the followers of Shaikh Ahmad Yasawi, show distinct influences from the original shamanism (SHAMAN) of the region. The progress of Islam was checked by the Russian advance across Siberia in the 17th century, and the last independent Muslim khanates of Turkestan came under Russian suzerainty by the late 19th century. Inevitably repressed by the Bolsheviks after 1920, with the vast majority of Muslim schools and MOSQUES abolished, it is difficult to evaluate the strength of religious feeling among contemporary Central Asian Muslims (estimated in 1970 at *c.* 37 million and increasing proportionally faster than other groups in the U.S.S.R.). Religious instruction has been virtually non-existent, and only a handful of the faithful have been allowed to perform the Pilgrimage (HAJJ) each year. However, official attitudes seem to have softened recently; thus a trickle of Muslims have been allowed to go to the Middle East as students, and public worship and celebration of festivals are allowed. [6: VII]

China, The People's Republic of, Chinese Religion in [X] The fall of the Ch'ing dynasty in 1912 meant the end of the great Sacrificial Rites (*Chi Li*) of imperial religion in China, and the official examination system based on the CONFUCIAN CANON had been abolished in 1905. The traditions of religious Taoism (TAO CHIAO) and CHINESE BUDDHISM and many features of popular or diffused religion in China continued to survive. [105: XII, 294–330]

After the establishment of the People's Republic of China in 1949, public acts of ritual and worship were actively discouraged (even though freedom of religious belief was included in the Con-

stitution). In the 1950s official religious organizations such as the Chinese Buddhist Association, the Chinese Muslim Association, and eventually the Chinese Taoist Association were founded, under the auspices of the Bureau of Religious Affairs. These were primarily intended to establish control over the religions and ensure political conformity. Such state control of religion is by no means a new phenomenon in China.

During the mid and late 1960s anti-religious campaigns were pursued as part of the general policy of eradicating old values and customs. By 1970 many urban temples and monasteries had been closed down. Reports began to appear about violent anti-religious acts carried out by the Red Guards of the Cultural Revolution. Homes were searched for religious objects and monks and priests were publicly humiliated. More recently, official attitudes to religion appear to have relaxed. Many monasteries and temples have reopened, ostensibly as places of historical and cultural interest. As recently as October 1981 official concern was expressed at the attitudes of prayer and reverence adopted by some visitors to the temples. Sections of the Chinese press reiterated that while freedom of religious belief was protected under the Constitution, people should be actively discouraged from practising religion.

Probably the most resilient traditional religious values and practices are those which have never been centrally organized. It is clear that many aspects of popular or diffused religion in China, such as reverence for ancestors, family and even communal festivals, and belief in local deities and spirits continue to survive, albeit in restricted forms in the rural areas of mainland China. (AN-CESTOR CULT (CHINESE); CHINESE PANTHEON; CHINA, THE REPUBLIC OF (TAIWAN), AND HONG KONG, CHINESE RELIGION IN; FESTIVALS (CHINESE)) [6A; 85: XXVIII, 231–41; 86: VIII, 114–22]

China, The Republic of (Taiwan), and Hong Kong, Chinese Religion in [x] Many features of traditional Chinese popular or diffused religion flourish in Taiwan, Hong Kong, and the New Territories, in spite of the influences of industrialization and secularization. One aspect of traditional Chinese life, the practice of FENG-SHUI (geomancy), has actually increased with the extensive building programmes in these areas. The annual cycle of communal and family festivals, such as New Year, the Bright and Clear Festival, and Serving All Souls, and the birthdays of particular deities are still celebrated with enthusiasm and sincerity (FESTIVALS (CHINESE)). [86: VII, 108–13] The traditions of family religion, such as reverence for ancestors and the honouring of gods on the family altar, continue to be observed, particularly by the elderly (ANCESTOR CULT; FUNERAL RITES). [1; 46]

The two most popular deities in Taiwan are the Heavenly Empress, known familiarly as 'Granny' (Ma tsu), and the Goddess of Mercy (KUAN YIN). Other important deities include the Jade Emperor (Yu Huang), the God of War (Kuan Kung), the local earth-god T'u Ti Kung, AMITABHA Buddha, and Sakyamuni BUDDHA (see CHINESE PANTHEON). [46; 85: XXV, 198–209; 86: IV, 56–68]

The majority of Chinese see no conflict or disharmony between the three great traditions of Confucianism, Taoism (TAO CHIAO), and BUDDHISM. Most people accept ideas and practices from all three. In general the values of Confucianism provide the framework for public life and for family and social ethics, emphasizing qualities such as loyalty, propriety (LI), and filial piety (CONFUCIAN CANON; CONFUCIUS).

The ostensible concern of the Taoist adept or priest is with the quest for immortality. In practice the Taoists have a much more important social role. They are the ritual manipulators of spirits, in healing and exorcism, and they regulate the important festivals which restore the balance of the Yin and Yang forces in nature and in society (YIN-YANG). One such festival is the elaborate festival of cosmic renewal (chiao) which takes place in most villages once every 60 years (TAO CHIA). [75–7]

For ordinary people Buddhism represents the virtues of abstinence and restraint, as exemplified by the relatively austere lives of the monks. It also offers the hope of salvation through rebirth in Amitabha's Pure Land (CHING T'U TSUNG). Buddhist monks frequently assist at funeral rites (CHINESE BUDDHISM). In many villages the temple (miao) is the centre of social and cultural life as well as a place of religious worship and ritual. Most village temples are administered by a lay committee of directors who usually employ a Taoist priest to officiate. [86: IV, 62–9]

Chinese Buddhism [x] There are various legends about the entry of Buddhism into China at very early dates, and there is some evidence of a Buddhist community in 65 CE at P'eng Ch'eng in northern Kiangsu [15: II, 27–32]. Buddhism entered China via the trade routes from CENTRAL ASIA. A memorial written in 166 CE criticizes Emperor Huan for worshipping at altars to Huang-Lao and the BUDDHA, and refers to a 'Sutra in Forty-Two Sections' [15: II, 34–6]. The close association between Buddhism and neo-Taoism (HSUAN HSUEH) is a distinctive feature of early Buddhism in China. It led to the interpretation and translation of key Buddhist terms with Taoist ones, and to the development of the ko i (Extending the meaning) method of expounding Buddhist teachings by referring to texts such as the I Ching (Classic of Changes), TAO TE CHING, and the CHUANG TZU. Many Chinese in the 2nd and 3rd centuries regarded Buddhism as simply a foreign form of Taoism (TAO CHIAO). [15: II, 48–53]

An Shih Kao was an important Buddhist teacher in China. He arrived in Lo Yang in 148 CE and effectively founded what became known as the DHYANA school, which emphasized the rules of discipline of the VINAYA (PATIMOKKHA) and meditation. One of his early translations was the *Sutra on Mindfulness of Breathing* (*An Pan Shou I Ching*). The other early interest in Chinese Buddhism was reflected by the PRAJNA school, based on the interpretation of the Perfection of Wisdom (PRAJNAPARAMITA), the earliest translation being of the *Perfection of Wisdom in 8,000 Lines* (*Ashtasahasrika Prajnaparamita*) by Chih Ch'an (Lokakshema) in 175 CE. This school was strongly influenced by neo-Taoist thought. [7: XX, 336–42; 15: III, 57–80; 32: VII, 237–58]

Hui Yuan (344–416), the most eminent Chinese Buddhist of his age, established a famous monastery at Lu Shan, engaged in a lengthy correspondence with KUMARAJIVA [74: 181–95], defended the right of the SANGHA to remain independent of the state [24: XII, 280–86], and founded a cult of AMITABHA [15: III, 103–12]. Hui's disciple Tao Sheng (360–434) studied with Kumarajiva for three years and developed his theories of the true self (*chen wo*) or Buddha nature (*fo hsing*) in man and sudden enlightenment (*tun wu*). [15: III, 112–20; 32: VII, 270–84]

The period between the 5th and 8th centuries CE was the time of the development and expansion of the major Buddhist schools and popular movements, such as CH'AN, CHEN YEN, CHING T'U, Chu She, FA HSIANG, HUA YEN, LU, SAN LUN, and T'IEN TAI [7: XXII–XXVI; 15: XI, XII; 24: XIII, XIV; 81: X, 124–39]. By the Sung dynasty (960–1126) Buddhism had declined and only the Ch'an and Ching T'u schools remained active and popular. [15; 16; 72; 104; 106]

Chinese Pantheon [x] The Chinese pantheon is so extensive that it is im-possible to count all the gods and spirits in it. The regional and historical variations, the influence of gods from BUDDHISM, and religious Taoism (TAO CHIAO) make systematic classification difficult. Even the apparently obvious distinction between a Buddhist pantheon and a Taoist pantheon is problematic because of the extent of the early interaction between these two traditions. [105: I, 23–5]

From Chou times (1027–402 BCE) the official or state religion of China focused upon the abstract deity Heaven (T'IEN), and its counterpart Earth (*Ti*) and the Royal Ancestors (*Tsu Tsung*). These were almost exclusively the concern of the ruler and the feudal lords or, in imperial times, the Emperor. [2; 4: III, 54–68; 63: 93–111; 84: V, 70–76]

The popular and anthropomorphic equivalent of Heaven was the Jade Emperor (Yu Huang), who received the full title 'Jade Emperor Lord on High', (Yu Huang SHANG TI) during the T'ang dynasty (618–907 CE). He came to be regarded as the ruler of the heavenly court and bureaucracy during the Sung dynasty (960–1126 CE). These were regarded as heavenly versions of the earthly institutions, with departments run by their appropriate gods and spirits. The most important of these include the Ministry of Thunder (Lei Pu) and the Heavenly Ministry of Healing (T'ien I Yuan), run by the legendary first three Sage Emperors of China: Fu Hsi, Shen Nung, and Huang Ti. The Ministry of Fire (Huo Pu) is run by a former Taoist sage and astral ruler of Mars, Lo Hsuan. The Ministry of Epidemics is run by another former Taoist, Lu Yo. The Ministry of the Five Sacred Mountains (Wu Yo) has the god of T'AI SHAN, the Great Divine Ruler of the Eastern Peak (Tung Yueh Ta Ti), as its chief minister. He is the Jade Emperor's grandson and chief assistant. He can determine a person's lifespan and their fortune and he assists Yama (VEDA) (Yen Lo Wang) in presiding over the fate of those in the hells. [25: 262–302; 102: 151]

Other major gods include the god of the ramparts or city-god Ch'eng Huang, whose duties made him the supernatural equivalent of the city magistrate. The god of the stove, Tsao Chun, had a vital role in domestic life by keeping records of each person's actions and reporting at least once a year to the Jade Emperor. Fu Shen the god of Happiness, Shou Hsing the god of longevity, and Ts'ai Shen the god of wealth are now among the most popular Chinese gods. [22; 23; 25; 42; 102]

Ching T'u Tsung [X] Pure Land school. Textually the school is based upon the *Larger Sukhavativyuha-Sutra* (translated in 252 CE), the *Smaller Sukhavativyuha-Sutra* (translated in 402 CE by Kumarajiva), and the *Amitayur-Dhyana-Sutra* (translated in 424 CE by Kalayashas). The *Sukhavativyuha-Sutras* contain a detailed account by the Buddha Sakyamuni (GOTAMA) of how the Buddha AMITABHA came to preside over the 'Land of Bliss' (*Sukhavati*) or 'Pure Land' (*Parisodhana-Kshetra*) as a result of his practice and devotion in a previous age as the monk Dharmakara. The *sutras* repeat the great vows taken by Dharmakara to enable those devoted to him and to the Pure Land to be reborn there and attain enlightenment. The BUDDHA then projects rays of light from his body and illuminates the Pure Land for the assembly to see (a detailed description is given in the *sutras*).

The tendency towards devotion focused on Amitabha and the Pure Land developed very early in China. In 402 CE Hui Yuan, the head of an important monastery near Lu Shan, founded a cult of Amitabha and vowed to be reborn in the Pure Land [15: IV, 106–8]. The organizer of Ching T'u as a separate school was T'an Luan (476–542). He emphasized the practice of *Nien fo* (Japanese: *nembutsu*), literally mindfulness or recollection of the Buddha, which was usually practised by devoted

repetition of the phrase, '*Namo Amitabha Buddha*' (Chinese: *Nan-mo A-mi-t'o Fo*; Japanese: *Namu Amida Butsu – see* AMIDA WORSHIP). Tao Cho (562–645) argued that the practice of *nien fo* was the only effective method of gaining rebirth in the Pure Land and hence enlightenment, because ignorant beings in the age of the DHARMA's decline were incapable of other religious practices or higher understanding. He advised the constant repetition of Amitabha's name and he developed the rosary for this purpose. Shan Tao (613–81), in his commentary on the *Amitayur-Dhyana-Sutra*, advocates primarily the practice of *nien fo* with a pure and undisturbed mind, together with the chanting of *sutras*, meditation upon Amitabha, worship of his image, and the singing of hymns in his praise. [15: XII, 338–50; 24: XIV, 334–45; 81: X, 125–7]

Chinvat Bridge [XXX] *Chinvato Peretu* (PAHLAVI *Chinvat Puhl*) The 'Bridge of the Separator', the Bridge of Judgement in ZOROASTRIANISM. It is believed that for three days after death the soul (*urvan*; Pahlavi *ruvan*) meditates on its life before proceeding to its judgement by the three YAZATAS, Mithra, Sraosha, and Rashnu. Its good and evil thoughts, words, and deeds are weighed in the balance. If the good predominate, then it is led by a beautiful maiden, the personification of its conscience (*daena*), across the bridge to heaven. If the evil predominate, then an ugly old hag leads the soul trembling across the bridge, which narrows so that the soul falls down into hell. This is the first judgement. The stay in heaven or hell is a temporary one for reward or corrective punishment for the soul until the day of the resurrection (FRASHOKERETI) when the whole person can be judged. [20: 60–66; 25; 35; 39: IX]

Chisungu [II] Dancing the *chisungu* is the ritual of female initiation – girls' puberty rites – among the matrilineal Bemba of northern Zambia and neighbouring peoples. The ceremony could take many weeks, involves the segregation of the novices, makes great use of clay figurines, and consists of a mass of symbolic usages whereby girls just prior to marriage are formally taught both 'the things of womanhood' and 'the things of the garden'. There is no form of circumcision. *Chisungu* is understood as a necessary handing on, sanctioned and required by the ancestors, of the norms required for marriage and good living.

The *chisungu* may be compared with the *nkang'a* of the Ndembu, another Zambian matrilineal people. For both peoples these are among the most important of rituals (*see also* NYAU). The Bemba have no male equivalent, but the Ndembu also have circumcision rites for their boys. Circumcision is part of the initiation of boys among many African peoples in all parts of the continent, but is by no means universal. Some, such as the Gikuyu, practise female circumcision (clitoridectomy) as well. For the Gikuyu, *irua* (initiation) provides entry at once into a particular age-set and to full maturity; it is the central ritual of personal and communal life. But just as other peoples, like the Bemba, have initiation rituals without circumcision so there are peoples, such as the GANDA, who have no puberty rites whatever. Where such rituals exist their meaning is closely related to the structures of society, but equally they are rich in a mass of often apparently obscure symbolism and may throw much light upon underlying religious concepts. [41; 43: 198–268; 44: 86–129]

Chöd [XXIX] The Chöd ('cutting') tradition of Tibetan Buddhism originated with the Indian Dampa Sanjay (d. 1117) and his Tibetan disciple the yogini Machik Labdron (1055–1149). Chöd combines the theories of the PRAJNAPARAMITA with the methods of TANTRA (2). By meditation on SHUNYATA and the visualized sacrifice of his physical existence to all sentient beings, especially those of a demonic nature, the Chöd practitioner 'cuts' or severs attachment to the notion of a truly existent self. Although Chöd no longer constitutes an independent sect its teachings have been preserved within the KAGYU and NYINGMA schools. [6]

Cholollan [XIX] (4th–16th centuries CE) At the time of the Spanish conquest (1521 CE), the city of Cholollan (also referred to as Cholula) was the religious centre of Mesoamerica, compared by the Spaniards to Rome and Mecca because of the great pilgrimages to its many shrines. [10: 119–20] This ceremonial and market city was one of the longest-occupied sites in Mesoamerican history and was organized around the Tlachihualtepetl, the largest pyramid temple in the world, which covered more than 16 hectares at the time of the conquest. This great shrine, famous as the oracle of QUETZALCOATL, was rebuilt at least four times during its existence. Historical records indicate that it was first settled by the Olmeca-Xicalanca, who constructed the early version of the ceremonial precinct. Following the fall of the great capital Teotihuacan in the 8th century CE, Cholollan became the pilgrimage and market centre *par excellence*, and drew pilgrims, merchants, nobles, and kings to its fairs and innumerable religious shrines. This expansion was partly brought about by the Tolteca Chichimeca, who resettled the city following the fall of their capital, Tollan Xicocotitlan. The Tolteca Chichimeca renamed the city Tollan Cholollan Tlachihualtepetl, revitalized the cult of Quetzalcoatl, and dispensed sacralized authority to the many rulers of the land who travelled to the shrine for investiture ceremonies. Cholollan was governed by two priestly rulers, the Acquiach, Elder of the Above, and the Tlalchiach, Elder of the Ground. Historical records show that the city was used as a periodic truce centre for warring factions, which celebrated there together on special occasions.

Christian Fellowship Church [xx]
The largest independent church in
Melanesia (MELANESIAN RELIGION),
founded about 1959 in New Georgia,
Solomon Islands, by Silas Eto (b. 1905),
who after education in the Methodist
Mission (METHODISM) had a series of
visionary experiences. An admirer of
John Wesley and J. F. Goldie the
pioneer missionary, Eto became
dissatisfied with local Methodism and
developed a well-organized church
with Pentecostal worship (PENTE-
COSTALISM), healing, prosperous
economic activities, and a holy village, Paradise (NEW JERUSALEM). In
the 1970s relations with Methodism
and other churches were being re-
established.

Christian Kabbalah [XVIII] The interpretation of KABBALAH as specifically
confirming Christian doctrine. Pico
della Mirandola (1463–94), who studied
Hebrew under Jewish teachers, argued
that Kabbalah proved the divinity of
JESUS CHRIST and that the triadic structure of the *sefirot* (SEFIRAH) confirmed
the TRINITY. His views influenced
scholars who saw in Kabbalah similarities to the Christian NEOPLATONISM
of pseudo-Dionysius. The Hebraist
Johannes Reuchlin (1455–1522) (notable
for his defence of the TALMUD against
Dominicans who demanded its
destruction) wrote influential dialogues
asserting the value of Kabbalah and
expounding techniques of *gematria*
(NUMEROLOGY), *notarikon* (alphabetical
symbolism), and *temurah* (mystical reinterpretation of words), which he applied
to confirm Christian doctrine. He
hoped such interpretations would aid
the conversion of the Jews, and indeed a
substantial number of conversions during the 16th and 17th centuries were justified by reference to Kabbalah. By the
mid 17th century most Christian scholars had some knowledge of Kabbalah,
but after 1700 its popularity waned and
views that Kabbalah 'proves' Christianity are now rare. [2]

Christian Science [XI.B] Mary Baker
Eddy (1821–1910) of New Hampshire,
U.S.A., developed a system of spiritual
healing based on the principle that mind
is the only reality and matter an illusion.
Right thinking is the answer to the illusion of illness. This system (and the
healing work of JESUS CHRIST) was explained in her *Science and Health with a
Key to the Scriptures* (1875). The movement has spread mainly in the English-
speaking countries, appealing more to
the relatively affluent than most SECTS.
It publishes the *Christian Science Monitor*
newspaper. Worship is simple, including readings from Mrs Eddy's works
and accounts of healings. [2: LX; 52; 98:
337–40; 144: 121–215]

Christianity (Early) [XI.A] Christianity is the religion which acknowledges
JESUS CHRIST as its founder. Every
variety of Christianity claims his authority in one way or another. Early
Christianity was based on his teaching
and even more on his death and resurrection in which, it was believed, God
had acted decisively for the salvation of
the world, and the kingdom of God
announced by Jesus had been inaugurated. Christianity first organized itself
in JERUSALEM (CHURCH) and was originally a movement within JUDAISM,
but within 20 years it took root among
Gentiles (ANTIOCH; PAUL) and began
to spread rapidly in the Mediterranean
world. Jewish Christianity remained
dominant, however, until the dispersal
of the Jerusalem church shortly before
the destruction of Jerusalem in 70
CE; after that its influence quickly
decreased.

When Gentile Christianity became
distinct from Judaism, its churches were
no longer *collegia licita* (permitted associations) in the eyes of Roman law. It
was therefore repeatedly the target of
attempts at suppression. After the great
fire of Rome in 64 CE Nero found in the
Christians of the capital convenient
scapegoats against whom the popular
anger might be turned. But Christianity

continued to spread, both upwards, socially (penetrating the imperial family by 96 CE), and outwards (reaching Britain by the end of the 2nd century). Its attractiveness was due in part to the Christian GOSPEL, which assured believers of immortality, pardon, freedom from the power of demons (DEMONOLOGY), and personal significance in God's sight, and in part to the warmth of the Christian fellowship in which discrimination on grounds of wealth, class, race, or sex was obliterated. In 313 CE its right to exist was at last confirmed by Constantine's Milan edict of toleration. In 381 CE Theodosius established it as the religion of the Roman empire. (BAPTISM; EUCHARIST; MINISTRY (CHRISTIAN); WORSHIP (BIBLICAL)) [3: 195–408; 5]

Christianity, History and Character of [XI.B] After the ministry of JESUS CHRIST in Palestine, Christianity spread through the Roman empire (CHRISTIANITY (EARLY)). It survived the fall of the Western Empire in 476 CE and converted the 'barbarian' invaders. The Eastern Empire survived as the Christian state of Byzantium until its fall to Islamic forces in 1453 CE. By the 11th century the Western and Eastern ORTHODOX CHURCH had divided. The Western church under the PAPACY contributed much to the development of Western civilization, partly through MONASTICISM. It also experienced conflicts with heresies (HERESY (MEDIEVAL CHRISTIAN)) and the STATE (CHRISTIANITY AND THE). The 15th-century CONCILIAR MOVEMENT challenged papal authority. The 16th-century REFORMATION and COUNTER-REFORMATION split the Western church into ROMAN CATHOLICISM and PROTESTANTISM; Protestantism further divided into many churches and SECTS. European expansion and MISSIONS from the 16th century spread Christianity to the U.S.A., AFRICA, ASIA, and LATIN AMERICA; but religious observance in Western Europe has greatly declined in the 20th century. Early Christian theology and medieval SCHOLASTICISM owed much to Greek philosophy as well as to the BIBLE. Even MYSTICISM has often been influenced by philosophical speculation. Later Western theology (unlike that of the Orthodox Church) has been much influenced by secular science and philosophy, especially in Protestantism. Despite a rich tradition of mysticism and asceticism, Christianity has shown strong activist tendencies in social and political life (SOCIAL MORALITY (CHRISTIAN)). Central to its teaching is the idea of GOD, as a TRINITY, who created the world and saves mankind through the work of the divine son Jesus Christ (CHRISTOLOGY; SALVATION, CHRISTIAN DOCTRINE OF). Historically, Christianity has emphasized its claims to exclusive religious truth, but these have been less marked in recent times. [5; 11; 20; 27; 38; 68; 69; 82; 83; 98; 128]

Numbers given for different Christian churches are difficult to compare as some count whole nations while others have restricted 'membership' but many 'adherents'. Claims are made for Christianity at 1,000 million to be the largest world religion. The following estimates (c. 1960) suggest the relative size of the larger bodies, without defining the degree of commitment: ANGLICANISM, 43,447,000; BAPTISTS, 23,967,000; CALVINISM, 46,943,000; LUTHERANISM, 79,491,000; METHODISM, 22,000,000; Orthodox, 141,875,000; Roman Catholicism, 539,225,000. [105 vol. 13: 678–82]

Christology [XI.B] Teaching concerning the person of JESUS CHRIST (cf. GOD; TRINITY). As Christians traditionally believe that Christ is both human and divine, the problem has been to defend the idea of distinct, fully divine and fully human 'natures' in a single, unified personality. Explanations owed much to Greek thought. Early theologians saw Christ as the eternal

Word (*Logos*) of God taking human form (Incarnation). In answer to the Arian view of him as a kind of subordinate being between God and man (ARIANISM; HERESY (MEDIEVAL CHRISTIAN)), the COUNCIL of Nicea (325 CE) defined him as 'of one substance with the Father' (*homoousion*). Theories proliferated in the 4th and 5th centuries, many views being condemned as heretical. Apollinarians emphasized Christ's divinity but saw his humanity as merely physical. Nestorians upheld humanity in Christ so distinct from his divinity as to suggest a split personality. Eutychians thought that there were two natures before the Incarnation and one 'mixed' nature after it. The Council of Chalcedon (451) [11: 51–2] defined the limits of orthodoxy: 'Jesus Christ . . . truly God and truly man . . . of a reasonable soul and body; of one substance with the Father as regards his Godhead, and . . . of one substance with us as regards his manhood . . . recognized in two natures, without confusion . . . without separation.' Dissident communities continued, including Nestorians. Monophysites taught that only one nature (divine) existed after the Incarnation. Monothelites taught that only one will existed in Christ. Early PROTESTANTISM remained 'orthodox' except for UNITARIANISM and later DEISM. From the 19th century onwards changing philosophies and views of human nature produced further speculation. In general (unlike the early church) the humanity of Christ has been readily accepted; the divinity has been more difficult. *Kenosis* theories see Christ as 'emptying' himself of divine 'attributes' (GOD, CHRISTIAN CONCEPT OF) to become man. The Chalcedonian definition has been widely criticized yet not replaced. [11: 35–52; 76: VI, XI, XII; 107: 281–2; 127]

Chthonian Religion [XXVIII] Devotion to GODS of the earth (ancient Greek *chthon*) as against those of the sky or heaven. The term is often used with specific reference to the nether-world (compare ANCESTOR-WORSHIP); but MYTHS, rites (RITUAL), and cults centred on the earth and its fertility may also be called 'chthonian' (contrasting with 'Olympian' in ancient Greek religion).

Chuang Tzu [X] The Taoist philosopher of the late 4th century BCE who provides the theme and inspiration for the treatise of the same name (TAO CHIAO). Only the first seven of its 33 chapters are thought to have been composed by Chuang Tzu. The work contains many of the same basic concepts and terms as the TAO TE CHING, but it gives a more detailed and systematic exposition of them. The *Chuang Tzu* embraces a much more personal and individualistic form of mysticism than that of the *Tao Te Ching*; in it one of the implications of naturalness (*tzu jan*) and non-doing (*wu wei*) is never to put oneself in a position in which one is called upon to govern or administer anything [96: VII, 93–4, XVII, 187–9]. Hence unlike the *Tao Te Ching* the *Chuang Tzu* is not addressed specifically to the sage ruler. Chapter Two of the *Chuang.Tzu* includes a detailed exposition of the arbitrary and indeterminate nature of names, language, argument, and all claims to valid knowledge. As an alternative its author recommends the embracing of all apparent opposites and contradictions [7: VIII, 179–90; 96: II, 36–76].

The work also devotes some attention to methods of mental discipline such as concentration, abandoning sense input and discriminatory thought, and achieving inner emptiness. These are summarized under the process called 'fasting the mind' (*hsin chai*). [7: VIII, 179, 201, 207; 96: IV, 57–8, VI, 90–91, VII, 97]

The *Chuang Tzu* advocates the value of yielding to change as part of the natural order of things, and this includes the sage's acceptance of his own death with equanimity. [7: VIII, 191–4; 19: VI; 21: I, II, III; 31: X; 96: VI, 77–80]

Church (**Christian**) [XI.A, B] (Greek
ekklesia) Both 'church' and SYNA-
GOGUE are used in the SEPTUAGINT of
the community of Israel and both are
used also in the New Testament of a
Christian community, but from an early
date 'synagogue' has been reserved for
Jews and *ekklesia* for Christians.

In its Christian sense the word
'church' has a twofold use in the New
Testament: (1) as the community of
Christians in a city (such as the church
in JERUSALEM or CORINTH) or the
church (meeting) in someone's house;
(2) as the world-wide community of
Christians. At first the local churches
were variously organized; in apostolic
times there was no overall organization
for the universal church. It comprised
Jews and GENTILES, although in some
places its membership might be entirely
Jewish or Gentile. By the end of the 1st
century it was predominantly Gentile
(CHRISTIANITY (EARLY)). [A.3: 195–
221; A.5: 45–56, 132–6; A.11]

Traditionally over the centuries 'the
church' has been interpreted as the
whole body of Christians, seen as one
holy, catholic (universal), and apostolic
(descended from the APOSTLES) body.
Separation from it involves HERESY or
schism. ROMAN CATHOLICISM, the
ORTHODOX CHURCH, and some parts
of PROTESTANTISM claim to be the sole
true church on earth. Others regard all
churches as partly defective. Some Protestants see 'true' Christians as members
of an 'invisible church' of the 'saved'
(both living and dead), which is imperfectly realized in existing organizations.
Christians also believe in the 'communion of saints', a spiritual communion
which binds individual Christians to
each other and to JESUS CHRIST. This
applies to those on earth ('church
militant') and in heaven ('church
triumphant'). (Cf. SECTS for 'church' as
a sociological term.) [B.1: 14–101; B.66;
B.76: XV]

Church Discipline [XI.B] Christian
regulations for religious and moral life

include systems of CANON law [107:
231]. This developed from rules of
early COUNCILS, bishops, and Popes,
later elaborated as in ROMAN
CATHOLICISM's *Corpus juris canonici.*
(The ORTHODOX CHURCH developed
its own system.) ANGLICANISM based
its canons on medieval material last
revised in 1969. Most churches have
developed rules administered through
hierarchies of church courts. Some, such
as Roman Catholicism, Anglicanism,
and PRESBYTERIANISM have at various
times made use of excommunication
[107: 490] – the ultimate penalty of
exclusion from the SACRAMENTS. This
formerly involved civil penalties as
well. The term *anathema* was formerly
used of exclusion from the church for
HERESY. 'Discipline' is also used to refer
to systems of rules in MONASTICISM. It
also refers to acts of physical self-denial
(like fasting) to assist spiritual progress;
and to the scourge, self-flagellation,
sometimes used for PENANCE.

Church Music (**Christian**) [XI.B] The
traditional music of the Roman MASS
was Gregorian chant ('plainsong') – a
single vocal line. But music for the mass
regularly adopted secular changes in
style and became increasingly elaborate.
Masses by classical and romantic
composers eventually entered the con-
cert hall, as did 'requiems' (for the
dead). The LITURGICAL MOVEMENT
encouraged simplification and congregational participation. (The ORTHO-
DOX CHURCH developed its own tradition [134 vol. 1: 201–8].) The 'motet'
(a polyphonal chant) was notably
developed by G. P. da Palestrina (*c.*
1525–94). From the 'cantata', a religious libretto with solos and choruses,
developed the more elaborate 'oratorio'.
This reached a popular climax with
G. F. Handel's (1685–1759) *Messiah.*
'Passions' (commemorating Christ's
sufferings) reached a summit in the
work of J. S. Bach (1685–1750). Div-
orced from its religious setting, much
of this music has become part of the

Western musical heritage. Psalms (from Hebrew scripture (BIBLE)) and hymns have had a more popular and congregational role. Both Eastern and Western churchmen wrote them to teach doctrine and inspire devotion; and they came to have an accepted place in the EUCHARIST. PURITANISM preferred psalms, as divinely inspired, but hymns eventually became a staple element in Protestant worship. Major contributors included Martin Luther (1483–1546), Isaac Watts (1674–1748) (CONGREGATIONALISM), and Charles Wesley (1707–88) (METHODISM). Their strong theology and felicitous language degenerated into 19th-century vagueness and sentimentality, notably in REVIVALISM. Religious songs of black Christians had stronger existential roots in slave experience. Modern church music and hymns reflect most levels of contemporary style and taste. [73; 113; 122 vol. 10: 97–134]

Church Organization [XI.B] ROMAN CATHOLICISM, ANGLICANISM, and the ORTHODOX CHURCH have a hierarchical organization. For the first two the basic unit is the parish (usually a village or area of a town) [107: 1032–3]. Parishes are grouped in 'dioceses' [107: 404] under a bishop; and groups of dioceses in a province under an archbishop as 'metropolitan'. (The Orthodox Church uses 'parish' for the bishop's area and 'diocese' for areas under autocephalous (AUTOCEPHALY) 'Patriarchs'.) The cathedral as the chief church of the diocese and 'seat' (*cathedra*) of the bishop is usually governed by a 'chapter' of 'canons' (always priests) led by a 'dean'. In Roman Catholicism the structure is headed by the Pope (PAPACY); but in the Orthodox Church the principle of autocephaly obtains. Systems of organization in PROTESTANTISM vary greatly. PRESBYTERIANISM and METHODISM have relatively centralized systems of local, regional, and national representative bodies. Some Lutheran churches

(LUTHERANISM), MORAVIANISM, and METHODISM in the U.S.A. have bishops, but without regarding them as a higher order of MINISTRY. CONGREGATIONALISM and the BAPTISTS have historically emphasized the independence of the local church. Most of the main Protestant bodies and Anglicanism have developed world representative bodies for consultation. (Cf. also COUNCILS.)

Circumcision (in Islam) [XIV] Though popularly regarded as one of the touchstones of the true believer, neither male circumcision nor female excision has any warrant in the QUR'AN. However, they were obviously ancient Near Eastern practices, and were soon hallowed by Muslim tradition as part of the SUNNA, so that male circumcision became regarded both as an initiation ceremony into the Islamic community and as a rite of passage into adult society. Normally, the operation is performed on boys after the age of seven or eight years and before the onset of puberty – in more advanced societies with a local anaesthetic – and is accompanied by festivities [21 'Khitān'; 29: 161; 39 s.v.; 45: II; 47: 251–2]

Circumcision (in Judaism) [XVII] The rite of circumcision, *berit milah*, performed on Jewish male children and converts to JUDAISM represents the sign of the COVENANT between God and the seed of Abraham (Gen. 17: 11). Circumcision takes place on the eighth day after birth, even if the day is a Sabbath (SHABBAT) or festival (CHAGIM), but may for health reasons be delayed. The child is placed momentarily on a chair set aside for the prophet Elijah, who is thought to attend every circumcision ceremony, and then on the lap of the person who holds the child, the *sandek* or godfather. Circumcision is performed by a *mohel* or trained circumcisor. He removes the foreskin of the penis with a sharp knife, then tears back the underlying membrane. The blood is sucked from the wound, either by mouth or in more modern times through the use of a glass tube to prevent infection. A celebratory meal follows. [9 vol. 5: 567; 48: 401; 52: 134]

Classic Maya [XIX] Among Mesoamerican cultures, the Classic Maya (200–900 CE) developed the most brilliant and complex religious traditions, expressed in elaborate networks of lavishly constructed ceremonial centres in southern Mesoamerica [9: VI, VII]. Classic Mayan cities were marked by a flowering of exquisite sculpture, monumental architecture, predictive sciences, and religious ritual [4: III, IV; 11: VII, VIII].

Mayan culture was run by priestly and royal hierarchies which directed the social order through an elaborate ceremonial system of temporal cycles and renewals. Among their most outstanding achievements were their writing system, mathematical precision, and astronomical observation. These developments were utilized in the worship of time, *kinh* (also signifying sun or day), which was measured in minute detail. *Kinh* and all important dimensions of life were recorded in a hieroglyphic writing system [13], still little understood, consisting of a hybrid mixture of pictographs, ideographs, and syllabic forms which narrated calendric, historical, and dynastic activities. This writing system survives in three codices, the *Codex Madrid*, the *Codex Dresden*, and the *Codex Paris* (CODEX (MESOAMERICAN)), and numerous temple inscriptions, and on ceremonial architecture. The Mayan priesthood developed a mathematical system based on the concept of zero and positional notation, which was developed to measure astronomical cycles with precision. [5: VII] Time was computed through the intermeshing of a 260-day calendar with a 365-day calendar, which were renewed every 52 years. In this larger calendar system, each day was named for its position in both calendars. The Mayan solar calendar was more exact than the

Gregorian year (brought from Europe in the 16th century). This great computation of sacred time had a fixed starting-point at 3113 BCE and prophesied the end of the universe in 2011 CE.

The Mayan cosmos was organized into 13 heavenly compartments and nine levels in the underworld where the nine gods of the underworld ruled. Horizontally, the earth had four quarters surrounding a central region (CEMANAHUAC). This universe had been destroyed and created a number of times. Among the most important deities reigning in this cosmos were Itzamna, the creator-god who fertilized the universe, Ah Kin, the sun-god, Ix Chel, the moon-goddess, and the Chacs, or rain-gods (TLALOC).

Codex (Mesoamerican) [XIX] (10th–16th centuries CE) One of the most important sources for the study of MESOAMERICAN RELIGIONS is the surviving picture books from the Mayan (CLASSIC MAYA), Mixtec, and Aztec regions which carry examples of the writing system, consisting of pictographs and ideographs with different degrees of phoneticism [17: XII]. These codices carry narrative drawings consisting of pictures of gods [19: 107, 135], processions, battles, sacrifices, buildings, places, and celestial events as well as ideograms associated with ideas and symbolic systems [11]. This writing system is also found in low-relief sculpture such as the Calendar Stone, the Tizoc Stone, and the Teocalli de la Guerra Sagrada (AZTEC SCULPTURE).

Mesoamerican codices include manuscripts called *tiras* (strips of animal skin or paper), or screenfolds called *amoxtlacuilolli* (which were folded *tiras*, long strips composed of sheets of animal skin or paper glued together), rolls and *lienzos* or canvas sheets on which paintings appeared. These manuscripts depicted a series of celestial or human events which were read and interpreted, with some flexibility, by oral specialists trained in the tradition. Every significant human event was influenced by consultation with the specialist in charge of these manuscripts. Surviving pre-Conquest codices fall into two categories: historical–genealogical books and ritual–divinatory books. Ritual–divinatory manuscripts like the *Codex Madrid*, *Codex Vaticanus B*, and the *Codex Borgia* depicted sacred almanacs (*Tonalpohualli*), divinities, divination, and prophecies of future events. One codex even covers such topics as bee-keeping, rain-making, crop care, and diseases. Historical–genealogical books like the *Codex Bodley* and *Codex Colombino* pictured the history of kings and dynastic genealogies. The native pictorial tradition was transmitted into the post-Conquest culture and appears in the *Codex Mendoza* which, accompanied by Spanish glosses, pictures the history, tribute, and daily life of the Aztec capital, Tenochtitlan. [15]

Communion [XI.C] A term used in several contexts in Christianity.

(1) A synonym for the EUCHARIST.

(2) The act of receiving the consecrated bread and wine.

(3) The communion of saints, the fellowship of all Christians in heaven and on earth.

(4) A specific Christian church or family of churches, e.g. ORTHODOX CHURCH or ANGLICANISM.

(5) To be in communion with a church indicates mutual recognition and acceptance of the SACRAMENTS and MINISTRY of respective churches.

Communist World, Christianity in the [XI.B] Marxist ideology maintains that religion will wither away when its economic basis is destroyed. In Eastern Europe, however, communist states face churches (notably Polish ROMAN CATHOLICISM, and the Bulgarian and Romanian ORTHODOX CHURCHES) which have been major sources of national and cultural identity. Romanian Orthodoxy still operates almost like an established church. Hence reli-

gious activity is generally allowed by law (in theory), and state subsidies are sometimes given where endowments were confiscated. (Albania, exceptionally, prohibits religion entirely.) In practice, however, there has been much communist indoctrination and persecution, especially in the 1950s and 1960s; and Christians suffer civil disabilities. Churchmen's reactions have varied enormously. Some resist openly; some passively conform; some support state social policy while criticizing its faults. To assume that only the first reaction is 'truly Christian' is an oversimplification. These reactions (and state policy) are partly conditioned by a past in which churches were often bastions of conservative privilege. Nor is religious decline due solely to persecution. Rapid industrialization and urbanization have produced similar effects to those in the West. (Cf. also CHINA and RUSSIA, CHRISTIANITY IN.) [9; 12; 83 vol. 4: XIII, XIX]

Conciliar Movement [XI.B] The Great Schism (1378 CE) between rival Popes (PAPACY) was ended by the COUNCIL of Constance (1417 CE). Several reforming Councils (which are collectively referred to as the Conciliar Movement) then upheld the doctrine that final authority in the church lies in a General Council. Though condemned by the Papacy, the tradition of questioning the final authority of the Pope persisted until Vatican Council I (1869–70). [11: 135–7; 26; 107: 326]

Confucian Canon [X] This achieved its present form (comprising the Five Classics and the Four Books) in the Sung dynasty under the direction of Chu Hsi (1130–1200 BCE). During the Former Han dynasty (206 BCE to 9 CE) controversy arose between the Old Character school (*Ku Wen Chia*), which used editions of the Classics that had purportedly survived Emperor Ch'in Shih Huang Ti's burning of the books in 213 BCE, and the New Character school (*Chin Wen Chia*), who used the editions of the Classics rewritten in the reformed script after the Ch'in persecutions. [32: II, III, IV]

The Five Classics are:

(1) The *Shu Ching* (Classic of History), which is a collection of documents, speeches, and counsels made by Chinese rulers and ministers purporting to date from the legendary rulers Yao and Shun to the early Chou dynasty (1000 BCE). Many of the supposedly older documents actually date from the Later Han dynasty (23–220 CE). [48; 58]

(2) The *Shih Ching* (Classic of Odes) is a collection of 300 poems and songs dating mainly from the early Chou dynasty (1027–402 BCE). [49; 59; 89]

(3) The *I Ching* (Classic of Changes) is a collection of texts on divination based on a set of 64 hexagrams made by various combinations of broken and unbroken lines reflecting the relationship between the two basic forces in nature and human society (YIN–YANG). Each hexagram is determined by casting 49 yarrow stalks, and each has a short cryptic interpretation. These have subsequently been expanded in the 'wings' or appendices, which are attributed to CONFUCIUS but which date from the Former Han dynasty. [103]

(4) The *Ch'un Ch'iu* (Spring and Autumn Annals) are extracts from the history of the state of Lu from 722 to 484 BCE, said to have been compiled by Confucius. They are accompanied by commentaries which date from before 200 BCE. [60]

(5) The *Li Ching* (Classic of Rites) is a collection of three books on the LI (Rites of Propriety): the *Chou Li* (Rites of Chou); *I Li* (Ceremonies and Rites), and *Li Chi* (Record of Rites). Although compiled during the Former Han dynasty, parts of these texts are much more ancient. [61; 83]

The Four Books are: the *Lun Yu* (Analects) of Confucius, the *Chung Yung* (Doctrine of the Mean), *Ta Hsueh* (Great Learning), and the *Meng Tzu* (MENCIUS). [44; 53; 54; 56; 86: 123–6]

Confucius [X] K'ung Fu Tzu (551–479 BCE). The best-known and probably most influential thinker in Chinese history. He was born of an impoverished noble family in the state of Lu, now Shantung Province. At the age of 20 he began his official career as keeper of the grain stores. According to most accounts he became prime minister of Lu in 501 BCE, although this is unlikely, and he is said to have resigned from office four years later because he disapproved of the ruler's policies. For the next 13 years he wandered from state to state attempting to advise different feudal rulers and gaining a small following of disciples. He eventually returned to Lu to spend the rest of his life teaching. [7: II, 14–48; 19: III, 39–59; 20; 31: IV, 43–75]

The most reliable source for Confucius's own ideas are the Analects or 'Selected Sayings' (*Lun Yu*), the earliest parts of which were composed shortly after his death. [91]

Confucius was primarily an educator and a transmitter of knowledge rather than a creative thinker. In accepting students he did not apply any class distinctions, accepting the poor as well as the rich [91: VII, 124]. One of his major contributions was the redefinition of key ideas in Chinese life and thought, along ethical and humanistic lines. The term *chun tzu*, literally meaning 'son of a ruler' or person of noble birth, was extended by Confucius to refer to anyone who was benevolent and modest of speech. Similarly he extended the use of the term LI (rites of propriety), which traditionally referred to the rules of proper conduct in anything from formal ritual procedure to detailed matters of etiquette. For Confucius *Li* referred primarily to the correct spirit in which ritual and social behaviour should be conducted, and this involved cultivating an attitude of respect and restraint [91: VIII, 132]. Confucius clearly regarded Heaven (T'IEN) as a positive and personal force in the universe [91: VII, 127, xiv, 189]: he was not, as some have supposed, an agnostic and a sceptic. His important contribution to political thought was his insistence on the identification of ethics with politics. He believed that government was primarily a matter of moral responsibility and was not simply the manipulation of power. [79; 82; 91: ii, 88, xii, 168]

Congregationalism [xi.b] Churches historically emphasizing government through officers elected by the membership, and the independence (hence 'Independents') of each local church. In later times associations of churches developed for cooperation. Membership was defined in terms of a 'gathered church' of believers bound by a 'covenant'. Congregationalism strongly influenced the founders of the New England colonies (notably the 'Pilgrim Fathers') and the u.s.a. has continued to be a major centre [2: ix]. English Congregationalists and Presbyterians (PRESBYTERIANISM) formed the United Reformed Church in 1972. Originally Calvinist (CALVINISM) in doctrine, later Congregationalism has often been open to influence from LIBERAL PROTESTANTISM. [71; 107: 332; 138]

Conservative Judaism [xvii] A modern movement within JUDAISM concentrated mostly in North America. Conservatism began with early 19th-century responses to modernity in Central Europe. Jewish intellectuals, like Z. Frankel (1801–75), who were unhappy with wholesale reforms of Jewish life, wished to preserve elements of the tradition. They founded the so-called 'Historical School', whose purpose was to introduce changes into Judaism which were consonant with Jewish historical development. This attitude was transferred to the u.s.a. by traditionally minded immigrants, who established the Jewish Theological Seminary (1887) in New York to train RABBIS in a modern approach to tradition. Solomon Schechter (1847–1915) was brought

over from England to head the seminary in 1902. An organization of Conservative rabbis, the Rabbinical Assembly of America, was formed at this time, followed by the association of Conservative congregations, the United Synagogue of America (1913). Conservative Judaism spread rapidly until it became the largest formal association of Jews, overtaking both REFORM and Orthodox JUDAISM [49: 254]. In 1922 a member of the seminary staff, Rabbi M. Kaplan, founded a more radical branch of Conservative Judaism known as 'Reconstructionism'. This has now become a completely separate religious movement [9 vol. 5: 901; 13: 285; 42: xiii, xiv].

Contemplation [xi.d] Prayer, the essence of which in central Christian traditions is the loving awareness of God. It involves no discursive thought (DISCURSIVE MEDITATION). As the 'prayer of quiet' it can be learned, as can other forms of prayer and meditation. Higher forms of contemplation are mystical states attained only by the free gift of God. They can involve rapture and ecstasy, as well as the purifying 'dark night' of the senses and of the soul. (HESYCHASM; MYSTICISM (CHRISTIAN)) [5; 19; 42]

Conversion (to Judaism) [xvii] Someone intending conversion to JUDAISM would at first be discouraged by a traditional Jewish law court (Bet Din). Should they persevere they would be expected to study Jewish teaching and familiarize themselves with religious practices. The ceremony of conversion (*giyur*) involves circumcision for the male and bathing (*tevilah*) in a ritual bath (*mikveh*) for both males and females. They are then considered as full Jews [9 vol. 13: 1182]. In REFORM JUDAISM conversion involves a simpler ceremony. [52: 15]

Corinth, Early Christianity at [xi.a] Corinth, refounded as a Roman colony in 44 BCE, was first evangelized by PAUL *c.* 50 CE. He spent about 18 months there and built up a large and gifted, if volatile, CHURCH. Most of the problems inherent in the Christianization of pagans were evident in Corinth and are treated in Paul's Letters to the Corinthians. Further problems arose *c.* 96 CE, when internal strife in the Corinthian church called forth an admonition from Clement, foreign secretary of the Roman church. [3: 296–308; 4: 248–79]

Corroboree [XXII] A term used in Australian English for any Aboriginal festive gathering involving singing and dancing (*see* SINGSING). The word was first used by 19th-century settlers in New South Wales, and was presumably borrowed from some local dialect. Because it covers sacred ceremonies and non-sacred entertainments alike, it is not a useful word in religious studies. In AUSTRALIAN RELIGION, religious ceremonies are ritual enactments of myths accompanied by song and dance, every movement being symbolic and meaningful, performed on sacred ground specially painted and marked for the occasion, as are the performers themselves. Non-religious dramatic performances with singing and dancing are for public entertainment and even instruction, as they sometimes include comment on social issues. The best-known instrument for musical accompaniment is the *didjeridu*, a long hollow drone-pipe with a wax mouthpiece [4: 367–87].

Cosmogony (Jewish) [XVII] The Pentateuch (BIBLE) begins with the account of the creation of the world by God, and there are scattered references to the topic in other biblical books. In rabbinical literature (RABBI) we already find some discussion of the idea that God created the world from nothing [9 vol. 5: 1059], and this theme of creation *ex nihilo* predominates in the work of the medieval theologians. Most of the latter reject the various notions of a pre-existing matter advocated by Greek philosophy [21: 94]. It is even stressed that creation *ex nihilo* is an essential part of

Jewish doctrine (THEISM) [19: 413]. Side by side with the philosophical interpretation of creation there were a number of medieval mystical teachings of a rather different nature. These see the created world as the end-product of a complicated process of emanation in which the unlimited Godhead, or *Ein Sof*, reveals Himself through 10 stages or *sefirot* [45: 25] (SEFIRAH). These stages represent continuity between the human and divine worlds.

Cosmology (Amerindian) [III] The wide variety of cosmogonic myths, the diversity of subsistence patterns, and the ever-present possibility of non-Indian influence upon aboriginal beliefs and practices, make it difficult to generalize regarding AMERINDIAN RELIGIONS and their world-views. One may note, however, that native American religions have usually placed greater emphasis upon action in this world than upon other-worldly speculations. The physical universe (although its origin is often a matter of conjecture) is generally accepted as the proper arena of human existence and the context in which man is to realize his fullest development (CREATION MYTHS). Yet inter-penetrating the visible, everyday world is its invisible, sacred, and powerful complement (MANITOU). Although conceptions of transcendent deities are not unknown (e.g. SIOUX), greater emphasis is usually placed upon the possibility of human interaction with the supernatural through the medium of this world (e.g. CALUMET). Man's life is conceived of as placed within a context of interlocking relationships wherein the divine, human, animal, and vegetative forms influence one another (e.g. OWNER OF THE ANIMALS). Thus there is a corresponding concern to discover these relationships and to establish correct patterns of behaviour in order to preserve the network and thereby realize fertility, long life, and social stability (CALENDAR ROUND). Rather than a sharp distinction between the sacred and

profane, Amerindian religions emphasize a continuity of existence; rituals, individual or collective, are thus directed
to the control of cosmic forces and the
influence of personal fate. [22: VIII, X,
XI, XIII]

Cosmology (Ancient Near Eastern)
[VI] SUMERIAN cosmology [24: 37–57]
became the foundation of many Near
Eastern concepts. The Sumerians specu-
lated that the major components of the
universe were heaven (a vaulted, hollow
space) and earth (a flat disc) which
existed, immovably, in a boundless sea
from which the universe had come into
being. Between heaven and earth was
the atmosphere, from which the sun,
moon, and stars were fashioned [16:
127–52]. The separation of heaven and
earth and the creation of the planets
were followed by plant, animal, and
human life. Invisible, immortal gods
guided and controlled this universe,
according to prescribed rules.

Deities were immortal and sustained
high moral values [16: 154], but they
could also be negligent, ill, wounded,
and even die [13: 157]. Whether city-
gods or state-deities, they tended to represent the elements of nature (moon,
sun, weather, agriculture) and the
underworld. Many early Mesopotamian
deities survived in Assyria or were introduced into the HITTITE pantheon
through the HURRIANS. All had human forms and were attributed with
human needs (ISLAND OF CREATION;
TEMPLES).

Cosmos [XII] Order; universe. The
Greeks believed that the universe was
ordered. Cosmic order, identified with
justice (*dike*), was a fundamental concept. Cosmogonic myths took the form
of theogonies. In the earliest (8th century BC) and most influential, the original entity was Chaos. Then came Gaia
(Earth) and other beings like Eros
(Love). Gaia had many children from
her son Ouranos (Sky), including the
Titans. One Titan, Kronos, castrated
and dethroned his father and became

world-ruler. He was himself dethroned
by his son Zeus (THEOI), whose rule
was to last for ever. It was challenged by
the *Gigantes* (Giants), Gaia's sons,
whom the 'new' gods, Zeus and his
contemporaries, defeated with Heracles'
(HEROES) help. Orphic (ORPHEUS) theogonies diverged from the mainstream.
Central was the murder by the Titans
of the future world-ruler Dionysos-
Zagreus, Zeus's son, later reborn as
Dionysos (THEOI). [10: 318–20; 12: 113–
19; 15: 73, 215–17]

Councils of the Church [XI.B] Official
meetings of bishops and others at
various levels of the CHURCH to settle
doctrine or discipline; at lower levels
usually called 'synods'. General (Ecumenical) Councils represent the whole
church. In ROMAN CATHOLICISM
they are considered valid and infallible if summoned and confirmed by
the PAPACY (but cf. CONCILIAR
MOVEMENT). They recognize 21 such
Councils. These include Nicea (325 CE),
on ARIANISM and the TRINITY; Chalcedon (451), which summed up the
limits of orthodoxy in CHRISTOLOGY;
Constance (1414–17), which settled the
Great Schism in the West; Trent
(1545–63), which was concerned with
the COUNTER-REFORMATION; Vatican
I (1869–70), which focused on the Papacy; and Vatican II (1962–5) [1], which
wrestled with the modernization of
Roman Catholicism. The ORTHODOX
CHURCH believes that Ecumenical
Councils cannot err, but recognizes none
after the seventh in 757; nor is papal
sanction necessary for them. ANGLICAN-
ISM and PROTESTANTISM recognize
the AUTHORITY of early Councils
in varying degrees, although it is believed that they could have erred. [67]

Counter-Reformation [XI.B] A 16th-
century movement of reform in ROMAN
CATHOLICISM as well as of defence
against the REFORMATION. Doctrine
was redefined and discipline reformed at
the COUNCIL of Trent (1545–63) [11:
261–9]. The PAPACY recovered respect

and authority. New religious orders (MONASTICISM), notably the Jesuits [11: 258–60; 107: 734–6], encouraged MISSIONS and pastoral activity. Notable mystics appeared in Spain, e.g. St Teresa of Avila (1515–82) and St John of the Cross (1542–91) (MYSTICISM). HERESY was repressed by the special tribunals of the Roman and Spanish Inquisitions [74] and the 'Index' (an official list of prohibited books) [107: 697]. Catholic princes strengthened the church politically against PROTESTANTISM. [20: VIII; 34; 64]

Covenant [XI.A] From the time of Moses (c. 1200 BCE) Israel considered itself to be a covenant community, bound to Yahweh by a solemn agreement in which he undertook to be their God and they undertook to be his obedient people. This covenant with Yahweh, which included the 'ten commandments', was their national constitution (TORAH). In form it resembled the treaties between Near Eastern kings and their vassals. From time to time the people were recalled (as by the prophets) to their covenant loyalty. The reformation under King Josiah (621 BCE), based on the law-code in the biblical book Deuteronomy, was a covenant renewal. The prophet Jeremiah's prediction of a new covenant (c. 587 BCE) was taken up both in the QUMRAN sect and in the Christian CHURCH, each of which regarded itself as the community of the new covenant. [1: 74–85; 19: 16–18, 35–8]

Cow [XIII.A] For Hindus the killing of a cow is a serious crime. The ARTHA-*shastra* refers to the killing of cattle as a crime worthy of death, but this may refer only to royal cattle [2: 196–7]. Nevertheless, reverence for the cow (whose five products, milk, curd, butter, urine, and dung, are regarded as purifiers) has grown steadily from the time of the BHAGAVADGITA, to the extent that Gandhi (1869–1948) regarded it as part of the essence of HINDUISM [25: 172–3, 243].

Creation Myths (Amerindian) [III] Cosmogony is one of the major themes of North American Indian mythology. The possibility of early European influence cannot be discounted. A survey of the more than 300 major variations reveals the presence of seven primary symbolic types: earth-diver; world-parent; emergence; spider-creator; creation by conflict or theft; creation from a cosmic giant; and the creator pair. [20] The earth-diver motif (most common throughout North America) attributes creation to an animal-like figure who dives to the bottom of a primeval ocean to retrieve mud or sand from which a somewhat fragile cosmos is shaped; its completion is usually left to a CULTURE HERO or TRICKSTER. The world-parent motif (limited primarily to the southwest), develops the sexual relationship of sky-father and earth-mother so common elsewhere. The sexual act is preparatory to true creation, which usually occurs after their separation. Emergence myths (mainly in the south-west, and among some Plains Indians) portray a gradual metamorphosis of mankind, animals, etc., as they progress through successive worlds to entry into the present or final world. 'Spider'-creation narratives identify this figure as the first being, who spins the web upon which the world is suspended. Conflict myths (primarily in the west and north-west) attribute creation to the actions of a trickster figure who 'steals' or fights to gain control of the elemental factors of creation (sun, fire, earth, water). Less frequent is the motif of creation resulting from the redistribution of parts from the body of a fallen giant (there is some occurrence in the north-east and north-west). A seventh type, widely occurring, ascribes creation to the cooperation or competition of two primordial agents (HERO TWINS), variously represented as twin brothers, sisters, father–son, uncle–nephew, etc.

Creeds (Christian) [XI.B] Short official statements of Christian belief, originally used at baptism (SACRAMENTS). They are arranged in sections on Father, Son, and Holy Spirit, with varying texts (TRINITY). The so-called 'Apostles' Creed' [11: 23] was accepted in the West for use in baptismal liturgies and ordinary WORSHIP in ROMAN CATHOLICISM and ANGLICANISM. It has also been acceptable to a wide variety of other churches. The more elaborate Nicene Creed (based on that of the COUNCIL of Nicea) [11: 24–7] has been used at MASS or EUCHARIST. (Its *Filioque* clause, stating that the Holy Spirit proceeds from the Father and the Son, was inserted later and is rejected by the ORTHODOX CHURCH.) The Athanasian Creed (of uncertain origin) is more elaborate in its CHRISTOLOGY and in modern times has been less used, because of its severe anathemas (formal exclusion from the church for HERESY). Early PROTESTANTISM produced 'Confessions of Faith' such as the Augsburg Confession (LUTHERANISM) [11: 210–12] and Westminster Confession (PRESBYTERIANISM) [11: 244–7]. The Thirty-Nine Articles has fulfilled a similar though more limited role for Anglicanism. Some Christian churches (e.g. BAPTISTS) have generally been reluctant to use formal creeds. [76: IX–XII]

Cremation (in Japan) [XVI] The priest Dosho (628–700 CE), an early introducer of Hosso sect (NANTO ROKU-SHU) practices who had studied under Hsuan Tsang in China, is the first recorded person to have been cremated in Japan, following a request made to his disciples. Cremation then received imperial sanction by Empress Jito, who was cremated in 704, a year after her death. In succeeding centuries the practice spread socially and geographically. Glass and inscribed gilt-bronze cinerary urns were later replaced as receptacles for the ashes by stone boxes and clay vessels. Following a medieval decline in the practice, perhaps because of the expense, it is now customarily carried out under Buddhist auspices, but is legally enforceable only in heavily populated areas.

Crusades [XI.B] European military expeditions to recover Christian holy places in Palestine from ISLAM. The first Crusade (1095 CE) captured JERUSALEM and established Christian states, which fell by 1291 despite further expeditions. Crusading motives included land-hunger and commerce as well as religion. The fourth (1202–4) was diverted to capture Constantinople from the ORTHODOX CHURCH. Others attacked heretics (e.g. the Albigensians–HERESY (MEDIEVAL CHRISTIAN)) and non-Christians in Europe. The Crusades also produced military 'orders' (MONASTICISM) such as Hospitallers (*c.* 11th century) and Templars (founded 1118 CE). [112; 117]

Culavamsa [IX.A] The 'Small' *vamsa* (or Chronicle), a Pali work which takes up the narrative of the Buddhist history of Sri Lanka from the MAHAVAMSA (Great Chronicle). The *Culavamsa* deals with the period from 302 CE to the beginning of the 19th century, and is the work of at least three successive authors [22: 142]. It was translated into German by W. Geiger, and from German to English by C. M. Rickmers.

Culture Hero (Amerindian) [III] Often the central figure in Amerindian myths, the culture hero continues the work of creation, transforming the landscape, regulating the cosmic patterns, and defining the dimensions of nature and human existence (CREATION MYTHS) [8: II]. The figure frequently provides a link between the primordial time of beginning (e.g. the golden age of the past) and the present human condition. His actions (including teaching mankind necessary arts and crafts as well as instituting laws and ceremonies) serve as a bridge between the two periods [23: IV]. Numerous accounts portray the culture hero as having the form of an animal-being (raven, coyote, and hare being common forms), while others speak of an anthropomorphic figure with SHAMAN-like powers, though the latter type is less frequent. Occasionally, the figure is placed in opposition to the supreme deity and through their interactions come the less desirable aspects of human life, including old age, disease, and death. The TRICKSTER-transformer presents a reversal of the more positive characteristics of this figure.

· D ·

Dagda [V] The Irish Dagda ('good god') is 'Father of All', a protective deity [26: IV, 38–42]. His huge club, supported on wheels, can both kill and restore to life, while his cauldron of abundance provides inspiration and rejuvenation. He is a rough, primitive figure, with a huge appetite, resembling the Gaulish mallet-god Sucellos [26: II, 19] and the Scandinavian THOR. He mates with the Morrigan, the war-goddess, and various river-goddesses. Oengus, a youthful deity, and BRIGIT are his children.

Daimon, Daimones [XII] The generic Greek meaning for *daimon* is 'divine power'. The word was used also to denote individual gods and, more narrowly, to mean 'intermediary being between men and gods', hence, 'individual destiny'. Some *daimones* received cult. There is one 5th-century reference to a *daimon* as an evil spirit, but it was Plato's pupil Xenocrates (*c.* 395–314) who developed the concept *daimon* (demon), as seen in the growing Hellenistic popular demonology, where philosophical speculation met rampant superstition. [2: III. 3.5, VII. 3.4; 6: 19–28, 50–56; 15: 282–4, 289–92; 17: 518–25, 871]

Dance [XXVIII] Rhythmic bodily movement. Ritual dancing has been a significant form of religious expression from ancient times (e.g. PREHISTORIC RELIGION and its hunting and fertility rites; Egypt and the ANCIENT NEAR EAST; ecstatic MYSTERY-CULTS). It has great importance for tribal peoples; in religions of Indian origin wherever they have spread; and e.g. in the Japanese dancing religion (Odoru Shukyo), the

Islamic order of dervishes (SUFI ORDERS), and some revivalist Christian groups. Indeed, the churches increasingly recognize its place in the liturgy, while theologians use the concept in some religious cosmology [19: p. xxxi; 23b: 106–8, 361–3 (where a Christian writer refers to the dance of SHIVA, and quotes some physicists); 28: 92–3, 168].

Darshana [XIII.B] One of the six salvation-philosophies of classical Hinduism. *Darshana*, literally 'seeing', means both 'view' and 'insight'. A world-view is implied, recognition of which will set one on the right path. As salvation results from overcoming a fundamental illusory understanding or ignorance (*avidya*), full recognition, as an experiential knowledge, is tantamount to liberation (MOKSHA). So *darshana* means not merely intuitive insight but also the system of thought which leads to this. The term has been used more widely. Jainism (JAINS), the LOKAYATA, the Buddhist schools, even grammar and ALCHEMY have been recognized as *darshanas*. Eventually the notion became accepted that there were six affirming (*astika*) *darshanas*, as opposed to those denying (NASTIKA) the authority of the VEDA (but other lists remained current in non-brahmanical circles). [General accounts of Indian philosophy: 5; 8; 10; 14; 17]

Although differing substantially on many points, the six orthodox Hindu *darshanas* accept the same social and ritual structure (orthopraxy) and the same general world picture (transmigration in SAMSARA). Listed with their subject-matter they are: (1) NYAYA, originally rhetoric and dialectic, later logic and epistemology; (2) VAISHE-SHIKA, ontology and metaphysics; (3) SAMKHYA, spiritual and 'occult' theory: (4) YOGA, spiritual practice; (5) MIMAMSA, ritual practice and requisite scriptural exegesis; (6) VEDANTA, the nature of the transcendent and appropriate scriptural exegesis. The first two differ mainly in subject-matter, but share the same general viewpoint. The same is the case with Samkhya and Yoga. From the medieval period the first five *darshanas* were widely regarded as approaches to the sixth. Viewed as different levels of truth serving particular purposes, the six *darshanas* were reconciled into a single very rich Vedantic system, requiring great subtlety of interpretation. [2: 325–31; 17: 23–148]

Dasam Granth [XXVII] In addition to its primary scripture, the ADI GRANTH, the Sikh PANTH recognizes a second collection, entitled the *Dasam Granth* or 'Book of the Tenth (Guru)'. Although the specific origins of this substantial work are obscure, its association with Guru Gobind Singh is well established (GURU (SIKH DOCTRINE)). The traditional view holds that the entire collection was written by the Guru. A more cautious and convincing interpretation attributes a small portion of it to him and the remainder to poets of his entourage [18: 314–16]. Among the works attributed to the Guru himself are *Jap Sahib*, the paean *Akal Ustat*, an autobiographical work entitled *Bachitra Natak*, and *Zafar-nama*. The bulk of the collection comprises a retelling of the KRISHNA legends and a lengthy series of diverting anecdotes, predominantly amoral stories concerning the wiles of women (the *Triya Charitra*). [14: 52–9; 23: 79–81] Most of the collection is written in Braj with little Punjabi (SIKH LANGUAGES). The script, however, is Gurmukhi [18: 317].

Daxma [XXX] (*dakhma, dokhma*) Popularly known as a 'tower of silence', a structure in ZOROASTRIANISM, in which the dead are laid for the flesh to be devoured by carrion-eaters (e.g. vultures). In ancient times the bodies were, it seems, simply exposed in a remote place with no structure. Death in Zoroastrian belief is the principal weapon of ANGRA MAINYU ('devil'), so that the locus of a dead body is considered a place where evil is powerfully present. To bury, cremate, or dispose of the body at sea would defile the sacred creations of earth, fire, and water (*see* AMESHA SPENTAS), hence the rite of exposure. [5: XII] Strict religious regulations direct the treatment of corpses. Nowadays PARSIS remove a corpse quickly to *daxma* grounds. There it is washed, a priest prays over it, and a dog and sacred FIRE are present to keep evil forces at bay. The corpse is carried in the funeral procession by corpse-bearers (*nasasalars*) who walk in pairs (in *paiwand*), as do the mourners, to protect themselves from the evil of Angra Mainyu, whose influence is greatest where death, his apparent victory, is triumphant (at least until the resurrection – FRASHOKERETI). Only *nasasalars* enter the *daxma*; the mourners remain praying outside [22: pt iii, 54–7]. Because they come into such contact with the impurity of death, *nasasalars* live apart and before re-entering society undergo the great nine-day purification ceremony, the *barashnum* [6: 111–38; 33: III, v].

Dayak Religion [XXII] 'Dayak' is a general name for the various tribal peoples of Borneo, notably the Ngaju in the south (in Indonesia) and the Iban or 'Sea Dayaks' in the north (in Malaysia). Borneo (or Kalimantan) has a long history of Hindu, Buddhist, and Islamic kingdoms (e.g. the Sultanate of Brunei). Such influences can be seen in the Iban word for god or spirit, *petara* (Indian *batara*, 'lord'), and the name of their creator-god, Raja Entala (Indian *raja*, 'king', plus Islamic *Allah*?). Similarly the two highest Ngaju gods are (male, upper world) Mahatala (Indian and

Islamic mixture?) and (female, under-world) Jata (Indian). The cosmos is governed by *hadat* (Ngaju) or *adat* (Iban), from the Arabic word for 'custom'; its observance ensures cosmic and social harmony. *Mali* (Iban) or *pali* (Ngaju) is the equivalent of Polynesian *tapu* (TABU). As in Bali (BALINESE RELIGION), the most lavish Ngaju ceremony is the second funeral, a few years after burial, but here the body is laid in a family shrine rather than cremated. A type of SHAMAN is found: the Ngaju *balian* (female, ritual prostitute) and *basir* (male, transvestite), and Iban *manang* (female or male transvestite); they procure healing with the help of their familiar spirits. [18; 24; 26]

'Death of God' Theologies [XI.C] The 'death of god' slogan is taken from Nietzsche's story of the madman in *Die fröhliche Wissenschaft* (1882) and used to label a number of very varied radical theologies developed especially in the U.S.A. in the 1960s. Among the claims advanced are (1) that language about a transcendent GOD is meaningless for modern secular man, (2) that God is not experienced today, (3) that God is not significant in contemporary culture, (4) that God is not a dominating presence but has 'withdrawn' to give man scope for responsible freedom, and (5) that God is not an enslaving threat but an immanent creative force within life. Few of the theologies were thoroughly atheistic. Most sought to identify a faith centred on JESUS CHRIST that would be appropriate to a mankind 'come of age'. [1; 18]

Deism [XI.C] originally referred to belief in one God, as opposed to ATHEISM and POLYTHEISM. During the 17th century the word came increasingly to be applied to positions which were regarded as less than fully orthodox forms of CHRISTIANITY. 'Deists' were often accused of rejecting belief in revelation, miracles, providence, and immortality. In fact the deism which flourished in the first half of the 18th century did not constitute a coherent movement. The so-called deists differed greatly over what they maintained, although they were united in seeking to hold only those religious beliefs which they considered to be rationally warranted. Generally they upheld the truth of some kind of NATURAL THEOLOGY. Among the leading deists are A. Collins (1676–1729) and M. Tindal (*c.*1657–1733) in England, F. M. A. de Voltaire (1694–1778), and J. J. Rousseau (1712–78) in France. Joseph Butler's *Analogy of Religion* (1736) was a classical reply to the English deists, arguing that revealed religion faced no greater problems than the natural theology accepted by the deists. Since the 18th century 'deism' has come to connote a belief that God created the world in the beginning but does not intervene in the course of natural and human affairs. [27; 28]

Dema Deities [XXII] The name *dema* comes from the Marind-anim peoples of south-west Papua and has been used to refer to similar concepts in MELANESIAN RELIGION and elsewhere. *Dema* gods and goddesses are mythological figures (animal, human, or superhuman) who have given to certain peoples their land, food-crops, totems, and knowledge (how to cultivate crops, raise pigs, make canoes, perform dances and sacred rituals). From their dismembered bodies, blood, etc., came the different tribes that are now in existence, together with their territory. Both local culture and the natural environment remain permeated with the supernatural power of these creative deities. [23]

Demon [XXVIII] A SPIRIT, below the status of GODS and subject to them, sometimes guardian of a human individual (Greek *daimon*; *see* DAIMON). The early concept was modified in a distinction between good demons (angels) and evil ones (devils). Sometimes, 'demon' was equated with 'evil spirit' (*see* DUALISM). However, the daimonic (an important notion in modern theology) has no necessary connection with malevolence or the negative aspects of existence. (*See also:* AHURA MAZDA; ANGRA MAINYU; JINN.)

Demonology (Biblical) [XI.A] In Judaism during the Hellenistic period there is a belief in individual demons, controlled by a hierarchy. The influence of ZOROASTRIANISM may easily be recognized. In the story of Tobit a sinister part is played by Asmodaeus (Zoroastrian Aeshma-daeva, the 'demon of Fury'). In the Enoch literature the demons are identified with the 'sons of God', who (according to Genesis 6: 2, 4) were attracted by the beauty of the 'daughters of men'. In the Synoptic GOSPELS the leader of the demons is Beelzebul. [16: XXXII; 19: 61–9]

Demythologizing [XI.C] The method of interpreting the New Testament put forward by R. Bultmann (1884–1976). An exponent of the Form-Critical method (BIBLICAL CRITICISM) of analysing the materials of the GOSPELS, Bultmann maintained that Christian belief was based on the Christ of faith rather than on the Jesus of history (JESUS CHRIST). He also held that since GOD's own nature was beyond man's apprehension, theology must confine itself to describing man's existence as it is confronted by God. His programme of demythologization is based on the claim that the New Testament does not merely contain specific elements which are untenable for modern man (such as the conception of a three-storeyed universe and stories of miracles), but that its presentation of the Christian faith is understood throughout in terms of a view of reality which is now unacceptable. Accordingly, Bultmann argues that if its content is to be grasped by modern man, it must be thoroughly and radically reinterpreted in terms of an appropriate conceptuality. This for Bultmann is largely provided by Heidegger's existentialist categories (EXISTENTIALISM). [2; 3]

Deva [IX.A] In Buddhist mythology, a 'heavenly being', literally 'one who shines'. *Devas* form a class of beings in opposition to *asuras*, and are thought of as living in happiness. They are, however, subject to rebirth, old age, and death, and can only find release from this by rebirth as humans, and thus eventually gaining nirvana (NIBBANA).

Dhamma (Pali) [IX.A] (Sanskrit *dharma*) (cf. DHARMA (HINDU)) In the Buddhist context *dhamma* refers either to the doctrine of the BUDDHA, proclaimed in every age by every Buddha, or to a mental event or phenomenon. As Buddha's doctrine it is summed up in (1) the three characteristics of existence, namely, ANICCA, DUKKHA, ANATTA; and (2) the Four Noble Truths (ARIYA-SACCA) and the Noble EIGHTFOLD PATH.

The second major meaning of *dhamma* in the Buddhist context, as a mental event or object of mind, can have past, present, or future reference, and can refer to both real and imaginary objects.

The word is used also in the general sense of 'the nature of things', or 'according to nature'. It occurs in this sense, for example, in a Buddhist text, the *Agganna Sutta*, where the evolution of the material world is described. Conze lists at least seven different and important meanings of *dhamma* [5: 92–6].

Dhammapada [IX.A] 'Verses on Doctrine', a book of the Buddhist Pali canon, consisting of 423 short verses. These deal with various aspects of Buddhist moral teaching and wisdom and are arranged under 26 headings, according to subject-matter. Some of the verses occur in other Pali canonical texts. A number of translations into English have been made, and the *Dhammapada* is generally one of the texts better known among lay Buddhists in Asia. [27A]

Dhammapala [IX.B] The name of two important THERAVADA Buddhist commentators. Dhammapala I (probably 7th century CE) was the South Indian author of PALI commentaries (*atthakatha*) on various canonical and semicanonical works, and adapted North Indian Buddhist ideas, especially those of Asanga, to accord with Theravada tradition. Dhammapala II (probably 10th century) was the author of numerous subcommentaries (*tika*) supplementing the works of BUDDHAGHOSA and Dhammapala I, notably the influential commentary to the *Visuddhimagga*. Later tradition and some modern scholarship identified the two. [41: 46ff, 254ff]

Dhanb [XIV] The general term for sin in ISLAM. The QUR'AN does not clearly propound a doctrine of original sin, but speaks of man's innate weakness and his sharing in Adam's sinfulness. All sins are regarded as disobedience to God and as ingratitude for His goodness. The supreme sin of *shirk*, polytheism and denial of God's unity (ALLAH), is unforgivable. Below this, the Qur'an and tradition distinguish lesser sins, which do not affect a man's faith, from grave ones, which God may pardon or punish for a certain period. There was much discussion by later theologians and sectarians about what constituted a grave sin (*kabira*); one Prophetic tradition posits seven, echoing the seven deadly sins of Christianity. The KHARIJITES and Mu'tazilites held that grave sins entailed permanent damnation. All authorities, however, admitted God's complete freedom to forgive sins (except *shirk*), and the Sunni (SUNNA) view came to be that this did not even require the sinner's prior repentance, for if God were to accept it, the divine pardon would be unnecessary. [10 'Sin (Islam)'; 39 'Sin'; 82 index s.v. 'Sin']

Dharma (Hindu) [XIII.A] A Sanskrit word of many meanings. It is formed from a root, *dhr*, which has a primary sense of 'self-subsistence', or independence of any antecedent being. *Dharma* is thus 'that which maintains' all other entities. In Hindu thought it has the sense of universal law, or norm. In this sense it has various applications: cosmic, moral, ritual, social, etc. It is also used to refer to the totality of what is otherwise called 'religion'. The characteristic term for what in the West is called 'HINDUISM', from a metaphysical point of view at least, is '*Sanatana* (eternal) *dharma*'.

For the individual, *dharma* is the moral norm, and this is specific to his social status and stage of life. For each VARNA (class) there is an appropriate *dharma*, or moral code. Further, for each of these there are four 'stages of life' (ASHRAMA) through which the individual passes. Each of these also has its appropriate *dharma*. The whole system of *varna* – and *ashrama*-specific *dharma* – is therefore referred to as *varnashrama-dharma*.

The word *dharma* is used in another sense. There are said to be, broadly, three characteristic types of human activity: *dharma* is the moral realm; ARTHA is the realm of material interest, including government; and KAMA (not to be confused with KARMA) is the realm of sensuous physical and aesthetic enjoyment. These three, if rightly ordered, lead to liberation or MOKSHA. Each of these realms of human activity has its special class of normative literature: *Dharma-sutra*, *Artha-sutra*, and the *Kama-sutra*. Based on these are secondary texts, the *Dharma-Shastras*, *Artha-Shastras*, and *Kama-Shastras*. [1: 114–15; 13: 294–8] (Cf. Buddhist DHAMMA.)

Dhimmis [XIV] 'Protected peoples', the term applied in pre-modern ISLAM to the Qur'anic 'People of the Book', those possessing written scriptures, originally Christians and Jews, but later extended to Zoroastrians (ZOROASTRIANISM), Hindus, etc. included within the Islamic empire. *Dhimmis* were accorded legal status within Islam, but as second-class citizens, liable to a poll-tax (*jizya*) instead of military service, and were forbidden to proselytize. Their legal disabilities were not removed in most Islamic countries till the 19th and early 20th centuries. [21 'Dhimma'; 73]

Dhyana Yoga [XIII.B] The way of meditation, one of four main routes of spiritual development (YOGA) widely recognized in Indian thought. It emphasizes purification and stilling of the mind by means of meditative techniques. Influential examples of this approach are the classical YOGA DARSHANA and Buddhist BHAVANA. The aim is to develop *samadhi* (ecstasy), a type of contemplative experience of alert absorption and unification. Different degrees and types of *samadhi* are elaborated in great detail in many Indian religious systems. *Dhyana* is more or less synonymous, sometimes used for an inferior stage, sometimes for a more advanced level. *Dhyana-yoga* usually involves systematic and intimate instruction from a teacher (GURU) and is often, but not invariably, associated with some kind of withdrawal from general social intercourse. It is sometimes associated with the development of PSYCHIC POWERS (*siddhi/iddhi*).

Di Deaeque [XXV] The gods and goddesses of Rome. These varied widely in character, from the high gods (such as Jupiter, chief of the state-gods, and Mars, god of war) down to the protectors of specific processes, such as one stage in the growth-cycle of corn [17: 1]. The names of deities were important to successful prayer, but formulae allowed for extra unknown powers. Even major deities had no kin relations, no adventures, and little personality, until later borrowing from Greek counterparts. This has led to theories that the early Romans had no gods, only spirits (*numina* – NUMEN) who developed personality late and under foreign influence [18]. The theories are incompatible with the Romans' INDO-EUROPEAN inheritance [6: 18–46], but rightly emphasize the range of types existing contemporaneously. The Romans recognized no intermediate category between men and gods; even the dead were seen as unindividualized, but divine (*divi*). There were various means by which the number of

gods and goddesses increased: they might be summoned from enemy cities by 'evocation' (as Juno from the Etruscan city of Veii) [9: 21–2]; or recommended by the SIBYLLINE BOOKS to be brought from abroad (as Apollo); or recognized as in the case of abstractions – Victory, Concord, or Piety [6: 397–441]. This preparedness to accept the new continues to be evident in imperial times, when cults from Asia Minor, Syria, and other parts of the East were accepted (SYNCRETISM) [7]. Roman gods were rarely thought to speak or intervene directly, but complex negotiations were undertaken through prayers and especially vows – which defined the conditions for fulfilment with quasi-legal precision [9: 14–16, 26–8]. The gods' response was thought to come through signs and PRODIGIA, but most importantly through success and victory.

Dialectical Materialism [XXVI] The name usually given to the outlook on human nature and on the world appropriate to MARXISM. The name did not originate with Marx (1818–83) or F. Engels (1820–95). Their account of the dialectical method was, however, expounded by Lenin (1870–1924) as 'nothing more nor less than the scientific method in sociology, which consists in regarding society as a living organism in a constant state of development, the study of which requires an objective analysis of the relations of production which constitute the given social formation and an investigation of its laws of functioning and development'. This statement by Lenin already implies a materialist standpoint, namely, that social change is governed by underlying material (economic) factors and not by ideas. So understood, dialectical materialism involves a hostile view of IDEOLOGY as a mere reflection of human social relations and an obstacle to basic changes.

Dialectical materialism has sometimes been taken to involve a particular view of what processes can take place in nature. The Soviet agriculturist T. D. Lysenko urged, in the 1930s, that the genetic theory favoured in the West was incompatible with dialectical materialism. The result of Lysenko's efforts was the suppression of the theory but not, as had been hoped, an increase in agricultural productivity. Dialectical materialism is now commonly interpreted by Marxists in such a way that a conflict between its principles and the findings of natural science is no longer possible. [17: II]

Digha Nikaya [IX.A] One of the main collections of Pali Buddhist discourses, and part of the SUTTA-PITAKA. The corresponding collection of Sanskrit discourses is the *Dirghagama* (AGAMA) [37: 7f]. The title indicates that it is the collection (*nikaya*) of long (*digha*) discourses or dialogues, 34 altogether, including the very long and important *Maha-Parinibbana Sutta* (Sanskrit *Maha-parinirvana Sutra*).

Din [XIV] The term used in ISLAM for 'religion' in general, so that one can have the *din* of Islam or earlier *dins* before the revelation of the faith. The term has connotations of indebtedness and obligation, i.e. of the believer's duties towards God. In Islamic theology, *din* comprehends both faith, *iman*, and the practice of the prescriptions of the law, the SHARI'A, and is often contrasted with the *dunya*, the sphere of secular life [32i: I]

Dinka Religion [II] The Dinka are a NILOTIC people in the southern Sudan; among their neighbours are the NUER and SHILLUK. Nhialic (literally, 'the Sky') is the Dinka name for God. In comparison with the Nuer Kwoth, he is encountered far more through the experience of powerful spirits (JOK), of which the most important are Deng, Garang, Abuk, and Macardit. They are known especially through possession. Deng, Garang, and Abuk (who is female) are the names of the first Dinka and remain very common today, but

the spirits are distinguished from the Dinka progenitors. Macardit (the great black one) is unique in being wholly bad and harmful. Oxen sacrificed to placate Macardit should be black.

Deng stands above all others so much that he seems almost to have the character of Nhialic. He is associated with rain, thunder, and lightning. It is significant for the identification of Deng and Nhialic that the great and ancient shrine known to Nuer as 'Luak Kwoth' is called 'Luak Deng' by Dinka.

The Dinka also respect totemic spirits, among whom may be noted *Ring* (flesh), the spirit of the priestly clans, the Masters of the Fishing Spear. It is incarnate within them. Dinka religion, like Nuer, centres upon ox-sacrifice, but here sacrifice is both more ritualistic and more sacerdotal, normally being executed by Spear-Masters. The powers of Spear-Masters derive from the rich myths relating to Aiwel Longar, the miraculous hero who led the Dinka to their present home (compare Nyikang of the Shilluk). He was conceived in the river and led his people across it, but frequently dealt them death as well as life.

The health and prosperity of the people are symbolized by, and indeed seen as dependent upon, the life of the Spear-Master. *Ring* enables them, furthermore, to lead the people and speak absolutely truthfully, above all when invoking in sacrifice. Great Spear-Masters, when old, choose death voluntarily, being buried alive after giving final advice to their people [36].

Dipankara [IX.A] A Buddha of a past age whom Shakyamuni Buddha, GOTAMA, the BUDDHA of the present age, met (in a previous life), and determined that, having honoured Dipankara, he would himself become a Buddha. Having so determined, he thereby became a BODHISATTVA, but had yet to pass through countless successive lives (some of which the JATAKA stories [14] are said to relate) before entering the

Tusita heaven (the fourth of the six heavens, or DEVA-worlds, in Indian cosmology, where one day corresponds to 400 years of human life [21: 1033; 23]) prior to his last birth (in Lumbini) as the Buddha [37: 335].

Dipavamsa [IX.A] One of the Pali chronicles (*vamsa*) (CULAVAMSA) which relate the Buddhist history of the island (*dipa*) of Sri Lanka. The *Dipavamsa* deals with the period up to the middle of the 4th century CE. It was probably composed during the succeeding 100 years, but incorporates much older historical traditions, and is 'the outcome of a fairly large number of previous works', all of which were the work of groups or schools, rather than of individual authors. [10A; 22: 131–8]

Disciples (Early Christian) [XI.A] Any founder of a school must have followers. The GOSPELS mention disciples of the PHARISEES and disciples of JOHN THE BAPTIST as well as disciples of JESUS CHRIST. Jesus had many disciples in addition to the APOSTLES whom he selected from their ranks. On one occasion he sent out 70 of them, two by two, on a preaching and healing mission. The disciples later formed the nucleus of the CHURCH, in which 'disciple' became a synonym of 'Christian'. [7: 91–7]

Discursive Meditation [XI.D] A Christian form of mental prayer which brings intellect, imagination, will, and emotions to bear on the teachings of the faith. The meditator will imagine events in the life of JESUS CHRIST, reflect on the significance of doctrines, draw moral and spiritual lessons, and turn to God in love and trust. There are many formal methods of this kind of prayer [22: 15], the best known being those contained in the *Spiritual Exercises* of St Ignatius Loyola (1491–1556).

Ditthi [IX.B] (Pali; Sanskrit *drshti*) 'Views', or 'wrong views', refer in early Buddhism to the one-sided or slanted attitude which underlies rigid opinions. This is seen as due to specific psycho-logical forces – drives or cravings (*tanha*) – which involve some kind of partial or incomplete understanding following loss of mental balance. The two extreme views of 'eternalism' and 'annihilationism' give certain conviction of eternal life or post-mortem annihilation respectively. Other types of *ditthi* include fatalism, materialism, theism, and views based upon a need to assert the self. Less frequent is the use of *ditthi* to refer to 'right view' as part of the EIGHTFOLD PATH. Various levels of understanding are mentioned. Fundamental is a basic knowledge of the law of action (*kamma*; Sanskrit KARMA) and result which alone allows true moral responsibility. Higher are various degrees of insight culminating in transcendent (LOKUTTARA) right view deriving from a permanent mental balance and contact with the unconditioned. [41]

Divination [XVIII] The use of magical means to discover information inaccessible to normal inquiry (about the future, lost objects, hidden character-traits, etc.). Divination exists in all societies, often under the auspices of religion (e.g. the Delphic oracle, the Tibetan state oracles), but sometimes outside or in opposition to it (as under Christianity, which has generally opposed divination). It takes two main forms: oracular, where the diviner enters a trance or other special state and relays the information; and interpretative, where random or enigmatic data are interpreted. The distinction is not clear-cut, however, for some interpretative systems (ASTROLOGY, TAROT) contain a powerful symbolism, others seem chosen to stimulate clairvoyance (PSYCHIC POWERS), and the sheer flexibility of interpretation normally admits an element of the 'oracular'. The diviner needs a shrewd knowledge of human nature as well as intuitive gifts because his role, however humble socially, is inevitably a priestly one, mediating between worldly concerns and mysterious but purposeful higher powers. [19]

Divination (African) [II] Divination is important for many African religions, and believed to be a reliable method for obtaining the answers to particular questions (by whom has one's child been bewitched, what spirit is troubling one, which practical course should one pursue over a specific matter, etc.). It takes two main forms (among many), the first being that of oracles, such as IFA or the ZANDE poison-oracle, the second that provided by a medium when possessed (*see* NGANGA and SPIRIT-POSSESSION). The former depends upon a certain mechanical and objective technique, the latter upon contact with spirits, though this will be preceded by careful interrogation of the client. Many peoples make use of both, oracle operators tending to be men while mediums are often women. [20; 21: 136–96; 26]

Divination (Ancient Near Eastern) [VI] Regarded as a supreme science, divination was used as a practical guide in all human affairs. Omens were consulted before battle, in personal matters, or to determine a god's anger, and omen texts are an invaluable source of political and other information [13: 160–64; 23: 20–22; 24: 346, 449–51]. Probably first devised by the SUMERIANS, divination became increasingly important in the Old BABYLONIAN period (*c.* 1700 BCE), and was inherited by the HITTITES. Augury (looking for signs in nature), lottery, and extispicy (the excision and examination of animal entrails to foretell events) were employed but, later, ASTROLOGY challenged extispicy as the favourite method.

Divination (Roman) [XXV] Elaborate methods existed to discern the attitudes of the gods towards human events, but this involved little or no prediction of the future. AUSPICIA took the form of asking the gods' approval for a particular course of action, such as joining battle. PRODIGIA were essentially bad signs, whose menace could be averted by the piety of the state and the skill of the priests. [12: 7–29; 17: IV] Some belief in divination is implicit in myths and in later poetry, and this may well have always existed at the popular level. In the late Republic (1st century BCE), the *haruspices* (diviners from Etruria, possibly representing a different tradition) began to be bolder in offering interpretations and this evidently reflects an increasing popularity of divinatory systems at the lower-class level. This tendency continued through the Empire when far more sophisticated systems of divination through magic and ASTROLOGY gradually established themselves at the highest levels of power and culture. [7: IX; 12: 119–39]

Divine Kingship (African) [II] Divine kingship can be well illustrated from Africa. Its characteristics are the relationship of dependence between the king and nature, the degree of seclusion imposed upon him, the primacy of ritual and sacerdotal over administrative action in his life, and the conceptual centrality of the kingship within the religious-belief system. Furthermore, the king may be seen as a reincarnation of a divine hero of the past and his death should be the effect of a deliberate choice on his own or his successor's part, not the consequence of sickness. Among the best examples are the SHILLUK *reth*, the LOVEDU Mujaji, the *lwembe* of the Nyakyusa [45: 17–48], and the *hogon* of the DOGON.

While the major monarchies of Africa, such as those of Ashanti, Benin, Dahomey, and Buganda (*see* AKAN, FON, GANDA), may not have fallen fully into this category, most still combined profound sacrality with secular political expertise. Rituals of kingship, especially the installation of monarchs, the renewal of king and kingdom in new-year ceremonies, and the cult at royal tombs are among the richest sources for African religious symbolism (examples of which are the Akan *odwira* and the Swazi NCWALA).

Divine Light Mission (DLM) [xxi] The movement achieved a rapid growth in the West after the then 13-year-old Guru Maharaj Ji went to London in 1971. Since then many thousands of his followers (known as 'premies') have 'taken Knowledge'. The Knowledge consists of four simple meditation techniques which are taught to the aspirant by a *mahatma* at a secret initiation and which, it is claimed, enable him to turn his senses within and perceive Divine Light, Divine Nectar, Divine Harmony, and the 'primordial vibration' which is the Holy Name or Word.

Some of the more dedicated premies live celibate, monastic-type lives in ashrams; the majority, however, follow a less rigid life-style, frequently sharing communal accommodation. Premies are expected to listen to and to give *satsang* (witnessing to their spiritual experiences), to give service, and to meditate. They also attend large festivals, held in different places around the world, in order to see their Perfect Master. [2: 53; 9; 11: VII; 14: III]

Dogon Religion [II] The Dogon of Upper Volta have a complex religious cosmology, much of it highly esoteric, and represent one of the most intricately sacralized societies in Africa. The basic belief is in the duality of Amma, the God creator, and Nommo, the totality of the universe, existing originally within an enormous egg. There is a basic male/female twinness in the Amma/Nommo relationship forever symbolized in subsequent relationships within Nommo. The perfect image of Nommo is, therefore, a pair of twins of opposite sex. The original ancestors of the Dogon were four pairs of twins, making eight into a particularly significant number in a vastly complicated NUMEROLOGY. The orderly development of the world was initially impeded by the bursting forth of Yurugu – the trickster or White Fox – the purely male part of an original Nommo. Yurugu, associated with death and night but also

with divination, remains the unpredictable element in life: at times apparently evil, at others inspirational. Order was restored through the sacrifice of Lebe, the first man.

The whole of social life, cultivation, the shaping of villages and homesteads, and particularly the life of the chief of each village, the *hogon*, is so arranged as to symbolize the intricacies of cosmological belief: villages are built in pairs, eight store-rooms preserve eight varieties of millet, the home of a living *hogon* contains eight stones for *hogons* of the past and eight for *hogons* of the future. The *hogon*, the high priest of Amma and successor of Lebe, controls all sides of life through his own ritualized existence, and stands as human symbol of the universal Nommo. [4: 83–110; 30]

Drama (Christian) [XI.B] Early Christians condemned the drama, because of its 'pagan' or immoral associations, until the medieval Mystery or Miracle plays developed (apparently from dramatized elements in the liturgy). These dramatized the Creation, Passion (sufferings) of Christ, and lives of SAINTS, mingled with popular comic elements. Some still survive, notably the Oberammergau Passion play in West Germany. PROTESTANTISM in general (notably PURITANISM) disapproved of drama, but religious drama is now widely used (as well as DANCE, which hitherto has played little part in Christian worship). [105 vol. 4: 1033–53; 107: 425]

Dreams and Visions in Modern Tribal Movements [xx] In most new tribal movements dreams and visions may have revelatory and mandatory qualities. Founders' visions often involve a visit to heavenly beings for a commission to found the new religion, together with details of its rituals, ethics, and sometimes a new script or language. All dreams are potentially significant, but many need interpretation by a leader, or the application of moral, biblical (BIBLE), or other critiques to eliminate those coming from evil spirits. Revelatory dreams can also be induced by sleeping in a sanctuary, by fasting, rolling on the ground, or by hallucinogenic drugs such as peyote (PEYOTISM) in the NATIVE AMERICAN CHURCH [19: 416–17, 430–32] or *iboga* in the Gabon Bwiti religion. For movements founded through visions or dreams *see* the CHRISTIAN FELLOWSHIP CHURCH, Alice LENSHINA's church, the NAZARITE CHURCH [16: 110, 112, 3245–7], the MAORI Ratana movement [9: 24–5], the HANDSOME LAKE RELIGION, and many CARGO CULTS. [4 vol. 2: 139–67; 14: 123–7, 130–31, 206–7; 16: 265–75; 19]

Druids [V] The Druids (the name is probably derived from a word meaning oak) were priests and learned men of Celtic Gaul and Britain. Many Greek and Latin writers refer to them, particularly Posidonius (1st century BCE) and his imitators [28: 14, III]. They taught young men, organized religious rituals, including sacrifice, and were skilled in healing, astronomy, calendric calculations, and consultation of omens [17: III, 94–108]. There is considerable argument as to their influence and the nature of their learning, which was not committed to writing [14: IV, 104–21]. The Romans set out to suppress them in the 1st century CE. Interest in Druids revived in the 17th century, and the antiquary John Aubrey mistakenly assumed that Stonehenge and other megalithic sites were Druidic temples [17: IV, 118–25]. A romantic, vaguely mystical picture of their ceremonies and secret wisdom was built up, and in 1819 Iolo Morganwg (Edward Williams) claimed an association with the National Eisteddfod of Wales, based on dubious evidence [17: IV, 143–50]. The Ancient Order of Druids began in 1781 as a secret society in London, developing into a friendly society, but strangely attired groups of self-styled 'Druids' have continued to meet to celebrate the summer solstice at Stonehenge, Tower Hill, and Primrose Hill in London, and other sites [17: IV, 155–7].

Druzes (Druses) [XIV] A sectarian Muslim group, today found in the mountainous regions of Lebanon, northern Israel, and southern Syria. Their numbers have been variously estimated at between 200,000 and 300,000. They stem from the Shi'i Muslim sect of ISMA'ILIS, as an offshoot in the 11th century of the Fatimid movement (*see* 'ALI, 'ALIDS, ISLAMIC DYNASTIES, and SHI'ISM). In belief and practice they are considerably aberrant from the main body of Muslims, rejecting many of the prescriptions of the SHARI'A and emphasizing e.g. metempsychosis (transmigration of the soul). The Druzes have maintained their identity through endogamy and through the social leadership of a class of ascetic initiates to the faith, the *'uqqal* ('sages'). [6; 10 s.v.; 21 'Durūz']

Dualism [XXVIII] (1) As a world-view, the belief that the 'real' is of two kinds, or in two ultimate controlling powers. Thus, metaphysical dualism (contrast MONISM) may oppose matter to SPIRIT, while dualistic religion involves belief in two eternally conflicting principles [8: 125–32]. Modified dualism holds God to be ambivalent, both benevolent and malevolent.

(2) A view of man as consisting of two substances, physical (flesh, body) and mental or spiritual (mind, soul, spirit).

Dukkha [IX.A] (Pali; Sanskrit *duhkha*) One of the three principal characteristics of all existence, according to the BUDDHA's teaching or DHAMMA. Variously translated as 'ill', 'suffering', 'unease', and 'evil', the central idea is of all that follows from ANICCA (*see also* ANATTA).

Durga [XIII.A] Literally 'she who is difficult of approach; the inaccessible', Durga is the mother-goddess of Hindu tradition. In some aspects she is fierce and terrible, the slayer of demons, whom she kills with her scimitar. An alternative name is Candi [3: 165f]; as such she is worshipped by village Hindus seeking for protection against wild animals. Other goddesses identified with Durga are Shitala, the protectress against smallpox, and Manasa, who protects against snakebite [2: 319]. Animal sacrifices to Durga have been made from medieval times, with some instances of human sacrifice [3: 339]. Her annual festival, Durga-puja, is celebrated in October–November, especially in Bengal and eastern India. In Brahmanical (BRAH-MANS) mythology she is regarded as the spouse of SHIVA, and sometimes worshipped as the virgin Kanyakumari [3: 164]. Another manifestation of this goddess is KALI.

· E ·

Ecumenical Movement [XI.B] A movement, originally mainly in PROTESTANTISM, to promote understanding and in some cases union between Christian churches. The modern movement was stimulated by the International Missionary Conference at Edinburgh (in 1910). It grew through organizations for doctrinal and social discussion in the 1920s. The World Council of Churches has met periodically since 1948. Participation by the ORTHODOX CHURCH, ROMAN CATHOLICISM, and PENTECOSTALISM makes it broadly representative of various forms of Christianity, but not of fundamentalism (AUTHORITY). Its recent selective support for liberation movements (LIBERATION THEOLOGY) has been controversial. Councils of churches are also common at regional and national levels. Increasing theological discussion, understanding, and practical cooperation have marked the relationships between the main Christian churches since the mid 20th century. Some church unions have been achieved (CANADA, INDIA). A projected union of English ANGLICANISM and METHODISM failed in 1972. Although achieved in India, reunion between episcopal and non-episcopal churches (MINISTRY) remains the most difficult to achieve. Optimistic reunion schemes characteristic of the U.S.A. and Britain during the 1960s appear to have given way to concern about political and social questions. Theological divisions today often cut across those traditionally dividing churches. Divisions are now often between radicals and con-servatives both within and across churches rather than between them. [1: 341–66; 115]

Edda [V] The title given to two Icelandic books providing most of our information about Norse mythology. Snorri Sturluson, poet, historian, and politician (1179–1241 CE), retold in superb Icelandic prose many northern myths, with quotations from poems and explanations of mythological imagery [20: 6, 1; 30: 1, 21–7]. He intended to provide a handbook for poets so that the ancient lore would not be lost. The book is called *Edda* in one MS, and therefore known as Snorri's Edda or the Prose Edda. The word *edda* means 'great-grandmother', but the title may have been derived from Oddi in Iceland, where Snorri was brought up. In 1643 a 13th-century manuscript book known as the *Codex regius* was found in an Icelandic farmhouse, containing poems on gods and heroes. This collection, together with a few poems from other MSS, is called the Elder, Poetic, or Saemund's Edda, after an 11th-century scholar [18; 30: 1, 17]. Various dates from 800 CE upwards have been suggested for the poems, a number of which appear to be pre-Christian and may have been composed in Norway [30: 1, 8–14]. Some deal with the exploits of Freyr, LOKI, ODIN, and THOR, and they include riddle contests between gods and giants, and much about the creation and destruction of the worlds of gods and men.

Eightfold Path [IX.A] That there is a path, or way, by which human beings can reach enlightenment is the fourth of

the four 'noble truths' (ARIYA-SACCA)
taught by the BUDDHA (GOTAMA). The
path is eightfold, and consists in:
(1) right understanding; (2) right aspir-
ation or purpose; (3) right speech; (4)
right bodily action; (5) right means of
livelihood; (6) right endeavour; (7) right
mindfulness; and (8) right concentration. These eight aspects of the way are
all fully analysed and expounded in the
Buddha's teaching. The first item in the
list refers to the adoption of that understanding of the world and of the human
condition which is set out in the
teaching of the Buddha. The second
refers to the necessary moral resolve; the
third entails the avoidance of false or
defamatory speech; the fourth, avoidance
of excessive sensuality, dishonesty, and
actions injurious to other beings. Right
means of livelihood means the pursuit
of an occupation or trade which does
not entail violence or hurt to others;
occupations such as butcher, fisherman,
soldier, dealer in liquor, or trader in
slaves are to be avoided. Right endeavour, or effort, means the effort to
avoid morally unwholesome states of
mind and to cultivate morally wholesome states. Right mindfulness means
the constant awareness of one's actions,
intentions, and feelings; and right concentration refers to the practice of bringing the consciousness to a single point in
the practice of meditation (SAMADHI).
[20A: 90–92]

Elamites [VI] Before the migrations of
the Medes and Persians *c.* 1000 BCE, the
history of religious development in Iran
(ZOROASTRIANISM) concentrated on
the Elamite kingdom (Old Elamite
kingdom, *c.* 2550–1860 BCE, Classical
period, *c.* 1330–1000 BCE) [21: III, 21–32;
22: III, 23–40]. Elam was regarded as a
religious centre which always retained
a distinct religious tradition [15],
although the pantheon included Babylonian as well as native deities and
there were many features in common
with other Mesopotamian religions

(BABYLONIANS; SUMERIANS). Sources
include dedicatory inscriptions, god
lists, monuments, reliefs such as the
famous religious procession· at Kuran-
gun, sculpture and seals, but these give
an inadequate understanding of the
essentials of the religion.

The kingdom was basically a tribal
federation. Each tribe retained its
deities, and each city-state worshipped a
patron deity and consort. Only the
strongest rulers sought to give the state
a religious cohesion, elevating certain
local cults to national status and making
the capitals – Susa and Dur-Untash –
sacred centres where the tribal gods had
shrines, or 'resting-places'. Choga-
Zanbil was also a great centre.

A divine ruler, who performed priestly duties (TEMPLES), the king held his
authority from the gods. Royal descent
passed through the female line; the society was characterized by matriarchal
traditions; and the earliest pre-eminent
deity was a mother-goddess, recognized
for her powers in MAGIC and in the
underworld. A male god, Khumban,
later became supreme, and the great
national god, In-Shushinak (originally a
local god of Susa), finally achieved
prominence.

No temple or foundation has survived, but cylinder seal representations
indicate that they followed the Babylonian type; however, a distinctive feature
was the huge horns which decorated the
tops of the temple walls. The temples
employed many priests and servants,
and housed votive statues and gifts
made to the gods. Daily animal
sacrifices were made, and an oracular
priest probably read the omens
(DIVINATION).

Elam was regarded as the home of
witches and demons. The most important and distinctive Elamite symbol was
the serpent, which represented an
ancient god and perhaps the dark powers
of the earth (ART AND SYMBOLISM
(ANCIENT NEAR EASTERN)). Religious

art and inscriptions of gods' names indicate some features of this religion and its close association with Mesopotamian beliefs, but many of its essential and unique elements remain obscure.

Emblems (Sikh) [XXVII] Two devices are regularly used by Sikhs as auspicious emblems. The earlier of the two, a combination of the Gurmukhi figure 1 and letter O (*see figure*), is taken from the ADI GRANTH, where it is used as an invocatory symbol representing the unity of God (the 'One *Oankar*' or Primal Being). The second popular device is the KHALSA emblem, comprising a steel quoit flanked by two daggers (*kirpan*) with vertical two-edged sword (*khanda*) superimposed.

Emin [XXI] An esoteric group founded by 'Leo', who is said to have studied the underlying nature of the human body by himself for 30 years. The movement grew in England during the 1970s, developing branches in North America, New Zealand, and Israel. Group study covers a wide range of subjects associated with the HUMAN POTENTIAL MOVEMENT, including ASTROLOGY, the TAROT, sacred dance, massage, and healing. [2: 142]

Emperor-Worship (Roman) [XXV] Alexander the Great (336–323 BCE) and his successors provided the model for the deification of Roman emperors, though man becoming god is not wholly alien to Roman tradition [20]. In the Eastern provinces, the living Emperor

was worshipped as such, but in Rome itself, deification (*consecratio*) was a distinct ceremony decreed after death for the Emperor, if he was thought deserving [8: 3–25]. Complex in its origins, the institution was never imposed from the centre, except to some extent in the Latin West. Its diversity and wide extension suggest that it provided a symbolic resource of value to local city élites (who provided the priests and benefactions) and to the central authorities [7: VI]. Jokes, some attributed to the emperors themselves (one allegedly died saying, 'I feel I am becoming a god'), and even more the silence of literature suggest scepticism among intellectuals [8: 177–206]. However, the silence may indicate simply that the institution, after initial awkwardness, became routine. For, although emperors did not manifest divinity by performing miracles, they were certainly recognized as gods both in language and ritual (in spite of the ambiguities of their position), the more so as time went by. [12: 238–44; 16: XLIX]

Empiricism [XXVI] The doctrine that there is no knowledge of the world except what is derived from sense experience. Philosophers who have been empiricists, like David Hume (1711–76) and Bertrand Russell (1872–1970), have commonly been led into SCEPTICISM about religion. An extreme form of anti-metaphysical empiricism is LOGICAL POSITIVISM. In a

IK-ONKAR: SYMBOL OF GOD

KHALSA EMBLEM

See EMBLEMS (SIKH)

broad sense, however, empiricism has by no means always been antagonistic to religion. Many theologians, including F. R. Tennant [21], have adopted an empiricist standpoint.

Emptiness [IX.B], or voidness (Sanskrit *shunyata*; Pali *sunnata*), is an important Buddhist concept. It may be used in reference to the successive meditations (*see* SAMATHA) to show their peaceful nature, quite empty of noisy distraction or subtle disturbance. Sometimes it refers to insight (VIPASSANA), where phenomena are seen as empty of self (ANATTA) or anything similar, and sometimes to NIBBANA or transcendent (LOKUTTARA) mind, as empty of greed, hate, and delusion. In MAHAYANA Buddhism emptiness is frequently stressed, especially in the SHUNYATA-VADA, signifying initially freedom from views and proliferating concepts. The realization that phenomena are empty of any substantial existence is distinguished as more profound. This should not be interpreted as nihilistic or as asserting the non-reality of ordinary experience; this would itself be a position and hence not 'empty'. What is envisaged rather is some kind of profound transformation of the understanding, leading to a type of relaxed fluidity of action. [5: 242–50]

Ennin [XVI] (792–864 CE), posthumously known as Jikaku Daishi, was a priest of the TENDAI sect from Tochigi prefecture who trained under SAICHO on Mt Hiei from the age of 14. He travelled with Fujiwara Tsunetsugu to China when 46, keeping a detailed account, *Nitto guho junrei koki*, returning about 10 years later. His commentary on T'ang China is a valuable firsthand record. He became chief priest of the Tendai sect in 854, sponsoring *nembutsu*, chanting the name of Amida (AMIDA WORSHIP). His followers split into two opposing groups, each vying for power within the sect.

Ephesus, Early Christianity at [XI.A] Although CHRISTIANITY had reached

Ephesus before PAUL resided there (52–55 CE), it is to him and his colleagues that the thorough evangelization of the city and its hinterland is due. But in the Christian tradition of Ephesus the outstanding name is John, 'the disciple of the Lord', who is said to have settled there in old age and is commemorated by the ruined basilica of St John on the hill Ayasoluk (a corruption of *hagios theologos*, 'the holy divine'). [3: 309–13, 356–7; 4: 287–99]

Eschatology (Biblical) [XI.A] The doctrine of the 'last things' (Greek *ta eschata*), whether personal or cosmic. In early Israel the dead were pictured as sharing an undifferentiated existence in Sheol. In post-exilic times, particularly from the 2nd century BCE onwards, the belief in bodily resurrection, especially for the righteous, was held by many Jews (not by the SADDUCEES). This belief was inherited by the Christians, who held that the first stage in the expected resurrection had been reached with the resurrection of JESUS CHRIST, and that the resurrection of his people would take place at his return in glory.

Along with the hope of resurrection went the expectation that at the end-time God would vindicate the cause of righteousness, creating a new order and establishing the rule or kingdom of God. (Cf. FRASHOKERETI, RAGNAROK.) [5: 181–97]

Eskimo–Aleut [III] Together, the Eskimo–Aleut (the latter a branch of the former, but having a distinctive culture of their own) occupy an area extending from the islands south-west of Alaska to the south-east of Greenland, including Newfoundland and Labrador. Little is known of early Aleut religion, missionary work having begun almost immediately after outside contact. Eskimo–Aleut religion is greatly influenced by a hunting and fishing economy. The powers of the universe, *inua* (also *yua*, *tayaruu*), are conceived of as anthropomorphic beings. In Alaska these are identified as personal GUARDIAN

SPIRITS and/or 'owners' or 'persons' of the animals. In central and eastern areas they are viewed primarily as female deities and as *tupilaks* (composite animal figures, OWNER OF THE ANIMALS, helpers of SHAMANS). The cosmos is perceived as naturally harmonious, or at least neutral, calamities befalling mankind through its negligence or disobedience. [23: VII–VIII] Chief among the spirit powers are those ordering the forces of nature (COSMOLOGY). A masculine power is associated with the sky and upper regions, and a feminine power is associated with the sea and land. The latter, often designated Sedna (or Siitna), is the irascible ruler of the undersea world and the one who gave rise to all creatures of the sea. Myths relate that while escaping a seducer she was cast out of her father's boat. As she attempted to cling to its side, her father, in fear for his life, struck at her hands with an ivory axe, cutting off her fingers, which were transformed into seals, walruses, and other sea animals. Sedna, herself, retreated to the depths where she now resides, visited on occasion by the ANGAKOK (or shaman) who seeks to persuade her to grant mankind good fishing. [22: II] Shamans also influence the movements of SOULS (*tarneg*), directing them back to their owners, who have suffered illness during their absence, or to the kingdom of the dead in the case of permanent separation. The autumn ceremonial, held among the Central Eskimo, seeks to placate Sedna and to establish the cosmos on a favourable course.

Ethike [XII] Morality, in Greek religion. The gods, especially Zeus, were thought to protect justice. 'Bad' behaviour was punished, directly e.g. through plagues etc. which would affect the community unless the offender were punished, or through action from inside the human mind leading to catastrophe. The Erinyes (Furies) were thought to punish certain crimes. But bad men often flourish, so the notion arose that

one could be punished in one's descendants, an idea later replaced by a belief in post-mortem punishments. Some believed in retribution through reincarnation. *Nemesis* (divine retribution personified) was thought to punish presumption (*hybris*). Mortals must, above all, worship the gods, respect their parents, honour their oaths, and behave well to guests, suppliants, heralds, and the dead. The moral content of religion – and especially of Orphism (ORPHEUS) – increased progressively, especially in Hellenistic times, when philosophy and the cults of Asklepios and the oriental gods posited a higher ethical standard. This included the spiritual purity which had first been propounded at Delphi (MANTIKE) (Delphi, like Eleusis (MYSTERIA), was a centre of moral teaching). [2: V, 3, 1; 7: 150–52; 8: 246–68; 13; 17: 54, 64–7; 18: 99–100, 152]

Ethiopian Churches [XX] African independent churches appearing from the 1880s, first in Ghana, Nigeria (here called 'African churches'), and South Africa, often through secession from a mission or older church which they resemble in worship, polity, and doctrine, with some African variations and cultural features such as polygamy. The term 'Ethiopian' used in southern Africa and as a classificatory term derives from biblical references to Ethiopia and from its ancient church regarded as a model for independency. [12: 40–41, 45; 16: 53–9]

Eucharist [XI.B] The chief SACRAMENT and central act of Christian WORSHIP (also called Holy Communion, Lord's Supper, and MASS). JESUS CHRIST at his final meal or 'Last Supper' with his disciples blessed bread and wine with the words 'this is my body', 'this is my blood'. Debate has centred mainly on the nature of the 'presence' of Christ in the rite; and its character as a Christian 'sacrifice'. In ROMAN CATHOLICISM 'transubstantiation' teaches that after consecration the 'substance' (inner reality) of the bread (the 'host') and wine becomes 'sacramentally' the Body and Blood of Christ, while the 'accidents' (their physical characteristics) remain unchanged. The ORTHODOX CHURCHES and many Anglicans (ANGLICANISM) believe in this change without attempting to define it. LUTHERANISM teaches 'consubstantiation' (coexistence of the complete physical elements with the Body and Blood). Calvin (CALVINISM) and some Anglicans deny any physical change but believe that the power of the Body and Blood is received (Virtualism). Some Protestants (e.g. Zwingli, 1484–1531 CE) see the rite as a memorial aiding faith. PROTESTANTISM rejected the notion of sacrifice in the Eucharist, but Roman Catholicism, the Orthodox Church, and Anglo-Catholics see it as at least realizing and applying the original sacrifice of Christ's death for the living and dead. Eucharistic worship ranges from the elaboration of the Mass and the Orthodox Church liturgy to the simplicity of the typical BAPTISTS or the PLYMOUTH BRETHREN and their 'Breaking of Bread'. QUAKERS and the SALVATION ARMY do not use it. Roman Catholicism gives only the bread (communion in one kind) to the laity. The ECUMENICAL MOVEMENT and LITURGICAL MOVEMENT have reduced many of the traditional eucharistic differences between Christians. [30: 222–45; 76: 211–16, 440–58; 107: 475–8; 109]

Europe, Christianity in [XI.B] After the fall of the Western Roman empire, and during the Middle Ages, Christianity became a predominantly European religion. The REFORMATION split in the Western Church left northern Europe dominated by PROTESTANTISM, southern by ROMAN CATHOLICISM; while the east was dominated by the ORTHODOX CHURCH. Close relationships were established with the STATE. European conflicts and empires (Spanish, French, British) have been reflected in the expansion of their brands of Christianity to the rest of the world. Christian theology, WORSHIP, and CHURCH ORGANIZATION are still strongly marked by the European phase of world history. European-influenced Christianity has been extended and modified in the U.S.A. and thence to the rest of the world. (Cf. also COMMUNIST WORLD.) [5; 20 vols. 2–5; 68; 83 vols. 1, 2, 4]

European Jewry [XVII] There are records of Jews on the European mainland several centuries before the Christian era, but it was only after the Roman conquest of Palestine in the 1st century BCE that the Jewish population of Europe grew substantially. From the 4th century the Christian church imposed various discriminatory restrictions on Jews, and these have shaped the history of the Jews in Christian Europe up to the modern period. The Jews were expelled from England in 1290 [39: IV], from France in 1394, from different parts of Germany in the 14th and 15th centuries, from Spain in 1492, and from Portugal in 1499 [9 vol. 6: 1069]. Despite pogroms (organized attacks against Jews), persecution, and expulsion (ANTI-SEMITISM), European Jewry flourished spiritually, in particular in Poland and Lithuania (ASHKENAZI). Great centres of Jewish scholarship were set up, and the Jewish community was a self-governing state within a state in the late Middle Ages [31: LXXI]. The Nazi massacres destroyed the old European communities (HOLOCAUST), and the centre of Jewish cultural life has shifted to ISRAEL and the U.S.A. since 1945.

Evangelical [XI.B] A word derived from the Greek for GOSPEL (the Christian 'Good News' of SALVATION) and used today of groups in PROTESTANTISM claiming to declare this with special fidelity. In German-speaking lands an alternative name for LUTHERANISM. The term has been used in English-speaking countries since the

18-century Evangelical Revival (RE-VIVALISM) to denote those emphasizing such teachings as the infallibility of the BIBLE, justification by faith, and personal conversion (SALVATION). They are generally hostile to ROMAN CATHOLICISM and Anglo-Catholicism (ANGLICANISM). But some Evangelicals adopt more liberal views on the Bible and social questions.

Evil (Ancient Near East) [VI] MAGIC was used to combat evil forces, which were often personified as demons. Sometimes a sick person was identified with an animal, which was then killed [23: 21]. Myths and ritual combats (ANCIENT NEAR EASTERN RELIGIONS; FESTIVALS) depicted the victory of good over evil, but man's own sin and not the god's vengeance was regarded as the cause of his suffering. No human troubles were therefore considered unjust, and a renewal of the god's favour was sought through prayers and lamentations [16: 166].

Misfortune was regarded as the result of divine negligence or of a man's sin, or even that of his forebears; however, blame was never attributable to the gods, and prayer could gain salvation [16: 153–66].

Evil, Christian Doctrine of [XI.B] Christians have endeavoured to explain the origin and meaning of evil and suffering, but especially to defend the goodness and omnipotence of God against objections arising from the existence of evil. Christian MONOTHEISM has been resistant to DUALISM and PANTHEISM, although these have sometimes influenced Christian philosophies and SECTS, e.g. the Albigenses (HERESY (MEDIEVAL CHRISTIAN)). Satan as an evil power is ultimately subordinated to God (cf. AFTERLIFE). Origen (c.185 to c. 254 CE), St Thomas Aquinas (c. 1225–74 CE) (THOMISM), and many others have explained evil as an abuse of human freedom necessarily allowed to achieve good. Leibniz (1646–1716) (who coined the term Theodicy for these matters) [107: 1358] saw the world as the best of all possible worlds with evil a necessary shadow to highlight its attractions. Modern treatments [60] have oscillated between optimistic and pessimistic views of human capacity for good and the possibility of overcoming evil in the world. These different views are partly related to changing views of MAN and of SIN. Suffering has also been treated as an occasion of spiritual development in submission to God, following JESUS CHRIST's example.

Exile (Jewish) [XVII] The experience of exile is central to Jewish self-consciousness. The pattern of exile began when the Babylonian empire carried off the inhabitants of the Judaean kingdom in the 6th century BCE (BIBLICAL HISTORY). That exile was only short-lived, and many Jews returned to rebuild their TEMPLE in JERUSALEM and live once again in their homeland. After the destruction of the second temple (70 CE) and the crushing of the Bar Cochba revolt against Roman rule (135 CE), Jewish life in Palestine deteriorated. The demographic centres of Jewry during the Middle Ages were in different parts of the Diaspora (dispersion) [9 vol. 6: 8]. Since Jews saw themselves as the people of God, to whom the HOLY LAND had been promised, they interpreted their suffering in the Diaspora as a consequence of the condition of exile itself. At the centre of their liturgy was the hope of a return to Zion in the messianic age (MESSIAH; ZIONISM) [48: 51].

Existentialism [XI.C] A philosophical doctrine which largely derives from Kierkegaard, although its standpoint of radical concern for the individual person is foreshadowed in Pascal (1623–62). Søren Kierkegaard (1813–55) was a Danish philosopher and theologian who attacked the prevailing Hegelian metaphysical system and the interpretation of CHRISTIANITY as a dogmatic system. Affirming the essential link between authentic truth and its subjective appropriation, he rejected attempts to produce an objectively inferred system of belief, and emphasized the necessity of a leap of faith by the individual as one who stands alone before GOD. In the 20th century existentialist positions have been developed in various ways. Heidegger (1889–1976) and J.-P. Sartre (1905–80) maintain that the fundamental principle that 'existence precedes essence' (i.e. that the individual does not have an imposed nature but must decide his character for himself) is necessarily atheistic while G. Marcel (1889–1973) and K. Jaspers (1883–1969) have developed Christian interpretations of the doctrine, stressing that faith is committed trust in a person rather than assent to dogmatic propositions. [23]

Exodus (in Judaism) [XVII] The redemption of the Israelites (c. 15th–13th centuries BCE) from slavery in Egypt, known as the Exodus from Egypt, is a fundamental motif of Jewish ritual. The major festivals – Passover, Pentecost, and Tabernacles (CHAGIM) – are built round events associated with the Exodus [44: IX, X, XX]. The belief in a Messianic age (MESSIAH) to come is dependent on the idea of divine salvation, and this is represented in Jewish consciousness by God's acts in Egypt (BIBLICAL HISTORY; MOSES) culminating in the Exodus *en route* for the Promised Land. [9 vol. 6: 1042]

· F ·

Fa Hsiang Tsung [x] The DHARMA Characteristics or 'Consciousness Only' (*Wei Shih*) school. This was the Chinese YOGACARA or *Vijnanavada* teachings, which were systematically developed in India by Asanga and Vasubandhu (d. 500 CE), and in China by Hsuan Tsang (596–664 CE). The last-named translated Vasubandhu's *Treatise in Thirty Verses on Consciousness Only* (*Ch'eng Wei Shih Lun*) with commentaries [52], and his *Treatise in Twenty Verses on Consciousness Only* (*Wei Shih Er Shih Lun*) [41]. (ALAYA-VIJNANA) The school was never popular in China. (*See Hosso in* NANTO ROKUSHU.) [7: XXIII, 370–95; 15: XI, 320–24; 32: VIII, 299–338]

Fa-Hsien [IX.A] One of the best known of the Chinese Buddhist monk-pilgrims who journeyed to the Buddhist holy land, India, in the early years of the 5th century CE, to visit the many sacred complexes and famous places associated with GOTAMA. Such pilgrims provide valuable data, through those of their travel diaries that have been preserved, concerning the Buddhism of their time. Other famous monk-pilgrims were I-Tsing and Hsuan-tsang, in the 7th century. On their travels they collected many Buddhist literary works and translated them into Chinese. [15: 424ff]

Falsafa [XIV] The Islamic term for philosophy. Orthodox ISLAM was always uneasy about the utility of philosophy, often viewing it, because of the extraneous forces which moulded it, as inimical to faith and conducive to heresy and unbelief. Hence when philosophy developed in Islam through translations from Greek – Plato, Aristotle, NEO-PLATONISM, etc. – it tended to be cultivated by scholars from trends of thought and sects outside Sunni orthodoxy (SUNNA), such as the Mu'tazilites, Twelver Shi'is (SHI'ISM), ISMA'ILIS, etc. Such philosophical questions as the difference in created beings between essence and existence, God's knowledge of particulars, the materialness or spirituality of punishment and reward in the next life (*see* AKHIRA), and whether creation was *ex nihilo*, were discussed by al-Farabi (*c.* 870–950), Ibn Sina (Avicenna) (980–1037), and others. The orthodox reaction came through the practitioners of KALAM and through the towering figure of al-Ghazali (1058–1111), whose refutation of the philosophers was in turn combated by Ibn Rushd (Averroës) (1126–98). Philosophy declined after the 13th century as the intellectual aspect of Islam became increasingly ossified. [21 'Falsafa'; 61: VII; 77]

Fasts (Jewish) [XVII] The most important of the Jewish fast days (*tzom* or *ta'anit*) is the Day of Atonement or Yom Kippur [52: 178]. This lasts for 25 hours, beginning at sundown on the previous day and continuing until nightfall. Jews spend most of the time in the SYNAGOGUE in prayer, and refrain from all food and drink. The only other fast of similar duration is the 9th of Av (Tishah Be-Av), remembering the TEMPLE destruction. Day-long fasts (sunrise to nightfall) are the 17th of Tammuz, when the events leading to the Temple's destruction began; the 10th of Tevet, remembering the siege of Jerusalem by the army of Nebuchadnezzar; the 3rd of Tishri or Tzom Gedaliah, when the Babylonian appointee as

governor of Judah was assassinated in
the 6th century BCE (BIBLICAL HIS-
TORY); and the 13th of Adar (Ta'anit
Ester), in memory of the events recorded
in the Book of Esther [44: XI, XIV].
The essence of all fasting is repentance.
[9 vol. 6: 1189]

Fatalism (in Islam) [XIV] There was a
persistent strain of fatalism in older
Near Eastern religions which was carried into early Islam [62]. The QUR'AN
speaks of God's eternal decree (qadar),
but elsewhere it allows a place to man's
free will. It was the task of later theologians to formulate a doctrine which
to some extent harmonized the two
opposed views, so that orthodoxy came
to allow man a certain liberty to acquire
actions broadly foreordained by God
(ALLAH) [82: 49–57]. The idea of res-
ignation to the divine will (see ISLAM)
has strengthened these tendencies towards a determinist emphasis on God's
sovereignty. The term kismet stems
from a Turkish form of Arabic qisma
'sharing-out', i.e. 'allotted fate' [39 'Predestination'].

Fatiha [XIV] The short opening sura of
the QUR'AN, beginning, 'In the name of
God, the Merciful, the Compassionate.
Praise be to God, the Lord of the
Worlds . . .'. It is held in special reverence by Muslims and much used liturgically, in some ways forming a parallel to
the use of the Lord's Prayer in Christianity. It is an indispensable part of the
worship or SALAT, being recited at the
beginning of each prostration, and is
further used as a prayer for the sick, the
dead, etc., as an exorcism formula, and
as a component in the wording of amulets and talismans. [10 S.V.; 21 S.V.; 81: 46]

Feng-Shui [X] Literally 'wind and
water', usually interpreted as geomancy.
Feng-Shui is the Chinese practice of
determining auspicious sites for buildings and graves, in accordance with the
natural forces and currents (ch'i) of the
landscape. The yin force (YIN–YANG) in
nature is identified as the White Tiger,
which should be found to the left of a

proposed site; and the yang force is the
Azure Dragon, which should be to the
right. [29: 86, II, 21–5; 68: XIV, 359–63]

Fenriswolf [V] The wolf Fenrir (Fenriswolf) is one of LOKI's monstrous sons.
The tale of his binding by Tyr, who
sacrificed his hand in Fenrir's jaws to
save the AESIR, is probably an ancient
Germanic myth [20: 57–8; 30: VIII, 180–
81]. Fenrir breaks loose at RAGNAROK
and devours ODIN, but is slain by
Odin's son Vidar. He may possibly be
identified with the hound Garm at the
entrance to HEL, and with the wolf pursuing the sun [6: II, 59; 20: 86–7].

Festivals (Ancient Near Eastern) [VI]
Cult-centres held periodic festivals
which included sacrifices and libations
to the deities (ANCIENT NEAR EASTERN
RELIGIONS). Some were local celebrations; others, probably performed by
the king (KINGSHIP) at the centre of the
state-cult, were intended to benefit the
whole country. Particularly important
were the new year FESTIVAL and the
spring festival, at which in some
instances a mock combat was enacted
(HITTITES) [13: 152]. This celebrated
the annual victory of life over death, and
of good over EVIL.

Festivals and Rituals (Hindu) [XIII.C]
The life of the high-caste Hindu involves a series of life-cycle rituals or
samskaras, the exact number of which
varies between different sources [2: 23].
Of these the most commonly practised
are: birth-rituals (jatakarma); the naming
of the child (namakarana); putting on the
sacred thread signifying a second birth
(upanayana); marriage (vivaha); and
funeral rites (antyesthi) [XIII.B.2: 160; 2:
74, 84, 126, 207, 234; 3: 1, 13, 27, 58,
135]. The offering of rice balls (pinda) to
the dead for the first 10 days after death
and periodically thereafter (shraddha) is
also faithfully maintained [XIII.B.2: 178;
2: 265; 3: 290; 4: 63].

The Hindu sacred year consists of 12
lunar months, with a leap month intercalated every two and a half years to
align it with the solar year. The month

is divided into the bright, auspicious fortnight when the moon is waxing, and the dark, inauspicious fortnight when it is waning [XIII.B.2: 494; 3: 260]. The months begin at full moon in North India and at the new moon in South India. The new year is considered to begin in spring or in late autumn in different locations. There is no universal festival calendar, each area and each deity having its own festivals. The more widespread festivals are: Holi, a spring festival of a carnival nature when coloured powder is thrown over passersby [1: 88; 3: 280]; Shivaratri, a festival devoted to SHIVA held in late February [1: 214; 3: 266; 4: 65]; Janmashtami, KRISHNA's birthday, celebrated at the end of summer [1: 94; 3: 317; 4: 74]; Dasera, in late autumn, commemorating the victory of RAMA over the demon army [1: 181; 3: 332]; and Divali, a festival of lights held at the onset of winter [1: 36; 3: 335].

Festivals (Chinese) [x] The great family and communal festivals (*Chieh Chi*) which were observed in traditional China and which are still observed in Taiwan and Hong Kong reflect many of the distinctive features of Chinese popular religion. [105: IV, 86–99; 86: VII, 108–13]

Among the most important domestic celebrations and rites are those associated with the new year (*Hsin Nien*). The end of the old year and the expelling of the dark *yin* force (YIN–YANG) is signified by cleaning and repainting the home. Two or three days before the end of the year the god of the stove Tsao Chun is dispatched to the heavenly court of the Jade Emperor (Yu Huang) (CHINESE PANTHEON) to report on the behaviour of his hosts during the year. This act is signified by burning Tsao Chun's picture and making offerings of sweet rice and wine in order to sweeten his reports. His return on New Year's Eve is signified by mounting a new picture and setting off fire-crackers. On New Year's Eve, Heaven, Earth, and the household gods and ancestors are

honoured by the family with offerings of food, incense, candles, spirit money, and many bows. On the third day the festival of Ts'ai Shen the god of wealth is celebrated in the home by placing offerings of meat and fish before his picture. Another important New Year festival is the Li Ch'un, beginning of spring. In imperial times this involved the Emperor's symbolic ploughing of a field in the capital, followed by a procession led by the 'spring ox', which was then sacrificed. In modern times the procession is led by a paper ox.

The Ch'ing Ming (Clear and Bright) festival is celebrated in the third month of the year by visiting and repairing ancestral graves, and offering food and spirit money to the *p'o* (souls of the ancestors). A special offering is also made to the Lord of the Soil (T'u Ti Kung), who protects graves. On the eighth day of the fourth month the birthday of the BUDDHA is celebrated at Buddhist temples by chanting sutras and washing the BUDDHA IMAGES. Traditional Chinese and Buddhist beliefs and practices combine in the P'u Tu or 'Saving All Souls' festival in the seventh month when the ghosts (*Kuei*) of those who died without descendants, or who were not properly buried, wander in search of food. The gates of hell are believed to be open for most of this month. On the 15th day the ghosts and their nearest Buddhist equivalents the *pretas* are offered food, drink, and prayers and in the Yu Lan Hui (Avalambana) festival are saved, at least temporarily, from their torments. [3: 4; 42; 75: 1, 16–31]

Fideism [XI.C] A term (from Latin *fides*, faith, belief) used to describe that kind of theological understanding which fundamentally denies that it is possible to establish the truth or reasonableness of religious beliefs by unprejudiced arguments and which consequently stresses the primary role of the commitment of faith in providing the basis for theological understanding. Initially the word was adopted by A. Sabatier (1839–1901) and E. Ménégoz (1838–1921) to describe their Protestant interpretation of Christianity (PROTESTANTISM) as 'the religion of the Spirit' and of SALVATION being by faith alone. The term is now generally used in a pejorative manner, particularly with reference to those views which have taken up the notion of a 'language-game' put forward by L. Wittgenstein (1889–1951) to argue that a religious or theological position is a self-contained system of understanding with its own presuppositions and rules that cannot be validly criticized or justified from outside the system. [13; 21]

Fijian Religion [XXII] The Fiji islands have a mixed population of (1) Indian immigrants (mainly Hindu, but also Muslim and Christian) and (2) native Fijians (predominantly Christian, particularly METHODIST). The Fijians and their religion are said to exhibit a mixture of MELANESIAN and POLYNESIAN features. (Fiji stands on the dividing-line between the two regions and had trading relations with Tonga.) The supreme god was Ndengei (a serpent, a Melanesian trait), who lived in a cave on the north-east end of Vitilevu island; earthquakes occurred when he turned over; he received food offerings and replied to requests brought to him by priests. Some priests were possessed by other deities (*kalou*) and in trance gave revelations on warfare, weather, and healing (as in Polynesia). MALE CULTS relating to ancestors (as in Melanesia) were associated with stone enclosures (reminiscent of the Polynesian MARAE). Ritual cannibalism was sometimes practised against enemies (*see* MANA). *Mburu* was the land of the afterlife, under the sea. [21; 22]

Fiqh [XIV] 'Knowledge', the technical term for the science of Islamic law, covering all aspects of human activity, from the religious cult to personal, criminal, and constitutional law, hence including the SHARI'A proper and other

sources of legal knowledge. After the 8th century, several schools of religious law (*madhhabs*) grew up, of which the four most important ones, still surviving today, are those of the Hanafis, Malikis, Shafi'is, and Hanbalis. A Muslim should follow one of these systems exclusively; only in recent decades have legal reformers selected items from different schools and combined them for modern legal proposals. In fact, the differences between the schools are slight. The Shi'is have their own body of law, again not greatly different from that of the Sunnis (*see* SHI'ISM, SUNNA). [21 'Fiḳh'; 47: 180–91; 61: IV]

Fire (Zoroastrian) [XXX] (*Adur*, older *atar*) One of the seven creations of AHURA MAZDA, protected by the AMESHA SPENTA of righteousness. Fire in all its forms, from the sun to the household fire, is sacred. The living warmth of the element of fire is thought to pervade all other creations. It has a unique ritual place in ZOROASTRIANISM, much of which derives from its role in Indo-Iranian tradition (INDO-EUROPEANS), as recipient of the sacrificial offering and conveyor of it to the gods (cf. AGNI in Hinduism). Prayers were addressed to the fire itself [translation 11: 134–87]. In ancient times ritual offerings were made to the household fire but in Achaemenid times (*c.* 4th century BCE) the temple cult of fire was introduced [7: 60–65, 85–90]. It is the fire not the temple which is the focus for worship. Fires may be moved from temple to temple, but they may not be extinguished. The three most famous ancient fires were those of Farnbag, Gushnasp, and Burzen-mihr. All were centres of pilgrimage. Gushnasp was the object of lavish royal patronage and the only one whose ruins (Takht i Suleyman) have been identified [19: 113–18].

In modern Zoroastrianism, especially among the PARSIS, temples have become increasingly important as they provide pure shrines for the sacred fires. Ritual fires are consecrated for private devotion and they are used in higher liturgies but they are not used for congregational worship (YASNA) [23: 55–64]. Essentially they consist of a sanctuary for the fire, a prayer-room, and a separate room (*urvisgah* or *yazishngah*) for the higher liturgies. There is no distinctive architectural style. The highest grade of fire is *Atash* (= fire) *Bahram* (*see* YAZATAS), the installation of which is so complex that it takes a year [33: ix]. Once installed it is enthroned and served with royal dignity. Two such temples exist in Iran, eight in India. The second grade is the *Adaran* fire, which is used in 'ordinary' temples, often called by the Persian name *dar-i Mihr* (Court of Mithra), or in India by the Gujarati term *Agiary*, meaning 'house of fire'. The lowest grade of fire, *dadgah*, can burn in the home but if it burns in a temple then it, like the others, must be ritually tended. The differences between the grades of ritual fires is determined by the rites of consecration. Worshipping before the fire, considered the son or representative of God, Zoroastrians believe they are standing in the presence of God. A fire is present at all Zoroastrian rites. [13: II; 22: pt III, 44–53]

Firqa [XIV] 'Sect' in ISLAM. In early Islam, there were intense struggles over such basic theological and political questions as predestination and free will, the nature of God's attributes, gradations of sinfulness (DHANB), the createdness or uncreatedness of the QUR'AN, the nature of the caliphate (CALIPH), etc., and corresponding sects formed, some purely theological and philosophical, others political and activist (e.g. ISMA'ILIS, KHARIJITES, SHI'ISM). Basing themselves on a tradition of the Prophet that 'differences amongst my community are a mercy from God', Muslim authorities did not regard the existence of sects as necessarily inimical to the basic unity of Islam, and despite their proliferation, Islam has always remained an essentially unified faith and institution. [31: VII; 46]

Folklore [XXVIII] Traditions, customs, and beliefs of the 'folk' or common people. Much that is studied by anthropologists in small-scale societies (rites (RITUAL), tales, songs, sayings) would, as a survival in technologically advanced society, be placed in this category. The study of such traditional material has formed an important aspect of RELIGIONSWISSENSCHAFT [18: 172–4; 25: 51].

Fon Religion [II] The Fon, principal people of Dahomey (now the People's Republic of Benin), were organized under the powerful monarchy of Abomey, which developed after the 16th century. Their exceptionally complex religion borrowed much from neighbouring societies (particularly the YORUBA) without fully synthesizing the borrowings, so that the variations remain great in different parts of the kingdom and cult centres. The monarchy, a relative latecomer, influenced, but was hardly central to, Fon religion, which in this and other ways may be compared with GANDA.

Its most striking character lies in its sexual duality. The creator god is seen as double – Mawu and Lisa – though behind these is a shadowy Nana Buluku, recognized but seldom mentioned. Mawu is female, symbolized by moon and night; she stands for rest and the first stage of creation – fertilization. Lisa, the male partner, has as his symbols sun and day; his field is work, and the second stage of creation, its ordering. (Among Ewe peoples west of the Fon, Mawu is male and Lisa a little-used praise name for Mawu.)

Mawu is assisted in creation by Da, a demiurge symbolized by rainbow and serpent; Lisa is assisted by Gu, the heavenly blacksmith. These are but two of a vast pantheon, the Vodun, the progeny of Mawu/Lisa, hierarchically responsible for every aspect of the world's ordering. The basic model of pairs of twins of opposite sex runs throughout the heavenly hierarchy and is seen as the ideal human condition. *Fa*, word of Mawu and symbol of destiny, is patron of a complex system of divination (IFA to the YORUBA).

The Fon are divided into clans, each of which has a divine founder, the Tohwiyo. Fon worship includes temples for Mawu/Lisa and also a remarkable system of convent initiation. [4: 210–34]

Frashokereti [XXX] (PAHLAVI *Frashegird*) The 'making wonderful' or renovation of creation at the end of the historical process in ZOROASTRIANISM. Because the world is the good creation of AHURA MAZDA, Zoroastrians do not look for 'the end of the world', instead they look forward to the time when it will be cleansed from all the unnatural impurity with which evil has afflicted it (BUNDAHISHN). The earliest traditions divided time into three great eras: creation, *bundahishn*; the period when good and evil are 'mixed together' (Pahlavi *gumezishn*); and the final state after the renovation, the time of separation (*wizarishn*) of good and evil. But in the scholastic theology of the Pahlavi books the history of the world is divided into four periods, each of 3,000 years, the last of which, it is believed, began with Zoroaster (i.e. the present time is 'in the last days'). Zoroastrianism traditionally awaits the coming of a saviour (*Saoshyant*; Pahlavi *Soshyant*), who will be born of a virgin, but of the seed of the prophet Zoroaster. He is expected to raise the dead and introduce the universal judgement. The first, or individual judgement, immediately after death (*see* CHINVAT BRIDGE) is for the soul only, but because the whole man is considered the creation of Ahura Mazda a second judgement after the resurrection is essential so that man may be judged, rewarded, or corrected in body as well as in soul.

Many scholars believe that this teaching, together with the idea of evil (*see* ANGRA MAINYU), heaven and hell, and the details of how evil attacks the world before the 'end' (e.g. earthquakes, wars, social and cosmic upheavals), all influenced Jewish, Christian, and Muslim doctrines [22: pt III, 24–38]. After the resurrection the heavenly and demonic forces will pair off in final conflict. The world and men will pass through a river of molten metal as a final test of purity. Then, when evil is finally defeated, heaven and earth will merge in what is literally the best of both worlds and mankind will dwell in perfection in the kingdom of Ahura Mazda for eternity. [5: IX; 7: 42f; 20: 66–9; 49: X; 50: XV]

Fravashi [XXX] (PAHLAVI *Fravahr*) Man's eternal spirit, which according to ZOROASTRIANISM remains in heaven even during his life on earth. In the creation myth (BUNDAHISHN) it is said that when AHURA MAZDA created the material world the *fravashis* of all men were consulted to see whether they chose to assume material form, and so take part in the battle with evil, or to remain in spiritual form and therefore stand apart from the conflict. The *fravashis* collectively chose to assume material form. The doctrine of free will is basic to Zoroastrianism and is developed to its logical conclusion in this myth, asserting that men have chosen to live in the material world. [5: index]

Freemasonry [XVIII] An international all-male movement with a membership of some 6 million, devoted to charitable and social activities and the secret practice of certain rituals. Freemasonry is not a religion, although in most countries masons must acknowledge a Supreme Being, venerated as 'the Great Architect of the Universe'. Members of a masonic 'lodge' take three 'degrees' (Entered Apprentice, Fellow Craft, and Master Mason), which are conferred with impressive rituals dramatizing the soul's progress from darkness to spiritual light and rebirth. (There are also many 'side degrees' to which a Master Mason may proceed.) In each degree the candidate is presented with 'working tools' symbolizing moral qualities he is expected to cultivate. Masonic teachings consist mainly of moral allegorization of the traditional implements of building and geometry, supplemented by legendary material imaginatively elaborated from the Hebrew scriptures (BIBLE). [7]

Freemasonry derives from the craft organizations of the medieval British free-stone masons. In the late 17th century declining lodges of such 'operative masons' accepted as members antiquarians interested in architectural traditions. These 'speculative masons' took over the lodges, refurbishing their traditional rituals and ethical teachings. During the 18th century freemasonry spread widely in Europe and North America, and it has since proliferated into a wide variety of forms. In Europe it attracted radicals and DEISTS; it has generally been viewed with suspicion by both the Communist parties and ROMAN CATHOLICISM. Orthodox freemasonry, however, has been remarkable mainly for its generous charities and its respectability (13 presidents of the U.S.A. have been masons, and since 1747 all Grand Masters of England have been noblemen). Masonic teachings and rituals have often been reported, but they remain little known among non-masons, and their aura of secrecy is an important source of their imaginative and emotional power.

Friday (in Islam) [XIV] This 'day of assembly' (*jum'a*) (ISLAM) has religious significance in that congregational worship at the midday SALAT, provided that there is a quorum of 40, is obligatory. It is not in origin a Sabbath or day of rest, but in the modern Islamic world it has become an official holiday. [10 s.v.; 39 s.v.]

Frost-Giants [V] Germanic mythology differs from Celtic in its greater emphasis on the adversaries of the gods. The AESIR were under continual threat from the frost-giants, apparently representing cold, chaos, and sterility, and

distinct from the fair giants, the VANIR. The EDDAS have many stories of their attempts to steal the gods' treasures, particularly THOR's hammer, the only weapon they feared, and the goddess Freyja (one of the Vanir [6: 1, 39–45, 89–91]). Individual giants are Hrungnir, who fought a duel with THOR; Thiazi, who stole the apples of youth; Thrym, who hid Thor's hammer; Suttung, from whom ODIN stole the mead of inspiration; Geirrod and his daughters, who tried to destroy Thor; and Hymir, a sea-giant. These, with others whose stories are lost, were killed by Thor, but many giants survived to attack Asgard (the Aesir dwelling-place) at RAGNAROK, although they perished in the final conflagration. Their allies were LOKI and his monstrous sons, FENRISWOLF and the World-Serpent.

Functionalism [XXVIII] (1) A mode of explanation, based on understanding of what something does or of the effects it produces rather than of what it is [2: 23; 18: XII]. RELIGION has been defined functionally (as that which promotes social solidarity or gives confidence). The SCIENCES OF RELIGION have sought to explain functionally the ORIGIN OF RELIGION or its persistence [1: 12–24, 106–22; 3: VIII; 4: II; 24: 20–24, 38–42].

(2) A way of understanding religious beliefs. Its objects (e.g. GODS) are regarded as SYMBOLS for functions or aspects of the divine or of ultimate reality.

[General survey in 30: 167–215]

Funeral Rites (Chinese) [X] The Funeral Rites (*Sang Li*), mourning, and continued offerings are essential elements in the traditional Chinese ANCESTOR CULT. Generally the procedures follow those described in the Classic of Rites (CONFUCIAN CANON; LI) [61; 81: VII, 88–91]. The elaborateness of the rites is determined by the status of the deceased in the family and the lineage. Their main intention is to assist the spirit (*shen*) of the *hun* soul on its dangerous journey through the underworld, and its safe transference to the spirit or ancestor tablet (*shen chu*). Only the very worthy *shen* can ascend to Heaven. The *p'o* soul, which normally resides in the grave, must also be ritually sustained and pacified to prevent it becoming a dangerous ghost (*kuei*). (FENG-SHUI; FESTIVALS (CHINESE)) [1; 38; 43; 66; 85: XXI; 86: III, 34–65; 105: II, 28–57]

Funerary Practices (Ancient Egyptian) [IV] At all levels of society, the dead were supplied with funerary goods for the AFTERLIFE. For the wealthy, these included anthropoid and rectangular coffins, face-masks, canopic jars (containing viscera), funerary jewellery, amulets, furniture, clothing, toilet equipment, and food and drink [6]. Also, there were model brewers, butchers, and bakers to prepare a continuing source of victuals. Hundreds of *ushabtis* (mummiform figurines representing agricultural labourers) provided the deceased with a MAGIC work-force.

A specialized literature, read at funerals and during mortuary rites (MANSION OF THE KA), relied on magical efficacy to overcome evil and to ensure the deceased's survival. First devised to obtain the king's immortality (the Pyramid texts, Old Kingdom *c.* 2500 BC [11]), democratization of religious customs made them available to wealthy commoners (Coffin texts, Middle Kingdom *c.* 1900 BCE). Later, New Kingdom texts (*c.* 1500–1100 BCE) include the Book of the Dead [1], and the cosmographic texts in the Valley of the Kings: the Books of Gates, Caverns, the Day and the Night, and *Am-Duat*. (*See also* MUMMIFICATION, PYRAMIDS.)

Fylgja [V] This term is used in early Icelandic literature for a shape accompanying a man through life. It resembles an external soul, often in animal form, visible in dreams or to those with second sight, and is capable of journeys away from the body. *Fylgja* is also used, together with the term *hamingja*, for a female guardian spirit attached to a family, passed on through the generations and sometimes seen as a supernatural bride [30: XI, 221–7]. VALKYRIES may appear in this role, and the term *disir* (goddesses) is also used for such guardian figures. In the Icelandic legendary sagas a giantess may be represented as both foster-mother and bride of the hero, helping him in time of need. Such beliefs may originally have been associated with the VANIR goddesses, and with the MATRES of Celtic tradition. The conception of the guardian spirit has left a considerable mark on heroic tales and poems, in both Irish and Icelandic literature.

· G ·

Gahambars [XXX] The six seasonal festivals of the religious year in ZOROASTRIANISM, which, together with New Year's Day (*No Ruz*), comprise a sequence which all Zoroastrians are required to observe. Each festival is held in honour of an AMESHA SPENTA and the respective creation. They are: 'Midspring' (*Maidhyoi-zarema*), honouring Khshathra and the sky; 'Midsummer' (*Maidhyoi-shema*), honouring Haurvatat and water; 'Bringing in the corn' (*Paitishahya*), honouring Armaiti and earth; 'Home-coming' (*Ayathrima*), honouring Ameretat and plants; 'Midwinter' (*Maidhyairya*), honouring Vohu Manah and cattle; and *Hamaspathmaedaya* (meaning uncertain), which is in honour of AHURA MAZDA and his creation, man – a time for joyfully welcoming back to earth the FRAVASHIS of the departed. This last festival is known among the PARSIS as Muktad, a Gujarati term. *No Ruz*, New Year's Day, was celebrated in honour of Asha and fire.

The rites for each festival are similar, beginning with the ceremony of the YASNA in the morning, followed by feasting where all who have the means are bound by the traditional Zoroastrian duty to give charitably to others [6: 11; 23: 51–5, 72; 33: 419–27].

Ganda Religion [11] The Baganda live north-west of Lake Victoria, in Uganda. They formed for centuries one of the most powerful monarchies in the region of the great lakes. While the king (*kabaka*) closely controlled religious institutions, as all other sides of life, and the dead kings were venerated, each with his own shrine-tomb, Ganda religion was not intellectually centred upon the kingship, itself a secular rather than religious institution.

Ganda religion shares the common BANTU characteristics: KATONDA, the creator-god; MIZIMU, ancestral spirits; *mayembe* (horns, of cow or buffalo), fetishes or objects with magical power (NKISI); *musezi*, the night-witch. Yet magic and witchcraft appear less important than among many peoples. Many proverbs show the strength and antiquity of belief in the one supreme Katonda. In practice organized Ganda religion came to pay little attention to Katonda, and was rather characterized by worship of the Lubaale, an extensive pantheon of nature heroes, similar to the Cwezi of the neighbouring Nyoro. In this it contrasted with the more emphatically monotheistic belief (in Imana) of two other nearby monarchies, Rwanda and Burundi.

The most powerful Lubaale were Mukasa (the lake-god) and Kibuka (war). Mukasa, god of water, fertility, and healing, sustained life in all its forms and was wholly benign. In marked contrast Kibuka frequently demanded human sacrifice. All the Lubaale had main and secondary temples (*kiggwa*), each with priest (*mukabona*) and medium (*mmandwa*). The royal tombs (*masiro*) had *mmandwa* but no *mukabona*, a dead *kabaka* seeming to stand somewhere between *mizimu* and Lubaale [35: 42].

Ganesha/Ganapati [XIII.A] An elephant-headed, popular deity of the HINDUS, son of SHIVA and PARVATI. He is the god of wisdom, and the remover of obstacles; hence is invoked at the outset of new undertakings. His one-tusked elephant-head symbolizes his sagacity, and his association with success is denoted by his paunch [15: 343]. His name indicates he is lord of the Ganas, who are demigod attendants of Shiva, and his status is that of a humble, important, and relatively recent addition to the Hindu pantheon. He has now come to be regarded as the patron of business activity, and at the start of the year business men hold a ceremony over their ledgers in his honour. Where business men abound this becomes a popular festival. [2: 317]

Ganga [XIII.A] The river most sacred to the Hindus (known to Europeans as 'the Ganges'). Many other rivers in varying degrees share the quality of sacredness attributed to the Ganga, which is regarded as flowing from the foot of God. With the other major river of the north Indian plain, the Yamuna (Jumna), the Ganga is regarded as a goddess. So also is the Sarasvati. The confluence (*sangam*) of these three is particularly sacred, and is known as a TIRTHA.

Gelug [XXIX] The Gelug tradition of Tibetan Buddhism was founded by the great scholar Tsongkhapa Lozang Dragpa (1367–1419 CE). In early life Tsongkhapa studied with masters of all the major Tibetan lineages, and received extensive training in philosophical and meditational teachings. Subsequently he attracted many disciples and founded the monastery of Ganden, which became one of the three principal seats of the Gelug tradition. The chief characteristics of the tradition are its strict adherence to the VINAYA rules of monastic discipline, and its emphasis on the 'graded path' (*lam-rim*) to enlightenment, which was inherited from the KADAM school [23; 25]. In philosophy the Gelugs have upheld the viewpoint of the Prasangika MADHYAMIKA as interpreted by Tsongkhapa, in which emptiness is referred to as 'the negation of all predicates' (*med-gag*).

Although the hierarch of the Ganden monastery is officially the head of the Gelug school, the office of the Dalai Lama, hierarch of the Drepung monastery, has attained pre-eminence. This is due to the Dalai Lama's position as head of the Tibetan state, a position attained in the lifetime of the fifth Dalai Lama, Ngawang Lozang Gyamtsho (1617–82), who unified the country under the authority of the Gelug sect [18]. The title Dalai Lama ('ocean-like guru') was conferred by the Mongol, Altan Khan, on his GURU Sonam Gyamtsho (1543–88), who was retrospectively recognized as the third in the line of incarnations. The political power of the tradition continued until 1959 with the exile of the 14th Dalai Lama, Tenzin Gyamtsho, as a result of the communist Chinese invasion and suppression of Tibetan independence.

Gentiles [XVII] The term Gentile is a translation of the Hebrew word *goi*, meaning member of a non-Jewish people. The Jews, seeing themselves as the children of Abraham with whom God had entered into a special COVENANT, made a sharp distinction between themselves and other nations. Their attitudes toward Gentiles have varied, depending partly on the attitudes of Gentiles themselves to the teachings of JUDAISM and to Jews. [9 vol. 7: 410; 25] The Gentile or Son of Noah has, according to Jewish teaching, to keep the seven Noachian laws: to maintain the rule of law; not to practise idolatry, blasphemy, homicide, sexual immorality, and theft; and not to eat a limb torn from a living animal. The pious of the Gentiles have a portion in the OLAM HA-BA or world to come. The opinion of the RABBIS about Muslims was that they were ethical monotheists, but considerable reservations were felt about Christian monotheism (TRINITY). [52: XIV]

Germanic Religion [V] Information about the religion of the Germanic peoples, in the area bounded by the Rhine, Vistula, and Danube, comes from Julius Caesar (1st century BCE [5]), Tacitus (1st century CE [27: 101–41]), and other Latin writers, of varying reliability [29: 1,

VI]. Anglo-Saxon England was settled in the 5th century and converted to Christianity by the 7th, but Scandinavia not until the 10th century. Evidence from missionaries, place-names, cult objects, amulets, grave goods, and other archaeological finds (SHIP-FUNERAL, SUTTON HOO) adds to our knowledge. The Icelanders retained an interest in earlier myths, and the Poetic and Prose EDDAS are the richest source for these, together with early skaldic verse [30: I]. In the Viking Age (9th/11th centuries) there were four main deities [6: II–IV]. ODIN (Germanic Wodan) was god of magic, poetry, riches, and the dead, and ruler of VALHALLA. THOR (Germanic Donar), armed with his hammer, was widely worshipped as a sky-god, controlling the weather and protecting law and the community. Freyr and Freyja were fertility deities, with many different names (VANIR). Earlier gods might be remembered as minor deities, like Tyr (Germanic Tiwaz [6: II, 59–60]). Numerous names of supernatural beings (FROST-GIANTS, FYLGJA) are preserved in Icelandic mythological poetry. There was an elaborate system of nine worlds of men and other beings round the World-Tree (YGGDRASIL), doomed to destruction at RAGNAROK [2: VII]. Powerful religious symbols in poetry and art were the horse, boar, wolf, eagle, and raven, as well as ship, spear, and hammer [10: II, 139–76], and the mead of inspiration provided for the gods [6: I, 40–41].

Gesar [XXIX] King Gesar of Ling is the greatest culture hero of Tibet. Traditionally he is venerated as an emanation of Padmasambhava and vanquisher of all the forces inimical to religion. [5] However, modern scholarship, while unable to date him, has suggested that Gesar might be a pre-Buddhist figure. His epic cycle, which was only finally systematized in written form in the 19th century by the great scholar Ju Mipham (1848–1914), spread in Tibet and Mongolia by the agency of wandering bards. A messianic hope has been inspired by the notion of King Gesar's triumphant return to rescue Tibet from her enemies and establish Buddhism throughout the world.

Ghost Dance [III] A revivalistic, prophetic movement among Amerindian tribes of the Great Basin and Plains of North America in the late 19th century. The founding prophet, a Paiute Indian, Wovoka, claimed it had been revealed to him in a vision that, if the Indians would dance, the dead would return and all native peoples would be restored to the happy way of life they had before the arrival of the white man [22: V]. As the movement spread among oppressed Indian groups, its eschatology was greatly embellished and its latent anti-white militarism blossomed [8: II]. Fanatical belief that 'ghost shirts' would protect wearers from the harm of enemy bullets prompted still further confrontation with whites. The movement subsided rapidly following the tragic massacre of Sitting Bull and his people at Wounded Knee in 1890.

Gilgamesh, Epic of [VI] During the first dynasty of Babylon (c. 1760 BCE), myths about Gilgamesh were combined as a single epic (ANCIENT NEAR EASTERN RELIGIONS). He was a preeminent figure in these accounts, which include tales of ancient kings and heroes of Sumer [24: 72–9]. This epic tells of his search for eternal life and of the origin of KINGSHIP. The introductory passage provides our main source for the SUMERIAN concept of the creation of the universe (COSMOLOGY). The epic also gives the earliest-known account of a universal flood [16: 200–205], which is thought to have influenced the flood narrative in the BIBLE.

Gnosticism [XI.A] The doctrine that knowledge (Greek *gnosis*) is the way to salvation, especially for human spirits, particles of light from the upper world which have fallen into prison-houses of flesh. Those who are worthy receive the saving knowledge from a redeemer-revealer. This basic scheme was variously elaborated in the Gnostic schools of the 2nd century CE, most, but not all, of which had associations with CHRISTIANITY. The possibility of a pre-Christian Gnosticism is not ruled out.

The variety of Gnostic schools was such that Irenaeus of Lyons (c. 180 CE) could say that there were as many systems of redemption as there were Gnostic teachers. But they shared the basic principle that the material world is evil, while the world of spirit is good. This led to the belief that the two worlds owed their existence to two different creators, the creator of the material order (the demiurge) being an opponent of the supreme God of truth. This cosmological dualism was variously set forth in mythological narratives and genealogical schemes.

Some Gnostic schools, e.g. the followers of Valentinus (c. 140 CE), were not far removed from church orthodoxy. Others were directly opposed to it, in ethics and theology alike; such were the followers of Carpocrates (c. 140 CE), who are alleged to have practised community of wives as well as of property (SIN; WOMEN). Such libertine Gnosticism was a deviation from the norm. Another group of the same period, the Naassenes, took their name from the serpent (Hebrew *nahash*), which they regarded as the embodiment of wisdom. Several of the NAG HAMMADI texts are of Naassene origin. [20]

God (in Hebrew and Christian Scriptures) [XI.A] From the beginning of Israel's history the God of Israel was known as Yahweh. He was not only the God of Israel; he was acknowledged as the creator of the universe, 'maker of heaven and earth', and as the judge of all nations. It was their common worship of Yahweh that gave a consciousness of unity to the tribes of Israel. One of his fuller titles was Yahweh, the God of

hosts (i.e. the hosts or armies of Israel; later the hosts of heaven).

The Israelites identified Yahweh with El, the head of the Canaanite pantheon (BIBLICAL HISTORY). More particularly, after David's capture of JERUSALEM (about 1000 BCE) Yahweh was identified with El Elyon ('God Most High'), who was worshipped in Jerusalem and had as his priests the pre-Davidic kings of that city. To this royal priesthood David and his heirs succeeded, and the MESSIAH of David's line was hailed as 'a priest for ever after the order of Melchizedek' (Melchizedek being an ancient Jerusalemite priest-king).

The documentary evidence that Yahweh's worship was aniconic (ICONOGRAPHY) is confirmed negatively by the absence from the archaeological record of any object which could be recognized as his image.

The prophets of Israel emphasized Yahweh's ethical character (which indeed had been explicit in the Mosaic COVENANT): he was pre-eminently a God of righteousness and mercy, and required those qualities in his people. If they were unjust or merciless, he would deal with them more severely because they were his people and ought to know better.

The God of the New Testament is identical with the God of the Hebrew Bible. Jesus had an intense awareness of communion with God: he habitually called him 'Abba' (the domestic word for 'father') and taught his followers to do the same. According to PAUL, the invocation 'Abba' on the lips of Christians is a token that they have received the same Spirit (HOLY SPIRIT) as indwelt Jesus. [2: 11–31, 55–9; 3: 161–5]

God, Christian Concept of [XI.B] Christianity formally teaches MONOTHEISM, rejecting both DEISM and PANTHEISM. (Elements of POLYTHEISM have, however, been common at popular folk level in various countries.) God has created the world distinct from himself, while remaining active within it. His attributes include eternity, unchangeableness (immutability), unlimited knowledge (omniscience) and power (omnipotence). This monotheism is complicated (but according to Christian belief enriched) by the teaching that God shows himself to be a TRINITY in unity of Father, Son (JESUS CHRIST), and HOLY SPIRIT.

Gods [XXVIII] Beings figuring in MYTHS or as objects of religious RITUAL, worship, or belief, which in significant ways resemble humans but are greater than they (e.g. in power, intelligence, or worth) [8: 132; 20]. It is misleading to confuse the singular (a god, a superhuman being) with the word 'God' used philosophically (for the supreme being in THEISM) or religiously (for the object of faith in MONOTHEISM). The gods named in myths and approached in rites (e.g. by tribal peoples) are a species of the class of SPIRITS. The gods of ancient national religions (ANCIENT EGYPTIAN RELIGION; BABYLONIANS; GREEK RELIGION; ROMAN RELIGION; SUMERIANS), although superhuman (notably as regards immortality), were not thought of as perfect, eternal, or infinite in the senses in which such terms are applied by philosophers or theologians to 'God'. In some religions with many gods (e.g. in India), their names may be interpreted as aspects of a single ultimate reality; or only one may be the object of active devotion (HENOTHEISM). The relation between such beliefs and prophetic monotheism or the various kinds of PANTHEISM is not simple or of only one kind. [8: V; 12: VIII; 32]

Goeteia, Mageia [XII] Witchcraft. The Greeks disapproved of witchcraft, whose goddess was Hecate, but made use of it (the earliest evidence dates from the 5th century BCE). *Mageia* boomed in Hellenistic times, enriched as it was by new, oriental material. Clients – of all classes – sought to win somebody's love, or to harm their enemies, etc. The means used included spells (*epodai*) and curses (*katadeseis*, *katadesmoi*), which were inscribed on tablets and buried, preferably in graves. In addition, wax figurines were melted or stuck with pins, or bound lead figurines were placed in graves. [10: 270–74; 17: 309–23]

Golden Dawn, Hermetic Order of the [XVIII] The most influential Western magical organization of modern times. Founded in 1888, it established 'temples' at London, Paris, Edinburgh, and elsewhere whose members pursued an extensive programme of esoteric studies, including ASTROLOGY, KABBALAH, TAROT, meditation, and ritual MAGIC. Its dominant figure was S. L. 'MacGregor' Mathers (1854–1918), an occultist of forceful personality and vivid imagination. The order had a 'grade' structure derived from the 'degrees' of FREEMASONRY, a member's progress through the grades being marked by a series of colourful initiation rituals drawing on Christian, Egyptian, and ROSICRUCIAN symbolism. Membership figures are unknown, but between 1888 and 1896 over 300 people joined. In 1900 Mathers's autocratic rule aroused resistance and thereafter the order disintegrated into factions. Central organization lapsed during the 1920s but several temples continued independently as late as the 1950s. Numerous organizations deriving from these or the original order still exist and the Golden Dawn's integration of magical lore from diverse sources contributed significantly to the modern revival of interest in the OCCULT. [13]

Gosala [XIII.B] The founder of the AJIVAKA religion (*fl. c.* 500 BCE), often referred to as Makkhali ('staff-bearer'). Gosala probably predeceased both his close associate MAHAVIRA (the founder of Jainism – JAINS) and the BUDDHA. Believed to have attained both omniscience and liberation, Gosala taught that everything is predetermined by fate (*niyati*) and that final liberation (MOKSHA) is inevitable for all at the end of a long period of transmigration. [1: 27–79]

Gospel [XI.A] An Old English word meaning 'good tidings', corresponding to Greek *euangelion*. In Christianity it is used first of the message of JESUS CHRIST, then of the message about Jesus, and finally of the written record of Jesus' ministry.

When Jesus bade his hearers 'repent and believe in the good news', he did so against the background of passages in the Book of Isaiah which announce the good news of the Jews' impending restoration after the Babylonian exile (BIBLICAL HISTORY). One such passage is Isaiah 61: 1, where an anonymous speaker claims that Yahweh has 'anointed' him with his Spirit to proclaim 'good tidings to the poor'. Jesus regarded his ministry as fulfilling this scripture. The 'good news' which he proclaimed to the poor was that, with the near irruption of the kingdom of God, their liberation was at hand.

The good news about Jesus declared that in him, and especially in his death and resurrection, God had acted decisively for the redemption of mankind (SALVATION). Various preachers had differing emphases, but this was basic: this, they agreed, was the one true gospel.

The true gospel might be spoken or it might be written. When four 1st-century records of Jesus were first collected in the New Testament CANON, they were referred to comprehensively as 'the gospel' (according to Matthew, Mark, and the other evangelists). Later came the practice of designating each of the four records as 'a' gospel or referring to them together as 'the gospels' (plural).

On the model of these canonical gospels a considerable number of other 'gospels' (sometimes called 'apocryphal gospels') appeared from about 150 CE onwards. While the canonical gospels are anonymous, those which appeared from the mid 2nd century onwards

claimed to be written by apostles and other associates of Jesus, or indeed to be transcripts of his teaching given privately to one or more of these. [3: 161–9; 4: 325–38; 6: 1, 232–84]

Gotama [IX.A] (Sanskrit *Gautama*) The clan name of the BUDDHA of the present age. He is known also as the sage (*muni*) of the Shakya people, hence as Shakyamuni. His personal name was Siddhattha (Sanskrit *Siddhartha*). In the Buddhist texts he is most usually referred to as Bhagavat (Master).

The PALI texts, which in the THERAVADA tradition are held to be early and historically reliable, provide no continuous account of Gotama's life. The longest consecutive period which is narrated is that of the last days, covering his journey on foot, with his disciples, from the capital city of Rajagaha across the Ganges (GANGA) towards the Nepal border to the obscure village of KUSINARA. Here the PARINIBBANA (final NIBBANA-ization) took place, after which his followers cremated the remains and, dividing the ashes, built a number of STUPAS, or reliquary mounds, placing some of the ashes in each. The period of public teaching and controversy which preceded the last days, approximately 40 years from the Enlightenment at BODHGAYA, is represented by the bulk of the contents of the SUTTA-PITAKA, but in no historical or systematic order. His birth, with its attendant wonderful events in heaven and earth, is described in the *Acchariyabhuta-dhamma Sutta* (*Majjhima Nikaya*). The first half of his life, before the Enlightenment and when he was still a BODHISATTVA, has still to be reconstructed from a variety of sources, so far as the Pali tradition is concerned. The Sanskrit literature contains some longer, continuous accounts, such as the MAHAVASTU or 'Great Event' (*c.* 2nd century BCE) and the 'Acts of the Buddha' (*Buddhacarita*) by the poet Ashvaghosha (2nd century CE). There are more data for the reconstruction of the history of Buddhist doctrine than there are for the life of Gotama [37: 14]. It has to be remembered that in the Buddhist view it is the DHAMMA, or doctrine, which is pre-eminent. Many Buddhas have proclaimed it, in every era of the unaccountable ages that are past, and many will in the unaccountable ages to come. The historical events of each Buddha's life are important only in relation to *dhamma*, which is, in the Buddhist view, eternal. [17: 105–29; 18; 35A; 37: 43–80]

Greek Religion [XII] 'Historical' Greek religion began in the 8th century BCE. The preceding Dark Age, starting when Mycenaean civilization collapsed (*c.* 1100), reshaped earlier religion and encouraged local divergences. In the 8th century Panhellenic sanctuaries (TEMENOS) and the epics of Homer and Hesiod became vehicles for crystallizing and systematizing belief, and radiated a Panhellenic religious dimension transcending local differences. This influenced, without suppressing, local variants (THEOI). Greece had no canonical body of belief or myth: there were no structures to support it – no clergy or scriptural texts, except for sects (ORPHEUS) and MYSTERIA. Few cults had professional priests. Most priests/priestesses were ordinary citizens elected for a year or for life, sometimes from within a *genos* (INSTITUTIONS) with hereditary rights in the cult. Myth (MYTHOS) was constantly reshaped by the poets. Piety was primarily expressed in cults (HEORTAI; INSTITUTIONS; RITES), some of which cut across civic groupings (*mysteria*, certain women's cults, especially Dionysiac cults). Healing and oracular cults involved private devotion. Alexander's Eastern conquests created new circumstances, mirrored in Hellenistic (323–31 BCE) religion. The popularity of the cult of Tyche (Fortune) reflected belief in life's unpredictability. Mostly, trends begun earlier were intensified. Civil cults continued, often accommodating new

needs, as the Tyche-cult did. A festival sometimes imported notions from STAR-WORSHIP. Gods acquired epithets denoting benevolence and/or protection. Remote and rural areas preserved traditional piety. A ruler-cult was important (POLITIKE). Because meaningful devotion was personal, voluntary cult associations flourished, some involving *mysteria*, which thrived in Late Hellenistic times, when traditional cults also enjoyed a revival. Oriental *theoi* were adapted to Greek needs (a superficial syncretism related them to Greek deities). Eschatological salvation was a central preoccupation of the Late Hellenistic period. These trends came to fruition under the Roman empire. [2; 4; 9; 15; 17: 16–17, 51–67, 129–32, 327]

Green Corn Festival [III] Known among the North American Seneca Indians as the *notekhwe'es* (literally, 'they gather food'), Green Corn is a major agricultural festival, especially among north-eastern Amerindian groups [23: XII]. Typically occurring in August, when the first corn is ripe, the ceremony is held in the Longhouse (council-house) and lasts three days or longer. Recurring elements of the ritual include a thanksgiving prayer, a tobacco invocation (CALUMET), recognition of the first appearance of the corn, dancing, and a repetition of the thanksgiving prayer. The ceremony ends with a feast.

Guardian Spirits (Amerindian) [III] Belief in guardian spirits is widespread throughout North American Indian peoples, save those in the south-west. Typically, the term refers to a complex of beliefs and rituals regarding the acquisition of personal guardian spirits through dreams or visions. Such spirits are usually sought through VISION QUEST, and although they appear in a variety of animal forms, are seldom to be identified with a particular species [8: v]. They usually bestow special power upon their devotee, often providing a tangible sign in the form of a MEDICINE BUNDLE.

Guna [XIII.B] As a term in Indian thought *guna* basically means a constituent strand or part, but it acquires the senses of 'quality' in VAISHESHIKA and 'modification' in grammar. VEDANTA distinguishes between *saguna* and *nirguna* BRAHMAN, i.e. the divine with and without attributes, but the most important use is in the originally SAMKHYA idea of the three *gunas* or modalities which constitute the primal ground or nature (PRAKRTI) from which the experienced universe evolves: *sattva* (goodness), *rajas* (passion), and *tamas* (darkness). Psychologically *sattva* makes lucid and gives joy, *rajas* arouses activity and gives misery, while *tamas* restrains and gives dullness. *Sattva* makes the body light and the faculties clear, *rajas* makes the body mobile and stimulates the faculties, while *tamas* makes the body heavy and clouds the faculties. Cosmologically *sattva* predominates in the realm of the gods (*deva*), *rajas* among men and *tamas* among animals and plants. One leads on to another and they act together in a multitude of ways in order to bring about through their transformations the complexity of the ordinary world. In the intervals between world cycles (*kalpas*) the three *gunas* are in equilibrium and nature is undifferentiated. [17: 77–80]

Gurdjieff, Georgei Ivanovitch (1874–1949) [XVIII] A highly unconventional religious teacher whose system, expressed in his own idiosyncratic terminology, was apparently synthesized from diverse sources including BUDDHISM and KABBALAH. Born at Alexandropol, in Armenia, Gurdjieff spent several years in Central Asia and Tibet before teaching in Russia and, after 1922, at his Institute for the Harmonious Development of Man at Fontainebleau, France. Ordinary man, Gurdjieff taught, is 'asleep' – he acts mechanically according to ingrained habit-patterns, and the three 'brains' which govern his activity and consciousness ('Thinking, Feeling and Moving Centres') are unco-ordinated. He has neither a soul nor a true will. He must remedy these defects by 'conscious labours and intentional sufferings' – the strenuous practice of exercises designed to develop self-awareness and release untapped reserves of mental and physical energy. [27] Versions of Gurdjieff's system are taught by several organizations in Europe and America established by his followers or those of his associate, P. D. Ouspensky (1878–1947).

Gurdwara (Dharamsala) [XXVII] In the Sikh JANAM-SAKHIS there are frequent references to rooms or buildings called *dharamsalas*. The *dharamsala* was the cult centre of the early PANTH. Each local community (*sangat*) gathered there as a conventicle (*satsang*) for pious discourse (*katha*) and singing of the Gurus' hymns (*kirtan*) [24: 107–8]. Early sources occasionally refer to the *dharamsala* as a *gurdwara* ('Guru's door'), and eventually this name became general. The shift was evidently associated with a developing belief that the GURU was mystically present wherever Sikhs gathered in *satsang*, a belief greatly strengthened by the custom of placing a copy of the ADI GRANTH in a *dharamsala* whenever practicable. [22: 82; 24: 261–2] Today the strict definition of a *gurdwara* is any place where the scripture is installed (RITUALS (SIKH)). The *gurdwara* is, however, much more than a place of worship. Although its prime focus is the sacred volume and its principal function *kirtan* [17: 3–8], it is also a community centre in the wider sense. Every *gurdwara* should include a hospice and a refectory (*langar*) at which meals are served free to all comers. The presence of a *gurdwara* is marked by a triangular flag (*nishan*) coloured saffron or dark blue. The functionary in charge is called a *granthi* (reader). [4: IV; 15: V; 26: 101–6, 112–17]

Gurdwaras (Historic Locations) [XXVII] The number of SIKH holy places is very large. Most are concentrated in the Punjab, but several are scattered over other parts of India/Pakistan and beyond. Almost all are associated with incidents from the lives of the GURUS, beginning with Nanak's birth (Nankana Sahib, Pakistan) and ending with Gobind Singh's death at Nanded in the Deccan. With few exceptions all are marked by *gurdwaras* or clusters of *gurdwaras*, the more important of them bearing the honorific 'Sahib'. The most famous centre is Amritsar, founded by the fourth Guru and developed by his successor. Pre-eminent among all *gurdwaras* is its Golden Temple (Harimandir Sahib). [15: 159–73] Many shrines mark places which the JANAM-SAKHIS record as places visited by Nanak on his travels. These include Panja Sahib near Rawalpindi [24: 92–3]. Among the prominent shrines of the Delhi area are Sis Ganj and Rakab Ganj, commemorating the execution and cremation of Guru Tegh Bahadur. Second only to the Golden Temple in importance is Kesgarh Sahib, Anandpur, which marks the founding of the KHALSA. Other important *gurdwaras* associated with the tenth Guru are Harimandir Sahib in Patna and Hazur Sahib in Nanded. [15: XIII–XVII] Since 1925 the principal Punjab *gurdwaras* have been controlled by the statutory Shiromani Gurdwara Parbandhak Committee.

Gurmat [XXVII] 'The teachings of the GURU', the correct and preferred term for what in English is called Sikhism. The two sources of Gurmat are scripture and tradition. The first of these includes the DASAM GRANTH but in practice the substance of scripture-based doctrine derives from the ADI GRANTH. This component comprises the teachings of Nanak, confirmed and reinforced by the other GURUS whose works have been included in the *Adi Granth*. In their many hymns the Gurus repeatedly stress the need to recognize the divine in the created world (AKAL PURAKH) and to appropriate God's proffered grace by meditating on his immanent presence (NAM

SIMARAN). [3: XX; 25: V] It is safe to assume that all who call themselves SIKHS accept Nanak's insistence on *nam simaran* and virtuous living. The same cannot be said, however, for the component which derives from tradition. Later tradition stresses the need to accept initiation into the KHALSA and to act according to its code (RAHIT). This requires observance of external symbols (most visibly the uncut hair) and a distinctive rule of living. The Khalsa order was established by the tenth Guru and those who accept its discipline normally insist that it is an essential part of Gurmat [17: 8–9].

Gurpurab [XXVII] Anniversaries of events associated with the SIKH GURUS are known as *gurpurabs*. Three of particular importance are the birthdays of Guru Nanak (November) and Guru Gobind Singh (December), and the martyrdom of Guru Arjan (May/June). Three other major festivals celebrated by Sikhs have Hindu antecedents but distinctly Sikh associations. These are Baisakhi (April), Divali (October/November), and Hola Mahalla (held during February/March on the day following the Hindu Holi festival). [4: 129–35]

Guru [XIII.A] In Hindu tradition, a teacher. The term, which originally indicated especially a BRAHMAN who instructed young *brahmans* in the sacred lore, has come to mean a religious teacher of any kind who has undertaken to give personal instruction to a pupil or disciple (*chela*). The guru–*chela* relationship is a very close one, and requires the utmost reverence and obedience towards the guru from the *chela*. [1: 164–5]

Guru (**Sikh Doctrine**) [XXVII] The word *guru* means 'preceptor' and in Hindu society that has normally meant a human teacher. Within the SANT TRADITION OF NORTHERN INDIA, however, Guru came to be identified with the inner voice of God. This view was inherited and transmitted by

Nanak, for whom the guru or satguru represented the divine presence, mystically apprehended and inwardly guiding the truly devout along the path of *mukti* (SACH-KHAND). Because Nanak communicated this essential truth with unique clarity he, as human vehicle of the divine guru, eventually received the title of Guru [24: 251–3; 25: 196–9]. This role was transmitted to each of his nine successors (GURUS) in turn, the divine spirit successively inhabiting 10 enlightened individuals. The death of the 10th Guru ended the personal transmission, but the immortal guru remained. According to Sikh doctrine the guru dwells eternally present in the sacred scripture (which thus became the *Guru Granth – see* ADI GRANTH) and in the corporate community (the Guru PANTH). [3: 297–301]

Gurus (Sikh Masters) [XXVII] The Sikh community (the PANTH) with its distinctive doctrines (GURMAT) derives from a succession of 10 Gurus who taught in the Punjab during the 16th and 17th centuries. Nanak (1469–1539 CE), first of the 10, was born a Hindu in an area ruled by Muslims. His teachings, delivered in hymns of superb quality, bear the characteristic Sant impress with little evidence of Muslim influence (SANT TRADITION OF NORTHERN INDIA) [25: V]. An extensive hagiography (the JANAM-SAKHIS) describes his childhood and missionary travels [25: IV]. Eventually he returned to the Pun-

jab and there attracted disciples, one of whom succeeded him as Guru Angad (1504–52). The third Guru, Amar Das (1479–1574), consolidated the Panth, particularly in terms of pastoral supervision. [23: 7–9, 41–2] His son-in-law, Guru Ram Das (1534–81), founded the town of Amritsar (GURDWARAS) and at his death confirmed the succession in his own family by choosing his youngest son Arjan (1563–1606) as fifth Guru. Arjan's term was important, partly because he compiled the principal scripture (the ADI GRANTH) and partly because the Mogul authorities began to take an unfriendly interest in the Panth. Guru Arjan died in Mogul (ISLAMIC DYNASTIES) custody and the skirmishes which followed in the time of Guru Hargobind (1595–1644) strengthened those elements within the Panth which favoured a more militant policy. [18: 56–7] Guru Hari Rai (1630–61) enjoyed a peace which continued precariously through the brief term of the child Guru Hari Krishan (1656–64). Mogul hostility revived, however, and eventually led to the execution of the ninth Guru, Tegh Bahadur (1621–75). Open warfare followed during the period of his son Guru Gobind Singh (1666–1708). Meanwhile, Gobind Singh had formally instituted the KHALSA order (1699), conferring on the Panth its visible and distinctive identity. [9: VI] With his death in 1708 the line of personal Gurus came to an end. [4: 11]

· H ·

Hachiman [XVI] A KAMI of fishermen and cultivators, the cult starting at Usa in Kyushu, Hachiman is popularly known today as the god of war [17: 426–40; 32: 41–5; 33: 23–4]. This deity, probably at first pronounced *Yawata* (Eight Banners), became associated with military men after being patronized by the Minamoto family in the 12th century, and was then identified with Emperor Ojin of the 4th century CE. From the 8th century, in the early blend of SHINTO and Buddhism, Hachiman was titled *Daibosatsu Hachiman* by the court, the Great Bodhisattva Hachiman (JAPANESE BUDDHAS AND BODHISATTVAS), or *Hachiman Daimyojin*, Great Deity Hachiman. About one-third of all SHINTO SHRINES are dedicated to Hachiman.

Hadith [XIV], 'story', is the body of traditions in ISLAM, i.e. the sayings of the Prophet MUHAMMAD, his Companions and other prominent early Muslims, the whole constituting the SUNNA and being regarded as a source of law only second to that of the QUR'AN; the *hadith* literature thus provided guidance on aspects of law and life where Qur'anic warrant was lacking [47: 170–77; 61: III]. The form of the individual *hadith* is one of subject-matter (*matn*) preceded by a chain (*isnad*) of oral repeaters and guarantors of the tradition. The traditions were later written down in collections, for, since fabrication of *hadiths* to justify particular sectarian or political doctrines became a flourishing industry, such scholars as Muhammad al-Bukhari (810–70) and Muslim (*c.* 817–75) had to sift through and critically evaluate an immense corpus, said to number

600,000, reducing them to collections of about 4,000 *hadiths* each. These are known as 'the two *Sahihs*', i.e. sound collections, and are accorded complete credence. To these, four others, of slightly less reliability, were added, the whole achieving canonical status. [3; 21 s.v.; 29: 65–6; 32: II; 35; 43: 79–250]

Hajj [XIV] The Islamic Pilgrimage, accounted one of the PILLARS OF ISLAM. The modern ceremony in the month of Dhu 'l-Hijja is a conflation of two earlier ceremonies held in western Arabia, the *hajj* and the *'umra*, and is centred on Mecca and its shrine the Ka'ba, considered to be Abrahamic in origin (*see* HARAMAIN), with certain ritual acts done outside the city. Every adult Muslim should perform the Pilgrimage at least once in his lifetime. The pilgrim wears a special, ritually clean garb (*ihram*), and observes certain TABUS during the days of the Hajj ceremonies. It has long been an occasion for Islamic solidarity and strengthening of brotherhood within the faith, and modern transport methods have meant that increased numbers of believers can fulfil this obligation ('ID). [10 'Pilgrimage (Islam)'; 21 'Ḥadjdj'; 28; 29: 81–102; 39 s.v.; 47: 161–2]

Halakhah [XVII] The legal side of JUDAISM, the texts dealing with Jewish law and ritual being known as *halakhic* literature. The term *halakhah* is of unknown origin, and usually taken to mean 'the way of going' from a root meaning 'to go'. It has been explained as that which comes from the past and goes on, i.e. a traditional rule, or as that in which Israel goes, i.e. a religious norm. In more recent times it has been argued that the term originated with the name for a fixed land tax, which then came to mean a fixed religious rule [29: 83]. The term *halakhah* is used in the TALMUD and MIDRASH, where certain rules are described as 'halakhah going back to MOSES at Sinai' or as 'a *halakhah* which is not publicized as a practical decision'. In the many cases of legal dispute it is often said that 'the *halakhah* is like RABBI X', 'the *halakhah* is like the later authority', or that 'this is a *halakhah* for the times of the MESSIAH', i.e. it has no practical application before then. *Halakhah* is contrasted with non-legal material, Aggadah [9 vol. 7: 1156; 50: 248, 253; 52: VII]. There is some discussion of the relative weight to be given to a *minhag*, or customary practice, where this prescribes a different norm of behaviour from the *halakhah*. The traditional Jew is bound by codified halakhic decisions, while the GENTILE is thought to be commanded by God only to keep the seven Noachian laws. REFORM and CONSERVATIVE JUDAISM have introduced modifications into halakhic rulings which are generally not accepted by Orthodox Jews.

Hammurabi's Code [VI] The gods, as guardians of Mesopotamian cities (BABYLONIANS; SUMERIANS), gave laws to mankind; their role is made clear in Hammurabi's Code, where the king enacts their instructions [7]. Hammurabi, king of the first dynasty of Babylon (1792–1750 BCE), is attributed with the compilation of the famous Code of Laws [23: 99–101], the most important single written document from Mesopotamia. Preserved on a black stone stele, the code states that the gods of Sumer had exalted MARDUK, and instructed Hammurabi to create justice in the land. He is shown before Shamash, the sun-god, who was also god of justice. Among laws governing society, the code also recognizes the social obligations of the TEMPLE [23: 18].

Handsome Lake Religion [XX] Also known as the Longhouse religion or Gai'wiio ('Good Message'), founded by an alcoholic Seneca chief, Ganioda'yo ('handsome lake') (1735–1815), whose heavenly revelations in 1799 transformed himself and the demoralized Seneca. Quaker beliefs were combined with traditional rituals and a puritan and modernizing ethic. The movement spread among the Iroquois tribes. Authorized preachers of the Code of Handsome Lake still serve some 5,000 adherents in Upper New York, Ontario, and Quebec, and maintain Indian identity. [12: 101–7; 18: VIII–X; 19: 387–97]

Hanif [XIV] (adj. Hanafi) In early Islam a term for one who follows the original, pure monotheistic religion, that of ABRAHAM and the first men. It is regarded in the QUR'AN as the religion to which mankind has an innate, natural propensity, and is contrasted with polytheism and idolatry and the corrupted monotheism of the Jews and Christians. Subsequently, it was often used as a synonym for 'Muslim', and Islam often called the 'Hanafi religion'.

Hanuman, Hanumat [XIII.A] A popular Hindu deity, the monkey-god. Famous for his part in the RAMAYANA epic as the brave and loyal helper of RAMA, he is worshipped in Hindu shrines in a half-human, half-monkey form. The inviolability of monkeys among Hindu people is associated with the cult of Hanuman. His name means 'having large jaws', and as the son of the wind he is reckoned able to wield rocks, remove mountains, fly in the air, and seize the clouds. [1: 317]

Harae [XVI] Purification by exorcism – *harae*, *oharae*, or *harai* – is the oldest of the current SHINTO practices. It is first mentioned in the 8th-century books (SHINTO LITERATURE): when Izanagi was attacked by evil spirits while trying to extricate his wife from the land of the dead, Yomi-no-kuni, he retired to wash himself in a river (SHINTO MYTHOLOGY). Purification was officially practised twice a year in early times, when the antisocial evils represented by Susano-o were washed away. *Harae* ceremonies (MATSURI) are now performed to exorcize those evils which are thought to disrupt normal social behaviour, and to nullify the stigmas accompanying disasters, diseases, childbirth, death, sorcery, bad dreams, and omens [general: 17: 79–91; 30: 51–2]. Running water or a neutralizing detergent is the preferred agent. The supplicant may also obtain purification by walking through a miscanthus ring; sprinkling salt at home or elsewhere; disposing of a small human effigy; or by participating in or witnessing dramatic performances in which symbolic malign spirits are destroyed. Cleansing (*misogi*), at the entrance to a shrine or temple, is done by washing the hands and rinsing the mouth with water at a basin. In the shrine, the priest waves a *gohei*, a short stick bearing strips of white paper. Abstention (*imi*), once followed by the community as a whole, then by a designated family, is now practised only by the priests, and, like *harae*, is intended to enable the supplicant, thus purified, to appear clean before the KAMI.

Haramain [XIV] The two sacred cities of ISLAM in western Arabia, Mecca and Medina, in which the Prophet MUHAMMAD received the divine revelations and successfully launched the new faith. Mecca had long been a trading town with an important shrine, the Ka'ba, which Muhammad now cleared of idols and made the pilgrimage centre of the purified Islam (*see* HAJJ). It had always had a sacred enclosure (*haram*) around it, which could only be entered at times of pilgrimage, in a state of ritual purity. Mecca therefore continues to be the most sacred site of all for Muslims. Medina was the town where Muhammad established his base after the migration of 622 CE. For over 30 years it was the capital of the new Arab caliphate (CALIPH), and always a centre of scholarship and piety, in particular for the study of law and HADITH. The location

there of the Prophet's MOSQUE and his tomb makes it a goal of veneration, often visited by pilgrims who have made the Hajj to Mecca, though the Medina shrine may be visited at any time. Both remain closed to this day to non-believers. [22]

Hare Krishna Movement [XXI] The International Society for Krishna Consciousness (ISKCON), founded on his arrival in America in 1965 by His Divine Grace A. C. Bhaktivedanta Swami Prabhupada (d. 1977), was to become one of the most visible of the NEW RELIGIOUS MOVEMENTS that came from the East. Bands of devotees became a familiar sight on the streets as they sang and danced their way through many of the larger cities, selling records, books, or the magazine *Back to Godhead* in their saffron robes, the young men with their heads shaved, apart from a topknot (with which, they believe, KRISHNA will pluck them up when he rescues them at the time of the deliverance of the world). ISKCON received additional publicity (and financial support) through the interest of the 'Beatle', George Harrison.

It is through the frequent chanting of their main MANTRA (Hare Krishna, Hare Krishna, Krishna Krishna, Hare Hare, Hare Rama, Hare Rama, Rama Rama, Hare Hare) that the devotees have become popularly known as Hare Krishnas (*see also* RAMA). The theological basis of the movement is the BHAGAVADGITA (as translated by their Master).

Many of the members in the early days came from the hippy counterculture. Serious devotees, however, on moving into a Temple, have to give up drugs and alcohol, can only eat specially purified vegetarian food, and must lead celibate lives (apart from the procreation of children within marriage). [2: 51; 3; 11: I; 14: II; 19; 25: II; 35; 51: IV]

Hari [XIII.A] An alternative name for KRISHNA, perhaps meaning 'saviour', from *hr* (to take away evil). He is said to favour worship which is offered with purity [3: 355]. His name is sometimes combined with Hara, one of the names of SHIVA; thus 'Hari-Hara' is a way of referring to both VISHNU and Shiva together. The *Hari-vamsa*, or 'chronicle concerning Hari', is a kind of Krishna-PURANA, the life story of a divine-human hero (cf. RAMAYANA).

Harijan [XIII.A] Literally, 'the children of HARI', that is, of God, the title was applied, with the best of intentions, by Mahatma Gandhi to the lowest class in Hindu society, commonly known as 'Untouchables' [25: 229]. The name has, however, another connotation: children of temple-prostitutes, whose paternity, being unknown, is ascribed to the deity of the temple, referred to by the general name *Hari*. Many of this class therefore prefer the name 'Untouchables', as it calls attention to the social stigma under which they suffer as poor, low-class people. In traditional Hindu orthodoxy they are regarded as a source of pollution, and even the contact of their shadow falling upon a person of Dvija, or 'twice-born', CASTE is thought to defile. Such distinctions are forbidden under the Constitution of India, although the ban is often ignored in practice. An ancient name for this class is Candala ('the worst' or 'wild' people).

Harris Movement [XX] The largest mass movement towards Christianity in West Africa. It stemmed from William Wade Harris (c. 1850–1929), a mission catechist in Liberia who led some 120,000 people in the Ivory Coast and western Ghana to abandon traditional religion and adopt an elementary Christianity between 1913 and 1915, when he was deported back to Liberia. British Methodist missionaries, who discovered the movement in 1924, attracted many adherents in building up the large Methodist Church, but some 100,000 followers continue to practise in Harris churches (METHODISM). [2: 20, 53; 8; 12: 55–6; 19: 174–5]

Hatha Yoga [XIII.B] The branch of YOGA which specializes in methods of physical training. Its earliest surviving manuals (e.g. the *Hatha-yoga-pradipika* of Svatmarama) are not earlier than the medieval period, but many Hatha Yoga techniques are of much older origin. Hatha Yoga claims to be a beneficial preliminary to the more difficult mental training of the YOGA-DARSHANA. A basic moral and religious discipline was originally required for Hatha Yoga, but in some more modern forms the undertaking of bodily purification exercises is considered a sufficient prerequisite. Suppleness, flexibility, and physical control are emphasized more than muscular development or speed of movement. The main methods are postures (*asana*), some very difficult, systematic tensioning and relaxation of particular areas (*bandha*), breath control (*pranayama*) of various kinds, and the use of imagination and attention in order to control various bodily phenomena. More advanced is a colourful visualized physiology derived from TANTRA (1), involving the arousing of fundamental vital or sexual energy (*kundalini*) and the activation of various channels (*nadi*) and centres (*cakra*). Eventually this should lead to *samadhi* and DHYANA YOGA practice. [4: 17–75; 7: 175–93; 18: 148–50]

Haus Tambaran [XXII] A spirit-house of the Tambaran ancestor cult (Sepik area, northern New Guinea), but used generally to refer to ceremonial MALE CULT houses throughout Melanesia (MELANESIAN RELIGION). In these, young men are secluded during initiation, taught the secrets of ritual and folklore, and admitted gradually to full status as adults. [2] In the past, a traditional *haus tambaran* (or *eravo* in the Papuan Gulf region) could tower to over 15 metres in height. [29]

Hawaiki [XXII] The legendary homeland of Pacific island peoples. Modern Hawaii, though named after it, is not the Hawaiki of old. A more likely dispersal point for early migrations is Savai'i (i.e. Hawaiki) in Samoa. But in most island genealogies Hawaiki simply represents the distant birthplace of gods (ATUA), chiefs, and men, from which great ancestors set sail. Spirits of the dead, seeking a resting-place, return there along the path of the setting sun. [3; 7; 15]

Head Cult (Celtic) [V] The taking of enemy heads in battle, to be preserved and set up in houses or fortresses, is frequently mentioned in early Irish literature. The Roman writers Diodorus Siculus and Strabo, deriving information from the Greek Posidonius (2nd century BCE [28]), describe similar practices among the continental Celts, and this is confirmed by art and archaeology [22: III, 71–4; 23: II]. In sanctuaries of the 2nd century BCE, such as Entremont and Roqueperteuse in southern Gaul, there were carvings of heads, and human skulls were displayed [17: II, 40]. Many stone heads from the Celtic period, some with horns, some with three faces, have been found in the British Isles [23: 11]. Heads were apparently associated with sacred springs, and were revered by the Celts as a source of supernatural power, providing inspiration, fertility, and healing. The head clearly played an important part in many rites of CELTIC RELIGION over a wide area and a considerable period of time.

Healing (in New Tribal Movements) [XX] Because interaction with Western societies usually results in more sickness for tribal peoples, already lacking adequate medical care, and because religion and healing have always been closely associated, many new tribal movements offer spiritual healing based on faith, prayer, vows, exorcism, or laying on of hands. The methods include physical treatments (holy water or oil, fasting, herbs, purgatives, or emetics) and psychological components (confession, reconciliation, community support). Some folk-healers, with varying degrees of religious syncretism, cater for the physically and mentally sick, as in the 'balmyards' of lower-class Jamaica, the AFRO-BRAZILIAN CULTS, the 'healing homes' of Nigeria, and through the rural folk-healers of the Philippines (PHILIPPINES RELIGION). Many healers such as Babalola in the ALADURA, Kimbangu in the KIMBAN-GUIST CHURCH, and Ratana in a MAORI MOVEMENT have contributed to numerically large groups, and most of the movements contribute a valuable medical service for certain kinds of sickness. [4 vol. I: 230–33, vol. 2: III; 9: 25–6, 31–6; 14: 175–7; 16: 220–37; 19]

Hel [V] In Scandinavian tradition the name for both the realm of the dead and the sinister giantess ruling it, said to be LOKI's daughter. Hel is a vague image for death rather than a clearly defined concept, existing alongside the tradition of the dead dwelling in mounds and the warrior paradise VALHALLA [6: I, 32, VI, 149–62]. The emphasis is on the long road leading there, with dangerous rivers to cross and a great gate which the living cannot pass.

Hellenistic Judaism [XI.A] The culture and religion of Jews in the Greek-speaking world after Alexander the Great (d. 323 BCE). Jews occupied one of the five wards of ALEXANDRIA; many settled in Cyrenaica. There was a large Jewish colony in ANTIOCH; others settled in Phrygia, Greece, and Italy.

Hellenistic Judaism tended to be more universalistic in outlook than Palestinian Judaism, especially in Alexandria, the home of the greatest Hellenistic Jewish thinker and writer, the philosopher Philo (20 BCE to 50 CE). [16: XXII, XXIII]

Hells (Buddhist) [IX.A] In Buddhist literature, one of the six levels of existence (*see* ASURA). Some hells are hot, some cold; in either case they are not eternal destinies (rebirth goes on), and are more like the Catholic purgatory [4: 51].

Henotheism [XXVIII] Concentration of attention upon a single GOD where many gods figure in belief or MYTH. 'Kathenotheism', roughly equivalent, is, more precisely, concern with one god at a time; the god worshipped is effectively the only one to the worshipper. 'Monolatry' is also used for the worship of only one god, while the existence of other gods is admitted or not questioned.

Heortai, Panegyreis [XII] Greek festivals, in honour of one or more deities. *Panegyreis* were of inter-state importance whereas *heortai* were festivals within the city-state, state festivals, phratry (kinship) festivals, etc. (INSTITUTIONS (GREEK)). Many festivals had an agrarian dimension. Cities sent embassies to each other's festivals and the *panegyreis*. Religious calendars varied between cities. Some *heortai* were peculiar to one city, others were celebrated by all (e.g. Thesmophoria), and yet others were celebrated by certain ethnic groups (e.g. Karneia celebrated by the Dorians). Each festival was a nexus of RITES spread over one or more days. These always included sacrifices, with feasts, processions, dances, and songs (mostly narrating myths). In addition they often included *agones*, competitions, musical and/or sporting. Tragedies were produced at dramatic competitions during the Athenian city festivals of Dionysos. There were many other rites (e.g. offering a robe to a deity, cleansing a temple and statue, sacred ploughings, obscene behaviour). The greatest *panegyreis*, attracting large crowds, were the Panhellenic *agones*: Olympia (Olympic Games), the earliest and greatest, were in honour of Zeus and involved a Panhellenic truce. Other games were the Pythia (founded in 582 BCE and held at Delphi); Isthmia (founded 581); and Nemea (founded 573). [2: II, 7; 5: V, 2; 15: 253–60]

Heresy (**Medieval Christian**) [XI.B] Medieval Christian dualist sects (DUALISM) included the Cathari ('the pure'), called Albigenses in southern France. They rejected the flesh and material creation as evil. The soul's salvation comes by liberation from the flesh, marriage and the eating of animal matter being forbidden for the 'perfect' minority. The rest postponed baptism into 'perfection' until near death. This movement (linked with a distinctive civilization in southern France) was suppressed by a CRUSADE and inquisition (i.e. special court for the trial of heretics) in the 13th century. The Waldensians in 12th-century France somewhat resembled later PROTESTANTISM and still exist today. The rather similar English Lollards originated with John Wyclif (*c.* 1330–84). His emphasis on predestination and a purified church influenced the Hussites (John Huss, *c.* 1369/72–1415) [26]. This movement, affected by nationalist feeling, weakened Catholic influence in Bohemia. Some ('Bohemian Brethren') later linked up with the REFORMATION, and a remnant was revived by the MORAVIAN BRETHREN. [107; 135]

Heresy, Orthodoxy, Schism (**Christian**) [XI.B] 'Orthodoxy' is Christian belief adjudged correct by a CHURCH authority. 'Heresy' is denial of an officially defined doctrine of the Church. ('Heretics' sometimes, naturally, denounce the official church as heretical.) ROMAN CATHOLICISM nowadays allows for the relative innocence of those brought up in a heretical environment. 'Schism' is deliberate separation from the Church without the involvement of doctrinal error [56]. For Roman Catholicism this means those out of communion with the PAPACY (the severity of this view was mitigated by Vatican COUNCIL II) [1: 355–66].

Hermeneutics [XI.C] The theory of understanding or interpretation, especially of biblical (BIBLE), philosophical, and literary texts. Although interpreters had long been aware of the need to determine rules for valid exegesis if alien meanings were not to be read into texts, the development of historical consciousness, from the 18th century onwards, added a new dimension to the problem. It came to be questioned whether a person of one culture could grasp the original meaning of texts produced in a different culture. The classical hermeneutic response argues that an interpreter can re-experience the mental processes of a text's author and so apprehend the meaning of his text because both author and interpreter share a common humanity. Recently this hermeneutic principle has been questioned on the grounds that it may fail to reflect adequately the fundamental differences of awareness produced by different cultures. Other studies have argued that understanding is an art: it cannot be produced simply by observing rules, because of the so-called 'hermeneutical circle' – namely the recognition that the meaning of a text as a whole and the meaning of each of its parts are reciprocally related since the apprehension of the one depends upon the apprehension of the other. [19]

Hermetica [XI.A] A body of Hellenistic mystical philosophy of the 2nd–3rd centuries CE, called after Hermes Trismegistus, 'Thrice-Greatest Hermes' (the Egyptian god Thoth). Hermes and others reveal this teaching to mortals as the way of wisdom and life. Some of the 18 treatises have the form of Socratic dialogues; others are epistolary in style. There is an element of Egyptian thought (ANCIENT EGYPTIAN RELIGION) in their background. The Greek sources are partly Platonic, partly Stoic (GREEK RELIGION); the SEPTUAGINT has also been drawn upon, especially for cosmogony. [15: 292–7, 300–307]

Hermetism [XVIII] Traditions derived from the HERMETICA, influential on European MAGIC, ALCHEMY, and MYSTICISM. Texts of the *Hermetica* reached Europe in the late 15th century, when it was supposed that their legendary author, Hermes Trismegistus, was a real person, an Egyptian sage roughly contemporary with Moses. Elements from NEOPLATONISM and GNOSTICISM in the texts were mistaken for evidence that Trismegistus had anticipated Plato and foretold the coming of JESUS CHRIST. Hermetic discourses on talismans, astral magic, and mystical gnosis thus became acceptable to some Christians. Hermetic cosmology, assuming a hierarchy of gods under the one supreme God and an elaborate structure of symbolic correspondences throughout nature, blended easily with Neoplatonist or kabbalistic (KABBALAH) views and stimulated the growth of Renaissance Christian occultism (OCCULT). Although shown in 1614 to be post-Christian, the *Hermetica* retained their authority for devotees of magic, and a fascination with ancient Egypt has characterized Western occultism ever since. [30]

Hero Twins [III] One of the most common and basic motifs of North American Indian mythology is that of the primeval hero twins. Usually conceived of as lesser divinities or as culture heroes, the twins are often the subjects of a miraculous birth (e.g. the NAVAJO and HOPI twin war-gods). In some versions of the myth, their mother is killed after their birth and their consequent exploits are to avenge her death. In still others, their father is portrayed as the sun-god, and their youth a period wherein they seek to learn his true identity. The twins may exemplify opposing characteristics (e.g. the one bringing benefits to mankind, the other introducing disease, old age, and death), perhaps representing conflicting aspects of the more general figure of CULTURE HERO [8: III, 38–43]. In many accounts, the twins complete the process of creation by ridding the world of monsters, by shaping the physical landscape, or by contributing to man's socialization.

Heroes [XII] A heterogeneous category of Greek cult-recipients. They were mortals who after death became 'semigods', able to help or harm mankind. Some heroes remained unnamed, being referred to simply as 'the hero'. Many heroes, named or not, did not figure in heroic myth. Most great mythological heroes were connected with cities as founders or kings, or were appropriated as ancestors by the great aristocratic families. They also received cult. Some had mortal parents, most had one divine and one mortal parent. A hero's power was centred on his grave. Cult was offered at alleged graves of heroes (which were often rediscovered Mycenaean tombs). Sometimes these were situated within *temene* (TEMENOS), or at shrines. Cult practice involved *enagisma* (RITES), libations, prayers, votive offerings, and sometimes lamentations. Herakles/Hercules (the greatest hero), Asklepios, and the Dioskouroi received cult both as heroes and gods. Some exceptional men were posthumously heroized. Heroization of the recent dead became routine in the Hellenistic period, a change which reflected a different social order and new hopes for immortality. [2: IV, 3, 4, 5; 12: 145–219; 15: 233–5; 16: 29–32; 17: 575–602]

Hesychasm [XI.D] A form of contemplative (CONTEMPLATION) spiritual practice developed by the monastic order of the ORTHODOX CHURCH. The essence of the practice lies in drawing the consciousness into the heart, and becoming aware of God's presence there [28: 140], and in the practice of pure prayer. Pure prayer is the spontaneous intercourse of the human spirit with God. The first theorist of pure prayer was Evagrius of Pontus (d. 399) [28: 204]. He thought of prayer as the perfect activity of the intellect, and gave no place to the body. This Platonistic approach was changed under the influence of pseudo-Macarius (5th century CE) [28: 24–9], who speaks of the heart rather than the mind as the focus of prayer, affirming that prayer involves the whole person.

The hesychast practice as developed by St John Climacus (d. 650), Nicephorus the Hesychast (d. *c.* 1285),

and Gregory Palamas (d. 1359) uses no mental images, no concepts, no rational considerations, no imaginings. It uses the recitation of the Jesus Prayer, 'Lord Jesus Christ have mercy on me a sinner', to attain the prayerful awareness of God. The hesychast usually prays sitting, head inclined, gaze lowered. Often the prayer flows with the rhythm of the breath [31; 36; 48].

Hesychasts claimed to experience the Uncreated Light of Tabor (MYSTICISM). This led to bitter controversy, resolved by the acceptance of the teaching of Gregory Palamas that this experience is indeed of God, but of his energies not his essence [28: 75ff; 29].

Heyoka [III] A category of ritual specialists or intermediaries, found primarily among North American (Plains and some Eastern Woodlands) Indian tribes, who, by virtue of a vision of the 'thunder beings' (THUNDERBIRDS), are obliged to assume clown-like, antinatural behaviour [17: VI]. Named after a minor deity, the adherents of this ancient, although still extant, form of the 'contrary' cult of the Plains characteristically engaged in such 'reverse' activities as masking, dressing warmly in summer, wearing no clothing in winter, backward speech, and other shamanic (SHAMAN) feats [22: VII]. Failure to behave in an atypical manner, it was believed, would be punished by lightning. Although much degenerated today, the cult survives in more conservative communities, providing, at the very least, an outlet for individual variation.

Hieroglyphs [IV] Egyptian hieroglyphs (consisting of phonograms and ideograms) first appear *c.* 3100 BCE, apparently already fully developed as a writing system. It was used for more than 3,000 years throughout Egypt and her empire, particularly for inscriptions on tombs, TEMPLES, and religious objects. Two cursive scripts were derived from hieroglyphs: hieratic, used by the priests in compiling religious books, and also for literary and business texts;

and demotic, evolved from hieratic from *c.* 700 BCE, and used in the Graeco-Roman period for ordinary, non-religious writing requirements. The earliest body of religious writings was the Pyramid texts (Old Kingdom, *c.* 2500 BCE) (FUNERARY PRACTICES [11]).

Hilal [XIV] Arabic 'crescent'. Now regarded as the quintessential symbol of ISLAM, it appears early in Islamic ART and architecture as a decorative motif, probably taken over from Sasanian Iran (ZOROASTRIANISM) and subsequently used on blazons, flags, etc. of the Egyptian Mamelukes and Ottoman Turks (ISLAMIC DYNASTIES). Western Christendom viewed it as the Islamic counterpart to the emblem of the cross, but only towards the end of the 18th century did the Islamic world gradually adopt it as a religious symbol. It now appears, together with a star, on the flags of many Islamic countries, and the Red Crescent is the Islamic equivalent of the Red Cross. [10 'Crescent'; 21 s.v.]

Hinayana [IX.A] A Sanskrit word, made up of two parts: *hina* (low or inferior) and *yana* (a vehicle or means of salvation). The combination of these two was applied by a Buddhist school of thought that called itself MAHAYANA, i.e. 'great or superior means of salvation' – superior, that is, to all 18 of the older Buddhist schools. The latter were regarded by the adherents of Mahayana as being too narrow in their concern for the attainment of the Buddhist goal and as pursuing a way which could not be followed by the majority of ordinary people. As a derogatory nickname the title Hinayana is not regarded as appropriate by the one remaining school of the 18 today, the THERAVADA, but is loosely used by Western writers as interchangeable with Theravada. Those who use it thus imply a Mahayana point of view. [4: 121f]

Hinduism [XIII.A] A term used by Europeans in the modern period to refer to the religious beliefs and practices of the HINDUS. The range of belief and practice thus covered is very great, from village goddess cults such as that of Manasa, the protectress against snakes (DURGA), to that of modern GURUS such as SAI BABA, and the doctrines of classical philosophers such as SHANKARA. What is common to most of the philosophical schools of thought is belief in MOKSHA, or 'release' from the round of repeated birth and death. It has been customary to regard this belief, and the theory of KARMA which is integral to it, as a characteristic of unsophisticated, low-CASTE Hindus also, but recent field-work has thrown doubt on this [22: 207]. At this end of the spectrum Hinduism consists of local village cults and beliefs which have, in some cases quite recently, been brought within the Hindu tradition and related to classical Brahmanical culture in a process which has been described as 'Sanskritization'. This is a reference to the bestowing of dignified Sanskrit names on village deities and practices, and the formal acknowledgement by the village people of the high status of the Brahman caste and the authority of the sacred texts of which the BRAHMANS are traditionally the custodians, that is the VEDA and the PURANAS.

A complementary process, which may be described as 'Dravidianization', was the gradual absorption by the invading Sanskrit-speaking Aryans (INDO-EUROPEANS) of certain cultural elements from southern India. The word 'Dravidian' refers to the people whose languages are now known as Tamil, Telugu, Kanarese, Malayalam, and Tulu. The cults of these people have probably contributed to Hindu cults now found in northern India, such as, for example, that of KRISHNA. The 'Dravidian' peoples have in modern times expressed great opposition to the social and religious pretensions of the BRAHMANS, and to the imposition of the Sanskritic language of Hindi upon South Indians. The Shaiva–Siddhanta

(SHIVA/SHAIVA) school of Tamil
Hinduism found in Sri Lanka and Tamil
Nadu holds that the life of the Brahman
is a life of pleasure and relates to the
world of the senses.

Within India 'Hinduism' thus varies
in its nature from village to village. It
varies also, often in significant details,
from one major region of India to
another. There are considerable differences in the deities worshipped, the
scriptures used, the caste structure, the
festivals, etc., between Kerala, Kashmir, Madras, Bengal, Punjab, and so
on. [4A; 6: 203–366, 602–59; 21; 25]

Hinduism is also found outside India
in countries to which Hindus have
migrated, such as Bali and some
countries in the Caribbean, East Africa,
and SOUTH-EAST ASIA.

Hinduism (Modern Movements)
[XIII.A] Central to Hindu religion is the
GURU. What Lannoy has called 'the
guru's magic circle' [13: 357] provides
the key to the understanding of the multitude of Hindu religious movements,
both medieval and modern, some of
which persist for a century or two,
while others prove short-lived. An example of the medieval kind is that of
Chaitanya and the Bengal Vaishnavas
(VISHNU, VAISHNAVA). Examples of
the modern kind [14: 364–70] are those
associated with Sri Ramakrishna (1834–
86) and Vivekananda (1863–1902) (also
of Bengal) [1: 637–59], from which has
grown the Ramakrishna Mission, which
now has religious, educational, and
social welfare centres throughout India
and beyond; the Brahma Samaj (the
God Society, which developed out of
the British India Unitarian Association,
founded in 1827) [1: 603–14; 25: 197–
206], also of Bengali origin, associated
with the Tagore family, having a
strongly Unitarian bias (UNITARI-
ANISM, and now almost defunct;
the Arya Samaj (the Aryan Society),
founded in western India in 1875,
and still active in missionary and Hindu
reformist activities in India and beyond

[1: 628–36; 25: 206–10]; and the integral
philosophy of Sri Aurobindo (1872–
1950), whose ashram at Pondicherry has
grown into a miniature city [1: 725–32].
In the south of India Narayan Guru
(1856–1928), who was born in Trivan-
drum (Kerala), became the leader of a
religious and social reform movement
(in terms of opposition to CASTE and
untouchability), a movement which is
still strongly supported by Keralan
Hindus in India and elsewhere. Possibly the most famous Hindu reformer,
the Mahatma (great-soul) Mohandas
Karamchand Gandhi (1869–1948), was
regarded as primarily a politician. He
said of himself that he wore the guise of
a politician, but was 'at heart a religious
man'. [1: 799–826; 25: 224–46] Of the
many Hindu gurus who at any one time
are well known to a wider circle than
that of their own disciples few achieve
lasting fame; since the Second World
War many such have arisen in India
or the West (e.g. MEHER BABA,
RAJNEESH). It would be rash to assume
that any of them, or the movements
associated with them, are of the same
order as those that have been mentioned
here.

Hindus [XIII.A] Inhabitants of the 'land
beyond the Indus river' were called
'Hindus' by the invading Muslims who,
in the 8th century, entered India from
the north-west. The term therefore designates primarily an inhabitant of India
[14: 142]. Some of these inhabitants
(fewer than 20 per cent in 1971) follow
religious traditions (mostly foreign to
India) which require their adherents to
differentiate themselves by the use of
such terms as Muslim, Christian, Sikh,
etc. Those who do not specifically so
designate themselves constitute the
'Hindu' population, both of India and of
those territories elsewhere to which
such Indians have migrated (HINDU-
ISM). Hindus follow a number of different cults: of DURGA, KALI, KRISHNA,
RAMA, SHIVA, VISHNU, and many
others. A distinctive feature of Hindu

cults is that many of the deities are female (*devi*). In India, Hindus constituted 83 per cent of the total population at the census of 1971.

Hittites [VI] The Hittite empire equalled the power of Egypt, Babylonia, and Assyria for some 200 years in the 2nd millennium BCE (Hittite Old Kingdom, *c.* 1740–1460 BCE, Hittite empire, *c.* 1460–1190 BCE). There is indication of an INDO-EUROPEAN strain in the language and physical appearance of some of the population, but the religion mainly incorporated elements of the original tradition. Isolated city communities were unified under the king at Hattusas (KINGSHIP), but independence in local religious matters was preserved [12; 13]. Civil and military concerns were centralized at Hattusas, but the king allowed virtual religious autonomy, although he was regarded as the great chief-priest.

Some syncretism occurred, however, and the state and kingship were placed under the protection of a group of national deities who received elaborate rituals (FESTIVALS) at Hattusas. The sun-goddess, 'queen of heaven and earth', was supreme patron of the state, and the sun-god, the 'king of gods', was lord of righteousness and justice. The weather-god of Hatti was the official consort of the sun-goddess. The nearby shrine of Arinna was an important cult-centre. The myths reveal something of the character of the state-gods (e.g. storm-gods and elemental forces), and monuments show their physical attributes (e.g. dress) [8; 24: 120–26, 346–58]. Local cults are less well documented, but a weather-god appeared in many cities, symbolized by a bull (ART AND SYMBOLISM) and the winged goddess Shauska was another prominent deity.

The Hittites [13: 88] enlisted the aid of their gods as witnesses and guardians of contracts made on earth, and this included peace treaties drawn up with foreign powers such as Egypt (*c.* 1250

BCE) [24: 201–6]. The law was enacted by men on the gods' behalf.

There were many places of worship, including open-air rock-sanctuaries and the temples at Boghazköy (*c.* 1740–1460 BCE). The Hittites established a special holy place at Yazilikaya, where all the deities were represented; this symbolized centralized political power [13: 38]. In some cities, the TEMPLE was the centre of civil administration and had a large staff, whereas elsewhere it consisted of several small shrines. The temple was the god's home, and he was represented by either a statue or a cult-object such as a *huwasi* stone. His priests were servants who attended to his daily needs. The gods, invisible and immortal, had human failings which could result in human misfortune (EVIL). Divine will could be ascertained through extispicy or augury (DIVINATION), which the Hittites inherited from BABYLONIA. Also, MAGIC played an important role in society.

Burial customs (AFTERLIFE) included cremation and inhumation for both rulers and commoners from earliest times. Myths and legends (ANCIENT NEAR EASTERN RELIGIONS) [24: 120–26] included only a few of Hittite origin; one myth – 'Slaying the Dragon' – dealt with the ritual combat between a divine hero and his opponent, and was performed at an annual festival to reinvigorate the earth and to confirm the victory of good over evil. The second dealt with the disappearance of the fertility-god and the consequent loss of the land's abundance, which was only restored when the god returned.

Holocaust [XVII] The consequences of the anti-Jewish policies of Nazi Germany and its fascist allies from 1933 to 1945, culminating in genocide. It is estimated that close to 6 million people of Jewish origin died in the Nazi extermination programme, the 'Final Solution of the Jewish Problem', the most notorious part of which involved the mass gassing and cremation of victims in death camps like Auschwitz and Treblinka [37]. Most of the Jews killed by the Nazis came from central and eastern Europe (EUROPEAN JEWRY). Polish Jewry, which before the war numbered more than 3 million, was almost completely destroyed. The basis of the policy behind the Holocaust was the racial theory of the Germans as a master race and the Jews as a sub-human group who corrupt pure Aryan peoples and have to be eliminated. These theories were put forward by 19th-century European racists, e.g. J. A. Gobineau and H. S. Chamberlain, but it was Hitler and his Nazi propagandists who turned racist theory into an active social programme. Jews were discriminated against economically, made to wear a distinctive badge, the yellow star, were herded together into ghettoes, used as slave labour, were experimented on by Nazi doctors, and were killed by mass shootings or gassings [14; 27: XXVII, XXVIII; 41: XXXI; 43: XX, XXI].

Holy [XXVIII] Set apart for a sacred purpose, or possessed of a peculiar quality deriving from relationship with a GOD or God. 'Holy' and 'sacred' are sometimes used synonymously [8: IV]. The concept of the sacred (Latin *sacer*) contrasted with the profane (*profanus*, literally, 'outside the temple'; so, 'what is for common use') is a key one for the specification of religion in the SCIENCES OF RELIGION and for RELIGIONSWISSENSCHAFT [9: 10]. Sacred things, places, times, events, actions, persons, communities, even life as a whole, may be holy, though for some religions holiness appertains in a primary sense only to the objects or object of devotion [28: V]. Rudolf Otto (1896–1937) analysed 'the holy' as a category of interpretation and evaluation peculiar to religion, required by that kind of experience for which he invented the term 'numinous' (from Latin *numen*) [23]. For Otto, the quality of what is so experienced (the ultimately real) is *mysterium tremendum et fascinans*. In his view, it is only in a derived sense

(yet inevitably) that 'holy' comes to mean 'completely good', 'morally perfect'.

Holy Land [XVII] The biblical Canaan was, in Jewish belief, promised by God to Abraham and his 'seed' as an 'everlasting possession' (Genesis 17: 3), and again to the 'Children of Israel' while in slavery to the Egyptians (Exodus 6: 4) (COVENANT; EXODUS). Its borders are variously described (Genesis 15: 18–21, Deuteronomy 1: 7–8, 11: 24, Joshua 1: 4, 13: 2–5), and Israelite settlement there reached its maximum during the reign of King David (BIBLICAL HISTORY) [9 vol. 9: 112]. The name Palestine (derived from (country of) the Philistines), in common use for the past two millennia, was introduced by the Romans. From Mishnaic times (2nd century CE) it has been known among Jews as 'Eretz Yisrael'. Although there has been continuous Jewish settlement in the Holy Land since the time of the second TEMPLE the majority of Jews have lived in the various countries of the Diaspora from about the 3rd century CE. Traditional Jews have always taken the biblical account of the divine promise seriously, and Palestine is the Holy Land of JUDAISM. [18; 21: XX; 26: XVI]

Holy Spirit [XI.A] In the Hebrew BIBLE, GOD exercises his creative power by his spirit ('breath') and speaks through prophets and sages. In the New Testament JESUS CHRIST accomplishes his ministry by the power of the Spirit and after his death endows his followers with the Spirit, which is spoken of in personal terms and functions as Jesus' *alter ego*, making his continuing presence real to them and enabling them to fulfil their charge as Jesus' representatives on earth. [12]

Honorifics, Titles, and Styles of Address (Sikh) [XXVII] Among the titles current in the Sikh PANTH the Arabic *Sahib* covers a particularly wide range. Used by the GURUS as a name of God it is now attached as an honorific postposition to personal names, the scripture, sanctified towns or villages, and important GURDWARAS. Other styles are prefixed and are more specific. Nanak, originally addressed as *Baba* (Father), is now (with his successors) generally known as Guru [24: 251–3]. *Bhagat* designates any poet (other than the Gurus) whose works appear in the ADI GRANTH [23: 60–61]. *Bhai* (Brother) is applied to male Sikhs of notable piety or religious learning, and is also used for a *granthi* (*gurdwara* custodian), *ragi* (*kirtan* singer), or *dhadi* (itinerant narrator of Sikh tradition). *Giani* designates a learned person; *Sant* a teacher of Sikh doctrine who attracts a following; and *Jathedar* the commander of a *jatha* (military or political unit). *Kesdhari* Sikhs (those with uncut hair) are addressed as *Sardar* for men and *Sardarni* for women.

Hopi [III] The westernmost of the Pueblo Indians of North America, and members of the Uto-Aztecan linguistic group, the Hopi (from *hopituh shinu-mu*, literally 'the peaceful people') inhabit lands within the NAVAJO reservation. Their myths recount the gradual progression of the ancestors through four successive underground worlds before emerging and eventually settling in their present home on the Black Mesa of the Colorado plateau (CREATION MYTHS) [25: I–v]. Central to Hopi religion is the concept of a dual division both of space and time between the upper and lower worlds, and a corresponding concern for cooperation between the two realms. Harmony between these realms is critical to the maintenance of health, food supply, and social stability [2: III]. The ceremonial cycle reflects both the cosmic pattern and the origin myth. Major divinities include Sotuqnangu (a type of sky-god), Masua (deity of earth and death), Tawa (father-sun), Kokyang Wuuti (spider-woman), and the twin war-gods (HERO TWINS). KACHINAS (spirits of the ancestors, vegetation, and animal life) figure prominently in ceremonies held from June to December [3]. Other major festivals include Wuwuchim (new year and principal initiation rite), Soyal (winter-solstice ceremony), and Powamu (bean dance) which marks the appearance of the chief *kachinas*. Myths also relate the origin of clans and secret societies that play central roles in Hopi rituals.

Horoscope [VIII] In ASTROLOGY, an interpretation of an individual's (or group's, e.g. nation's) fate and character based on the positions of the heavenly bodies at a particular moment, usually birth. The horoscope has as its basic frame of reference (I) the zodiac, which is the circle of twelve 'signs' (Aries, Taurus, Gemini, Cancer, Leo, Virgo, Libra, Scorpio, Sagittarius, Capricorn, Aquarius, Pisces) traversed by the sun, moon, and planets in periods of, approximately, 27 days (moon), one year (sun, Mercury, Venus), two years (Mars), 12 years (Jupiter), 30 years (Saturn), etc., and (2) a relatively fixed circle of 12 numbered 'houses', against which, as a result of the earth's daily rotation, the entire zodiac with the sun, moon, and planets appears to turn once every 24 hours. Casting a horoscope is thus like reading a number of pointers on a clock which itself turns quite rapidly against a second dial. A difference of an hour, even of a few minutes, can effect a considerable change; moreover, each horoscope is specific to a particular locality. Significant data are: (1) the positions of sun, moon, and planets within the zodiac (e.g. sun in Aries); (2) the 'aspects', i.e. the angular distances, of the sun, moon, and planets to each other (e.g. Venus in 'square' or 'quartile' aspect, i.e. at an angle of 90°, to Mars); (3) the positions of the sun, moon, planets, and signs against the circle of houses and its four cardinal points (*see figure*), especially the 'ascendant' and 'midheaven' (i.e. what sign, etc., is rising in the east or culminating to the south at the given moment), e.g. moon in the seventh house, Scorpio rising. For interpreting horoscopes certain values have traditionally been assigned to the planets, signs, aspects, and houses. The houses are each associated with particular areas of life or activity (e.g. the second with money-making, the eleventh with friends), the planets with activities and characters (e.g. Venus with love, 'mercurial' characters with Mercury), and the aspects with favourable or unfavourable situations (e.g. planets in opposition or square/quartile aspect tend to have sinister implications). Casting and interpreting horoscopes has been for more than 2,000 years the focus of the 'science' of astrology. Though widely discredited, especially in the West, it is an exacting art demanding considerable expertise [techniques: 11: VIII; 12; 14].

Hsuan Hsueh [x] 'Dark learning.' Sometimes referred to as Neo-Taoism by modern scholars, an intellectual movement which developed in the 3rd and 4th centuries. The main exponents were Wang Pi (226–249 CE), Ho Yen (d. 249), and Kuo Hsiang (d. 312). Wang Pi was a former minister who wrote commentaries on the TAO TE CHING and the *I Ching* (Classic of Changes), emphasizing the ontological aspects of Taoist philosophy (TAO CHIA). According to Wang Pi, *wu* (Non-Being) is the source of all things and is equivalent to the *tao* of the *Tao Te Ching* and the *t'ai chi* (Supreme Ultimate) of the *I Ching*. *Wu* is the source and substance (*t'i*) of

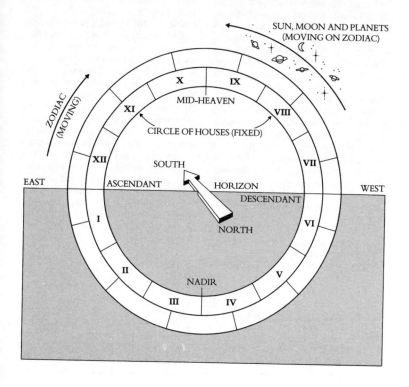

SUN, MOON AND PLANETS
(MOVING ON ZODIAC)

ZODIAC (MOVING)

X   IX

XI   MID-HEAVEN   VIII

CIRCLE OF HOUSES (FIXED)

XII   VII

SOUTH

EAST   ASCENDANT   HORIZON   WEST
DESCENDANT

I   VI

NORTH

II   V

NADIR

III   IV

reality, but its function (*yung*) can only be manifested through *yu* (Being). Wang Pi's distinction between substance and function and his relating of it to the distinction between Being and Non-Being had an important influence on later Taoist thought, on NEO-CONFUCIANISM, and even on CHINESE BUDDHISM. Ironically, exponents of Hsuan Hsueh honoured CONFUCIUS as a greater sage than Lao Tzu because Confucius was at ease in the world of Being, and did not attempt the impossible by trying to speak of Non-Being. [7: XIX, 314–35; 32: V, 170–72]

Closely associated with Hsuan Hsueh was the movement known as Ch'ing T'an (Pure Conversation), which probably started in the Later Han dynasty (23–220 CE) but was adopted by the Neo-Taoists for metaphysical discussion and speculation. The Seven Sages of the Bamboo Grove in the 3rd century CE were typical exponents. Eventually Buddhist concepts were introduced into the discussions. [15: III, 61–76; 64: 59–69; 100: 123–6]

Hsun Tzu [x] 300–230 BCE. A naturalistic and rationalistic Confucian philosopher who argued that human nature is basically evil and that goodness must be produced by moral training and, if necessary, formal constraints. He interpreted Heaven (T'IEN) in purely naturalistic terms as the process of natural laws. He was sceptical about the existence of ghosts (*kuei*) and spirits (*shen*), but defended the FUNERAL RITES and the ANCESTOR CULT in terms of their benefits for the living. [7: VI, 115–35; 26; 31: XII, 279–311; 97]

Hua Yen [x] A scholastic and eclectic school of CHINESE BUDDHISM founded by Fa Tsang (643–712 CE) and based on the *Avatamsaka-Sutra* (*Hua Yen Ching*). In an attempt to elucidate the essential teachings of Hua Yen to the Empress Wu, Fa Tsang composed his *Treatise on the Golden Lion*, which remains one of the clearest expositions of Hua Yen teachings. Fa Tsang accepted

the basic SAN LUN (SHUNYATA-VADA or MADHYAMIKA) teaching on the EMPTINESS and consequent non-differentiation of DHARMAS and develops this into a doctrine of the mutual implication of *dharmas*, in which the coming into existence of any one *dharma* implies the simultaneous existence of all others. There are clear similarities between Hua Yen and the earlier T'IEN TAI teachings, the differences being largely matters of emphasis. Like the T'ien Tai school, Hua Yen classified Buddhist teachings according to their nature and the capacity of the BUDDHA's audience. The 'five doctrines' are also described in the *Treatise on the Golden Lion*. (*See Kegon in* NANTO ROKUSHU.) [7: XXV, 406–24; 12; 15: XI, 313–20; 18; 24: XIII, 328–33; 32: VIII, 339–59]

Huehuetlatolli [XIX] The most formal and influential form of sacred instruction in Nahuatl culture (MESO-AMERICAN RELIGIONS) was the *huehuetlatolli*, 'ancient word'. [8: IV] These teachings consisted of polished rhetorical orations which transmitted the cultural traditions in a society where the writing system was not adequate for their verbal communication. *Huehuetlatolli* were delivered in the schools (CALMECAC), as prayers to the gods on ceremonial occasions, at the investiture of a king, for the departure and return of merchants, and at ceremonies associated with the life-cycle. These ancient truths, which were delivered in an elegant, florid, intensely metaphorical style, aimed to instruct, inspire, and illuminate the traditional values and meanings of the culture for the listeners.

Huitzilopochtli [XIX] One of the most important gods in MESOAMERICAN RELIGIONS was Huitzilopochtli (Humming-bird of the South), the tribal god of the wandering Mexicas who became the patron deity of the Aztec capital city, Tenochtitlan. The spectacular religious development that was founded on him is symbolized in two mythical episodes which were ritually celebrated by the Aztecs, one concerning the origin of the capital, the other telling of the birth of the ideal warrior, Huitzilopochtli, and the origin of massive HUMAN SACRIFICE. Aztec sacred history tells that Huitzilopochtli led his people, the Mexicas, from Chicomoztoc (the Place of Seven Caves), into the valley of Mexico, where he appeared in the form of a giant eagle landing on a cactus growing in the centre of Lake Texcoco (1325 CE). This event marked the foundation of the new community and a shrine was built on the spot to celebrate Huitzilopochtli's power and authority. This shrine, which became the TEMPLO MAYOR of the Aztec empire, and the ritual activity associated with it, were modelled after the myth of Huitzilopochtli's birth as a ferocious solar warrior at the cosmic mountain, Coatepec, and the slaughter of his 400 brothers and sisters. [14: 42–6]. Huitzilopochtli's supreme power was commemorated at the festival of Panquetzalitzli (Raising of Banners), which involved special human sacrifices following the opening ritual called Ipaina Huitzilopochtli (the Swiftness of Huitzilopochtli). [7: 457–62] In this ritual, a swift runner carried a dough image of the god through the lavishly decorated streets of the city, pursued by a multitude of revellers who never managed to catch the lead runner. This signified that the Aztec patron god was never captured in war, but was always triumphant over his enemies, whom he destroyed at the Templo Mayor. Historically, following the formation of the Aztec state in 1428 CE, the cult of Huitzilopochtli grew to include massive human sacrifices of captured warriors, women, and children, which, it was thought, contributed to the consolidation of Aztec power, cosmic stability, and Huitzilopochtli's dominance. [10: 156–72]

Human Potential Movement [XXI]
An umbrella term covering a wide range of groups whose beliefs and practices

are designed to promote 'wholeness', self-awareness, self-development, or self-realization for the enlightened individual. Its roots go back at least as far as GURDJIEFF, but during the 1960s and 1970s the movement expanded rapidly throughout the West, particularly in California, to encompass a multitude of techniques which could be ancient (such as various types of YOGA), esoteric (such as some meditation MANTRA), or entirely novel (such as 'bio-feedback'). Included under the umbrella one can find massage, dance, the martial arts, dietary rules, psychodrama, humanistic psychology, *gestalt* therapy and the more mystical forms of psychoanalysis. 'Encounter' groups have been particularly prominent since the late 1960s (one of the most notable being the Esalen Institute in California). In these groups people are meant to release repressed emotions and talk about problems with the help of others. [33; 41: 103] There is considerable variation in the methods used to achieve such goals. Innumerable Americans and Europeans have 'graduated' from 'est' (Erhard Seminar Training): they are shut up for a weekend, during which abuse is hurled at them to enable them to achieve personal growth [37: 49]. Large sums of money have been paid out by individuals seeking to release pent-up emotions by re-experiencing their own births (in a deep tub of hot water with Leonard Orr's 're-birthing' [37: 118] or by learning to emit the 'primal scream' in Arthur Janov's Primal Therapy [37: 133]).

The range of spiritual and mystical meanings that such therapies may have for their practitioners has led to many of the groups being attacked as quasi-religious and/or harmful by the ANTI-CULT MOVEMENT. At the same time, many of the techniques, especially those developed in some encounter groups, are used by Christian clergy, in prisons, hospitals, and for training in a number of socially respectable institutions. [General descriptions of movement: 3; 10; 14:

v; 30; 31; 32; 37; 38; 48; 51; 56; 57;
guides for contacting groups: 2; 20; 41;
42]

Human Sacrifice (Aztec) [XIX] Human
sacrifice, called *tlamictiliztli*, was a
widespread MESOAMERICAN RELI-
GIOUS practice which proliferated during the expansion of Aztec power. Its
stated purpose was the constant renovation of cosmic order and the nourishing
of the gods, who were fed the blood
and hearts of the *ixiptla*, or representative of the gods, in the form of the
sacrificed victim. Aztec myths relate
that the Fifth Sun (TEZCATLIPOCA)
was created through the sacrifice of
the gods [12: 44–5], who subsequently
created warfare among humans so
that captured warriors could be ritually
killed to feed the sun and other deities.
Aztec warfare was carried out in part
to supply the major temples with
sacrificial victims.

The most-valued sacrificial victims
were captive warriors, who were

Aztec arrow and gladiatorial human
sacrifice

treated with elaborate care and ceremony
because they were considered the living
representatives of the deities. [2: IX]
Women, children, and slaves paid as tribute from enemy provinces were also
ritually sacrificed. The variety of sacrificial methods included shooting with
arrows (*see figure*), beheading, immola-
tion, and, most commonly, heart extraction. In the latter case, the victim
was killed with the *tecpatl*, a jewelled
flint-knife wielded by the QUETZAL-
COATL priest or the TLATOANI (Ruler).
The victim was stretched over the *tech-
catl* (sacrificial stone), located at the top
of the temple pyramid's steps (TEMPLO
MAYOR) so that the body could be
rolled down and dismembered at the
bottom following heart extraction.
This action represented the descent of
the sun into the underworld, now ener-
gized by the blood of the warrior
(CEMANAHUAC). Specific parts of the
body, usually the thighs, were cut up
into portions for sacrificial meals by the
nobles, warriors, and merchants into
whom the divine energy passed.
The skull was placed on the *tzomp-
antli*, or skull-rack, in the ceremonial
centre.

The intense political struggles of rival
cities in late 15th and early 16th century
CE central Mesoamerica resulted in the
escalation of warfare, sacrifice, and
ritual cannibalism. [10: X] In Tenochtitlan alone, major Aztec building
renewals or inaugurations of kings
were accompanied by the sacrifice of
thousands of captured warriors to
ensure the stability of the Aztec state and
the motion of the cosmos. (NEW FIRE
CEREMONY)

Humanism [XXVI] Since the 16th century the word 'humanist' has been used
to distinguish students of subjects like
poetry, history, and moral philosophy
from students of other kinds (e.g. of
THEOLOGY). This remains one special
use related to the word 'humanities'.
More commonly, however, the word
'humanist' is used to mean a person

with a set of entirely non-religious beliefs and values. MARXISM, UTILITARIANISM, and other SECULAR ALTERNATIVES to religion can be regarded as forms of humanism. Marx himself accepted the label, although it is often repudiated by 20th-century Marxists because it is a label commonly claimed by non-Marxists.

The tradition of 'liberal' or 'ethical' humanism associated with the Ethical Societies founded in the late 19th century emphasizes what, from a Marxist point of view, is called 'bourgeois individualism'. There are no set doctrines attached to this form of humanism and, although humanists believe in the importance of political reforms, they are not committed to any particular political programme. They have been most active in defending the individual against imprisonment for political belief and in causes like abortion and euthanasia. Their position has been summed up as a belief in an 'open mind' and an 'open society' [3: 186] – a formulation due to the philosopher Karl Popper (b. 1902) [16].

Liberal or ethical humanism can be distinguished in theory, if not always in practice, from scientific humanism. The emphasis of the former is on political reform, the latter on science, as the means of improving the human condition. The former emphasizes the freedom and dignity of the individual; the latter may deny, as the well-known American psychologist B. F. Skinner (b. 1904) [19] does, that such terms have any place in a scientific view of man. It may be better to refer to an exclusive emphasis on science for the solution of all problems as *scientism*. There are those, like Bertrand Russell (1872–1970) [18], who have attached importance to both science and social reform.

In the 19th century humanism took various church-like forms [22: 195], which gave it the character of a secular religion. These do not flourish in the same way today and the quasi-religious

forms of humanism tend to be those which find a panacea for human ills in a particular theory of human nature such as Freudianism or Existentialism. [*See* 20]

Hurrians [VI] Hurrian peoples, who inhabited the mountainous regions south of the Caspian sea from *c.* 2300 BCE, moved gradually southwards and westwards, forming important elements in several kingdoms including Mitanni, where they were dominated by a ruling caste of Indo-Aryans (INDO-EUROPEANS). They also contributed substantially to the Hittite empire (HITTITES), where their language and religion were important elements.

The theologians of the Hittite capital adopted Hurrian deities [13: 140–41], and some Mesopotamian gods were introduced to the Hittites in this way. The great rock-sanctuary of Yazilikaya, about 3 km from Boghazköy, was a state monument, carved in relief, showing not only deities of the Hittite kingdom (ART AND SYMBOLISM), but also some Hurrian deities that had been officially accepted into the Hittite pantheon.

In areas where Hurrians formed the main element in the population, Hurrian deities such as Teshub, the weather-god, and his consort, Hebat, were worshipped. They were prominent at Aleppo, Samuha, and elsewhere. With increasing Hurrian influence on the state religion, Hebat was eventually identified with the sun-goddess of Arinna.

The most elaborate myths and legends in the Hittite archives were also drawn from the Hurrian religion, although many are only partly preserved [24: 120–26]. Two of the most important concerned the god Kumarbi, who was the father of the gods. One tells of the struggle for divine KINGSHIP and the creation (COSMOLOGY); it has been compared with the Theogony of Hesiod [1]. Kumarbi, originally a wise king, was impregnated by Anu, the great god, with three terrible gods, the weather-god, the Tigris, and Tasmisu (a minion of the weather-god), whom he spat forth, impregnating the earth with them, and the earth in turn gave them birth.

The other – the 'Story of Ullikummi' – is fragmentary, but deals with the conspiracy by Kumarbi against Teshub. Kumarbi begat Ullikummi, who fought on earth against the gods; the conclusion (now missing) probably saw the restoration to power of Teshub and the defeat of Kumarbi and Ullikummi (ANCIENT NEAR EASTERN RELIGIONS).

· I ·

Icon [XI.D] A symbolic sacred image
[12; 17]. Icons are venerated and used in
religious ceremonies by Orthodox
Christians, and form an integral part
of the decoration of their churches
(ORTHODOX CHURCH). The second
COUNCIL of Nicea (787 CE) approved
the veneration of icons as a sign of faith
in the Incarnation (CHRISTOLOGY).
The Divine Logos has become fully
human as JESUS CHRIST, and can be portrayed. [47: 38ff; 27: 132ff, 203]

Orthodox theology sees redemption
as involving the whole of creation.
Icons are material embodiments of spiritual meaning and of spiritual power.
They represent the return of the material creation to God; they are access
points to the realities of the Divine
Kingdom (ESCHATOLOGY). [33; 35:
153ff; 45] (ARCHITECTURE (CHRIS-
TIAN); ICONOGRAPHY)

Iconography [XXVIII] Description and
systematic study of portraits, and so, by
extension, of any embodiment of visual
art. A distinction is made between
'iconography' as descriptive analysis of
the subject-matter of works of art, and
'iconology' as interpretation of their
meaning. There is a further distinction
between 'iconic' art, having some
likeness to what is represented, and
'aniconic', symbolizing without visual
resemblance. For RELIGIONSWISSEN-
SCHAFT, paintings, sculpture, architecture, dress, indeed any objects used in
worship and ritual, can provide
important and often indispensable
information about beliefs and practices,
as well as a means of entry for the
phenomenologist (PHENOMENOLOGY
OF RELIGION) trying to share the inner
perspective of those who participate in a
religion other than his or her own.
From the prehistoric cave-paintings of
France and Spain to the form and
decoration of existing temples, cathedrals, mosques, and shrines, the range
of iconographic material bearing upon
religion is immense [21], and much of
its symbolism (SYMBOL) would remain
obscure apart from this source of
knowledge and understanding. [12: VIII;
17: VII, XIII; 28: XII]

Iconography (**Christian**) [XI.B] St
Thomas Aquinas (c. 1225–74 CE)
(THOMISM) justified reverence to
images, arguing that worship is directed
to the reality symbolized. PROTEST-
ANTISM generally reacted violently
against images, although Luther
(LUTHERANISM) allowed the crucifix
(image of JESUS CHRIST on the cross).
Anglo-Catholics (ANGLICANISM) allow
for the use of images. The ORTHODOX
CHURCH reverences ICONS. The chief
Christian symbol is the cross, referring
to the crucifixion of Jesus Christ, and to
SALVATION. The early 'fish' symbol
used of Christ and the EUCHARIST has
recently been revived. (It supposedly
refers to the Greek word for fish –
ichthus – standing for the initials of 'Jesus
Christ, Son of God, Saviour' in Greek
[107: 514].) Other symbols have been
drawn from animals, colours, numbers,
and objects connected with Christ,
MARY, and the SAINTS. People from
Hebrew scripture (BIBLE) were used, as
prefiguring Christ. Statues and other
imagery proliferated in Western medieval churches (ARCHITECTURE). Eastern images of Jesus characteristically
represented him in majesty (*Pantocrator*).

Western ones gradually shifted to realistic emphasis on his humanity. COUNTER-REFORMATION images reinforced devotions attacked by Protestantism. Modern Christian images reflect the variety of contemporary artistic styles, although applied to traditional subjects. [43; 99: VIII]

'Id [XIV] The general term in ISLAM for 'religious festival' (Turkish equivalent, *bayram*), used especially for the two great festivals. The first, the 'Id al-Adha ('of sacrifice'), falls on 10 Dhu 'l-Hijja during the Pilgrimage period (HAJJ) and is traditionally associated with ABRAHAM's intended sacrifice of his son. The second, the 'Id al-Fitr ('of breaking the fast'), falls on 1 Shawwal, the end of Ramadan, the month of fasting (SAUM). Both are occasions for general rejoicing, the wearing of new clothes, etc., and the latter has become a major public holiday. The occasion of the Prophet's birthday (12 Rabi' I) or *maulid*, has over the centuries become a major festival, as have the birthdays of many local holy men (WALI) [45: XXIV–XXVII; 54]. Among the Shi'is (SHI'ISM), the anniversary of al-Husain's killing (10 Muharram) releases a great outpouring of passion and emotion (*see* 'ALI, 'ALIDS *and* PASSION PLAY). Shi'is also celebrate the festival of Ghadir Khumm (18 Dhu 'l-Hijja), when, they hold, MUHAMMAD designated 'Ali as his divinely ordained successor. [21 s.v.; 29: 168–9; 74]

Ideology [XXVI] A system of beliefs shared by a group of people which affects the kinds of behaviour of which they approve and disapprove. In a broad sense a political party will commonly have an ideology which sets limits to the kind of policy it can be expected to pursue. But the word is also commonly used for sets of belief where particular importance is attached to profession and where the relation to practice may be obscure.

Marx (MARXISM) and M. F. Engels (1820–95) regarded ideologies as im-positions by the ruling class upon society as a whole of ideas which reflect and appear to confirm existing economic relationships. They are a kind of deception which, if successful, produces a 'false consciousness' among the people and a corresponding complacency about the established order of society. Religions, according to Marxism, are ideologies in this sense. [11; 12]

Marx's conception of ideology has proved very influential, and non-Marxists have adopted it in a modified form. The U.S. sociologist Peter Berger, for example, follows Marx in reserving the word 'ideology' for cases where a particular idea serves a vested interest in society. [2: 130ff] The function of an ideology, as he sees it, is to preserve a vested interest by interpreting social reality so as to provide an appearance of justification for behaviour that would otherwise seem indefensible. Berger allows that the ideologist may himself be taken in by the deception which he practises on others. It is in this way that he thinks that religious persuasions can function as ideologies.

One example given by Berger is the role played by Protestant fundamentalism (AUTHORITY (CHRISTIAN)) in maintaining the racialist social system of the Southern U.S.A. Berger claims that revivalist preachers, by identifying morality with private acts and public morality with the private acts of public persons, contribute to the maintenance of a social system whose central social arrangements are morally dubious. It is not that segregation is proclaimed as a God-given natural order but that attention is diverted from social evils which it would otherwise be difficult to ignore. In this way an ideology can help to preserve the existing social order without explicitly condoning it.

Ifa [II] Ifa is the chief YORUBA system of divination and probably the most complex in Africa. Originating in the city of Ife, its use has spread to other West African societies (Benin, FON, and the

Ewe of Togo and eastern Ghana) and
also to Brazil and Cuba. Its characteristics are the precision of the system, its
vast corpus of related verse, and its religious foundation in the worship of the
ORISHA, Ifa, or Orunmila. Orunmila is
the divine patron of divination, the
communicator to mankind of their
destiny as decreed by Olodumare.
Through Ifa one's destiny is revealed.

Ifa depends upon the manipulation of
16 palm-nuts or the toss of a chain from
which – as in many systems of divination – 16 basic permutations are possible. Upon these depend 256 figures, for
each of which Ifa provides a considerable number of verses. The *babalawo*
(diviner) recites the relevant verses until
the client chooses one. The verses constitute a vast corpus of unwritten scripture. Each provides guidance, including
instructions to offer sacrifice, normally
at the shrine of Eshu.

The Ifa diviner is called *babalawo*
(father of secrets). Always a man, and a
priest of Orunmila (Orisha), the *babalawo* has had years of apprenticeship and
is required, especially, to memorize the
verses. He may rise in honour through
various initiations. The 16 diviners of
the king of Ife, the Awoni, are the highest. [18; 20]

Iglesia ni Cristo [XX] The largest independent church in the PHILIPPINES,
founded in 1914 by Felix Manalo (1886–
1963) after experience in five mission
churches. Manalo's son Eraño now
presides over the movement, which is
strongly anti-Catholic and well organized, with up to 1 million members. It
is characterized by splendid and distinctive church buildings, a dogmatic
Unitarian interpretation of the BIBLE
(UNITARIANISM), and a fondness for
public debate. The church, which supports President Marcos, has had several
secessions. There are branches among
Filipinos in many parts of the world. [5:
49–50]

Ijma' [XIV], 'consensus', is one of the
bases of classical Islamic religious law

for the Sunni mainstream (SUNNA).
Only the sectarian KHARIJITES rejected
it, as also the Shi'is (SHI'ISM), the latter
substituting for it obedience to the authoritative IMAM. The consensus of the
early Muslims, that of the Prophet
MUHAMMAD's companions at the outset, which later broadened out to
include that of all believers (or at least of
all qualified ones), supplemented the
QUR'AN and HADITH as sources of law
when these two gave no clear guidance.
It was founded on a tradition from the
Prophet, 'My community will never
agree upon error.' [21 'Idjmā'; 47: 178–
9; 83: 33–9]

Illuminati [XVIII] A secret society devoted to anti-priestly and democratic
ideals, founded in 1776 at Ingolstadt,
Bavaria, by Adam Weishaupt (1748–
1830). Initiates were trained in materialist philosophy under the guidance of the
Areopagus (inner directorate). Having
established the organization in Bavaria,
Weishaupt decided in 1779 to infiltrate
continental FREEMASONRY, where the
order spread rapidly until 1784, when
internal quarrels led to publicity and it
was suppressed by the Bavarian and
other governments. [22: V]

Imam [XIV], literally 'exemplar, model', hence 'leader', denotes, first, the
leader of the Muslim worship (*see* SALAT)
in the MOSQUE. He may be any adult
male Muslim of good character and
standing in the community, and is not
in any sense an ordained priest or minister, though larger mosques may employ
a salaried IMAM. Second, it denotes the
charismatic leaders of the Shi'a (SHI'-
ISM), who hold that God has designated a line of the immaculate members
of the family of 'ALI to act as the sources
of spiritual and secular guidance for the
community; hence knowledge of the
Imam of the time is a prerequisite of all
true believers. Since the disappearance
of the 12th of the line in the later 9th
century, there has been a period of
occultation of the Imams; but the Shi'is
now await the return (*raj'a*) of the

expected Imam, who will re-establish a reign of justice and peace on earth (*see* MAHDI). Third, it can refer to the secular head of the community as a virtual equivalent of CALIPH. [10 s.v.; 21 'Imāma'; 41: XI]

Iman [XIV] 'Faith' in ISLAM, connected also with *mu'min* ('believer'). Most Islamic theologians agreed that faith involved the three elements of intention or conviction (NIYYA), external profession (*qaul*), and performance of works ('*amal*), but differed on their relative proportions and/or importance. One school, the Ash'aris (*see* KALAM), laid greatest stress on conviction in the heart. Degrees of faith were recognized, with emphasis on essential articles of faith (as opposed to those without which a person does not necessarily cease to be a Muslim). All authorities agree that faith is required for salvation. (*See also* 'AQIDA, DIN, SHAHADA) [10 'Faith (Islam)'; 21 s.v.; 29: 47–8; 82: 111]

Imhotep [IV] The vizier of King Djoser (3rd dynasty, *c*. 2800 BCE), Imhotep was the architect of the world's first major stone building – Djoser's Step PYRAMID at Saqqara [8: II, 53]. He also achieved a reputation as a sage, and was deified and worshipped in the Late Period (*c*. 600 BCE) as a god of healing. He was renowned among Egyptians and Greeks, who named his chapel at Saqqara the Asklepieion where people from all parts of Egypt sought miraculous cures.

Inari [XVI] Popularly called fox-shrines, especially numerous in rural areas of Japan, *inari* have seated stone images of foxes at the entrance, the 'messengers' of the KAMI of agriculture, food, and fertility [32: 194–5]. The SHINTO SHRINES are often dedicated to other *kami*, particularly Uga-no-mitama, the female *kami* of agriculture. The cult is very old and, among other explanations, was said in early times to appease foxes from damaging crops, or to neutralize fox-possession. The head shrine,

Fushimi Inari in south-east Kyoto city, traditionally built in 711 CE, is noted for its thousands of votive *torii* (sacred gates) in long tunnels, covering the hill behind. The chief festival is Hatsu-uma, the 'first horse day' after the official first day of spring, welcoming back the agricultural *kami*.

India, Christianity in [XI.B] Tradition claims that the APOSTLE Thomas reached India, and several churches survive from 4th-century CE Nestorian origins (CHRISTOLOGY). They are the Malabarese and Malankarese Catholics, Syrian Orthodox, Jacobite and Nestorian (Mellusian) Churches, and the Mar Thoma church. Western Christianity arrived with the Portuguese and notably the Jesuits (MONASTICISM) St Francis Xavier (1506–52) and Robert de Nobili (1577–1656). De Nobili influenced high-CASTE Indians by acting like a Hindu guru. The English East India Company was hostile to MISSIONS but the BAPTIST William Carey (1761–1834) landed in 1793. In 1813 the influence of the 'Clapham Sect' (REVIVALISM) opened India to PROTESTANTISM. Alexander Duff (1806–78) initiated educational missions to the higher castes and, by the end of the 19th century, although all religions were tolerated by the government, American and European Protestant missions were numerous. Mass conversions occurred among the poorer castes. Political independence (1947) hastened the independence of local churches. Christianity in India, although more successful than in Pakistan, amounts to only 3 per cent of the population. Westernization in India, however, has probably helped it to become more influential than in CHINA. The Church of South India (1947) incorporates ANGLICANISM, CONGREGATIONALISM, METHODISM, and PRESBYTERIANISM. The Church of North India (1970) includes BAPTISTS too. [65: V, XVI; 82 vol. 3: VIII, vol. 6: III, vol. 7: XI; 83 vol. 3: XVII, vol. 5: XI; 103]

Indian Shaker Church [xx] In 1881 a Squaxin Indian near Puget Sound (Washington), John Slocum, received a revelation during a coma. The next year a shaking paroxysm of his wife Mary was regarded as the spirit of God curing John of an illness. The Shaker Church they founded replaced SHAMAN healing by the new shaking and dancing rituals, along with Christian elements. In the 1970s over 20 congregations in northwest U.S.A. embraced perhaps 2,000 adherents in this Indian Christian syncretism. [1; 12: 124–7; 19: 353–64]

Indo-Europeans [xxx] In *c.* 5000 BCE there were groups of peoples living (probably) in eastern Europe which began to fragment, with groups migrating in different directions. Over two millennia or more, some travelled east and eventually settled in India (*c.* 2000–1500 BCE) where they overpowered the civilization of the INDUS VALLEY. *En route* a few apparently settled in Iran, and a later 'wave' of these nomadic peoples colonized that country. They spoke of themselves as the 'Aryans', the noble ones. Scholars generally refer to the 'proto-Indo-Iranians' (the ancestors, on the South Russian steppes, of the Iranians) and the 'Indo-Aryans' (the Aryans who invaded India). These invaders brought with them a rich oral tradition, much of which is preserved in the HINDU *Rig*-VEDA and the AVESTA of ZOROASTRIANISM. Some Indo-Europeans, the Tocharians, travelled further east. Other Indo-Europeans travelled south, settling in Greece and Rome, while others migrated west and settled in various North European areas, e.g. Scandinavia. The existence of the parent groups of peoples can be established by the similarity of the respective descendent languages (e.g. Sanskrit, Greek, and Latin). Certain rituals are similar in the religions of the countries in which the Indo-Europeans settled, which suggests an original common practice (e.g. the veneration of fire). The Indo-Europeans considered certain natural phenomena, such as the sun and sky, to be deities. G. Dumézil (b. 1898) (TRIPARTITE IDEOLOGY) has attempted to reconstruct a common structure behind the various mythologies of the different religions which are of Indo-European descent. [5]

Indus Valley [XIII.A] The site of an early Indian civilization dating from at least 2500 BCE, evidence of which began to be found from 1920 with the excavation of two sites, Harappa and Mohenjo-Daro. The findings from these sites suggest that many features of 'modern' Hinduism are ultimately derived from this early period. The most notable examples are: the popularity of the cult of the mother-goddess; the yogic posture; the fertility deity (who seems to be a form of SHIVA), who is also lord of the animals, and associated with meditation; the worship of the pipal-tree; the generally domestic-centred nature of popular cults; and the large part played by animals, especially the bull [2: 14–24; 14: 10–12], although not the COW. The archaeological evidence has been interpreted as an indication of the existence of great baths and possibly water rites.

Insan [XIV] (Arabic 'man'). The doctrine of man in ISLAM. Islamic theology concentrated more on defining God and his attributes (ALLAH) than on man. The QUR'AN regards man as God's noble work, created from clay as his representation on earth and to serve and glorify him (*see* KHALQ). He is endowed with a soul (*see* RUH), which will return to God when the body perishes. The Qur'an is ambiguous about man's free will (FATALISM (IN ISLAM)), but many traditions stress how man should act, in effect according him free will. While orthodoxy regards man as altogether different from the transcendent God, Sufi mystics (SUFISM) have sought nevertheless to achieve closeness to, and even union with, God. (For women in Islam, *see* MAR'A.) [10 'Man (Islamic doctrine)'; 21 s.v.; 29: 32–3]

Institutions (Greek) [XII] Until Hellenistic times (GREEK RELIGION) most cultic activity was channelled through institutions. Individuals mostly worshipped as a member of one of the following groups: *oikos*, a household; *demos*, a commune; *phratria*, a group of families; *phyle*, the tribe; *genos*, an aristocratic descent group; or as a member of the city-state. For certain rituals age, sex, or occupation were the distinguishing criteria. Institutions regulated inter-state activities. The most important was the Amphictyoniai, the League of States, which was responsible for inter-state sanctuaries. [2: V, 3.3; 9: 103–11; 11: 256]

Intertestamental Literature [XI.A] Jewish literature which appeared in the last two or three centuries BCE and provides a background to the New Testament. It includes most of the 'apocryphal' books (mainly books found in the SEPTUAGINT but not in the Hebrew Bible (CANON)) and the pseudepigrapha, works of later date ascribed to ancient authors like Enoch, the patriarchs, and MOSES. The volume of extant intertestamental literature has been greatly amplified by the discoveries at QUMRAN.

The intertestamental writings embrace APOCALYPTIC works, 'wisdom' books (e.g. the *Wisdom of Ben Sira, c.* 180 BCE), and the so-called Wisdom of Solomon, *c.* 100 BCE), histories (e.g. 1 and 2 Maccabees), and edifying fiction (e.g. Tobit, Judith). They reflect Jewish conditions at the time when they were composed and provide valuable source material for the development of Jewish thought in the Hellenistic age. [16: XXXII, XXXIII]

Io [XXII] The supreme being in New Zealand Maori belief, barely traceable elsewhere in POLYNESIAN RELIGION. Io's identity was a secret known only to TOHUNGAS in a few Maori houses of learning (*whare wananga*). All life and power (MANA) comes ultimately from Io. He exists eternally in the highest of 12 heavens, acting through a hierarchy of gods and guardian-spirits superior to the classic ATUA. No image of Io is known, and mention of his name in prayers and chants is rare. [6; 7; 16]

Iroquois [III] A general designation for five North American Indian tribes (Mohawk, Seneca, Onondaga, Cayuga, and Oneida) of Hokan–Siouan linguistic stock. Cosmogonic myths recount the birth of twin brothers, Ioskeha and Tawiscara (the principles of good and evil respectively) from the daughter of sky-woman (CREATION MYTHS). Ioskeha, the CULTURE HERO, ultimately creates mankind, with divisions into moieties (or tribal subgroupings). A return of Ioskeha occasions the 'False Face' society: a group of medicine-men, whose masks represent spirits benevolent to mankind, seek the prevention and cure of illness [23: XVII]. Aboriginal religion was transformed and renewed by the Seneca prophet HANDSOME LAKE.

Iruva [II] Iruva (with parallel forms of the word, Izuwa, Ilyuva, Lyuba, Luba, Loba, etc.) is one of the most widely spread names for God in Africa. It is mainly found in Tanzania (Chagga and Meru in the east, Kimbu, Nyamwezi, and Sukuma in the west) and among neighbouring peoples; but it is also to be found in Congo (Brazzaville) and southwest Cameroon. The word means 'sun' in each language, though in some (Sukuma, for instance) there is now another secular word for sun too. These religions do not, however, identify God and the physical sun, but recognize a clear distinction. Iruva represents a basic, and certainly ancient, aspect of Bantu theology: God in the sky, symbolically male, life-giving. [31]

Ise Jingu [XVI] The grand shrines of Ise in Japan. These are two shrines, at Uji-Yamada and Ise in Mie prefecture (SHINTO SHRINES) [2: I, 176–8; 17: 110–15; 32: 28–47]. They are 6 km apart, separated by the Isuzu river. The original shrine, the Naiku (inner shrine), was dedicated to AMATERASU-OMIKAMI, the sun-goddess, and according to tradition was founded in 4 BCE (perhaps actually in the 3rd century CE) after Emperor Suinin wanted to move the sacred mirror from his residence. The other shrine, Geku (outer shrine), was dedicated to Toyouke-omikami, the grain-goddess (KAMI), and is said to have been founded by Emperor Yuryaku in 475 CE (perhaps actually c. 490). As a union of sky and earth deities, the site became the most revered spot in Japan, and pilgrimages and special imperial visits were made throughout the centuries. All persons nowadays hope to go once in a 60-year span. An imperial family daughter was for long dispatched as the chief priestess (*saigu*) at the shrines. At great expense and in an exceptionally elaborate ritual, the shrines are rebuilt on adjoining lots every 20 years. The *shintai* (or *go-shintai*: god body) is transferred in the Sengushiki ceremony, and the old shrines are dismantled. The last rebuilding was in 1973–4.

Ishvara [XIII.A] In Sanskrit 'the one who is able'; thus, a lord or king, and in Hindu tradition, the supreme god. Whereas specific names are used for the gods (e.g. SHIVA, VISHNU, etc.), this is the word which indicates 'God' in the general sense.

Islam [XIV], the name of the faith, means 'submission [to God]', the adherent or Muslim being therefore 'one who submits himself to God' (ALLAH), i.e. surrenders himself unconditionally to the divine will. Tradition regards Islam as the final unfolding of God's revelation to mankind, a complete system of faith and behaviour whose archetype is preserved in heaven with God, whereas earlier versions of the revelation, such as those given to the Jews and Christians, had been imperfect ones. The Prophet MUHAMMAD was the channel only for this revelation, hence it is misleading to speak of the faith as 'Muhammadanism'. Islamic theologians

distinguished between the verbal profession of adherence to Islam (SHAHADA) and inner faith (IMAN), but connected them closely in that true intention in the heart leads inevitably to performance of the external duties of Islam (*see* PILLARS OF ISLAM) and overt profession of the faith. No distinction between the religious sphere and that of practical life is possible, and the all-embracing law of Islam (SHARI‘A) covers all facets of human activity [21 s.v.; 29: IV; 80].

Islam spread rapidly from its birthplace in western Arabia (*see* HARAMAIN) in the early 7th century CE, so that, by 713, Arab believers stood on the Atlantic coast and the Indus river banks. Its actual penetration among the peoples of the intervening lands was naturally a slower process; in such regions as sub-Saharan AFRICA, Islamization is still proceeding. In some areas (e.g. the Arabian peninsula, North Africa), older faiths have been totally overlaid; in some (e.g. Egypt, Syria, Lebanon, Indonesia), significant non-Muslim minorities survive; in some (e.g. the Indo-Pakistan subcontinent, China), Islam is still a minority; and in some (e.g. Spain, the Balkans, South Russia), Islam has receded. Statistics for numbers of Muslims today are only approximate, in the absence of reliable censuses in many countries, but the total perhaps approaches 600 million. (*See also*: AFRICA, ISLAM IN; CHINA AND CENTRAL ASIA, ISLAM IN; DIN; ISLAMIC DYNASTIES; SOUTH ASIA, ISLAM IN; SOUTH-EAST ASIA, ISLAM IN; WEST, ISLAM IN THE.)

Islamic Dynasties [XIV] In its early days, the Islamic community was directed by the CALIPHS of the 'Rightly guided' or 'Orthodox' line (632–61) of Medina; then by the Umayyad line (661–750) of Damascus; and then by the Abbasids in Baghdad (750–1258), latterly as puppet rulers only in Cairo (1261–1517). The central authority of the caliphate declined from the 9th century onwards, and various lines of provincial governors or local potentates, from Morocco to Central Asia, became autonomous and then virtually independent. In North Africa, Egypt, and Syria a powerful rival caliphate, that of the Fatimids (909–1171), arose under Shi'i leadership (SHI'ISM), and in Iraq and the Iranian world there arose the Sunni (SUNNA) Turkish Seljuk dynasty of sultans or secular rulers (1038–1194). The reassertion of Sunni orthodoxy over political Shi'ism led to the triumph in 1260 of the Turkish Mamelukes in Egypt and Syria as independent sultans. But their authority declined after the Ottoman Turkish conquest in 1517, as this latter dynasty (1342–1924) expanded across the Near East as far as the Persian Gulf and into Christian Europe as far as Hungary. The eastern Islamic world, however, suffered in 1217 and again in 1256 the cataclysmic invasions of the Mongols from inner Asia, and then likewise the ravages of the military conqueror Tamerlane (1336–1405). Eventually, new Turkish-directed empires arose in Muslim India, above all that of the Mughals (Moguls) of Delhi (1526–1858), and also in Persia, above all those of the Safavids of Isfahan (1501–1732) and the Qajars of Tehran (1779–1925). European economic and political encroachments, accentuated in the 19th century when Egypt broke away from Ottoman control, caused much of the Islamic world to fall under the domination of empires like those of Russia, Holland, Britain, and France. Turkey and Persia alone preserved their independence, although the Ottoman empire was dismembered after the First World War and the Arab provinces formed into various, largely new, separate states. [9A; 10A; 36A; 37]

Islamic Modernism [XIV] has been called into existence by the material and intellectual challenge of the West, and the impelling need to adapt the faith to present conditions. Figures like Muhammad 'Abduh (1849–1905), rector of AL-AZHAR, sought to modernize

traditional education, and his disciple Rashid Rida (1865–1935) and the Salafis (literally, 'those going back to the first Muslims') made the journal al-Manar a vehicle for a reformism which involved getting back to the original, pristine Islam, purged of accretions [6: II; 14: III; 46: XI; 67: 68–87]. Out of such trends sprang the Muslim Brotherhood of Hasan al-Banna' (1906–49), which emphasized social amelioration [14: VII; 57] (the increasing political activism of its adherents has made it suspect to several Islamic governments). [General surveys in 14: V–VII; 21 'Iṣlāḥ'; 27; 31: X; 61: XII–XIII; for legal aspects, see 13: 149–225]

Island of Creation [IV] Various Egyptian myths explained the creation of the world, the gods, mankind, and religion. Each myth incorporated the belief that an 'Island of Creation' had emerged from the primeval waters and had become the first god's home [7: I]. By the Old Kingdom (c. 2600 BC), the priests of Heliopolis, Memphis, and Hermopolis promoted the most important of these, stressing their own deity's primal role in the creation. Later, the cosmogony of Thebes was added (AMUN).

Isma'ilis [XIV] A subsect of SHI'ISM, which branched off from the main body in the later 8th century. Their adherents held that Isma'il, son of the sixth IMAM, should rightfully have been designated seventh Imam of the Shi'a (hence their alternative name of 'Seveners'). The Isma'ilis came to stress the internal, esoteric aspect of the QUR'AN and the teachings of Islam, by means of which they derived 'authoritative instruction' (ta'lim). This esoteric interpretation also involved a distinct cosmology, and the sect's followers made many valuable and subtle contributions to Islamic philosophy and theology [general survey in 21 'Ismā'īliyya']. With the establishment of the Fatimid dynasty in Egypt and Syria (ISLAMIC DYNASTIES), whose Imams or CALIPHS claimed descent from Fatima, wife of 'ALI and daughter of the Prophet, the Isma'ilis achieved their greatest political success. Other groups in Syria and Persia became notorious in the 12th and 13th centuries as the 'Assassins', for their activism in politics and warfare [43: 25– 79; 46: V–VII; 48]. Isma'ilis survive today, substantially prosperous as a community and having shed their earlier radicalism, in the Khoja communities of India, Syria, Iran, and East Africa and the Bohoras of India. The Imams of the former group bear the title 'Agha Khan'. [2: II]

Israel, State of [XVII] The modern Jewish state founded in the ancient HOLY LAND of JUDAISM on 14 May 1948. [9 vol. 9: 301]. Mass Jewish return to Palestine began at the end of the 19th century under the influence of the ideals of ZIONISM [18; 28]. The Balfour Declaration of 1917, issued by the British government, promised the establishment of a Jewish national home in Palestine, which was then a British mandate territory. Nazi ANTI-SEMITISM gave a new impetus to Jewish nationalism, and to the immigration or *aliyah* to Palestine. The United Nations partition plan of 29 November 1947 envisaged two states in Palestine, one Arab and one Jewish. The Arab states refused to accept the idea of a separate Jewish state, and declared war on the fledgeling Jewish state in 1948 [41: 448–68; 43: XXII, XXV]. An armistice was agreed in 1949, but a state of war has continued between Israel and her neighbours, except for Egypt which signed a peace treaty at Camp David in the U.S.A. after Presi-

dent Sadat visited Jerusalem in November 1977. The state of Israel has a mixed legislature; most of its laws are dealt with in secular courts but issues of personal status come under the jurisdiction of religious courts. Jews, whether religious or secular, have to undergo MARRIAGE and divorce under the control of the Orthodox rabbinate (RABBI).

Ius Divinum [XXV] The sacred law of Rome, consisting essentially of traditional norms expounded by the priests (SACERDOTES) in the light of their written records of past incidents and the comments (*responsa*) of their predecessors. It was never codified, as were other areas of Roman law, but remained a priestly preserve, almost never giving rise to coercive legal action – coercion was left to the gods. The emperors, as members of all colleges, eventually inherited authority from the priests. [1: 100–102; 11: 195–200]

Izumo Taisha [XVI] Izumo grand shrine; the chief shrine outside the official mythology of the Yamato tribe. It is located in Shimane prefecture on the Japan Sea side (SHINTO SHRINES) [2: I, 79–81; 17: 326–53; 32: 6–7, 184–7]. It is dedicated to Okuninushi-no-mikoto, KAMI of fishing and sericulture, whose anti-Yamato hostility was mitigated by the gift of a palace and generous annual tribute, and who was traditionally given authority over the religious affairs of the country. Although rebuilt on a smaller scale after a sudden collapse in 1031, the shrine is still the largest in Japan. It has a high, raised floor, *taishazukuri* in style.

· J ·

Jahiliyya [XIV] ('time of ignorance, barbarism'), the name given in post-Islamic times to the period of mankind preceding the Prophet MUHAMMAD's mission and the proclamation of the new faith of ISLAM. Hence in the QUR'AN the Jahiliyya is contrasted, as an age of violence, lawlessness, and idolatry, with the enlightenment of Islam, the new ethical dispensation under the divine law, and the worship of one God. [10 'Ethics (pre-Islamic)'; 21 Djahiliyya'; 32 vol. I: 201–8; 37 vol. I: I]

Jains [XV] The Jain, or *Jaina*, religious tradition of India is derived from the ancient *jinas*, or 'those who overcome'; another name for the latter is TIRTHANKARAS. Although the tradition refers to 24 of these, the Jain community of India can be traced back to the life and work of Vardhamana, also called the MAHAVIRA (Great Hero), who is said to have been the most recent of the Tirthankaras. From eastern India (approximately modern Bihar), where the Mahavira lived, the Jain community migrated in the 3rd century BCE to Gujarat and Rajasthan in western India [3: 201]. Like the Buddhists, the Jains who were seriously dedicated to the quest for MOKSHA lived as ascetics, devoting their whole lives to the task. A division arose among them at the time of the migration on the matter of how far their austerities should go. One section held that no clothing at all should be worn, and these came to be known as *digambaras* (that is, 'sky-clad', or naked); those who disagreed on this point were known as the *shvetambaras*, or 'white-clad', from their plain white robes. In modern times even the former section

have taken to wearing robes in public, but the traditional division persists. Each developed its own corpus of literature, much of which was devoted to exposition of the theory of KARMA. The community has not spread outside India, but it has had a more or less uninterrupted history in India, unlike BUDDHISM. The Jains have maintained a strict vegetarianism in matters of diet, and the practice of AHIMSA, with which this is connected, is a cardinal doctrine. Mahatma Gandhi, himself from Gujarat, was influenced by their doctrine and practice. At the time of writing there are about 3¼ million Jains in India, and their numbers have been growing at a rate very slightly above the national average growth rate. [3 passim; 4]

Janam-Sakhis [XXVII] Hagiographic accounts of the life of Nanak (*see* GURUS) [23: II]. Beginning with stories of Nanak's childhood they take the reader through a narrative of early adulthood in the town of Sultanpur, extensive travels within and beyond India, and a final period of teaching back in the Punjab at Kartarpur. The characteristic form is the anecdote (*sakhi*), and most *janam-sakhis* comprise collections of anecdotes loosely organized in varying chronological patterns. These anecdotes follow earlier SUFI forms and it is evident that they circulated orally before being recorded. Some are simple borrowings from Hindu and Muslim sources. Others are the complex results of extended growth processes within the PANTH [24: V]. Wonder stories are prominent in all collections. Several manuscript *janam-sakhis* have survived from the mid 17th century onwards and these may be grouped as distinctive families or traditions [24: X]. The better-known are the *B40 Janam-sakhi*, the *Adi Sakhis*, and the *janam-sakhis* of the Puratan and Bala traditions. A different style is followed by the *Miharban Janam-sakhi*. This uses the narrative structure of the *janam-sakhi* form, but concentrates on exegesis of Nanak's works [24: III]. The language of most *janam-sakhi* is Punjabi (SIKH LANGUAGES). A late representative of the Bala tradition dominates the market in published *janam-sakhis*.

Jansenism [XI.B] A movement in ROMAN CATHOLICISM named after Cornelius Jansen (1585–1638 CE), Bishop of Ypres, who promoted St Augustine's (AUGUSTINIANISM) severe doctrines of God's grace (SALVATION). Their severe MORAL THEOLOGY was opposed to Jesuit casuistry (MONASTICISM). Condemned by the PAPACY in 1653 [11: 269] and 1713, its influence continued in moral severity and resistance (sometimes political) to papal authority. [22; 34; 102]

Japan, Buddhism in [XVI] Japan adopted Buddhism and used it to complement the native SHINTO religion [general: 8: 44–7; 11; 13; 15; 19: 46–69, 191–213; 24; 34]. The formal advent of Buddhism is recorded in the *Nihon Shoki* in 552 CE as the gift to Emperor Kimmei of some Buddhist objects from Paekche, the kingdom of south-west Korea [2: II, 65–7]. Other texts imply the year 538. The Soga family were willing to use the scriptures, banners, and one or more images, but they did so in the face of strong opposition from other leading families, especially the Mononobe, the professional Shinto priests, and a plague was attributed to the anger of local gods. But since Buddhism was associated with literacy and other cultural advances, it proved irresistible. In a family power struggle the Soga destroyed the Mononobe in a battle of 587, securing the future of Buddhism. Emperor Yomei (r. 586–7)

was the first ruler to profess Buddhism (JAPANESE BUDDHAS AND BODHISATTVAS).

Major strides were made under Crown Prince SHOTOKU [2: II, 122–48; 23]. Architects, tile-makers, bronze-casters, and sculptors were invited to build and decorate temples. Koreans taught the Japanese to read the Chinese *sutras* (scriptures) (CHINESE BUDDHISM), making Chinese the basis for all Buddhist terminology, the Japanese using phonetic equivalents in most cases. The prince analysed the *sutras* and propagated their moralistic content. As additional *sutras* were introduced, 'schools' of studies (NANTO ROKUSHU) formed, such as Jojitsu, Sanron, and Kusha. By the 8th century, the Hosso, Kegon, and Ritsu schools had assumed sectarian characteristics [11]. Archaeologists and historians have identified the existence of about 900 temples by the end of the 8th century, including the provincial temples ordered in the 66 provinces by Emperor SHOMU in 741, an edict which had the effect of making Buddhism the state religion. The temples of the Nara capital (710–84) accumulated such formidable wealth and power, dominating national policy, that the Emperor KAMMU moved the capital to another location, thereby greatly changing the course of Buddhist history.

Non-exclusiveness is typical of Japanese religion, the pluralistic nature of thought allowing borrowing, mixing, and rationalization (SYNCRETISM). Even today it is not clear whether some deities are Shinto or Buddhist. This was more and more apparent once the intellectualized, abstruse 9th-century esoteric sects were brought in, both TENDAI and SHINGON having much beyond the reach of the ordinary man [37]. Tendai, however, proclaimed the Buddha-nature of the individual and had a versatile appeal, while Shingon joined forces with traditional Shinto holy spots (RYOBU-SHINTO), introducing

Buddhism to rural areas and rural people to additional mystical ceremonies [29: 54–61]. An increasing overlap of Buddhist and Shinto ideas and practices indigenized Buddhism, without which it may never have been more than a religion of the educated and the upper classes. Buddhism became responsible for the affairs of the dead, and AMIDA WORSHIP in Tendai spread widely to dominate the 10th to 12th centuries, offering the Fujiwara aristocracy the 'Easy Path'. The Pure Land sect with its teaching of an assured afterlife of eternal bliss was popularized by writers and street preachers in the Kamakura period (1185–1333) [29: 61–7]. ZEN was acceptable to both the ruling class and the samurai (warriors) from the 13th century, the northern and southern Chinese versions represented in the Japanese Rinzai and Soto. Stressing sudden enlightenment and meditative discipline, they attracted upper and lower social levels [36]. The impact of Zen was far-reaching. It helped to produce a strong warrior class which based its principles on Zen discipline and Confucian concepts of loyalty (CONFUCIUS) and abetted 200 years of civil war, finally resolved by the Tokugawa family ascendancy in the 17th century. These same principles were used to stratify the society as a device to stay in power, while the shoguns supported selected temples and sects.

The most difficult period for Buddhism was in the early Meiji era (1868–1912) when the clergy was regarded as a deterrent to the modernizing process and Shinto was manipulated for nationalistic ends [17: 49–52]. Temples were destroyed and many priests forced out. Some priests voluntarily converted to become officials at Shinto shrines, as many were ordained in both religions. Relief came around 1877 with more even-handed treatment.

Despite extreme fragmentation today into sects and smaller associations, Buddhism and its temples now enjoy the affluence of the Japanese economy. Some thrive exclusively on the financial benefits of legislated Buddhist funerals. Those with historical treasures, where 'donations' are required at the entrance, have a new-found wealth and the political power which goes with it.

Japan, Christianity in [XVI] St Francis Xavier arrived in Kagoshima in 1549 and many converts were made to Catholicism before the missionaries were abruptly ordered out in 1587 [19: 71–87, 215–23; 26]. Persecutions started in 1597 and the exclusion policy almost succeeded in eliminating Christianity, the exception being the 'hidden' groups on Kyushu island. The first Protestants (PROTESTANTISM) arrived in 1859, a few years after the country was opened again to Western contacts by Commodore Perry in 1854 [7; 12; 20]. Traditional Christian denominations were represented, and were noted especially for supporting many schools, universities, and hospitals. Just prior to the Second World War, in order to centralize control, the government obliged more than 30 denominations to unite in an organization called the Nihon Kirisuto Kyodan (United Church of Christ in Japan). It still exists, but many denominations and groups do not belong to it. Christians in Japan tend to come from the educated classes. Less than 1 per cent of the population is Christian.

Japanese Buddhas and Bodhisattvas [XVI] Japanese Buddhist terms were taken from Chinese or the original Sanskrit (i.e. Buddha = *butsu*; bodhisattva = *bosatsu*) [general: 8; 13; 15; 19: 47–69, 191–213; 24; 34]. Shakyamuni is the first recognized BUDDHA, the oldest Japanese image being one of 606 CE. THERAVADA JATAKA stories appeared only briefly before 650. By the 9th century the importance of Shaka had been eclipsed by esoteric introductions and TENDAI's interest in Yakushi (*Bhaishajya-guru-vaidurya-prabhasa*) and Amida (Amitabha) (AMIDA WORSHIP), but Shaka worship was temporarily revived by NICHIREN [1] in the 13th century. Yakushi assumed early popularity as a healer and by the 8th century came to be the eastern earthly counterpart of the western, distant Amida [11]. The Hosso sect (NANTO ROKUSHU) promoted the worship of four Buddhas: Shaka, Yakushi, Amida, and Miroku (MAITREYA), the latter coming into Japan as a BODHISATTVA and identified with Prince SHOTOKU as a reincarnated Siddhartha. Yakushi almost disappeared from public interest after the 13th century under the growing impact of Amidism and ZEN. Except for some revived popularity around the time of Mappo in the 11th century, Miroku slipped into oblivion in later centuries. The monumental images in the large 8th-century temples are of Roshana (or Birushana; Sanskrit *Vairocana*), the universal symbol of light, but this Buddha is better known in its more Japanized esoteric form as Dainichi Nyorai (The Great Illuminator Buddha). In SHINGON he is accompanied by a host of esoteric Buddhas and the Godaimyo-o (Five *Vidyarajas*, Great Kings), the chief of which is Fudo (*Acala*) [37].

Sho Kannon, from the Chinese KUAN-YIN (AVALOKITES-VARA), a Bodhisattva of Amida, is known in eight fundamental forms, for instance, the Thousand-armed (*Senju*), Eleven-headed (*Juichimen*), and Horse-headed (*Bato*). Now referred to in English as the Goddess of Mercy, the feminization of Kannon is relatively modern in Japan. Classified with Kannon is Jizo (*Kshitigarbha*), represented as a monk with shaved head, often in a row of six (*Rokujizo*) for six classes of creation. He is still popular today as the patron saint of children, expectant mothers, and travellers (JAPAN, BUDDHISM IN).

Jataka [IX.A] Buddhist collections of stories which are held to refer to earlier existences of the BUDDHA. Each narrative consists of verses and a prose narrative; only the former were held to be canonical. The number of stories in the collection varies from one Buddhist country to another. The oldest and most complete collection has 547 stories [14: VII]. The legendary style and content of the stories differs considerably from that of the teaching of the Buddha contained in other Buddhist texts, especially of the THERAVADA. Attempts at critical comparison of the materials found in the *Jatakas* with that of other texts are now in their early stages. [14]

Javanese Religion [XXII] The religion of Java (an island of Indonesia) is officially ISLAM (Sunni (SUNNA), Shafi'ite school), but traces of the earlier Hinduism and Buddhism are detectable, together with indigenous features relating to agriculture and local spirits. Solid reminders of the Indian era of Javanese religious history are the stone monuments of central Java (8th/9th century), notably Borobudur (a massive, multi-tiered STUPA, MAHAYANA Buddhist) and the group of three temples at Prambanan (dedicated to the Hindu triad of BRAHMA–VISHNU–SHIVA), on which are portrayed countless scenes from the life of the BUDDHA and the epic of RAMA (*Ramayana*) respectively [5]. Before Islam caused the fall of the Majapahit empire of Java in the 16th century, Shiva and the Buddha were worshipped side by side, or even jointly, as Bhairava Buddha [26]. The Hindu deities LAKSHMI and Vishnu survive as Sri and Sadono in fertility ceremonies for rice cultivation [1]. Central to Javanese religion is a simple communal feast held on such occasions as birth, circumcision, and marriage, known as the *slametan*. Its aim is community solidarity (*slamet*, from Arabic *salam*, 'peace'); there is Islamic prayer to ALLAH, but also the belief that the incense and the food aid in placating spirits. The *dukun* is a functionary practising healing, divination, and sorcery [13]. Mysticism is widespread, sometimes SUFI, sometimes Javanese (and owing much to the Hindu–Buddhist past). [26]

Jehovah's Witnesses [XI.B] Charles Taze Russell (1852–1916 CE) of Pittsburgh (U.S.A.) founded this MILLENARIAN movement or SECT. He was succeeded by Joseph Franklin ('Judge') Rutherford (1869–1941). Witnesses interpret the BIBLE literally, reject the TRINITY and understand JESUS CHRIST in ARIAN fashion. The millennium has begun and a final battle (Armageddon) is imminent, after which the Witnesses will rule with Christ. Other churches are rejected as ruled by Satan. Refusal of military service and hostility to earthly institutions has led to clashes with governments. Witnesses live plainly, refusing stimulants and blood transfusions. They are active propagators of their faith, publishing the *Watchtower* magazine. [98: 341–7; 114; 125]

Jerusalem, Early Christianity at [XI.A] Although Jesus made many DISCIPLES in Galilee, the first Christian CHURCH was formed in Jerusalem, seven weeks after his death. It speedily numbered some thousands, and met in several groups, some led by APOSTLES, others by Jesus' relatives, especially his brother James. Other groups, comprising Hellenists, renounced the TEMPLE order and, being soon forced to leave Jerusalem, promoted Christian advance in neighbouring provinces. The Jerusalem church became increasingly conservative. Demoralized by the execution of James in 62 CE, it left Jerusalem before the Roman siege eight years later. [3: 195–215, 349–72]

Jerusalem (in Islam) [XIV] To Muslims, this is the third most sacred city, after Mecca and Medina (*see* HARAMAIN). Occupied by the Arab armies in the time of the second CALIPH 'Umar (634–44), it was considered by the Muslims as holy because of the traditional interpretation of *sura* XVII, 1, in the QUR'AN, which speaks of the Prophet MUHAMMAD's night-journey (*mi'raj, isra'*), in the company of an angelic visitant, to 'the farthest place of prostration'. This became identified with the

site of Solomon's temple in Jerusalem, certainly during the rule of the caliph 'Abd al-Malik (685–705), who in 691 built the Dome of the Rock on the site and seems, perhaps for political reasons, to have encouraged pilgrimage (HAJJ) to Jerusalem in addition to that to the Haramain. Muhammad probably followed Jewish practice in making Jerusalem the direction of prayer (*qibla*) in the first year or so after the migration from Mecca to Medina, before the Ka'ba at Mecca was made the devotional focus of the Islamic faith. Over the centuries Jerusalem has remained a place of veneration for Muslims, above all for those of the Syro-Palestinian region. [19; 21 'al-Ḳuds']

Jerusalem (in Judaism) [XVII] City in the Judaean hills and capital of the state of ISRAEL. Jerusalem became the centre of Israelite religion after its conquest from the Jebusites by King David (11th/10th centuries BCE) (BIBLICAL HISTORY) and the building of the first TEMPLE there by his son Solomon. During the brief Babylonian captivity (6th century BCE) the holy city of Jerusalem was at the forefront of the captives' thoughts ('If I forget you, O Jerusalem . . .' – Psalm 137: 3–6). The revolt against Rome of 67–70 CE ended with the destruction of Jerusalem by the besieging Roman army [31: XXXII]. In the Middle Ages, under Christian and Muslim rule, the Jewish population of the city was small, but for the Jews of the Diaspora it remained the holy city towards which all Jews turned in prayer (HOLY LAND). After the war of 1948 the old city of Jerusalem was in Arab hands, the new and old sections only being united after the 1967 war. [9 vol. 9: 1378]

Jesus Christ [XI.A] The founder of CHRISTIANITY, who was born in Bethlehem about 5 BCE and lived in Nazareth (Galilee) until 27 CE, when his public career began with his BAPTISM by JOHN THE BAPTIST. After John's imprisonment Jesus proclaimed in Galilee the imminence of the kingdom of GOD.

This new order, that he and his followers held to have been foretold in Hebrew PROPHECY, took its character from the God whose kingdom it was. Jesus presented him pre-eminently as Father, and urged his hearers to promote God's will above all else and trust him to supply their daily needs. God's kingdom involved a reversal of accepted values: humble service was true honour and the poor and meek were most worthy of congratulation. (PARABLES)

Jesus' preaching was accompanied by a healing ministry, including especially the exorcizing of demons (DEMONOLOGY). He gathered many DISCIPLES; from them he selected 12 APOSTLES to share his ministry.

After a year's activity in Galilee, he came south to Judaea, to offer JERUSALEM also the way of peace, without which it would experience total disaster. Despite this pacific emphasis, the authorities feared that he would precipitate a revolt against Rome. He was arrested during Passover week, 30 CE, and sentenced to crucifixion by Pilate, Roman governor of Judaea. Shortly afterwards his followers proclaimed that he had risen from the dead and appeared to them alive.

They generally identified him with the expected 'Son of David' – the MESSIAH (anointed one) or Christ. There is no record that he himself claimed Davidic descent. He preferred to speak of himself as the 'son of Man' – a title not in current use and capable therefore of being filled with the meaning he chose to put into it. After his death and resurrection belief in his divine authority and exaltation was expressed in the titles 'Lord' and 'Son of God'. In his ministry and death he was believed to have embodied the figure of the Servant of the Lord in the Book of Isaiah. The designation 'Lamb of God' conveyed the redeeming efficacy of his death, with an allusion to the sacrificing of the Passover lamb by Israel in Egypt. [3: 155–94; 7; 8; 19]

Jesus Movement [XXI] The Jesus Movement, or 'Jesus Revolution', is an umbrella term used to describe the large number of conservative EVANGELICAL Christian groups that emerged in the late 1960s and spread throughout North America and Europe during the 1970s [2: 1; 36]. The term 'Jesus freaks' [8: II] was used to describe the members of these groups who, partly in reaction to the counterculture of the 1960s, publicly displayed their 'rediscovery' of Jesus with Jesus posters, Jesus bumper stickers, and 'Jesus Loves Me' sweatshirts. Much of the movement was contained within the more Evangelical or PENTECOSTAL branches of traditional Christianity, but several new groups and communities were formed, some of these being viewed with utmost suspicion as dangerous heresies by more orthodox Christians [11; 12] and the ANTI-CULT MOVEMENT (e.g. the CHILDREN OF GOD). One of the original movements, which was militantly active in California, was the Christian World Liberation Front (CWLF) [14: VII]. Associated by some with the general trend were other movements such as the Catholic Charismatic Renewal [14: VIII] and the Jews for Jesus, a movement which, through the Christianization of Jewish youth, has caused some concern among orthodox Jewry [14: XII].

Jihad [XIV] (literally 'struggle') The term used in ISLAM for 'holy war', warfare against unbelievers, the underlying idea being that, since Islam is a universal religion, force may be used to expand its borders. *Jihad* ceases when DHIMMIS agree to accept the political authority of Islam, but continues against idolaters till they submit. It is a duty incumbent on all Muslims, hence usually considered as one of the PILLARS OF ISLAM. Increasingly, *jihad* has also been interpreted as warfare for the defence of Islam or else (especially in SUFISM) as a spiritual struggle against the evil in oneself. [10 s.v.; 21 'Djihād'; 60; 83: V]

Jingi-kan [XVI] The 'Office of Divine Affairs', first set up after the Taika Reform (646 CE), later defunct, and revived in 1871 by Emperor Meiji in order to control the SHINTO SHRINES and their property, which was then placed under national, prefectural, or local jurisdiction [8: 27–32]. Priests were appointed as government officials, the emperor the official head of the Shinto state (KOKUTAI SHINTO). Short but violent suppression of BUDDHISM between 1868 and 1872 through a movement called Haibutsu Kishaku ('Throw out the Buddhas'), brought strong reaction, and resulted in a new bureau (1877) to accommodate both SHINTO and Buddhism. After the Second World War the Japanese constitution separated Shinto from the state and enforced the principle of religious freedom, a clause which was actually written into the constitution of 1889 [17: 48–52].

Jingu-ji [XVI] Japanese shrine-temples. Variously called *jingan-ji*, *jingo-ji*, *jinkyo-ji*, *jingu-in*, these were Buddhist temples, usually of either the TENDAI or the SHINGON sect, built to protect SHINTO SHRINES [18: 37–8; 33: 305] where Buddhist priests could chant *sutras* to enlighten the KAMI [19: 18]. They were often built within the precincts of the shrine itself. Their deities were mountain-spirits (*gongen*), their priests called *shaso* (shrine-priests). The oldest dated *jingu-ji* was built at Ise (ISE JINGU) in 698, the home of Shinto. Once accepted there, hundreds were built elsewhere. By the 9th century they were ranked in importance just below the provincial temples, for imperial favours. None is recorded as being built after 1627 and all were destroyed or renamed in the Meiji period (1868–1912) because it was thought that they disgraced the concept of the original *kami* of Japan.

Jinn (sing. *jinni*, English *genie*) [XIV] In Islam, spirit-beings originally created from fire. According to official doctrine, going back to the QUR'AN, they form an intermediate creation between mankind and the angels. They may be believers in Islam or unbelievers; the latter are therefore demons (*see* SATAN (IN ISLAM)). King Solomon is regarded as having commanded cohorts of *jinn* to build the Temple. Classical Islamic law defined the status of the *jinn* and even considered the question of intermarriage between humans and *jinn*. In popular lore, they represent the untamed spirits of wild and desert places, normally invisible but capable of assuming corporeal form as men or animals, and are associated with the practice of magic and the service of talismanic formulae. [10 s.v.; 21 'Djinn'; 29: 50; 39 'Genii'; 45: X; 53; 64: 41–2]

Jnana Yoga [XIII.B] The way of knowledge: one of three or four alternative routes of spiritual development (YOGA) widely recognized in Indian thought. New ways of understanding human experience are intended to bring about some kind of transformation of fundamental motivation. Most of the Hindu DARSHANAS as well as the more wisdom-oriented forms of Buddhism would come into this category. Usually other forms of *yoga* would have an auxiliary role. [4: 101–4; 18: 143–5]

John the Baptist [XI.A], who figures in the New Testament (BIBLE) as precursor of JESUS CHRIST (whom he baptized), was a religious leader in his own right. Born into a humble priestly family about 5 BCE, he was brought up in the Judaean wilderness. There, about 27 CE, he launched his preaching campaign, calling for national repentance and simple living because of the imminent arrival of the 'Coming One' to execute divine judgement on Israel. His many hearers recognized him as a prophet; he urged them to be baptized in the Jordan and thus form a new community 'prepared for the Lord'. His popularity excited the suspicion of Herod Antipas, tetrarch of Galilee and Peraea, who had him imprisoned and later put to death. His DISCIPLES survived as a distinct group for several decades. [3: 145–54]

Jok [II] (*Juok*) is the ancient NILOTIC name at once for God, for spirit, and for spirits. Its use developed differently among the various Nilotic peoples. For some it has retained a monotheistic sense, as with the SHILLUK. With others, a basic monotheism has remained, but God is generally now known by another name: Nhialic (DINKA), Were or Nyasaye (southern Luo). *Jok* has in these cases retained rather its generic sense: spirit. The central Nilotic peoples (Acholi and Lango), conversely, continue to use the word *Jok*, but either lost or never had the strong monotheism characteristic of the NUER to the north and the Luo to the south. For them *Jok* refers only to a multiplicity of very limited and localized spirits, ancestral or otherwise, without any sense of unity or a pre-existing *Jok* (creator). Among the Nuer, Dinka, Padhola, too, evidence suggests a tendency away from the one creator towards 'spirits', though not comparably with Lango or Acholi. [4: 154–7; 11: 122–4; 39]

Jon Frum [xx] A diffused CARGO CULT on Tanna and adjacent islands in the New Hebrides (now Vanuatu) appearing intermittently since 1940. It focused on a mysterious Jon Frum, sometimes identified as the god of Tanna's highest mountain, or (owing to contact with U.S. troops) as the 'king of America', whence the cargo would come. The movement restored traditional customs, was anti-white and anti-mission (Presbyterian), in frequent conflict with the government, and was still active at independence in 1980. [12: 171; 19: 322–6; 20]

Jonang [XXIX] The Jonang tradition of Tibetan Buddhism was founded by Dolpopa Sherab Gyaltsen (1292–1361), a philosopher who propagated the controversial doctrine known as 'empty of any other' (Tibetan *zhen tong*). Dolpopa was especially influenced by the notion of the 'BUDDHA-nature' (Sanskrit *tathagatagarbha*, Tibetan *desheg nyingpo*) inherent in all sentient beings, which is elaborated in the *Uttaratantrashastra*, a philosophical work attributed to MAITREYA. According to Dolpopa's theory, the *Prasangika* MADHYAMIKA view that the true nature of reality is itself empty (*rang tong*), being neither existent nor non-existent, is only correct at the level of relative truth. In ultimate truth the nature of reality is empty of anything apart from itself (*zhen tong*) and may therefore be described as ultimately existent. [16]

The Jonang tradition was proscribed in the 17th century CE by the GELUG authorities, but their doctrines have been maintained by certain scholars of the KAGYU, SAKYA, and NYINGMA schools.

Josephus [XVII] A 1st-century CE Jewish historian, Josephus Flavius was commander of the Jewish rebels in Galilee during the war against Rome, 67–70 CE. He defected to the Romans when he became disillusioned with Zealot ideology. He wrote a detailed account of the war in *The Jewish War*; an autobiographical sketch; a history of the Jews, *Jewish Antiquities*; and a work of Jewish apologetics, *Against Apion* [13: 52]. Josephus' writings were preserved by the Christian church. [9 vol. 10: 251]

Judaism [XVII] The religion of the Jewish people in the period following the destruction of the second TEMPLE in 70 CE, to be distinguished from the religion of the biblical and late second Temple periods which centred round the sacrificial cult (BIBLICAL HISTORY). The form which the religion of the Jews took in the era after 70 CE differed substantially in its ritual from that of the BIBLE. The basis of the new religious institutions developed by the councils of sages held first in Yavneh (70–132 CE) and then in Usha (post-140 CE) was the outlook of the PHARISEES [11: 1–XII]. The shift in emphasis from Temple cult to a religion of the home and

SYNAGOGUE is characteristic of these councils. The role of the priest virtually disappeared and the religion became almost totally laicized – the RABBI being a teacher and authority on the HALAKHAH. The main ideas are of a teaching of divine origin, TORAH, contained in the Pentateuch and developed in the other books of the Hebrew BIBLE, which is accompanied by an oral teaching explaining the texts. This oral teaching is open to growth through biblical exegesis and MIDRASH. The commandments of God (MITZVAH) contained in Torah determine Jewish norms, and extend into every facet of the life of the individual and the community (KEHILLAH) [13: XI; 52: VIII–XII]. The belief in one god (THEISM) who will send a MESSIAH to usher in the redemption, who judges man's actions, and who rewards and punishes man are integral themes of Jewish belief [9 vol. 10: 383]. In the 19th century reform movements sought to modify some of the beliefs and practices of traditional Judaism, which led to the setting up of REFORM and CONSERVATIVE Judaism as separate religious movements.

Juggernaut [XIII.A] The English pronunciation of Jagan-natha, meaning 'protector of the world', the name of a Hindu deity who is equated with VISHNU, and whose temple is at Puri, in eastern India. It is famous for its annual festival, when the *murti*, or 'material form' of Jagan-natha, is taken in procession in a huge carriage through the streets, and over-enthusiastic pilgrims have been known to be crushed beneath the wheels.

Junrei [XVI] Medieval Japanese pilgrimages. Pilgrimages from Kyoto to Nara, the 'southern capital' (JAPAN, BUDDHISM IN), increased in popularity through the Mappo (End of the Law) period (1052 for Japan) and into the 13th century, as both SHINTO and Buddhist holy spots were visited, in particular the shrines at Kumano and the Nachi waterfalls and, later, Ise shrine (ISE JINGU; SHINTO SHRINES). A contemporary writer said the roads were so thick with people they looked like ants. Internal peace in the Edo period (1615–1868) encouraged a revival of the practice, especially visits to the Kobo Daishi-related (KUKAI) 88 temples of Shikoku, which required about two months, the 33 Kannon temples of the Kansai, and other routes. The physical effort was thought to induce communion with the BUDDHA, cures were sought, and even death on the trip was considered desirable for the aged. Buses and cars are used today.

· K ·

Kabbalah [XVII] The 'received tradition' of Jewish mysticism, particularly those forms of mystical teachings which were developed in the Middle Ages in south-west Europe, and later on in the Galilean city of Safed in Palestine [9 vol. 10: 489]. The main text of the Kabbalah is the ZOHAR, written down in 13th-century Spain [45: v]. Unlike exoteric Judaism the Kabbalah teaches that the creation of the world took place through a series of emanations from the Godhead or Ein Sof (COSMOGONY). These emanatory structures, the 10 *sefirot* (SEFIRAH), are the inner constitution of all reality as well as of the divine manifestation. They represent a finely balanced harmony enabling the flow of divine energy to sustain man and nature. Man's sins affect this harmony, disturbing it and allowing the potential for evil within it to become active. The Kabbalah reinterprets all the main beliefs and rituals of JUDAISM in terms of its esoteric theology, which has pantheistic overtones. Its powerful images appealed to mystics and non-mystics alike. The most important development of Zoharic ideas was the Kabbalah of Isaac Luria (1534–72), which introduced a strong messianic (MESSIAH) element, and led to messianic movements of a mystical type. (*See also* SITRA ACHRA.) [45: VII, VIII; 46: 37; 52: VI]

Kachinas [III] Among PUEBLO Indians of the North American south-west, *kachinas* serve as the symbolic representations, often in human form, of the many powers and manifestations of nature and of the ancestors [3]. Myths relate that, in primordial times, man-

kind and the *kachinas* lived together, the latter freely bestowing their blessing of rain and general prosperity. Now, through the agency of human impersonators who dress and don masks to represent them, the *kachinas* return for part of the year to serve as intermediaries between man and the principal Pueblo deities [25: III]. The HOPI and the Zuni tribes have the greatest number of distant *kachinas*, who appear at specific annual celebrations.

Kadam [XXIX] The Kadam tradition of Tibetan Buddhism originated in the 11th century CE from the teachings of the Indian master Atisha (979–1053) and his Tibetan disciple Dromton (1005–64) [3]. During his residence in Tibet from 1040 till his death in 1053 Atisha emphasized the practice of *sutra* and TANTRA doctrines in a 'graded path' (*lam rim*) and transmitted a series of instructions on *bodhicitta* ('thought of enlightenment') known as 'mind-training' (*lobjong*). Although the Kadam sect ceased to exist after the 14th century these teachings have been preserved within the GELUG and KAGYU schools.

Kagyu [XXIX] The Kagyu (more correctly, Dagpo Kagyu) tradition of Tibetan Buddhism was established in the 11th and 12th centuries CE by the three successive masters, Marpa the translator (1012–97), who studied TANTRA (2) in India; his student, Milarepa (1040–1123) [12]; and the latter's disciple Gampopa (1079–1153), who was heir both to Marpa and Milarepa's lineage and also to the *sutra* teaching of the KADAM lineage. [17] After Gampopa's death the tradition split into four principal branches, Karmapa, Baram, Tshalpa, and

Phagmo Drupa, from the last of which eight subsects subsequently emerged. Under the leadership of the 16 incarnations of the Karmapa Lama the Karma Kagyu branch has been the most extensive of the four chief lines. [21]

The most prized teaching of all the various Kagyu sects is the system of theory and meditation known as 'the great seal' (Sanskrit *mahamudra*, Tibetan *chag chen*), which Marpa received from his Indian GURUS Naropa and Maitripa. The term 'great seal' is derived from the TANTRAS and refers to the meditative realization that the world of appearances and mind itself are inseparable and naturally empty. Thus all phenomena of SAMSARA and NIRVANA are 'sealed' with emptiness. [2]

Although the Kagyu tradition is especially famed for its emphasis on devotion and meditation, it has also produced talented scholars such as the eighth Karmapa, Mikyo Dorje (1507–54), and Jamgon Kongtrul (1811–99), both of whom upheld the theory of 'the great middle' (Tibetan *uma chenpo*), which represents a synthesis of the MADHYAMIKA and YOGACARA philosophies.

In recent years the Karma Kagyu sect, under the direction of the 16th Karmapa, Ranjung Rigpe Dorje, has established numerous centres in the United Kingdom, France, and North America.

Kakon [XII] (Greek: 'evil') Death is an inescapable evil, part of the human condition. But other evils, disease, painful old age, harsh toil, etc., it was thought, might have been avoided. One version of their origin tells of five successive 'races' of generally deteriorating merit and circumstances, the last one being 'our own'. In another version a quarrel between Zeus (THEOI) and Prometheus (THNETOI ANTHROPOI), who tried to cheat the gods on behalf of mankind, resulted in the estrangement between men and the gods. The latter created the first woman, Pandora, who brought evil

to men just by her presence. In another version Pandora opened a jar and released diseases and banes upon the world. In Orphism (ORPHEUS), mankind sprang from the Titans' ashes and carries the guilt of the Titans' murder of Dionysos–Zagreus, for which it must atone. [12: 131–43]

Kalam [XIV] The medieval Islamic term for scholastic and apologetic theology, literally meaning 'discourse' but early acquiring the sense of 'disputation, controversy'. The defence of the faith by rational arguments, the stilling of believers' doubts, and the strengthening of their belief were thus the aims of what became a highly sophisticated dialectical system employed, for example, against the Mu'tazilites (*fl.* later 8th–10th centuries), the conservative literalists, and the Hellenizing philosophers. Two main schools of *kalam*, the Ash'ari and the Maturidi, emerged from the 10th century onwards [43: 375–515]. In recent times, its *raison d'être* has virtually disappeared, and Islamic modernists have tended to be practical men and reformers rather than apologetic theologians. [21 s.v.; 52: 153–242; 61: V]

Kali [XIII.A] 'The black one'; the name of a Hindu goddess, a form of DURGA, whose cult is particularly popular in eastern India. She is represented as fierce and bloodthirsty, the destroyer of evil, but is also venerated as the Mother. [6B: 86–8]

Kama [XIII.A] The name of the Hindu god of love [2: 317f], and also, together with ARTHA, DHARMA, and MOKSHA, one of the four goals of life in Hindu tradition. Kama represents 'the pursuit of love of pleasure' [1: 258], both sensual and aesthetic. It relates closely to the way of life (ASHRAMA) of the married householder. Provision is therefore made 'for its regulated enjoyment, rather than its suppression, and thus for the development of a well-rounded personality' [1: 258]. The texts in which the necessary guidance and techniques are set out are the *Kama-Shastra*, and *Kama-*

Sutra of Vatsyayana, the latter written in the early centuries of the Christian era [2: 172]. These are represented as having been originally promulgated by the gods and sages, long ago, as part of a 'comprehensive code of conduct'. A close relationship between cosmic creation (envisaged in terms of the union of gods and goddesses) and human procreation is characteristic of Hindu religious ideas. The importance of sexual activity and erotic technique for the satisfaction of both husband and wife is the basis of the classical texts.

Kami [XVI] SHINTO deities. Sacred objects, divine beings, natural phenomena or venerated symbols [13: 5–6; 17: 441–514; 30: 6–9], the *kami* are described as having a parent–child (*oya-ko*) relationship to people or, better, an ancestor–descendant relationship [19: 14–15]. Eighteenth-century writers were the first to attempt a definition: Motoori Norinaga (1730–1801) said that they were extraordinary, endowed with high virtuosity, and inspired awe [19: 37–8]. While omnipresent in nature, associated in particular with specific mountains (SACRED MOUNTAINS), rocks, waterfalls, and other features, they are not all-powerful nor are they all benign.

The *kami* have been classified as *amatsu-kami* and *kunitsu-kami*, celestial spirits which remain eternal and above, and terrestrial spirits which dispense benefactions to, or discipline, people on earth. They are variously said to have nomadic and agricultural sources, or Yamato tribal and Izumo tribal origins. But the classification copes with only the small number – traditionally, there are 8 million – which have been identified by name and with specific activities and human needs. The chief *kami* is AMATERASU-OMIKAMI, the sun-goddess, enshrined at ISE JINGU. Historical conditions have continued to produce more *kami*, such as deified statesmen and military figures and, since the Meiji period (1868–1912), all

the soldiers killed in wars are now buried at Yasukuni shrine in Tokyo and referred to as *kami* [17: 441–59].

Kamma-tthana [IX.B] In THERA-VADA Buddhist meditation practice (BHAVANA) *kamma-tthana*, originally an occupation such as trade or agriculture, may mean either the particular mental object which is the subject of practice or a given meditational path. In the first sense BUDDHAGHOSA lists 40 *kamma-tthana* for SAMATHA meditation practice, classified according to their potential for development and their suitability for differing psychological types [45: 116–21; 64: 29–30]. Similar notions are found in North Indian Buddhist writings; the *Abhidharma-kosha*, for example, recommends developing awareness of ugliness for the passionate, loving-kindness (*maitri*; Pali *metta*) for the aggressive, and mindfulness of breath for the thought-ridden.

Kammu [XVI] The Emperor Kammu (736–806 CE) was Prince Yamabe, the first son of Emperor Konin, who ascended the Japanese throne in 781 and moved the capital to break the power of the Nara clergy (JAPAN, BUDDHISM IN) [21: 40–41]. As the last of the strong early emperors, he cut the income of the temples, defrocked and disciplined many priests, and built new cities, first Nagaoka in 784, then Heian (Kyoto) in 794, obliging the temples to remain behind. Kammu was head of the Confucian academy (CONFUCIUS) and supported the Buddhist temples of his choice, sending SAICHO and KUKAI to China. He successfully concluded the century-old war with the ancient, non-Japanese people, the Emishi (now called Ainu) in north Japan.

Kanjur [XXIX] The Tibetan canonical collection of the teachings of BUDDHA, numbering 108 volumes and arranged and edited by the historian Buton (1290–1364). It contains the three *pitakas* of *sutra*, *abhidharma* (ABHIDHAMMA) and VINAYA as well as various TANTRAS (2) revealed by Buddha. The *sutra-pitaka* (SUTTA-PITAKA) includes both HINAYANA and MAHAYANA discourses.

The tantric collection preserved in the Kanjur only includes the 'new' *tantras* diffused in Tibet from the 10th century onwards. The 'old' *tantras* of the Nyingmapa (NYINGMA) tradition are collected in the series known as *The One Hundred Thousand Tantras of the Old Tradition*, edited by Jigme Lingpa (1729–97). The companion collection to the *Kanjur* is the *Tenjur*, a collection of 225 volumes of treatises and commentaries composed by various Indian masters.

Karah Prasad [XXVII] The 'sacramental' food distributed in GURDWARAS and at the conclusion of important Sikh RITUALS. The food (*prasad*), which should be prepared in a large iron pan (*karah*), comprises equal parts of coarsely refined wheat-flour, sugar, and ghee [13: XII]. The procedure to be followed in preparing it is detailed in *Sikh Rahit Maryada*, the current version of the KHALSA code (RAHIT-NAMA). [4: 173–4; 17: 7–8] When distributed it must be offered to all, regardless of caste, creed, or status. [23: 67–8, 86–7]

Karma [XIII.A] In Indian tradition *karma* means primarily action, work, or deed. In its secondary sense it signifies the 'effect' of an action, or the sum total of the 'effects' of past actions. Thus, it is stated in the *Chandogya Upanishad* (VEDA) that those whose past deeds have been good will after death be reborn from the womb of a Brahman woman, whereas those whose deeds have been evil from the womb of an outcaste woman (CASTE). According to the Veda, sacred acts, or religious rites, are productive of good effects, and the result can be in accordance with the intention with which the rite (such as sacrifice) was performed. [25: 77] Regarded as a 'law' of the universe, the notion of *karma*, especially with reference to rebirth, is specially characteristic of Indian culture. However, although it is

a Brahmanical doctrine (BRAHMANS), it cannot necessarily be regarded as universally accepted among Hindus (HINDUISM) of all classes, especially as an explanation of present low social status. Alternative explanations range from the ancient Buddhist denial of the 'Brahman-by-birth' to the many modern examples of anti-Brahman movements which explain Brahmanical claims to superiority as historical fiction. [1: 244–5]

Karma (**Jain Doctrine**) [XV] Among the JAINS the KARMA theory, found in almost all Indian religious thought, has certain features which are peculiar to this tradition. Even in terms of the literature devoted to it, the Jain version of the theory is outstanding: the Shvetambara school have a large number of *Karmagrantha* or sacred texts devoted to *karma*, and the Digambara school have 38 volumes in their *Shatkhandagama*, *Kashaya-prabhrta*, and commentaries. Four aspects of *karma* are dealt with: influx, bondage, duration, and fruition. The fundamental difference between the Jain and the BRAHMAN theories of *karma* is that whereas the latter hold that the soul cannot change, the Jain view is that the soul (or *jiva*, literally, 'a life') can expand, contract, and move into various shapes [2: 220]. It was on this point that 'the model of a karmically ordered universe, in which the soul's position could be improved or worsened by action' [1: 228f] prevailed over the fatalistic and deterministic doctrine of another ancient Indian school contemporary with the Jains, i.e. the AJIVAKA. The Jain theory was that the effect of action (*karma*) was to 'engross' the soul, that is, make it thick, or heavy. From this it followed that release (MOKSHA) from the round of rebirth is achieved by the slow and difficult practice of a life of austerity in order to dispel such karmic grossness as had already surrounded the soul, and to prevent the addition of any new karmic grossness. [1: 293f; 3: 201]

Karma Yoga [XIII.B] The way of action: one of three or four alternative routes of spiritual development (YOGA) widely recognized in Indian thought. The word *karma* means originally sacrificial or ritual action (cf. MIMAMSA), then performance of one's CASTE duties and worldly activities in general. *Karma yoga* is the path of development, either through perfect performance of religious activities or through the carrying out of affairs without concern for the fruits of action, i.e. motiveless and spontaneous undertaking of one's duties. [19: 16–20]

Kashrut [XVII] A general term for Jewish dietary requirements [9 vol. 6: 26]. JUDAISM considers the following categories as *kosher*, or fit to be eaten: (1) animals which chew the cud and have cloven hoofs, e.g. cattle, sheep, goats, deer; (2) birds which are not birds of prey, and about which Jews have a tradition of their being eaten; (3) fish having fins and scales; (4) locusts of certain types. Before being eaten animals and birds have to be ritually slaughtered, examined to ensure they are not diseased, and animals have to have the sciatic nerve excised (ANIMAL SLAUGHTER). Domesticated animals have the hindquarter fat removed. The blood must be removed from all meat by washing and salting, and meat cannot be cooked or eaten with milk [52: 201]. Indeed, different crockery and cutlery are used for meat and milk, and a time interval must elapse after eating meat before milk products can be eaten. [16] On Passover (CHAGIM) all food containing leaven is forbidden.

Katonda [II] This, the chief GANDA name for God, means 'creator'. Similar forms are widely used among other Bantu peoples as a secondary God-name, e.g. Matunda among Kimbu, Nyamwezi and Sukuma in Tanzania. Unlike some African God-names, whose meaning is lost or is strongly symbolical, Katonda has a high theological sense and goes with an absence of anthropomorphic myth. It represents one basic theme of Bantu theology, as IRUVA with its sun symbolism represents another.

Kehillah [XVII] The Jewish community, usually centring round a SYNAGOGUE [1: III]. The lay leadership are elected to office by the members, and usually comprise a president, treasurer, and wardens. In a traditional community only males are eligible for office. The RABBI of a *kehillah* is employed to teach, preach, supervise ritual requirements, and perform pastoral duties. The CANTOR will lead the prayers in the synagogue and officiate with the rabbi. The community might also employ a ritual slaughterer (ANIMAL SLAUGHTER; KASHRUT); a scribe to write and mend TORAH scrolls, and teachers for the religion school (*cheder*). Although the family is the most important unit of Judaism much of the religion is dependent on communal life [9 vol. 5: 808]. All committed Jews would belong to a *kehillah* of one type or another, and traditional Jews will live within walking distance of fellow community members to be able to attend synagogue services on Sabbaths (SHABBAT) and festivals (CHAGIM). [52: 207]

Khalq [XIV] Creation, in ISLAM. The orthodox, Qur'anic view is of a creation *ex nihilo* and in time by the pre-existing and eternal God, fashioning heaven and earth within six days (ALLAH). Authorities vary on what was the first thing created, whether the Pen, which set down the divine decree and all that could be brought into being, or the light and the darkness. Some later theologians put forward the idea of continuous creation, that God's sustaining power requires a fresh creative act at each moment of his creatures' existence. Others, influenced by NEOPLATONISM, regarded creation as an act of emanation from God, an epiphany of him, so that beings are mirrors of the divine essence. SHI'ISM introduced the idea of a pre-eternal creation of forms of light, whose temporal manifestations became the Prophet MUHAMMAD and the IMAMS. An important theological controversy of medieval times revolved round the question of the createdness or otherwise of the QUR'AN. The orthodox view, which came to prevail, was that it was eternally pre-existent with God himself. [21 'Khalk̲'; 39 'Creation']

Khalsa [XXVII] The SIKH order instituted by Guru Gobind Singh and inaugurated with an impressive ceremony held at Anandpur in 1699 (*see* GURUS) [9: VI; 10: VII]. The traditional reason given for the founding of the order has been the Guru's decision to provide his followers with a militant and highly visible identity, needed in order to nerve them for imminent trials. Although this explanation may still be valid it must be supplemented. Recent research has shown that although the word *khalsa* derives from the Arabic/Persian *khalisa*, 'pure', it relates to a secondary meaning, namely lands under direct crown control. The Guru's concern was to demolish the authority of the *masands*, deputies appointed by earlier Gurus to supervise an increasingly scattered flock of disciples. The *masands* had become corrupt and it was to break their power that the Guru summoned all Sikhs to come under his direct personal control (*khalsa*). [7: 60–61; 9: 113–15] Entry into the Khalsa is effected by an initiation rite (*amrit sanskar*) in which five devout Sikhs (*panj piare*) administer baptism using water stirred with a two-edged sword (*khande di pahul*). All who accept baptism must vow to live according to the RAHIT (the Khalsa code). Male initiates add *Singh* to their given names and women add *Kaur*. [17: 13–16]

Kharijites [XIV] A sect which arose in early ISLAM, diverging after 657 from the Sunni majority (SUNNA) over the question of politico-religious leadership in the community and such theological issues as the definition of the true believer and the relative importance of faith and works. A violent and radical force in the first centuries of the caliphate (CALIPH), at times posing a threat to its stability, this activist aspect gradually subsided and left only an intellectual strand in Islamic thought [21 s.v.; 46: II; 79: V]. However, some small groups stemming from the Kharijites have survived into modern times, notably the Ibadi communities of certain parts of North Africa, the East African coastlands, and Oman. [6: XVI; 21 'Ibādiyya']

Kimbanguist Church [XX] A movement known officially as L'Église de Jésus Christ par le Prophète Simon Kimbangu. It stems from the brief ministry of Simon Kimbangu (1889–1951), a Baptist catechist in the Lower Congo in 1921. He was wrongly sentenced to death for sedition (a punishment commuted to life imprisonment). Despite persecution for over 30 years the movement is now the largest independent church in Africa, claiming 3 million members in Zaire and adjacent countries, and led by Kimbangu's three sons. [21: 25–7; 13; 19: 366–82] In 1970 it became a member of the World Council of Churches.

Kingship (Ancient Near East) [VI] The kings of the ANCIENT NEAR EAST ruled by divine consent; leaders in war, law, and religion, their prime obligation was to serve the national god. The king, whose victory on earth merely reflected his god's success in heaven, was the god's high priest (TEMPLES (ANCIENT NEAR EASTERN)), and in Babylon, in an annual ceremony (part of the New Year FESTIVAL), he had to 'grasp the hand of MARDUK', the national god, in his temple, thus affirming his right to rule.

The king was the least static element in SUMERIAN society [23: 23–5] – the ruler of the most powerful city seized overall leadership until replaced by another – but Sargon of Agade (ASSYRIANS) made provincial rulers accountable to him as overlord, establishing a centralized authority. Later, Hammurabi of Babylon (HAMMURABI'S

CODE) [7] drew up his code at the chief god's behest. In Elam (ELAMITES) [15; 17], the kings were priests who held authority from the gods; descent passed through the female line and, if a king died, his brother usually inherited the throne and the royal widow. King and queen made daily donations at the temple. In-Shushinak was the royal god. Rival rulers of this period depended on omens (DIVINATION) in military action, the armies moving only under the leadership of a 'seer', who preceded them into battle.

The kings of Assyria, modelling their empire on Sargon's concept of centralized rule, were priests of Ashur. Seal impressions show the king receiving divine commands from the god [5], for it was believed that a ruler held power from the deity whose turn it was to rule the world. The kings had large harems, but one queen became chief consort, albeit any son could be chosen as heir. Several rulers built up libraries of religious and other texts [11].

The kings of Hattusas (c. 1740–1460 BCE) welded together isolated city communities, creating the 'Land of Hatti', later to become the centre of the Hittite empire [12]. Originally elective, the kingship was endowed with superhuman powers in the Empire period (c. 1460–1190 BCE). Ancestral rulers received cults, but kings were not deified while alive. Queens had strong, independent roles, the queen mother retaining pre-eminence until her death [13: 63–6]. As chief priest, the king visited the main religious centres of his realm, and performed a royal ritual for the national god in his temple, preceded by a royal toilette.

Kingship, Sacral (Jewish and Early Christian) [XI.A] The kings of Israel were sacral in the sense that they were anointed by Yahweh (GOD) (through priestly or prophetic agency) and were theoretically sacrosanct; but they were Yahweh's servants, subject to his law, not divine kings, like some ancient Near

Eastern rulers (KINGSHIP (ANCIENT NEAR EAST)). They originally exercised priestly privileges, but eventually lost these. The ideal of sacral kingship survived in Israel's expectation of the MESSIAH. JESUS CHRIST claimed no royal status, but many of his followers later acknowledged him as the Davidic Messiah and as successor to Melchizedek, an early Jerusalemite priestking. [2: 28–34; 16: XXIX]

Kitawala [XX] A widespread movement in central Africa under the influence of American JEHOVAH'S WITNESSES, or the Watch Tower (hence *tawala*) Bible and Tract Society. African versions arose in northern Nyasaland (now Malawi) under Elliott Kamwana from 1907 until he was deported in 1909, and in the then Northern Rhodesia (now Zambia) and Belgian Congo (now Zaire) under Nyirenda, who claimed to be Mwana Lesa (Son of God) and was executed in 1926. In spite of frequent persecution, the movement persists. [2: 57–8; 12: 37–9; 19: 83–4, 253–4]

Knights Templars [XVIII] A religious military order founded in 1119 at Jerusalem to protect Christian pilgrims against Muslim attack. Quartered originally near the site of the TEMPLE, they lived under monastic rule, but their activities were mainly military and administrative. Important in maintaining the Latin kingdoms in the Holy Land, they also held property in Europe and acted as international bankers, conducting their internal affairs in strict secrecy. After the Crusades they lost their military importance and in 1312 Philip IV of France, jealous of the order's wealth and power, persuaded Pope Clement V to suppress it. The Grand Master Jacques de Molay and others were accused, probably falsely, of homosexuality, blasphemy, and idolatry, and were executed in 1314. [1] The mystery surrounding the Templars' beliefs and practices, and speculation aroused by their remarkable circular churches, have led to their being claimed as ancestors by several modern OCCULT and Masonic groups (FREEMASONRY).

Kokutai Shinto [XVI] Emperorworship in Japan had its recognizable beginning in the claims made by 8th-century writers for the divine origins of the earliest rulers, the Sun line [17: 389–425]. This ultimately led to veneration of the places where certain rulers lived, such as the Kashihara shrine (SHINTO SHRINES) in Nara prefecture for 'emperor' Jimmu, and a few emperors became the object of particular cults, such as Emperor Ojin, known as HACHIMAN. By the 19th century all of the tombs identified with the royal family had come under the jurisdiction of the Imperial Household Agency and have since been treated as sacred. Westerners speak of Tennoism (*tenno* = emperor). Officially in Kokutai Shinto (National Structure Shinto), the emperor, as the direct descendant of the sun-goddess AMATERASU-OMIKAMI, embodied the *kami* spirit as head of the SHINTO state and spoke with infallible authority. The concept suffered historically through enfeeblement of the imperial system, but was revived by a rising nationalism among 17th-century writers, coming to a climax after Emperor Meiji took power from the Tokugawa in 1868, and was given moral validity in the Imperial Rescript on Education in 1890 [8: 108–10]. In 1945 the emperor publicly renounced his divinity.

Krishna [XIII.A] An AVATARA of the Hindu deity VISHNU. Like other divine human heroes he is said to have been miraculously born. After his birth he was secretly abandoned in some cowherds' dwellings at Mathura, in order to divert the search being made for him by Kamsa, an oppressor whom Krishna had been born to destroy, and who had been forewarned of his fate. The youthful amorous adventures of Krishna with the female cowherds (*gopis*), among whom was Radha, is a well-known feature of

the story, and is taken as an allegory of the devotees' love for their divine lord. The sound of Krishna's flute, calling the young women to come and dance in the moonlight, is said to symbolize the voice of God calling those who hear it away from earthly to divine pleasures. Krishna's subsequent career includes the destruction of oppressive kings and demons in various parts of India, and the climax of the story, as told in the MAHABHARATA, is the battle of Kurukshetra. It was on the eve of this battle that he preached to Arjuna the great moral discourse of the BHAGAVADGITA (the Song of the Lord). Krishna is thus a figure with an appeal to all: to men and women, to young and to old. [2: 306–8] The worship of Krishna usually includes also that of Radha, his lover, as the joint cult of Radha–Krishna. It is probable that the story has some historical basis in a folk-hero of the Brindavan region, upon which it centres, in north India. Brindavan is the principal pilgrimage centre for devotees of Krishna. [1: 306–9; 16a: 204–31]

Kshatriya [XIII.A] The name of one of the four VARNAS or classes in Hindu society. The original meaning is 'endowed with sovereignty' (or supremacy, or power), whether human or superhuman. The name, as well as other ancient evidence, raises the possibility that originally the rank-order of BRAHMAN and Kshatriya may have been Kshatriya first, rather than second to Brahman, the accepted order of later times. [2: 142f]

Kuan (Shih) Yin [X] The Chinese term for AVALOKITESHVARA, the BODHISATTVA of compassion. *Kuan Shih Yin* means 'Hearer of the sounds (prayers) of the world'. In India Avalokiteshvara was represented as male, but in 8th-century China he came to be represented as female. [15: XII, 340] Kuan Yin was adopted into the popular Chinese pantheon as the 'Goddess of Mercy', the protector of women and children, and patroness of sailors.

[4: VI, 180–200; 23: V, 47–57; 42: IX, 68–77]

Kukai [XVI] (774–835 CE), post-humously known as Kobo Daishi, was the priestly founder of the Japanese Buddhist SHINGON sect (JAPAN, BUDDHISM IN) [21: 45–6]. He was trained early in Kegon *sutras* (NANTO ROKUSHU) at the Todai-ji in Nara (NANTO SHICHIDAI-JI). His trilogy *Sankyoshiki*, describing his conversion as a result of a discussion between a Buddhist, a Taoist (TAO CHIAO), and a Confucian (CONFUCIUS), received imperial recognition and he was sent to China in 805. He introduced esoteric doctrines on his return and, after being welcomed by the mountain-spirits (SACRED MOUNTAINS), he built a Shingon temple on Mt Koya in Wakayama prefecture which grew into the Kongobu-ji and an immense complex of other esoteric temples. Through tireless activity and exposition of Shingon, he became the most revered and mythologized saint after Prince SHOTOKU. Appointed to high posts by the court, he was given his posthumous title in 921, and is called 'the Daishi' (Great Master) in popular sentiment today. The Japanese have taken over the practice of CHINESE BUDDHISM of giving posthumous names to outstanding priests. Since it is the most reverent way of referring to them, most people call them today by their posthumous names.

Kumarajiva [x] (344–413 CE) Probably the single most important figure in the history of CHINESE BUDDHISM. He was taken to China as a prisoner in 383 when Kucha in central Asia was raided by a Chinese expeditionary force. He spent 17 years as a captive in north China, during which time he mastered Chinese. In 401 he was taken to Ch'ang An, where he carried out his translation work and was honoured with the title, 'National Teacher'. His major contribution was in the area of translation and the clarification of terms. He translated several important texts, including the 'Three Treatises' of the SAN LUN school, and the *Mahaprajnaparamita-shastra* (Great Perfection of Wisdom Treatise), the *Saddharmapundarika-sutra* (The Lotus of the True Dharma), the *Smaller Sukhavativyuha-sutra* (*see* CHING T'U TSUNG), the *Vimalakirti-nirdesha-sutra*, and the *Shurangama-samadhi-sutra*. [15: III, 81–7; 74: III, 71–95]

Kusinara [IX.A] The small town in northern India where the BUDDHA'S PARINIBBANA took place (modern Kusinagara, or Kasia, on the eastern border of Uttar Pradesh), according to the account in the Pali text [17: 104f]. In Sanskrit texts the place is known as Kushigrama and Kushinagari. It is one of the four sacred places to which Buddhists from many countries make pilgrimage, together with LUMBINI, BODHGAYA, and Sarnath. [37: 77–80]

Kwakiutl [III] A Pacific north-west North American coastal group, along with the Bella Bella and Nootka, belonging to the Wakashan linguistic family. The group occupies both shores of Queen Charlotte Sound and the northern portion of Vancouver Island. The term *kwakiutl* (literally 'smoke of the world') is probably a reference to their mythic place of origin (CRE-ATION MYTHS). They were contacted early by Europeans, and trade with the latter gradually undermined their rigid-ly hierarchical society. Divided into clan groups (*numayma*) within villages, each clan traces its ancestry to a mythic ani-mal ancestor who, in primordial times, became human. Priority among mythic forebears (e.g. the time of their trans-formation) yields a ranking of Kwakiutl clans. The primary religious concern is for man to occupy his proper place in the cosmic scheme and thereby acquire the necessary supernatural power, *nawa-lak* (COSMOLOGY). SHAMANS (*pexala*) acquire *nawalak* in excess of ordinary mortals, often through virtual identi-fication with a granting spirit. Baxba-kualanuxsiwae (the great Man-Eater), chief among Kwakiutl deities, is central to the *hamatsa* cult (the principal secret society), whose dancers hold the highest rank in the winter ceremonial (CALENDAR ROUND) [8: VIII]. Their ritual, performed at the time of year known as *tsetsaequa* ('full of secrets'), recreates for the initiate the death and reconstitution by the cannibal-god and is believed to facilitate the initiate's metamorphosis into full membership. The *potlatch* ('a giving') was a ceremonial distribution of wealth, probably linked originally to a death–rebirth motif present elsewhere in Kwakiutl practice. [7]

· L ·

Lakshmi [XIII.A] Sanskrit word meaning 'wealth, beauty, splendour', qualities which are personified in the Hindu goddess of prosperity, wife of VISHNU, and sometimes referred to as 'the lotus-goddess' [17: 153].

Land of Youth [V] Tir na n-Og (Land of the Young) is one of several Irish names for a realm of bright beauty and fair women, free from death or suffering, which in Irish literature lies across the sea or within the *sid* (burial mound). Kings and heroes visit it to find LUG or Manannan ruling there [21: XVI, 314–25]. The Norse equivalent may be Odainsakr (Field of the Not-Dead) or Glasisvellir (Glittering Plains), ruled by the legendary King Gudmund, sometimes visited by men.

Languages (Jewish) [XVII] The sacred language of JUDAISM is Hebrew, a North-West Semitic language. The Hebrew of the BIBLE is written in a consonantal form, the vowel system in general use today being the work of the Tiberian Masoretes of the 9th and 10th centuries, who formalized the traditional vocalization. Around the beginning of the Christian era Hebrew was replaced as a spoken language by Aramaic, and became a literary language. Aramaic is also of North-West Semitic origin, and some sections of the Bible, in the Books of Daniel and Ezra, are written in it. The Jerusalem and Babylonian TALMUDS, the TARGUM translation-commentaries on the Bible, parts of Midrashic (MID-RASH) literature, and the ZOHAR are all in Aramaic. In the Middle Ages Jews used Hebrew and Aramaic for composing religious texts, for corres-

pondence with Jews in other countries, and for prayer [3 vol. 7: XXX]. They usually spoke the native language of their host countries. As Jews were expelled from various European countries between the 13th and 15th centuries (ANTI-SEMITISM; EUROPEAN JEWRY), they took with them these native languages, which they continued to speak as Jewish dialects. The most important of them are Yiddish, a medieval German dialect, and Ladino, a form of late medieval Spanish. [1: 359; 9 vol. 10: 66]

Lapps, Religion among the [VII] The Lapps are a nomadic people, herders of reindeer in northern Scandinavia, whose traditional religious outlook resembled that of the ESKIMO [8: 84–8; 9: 118–21]. Lapp beliefs were influenced by Nordic mythology (ANCIENT EUROPE; *and see* SYNCRETISM) and later by CHRISTIANITY. Correspondence between their deities and those of the EDDAS, and the fact that western Lapps have a more developed cosmogony than those of Finland do not necessarily imply extensive borrowing. Lapp gods represent elements and forces of the environment. such as the sun as cosmic primordial being, Pieve. This is a less clearly personified concept than those of the supporting gods (thunder, wind, moon). With the Eskimo Selna (Woman of the Sea) may be compared Væralden-olmai (Man of the World), associated with fertility, and, merged with him, Ratien-attje (ruling father for the Swedish Lapps). Many cult-sites (*seide, saivo, passe*) have been found, especially in Sweden, often associated with awe-inspiring natural features (trees, rocks). Large stones and platforms were used for SACRIFICE (e.g. of a white reindeer to Pieve). The role of the *noaide* (SHAMAN) is as significant for Lapps as for other Arctic cultures [8: 84–5; 9: 121–3], and their use of drumming to achieve a state of ecstasy is a salient feature. The drums were often decorated to represent gods or spirits [9: 120–24]. Lapp behaviour was ruled by TABUS, many of them governing the pursuit, slaughter, and consumption of food animals. Those to do with the bear (the largest animal hunted) were of such importance that accounts of Lapp religion usually give prominence to what is called 'the bear cult' [8: 98–100]. The use of special 'bear language', rituals of capture and disposal, rules for the removal, placing and use of the skin, and, when all other parts had been eaten or ceremonially buried, a final festival of purification show how great was the Lapps' respect for the bear and its spirit. With similar behaviour towards other animals, this pattern of activity is evidence for a world-view in which no sharp distinction is made between humans and all that is living. Appreciation of this sense of unity and interaction with the whole visible environment and, through the shaman, with the world of spirits, is indispensable if one is to understand the place and function of the sacred among the Lapps.

Latin America, Christianity in [XI.B] South America, Central America, and parts of North America were colonized by the Spanish and Portuguese in the 16th century. Conversion to Roman Catholicism, often forcible and accompanied by slavery, was part of official policy. Missionary work was largely by the religious orders, notably friars and Jesuits (MONASTICISM). Bartolomé de las Casas (1474–1566) defended Indian rights, and the Jesuits in Paraguay protected converts from exploitation in paternalistically run villages (*Reducciones*). The colonies won independence from Europe during the 19th century and republican anticlericalism some-

times resulted in disestablishment and persecution of the church (as in Mexico). Church influence nevertheless remains strong and the inclination to support conservative regimes has invited hostility from revolutionary movements. However, LIBERATION THEOLOGY and radical social reform have developed, especially among younger, European-influenced clergy. ROMAN CATHOLICISM at the popular level has often syncretistically incorporated pre-Christian religious belief, in festivals and devotions to MARY (AMERICAN INDIANS, NEW RELIGIOUS MOVEMENTS). Recently, evangelical PROTESTANTISM, partly Christian cults, and PENTECOSTALISM [61: VI–VIII] have increased [5: 321–81; 82 vol. 3: III, IV, vol. 5: IV; 83 vol. 3: XII, vol. 5: V; 94]

Lenshina, Alice [xx] A Bemba woman, born Alice Mulenga Lubusha in a Church of Scotland mission in northern Zambia, Alice Lenshina experienced a mystic call in 1953 and proclaimed a new way, which elicited a mass response in areas strong in PROTESTANTISM and ROMAN CATHOLICISM. Her new Lumpa ('best of all') Church, with herself as Lenshina (i.e. 'Queen'), lost some 600 lives in a clash with the Kaunda government in 1964, following which the church was banned and she was detained. She died in 1978. [19: 94–100]

Leza [II] (or Lesa) is the name for God of a large number of African peoples in Zambia and neighbouring countries, among them the Bemba, Ila, and Lala. The etymological meaning is uncertain. Leza is the creator of the world, held immediately responsible for natural phenomena, especially when unusual, and seen as a loving if somewhat remote and incomprehensible father of men. West of the Leza area the major Godname is NZAMBI; in the east MULUNGU or (in Malawi) Chauta; and in the north IRUVA. These together provide the core of BANTU theological nomenclature, but many tribes use other names, despite an apparent tendency for ones like Leza to spread from people to people. The division between names is not necessarily one between theologies – equally the same name may carry rather different connotations among different peoples – yet Leza, Mulungu, and Nzambi all seem to speak of essentially the same belief in one God (associated with the sky and with thunder and lightning) quite unlike the ancestral spirits, creator of all things and ultimate source of morality, yet somewhat withdrawn and seldom the object of regular worship. [15; 22]

Lha–Dre [XXIX] The *lha* (gods) and *dre* (demons) are the supernatural beings of indigenous Tibetan folk-religion. According to Buddhist doctrinal classification they are 'deities of the world' (*jigten-pa*), distinct from the symbolic deities of Buddhism which embody the various qualities of enlightenment. By classifying the *lha* and *dre* in this manner and assigning them duties as 'oathbound' protectors of religion, Buddhism in Tibet was able to assimilate their cults. The Tibetan religion is rich in such supernatural beings, both beneficent and malign. Especially significant are the deities who personify elemental and environmental forces, such as the *sa-dag* ('lords of the soil'), who are placated before any construction or farming is carried out, and the *lu*, spirits dwelling in watery environments who also require placation. Alongside these and numerous other autochthonous deities Buddhism has brought to Tibet its own 'worldly gods', namely such Indian deities as SHIVA, VISHNU, and BRAHMA, who now serve as oathbound protectors of the Buddhist faith. [14; 24]

Li [X] ('Rites of Propriety') The two components of the Chinese character *Li* mean 'spirit' and 'sacrifice', although in some contexts the term can be translated simply as 'religion' or 'morality'. Generally *Li* refers to formal rituals and

sacrifices, which may be the rites of the official or state religion, communal and agricultural rites, or domestic rites such as FUNERAL RITES (*Sang Li*). *Li* also refers to the rules of proper conduct and the behaviour appropriate to specific circumstances. The detailed regulations of the *Li* are found in the Classic of Rites (*Li Ching*) [61; 83]. Through most of Chinese history from Chou times (1027–402 BCE) the Ministry of Rites (*Li Pu*) was responsible for determining and regulating the sacrificial rites (*Chi Li*) of the official or state religion.

By the Ch'ing dynasty (1644–1911 CE) these were classified into three groups. The Great Sacrificial Rites were the offerings to heaven (T'IEN), earth (*Ti*), and the royal ancestors (*Tsu Tsang*) and the gods of the soil and grain (*She Chi*). The Medium Sacrificial Rites were the offerings to the sun and moon, representing the *yang* and *yin* (YIN–YANG) principles, the kings and emperors of former dynasties, the Sage Emperor Shen Nung and god of agriculture, and Lei Tsu the goddess of sericulture. The Great Rites were almost exclusively the concern of the emperor, who performed them on behalf of the people to ensure the perpetuation of the political and the natural order.

The Lesser Sacrificial Rites date mainly from after the end of the Han dynasty (221 CE) and were usually conducted not by the emperor but by local officials in state temples. They include offerings to the Sage Emperor Fu Hsi, the god of war (Kuan Ti), the god of literature Wen Chang, and various local gods associated with the Ch'ing capital Peking. [2; 4: III, 54–68; 20; 30; 86: V, 70–76]

Liberal Protestantism [XI.C] A somewhat diverse movement in Protestant theology which arose in the second half of the 19th century (PROTESTANTISM). Negatively, it is characterized by a rather critical attitude to naïve biblicism (e.g. to a simplistic affirmation of statements in the BIBLE) and to traditional dogmatic formulations of the Christian faith. Positively, it is concerned to present the spirit of the Christian GOSPEL in contemporary terms and to assert the importance of the individual's religious experience. Its early development was considerably influenced by Albrecht Ritschl (1822–89) and his followers. Ritschl insisted that religion is not reducible to other forms of experience, that religious knowledge is a matter of 'value judgements', that CHRISTOLOGY must take seriously the results of historical research into the life of JESUS CHRIST, and that reconciliation with God must be expressed in moral activity in the world (SALVATION). The classical expression of the liberal Protestant position was produced by Adolf Harnack (1851–1930). In *What Is Christianity?* he expounded the Christian faith popularly in terms of the fatherhood of God, the brotherhood of man, the higher righteousness, and the command of love. [22]

Liberation Theology [XI.C] A term covering various theological movements which have developed since the mid-1960s and which are concerned to understand the Christian GOSPEL in terms of current needs for establishing human freedom. Four areas of oppression particularly treated by these movements are the economic exploitation of the less-developed countries, sexual prejudice against women [24] (WOMAN (IN EARLY CHRISTIANITY)), racial discrimination, and political tyranny. The liberation theologies, which often adopt analyses of social situations from MARXISM, interpret redemption as liberation, see JESUS CHRIST as identified with the oppressed, and challenge the male-dominated conceptualities of theology and culture. [9; 16]

Lila [XIII.B] 'Joyful play': God's motivation for periodically creating the universe, in VEDANTA thought. It is sometimes mistakenly interpreted as capriciousness. A divine power free from all imperfection or defilement could not have motivated action based upon any need or partiality, otherwise it would be subject to the law of KARMA. So the act of creation is explained as joyful spontaneity or fun. [3: 117ff; 15: 361–3]

Lingayata [XIII.A] A Hindu movement of somewhat puritanical character among the Shaivas (SHIVA/SHAIVA) of South India. Its members are strict vegetarians and abstainers from alcohol. Disregarding CASTE distinctions they do not accept the idea of the high status of BRAHMANS. The movement is said to have been founded in the 12th century CE [14: 268].

Literalism [XXVIII] A term with two meanings. (1) In the interpretation of sacred scripture, acceptance of statements at their face value or 'according to the letter', as opposed to interpreting them symbolically or metaphorically. (2) In theories of religion, a method of explanation which regards RITUALS and other religious actions as accounted for by beliefs about the world (for example a DANCE occurs because the participants believe that SPIRITS can be induced by it to give rain), and as functioning as instruments of control of the conditions of life, rather than as symbols. [26: 11–12]

Liturgical Books (Eastern Orthodox [IX.D] Books containing the order of services and texts to be used [25: 535–43]. The *Typikon* lays down when and in what manner services are to be held. The *Euchologion* contains the priest's part of morning (*Orthros*) and evening (*Hesperinos*) prayer, the MYSTERIES, and other services.

The *Horologion* contains the fixed parts of offices for the reader (*anagnostes*) and singers (*psaltai*). Variable parts of services are contained in a number of different books: the *Menaia* contains texts for each date; the *Triodion* gives texts for the 10-week period before Easter (LITURGICAL YEAR), especially the texts for Great Lent and Holy Week; the *Pentekostarion* covers the period from Easter Sunday to the feast of All Saints, which in the Orthodox calendar is the Sunday after Pentecost. The weeks of the year from the Sunday after Easter (St Thomas Sunday) onwards fall into cycles of eight, each using one of the eight Byzantine musical tones. The texts for these cycles are contained in the *Oktoechos* or *Paraklitike*.

The Book of Psalms (Psalter) (BIBLE) and a book of GOSPEL readings are used, and a book of epistles and readings from the Acts of the Apostles called the *Apostolos*.

Liturgical Movement [XI.B] A movement in ROMAN CATHOLICISM from the early 1900s to encourage congregational participation in the MASS, after a long period during which passivity or engagement in individual devotions had been customary. Results include: more frequent communion; simplified services; and translation of the MASS out of Latin, especially since the second Vatican COUNCIL (1963) [1: 137–78]. Similar concerns have affected ANGLICANISM and other churches. Modern church plans show the movement's influence (ARCHITECTURE). [30; 57; 78]

Liturgical Year (Christian) [XI.B] The Western 'liturgical year' begins with the four Sundays (Sabbaths: SHABBAT) of Advent which prepare for JESUS CHRIST's 'coming' at Christmas. Advent is followed by Epiphany, celebrating his revelation to the Gentiles. Several weeks later, Ash Wednesday introduces the 40 days of fasting in Lent. This leads to Good Friday (commemorating Jesus' crucifixion) and Easter Sunday (celebrating his resurrection). Five Sundays then lead to Ascension Day (commemorating Jesus' reception into heaven). Next comes Whit Sunday (Pentecost, the day of the reception of the HOLY SPIRIT by the APOSTLES) and the following Sunday celebrates the TRINITY.

The liturgical year of the ORTHODOX CHURCHES has certain differences: (1) It begins on 1 September. (2) Epiphany commemorates the baptism of Jesus. (3) Great Lent (one of several such seasons which prepare for Great Feasts) begins on 'Pure Monday'. (4) Pentecost is the feast of the Holy Trinity as well as of the Descent of the Holy Spirit.

To these festivals commemorating Jesus' life and work are added others for the Virgin MARY and a large number of SAINTS. Official worship at these festivals has been accompanied by many other ancient customs of non-Christian origin, particularly at Christmas (e.g. Christmas trees) and Easter (e.g. Easter eggs). These, however, are often given a Christian significance [30; 105 vol. 8: 915–19]. Other festivals and customs in Christian lands reflect the survival of folklore and MAGIC [128].

Liturgy (Jewish) [XVII] The thrice-daily recital of prayers in JUDAISM is modelled on the sacrificial ritual of the TEMPLE. The central part of the morning liturgy (*shacharit*) is the recitation of the SHEMA with its accompanying benedictions, followed by the AMIDAH, a prayer of 19 benedictions said standing and facing JERUSALEM. For certain parts of these prayers a quorum (*minyan*) of 10 adult males is necessary. Various benedictions, psalms, and hymns have been added over the centuries. On Sabbaths (SHABBAT) and festivals an extra *amidah* (*musaf*) is said commemorating the extra sacrifice brought on those occasions in the Temple. The afternoon prayer (*minchah*) consists of a psalm, the *amidah*, and a short concluding prayer. The evening service (*maariv*) consists of the *shema* and *amidah* with some short additional pieces [9 vol. 11: 392]. The traditional prayers are in Hebrew, although REFORM JUDAISM has introduced many vernacular prayers since many modern congregants cannot understand the Hebrew LANGUAGE [20; 42: VII, XII].

Logical Positivism [XXVI] A view, hostile to metaphysics and much traditional theology, according to which there are only two classes of genuine statements. There are statements, like those of logic and mathematics, which are known to be true or false independently of experience (but which can, if true, be reduced by analysis to tautologies). The only other genuine statements, including those of natural science, are those which are verifiable by sense experience. Metaphysical or religious assertions which purport to make claims about the nature of the universe but which do not meet the criterion of verifiability are held to be strictly 'meaningless'. They might express feelings but they do not convey any information.

This view is associated with a group founded in the 1920s by Moritz Schlick. The group, consisting of mathematicians, scientists, and philosophers, came to be known as 'the Vienna circle'. A forceful, though modified, version of logical positivism was introduced to the English-speaking world by A. J. Ayer (b. 1910). [1] Ayer reformulated the criterion of verifiability so that it would not, as had the stricter version of the Vienna circle, exclude important scientific statements as meaningless. Many, following Karl Popper (b. 1902) [15: 1], take the view that falsifiability rather than verifiability is a more appropriate criterion for distinguishing scientific statements. This requirement is a more problematic one so far as religious affirmations are concerned. 'God is love', for example, would be verified by some kind of beatific vision in an afterlife. But it has been claimed, by A. G. N. Flew (b. 1923) [8: VI], that 'God is love' is not falsifiable and therefore is not a genuine statement. The critique of religious utterances as 'meaningless' has been questioned by P. E. Winch (b. 1926) and other philosophers influenced by the writings of Ludwig Wittgenstein (1889–1951) [e.g. 5: X–XII].

Lokayata [XIII.B] A system or movement in Indian thought which denied life after death and adopted a materialist standpoint. Classical Indian verse, drama, and story refer not infrequently to materialist views of a popular kind; indeed, such notions are already present in the literature of the VEDA. More systematic materialist theories are first known from the period of the foundation of BUDDHISM and Jainism (JAINS) (c. 500 BCE). Eventually, a coherent philosophy of life with systematic expression and literature came into existence (by the 1st century CE, perhaps much earlier). Its foundation was mythologically attributed either to Brhaspati or to Carvaka. Little Lokayata literature survives, but the system appears to have held that sense experience is ultimately the only source of knowledge (pramana). Some sources portray it as recommending enjoyment of pleasure or advocating a hedonistic ethic. The Lokayata was strongly opposed to CASTE, the cult of deities, and the support of religious professionals. [5: III, 512–50; 10: II, 215–26; 14: 27–35; 16: 227–49]

Loki [V] Loki is found among the Scandinavian AESIR, sometimes accompanying ODIN and THOR on journeys. In the EDDAS he is represented as a trickster figure, expert at taking on bird or animal shapes, performing acts of mischief, and getting in and out of dangerous and ridiculous situations. He helps the giants to steal the gods' treasures, and then uses his creative skills to win them back (FROST-GIANTS [6: VII, 176–82]). In the poem Lokasenna [18: 90–103] he bitterly abuses all the Aesir and VANIR in turn, and is said to be responsible for BALDER's death and to have been bound under rocks as a punishment. HEL, FENRISWOLF, and the serpent encircling the world are all said to be the children of Loki. He and his sons fight against the gods at RAGNAROK. His relationship with the huge and sinister giant skilled in magical deceptions, Utgard-Loki ('Loki of the Outer Regions'), is not clear [6: 1, 32–3, 182].

Lokuttara [IX.B] A technical term of the ABHIDHAMMA. The earlier Buddhist literature describes four grades of saint, collectively known as 'nobles' (*ariya*; Sanskrit *arya*): stream-enterer, once-returner, never-returner (ANAGA-MI), and ARAHAT. Having perfected the training in external morality (SILA), all are free from the danger of an unpleasant rebirth. All have seen the Buddhist goal and are as a result free from doubt and opinion (DITTHI). In *abhidhamma*, *lokuttara* (Sanskrit *lokottara*) (literally 'supramundane', i.e. transcendent) refers to the type of consciousness, occurring initially as a momentary flash, which transforms the individual permanently into a 'noble'. It is the culmination of Buddhist meditation practice (BHAVANA), uniting in a harmonious balance the two aspects of calm and insight. *Lokuttara* mind involves a direct realization of the unconditioned and, being quite free of any trace of defilement, cannot give rise to any attachment and necessarily erodes unskilful tendencies (cf. SKILFUL MEANS). The four grades of saint are the result of different degrees of clarity in this realization. [42: 785ff]

Lotu [XXII] A Tongan word for prayer or worship used by 19th-century Christian converts to refer to mission teachings and church services. When they in turn became missionaries to other Pacific islands the word was used generally for the Christian teaching. In modern Melanesian pidgin it can include any religion, Christian or otherwise.

Lovedu Religion [II] The religion of the Lovedu, who live in the Transvaal, is centred upon Mujaji, their divine queen, and ancestral spirits. They have no interest in cosmological myths, and belief in Khuzwane, the creator, is shadowy. They do not pray to him, nor do they see their ancestors as intermediaries. Both the control of nature, especially rain, and the whole life of society depend principally upon the queen, her physical health and emotional happiness. She herself depends not only upon

her inner divine power, but also on special rain-medicines and the royal ancestor spirits. The queen's holiness requires seclusion and, finally, death at her own hands, but not a continuously ritualized life. Her death is followed by a period of natural and social confusion.

Throughout Lovedu society women are important. Many rituals are conducted by them and no ancestor spirit is more powerful than a mother's mother. Rain symbolizes the good life, coolness, fruitfulness, moderation, social reconciliation; heat symbolizes what is evil, sorcery, witchcraft, passion, fighting [4: 55–82; 33].

Lu Tsung [X] The Chinese VINAYA School, founded by Tao Hsuan (596–667 CE). It was based on the 'Vinaya in Four Parts' (*Ssu Fen Lu*), which was translated in 412 CE. The school emphasized the rules of monastic discipline. (PATIMOKKHA: *see also Ritsu in* NANTO ROKUSHU.) [15: XI, 301]

Ludi [XXV] Roman games, which included a wide range of public spectacles – racing, drama, displays of wild beasts, fighting, etc. – always presented in a religious context, preceded by rituals and processions and dedicated to a god or goddess. The great *ludi* (*plebeii* and *Romani*) seem to go back to the 6th century BCE, though there are ludic elements in older festivals, perhaps deriving from initiatory rites. Their frequency, popularity, and extravagance increased as the empire grew. [1: 134–7; 6: 571–5]

Lug [V] The Irish Lug (Shining One), with the title 'Of the Long Arm', is thought to be related to the Celtic deity equated with Mercury in Gaul. He appears in a medieval Welsh story in the *Mabinogion* as the hero Lleu Llaw Gyffes [15: 63–75]. Lug has much in common with the Germanic Wodan/ODIN, since he is a god of many skills, including music and poetry, who brought wealth, was skilled in magic and warfare, carried a huge spear, and was associated with the raven. He was said to have been fostered by Manannan Mac Lir, 'son of the sea' [26: IV, 42–6]. He joined the TUATHA DE DANANN and led them to victory at the battle of Mag Tuired, when he slew his grandfather, Balor of the baleful eye, with his sling [21: II, 33–8, VI, 142–5]. He is represented as reigning as a king in the other world. His festival was Lughnasa, marking the beginning of harvest (SAMHAIN), still remembered in popular tradition [16: I].

Lumbini [IX.A] The birthplace of Shakyamuni BUDDHA (GOTAMA); one of the four places of pilgrimage for Buddhists. Just within the southern border of Nepal, the place is marked by a stone pillar set up by the Indian emperor ASHOKA, which records his own visit there to reverence 'the place where the Buddha was born' [17: 160].

Lutheranism [XI.B] Martin Luther (1483–1546) [8] was the father of the German REFORMATION. His *Ninety-Five Theses* (1517) against 'Indulgences' [11: 182–91] (PENANCE) provoked a general revolt against the PAPACY. His key doctrines [40] were that justification is by grace through faith alone, not by works (SALVATION), and that the AUTHORITY of the BIBLE is supreme over CHURCH tradition. Lutherans [107: 848–50] came to dominate parts of northern Europe and there are substantial groups in the U.S.A. through German immigration.

European Lutheranism has commonly been organized in established churches with a tendency to Erastianism (STATE). The Augsburg Confession (1530) [11: 210–12] is the chief Confession of Faith. A form of Lutheran 'SCHOLASTICISM' in the 17th century provoked PIETISM in reaction. Lutherans have been prominent in BIBLICAL CRITICISM and LIBERAL PROTESTANTISM, but in liturgy and eucharistic theology (EUCHARIST) sometimes closer to ROMAN CATHOLICISM than other branches of PROTESTANTISM. [10]

· M ·

Madhyamika [IX.A] One of the major Buddhist schools of philosophy (known also as SHUNYATAVADA), founded by NAGARJUNA. It has been described as 'the central philosophy of Buddhism' [24], or the synthesis of the pre-Buddhist doctrine of the ATMAN (thesis), and the Buddhist *abhidharma* (ABHIDHAMMA) position (antithesis), and thus 'the maturity of the critical consciousness within the fold of Buddhism' [24: 76]. (*See also* NANTO ROKUSHU *and* SAN LUN.)

Madrasa [XIV] A higher institution of learning in traditional Islamic education. The MOSQUE was (and still is) a place of instruction and often the depository for a library. Children normally spent several years on the QUR'AN in a primary school attached to a mosque before joining the teaching circle of a prominent scholar for instruction in the Islamic sciences. *Madrasas*, or colleges, were founded, often with sectarian affiliations, from the 11th century onwards. The *madrasa* teacher, who was known as a *mudarris*, gave his students certificates of attendance and qualification to teach, in turn, the texts which had been studied [72: VI]. In the last century, these institutions have tended to be replaced by colleges and universities with curricula and teaching methods more approximating to those of the West. (*See* AL-AZHAR *and* ISLAMIC MODERNISM.) [General surveys in 10 'Education (Islam)'; 61: XI; 67; architecture: 56: I]

Magen David [XVII] The six-pointed star of David, which has come to be identified as a typically Jewish symbol and appears on the flag of the state of ISRAEL. Its use as a uniquely Jewish symbol only dates back several centuries, prior to which it was used as a decorative motif by non-Jews as well [46: 257]. It is often found today on Jewish tombstones, and worn as an ornament round the neck by young Jews.

Magi [XXX] A priestly tribe among the ancient Medes [15: 82–5]. They became the official priesthood of western Iran and thereby acted as the transmitters of ZOROASTRIANISM, even though ZOROASTER and his immediate followers were not part of the Magian tradition [5: 10f]. Zoroaster referred to himself as a *zaotar*, a fully qualified priest, and as a *manthran*, a composer of MANTHRAS [5: 183f]. In the AVESTA the general term for priest is *athaurvan*. But throughout the recorded history of western Zoroastrianism it is the *magi* who appear on official state records as the priests of the religion. Western (e.g. Greek and Roman) writers commented on their discipline, dress, study, worship, ethics, practices of divination and prophecy, and their purity laws. Although magic is named after them there are no known practices of the Iranian clergy which really justify this. The *magi* were well educated, working as judges and scribes as well as royal advisers and 'chaplains'. In Sasanian times (3rd–7th centuries CE) a *mobadan mobad* (high priest of high priests) was appointed for the whole community.

Among PARSIS a high priest is called a *dastur*. Since the 16th century the senior *dastur* has been considered the *dastur* of the priestly city of Navsari. A *panthaki* has administrative responsibility over a specific region (*panthak*) and he employs *mobeds* (priests) to perform ceremonies within his area.

There is a two-stage initiation into the priesthood involving the rites of *navar* and *maratab* [33: VIII]. The Zoroastrian priesthood is hereditary, but the lineage lapses if three successive generations fail to take at least *navar*. One who proceeds no further than this first initiation is known as *ervad*. Women and lay persons (*behdin*) cannot be priests. Functionally, a Zoroastrian priest is a man of religious learning who can perform rites and who maintains the necessary ethical and ritual purity to do so, hence one term for a priest is a *yozdathrager*, the 'purifier'. As a man of spiritual power his actions, words, and gaze can consecrate objects (*manthras*). Ritual power ('*amal*) can only be actualized in a clean place, i.e. free from the dirt associated with evil's weapons of decay and death (ANGRA MAINYU), by a righteous priest who must recite with devotion and attention [27]. In ancient times the *magi* practised animal sacrifice; this is rare among modern Zoroastrians in Iran and has not been part of the Parsi practice for over 100 years [23: 55–65].

Magic [XVIII] Ritual activity intended to produce results without using the recognized causal processes of the physical world. Present in all cultures and ranging from folk-magic worked by simple traditional rules to sophisticated magical systems backed by complex metaphysics, magic generally depends upon a world-view in which things of one order are felt to correspond to things of another, so that operations performed symbolically in one realm will take practical effect elsewhere. The Azande (ZANDE RELIGION) sorcerer depriving a popular man of his friends by the use of twigs from a tree which loses its leaves rapidly when cut [9], and the Renaissance courtier-magician seeking to compel a lady's love by a talisman (an object ritually constructed to bring special powers to its possessor) of Venus,

constructed of copper at astrologically appropriate hours, both create a 'model' of a force which they seek to project.

Distinctions between magic operating 'mechanically' and magic inducing a spirit or god to act are not always useful. The man who ill-treats a lock of his enemy's hair to harm him probably expects automatic results; the Renaissance magician conjuring up a spirit to reveal celestial wisdom probably does not. But in medieval Europe holy water cured illness. Was virtue inherent in the consecrated substance, or were cures granted through faith and God's grace? Opinions differed. [24] Nor is magic altogether distinct from religious ritual, where symbolism helps evoke certain feelings and attitudes. It has been practised for the most exalted ends by deeply religious people (WESTERN MAGICAL TRADITION). Inherent to the non-logical and creative functions of the human mind, magic shades off into religion, psychotherapy, art, and technology, to all of which it has made fundamental contributions.

Magic (Ancient Egyptian) [IV] Important in daily life, Egyptian magic was based upon the 'sympathetic' principle, affirming that the spoken name or image of a living being or an object created the presence of the original. The magician could then control it, either by magical rites or the recitation of formulae [18: X, 229]. It was used as a protection against hostile forces: illness (MANSION OF THE GODS), ferocious animals, and Egypt's enemies. Potsherds were inscribed with enemies' names, and then ceremonially smashed (the Execration Texts). [6]

Magic (Ancient Near Eastern) [VI] Incantation priests (TEMPLES) recited spells as part of magical rituals which could drive out sickness, banish misfortune, curse enemies, protect property, or bring good luck and success. Illness was regarded as a demon (EVIL) to be driven out with magic, assisted by medicine [23: 20–21]. Probably originating in Babylonia (BABYLONIANS), although Elam (ELAMITES) was regarded as a centre for witchcraft, magic was disseminated to northern Syria and the HITTITES, through the HURRIANS. In the Hittite empire, black magic was recognized in law as a crime [13: 161].

Mahabharata [XIII.A] 'The Great Epic of the Bharatas', containing 90,000 stanzas, is a compilation of ancient Indian epic material made probably between the 2nd century BCE and the end of the 1st century CE. The scene of the story is the upper Ganges plain, and its central concern is the battle between the Kauravas and the Pandavas, the other branch of the Bharatas, a people who claim to have descended from an eponymous ancestor, Bharata. In origin probably a 'martial ballad' [2: 409] the epic, preserved and transmitted by the BRAHMAN class, has probably had considerable didactic and religious material incorporated into it in the course of transmission. 'Warlike narratives ... mingled with mythological scenes and moral discourses' [19: 11] reveal the ethical values of ancient Hindu society and especially such matters as the duties of the individual. The central and best-known part of the epic is the discourse delivered by KRISHNA to the hero, Arjuna, known as the BHAGAVADGITA (Song of the Blessed One), that is, of Krishna as the AVATARA of the supreme God, VISHNU. The discourse concerns primarily the DHARMA of the KSHATRIYA or warrior class (VARNA). Another of the component parts is the *Shanti Parvan*, a discourse on ethics and government delivered by the dying Bhishma. Another is the story of Nala and Damayanti, told as a warning against the evils of gambling [2: 412–14].

Mahasanghika [IX.A] The more democratic of the two wings in the early Buddhist community, the 'Great Assemblists', as distinct from the conservative Sthaviravada, or THERAVADA, which followed strictly the

doctrine of the elders, and was more exclusive in membership. The Mahasanghikas were probably the forerunners of what eventually became the MAHAYANA. [4: 119f; 37: 213–18]

Mahavamsa [IX.A] The 'Great Chronicle' (in Pali) of the Buddhist history of Sri Lanka, a poetic work 'worthy the name of a true epic' [22: 141]. It covers the entire period from the lifetime of GOTAMA to the 4th century CE. It has been translated into English prose by W. Geiger and M. H. Bode (CULAVAMSA; DIPAVAMSA) [10A; 22: 139–46]

Mahavastu [IX.A] The 'Great Event', that is, the life of GOTAMA, the BUDDHA, according to the Lokottaravada school of Buddhists. The Sanskrit text was edited by E. Senart (Paris, 1882–97) and an English translation by J. J. Jones (London, Pali Text Society, 3 vols., 1949–56) is available.

Mahavira [XV] The title of the Indian religious teacher of the 6th/5th centuries BCE, whose teachings are preserved by the JAINS. The traditional date for his birth is 540 BCE, and for his death 468 BCE, although these are not universally agreed. He appears to have been a slightly senior contemporary of GOTAMA and, like him, lived in the lower region of the Ganges (GANGA) valley in what is now called Bihar. He left home for the homeless life of the ascetic at the age of about 30, wandering from place to place, discussing and disputing with other such ascetic philosophers, and undergoing various austerities. His personal name is given as Vardhamana. He is said to have gained full enlightenment and thus to have become a *Jina* (one who overcomes), and to have died of voluntary starvation at Pava, in Bihar [1: 290ff].

Mahayana [IX.A] A development of thought and practice within Buddhism from about the 1st century CE which emphasized: (1) the supramundane personality of the BUDDHA as the essence of phenomena; (2) the BODHISATTVA ideal, against the more private emphasis of the older schools; and (3) the philosophy of *shunyata*, the 'voiding' of all the pluralistic and relativistic elements which the older schools had affirmed [24: 76]. Mahayana practice entailed a reinterpretation of the older discipline for monks, which had been adhered to with rigid literalism, and the development of 'skill in means' (SKILFUL MEANS) instead. This enabled Buddhist monks more easily to travel to and settle in territories and climates other than that of India, such as Nepal, China (CHINESE BUDDHISM), Tibet (TIBETAN RELIGIONS), and Japan (JAPAN, BUDDHISM IN). At the popular level the *bodhisattva* doctrine provided a popular, lay base through the opportunity it afforded for the assimilation of a variety of cults. [5: 195–274; 37: 352–422]

Mahdi [XIV] Literally 'divinely guided one': a term with millenarian and eschatological implications, used at various stages in Islamic history. It is the name given by mainstream Sunnis (SUNNA) to the periodic revivers of the faith when it has grown weak or when the Muslim community has fallen into an oppressed and impotent state. It is also believed that towards the end of the world, before the Last Day (QIYAMA), a Mahdi, often identified with the returned JESUS, will establish a reign of justice on earth. In SHI'ISM the Mahdi is a vital figure, identified with the Hidden IMAM who will reappear and rule by divine prescription. This idea of a messianic figure has often sustained Muslims through dark periods of their history, and religious leaders making such claims for themselves have frequently arisen; notable here is the Mahdi Muhammad Ahmad, who set up a theocratic state in the Sudan which endured from 1882 till 1898. [10 s.v.; 20 s.v.; 46: XI; 83: IV]

Maimonides, Moses [XVII] The greatest of medieval Jewish codifiers and theologians [9 vol. II: 754]. Maimon-

ides was born in Córdoba (Spain) in 1135 CE but had to flee his native land to escape from a fanatical Islamic sect and eventually settled in Fostat (Egypt) where he died in 1204. For the later part of his life he was a physician at the court of the sultan. His fame rests on his two major works: the *Mishneh Torah*, a codification of all of rabbinical law and ritual; and *The Guide of the Perplexed* [30], which synthesizes Jewish and Aristotelian thought [17: 152; 19: XIII]. He also wrote an important commentary on the MISHNAH, a survey of the 613 biblical commandments (MITZVAH), and medical treatises. Most of his writings, including his letters on legal and theological subjects to Jewish communities that had turned to him for advice, were originally in Arabic and were translated into Hebrew by others. Controversy surrounded many of his views. [22; 52: 60]

Maitreya [IX.A] In the Buddhist philosophy of history a BUDDHA appears from time to time to renew the knowledge of the Buddha DHAMMA among mankind. The Buddha who is next to come, and who will thus follow Shakyamuni Buddha (GOTAMA), is known as Maitreya, a proper name meaning the 'friendly one' or 'kind one' (Pali *Metteyya*). At present, in accordance with the BODHISATTVA concept, he is awaiting this future birth (as a human and a Buddha) in the Tusita heaven (DIPANKARA), and is referred to in Buddhist literature as the Bodhisattva Maitreya. [4: 116f; 37: 426–9]

Mala'ika [XIV] Angels, in ISLAM. In Islamic cosmogony, these form a part of God's creation; sometimes described as made of light, they are considered by theologians, on the basis of the QUR'AN, as superior to mankind in general but inferior to the 'messengers of mankind', i.e. prophets, who have to fight against the sinfulness of human nature. The Qur'an mentions by name Jibril (Gabriel), bearer of the revelation to MUHAMMAD, and Mikha'il. Others are also cited, such as the angel who will sound the last trump before Judgement (QIYAMA); those near to God's throne who hymn his praises; the angel of death; the keepers of heaven and hell; and the two recording and guardian angels over human individuals. Iblis, the rebel against God and tempter to evil of mankind, has an ambiguous position in Islamic lore; he behaves as a fallen angel, but is considered to be made from smokeless fire, like the JINN. (*See also* SATAN (IN ISLAM).) [10 'Angel(s) (Islam)'; 20 s.v.; 39 'Angels']

Male Cults (Melanesia) [XXII] Marking entry into adulthood in traditional Melanesian society are strenuous and painful rites (circumcision, bloodletting, tattooing) to purify young males from the weakening effect of contact with mothers and other women during childhood. Such public puberty rites are accompanied by secret initiations into male cults, during which tribal lore and ritual are gradually revealed. Novices are ceremonially washed, isolated from women and children, made to fast or eat special food, and teased and beaten by their elders. [2] All this takes place to gain the approval of ancestral spirits, who reside with the menfolk in the sacred cult house (HAUS TAMBARAN) and are invoked with chants and prayers, making themselves visible and audible through MASKS, flutes and drums, bullroarers, and other sacred media. Male-cult rites accompany births, initiations, marriages, and funerals. Cult specialists arrange ceremonial exchanges of goods and wealth, like the Papuan *kula* and *hiri* cycles [20; 25] and the New Guinea Highlands pig-feasts and ritual dances (SINGSING). [14; 23] Besides cults common to all adult males, there have also been bachelor associations, sorcerers' cults, and other secret societies. [9; 12]

Man, Christian Doctrine of [XI.B] The main Christian tradition has seen man as composed of two elements, body and soul, the latter being purely

spiritual. Together they constitute a complete human being. Christianity shares with other religions a belief in the immortality of the soul. It adds to this, however, the belief that the soul will ultimately be resurrected and 'clothed' in a spiritual 'body' (AFTERLIFE). The main Christian tradition on the origin of the soul (following St Thomas Aquinas (THOMISM)) has held that each soul is created separately by God (Creationism); though some have seen it as transmitted by parents to children (Traducianism). Man is created in the 'image of God' (*imago Dei*), which was partly but not wholly destroyed by the Fall and Original SIN. For ROMAN CATHOLICISM and the ORTHODOX CHURCH sufficient is left of the 'image' (including free will) to allow for receptiveness to God's grace (SALVATION). PROTESTANTISM originally saw the 'image' as completely destroyed. This has been greatly modified for many Protestants by the decline of CALVINISM and the rise of humanistic optimism since the 18th century. Developments in evolutionary theory, philosophy, and psychology have greatly complicated and modified traditional Christian views of man's nature, not always in an optimistic direction. [60; 76]

Man (**in Judaism**) [XVII] The biblical account of man being created in the image of God (Genesis 1: 27) was the basis of the Judaic understanding of his nature [7: III]. The medieval theologians were divided about whether or not man's status was above that of ANGELS, but most agreed that he was the goal of creation. Kabbalists (KABBALAH) saw man as a microcosm who played a central role in maintaining the harmonious function of all levels of reality. Man's task was to act with God as a partner in the continuing work of creation, and to bring about the Kingdom of God on earth by following the good inclination (*yetzer tov*) within him and overcoming the evil inclination (*yetzer-ha-ra*) [21: XVII]. The prohibition on homicide is explained in terms of the 'image of God' within man, as are a number of other halakhic laws (HALAKHAH). Man's free will is a cornerstone of Jewish thought. [9 vol. 11: 842]

Mana [XXII] Power and authority in POLYNESIAN and MELANESIAN RELIGION. In Polynesia *mana* comes from kinship with gods (ATUA) and famous ancestors. Tribal chiefs embody the *mana* of their people and land. All who are strong, wise, or skilful demonstrate *mana*. It is present in the orator's speech, the TOHUNGA's chant, the warrior's club and the craftsman's tool. [16: 26–34] Rules of *tapu* (TABU) preserve the potency and holiness of *mana*. A breach of *tapu* means a release of uncontrolled *mana*, dangerous to life and social order. The TOHUNGA uses water and cooked food to neutralize *mana* and restore right relations between sacred and profane things. Cooking and eating the bodies of slain enemies is the ultimate way to destroy their *mana* and that of their tribes. [7: 400–402; 16: 267–70] In Melanesia, possessing *mana* depends less on divine ancestry than on direct access to unseen powers, shown by success in warfare, ritual, or sorcery, and by the fertility of wives, gardens, and pigs. [9; 23]

Mandaeans [XXX] A small and declining religious community in Iraq and Iran claiming descent from JOHN THE BAPTIST, believing that their ancestors moved east after the fall of JERUSALEM in 70 CE. Their religion obviously descends from GNOSTICISM, teaching both a light/darkness dualism and the imprisonment of a spiritual soul in the evil material world. They believe that the soul will be saved by the saviour to come, Manda d'Hayye (The Knowledge of Life), from whose name the designation of the community is derived. [36A; 37]

Mandir [XIII.A] Literally, an 'abiding-place' or 'dwelling': the common word among Hindus for what in English is rendered by 'temple'. The *mandir* is re-garded as the dwelling-place of the deity and is accordingly usually identified as, for example, a SHIVA-*mandir*, a KALI-*mandir*, etc. The gods are thought to dwell where man worships them and abide in the image, making it a living image (*murti*), which is fashioned according to traditional canons of form and beauty, as well as posture (e.g. the *mudras*, or gestures) as laid down in the Shastra (Hindu sacred writings) and AGAMAS. The form need not be human: a dramatic vermilion-smeared stone may also be the dwelling-place of the divine. The small, village *mandir* is in essence a hut, or tiny house, in which the representation of the deity will be found. Larger temples are compounds of sanctuary (*garbha grha*, or womb chamber), courtyard, rooms for pilgrims, and a meeting-hall. The most elaborate temples, embellished with many statues and stone-carvings, were sometimes constructed as representations of Mount MERU, around which, in Hindu cosmogony, the gods dwelt. This was echoed in the structure of the spire or *shikhara*. The usual form of worship in the *mandir* for the layman is either *darshana* (seeing the deity and being in his/her presence) or *puja*, joining in an offering to the god. [14B] (*See also* FESTIVALS AND RITUALS (HINDU).)

Mani [XXX] A prophet (216–77 CE) born of a noble Parthian family (ZOROASTRIANISM) and brought up in Babylonia in a sect within GNOSTICISM. He had his first vision at the age of 12 and later taught that he brought the fulfilment of Zoroastrian, Christian, and Buddhist beliefs. He travelled on missions to India and after receiving royal protection from the Iranian monarch Shabuhr (in *c.* 240 CE) established his teaching in many parts of the Iranian empire. A later monarch imprisoned him and he was put to death, probably in 277, in prison, but by then his teaching had spread into the Roman empire. The Christian St Augustine

(354–430) was a Manichaean before he became a Christian and brought some of his old beliefs with him into his new faith. The main centre of the religion, however, remained north-east of Iran, until it disappeared from history in the 16th century. Mani accepted the Zoroastrian beliefs in God and a devil, heaven and hell, the concept of history (BUNDAHISHN), individual judgement, and a life after death. But he was un-Zoroastrian in his teaching (DUALISM) that matter is evil, in advocating asceticism and celibacy. He was labelled a heretic (*zandik*) by the Zoroastrian priests (MAGI) of the empire in which he mainly lived and worked. His myths of creation and of redemption and his understanding of human nature are typically Gnostic. The Manichaean community was hierarchically structured. Mani's successor, the Twin, resided in Babylon and below him were five grades: 12 teachers, 72 bishops, 360 elders, the body of the Elect (which included women), and the Hearers (the only grade allowed to marry). There was a written canon of scripture (with some fine illuminated manuscripts) and an organized cult using hymns and formal prayers. [40: 67–76; 47]

Manitou [III] An ALGONQUIN term roughly equivalent to 'mysterious' or 'supernatural', used as a noun to designate the supernatural world, and as an adjective to identify any manifestation thereof. In general, *manitou* may refer to: the supreme being; those spirits encountered in visions (VISION QUEST); lesser spirits; or the various powers of nature or other cosmic features [8: I]. Lesser entities exhibit or manifest the quality of *manitou*, as witness, for example, the Narragansett Indians, who used it to describe 'excellence' in men, women, birds, beasts, etc. The term suggests more the presence of a certain 'spirit' or 'disposition' rather than supernatural power, although the latter is frequently associated with a being that is *manitou*.

Mansion of the Gods [IV] The term for temple in ANCIENT EGYPTIAN RELIGION. In the 'god's mansion' the priests performed regular rituals. Solar temples of the 5th dynasty, *c.* 2480 BCE (RE'), and those built for the Aten (18th dynasty, *c.* 1360 BCE) (ATENISM), developed from a different tradition, but the New Kingdom cult temples (for the god) and mortuary temples (for the dead – and deified – kings) developed from *c.* 1500 BCE onwards from the primitive reed-shrines and symbolized the 'ISLAND OF CREATION' [7; 10].

Interior walls, decorated with registers of scenes, showed the king performing rites for the god. Ritual sequences were privately enacted by the high priest. In the daily temple ritual, he cleansed, clothed, offered insignia to, and fed the deity, while, in the ritual for the royal ancestors, the god's food was subsequently offered to the ancestral rulers of Egypt. Other rituals (FESTIVALS) took place periodically, amid public rejoicing, portraying special events in the god's life and mythology. The resurrection of Osiris was annually re-enacted at Abydos and elsewhere. Statues of male deities were carried in procession to the neighbouring temples of their consorts for a period of several weeks. This reflected the belief in the gods in human terms, with a need for food, clothing, and recreation.

Priests were involved in funerary and mortuary rites and in temple worship. The priesthood was hereditary in certain families [21: III, 60], and although it sometimes entailed permanent, powerful appointments, it was usually a subsidiary profession held by lawyers, doctors, or scribes, who spent three months annually in the local temple. As 'god's servants', they had no pastoral duties, but performed the rituals for the deity and instructed the young in the 'House of Life', an area of the temple used for education.

Mansion of the Ka [IV] The term for tombs in ANCIENT EGYPTIAN RELI-

GION. In predynastic Egypt (*c.* 3400 BCE), everyone was buried in simple pit-graves; then, brick-built mastaba-tombs ('bench-shaped') were introduced for royalty and the great nobles (*c.* 3100). These became the standard noble tombs of the Old Kingdom (*c.* 2700–2300 BCE), clustered around the royal PYRAMID and consisting of a superstructure and substructure (above and below ground), a *serdab* where a statue of the deceased stood, and an offering chapel [8: 1, 39].

With increasing democratization in funerary beliefs, provincial nobles built rock-cut tombs near their own capitals and, by the New Kingdom, royalty were themselves buried in deep tombs at Thebes (*c.* 1570–1087 BCE), cut into the Valleys of the Kings and Queens, while their nobles' tombs were scattered throughout the same area. Whatever the design, the tomb – 'Mansion of the Ka' – was regarded as a 'house' for the deceased and, at the burial ceremony, the 'Opening of the Mouth' ritual was performed to bring alive the mummy (MUMMIFICATION) and all the wall-scenes and contents of the tomb. [6]

Manthras [XXX] 'Sacred words', in ZOROASTRIANISM. Primarily these are the *Gathas* of ZOROASTER (*see also* AVESTA), but the term is also used to refer to all prayers. Zoroastrians should pray at the five religious divisions (*gahs*) of the day [5: 258–66]. Before praying, men (and women – there is no difference in the duty of the sexes in this regard) should wash all exposed parts of the body: face, hands, and feet. After untying the sacred cord (*kusti*) which all initiated Zoroastrians wear around the waist as a symbol of the religion after initiation (NAUJOTE), the worshipper faces the light and recites what are known as the '*kusti* prayers'. These involve the formal rejection of evil (ANGRA MAINYU) and the expression of allegiance to the good (AHURA MAZDA). There are a number of important traditional Zoroastrian prayers.

The *Ahuna Vairya* (PAHLAVI *Ahunvar*) is the first taught to any Zoroastrian child and was probably composed by Zoroaster himself. Others are the *Airyema isho*, *Yenghe hatam*, and *Ashem Vohu* [7: III]. The *Frcvarane* is a confessional giving assent to the key Zoroastrian teachings [5: 253–7]. All of these utterances are in Avesta, the sacred language. Zoroastrians believe that prayer in the language of revelation prevents thinking in merely human terms. Some PARSI reformists have called for vernacular translations to aid understanding – since few priests and virtually none of the laity understand Avesta. But the majority faithfully continue to use the language of their prophet, which is believed to create a unique spiritual aura. *Manthras* are thought to be words of power which is made effective through enactment, that is, through recitation. Unspoken, e.g. written, words, or those spoken by an unqualified person, e.g. a non-Zoroastrian (*juddin*), are dead *manthras*. Prayers to the heavenly beings (AMESHA SPENTAS, YAZATAS) effect their protective presence [27].

Mantike [XII] Greek divination. The aim of this was not so much to predict the future as to seek advice concerning a future action – at least until the appearance of Hellenistic astrological determinism (ASTROLOGY). Inquirers were individuals or states. There was both skill-based and inspirational divination. The first involved the interpretation of omens (signs or events) by a *mantis* (diviner) or *exegetes* (official interpreter) chosen by Delphi. Its commonest forms were interpretation of sacrificial victims' entrails (*hieroscopia*) and of the flight of birds (*oionoscopia*). In inspirational divination a god was thought to possess a person and to speak through their mouth. This was the main divination mode at Delphi (TEMENOS): Apollo's *prophetis* (prophetess), who was called Pythia, gave oracular responses while divinely inspired. Delphi was the most important oracle (*manteion/chresterion*), and was consulted as a higher authority transcending the city-states. Delphi played an important advisory role in civic and inter-state archaic (*c.* 700–480 BCE) politics. Other forms of divination included conjuration of ghosts at *nekyomanteia* (oracles of the dead). Oracle-mongers peddled collections of oracles attributed to legendary seers. [2: II, 8; 16: 123–42; 17: 538–42; 18]

Mantra [XIII.A] A mystical verse of Indian scripture, or one having some special significance, as for example the *guru-mantra*, given by a GURU to his pupil on the latter's initiation; in general, an incantation, charm, spell, or chant.

Maori Movements [XX] The oldest continuing movement (of some 30) in New Zealand since 1833 is Ringatu (Upraised Hand), founded by Te Kooti in 1868, with an oral liturgy based on the Hebrew Scriptures (BIBLE); Saturday worship and faith healing are practised. Its 5,000 members are moving in a Christian direction. The largest movement is the Ratana Church, stemming from Wiremu Ratana (1873–1939), a healer in the 1918 influenza epidemic. It rejects traditional religion, and emphasizes angels and Ratana as intermediaries. It has over 25,000 members and considerable political influence. [7; 9]

Mara [IX.A] The 'evil one' in Buddhist mythology. Literally, the name Mara denotes 'the killer'. References to such a being are frequent in the Pali literature [19: 96–163] and are even more extensive and elaborate in Sanskrit Buddhist literature [19: 144–9]. Nevertheless, in Buddhist thought Mara has no absolute ontological status, and like all compounded entities this figure also is resolvable into its constituent psychological and social components. Mara's function, like other elements in Buddhist mythology, is that of a bridge from the everyday understanding of ordinary phenomena to the insight into the nature of things according to Buddhist analysis. [19: 72–80]

Mar'a [XIV] Arabic for 'woman'. Classical ISLAM regarded. women as intellectually inferior to men and of subordinate legal status. Because of the development, at least in urban Islam, of female seclusion, women were virtually excluded from public life and had to exercise any influence from behind the scenes [45: XIII; 47: II]. The movement to open out women's lives and to give them greater rights is part of ISLAMIC MODERNISM, beginning with Qasim Amin (1865–1908), who both advocated a reinterpretation of the QUR'AN and tradition and also appealed to natural justice and individual freedom [38: VII]. In recent decades, secular legislation has in many Islamic countries been assisting this process, but much remains to be achieved at the local and internal family level (*see:* MARRIAGE AND DIVORCE (IN ISLAM); VEILING (IN ISLAM); ZINA). [75]

Marae [XXII] A sacred area in POLYNESIAN RELIGION containing a raised shrine (*ahu*) where priests (TOHUNGA) make offerings and recite chants (*karakia*). Gods and ancestors are sometimes represented by carved posts or stones. *Maraes* range from tiny paved clearings to massive stepped platforms (Society Islands) and walled enclosures (called *heiau* in Hawaii). [3] Among the New Zealand Maori, the *marae* was for communal gatherings, with the most *tapu* (TABU) activities of priests confined to small shrines (*tuahu*) elsewhere. [6: 272–8; 7: 477–84]

Marcionism [XI.A] The teaching of Marcion, a Christian from Asia Minor, who settled in Rome *c.* 144 CE. He maintained that Christianity was a completely new revelation, quite unrelated to the 'Old Testament' (BIBLE) or to Jewish religion. He published the first known CANON of Christian scripture, edited in conformity with his beliefs.

Marduk [VI] During the reign of Hammurabi (1792–1750 BCE) (BABY-

LONIANS; HAMMURABI'S CODE) [7], Marduk, the city deity of Babylon, emerged as supreme god of the pantheon. He was the last divine overlord and the custom of elevating to preeminence the deity of the paramount city-state now ceased [24: 23]. His significance was only finally eclipsed by Ashur, state-god of the ASSYRIANS [25: 39]. Marduk's powers included the ability to obtain medicines (MAGIC) which expelled demons (EVIL). The Epic of Creation, recited at Babylon, praised Marduk's victory over the dragon. (ANCIENT NEAR EASTERN RELIGIONS) [24: 60–71]

Marga [IX.A] A Sanskrit term (Pali *Magga*), meaning the 'way' or 'path', and the term used in Indian religion generally and in BUDDHISM especially for the way of life which the adherent is to follow. Buddhism, because of its avoidance of the extremes of asceticism and hedonism, is called the Middle Way. The Buddhist life is set out in detail in the *atthangika magga*, the noble EIGHTFOLD PATH.

Maria Legio [XX] Known also as Legio Maria, the largest African independent church from a background of ROMAN CATHOLICISM, founded in Kenya in 1963 by two Catholics of the Luo people, Simeon Ondeto and Gaudencia Aoko (b. 1943), and named after the Legion of Mary. Combining Catholic and pentecostal features (PENTECOSTALISM) with healing, exorcism, a strict ethic, and strong African emphasis, it initially attracted upwards of 80,000 adherents, but has since declined and Gaudencia Aoko has left it.

Marrano [XVII] Word of Spanish origin meaning 'swine' and applied to those Jews in the Iberian peninsula who were forcibly converted to Christianity in the 14th and 15th centuries but maintained a secret Jewish life [40]. The expulsion of the Jews from Spain in 1492 was partly intended to prevent Marranos having contact with their old co-religionists (EUROPEAN JEWRY). When Marranos were able to escape from Spanish-ruled territory and from the watchful eye of the Inquisition many of them reverted to JUDAISM. [9 vol. 12: 1022]

Marriage (Christian) [XI.B] Christian marriage has always been characterized by the practice of monogamy (one current wife only) and official resistance to divorce. Traditionally, marriage was justified primarily for producing children and avoiding fornication (SEX), with partnership in the background. Modern Western Christians and ORTHODOX CHURCHES, however, virtually reverse this order. ROMAN CATHOLICISM, the Orthodox Church, and some in ANGLICANISM class marriage as a SACRAMENT. Condemnation of marriage has usually been regarded as an error, except by extreme ascetics. Christian distrust of sex, however, has been a factor in the value placed on celibacy as an aid towards high spiritual attainment (as in MONASTICISM). Roman Catholicism forbids marriage for all clergy. The Orthodox Church permits the ordination (MINISTRY) of married men as deacons or priests but not as bishops. An unmarried priest or deacon cannot marry and one widowed after ordination cannot remarry. Divorce is forbidden by church law for Roman Catholics and (officially) for Anglicans; but decrees of nullity (declaring that a true marriage never existed) can be obtained. In practice many churches in PROTESTANTISM accept divorce under secular law while upholding lifelong marriage as the ideal. [1: 249–58; 93: 206–7; 107: 889–90]

Marriage and Divorce (in Islam) [XIV] Muslim marriage is essentially a civil contract. The partners should be of equal social status, and the bride receives a dowry. Child betrothal is possible, but minimum marriage ages have now been laid down in many Islamic countries by the secular law (e.g. 18 for the bridegroom and 16 for the bride in the Egyptian code of 1931), but marriage between minors remains valid in

the eyes of the SHARI'A. Polygamy retains its Qur'anic sanction, but is
becoming exceptional and is discouraged
by secular law codes. Unilateral divorce
by the husband likewise remains valid
according to Shari'a; modern law
has tried to mitigate this, but the
woman is still comparatively disadvan-
taged. (*See* MAR'A.) [21 'Nikāḥ'; 29: 127–
36; 39 S.VV.; 45: III; VI; 65: XXII]

Marriage (in Judaism) [XVII] It is a
positive duty for Jews to marry and
have at least two children (one male,
one female) in accordance with the commandment 'be fruitful and multiply'
(Genesis 1: 22, 9: 1) [12: III]. The marriage ceremony takes place under a
canopy (*chupah*) and consists in the
groom giving the bride a ring in front of
two witnesses and saying, 'Behold you
are sanctified to me with this ring
according to the law of MOSES and of
ISRAEL' [48: 396]. This is preceded by a
benediction over wine and over the
ceremony. The marriage document
(*ketubbah*) is read, followed by another
blessing over wine and the seven marriage benedictions. The couple then
retire to a room to be alone together
(*yichud*), which completes the marriage
ceremonies [11: 166]. For the marriage
to be dissolved the couple need to
undergo a religious divorce ceremony,
in which the husband presents a specially written bill of divorce (*get*) to his
wife. [52: IX]

Marxism [XXVI] A political creed
derived from the work of Karl Marx
(1818–83) which has been, since the 19th
century, the dominant creed of communism. Communists generally believe
in a society in which there is no private
property. Marxists further believe,
however, in the necessity and inevitabil-
ity of a proletarian revolution to bring
about a communist society. The underlying theoretical approach of Marxists is
generally known as DIALECTICAL
MATERIALISM.

Marxism is sometimes represented as
a SECULAR ALTERNATIVE to religion.

Marx himself held that the criticism of
religion is the beginning of all social
criticism. He saw religion as both an
expression of human distress and as a
means of disguising its true causes. It is
the opium of the people because it offers
them an illusory happiness. It is, in
Marx's sense, IDEOLOGY. It helps to
preserve the established order of society
by encouraging the people to look to
another world for their happiness. Revolution and religion were, for Marx,
alternatives. To secure the real happiness of men it is necessary to abolish
religion as their illusory happiness. [12:
250]

Marxism has sometimes been seen as
a kind of secular religion [22: 196ff].
The writings of Marx himself have
tended to be treated more like a sacred
text than a contribution to science.
Scientists whose views seemed incompatible with dialectical materialism were
once persecuted in the Soviet Union.
More positively, perhaps, former Marxists sometimes use words like 'conversion' and 'faith' [22: 197] to describe
what it was like for them to become a
Marxist. These and other similarities
with religions make it intelligible to
describe Marxism as the major secular
religion to have emerged in the last
century. But such a description cannot
be made without a good deal of qualification. Many would hold that it dis-
torts religion, or Marxism – or both.

Mary, Virgin [XI.B] Mary, as the
mother of JESUS CHRIST, is placed
above the SAINTS for devotion in
ROMAN CATHOLICISM, the ORTHO-
DOX CHURCH, and among Anglo-
Catholics. Special doctrines about her
include the teaching that she is 'ever-
virgin'; 'God-bearer' (*Theotokos*); and
that her body was taken into heaven (the
Assumption) [11: 280]. The Immaculate
Conception (that she was conceived
without sin) was defined dogmatically
for Roman Catholics in 1854 [11: 271].
This is generally rejected by the
Orthodox Church. Popular claims for

her as 'Co-Redemptress' with Christ have receded officially since Vatican COUNCIL II. Belief in the efficacy of her intercession with Christ has helped to encourage numerous special devotions and practices in her honour, such as the rosary cycle of prayers. The 'Sacred Heart' (iconographically represented as Christ opening his chest to reveal his heart as a symbol of his love for mankind) is an example ôf devotions to specific aspects of the person of Christ applied also to Mary. PILGRIMAGES are undertaken to places where she has appeared in visions (e.g. Lourdes). In some countries, e.g. Italy, and in LATIN AMERICA her images and festivals appear to be coloured by pre-Christian cults (SYNCRETISM). PROTESTANTISM has generally rejected this theology and devotion, but some Protestants now express more interest and sympathy. 'Mariolatry' is a Protestant term of abuse implying idolatrous worship of Mary. [3; 53; 95; 107: 882–4]

Masalai [XXII] A Papua New Guinea pidgin word covering a wide variety of animal and land spirits, demons, and minor deities dwelling in caves, streams, and forests. In MELANESIAN RELIGION *masalai* are commonly feared and their haunts avoided, but they are not worshipped or venerated as are spirits of the recent dead or clan ancestors (TUMBUNA). *Masalai* may adopt animal or human forms to attack or deceive people. They enforce TABUS by inflicting accidents or sickness on those who trespass or infringe. [14: 179–82; 22; 23]

Mashhad [XIV] A shrine in ISLAM, literally 'place of martyrdom, witness' (other frequent synonyms include *qubba*, *turba*, and, in the Persian world, *ziyaratgah*, 'place of pilgrimage'). The foremost shrine in Islam is, of course, the Prophet's tomb at Medina, usually visited after the Pilgrimage to Mecca (HAJJ), but lesser shrines are scattered all over the Islamic world, with those of the earlier prophets, Muhammad's companions, and the early Muslims especially concentrated in Palestine, Syria, and Iraq. The shrines of the Shi'i IMAMS and martyrs in Iraq and Iran (e.g. of 'ALI at Najaf, al-Husain at Karbala, 'Ali al-Rida at Mashhad in northeastern Iran and his sister Fatima at Qum) have been richly endowed by the Shi'i faithful (SHI'ISM), and are goals of pilgrimage for them. They are jealously guarded against non-Muslims, and even Sunnis (SUNNA) are unwelcome there. [12; 45: X; architecture: 56: 1]

Masks (Melanesian) [XXII] Masks are the most important man-made objects in MELANESIAN RELIGION. From the intricate carvings and costumes of the Malangan and Dukduk cults of New Ireland and New Britain [9; 23: 45–53] to the towering Hevehe and fantastic Kovave constructions of the Papuan gulf, masks illustrate the high point of traditional art and iconography. [22; 29] Central to MALE CULT rites, masks visibly dramatize the presence of powerful ancestors, gods, and spirit-beings on whom society's security depends. Bullroarers, *garamuts* (slit-gongs or drums made from hollowed logs), and bamboo flutes have a similar function, giving voices to the spirits. Housed in shrines, TABU to the uninitiated, these sacred objects are often destroyed after use, because of their dangerous MANA. Their ceremonial display is at times accompanied by elaborately rehearsed dancing, ritual fighting, fire dance, music and song, and vast communal feasts (SINGSING).

Mass [XI.B] A term used, mainly in ROMAN CATHOLICISM, for the EUCHARIST. PROTESTANTISM rejected it because of the association with the notion of eucharistic sacrifice, although Luther (LUTHERANISM) constructed a 'German Mass'. Anglo-Catholics have revived the term and the associated doctrines in ANGLICANISM. The 'Canon of the Mass' refers to the prayer consecrating the 'elements' (bread and wine). 'High Mass' involves elaborate ceremonial, music, and several assistants, by contrast with the more common 'Low Mass' – a distinction, however, which ended with Vatican COUNCIL II and the LITURGICAL MOVEMENT's emphasis on congregational participation. 'Dry Mass' was a shortened form without the reception of the bread and wine of the Eucharist, popular in the later Middle Ages. The Missal is a book containing the prayers and directives for celebrating Mass throughout the year. 'Requiem Masses' are for the dead at funerals and other occasions. These and other forms of Mass have provided the occasion for much CHURCH MUSIC. [1: 137–78; 30: 254–6; 105 vol. 9: 413–28]

Matres [v] The Celtic *Matres*, the Divine Mothers, are often represented in groups of three in Gaul and Britain. They are accompanied by fertility symbols such as horns of plenty, fruit, loaves, or children, and in Gaul by dogs, birds, and trees. They may appear singly under local names, and many individual Celtic goddesses, such as Epona, the horse-goddess, had a maternal aspect [26: III; 23: V, 204–13]. They have much in common with the VANIR of Scandinavian tradition.

Matsuri [XVI] SHINTO ceremonies and festivals. Shinto as a religion is known primarily for its ceremonies and festivals, which invoke the presence of the KAMI and obtain their approval [general surveys: 3; 17: 168–224]. Combining early shamanistic practices (MIKO) with agricultural rituals, these marked seasonal changes, aided fertility, and warded off plagues. The harvest festival (Niiname-sai) was traditionally the most important, thought of as the time when the male celestial *kami* descended to unite with the female terrestrial *kami*, terminating in a sacred feast. The national ceremonies (Kanname-sai and Niiname-sai) are today conducted by the emperor in private, since he has been formally deprived of his position as the public head of the Shinto state (KOKUTAI SHINTO). Two of the major festivals of Kyoto are anti-calamity

parades. The first is the 15 May Aoi (popularly, hollyhock) festival, when leaves of *Asarum caulescens* (a wild ginger) are offered to the *kami* of the Shimogamo and Kamigamo shrines (SHINTO SHRINES). This is said to have originated in the 6th century as an attempt to obtain relief from storms. The second is the July Gion festival, at the end of which large floats are washed and carried through the city, which traces back to a plague of 876 [3: 30–32, 44–55]. Some have fertility connotations, such as Tanabata, originally the seventh night of the seventh month of the lunar calendar, when two stars cross the sky to meet [9: 79–94]. Numerous festivals celebrate local events and invoke the neighbouring tutelary *kami*. These are accompanied by dancing and singing, the most popular being the *bon-odori*, connected with the return of the souls from their short visit to earth, and rice-planting, growing, and harvesting songs (*taue-uta*).

The order of ritual when conducted at a Shinto shrine in the presence of the *kami* follows a fixed pattern [30: 50–71]. It is done with great precision and deliberation. The priests purify (HARAE) the participants who are requesting a special blessing; all make obeisances in the direction of the *shintai* (or *go-shintai*: the god body); the door of the inner sanctuary is opened and offerings of food or drink are proffered. Prayers are recited, music and dancing follow, and a branch of the evergreen *sakaki* tree is offered. The offerings are then removed, the door of the shrine closed, the last bows made, and the group enjoys feasting and drinking. At most Japanese marriage ceremonies today offerings are made and blessings are received at a Shinto shrine.

Maui [XXII] A culture hero in POLYNESIAN RELIGION. It is believed that Maui was born to Taranga by miscarriage and thrown into the sea. He was saved by the gods (*atua*), who taught him skills and magic. He became

Maui-of-a-Thousand-Tricks, fishing up islands, slowing the sun, stealing fire, and showing mankind the use of barbed hooks and spears. He died while trying to gain immortality for mortals from the goddess of death, Hine-nui-te-Po. [15; 22; 30]

Maya (1) [IX.A] The mother of GOTAMA, the BUDDHA, who, according to Buddhist tradition, possessed all the qualities required in the woman who was to bear a Buddha. She was not passionate, took no alcohol, and observed the precepts of a lay Buddhist faithfully. According to tradition, on the day of her conception she had a dream in which the BODHISATTVA, in the form of a white elephant carrying a white lotus in his trunk, entered her right side; the scene is often depicted in murals in Buddhist temples. [21: 608f]

Maya (2) [XIII.B] An important concept in VEDANTA thought. *Maya* is originally the magical power of creating illusion or deceit, but in the ADVAITA VEDANTA it refers to the illusory existence of a world of multiplicity superimposed upon the single non-dual reality (BRAHMAN) by the power of ignorance (AVIDYA). *Maya* and ignorance may be identified, but, if distinguished, *maya* is the power of God (ISHVARA), which creates the illusion of a differentiated universe and conceals the divine unity behind appearances, while ignorance creates the seemingly separate self at the individual level. *Maya* is not hallucination. The world is seen under a false appearance like the snake on the path which is actually a rope; it is not purely imaginary. The power of *maya* is considered to be neither identical with *brahman* nor completely different. The term *maya* is sometimes used to refer to the SAMKHYA *prakrti* or the divine SHAKTI.

Mbona [II] One of the best-known territorial cults of central Africa. Its principal shrine is situated at Khulubvi by the Shire river in the far south of Malawi among the Mang'anja people. Over 500 years old, its character has changed with altered political and social circumstances; its basic function was rainmaking, but to this was added its role as the official cult of the Lundu paramount chieftainship (although Mbona in the central later tradition was a martyr figure killed by a Lundu chief). If the shrine was effectively dependent upon the political power, it had also a certain spiritual and moral independence. The organization of the shrine, besides 'Mbona's wife', priests, and medium, included representatives of many chieftainships and messengers bringing petitions from a wide area, including the Indian Ocean, far beyond Mang'anja territory. Lesser Mbona shrines were set up elsewhere with a varying theology. Mbona illustrates both the historical depth and the inter-tribal spread of African religious institutions. [11: 73–94; 13: 147–86; 16: 219–40]

Medicine Bundles [III] In North America, within the context of the VISION QUEST, it was common for the visionary to receive a talisman as a tangible sign of the supernatural power conferred upon him by his GUARDIAN SPIRIT [8: VII]. The sacred bag or pouch might contain such objects representative and evocative of power as eagle feathers, shells, animal parts, tobacco (CALUMET), herbs, or porcupine quills. Its conferment was often accompanied by instructions regarding its care and use, including certain prohibitions. A medicine song, often used in association with the medicine bundle, might also be added. The bundle thus served as an individual emblem, symbolizing the relationship between the visionary and his guardian spirit.

Medicine Man [III] General designation for a SHAMAN, diviner, or healer, among Amerindians [22: 1]. Although details of election, initiation, and role within the group vary, common elements may be observed. Among the Ogalala SIOUX, the *wicasa wakan* or *winyan wicasa* (literally 'man sacred', 'woman sacred') are distinguished from the *pejuta wicasa* (literally 'medicine man'), the latter being primarily concerned with conventional medicine [17: VI]. The general pattern for the former includes: some initial indication of spiritual election (e.g. childhood vision); additional omens; consultation with an established holy man (or woman); and, if so advised, embarkation on the VISION QUEST (*hanbleceya*, literally, 'crying for a vision') [22: III]. Those whose visions indicate a potential career undergo a period of apprenticeship wherein ritual and curing techniques are learned (*see* MIDEWIWIN). After his/her assumption of the role as visionary, healer, interpreter of dreams, and intermediary with the supernaturals, the *wicasa wakan* renews his/her power. Loss of power, especially with the advance of years, occasions retirement and replacement by younger practitioners.

Meher Baba [XXI] A relatively loose-knit movement of 'Baba-lovers' tries to follow the teachings of their Indian master, Meher Baba, who observed a silence from 1925 until his death in 1969. Western devotees are mainly, though not exclusively, to be found in the U.S.A. They accept that Baba was incarnated God, the AVATARA, and that the most direct path to self-realization is love and complete surrender to Baba. [2: 64; 28; 30: III]

Melanesian Religion [XXII] Melanesia comprises Irian Jaya, Papua New Guinea, the Solomon Islands, Vanuatu (formerly New Hebrides), and New Caledonia. Despite great regional diversity, general religious similarities exist and can be illustrated from Papua New Guinean examples. Oral traditions preserve stories and songs about the creators of local culture and bringers of knowledge and skills (DEMA DEITIES). More important, generally, are the tribal ancestors (TUMBUNA) and numerous land-spirits (MASALAI) inhabiting streams, trees, or animals, who regulate spiritual power (MANA) within the tribal territory. Through dreams,

possession, mediums, and prophets the living keep in touch with their deities and ancestors, forming a continuing community. Right relationships, maintaining life and prosperity, are established through rituals. Central among these are MALE CULTS of initiation and purification, usually associated with shrines or spirit-houses (HAUS TAMBARAN). Birth, marriage, and funeral rites also ensure peace and security. Elaborate festivals of ritual and dance (SINGSING) and complex trading exchanges renew bonds both with ancestor-spirits and with other social groups among the living. Birds, lizards, snakes, sharks, and certain plants as totems are recognized in local custom and folklore, and serve to unite clan groups with their natural habitat. Secret techniques for healing, magic, and sorcery (POISEN) are available for good or harmful use. Spiritual powers are believed to make themselves present on ritual occasions, in sacred MASKS, drums, flutes, and other artefacts. After widespread missionary influence during this century, traditional beliefs and practices have declined greatly. Yet they still lie beneath much Melanesian Christianity, and reappear from time to time in prophetic movements and so-called CARGO CULTS. [2; 14; 20; 23; 25]

Mencius [X] Meng Tzu (371–289 BCE), the Confucian philosopher who comes closest to the thought of CONFUCIUS himself. He had an official post in the state of Ch'i for a time, but he spent most of his life travelling from state to state, attempting to convert rulers to his teachings. He emphasized the Confucian values, goodness (*jen*) and righteousness (*i*), and believed knowledge of them to be innate in the human mind (*hsin*). Although he argued for the innate goodness of human nature he also stressed the need for moral cultivation and moral reflection in order to recover the 'lost mind' [7: III, 51–83]. He regarded such cultivation as conforming

Mende Religion

to the Will of Heaven (*T'ien Ming*).
Mencius insisted that rulers should govern in accordance with the Will of
Heaven (T'IEN) and for the benefit of
the people. He was on occasion quite
critical of certain rulers, particularly
King Hui of Liang. [19: V, 81–105; 31:
VI, 106–31; 54: 73]

Mende Religion [II] The Mende of
Sierra Leone and Liberia believe in
Ngewo, creator of the universe and all
spirits. The word's meaning is uncertain; an earlier name is Leve, 'the
high-up one'. The earth is sometimes
described as his wife. In emergency
Ngewo is invoked directly, but normally
through the ancestors: the near and
known ones, the Kekeni, and through
them the remote ones, the Ndebla. The
Mende practise a complex ancestor-cult,
including post-funeral grave-rites and
further routine offerings, but especially
sacrifices at times of misfortune.
However, much of Mende religion is
related to the major secret societies
which control various areas of life: the
Poro, male initiation and political
advancement; the Sande, female initiation, childbirth, and the maintenance of
womanly virtue; the Humoi, the laws of
marriage and sexual relationships. All
have their own rituals, initiations, and
sacrifices. Mende religion is characterized by the balance of ancestor-cult
and secret society, both subservient to
Ngewo, remote but never absent [4:
111–37].

Mendelssohn, Moses [XVII] The first
important Jewish thinker of the
Enlightenment, Mendelssohn (1729–
86) taught himself European languages
and launched on a career as a German
writer [9 vol. II: 1328]. He translated
the BIBLE into German, printed in
Hebrew characters to enable his coreligionists to learn that language, and
advocated educational reforms and religious tolerance for Jews in his book
Jerusalem. He claimed that the beliefs of
JUDAISM were not dogmas but the conclusions of a universal rational religion.
[2; 42: III; 52: 71]

Menstruation (in Judaism) [XVII] The
menstruant woman is considered ritually unclean in the BIBLE. In order to
become ritually pure she bathes in a bath
of living water (MIKVEH), usually
spring or rain water. In post-TEMPLE
times ritual impurity ceased to play a
major role in Jewish religious life. The
only surviving restrictions on the
menstruant (*niddah*) relate to the prohibition on sexual relations with her
husband until she takes a ritual bath a
week after menstruation has ceased [9
vol. 12: 1141]. These laws are known as
the laws of 'family purity' (*taharat
ha-mishpachah*), and are strictly adhered
to today by Orthodox Jews though not
by Reform Jews (REFORM JUDAISM).
The RABBIS of the TALMUD explained
the family-purity laws not by reference
to ritual impurity, but as necessary to
prevent the husband taking his sexual
relations with his wife for granted.
When they resume their sex life together, after menstrual separation, they
are like bride and groom once again.
[52: 155]

Merkabah Mysticism [XVII] The mystical tradition of the early rabbinical
period was known as Maaseh Merkabah, since the goal of this tradition was a
vision of the divine throne or chariot
(*merkabah*), depicted in the opening
chapter of Ezekiel [15: III]. In order to
attain to this vision the adept had to go
into a state of mystical contemplation
and then to pass through seven stages or
'halls' (*heikhalot*). Each hall is guarded
by an ANGEL, who will not allow anyone through who does not know the
correct mystical password. These passwords are meditational names made up
of letter combinations of the Hebrew
alphabet. The Merkabah tradition was
an esoteric one which could only be
passed on to a student who already had
some mystical understanding, and could
only be taught to one student at a time

[52: 91]. The TALMUD tells how four sages went on a mystical journey to Paradise, and only one emerged unharmed [45: 11].

Meru, Mount [XIII.A] The legendary mountain of Hindu cosmology which is the centre of the world; round it revolve sun, moon, and stars. On the four sides of Meru are four continents, separated from each other by oceans and identified by the trees growing on them at the point adjacent to the mountain. Thus the southern continent, having a rose-apple (*jambu*) tree, was called the island (*dvipa*) of *jambu* (Jambudvipa). This contained the Himalaya mountains, and to its south was the land called Bharata-varsha (the land of the sons of Bharata – the eponymous ancestor of the people of India, to whom the name MAHA-BHARATA also refers). In another version of the cosmology found in the PURANAS, Jambudvipa encircles Meru, and is surrounded by an ocean and another continent, forming a concentric circle. (*See also* MANDIR.) [2: 490f]

Mesoamerican City (200–1521 CE) [XIX] Mesoamerican culture from the middle of the 2nd millennium BCE on was organized at ceremonial centres which developed, during the Classic period (200–900 CE), into impressive sacred cities [18: 225–35; 19: V]. The earliest example of the elaborate ceremonial centres at which incipient urban institutions were organized was the Olmec culture, whose priestly élites operating in scattered ceremonial precincts controlled long-distance trade, exquisite artistic traditions, and widespread religious cults [10: 35–43]. Towards the end of the 1st millennium BCE new centres of culture developed in the central plateau of Mexico, the lowland Mayan region, and the valley of Oaxaca [10: V]. While village farming communities and hunting and gathering peoples prospered within their spheres of influence, it was the city and city-state (*tlatocayotls*) which set the style for

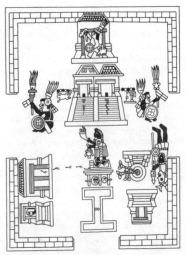

Aztec ceremonial centre (Great Temple of Huitzilopochtli, Tenochtitlan)

political organization, economic exchange, and religious patterns. The major ceremonial cities like Teotihuacan, Tikal, CHOLOLLAN, Monte Albán, Tula, Xochicalco, Tajin, Chichen Itza, and Tenochtitlan were characterized by hierarchically structured, functionally specialized social institutions which were the instruments for the creation of political, economic, social, and sacred space. [9: 11, III] Directed by organized priesthoods and divine rulers, these sacred cities were marked by pyramid temples, palaces, ceremonial courtyards (*see figure*), market-places, terraces, BALL COURTS, and platform mounds. Utilizing intellectual models from what could be termed cosmo-magical thought, which presupposed an intimate parallelism between the mathematically expressible regimes of the heavens and the biologically determined rhythms of life on earth [18: V], the sacerdotal élites organized their capitals around majestic shrines which linked the citizens to the supernatural world, tended to divide their kingdoms into four quarters conforming to the cosmological design, and strove to achieve precise parallels between ritual, ritual architecture, and cosmogonic dramas. Clear examples of this pattern were Teotihuacan, Tula Xicocotitlan, Chichen Itza, and Tenochtitlan. Special variations of this pattern of organization were utilized in the Mixtec and Mayan regions. [5: VI; 10: 55–72]

Mesoamerican Religions [XIX] Mesoamerican religions include those religious traditions developed in central and southern Mexico, the Yucatan peninsula, El Salvador, Guatemala, and parts of Honduras, Nicaragua, and Costa Rica between 2300 BCE and 1521 CE. Civilizations like the Toltec, Mayan (CLASSIC MAYA), Huastec, Mixtec, and Aztec shared such cultural and religious features as: monumental ceremonial centres (MESOAMERICAN CITY); complex ritual and solar calendars (TONAL-POHUALLI; CALENDAR STONE), which intermeshed to create 52-year cycles (NEW FIRE CEREMONY); writing (CODEX (MESOAMERICAN)); HUMAN SACRIFICE (AZTEC) and a cosmology designed in terms of four cardinal directions and the centre (CEMANA-HUAC) inhabited by complex pantheons of gods (HUITZILOPOCHTLI; OMETE-OTL; QUETZALCOATL; TETEOINNAN; TEZCATLIPOCA; TLALOC). These religious traditions flourished in major cities like Teotihuacan, El Tajin, Tikal, Monte Alban, CHOLOLLAN, Tula (TOLLAN), Chichen Itza, and Tenochtitlan, where organized priesthoods (TEOPIXQUE) and divine rulers (TLATOANI) organized community life around great ceremonial centres which connected the community to the supernatural realm and legitimated the authority of élite groups. Generally, these ceremonial centres consisted of pyramid temples, palaces, ceremonial courtyards, market-places, BALL COURTS, and platform mounds. Elaborate calendrical rituals, often culminating in

human sacrifices, of others or by self-immolation, were carried out within these ceremonial precincts.

Messiah (in Judaism) [XVII] Coming from the Hebrew *mashiach*, or 'anointed one'. The Messiah is the appointed one of God who will come in some future time at the beginning of the Messianic age [47: XXIX]. The Jewish exiles (EXILE) will be gathered in to the HOLY LAND and there will be a resurrection of the dead and the judgement of mankind. Biblical references to the Messiah and the Messianic age are couched in symbolic language, and were variously interpreted in rabbinical and medieval Jewish literature. The belief in the coming of the Messiah and the resurrection of the dead are two of MAIMONIDES' 13 principles of Jewish doctrine [22: XIII, XIV]. Throughout Jewish history the Messianic hope has helped the Jews to survive suffering and persecution. It has also led to Messianic movements which have at times generated a fever pitch of excitement among Jewish communities, and greatly enriched Jewish folklore with Messianic legends and stories [46: 1].

Methodism [XI.B] A section of the Evangelical Revival (REVIVALISM) led by John Wesley (1703–91) (ARMINI-ANISM) [6] and George Whitefield (1714–70) (CALVINISM). Wesley taught justification by faith and Christian, perfection (SALVATION), using lay preachers to develop a chain of fellowship societies. After separating from ANGLICANISM, English Methodism suffered many divisions, but it was largely reunited in 1932. Methodism is most numerous in the U.S.A [16], pioneered there by Francis Asbury (1745–1816). The largest body is the United Methodist Church (1968). CHURCH ORGANIZATION resembles that of PRESBYTERIANISM. WORSHIP combines formal and informal elements. Methodism does have a prayer book, historically derived from Anglicanism but recently revised under the influence of the LITURGICAL MOVEMENT. Its use is, however, not compulsory. Hymn singing is central and extemporary prayer customary. (*See also* CHRISTIAN FELLOWSHIP CHURCH, HARRIS MOVEMENT). [32]

Mezuzah [XVII] Parchment roll on which the first two paragraphs of the SHEMA (Deuteronomy 6: 4–9, 11: 13–21) are handwritten [48: 41–2]. A *mezuzah* is attached to every doorpost in the traditional Jewish home, usually inside a decorated case [52: 199]. This is in fulfilment of a literal understanding of the commandment, 'You shall write them on the doorposts of your house' (Deuteronomy 6: 9, 11: 20). It is customary for Orthodox Jews to kiss the *mezuzah* on entering or leaving a house. [9 vol. 11: 1474]

Midewiwin [III] Literally, 'mystic doings', an occult-medicine society in North America, primarily found among the Ojibwa or Chippewa Indians. Members (*mide*) of the Midewiwin, having paid the requisite entrance fee and received instruction from an elder *mide*, may progress through initiatory rites into the society's four levels. Initiates, usually seeking secret healing rituals and powers for themselves, first acquire a knowledge of medicinal herbs and techniques, as well as of the mythic precedent. In the medicine-lodge (*midewigan*), the neophyte undergoes a ritual death and rebirth, having first been shot with *migis* (small white clam shells) and then revived through contact with the same MEDICINE BUNDLES. The initiate may then progress to the status of MEDICINE MAN, at the highest of the society's levels. [23: IX]

Midrash [XVII] Jewish tradition of biblical exegesis found in rabbinical (RABBI) literature: the Palestinian and Babylonian TALMUDS, the Aramaic translations (TARGUM) of the BIBLE, and the various collections known by the name of Midrash. Midrash may be either Halakhic (HALAKHAH), interpreting and applying the legal and ritual norms of the Bible, or Aggadic (AGGADAH), expounding theological and ethical teachings on the basis of a biblical text [53: 18]. Midrashic exegesis does not, on the whole, seek the plain meaning of scripture but the relationship between a biblical idea or theme and the very different social and cultural context of rabbinical JUDAISM [47: 339; 50: 223; 51: XV]. One of the tasks of Midrash is reconciling texts which appear contradictory. It was the availability of Midrashic techniques which allowed Pharisaic Judaism (PHARISEES) to survive the destruction of the second TEMPLE in 70 CE, and to reconstitute Judaism at the rabbinical councils of Yavneh and Usha in the 1st and 2nd centuries CE.

Miko [XVI] Female shamans in SHINTO. Formally called *kamiko* and *ichiko*, these are the young women who are dedicated to the service of the KAMI and carry out duties at the SHINTO SHRINES [17: 137–9; 18: 181–215; 30: 43–6]. Traditionally selected from certain families, in a rigid regimen involving years of strict virginal life, the former are trained to assist the Shinto priests and perform the sacred dances (*kagura*) (MATSURI). They are seen at shrines wearing white blouses and red skirts, symbols of their vows. The *ichiko*, more properly SHAMANS, evolved spontaneously as mediums, who may become possessed and be in contact with spirits not normally encountered through shrine activities. Many female shamans are identified in early SHINTO LITERATURE, especially as wives or daughters of emperors, or ruling alone, allowing the emperor to devote more time to politics. In medieval times, when official support for shrines and temples was reduced, the *miko* system broke down and mediums scattered and travelled, practising divination and exorcizing through incantations (HARAE).

Mikveh [XVII] A pool or 'gathering' of natural water used for ritual purification in JUDAISM. It is usually constructed by allowing rain water to collect in a specially designed container; once the required minimum amount is present to constitute a *mikveh* a separate container of tap water is joined to the 'living water'. Ritual bathing takes place in the tap water which technically becomes an extension of the natural water, but can be changed by draining and refilling [52: 156]. The *mikveh* is used today by traditional Jews for a variety of purposes. Women bathe in it at the end of their period of menstrual separation (MENSTRUATION) and after childbirth before resuming sexual relations with their husbands. Converts (CONVERSION) to Judaism must immerse themselves (*tevilah*) in a *mikveh*, and vessels bought from GENTILES must be dipped in one before they can be used in the preparation of food. Pietistical Jews immerse themselves before prayers, or before the Sabbath (SHABBAT). [9 vol. II: 1534]

Milinda [IX.A] Ancient Indo-Greek king, of the city of Sagala (identified with modern Sialkot) [21: 1090], whose 'questions' concerning Buddhist teaching and practice, addressed to the Buddhist *thera* (THERAVADA), Nagasena, together with the latter's replies, constitute a Pali Buddhist classic, the *Milindapanha*, of which there was also a Sarvastivadin (SARVASTIVADA) version [37: 330]. A Sinhalese translation was made in the 18th century [22: 284], and an English translation by I. B. Horner published in 1963. [11B]

Millenarianism [XI.B] The belief in a future 1,000-year period of JESUS CHRIST's rule on earth. Pre-millennialists believe it will follow the Second Coming of Christ, post-millennialists that it will prepare for that coming by spreading righteousness over the earth. Millenarianism has produced special 'Adventist' SECTS, some specifically dating the 'End', such as the followers of William Miller (1782–1842) in the U.S.A. Millenarianism tends to increase

in times of political and social stress. [51; 107: 916; 120]

Mimamsa [XIII.B] ('investigation') is systematic HERMENEUTICS of the Vedic scriptures. This is very old, with origins in the period of the BRAHMANAS, but its surviving literature is much more recent. Two Mimamsas are distinguished, each of which is one of the six DARSHANAS or salvation-philosophies of classical Hinduism: (1) *Purva-mimamsa* (Investigation of the earlier portions of the Veda), also called *Karma-mimamsa* (Investigation of ritual action) or just *Mimamsa*; and (2) *Uttara-mimamsa* (Investigation of the later portions, i.e. the *Upanishads*), also called *Brahma-mimamsa* (Investigation of BRAHMAN), but usually known as VEDANTA. The classic text of the *Purva-mimamsa* is the *Mimamsa-sutra*, attributed to Jaimini (*c*. 2nd century BCE), with an authoritative commentary by Shabara (probably 6th century CE) [8: IX, 319]. The main concern was to expound the rules of interpretation of the VEDA, understood as eternal and authoritative. Vedic statements were explained as injunctions for the performance of sacrificial and other actions (KARMA) that would create a new potency capable of determining the individual's future after death. The Vedic gods were identified with the ritual words themselves.

More philosophically evolved Mimamsa systems were developed around the 8th century by Kumarila Bhatta and Prabhakara, drawing from NYAYA and Buddhist thought [8: IX, 324–5]. Distinctive views were set forth on the sources of knowledge (*pramana*), the nature of sound, and the way in which things are known. The notions of a supreme deity (ISHVARA) and of a periodical creation and destruction of the universe were attacked. The influence of the *Karma-mimamsa* has been very strong in ritual practice and some aspect of Hindu law. Its hermeneutics are central to the usual Hindu understanding of their scriptures as embodying eternal truths rather than historical accidents. [5: I, 367–405]

Ministry (Christian) [XI.A, B] The early Christian ministry was flexible and variable. The APOSTLES exercised some supervision over the churches, but some GENTILE churches strongly resisted the control of the Jerusalem apostles, while even in JERUSALEM they were soon superseded by a *sanhedrin* of Elders directed by James the Just.

In many churches the leadership was charismatic. Even where there were elders on the Jewish model their authority might be overruled by itinerant prophets. In the Corinthian church there was a tendency to be impatient of any control; in Philippi the church was administered by 'bishops' and 'deacons' (superintendents and ministers). In the 1st century CE the institution of the single bishop in each church had scarcely emerged. Nor was there any idea of a sacrificing priesthood; all church members shared in a common priesthood. [A9; 11]

Later, in ROMAN CATHOLICISM, the ORTHODOX CHURCH, and ANGLICANISM priests were 'ordained' (consecrated) to administer SACRAMENTS (*see also* MARRIAGE). Priestly orders and confirmation (sacraments) are administered by bishops in Roman Catholicism and Anglicanism. Confirmation is administered together with baptism by Orthodox Church priests. The bishops' authority is thought to descend from JESUS CHRIST's commission to the APOSTLES (apostolic succession). PROTESTANTISM reacted against the sacrificial implications of 'priesthood' and the MASS, and against the special status of bishops. Protestants generally use the terms ministry and minister. When bishops were retained (in LUTHERANISM, American METHODISM, and the MORAVIAN BRETHREN), they were seen mainly as useful traditional supervisory officials.

Some Protestants regarded other forms of ministry as of divine origin (PRESBYTERIANISM) but many adapted ministry according to need. The deacon originally assisted the priest and administered charity. This continues in the Orthodox Church, and with varying functions in Protestantism. Roman Catholicism and Anglicanism retain the office as a stage to the priesthood. Various other offices are used in CHURCH ORGANIZATION and oversight which may be regarded broadly as 'ministries'.

Anti-clericalism (hostility to the power and status of priests or ministers) has often occurred in Christian history [B119]. It was a factor in the REFORMATION which often reduced the status of the priesthood. Most churches now encourage a 'ministry' by lay people (i.e. those not ordained) [B139; I: 56–65, 489–522], although only Protestantism allows ordination of women. French Roman Catholics have experimented with 'worker-priests' [B121] engaged in secular occupations. [B.I: 532–76; 81; 107: 1004]

Mishnah [XVII] The first text of rabbinical Judaism, edited from previous collections by RABBI Judah the Prince and his colleagues at the end of the 2nd century CE [8; 29: 83]. The Mishnah is divided into six sections: (1) agricultural laws and benedictions; (2) festivals (CHAGIM); (3) laws relating to women; (4) civil laws; (5) holy things; (6) ritual purity laws. The Mishnah deals primarily with halakhic (HALAKHAH) issues and became the authoritative source for later Judaism [50: V; 51: III, IV].

Missions (Christian) [XI.B] Medieval Christianity became a largely European religion after the conversion of the Roman empire and its 'barbarian' successors (but cf. ASIA and RUSSIA, CHRISTIANITY IN; ORTHODOX CHURCH). ISLAM soon barred access to the East (cf. CRUSADES). Subsequent missionary history is related to (without being wholly determined by)

European trade and colonialism. Thus 16th-century Spanish, Portuguese, and French expansion, as well as COUNTER-REFORMATION zeal, encouraged missions to the Americas and Asia. PROTESTANTISM, struggling for survival (and perhaps inhibited theologically by the doctrine of predestination (CALVINISM)), lagged behind. The dramatic 19th-century development of Protestant missions relates to British colonial expansion, but even more to energies released by the Evangelical Revival (REVIVALISM). The missions of ROMAN CATHOLICISM also revived. Missions made Christianity a world religion, while revealing its limitations. BUDDHISM, HINDUISM, CONFUCIANISM, and in particular Islam proved culturally and religiously resistant to it; AFRICAN RELIGIONS much less so. Missionaries (especially Protestants) were reluctant to accommodate to other religions; looked down on non-Western cultures; and were slow to create churches independent of European control. Independence was accelerated by the shock of decolonization after 1945 and by communism in CHINA.

It remains difficult to assess the missionary achievement, which may have been as much cultural and political as religious. Missionaries did important pioneering medical and educational works, although reforming zeal often damaged societies and their culture (ECUMENICAL MOVEMENT). Non-Western styles of Christianity are only slowly emerging (along with syncretistic (SYNCRETISM) cults, perhaps in reaction against Westernization). But the future of Christianity may well lie outside Europe. [5:385–437; 20 vol. 6; 33; 65; 82; 83; 100]

Mithras/Mithraism [xxx] Mithras was a god popular in the Roman empire from the 2nd to the 5th centuries CE. His cult was strongest in the frontier regions, notably along the Rhine and Danube, also in Rome and her port of Ostia. It was socially respectable, being popular among the military and officials. The cult claimed descent from ZOROASTER. Mithras was an Indo-Iranian deity (INDO-EUROPEANS) and he is worshipped in both HINDUISM and ZOROASTRIANISM [17], but scholars are divided on whether the Roman cult had any real continuity with these religions [4; 14; 21]. The Roman temples were made to look like caves, to imitate the universe, the cosmic cave, as the Romans perceived it. Mithras was spoken of as the creator and father of all; his worshippers also believed that he saved men. The focal point of temples was a relief showing Mithras slaying the bull (*tauroctony*), a scene interpreted in different ways by scholars, and probably by different Mithraists: as the act of creation, or of salvation, or as having esoteric astrological significance. Other scenes which decorate many temples include a divine banquet shared by Mithras and Sol over the body of the bull, a myth scene which was re-enacted in the cult. Temples were small and fellowship was a central emphasis of the cult (although women were excluded). There were seven grades of initiation, each of which stood under the protection of a planet: *Corvus* (Raven), protected by Mercury; *Nymphus* (Bride), protected by Venus; *Miles* (Soldier), protected by Mars; *Leo* (Lion), protected by Jupiter; *Perses* (Persian), protected by the moon; *Heliodromus* (Runner of the Sun), protected by the sun; and *Pater* (Father), protected by Saturn. Progression through the grades was believed to correspond to the ascent of the soul through the planetary spheres [41: VI, XIV]. The religious life was disciplined, ascetic, and arduous [8; 26; 40].

Mitzvah [XVII] (literally 'commandment', plural *mitzvot*) According to rabbinical tradition there are 613 *mitzvot* (248 positive, 365 negative) in the Pentateuch (BIBLE) [9 vol. 5: 760] which God commanded the Jewish people to obey, and seven Noachian *mitzvot* applicable to the sons of Noah, i.e.

GENTILES. The best-known group of *mitzvot* is the ten commandments or Decalogue (Exodus 20: 2–14, Deuteronomy 5: 6–18), which is of central importance for JUDAISM. Care was taken, however, not to emphasize the Decalogue, to avoid creating the impression that only these ten *mitzvot* were divinely revealed. In the course of time all halakhic norms (HALAKHAH) built around the biblical commandments came to be thought of as *mitzvot*, since they drew their ultimate authority from God. This is based on the traditional Jewish exegesis of Deuteronomy 17: 9–11 ('According to the TORAH which they [i.e. the religious leaders] will teach you' [32: 160, 668]), implying that the rabbinical developments of ritual have divine sanction. Certain *mitzvot* play a major role in the life of the Jew and are determinants of Jewish identity: CIRCUMCISION for the male Jewish child; MARRIAGE and laws of sexual relations; the duty of Torah study; prayer; the dietary laws (KASHRUT); the MEZUZAH parchment attached to the doorposts of the Jewish home; contributions to charity or *tzedakah*; the Sabbath (SHABBAT) and festival (CHAGIM) rituals. Modern Jews may not keep all these commandments in quite the traditional way, and REFORM JUDAISM has modified many ritual details [42: VII] to adjust Judaism to modern life, but the essentials of the *mitzvot* still represent what is distinctive in Jewish religion. From the medieval period until modern times Jewish theologians have sought to find reasons for the *mitzvot* (*ta'amei ha-mitzvot*), and to explain their value in psychological, ethical, or mystical terms.

Mizimu [II] The spirits of the dead or ancestral spirits in many BANTU languages (singular: *muzimu, mudzimu, mzimu*). Linguistically this is one of the most widely extended words in African religion (cf. NGANGA); it is the normal word for the dead from the SHONA in Zimbabwe, northward across Zambia,

Malawi, and Tanzania to Rwanda, and to the Banyoro and Baganda in Uganda (*see* GANDA). It overlaps with many God-names: LEZA, Imana, MULUNGU, MWARI, Ruhanga, KATONDA, but is nevertheless far from universal in Bantu religions, seldom appearing in this form in the west or south (*but see* MODIMO). The *mizimu* can help or harm the living, and receive regular veneration (*see* ANCESTOR WORSHIP (AFRICAN)). The word itself indicates a status and power not possessed by living elders, and, significantly, is not in the normal nounclass for persons.

Mo Tzu [X] (*c.* 470–391 BCE). An anti-Confucian, pragmatic philosopher who argued that the validity of a theory, policy, or action should be determined by: (1) whether it was employed by the sage-rulers in history; (2) whether there were contemporary testimonies to its validity; and (3) whether it had any practical outcome, in increasing the health, wealth, and general wellbeing of the population [7: IX, 222–30]. His third criterion was the most central to his thought and he used it in condemning many Confucian values and practices (CONFUCIUS). He criticized the exclusive emphasis on filial piety (*hsiao*) and differentiated love, and condemned elaborate FUNERAL RITES, rites (LI) generally and music (*yo*). He emphasized the value of Universal Love (*Chien Ai*) in terms of the benefits it produces; and condemned offensive wars on similarly utilitarian grounds. Mo Tzu found a further sanction for his teaching on Universal Love in his doctrine of the Will of Heaven (*T'ien Ming*). [7: IX, 217–21]

Mo Tzu's advocacy of the policy of 'Agreement with the Superior' (*Shang T'ung*) on the political level seems to have favoured a disciplined and authoritarian theocratic state. His condemnation of offensive wars did not lead to pacifism but to the organization of a disciplined military force of loyal followers who were trained to defend weaker states against aggressors. [31: V, 81–105; 65: L, 257–9]

The later sections of the Mohist texts, written after Mo Tzu's death, are largely concerned with defensive military tactics and the systematic exposition of Mohist concepts [35]. As a movement Mohism flourished during the Later Warring States period (402–221 BCE), but it was practically extinct by the beginning of the Han dynasty (206 BCE). [7: IX, 211–31; 19: IV, 60–80; 31: V, 76–105; 65; 66]

Modimo [II] (sometimes Molimo, or Morimo) is the name for God among a number of southern African BANTU peoples: the Tswana, Sotho, Pedi, and others. The word is linked etymologically with *muzimu* (MIZIMU), the most common Bantu name for ancestral spirit. The ancestors are here called *Badimo*. This linguistic linkage between God and the ancestors has proved confusing to observers, but the deep distinction between the two remained clear enough in the minds of most users, even if this appears an area in which belief in the creator God had become more vague and ineffectual than elsewhere [15: 116–22].

Moksha [XIII.A] 'Release', 'liberation', or 'escape' are possible renderings of this Sanskrit word; it is the recognized goal of Hindu religious activity. It is also the fourth end of human life [1: 276–366], beyond DHARMA, ARTHA, and KAMA, all of which when properly followed culminate in this supreme goal, which is the final transcending of mortal existence.

Monasticism (Christian) [XI.B] Christian monasticism originated in loosely organized communities of hermits in the 4th century CE who had retreated to the Egyptian desert in search of perfection. The monk's original aim was personal SALVATION, although later his sanctity was also thought to benefit those in ordinary life. His central activities are the daily 'hours' of prayer (WORSHIP), and work (originally manual). He is supported by a life under special rules, including the vows of poverty, chastity, and obedience. The Rule of St Benedict (450–543 CE) [11: 116–27] has been of primary influence in Western monasticism. (For the ORTHODOX CHURCH *see* MONASTICISM (ORTHODOX CHRISTIAN).) Benedictine 'orders' of groups of monasteries include the Cluniacs and Cistercians. From the 12th century onwards orders of friars developed. In contrast to monks, friars were active in the world, preaching and teaching, but unlike ordinary clergy they lived under the 'rule' authorized for their order. They include Franciscans (St Francis of Assisi, *c.* 1181–1226 [11: 128–31]) and Dominicans (St Dominic, 1170–1221). The Jesuits (St Ignatius Loyola, 1491–1556) were even more flexible, being active in the COUNTER-REFORMATION and MISSIONS. The numerous female orders (nuns) were usually more strictly enclosed at first than were those for men. But in more recent times nuns have been typically involved in nursing, educational, and charitable work outside the confines of the convent (house for nuns). PROTESTANTISM rejected monasticism, but 19th-century Anglo-Catholics (ANGLICANISM) revived it. LUTHERANISM and French CALVINISM (at Taizé) have also revived monasticism. Monasticism has made large contributions to civilization, culture, education, scholarship, and the arts, and to missions. [1: 466–82; 72; 107: 930]

Monasticism (Orthodox Christian) [XI.D] All Orthodox monks and nuns belong to one spiritual family. There are no separate 'orders' as in the Western Church (MONASTICISM (CHRISTIAN)). Orthodox monastic life is centred on prayer (CONTEMPLATION; HESYCHASM) and self-discipline, and takes several forms.

Hermits are monks or nuns who live alone, following the tradition of St

Antony the Great (d. *c.* 355), in a life
of solitude and prayer. Communities
of hermits (*sketes*) exist, especially on
Mt Athos (Greece). Fully communal
monasteries (called coenobitic) developed, under the influence of St Pacho-
mius (d. *c.* 346), St Basil (d. 378), and St
Theodore (759–826) [35: 247ff; 26: 54
ff]. In the medieval period more relaxed
forms of community life appeared, in
the idiorrhythmic monasteries, in which
each monk organizes his own pattern of
work, and can possess a certain amount
of private property. From St Basil,
Orthodox monasticism inherited a
strong tradition of caring service.

Monks are of three grades. The
rasophoros takes no vows, but lives and
studies the monastic life. Monks of the
'lesser habit' and of the 'great habit'
undergo a form of ordination involving
vows of permanent commitment,
chastity, obedience, and willing endur-
ance. [35: 259ff] Sometimes a monk of
exceptional holiness and insight becomes a *staretz*, a spiritual father who makes
himself available to teach others. [20:
146ff; 41]. Mount Athos is still the
chief centre of Orthodox monasticism.
[1: 37]

Monism [XXVIII] As a world-view, belief that reality is of one kind (as against
DUALISM and pluralism). A monist may
hold that all is SPIRIT (one meaning of
idealism) or matter (materialism). As a
view of man, monism rejects any dualism of body and mind, or of flesh and
spirit. Neutral monism holds that the
material and the spiritual, the physical
and the mental, are aspects of one being
or substance. Some PANTHEISM is explicitly monist. [8: 133–4]

Monotheism [XXVIII] Belief that there
is one, but only one, divine being [20: 1]
(cf. GODS; HENOTHEISM; THEISM) [7:
4]. The term is often used more
specifically for belief in the supreme
personal creator-God of JUDAISM,
CHRISTIANITY, and ISLAM [5: 76–7],
although the Christian doctrine of the
TRINITY is monotheism modified (or

more than this, as e.g. some Jews and
Muslims see it). Theories of religious
evolution, which saw monotheism as
emerging from POLYTHEISM [25: 19,
52], were countered by arguments that
it was original or primordial [17: 98–9;
25: 63–4, 183–4], or that it arose historically by revelation through PROPHECY
in the context of protests against idolatry [17: 103–4].

Moral Re-Armament [XI.B] Movement founded by the American
LUTHERAN Frank N. D. Buchman
(1878–1961) in the 1920s which from
1929 called itself the 'Oxford Group'.
Concentrating on the affluent and
influential, it operated through small
groups cultivating the 'Four Absolutes'
(honesty, purity, unselfishness, love).
As 'Moral Re-Armament' (M.R.A.) its
interests expanded to political and social
regeneration from 1938. During the
cold-war period following the Second
World War, M.R.A. claimed influence
at high levels of political and industrial
life, with an anti-communist orientation, but has had less publicity in recent
years. [20a]

Moral Theology [XI.B] Love for God
and man may be said to be the root principle of Christian morality. It came to
be regarded as the chief 'theological virtue' (with faith and hope) as contrasted
with the 'cardinal (i.e. fundamental) virtues' (prudence, temperance, fortitude,
and justice) derived from classical
ethics. Moral distinctions and precepts
were elaborated in the medieval period,
still influenced by classical thought but
also by the development of PENANCE.
By the 17th century an elaborate casuistry (the science of cases of conscience)
had evolved. The Jesuits developed
'probabilism', a system favouring lenien-
cy to sinners, opposed by JANSENISM.
Early PROTESTANTISM reacted against
such complexities. They regarded them
as SALVATION by 'works' (i.e.
salvation achieved through man's own
actions), and thus as 'Law' rather
than GOSPEL. But they generally

resisted antinomianism (the rejection of a moral law). ANGLICANISM and PURITANISM developed a casuistry based on their own doctrines. Modern Christians have been influenced by the complexities of contemporary society; by concern for SOCIAL MORALITY; and by non-Christian moral reflection. Some simply apply the general 'law of love', liberally adapted to circumstances ('situation ethics'). [45] Others make fresh attempts to develop detailed guidelines between general principles and individual cases. In the U.S.A. especially, much use has been made of psychologically influenced 'pastoral counselling'. [93]

Moravian Brethren [XI.B] The Bohemian Brethren (cf. HERESY (MEDIEVAL CHRISTIAN)) were 'renewed' by the Lutheran Count Zinzendorf in Germany (1722) under pietist (PIETISM) influence and later became an independent church. Early Moravians developed economically self-sufficient communities (later dissolved); missions overseas; and devotional methods which influenced METHODISM. Their piety centres on special devotion to the humanity of Jesus. [85; 107: 938]

Mormons [XI.B] 'The Church of Jesus Christ of Latter-Day Saints.' The Mormons' visionary founder Joseph Smith (1805–44) in the U.S.A. claimed to translate the revealed *Book of Mormon*, which supplements the BIBLE. Brigham Young (1805–77) led the sect to Salt Lake City (1847). Early violence and polygamy (later abandoned) brought clashes with the government. Mormonism is a highly American form of MILLENARIANISM. JESUS CHRIST was, it teaches, revealed to early immigrants in America, and will found a new Jerusalem there. The church is ruled by an elaborate hierarchy. Baptism and marriage can be contracted vicariously for the dead to 'seal' them in the faith. Mormons avoid stimulants and give two years' free service to the church. [2: 501–9; 14; 98: 348–54; 106]

Moses (in Judaism) [XVII] Moses (c. 13th century BCE) is the central figure from the BIBLE for rabbinical JUDAISM, and is referred to as 'Moses, our RABBI'. According to MAIMONIDES' seventh principle of Jewish doctrine Moses was the greatest of the prophets [22: VIII], and the Pentateuch, which was revealed to him by God, is a unique, unchanging revelation [22: IX, X]. The oral traditions of Judaism are also thought to originate with Moses, who spent 40 days being instructed by God at Sinai. [9 vol. 12: 371; 11: 15]

Mosque [XIV] (Arabic *masjid*, 'place of prostration', or *jami'* '(place of) congregating together', used especially for larger mosques), the building in which Muslims can worship congregationally, often also used for educational and teaching purposes (MADRASA). Although the daily worship (SALAT) can be performed anywhere, it is especially meritorious when done in a mosque as an expression of solidarity with other believers, and must be so performed on a FRIDAY morning, when a sermon (*khutba*) is usually preached. Originally a place of public assembly, the mosque acquired more and more an atmosphere of sanctity, like a Christian church, so that a state of ritual purity (TAHARA) became necessary for all entrants, and the admission of women (MAR'A) was allowed only to a limited extent and reluctantly [10 S.V.; 29: 76–80; 39 'Masjid']. Mosques vary from simple, roofless constructions of palm trunks in Africa to the architectural splendours of the great mosques of Cairo, Istanbul, or Isfahan. Notable features include the provision of a fountain or cistern in the courtyard, for the performance of preparatory ablutions; an apsidal niche (*mihrab*) oriented towards Mecca (the *qibla* direction) (*see* HARAMAIN), which the believers face in rows under the leadership of the IMAM or prayer-leader; in larger mosques, a minaret, which the *muezzin* ascended (in pre-electrical-recording days) to give the call to prayer (*adhan*); a pulpit (*minbar*), from which the sermon is delivered; in larger mosques, again, a platform (*dakka*), used as a seat for the *muezzin*; and a stand (*kursi*) or lectern for the QUR'AN, used here liturgically [49: II; 56: I]. The floor of the mosque is often covered in carpets, and the walls may be decorated with Qur'anic texts in fine calligraphy and vegetal or abstract patterns (*see* ART IN ISLAM). [44]

Muhammad [XIV] The prophet of ISLAM. Born *c.* 570 in the west Arabian trading town of Mecca (*see* HARAMAIN), Muhammad spent his early life as a merchant. In middle life an interior conviction dawned on him that he was the prophet chosen by God (ALLAH) to convey the eternal message to his people the Arabs, just as MOSES had brought it to the Jews and JESUS to the Christians. The divine revelations to him continued from around 610 until his death in 632, and form the QUR'AN. Their original message, probably to the Arabs only in the first place, was eventually broadened out into a universal one, so that Muhammad becomes the prophet for all mankind, with a divine message superseding all previous ones (*see* NABI). The progress of his apostleship in Mecca was impeded by the hostility of his pagan fellow-townsmen, with their attachment to the ancient gods, so that in 622 he and his followers migrated to the town of Yathrib, now renamed Medina. This departure (*hijra*) came to mark the beginning of the Muslim era (CALENDAR (IN ISLAM)). At Medina, Muhammad organized his Meccan followers plus the Medinan converts or 'Helpers' into a dynamic religio-political group, whose authority was by his death extended over much of the Arabian peninsula, providing the basis for the future military expansion of Islam [10 s.v.; 37i: II; 39 s.v.; 43: 283–336; 63; 76]. Although Muhammad always protested that he was only a man, the channel chosen for God's revelation but not himself an angel or divine being,

later generations of the faithful erected him into a miracle-working figure and into the archetype of humanity, the Perfect Man. [4]

Mulungu [II] Mulungu (or a related word: Mlungu, Murungu, Mluku; in Swahili Mungu, Milunga) is one of the most widely used names for God in eastern Africa, from the Zambezi in the south to Kenya and peoples like the Kamba and Gikuyu in the north. This is the effect partly of Swahili influence on the hinterland, partly of the preference of Muslims and Christian missionaries for using Swahili. Yet the use of the word by many inland peoples certainly precedes this: it was noted on the middle Zambezi by Portuguese in the 17th century. The meaning and etymology are unclear. Among a few peoples (e.g. the Kinga) there may be a plural, *milungu*, meaning ancestral spirits, but in most languages Mulungu is emphatically singular, supreme, and non-ancestral. [15; 22]

Mummification [IV] A chemical method used by the Egyptians, from the Old Kingdom to the Christian era (*c.* 2600 BCE to *c.* 400 CE), to preserve the human corpse. Herodotus (*c.* 484–430 BCE) [15: 160] distinguished three grades of mummification. The most expensive method, available at first only for royalty but gradually adopted by all wealthy persons, involved removal of the viscera, dehydration of the tissues by means of natron, and subsequent anointing and bandaging of the body; amulets were inserted between the layers of bandages. [3; 4] It was believed to be important to preserve the body so that the soul, which left at death, might return to take food offerings. (*See also* ANIMAL CULTS.)

Music (in Islam) [XIV] Music has not been used liturgically as extensively in ISLAM as in certain other faiths, although its use is by no means lacking. Islamic theologians disagreed over the lawfulness of listening to music (*sama*'), and traditions exist supporting both sides;

but it is true that in many pious quarters the use of music was frowned on as frivolous. However, elegant cantillation of the QUR'AN (*tajwid*) existed from an early time, and the call to prayer in the MOSQUE (*adhan*) was in effect chanted musically. Dancing, instrumental music, and the chanting of poems or hymns in vernacular tongues became characteristic, above all, of much Sufi ritual and *dhikr* sessions (SUFI INSTITUTIONS), being viewed as inducements to ecstasy and an approach to the godhead. [45: XVIII–XIX; 49: VI]

Music (Jewish) [XVII] In JUDAISM sound takes precedence over ICONOGRAPHY as the main form of religious expression. Ancient Hebrew song is referred to on numerous occasions in the BIBLE, and in the TEMPLE the Levites were singers in the sacrificial cult [3 vol. 1: 123]. Percussion and stringed instruments are also mentioned. Music was used to induce the ecstatic trances of the prophets (PROPHECY), and David played for King Saul to soothe his troubled spirit (BIBLICAL HISTORY). Many of the biblical Psalms are preceded by instructions indicating their melodies. With the destruction of the second Temple Jewish music underwent a complete change. As a sign of mourning instrumental music was forbidden in the SYNAGOGUE liturgy. The Pentateuch and other biblical books were chanted according to traditional melodies, some of which have been preserved down to modern times. The synagogue CANTOR, whose original role was simply as prayer leader, has in the course of time become a musical performer with a distinctive style. Cantorial music has been influenced by European operatic traditions, folk-songs, and Israeli popular tunes, as well as by Chasidic melodies which CHASIDISM developed for the purpose of serving God through the joy of song and dance [36: XX]. Instrumental music is played at Jewish weddings, and on Sabbaths (SHABBAT) and festivals (CHAGIM) hymns are sung

by the Jewish family at meals. [9 vol. 12: 554; 20: I–III; 26:V]

Mwari [II] The name for the High God among the SHONA of Zimbabwe and the Venda of the Transvaal. Among BANTU theologies that of Mwari seems to possess a special, even ambiguous, character. For the Venda Mwari (or Mwali) was originally, it appears, a hero king. For the Shona he (or perhaps she, for Mwari has some strongly feminine attributes including the title Mbuya – Grandmother) is above all the giver of rain and fertility, whose greatest praise-name is Dzivaguru (Great Pool). The cult of Mwari seems to have been brought into Shonaland at some uncertain date, probably little by little replacing in name an earlier High God. Since the early 19th century at the latest it has centred on cave-shrines in the Matopo hills, the principal shrine being now at Matonjeni. The cult is significantly inter-tribal: when the Ndebele conquered western Shonaland in the 19th century they quickly adopted Mwari, and Venda lineages continue to be influential among the priests, but the chief area of influence is undoubtedly southern Shonaland. The cult organization includes priests, mediums, dancers, and messengers, who link the shrine with different parts of the country and bring offerings and petitions for rain.

Across several centuries and political changes the Mwari cult has retained a widely extended religious and political influence through an institutional, oracular, and ritual pattern notably different from that associated with the recognition of the one God among most other Bantu peoples. [13: 287–313; 16: 179–218; 23]

Mysteria [XII] Greek cults accessible only after initiation undergone by personal choice, often apparently involving closer contact with the divinity. They began as community agrarian rites, then acquired the initiatory aspect and soteriological functions, promising a blissful afterlife. Most important were the

Eleusinian mysteries, connected with the Athenian state-cult, honouring primarily Demeter and Kore (= Persephone) (AFTERLIFE (GREEK); MYTHOS; ORPHEUS; THEOI). In Hellenistic times mystery-cults multiplied. *Mysteria* became attached to the cults of certain oriental gods. These, like the Bacchic/Dionysiac mysteries (ORPHEUS), were not tied to a particular locality. [2: VI; 17: 792–80]

Mysteries (Eastern Orthodox)[XI.D]
The Eastern ORTHODOX CHURCH recognizes seven principal mysteries: BAPTISM, chrismation, confession, EUCHARIST, MARRIAGE, *euchelaion*, and ordination (SACRAMENTS). Baptism is by triple immersion in the name of the TRINITY. Chrismation, the 'seal of the Spirit', corresponds to confirmation. It is given by anointing with *chrism* (sanctified perfumed oil), usually at baptism. Marriages are consecrated by prayers and blessings, by the crowning of bride and groom, and by their sharing a common cup of wine. *Euchelaion* corresponds to the sacrament of extreme unction. It includes seven Epistle (BIBLE) and GOSPEL readings and seven blessings of oil which is used to anoint the sick or, on Wednesday in Holy Week, the whole congregation.

Monastic profession (MONASTICISM (ORTHODOX CHRISTIAN)) is often accounted a mystery, as are: the blessing of water at Epiphany (LITURGICAL YEAR) and of grapes at the festival of the Transfiguration; funeral and memorial services; and the *artoklasia*, a blessing of bread, wine, and oil usually celebrated at vespers (*hesperinos*). All these rites are in the *Euchologion* (LITURGICAL BOOKS (EASTERN ORTHODOX)).

The rite of the eucharist begins with a service of preparation (*prothesis, proskomide*) of the bread (*artos, prosphoron*) and wine. The 'Liturgy of the Catechumens' includes a long litany, the singing of antiphons (in the Russian use psalm verses, in Greek use short verses addressed to the Blessed Virgin MARY and

JESUS CHRIST), the hymns of the day (*apolitikia troparia*), and the 'Kontakion', the refrain from a verse-sermon once sung at this point. The Trisagion ('Holy God, Holy and Mighty, Holy and Immortal, have mercy on us') is sung before readings of the *Apostolos* and Gospel (LITURGICAL BOOKS (EASTERN ORTHODOX)).

The 'Liturgy of the Faithful' begins with further litanies, the 'Cherubic Hymn', and the great entrance of the clergy carrying the bread and wine. The Nicene CREED precedes the Anaphora, the prayer of offering and consecration which begins with the exhortation 'Lift up your hearts', a preface, and hymn 'Holy, holy, holy'. After the commemoration of the Last Supper the bread and wine are consecrated by the invocation (*epiklesis*) of the HOLY SPIRIT. After the communion and the dismissal prayers, *antidoron*, blessed but not consecrated *prosphoron*, is distributed to all.

For most of the liturgy the priest, as emissary of the people before the throne of God, stands at the holy table behind the *iconostasis*. This ICON-screen represents the COMMUNION of the saints; the altar behind it joins heaven to earth when the Holy Spirit descends to change the bread and wine into the body and blood of Christ. [26: XV]

Mystery-Cult [XXVIII] Devotion, often to a single god or goddess, in which secret RITUALS and doctrines have a place. Examples abound in the ancient Mediterranean world of religious societies, outside the 'civic' or official religion, which imparted their secrets only to initiates (Greek *mustae*). Initiation often involved purification ritual, instruction, and a revelation of the god, usually in a sacred drama. Of major importance among the Greek mysteries were the Dionysian (later Orphic) and Eleusinian (MYSTERIA); in the early Roman empire, Mithraism (MITHRAS); from Egypt, those of Isis and Osiris (MYSTERY-CULTS (ROMAN)); and further east those of Attis, Cybele, and Sabazius. [11A; 22A; 24A & B]

Similar cults are found down to our own times (e.g. FREEMASONRY, ROSICRUCIANISM) [28A: 101–39, 147–51, 257–80, 354–6], many of them exemplifying SYNCRETISM. Their rituals and related MYTHS played and probably still play an important role in personal religion, especially when official and established religions fail to satisfy individual needs. Such cults have no necessary connection with MYSTICISM, but many could be classified as SALVATION-religions of a sacramental (SACRAMENTS) kind.

Mystery-Cults (Roman) [XXV] Mystery-cults in the Roman world were always perceived as introductions from the East, but were in fact Greek, or Graeco-oriental, in origin. The earliest was the cult of Bacchus, which spread widely through Italy in the 3rd/2nd centuries BCE, until brutally persecuted by the authorities in 186 BCE [9: 53–8; 14: 14–21]. Mystery-cults presented new problems to authorities only accustomed to dealing with groups (*collegia*) providing for banqueting and the funerals of members; but the persecution was sporadic and short-lived. The most important cults (Bacchus from Greece, Isis from Egypt, Attis from Asia Minor – *see also* MITHRAS, MITHRAISM) had structural similarities: all constituted themselves as groups with their own authority-system, based on initiation into membership; and all claimed to offer secret knowledge and, through different rites and myths, created structures based on the reversal of received ideas on reality, morality, life, and death [4; 7: VII; 9: 222–8; 15: V–IX]. Mysteries, however, fitted stably into the pagan world – their innovativeness and interest in the afterlife have been exaggerated in many modern studies by anxiety to find anticipations of Christianity. But they did pioneer, at least for the West, the possibility of groups based on individual

choice, and hence led to an intensification of commitment and religious experience. [7: VIII; 12: 220–23; 16: XXXVIII, XLVII]

Mysticism [XXVIII] An umbrella term for practices, experiences, and writings in which direct awareness of and/or union with God or ultimate reality is the main focus [8: XII; 14; 15: XVI, XVII; 17: 48–50]. Mysticism may also denote the belief that there is a highest knowledge inaccessible to human understanding or through sense-experience, but attainable through disciplinary practices, in expanded states of consciousness, or intuitively [17: II; 28: VIII]. Many religious traditions prescribe techniques of contemplation and meditation as means to mystical experience, and offer descriptions of such experience (which is nevertheless said to be ineffable). Sacred scriptures may include what is claimed to be mystical knowledge. Some theories of religion claim that mysticism is 'the heart' of all 'true religion' and the key to a unity of all religions. These have been countered by scholars who argue that the mystical is only one aspect or type of religion, to be contrasted with 'the prophetic' or 'the devotional'. [17: XIX; 23: 21–3, 103–8, 197–207; 25: 117–18]

Mysticism (Christian) [XI.D] The spiritual quest for the most direct experience of God. Characteristically, Christian mysticism is centred on prayer. God is accessible through scripture (BIBLE), through the SACRAMENTS, and above all in the person of JESUS CHRIST. The mystic seeks to go beyond the concepts and images presented in scripture, theology, and tradition, and come to God himself. [9; 16; 45] Theologians disagree as to whether the experience of God the mystic attains is ever truly direct and immediate, or whether it always involves the mediation of concepts and ideas.

The attainment of God is symbolized in various ways: St Bernard (1090–1153), St Teresa (1515–82), and St John

of the Cross (1542–91) use images of
sexual love and spiritual marriage; St
Gregory Palamas (c. 1295–1359) speaks
of illumination by seeing the 'uncreated
light' manifested in the transfiguration
of Jesus on Mount Tabor; St Gregory
of Nyssa sees the mystic taken from
the revelation of God in light to the
'unknowledge' of him in darkness, as
Moses met God first in the burning bush,
and then in the cloud. [5; 24; 40]

Christian mysticism has many forms:

(1) There is a liturgical and sacramental mysticism which sees and uses
the sacraments as means of ascent to
God [7].

(2) There is a devotional mysticism
centred on meditation (DISCURSIVE
MEDITATION) on the person, life, and
teaching of Jesus. Many Franciscan
writers stand in this tradition.

(3) There is a tradition of CON-
TEMPLATION which takes different
forms in eastern HESYCHASM and in
western writers such as Meister Eckhart
(c. 1260–1327) and the author of *The
Cloud of Unknowing* (c. 14th century CE)
[8; 9; 13].

(4) There is a large family of schools
of mysticism, including the Carmelite,
the Ignatian, and the school of Berulle
(1575–1629), which use discursive
meditation as a means of preparation in
the earlier stages of the path, and then
move to contemplative prayer [18; 42;
43].

Myth [XXVIII] Narrative, usually traditional, in which events are described as
deeds of GODS, heroes, or other superhuman beings; i.e. events in the realm of
nature or history are attributed to causes
not acceptable in current scientific or
historical explanation. If all such
attribution is false, myths are indeed, as
popular usage has it, fictitious stories,
unfounded explanations. However,
'myth', an English word of recent (early
19th-century) invention, is now a technical term of the human sciences,

historiography, literary criticism,
THEOLOGY, and RELIGIONSWISSEN-
SCHAFT, with many shades of
meaning [8: VI; 10; 12: III; 14: XII;
18: XII]. 'Mythology' is older, meaning (1) the body of popular lore in
which the world-view and moral outlook of a group or tradition are embodied, or (2) the scientific pursuit of
collecting and studying such matter.

Myth is closely linked with RITUAL
[28: VI], but not all rites involve recital
of myths, nor do all myths appear to
have or to have had ritual expression.
Many myths concern origins, but they
are not all aetiological (i.e. intended to
describe or explain the cause of something). FUNCTIONALISM stresses the
role of myth (e.g. as a charter for a way
of life); STRUCTURALISM investigates
mythical thought as a means by which
unintelligible and random experience is
rendered intelligible and given pattern
[16]. In the study of religions, myths,
whether embodying facts or not, are
seen as SYMBOLS conveying profound
truths about human existence and/or
superhuman reality [2: II; 5; 7: 4]. Much
theological debate has concerned 'myth
in sacred scripture' and the significance
of DEMYTHOLOGIZING.

Mythos (peri Theon) [XII] Myths concerning the GODS in Greek religion. The
early history of the gods is that of the
COSMOS. There are myths concerning
individual Greek gods, mostly describing their birth, acquisition of functions,
and, as with HEROES, actions leading to
the foundation of a cult or ritual. Central to the Eleusinian MYSTERIA is the
myth of Persephone's abduction by the
underworld god Hades. Her grieving
mother Demeter (THEOI) (who was
responsible for agriculture) caused
famine, and it was eventually arranged
that Persephone would spend some
months each year in Hades and some
with Demeter. [3; 12: 119–31, 249–
52].

· N ·

Nabi [XIV] One of the Islamic terms for 'prophet', together with *rasul*, literally 'messenger'. The latter is sometimes considered to be the higher rank, as sent from God to a people with a specific version of scripture, and MUHAMMAD is often termed 'the messenger of God'; but in practice the terms are often interchangeable. Tradition mentions former prophets as numbering over 100,000, and the QUR'AN includes many prophets and patriarchs from the Hebrew scriptures, and New Testament (BIBLE) ones like JOHN THE BAPTIST and JESUS, in addition to certain native Arabian figures. All were forerunners of Muhammad, who is the culmination of the line, and all the scriptures which they brought are believed to confirm the final and fullest revelation, the Qur'an [10 'Prophet(s) (Islam)'; 29: 50–51; 39 'Prophet'; 42]. Hence later religious leaders in Islam whose claims have seemed to rank them with the prophets, such as Baha'ullah (BAHA'IS) and Mirza Ghulam Ahmad (AHMADIS), have been placed outside the pale of Islam by the orthodox.

Nag Hammadi [XI.A] A town of Upper Egypt, on the west bank of the Nile, near which was discovered in 1945 a jar containing 13 leather-bound papyrus codices, comprising some 52 Coptic documents of the 4th century CE, nearly all Gnostic (GNOSTICISM) in character. Many were translations of earlier Greek originals. In them the teachings of various Gnostic schools, previously known for the most part through the writings of their critics, are now directly accessible. Their publication has been entrusted to an international team of scholars. [15; 20]

Nagarjuna [IX.A] The name of more than one Buddhist teacher [37: 6, 388, 488], in the 2nd and 9th centuries CE. The most celebrated is the philosopher of the 2nd century, who is regarded as the founder of the MADHYAMIKA school [24], and one of the earliest writers of a class of Buddhist literature called Shastra, which consists in reasoned, philosophical argumentation of the ideas found in the words of the BUDDHA in the *Sutras* [5: 200]. (*See also* SAN LUN TSUNG.)

Nalanda [IX.A] A town in Bihar (India), scene of some of the Buddha's discourses (GOTAMA), and later one of the major centres of Buddhist learning, following the rise of MAHAYANA, attaining great prestige between the 8th and 12th centuries CE.

Nam Simaran [XXVII] Sikh meditation technique. GURMAT affirms that liberation (*mukti*) is attained primarily through the discipline called *nam simaran* or *nam japan*, 'remembering' or 'repeating' the divine Name. *Nam* signifies all that constitutes the being and nature of God (AKAL PURAKH) [25: 195–6]. For Nanak (*see* GURUS) *nam simaran* meant regular disciplined meditation on the manifold *nam*. The essence of *nam* is harmony, and they who sustain the discipline will progressively merge with the divine harmony, ultimately passing beyond the transmigratory round into the ineffable bliss (*sahaj*) which for Nanak is final liberation (*see* SACHKHAND). With this sophisticated technique there also continues literal *nam* *japan*, the practice of uttering a word, syllable, or MANTRA of particular religious import (e.g. *satnam*, *vahiguru*), either as a pious ejaculation or in extended repetition. For the latter procedure a *simarani* (rosary) is commonly used [24: 263]. A third method practised by Sikhs is the singing or chanting of *gurbani* (compositions from the sacred scripture). Daily NIT-NEM is thus a form of *nam simaran*.

Nanto Rokushu [XVI] These are the Six Sects (Jojitsu, Sanron, Kusha, Hosso, Kegon, Ritsu) of the Southern Capital, the term given by later writers to the religious distinctions of the Heijo (Nara) capital (JAPAN, BUDDHISM IN) [II]. The term 'sects' implies distinct beliefs and practices, but these were more philosophical schools, often more than one being studied at any one time [34: 105–33]. Jojitsu (*Satyasiddhishastra*, Chinese *Ch'eng-shih*, Treatise on the Completion of the Truth) and Sanron (MADHYAMIKA, Chinese SAN LUN, the Middle Path) are both attributed to a Korean priest, Ekan, who arrived in about 625 CE. Kusha (*Abhidharmakosha* VAIBHASHIKA; Chinese *Chu-she*, Treasury of Analyses of the Law) came in with a priest called Chitsu in 658. Kusha was absorbed by Hosso in the 8th century and Jojitsu and Sanron have also disappeared. The other three became sectarian and still have a substantial number of temples and adherents. Hosso was based on the *Yogacarabhumishastra* (YOGACARA school, Chinese FA HSIANG, Treatise on Yoga; or *Vijnaptimatra*, Japanese *Yuishiki*, Consciousness-only). Like Sanron, it was the Middle Path, with the Eightfold Negation. For the Japanese it was based on the Chinese sect founded by Tzu-en. Several priests venerating MAITREYA (Japanese *Miroku*) (JAPANESE BUDDHAS AND BODHISATTVAS) returned with variations from China, particularly Dosho in 654 and Gembo in 735. Many important early temples

belonged to Hosso, which by the 8th century venerated four Buddhas: Shaka, Amida (AMIDA WORSHIP), Yakushi, and Miroku. Kegon (*Avatamsaka*, Chinese HUA-YEN, Garland) has confused beginnings, but perhaps was propagated from around 736 by a Chinese priest called Dogen in Japan, who had settled in the imperially supported Todai-ji. Ritsu (*Vinaya*, Chinese *Lu*, Rules) was brought by the Chinese priest known as Ganjin in Japan who had been invited to ordain novitiates. He survived several shipwrecks and performed the ceremony at the Todai-ji in 754 (NANTO SHICHIDAI-JI), later building the Toshodai-ji. Like Jojitsu and Sanron inasmuch as it embodies both MAHAYANA and THERAVADA elements, Ritsu stresses prescribed rules and discipline. (*See also* SHUNYATA-VADA.)

Nanto Shichidai-ji [XVI] These are the Seven Great Temples of the Southern Capital (JAPAN, BUDDHISM IN), the chief temples of the old Nara capital which remained throughout Japanese history as the most popular pilgrimage from the Kyoto capital (JUNREI). They dominated 8th-century politics and were the cause of Emperor KAMMU moving the capital farther north. In 796 they were listed in the following order, believed to have been that of their relative importance [24: 55–148]: Todai-ji, built by Emperor SHOMU, finished about 752, the main hall containing the Great Buddha; Kofuku-ji, the Fujiwara family temple; Ganko-ji, the old Asuka-dera or Hoko-ji; Daian-ji, the old Daikandai-ji; Yakushi-ji, finished around 690; Saidai-ji, built by Empress SHOTOKU around 765 and rivalling Emperor Shomu's Todai-ji in splendour and size; and the Horyu-ji, built by Prince Shotoku in 607, but rebuilt after a fire in the late 7th century, the only one outside the old city of Nara. Most of them have been reduced by frequent fires, but some are still major attractions for both pilgrims and tourists today.

Nastika [XIII.B] ('a denier') A term of opprobrium in Indian thought; in orthodox Hinduism one who denies the authority of the revelation of the VEDA or (later) the existence of God, e.g. a follower of BUDDHISM or Jainism (JAINS). The latter understood it as meaning a denier of the law of KARMA and life after death, e.g. an adherent of the LOKAYATA, who in turn interpreted it as denying the authority of sense experience.

Nath Tradition [XXVII] The ascetic Nath or Kanphat tradition of India comprises a cluster of yogic sects (YOGA), all claiming descent from the semi-legendary Gorakhnath and all teaching the efficacy of HATHA YOGA as the means of spiritual liberation. Nath beliefs derive from esoteric Tantrism (TANTRA (2)) [25: 243–4]. The tradition figured prominently in early SIKH development for two reasons. First, the Sant movement (of which Nanak was a conspicuous representative – *see* GURUS) was significantly affected by Nath ideals (SANT TRADITION OF NORTHERN INDIA). Nath doctrine affirms that the rigorous application of *hatha yoga* induces a psychophysical process whereby the spirit ascends to mystical bliss [22: 97]. The Sants rejected the physical features of *hatha yoga* in favour of meditation technique, but accepted the concept of a spiritual ascent to ultimate bliss [25: 151–3; 28: 85–9, 120–43]. Second, the Naths were also important to the early PANTH in that they clearly provided powerful competition. JANAM-SAKHI anecdotes give considerable prominence to debates between Nath masters (called Siddhs) and Guru Nanak [7: IV; 24: 66–70, 144–57]. The tradition, though greatly weakened, still survives.

Native American Church [xx] This church includes some 100,000 adherents from over 50 North American Indian tribes (AMERICAN INDIANS (NORTH) AND ESKIMOS: NEW RELIGIOUS MOVEMENTS) loosely united through sacramental ingestion of the non-narcotic hallucinogenic buds of the peyote plant (PEYOTISM) in Saturday all-night rites, round an earthen altar and sacred fire. Despite being banned by Indian and white authorities since its inception a century ago, this peyote cult has gradually won religious freedom. It provides healing, an antidote against alcoholism, and claims to be an Indian Christianity. [11; 12: II; 19: XIII]

Natural Religion [XXVIII] A spontaneous and unargued religious response to the world, or religiousness which develops in human experience untaught [25: 39; 27: 40–43, 217–18, 226]. As such, it is contrasted with 'the positive religions' [27: 45] as specific traditions, or systems claiming authority for their doctrines. In 18th-century Europe, natural religion (as e.g. in David Hume's *Dialogues* thereon) denoted those beliefs supposedly common to all mankind, or at least attainable by human reason (one form of DEISM), a meaning for which 'NATURAL THEOLOGY' is now the widely accepted term. [3: 32–4]

Natural Theology [XI.C] The understanding of the nature and existence of GOD and of the duty, freedom, and immortality of man, which is held in Western thought to be obtainable through rational reflection on the world, taking account of human thought and experience. It is usually contrasted with revelation, i.e. that theological understanding which is held to have been given to man by God either through some quasi-verbal communication or through events discerned as disclosing God's nature. Some theologians (e.g. Barth – NEO-ORTHODOXY) hold that the only authentic knowledge of God is by divine self-revelation. Others (e.g. Aquinas – THOMISM) hold that some valid conclusions may be reached by reason but that revelation provides the norms of correct understanding. Especially since John Locke (1632–1704), other theologians have seen natural theology as the only acceptable foundation of theological understanding. 'Apologetics' is the use of the arguments of natural theology to defend the reasonableness of religious beliefs. [3; 15; 17]

Naujote [xxx] The PARSI term for the rite of initiation in ZOROASTRIANISM. (By Irani Zoroastrians it is called *sedre-pushan*.) The term is understood by most Parsis as meaning 'new birth'. The rite traditionally takes place at the age of puberty, but nowadays among Parsis usually at nine or eleven (even numbers are considered inauspicious). Essentially it consists of the donning, for the first time, of the sacred shirt (*sudreh*) and cord (*kusti*) [33: VII]. These are the traditional 'badges' of the religion, said to symbolize the 'armour of the faith' for the believer in the war against evil. The *sudreh* is a white cotton garment, worn next to the skin with a token purse at the v of the neck to symbolize the duty of storing up righteousness. The *kusti* is a length of plaited lamb's wool, tied three times round the waist to the accompaniment of prayers several times a day (MANTHRAS). Before initiation a child is thought not to be morally responsible for its actions, but thereafter its thoughts, words, and deeds are stored up for judgement (CHINVAT BRIDGE; FRASHOKERETI). Initiation and the wearing of *sudreh* and *kusti* are the duties of all Zoroastrians, men and women. [6: 236–40; 22 pt III: 42–4; 23: 41–4]

Navajo [III] Members of the Athapascan linguistic group, the Navajo migrated from the west of what is now Canada to the North American south-west prior to 1300 CE, gradually replacing a hunting economy with sheep-raising and agriculture [19]. Navajo myths recount the emergence of mankind into this, the fifth world, through four previous subterranean realms. The present world is inhabited by two classes of beings, the Yeis (or

'holy people') and the Earth-Surface People (humans). Begochiddy began the creative process in the first world and guided the Yeis through the successive worlds to this one. In the fifth world, the Navajo have been especially blessed by Changing-Woman, a holy person of miraculous birth, who acts kindly towards mankind. The Yeis are neither all-powerful nor supreme. Instead, each has responsibility for some aspect of this world (e.g. control of weather, movements of heavenly bodies, care of animals). Man, too, has specific responsibilities and together, through his moral and ceremonial behaviour, he and the Yeis preserve the harmony of existence [13: V–VII]. Myths relate that when the work of creation was complete, Begochiddy saw that it was 'beautiful', i.e. its parts were all in harmony. The central concern of Navajo religion is therefore to preserve 'beauty' at all levels, as witness the common refrain of prayers, 'May I always walk with beauty all around me.' [2: 1] (*See* SAND-PAINTINGS.)

Nazarite Church [xx] A large independent church, ama-Nazaretha, named from the biblical Nazarites and founded by Isaiah Shembe (1870–1935) among the Zulu in Natal in 1911. The great festivals of Tabernacles in July and New Year in January centre upon the holy centre of Ekuphakameni near Durban and the holy mountain, Nhlangakazi. After the death in 1976 of J. G. Shembe, who had succeeded his father, a leadership dispute arose between J. G. Shembe's son Londa and his elder brother Amos. [12: 46–7; 16: 110–11, 194–6, 227–32, 281–94, 328–30]

Ncwala [II] The name of the great annual festival of renewal of the Swazi king (*nkosi*), one of the more striking surviving expressions of sacred monarchy in Africa. It takes place immediately following the summer solstice. Its complex series of rites, with their stress on the king's liminal weakness and the popular chanting of songs of execration, provide a symbolic death followed by revitalization of the *nkosi* and so too of his people. The unity of the nation, despite the recalled divisions of past and present, is strengthened and symbolized by the ritual renewal of its king [34: 197–225].

Neo-Confucianism [X] Neo-Confucianism emerged as an identifiable movement during the Sung dynasty (960–1126 CE) as a Confucian (CONFUCIUS) response to teaching of Taoism (TAO CHIA) and BUDDHISM. Chou Tun I (1017–73) was an early contributor to the movement and his theories provide the basis for all later Neo-Confucian metaphysical and cosmological speculation. His influential *Explanation of the Diagram of the Supreme Ultimate* explains the generation of the YIN–YANG forces, the Five Elements (WU HSING) and all phenomena, including human intelligence and moral principles, from the *T'ai Chi* (Supreme Ultimate) or *Wu Chi* (Ultimate Non-Being). He states that by acting in accordance with these principles the sage can achieve tranquillity. [7: XXVIII, 460–80].

Eventually, two traditions of Neo-Confucian thought developed: the School of Principle (*Li Hsueh*), systematized by Chu Hsi (1130–1200), and the School of Mind (*Hsin Hsueh*), best represented by Lu Chiu Yuan (1139–93) and later by Wang Yang Ming (1472–1529). Chu Hsi's literary output was immense. He argued that all existence is composed of varying combinations of Principle (LI), which is unchanging and derives from the Supreme Ultimate; and Substance (*Chi*), which determines the change and differentiation of phenomena. He maintained that moral cultivation and the purification of *Chi* required detailed investigation into the nature of phenomena. [5; 6; 7: XXXIV, 588–653; 10]

The School of Mind was more monistic and idealistic in character, reducing all reality to the single Principle (*Li*), which is identical with the mind (*hsin*). Therefore *Li* was discovered by investigation of the mind, through meditation and moral reflection. Wang Yang Ming developed this view, suggesting that the mind is essentially pure and has innate knowledge of moral principles, such that if the mind is penetrated through meditation, good conduct is inevitable. [7: XXXV, 654–91; 8; 10; 17; 32: X–XV]

Neo-Orthodoxy [XI.C] A widely influential school of theology in PROTESTANTISM which shares the fundamental insights of Karl Barth (1886–1968). It is so called because it seeks to re-express the classical Protestant orthodoxy of the REFORMATION period. It is also known as 'kerygmatic theology' (since it sees theology as the proclamation – Greek *kerygma* – of GOD's saving and revelatory activity in Christ (CHRISTOLOGY; SALVATION)), 'dialectical theology' (since it holds that God so surpasses human understanding that descriptions of him inescapably involve paradoxical expressions), and 'crisis theology' (since it stresses the divine Word as a judgement – Greek *krisis* – on the world). Barth rejected attempts to derive a knowledge of God from nature and human experience (NATURAL THEOLOGY) on the grounds that man's reason has been hopelessly corrupted by the Fall (SIN). God, as the utterly transcendent and sovereignly free, is only to be known through his self-revelation to man, a revelation which is uniquely given in the 'Word of God' manifested in JESUS CHRIST and made known through the BIBLE. [3; 14]

Neoplatonism [XVIII] A version of the Platonic philosophy inaugurated by Plotinus (204–70 CE), who developed a mystical interpretation of Plato's teaching (PHILOSOPHIA). Starting from the Platonic doctrine of the Soul's ability to ascend by a purified love to contemplation of the 'forms' – perfect archetypes of which the sensible world is merely a flawed reflection – Plotinus postulated three 'hypostases' or levels of true reality beyond the material world. These were the Soul (*psyche*), the Intellect (*nous*), and the One or the Good; they could be viewed as metaphysical entities or as states which the philosopher might experience in contemplation. The Soul corresponded to mind in the individual: it was the agent of thought, memory, and sensory perception. It survived death, and if insufficiently purified from worldly desires would be reincarnated in a new body. The Intellect was the timeless repository of the 'forms': ascending to this level, man might perceive truth intuitively, without discursive thought. The One was God, the ultimate reality and hence indescribable. Union of the individual with the One was the goal of the philosophic life and was to be attained by the practice of virtue and contemplation. [26]

Plotinus's successors – Porphyry (*c.* 232–305 CE), Proclus (*c.* 412–85), Iamblichus (*c.* 250–350) and others – elaborated the hypostases into a complex hierarchy, some levels of which were identified with the Greek gods (THEOI); and advocated *theurgy*, a system of ritual magic, as a means of purifying the soul. Neoplatonism was prominent in the Near East until the 6th century, offering a coherent alternative to Christianity, on which it had a lasting influence, notably through the 6th-century Platonic school at Alexandria and the writings (*c.* 500 CE) attributed to Dionysius the Areopagite.

New Church [XVIII] The 'Church of the New Jerusalem': followers of Emanuel Swedenborg (1688–1772), a Swedish scientist who began in 1743 to experience visions and converse with angels. Swedenborg turned to theology, teaching that there is a 'correspondence' between the external universe and spiritual realities (the sun's heat and light, for example, correspond to the love and wisdom of God) and that the BIBLE has an 'inner' spiritual sense to be read in the light of such correspondences. The revelation of this inner sense is the Second Coming of JESUS CHRIST as the Word and inaugurates a new Church upon earth. Man must strive to open his 'interiors' to Heaven by repentance, virtue, and love of God. Evil states of mind are 'hells'; after death those accustomed to them gravitate there permanently. Others rise to Heaven, forming 'societies' of angels ranked according to their degrees of love and faith. [25] Members of Swedenborgian churches today are few in number: some 3,000 in Great Britain and 7,000 in the U.S.A.

New Fire Ceremony [XIX] The greatest renewal ceremony in Aztec religion (MESOAMERICAN RELIGIONS) was the New Fire Ceremony, called Toxiuhmolpilia, the Binding of the Years [2: 21–7]. It took place at the completion of a 52-year cycle called Xiuhmolpilli, and initiated another CALENDAR ROUND depicted in codex and stone as a tied bundle of 52 reeds (TONALPOHUALLI). The Toxiuhmolpilia took place at midnight on the Hill of the Star at the outskirts of Tenochtitlan, following the ritual extinguishing of all domestic and temple fires, the breaking of pots, and the sweeping of all homes in the realm. A distinguished war captive was ritually sacrificed and a fire was started in his chest after his heart was offered to the absent sun (HUMAN SACRIFICE). The fire was taken to all temples and towns in the Aztec empire, signifying the revitalization of the society and the heavens.

New Jerusalems or Holy Villages (Tribal Peoples) [XX] New tribal movements have created many 'holy cities' or villages, often with biblical names: Salem in Fiji, also in Nigeria (God's Kingdom Society); Paradise in the Solomon Islands (CHRISTIAN FELLOWSHIP CHURCH); Guta ra Jehova ('City of Jehovah') in Zimbabwe (Mai Chaza's church); Sione ('Zion') of Alice LENSHINA; and Nineveh of the African Israel Church Nineveh in

Kenya. Other notable examples include Aiyetoro ('happy city') of the Holy Apostles' Community in Nigeria; Nkamba in Zaire (KIMBANGUIST CHURCH); Ekuphakemeni of the NAZARITE CHURCH; and Amakokopai of the Hallelujah Religion in Guyana. There are also many in the PHILIPPINES. There may be administrative, economic, educational, and healing aspects to the religious activities in these cities or villages. Members come long distances on pilgrimages to major festivals, for example 100,000 or more gather every Easter at Zion City Moriah of the Zion Christian Church in northern Transvaal to share in the blessings of the new community as an outpost of heaven. [2: 174, 273; 16: 152–4]

New Religious Movements in Primal Societies [xx] For several centuries, but increasingly in the 20th, the tribal peoples of the Americas, Asia, Africa, and the Pacific have produced a wide range of new religious movements through interaction with more sophisticated and powerful cultures and religions – especially with Christianity, less often with Hinduism and Buddhism, and only occasionally with Islam. Since these movements show differences from the traditions upon which they draw they are commonly rejected by adherents of the contributing religions. Their variety is indicated by the range of names used for different movements: nativistic, revitalization, millennial, messianic, syncretist, separatist, adjustment, prophetic, or healing movements, independent churches or sects [19: 484–92]. There may be well over 10,000 such movements identifiable in the last 100 years, with 12 million or more adherents.

The movements commonly arise among confused, powerless, or disintegrating peoples whose needs are not met by either their traditional religion or the new invasive faith. The founders are often charismatic figures who claim to have had a mystic experience of communication with the spirit world and to have been charged with bringing the new religion to their people; even in cultures dominated by senior men founders may be young men or women. There is often a dramatic rejection of some traditional ways, especially of reliance on the ancestors, SHAMANS, the medicine bags (MEDICINE BUNDLES) or magic objects, and traditional rituals and divinities. Other traditional elements, especially reliance upon dreams as a means of revelation and polygamous marriage, are often retained. The new divinity is usually one supreme personal god who demands a reformed way of life with insistence on peace and love, sexual discipline, industry, and avoidance of alcohol and tobacco. This strict ethic is sustained by new rituals and songs, often with drumming or dancing, new symbolisms, and forms of worship of considerable creativity.

A very pragmatic religious blessing is offered, with healing, revelations, and power from the spirit world, protection from evil forces, the promise of a new order of freedom and prosperity, and a new community in place of the disrupted social order. The new hope, self-respect, and dignity contribute to the survival of a tribal people faced with the invasive and dominant society, and so may assist long-term accommodation to modernization and development. In so far as the hopes may be unrealistic and the ecstatic worship an escape from action, the new movements may be of no more than temporary benefit or even be deleterious. In either case they are authentic new religious forms of considerable extent and importance across the world of tribal cultures. [12; 17; 19]

New Religious Movements in the West [xxi] The current wave of new religious movements in the West began to be publicly visible in the mid-1960s, largely as part of the so-called 'counter-culture', but it can be seen, especially in its more theologically oriented forms, as a phenomenon of the 1970s. The groups have flourished throughout the whole of North America [10; 14; 15; 20], but particularly in California. They are also to be found in New Zealand, Australia, and Europe – particularly in England [2; 41; 42], West Germany, and Austria. They tend to be less visible, if not unknown, in Scandinavia and the Mediterranean countries and are almost entirely absent in Eastern Europe. Counts of several thousand movements have been made, but most of these have very few members: rarely more than two or three thousand, more often well under 100.

A variety of theories have been offered by way of explanation for the present rise of such movements: it is said that they exemplify a reaction to and/or a reflection of contemporary society [3]; that they meet the psychological and/or spiritual needs of inadequate and/or truly religious persons; that they achieve what success they do only through 'brainwashing' or mind-control techniques [11; 12]; or, in a more religious or cosmic vein, that they herald the dawning of a New Era, of the Age of Aquarius [38], or of the New Religious Consciousness [14]. Although the present situation is considered by many to be a unique occurrence in the West, comparisons can be usefully made [55] with contemporary Japan, India, and Africa (AFRICA, NEW RELIGIOUS MOVEMENTS IN; NEW RELIGIOUS MOVEMENTS IN PRIMAL SOCIETIES) and with other periods in history which have seen the proliferation of new religious movements or REVIVALISM (e.g. Rome in the 1st and 2nd centuries CE, North and Central Europe in the 1530s, England from 1620 to 1650, and, in North America, the Great Awakening of the late 1730s, which was followed by the second Great Awakening from 1820 to 1860). The contemporary movements are, however, somewhat different in that they tend to draw their adherents largely (although by no means exclusively) from the more

prosperous and educated sections of society.

Many of the contemporary new movements have a charismatic, sometimes a messianic, leader and several espouse millennial or Utopian beliefs in the perfectibility of society – or of the enlightened individual. What must be stressed, however, is that the groups do differ very widely in their beliefs and practices and the type of membership which they attract. Several groups owe their theological and ritual origins to India [7; 30; 31] (e.g. ANANDA MARGA, DIVINE LIGHT MISSION, HARE KRISHNA, MEHER BABA), while others are based (more or less loosely) upon the Christian tradition (e.g. CHILDREN OF GOD, PEOPLE'S TEMPLE, UNIFI-CATION CHURCH, and the WAY INTERNATIONAL). Yet other groups have developed from more secular belief systems designed to promote personal growth and development (e.g. the HUMAN POTENTIAL MOVEMENT, SCIENTOLOGY, and SYNANON). Membership of some of the movements involves only a partial commitment from all but a small group of core members, but in other movements complete, full-time devotion is called for, and members may frequently be required to live in a community centre and abandon careers and individual ownership of property (e.g. Hare Krishna, Children of God, Unification Church). It is these latter movements which have received the greatest attention and criticism from the media and from the ANTI-CULT MOVEMENT. [44] [Guides for contacting groups: 2; 20; 41; 42; general books on new religious movements: 3; 7; 10; 14; 15; 30–32; 38; 51; 55–7; 59; critical evaluation: 8; 11; 12; 25; 26; 37; 47: *see also individual movements for specific reading*]

Nganga [II] Probably the most widely extended of all African religious terms, found in societies all across Bantu Africa from the Bakongo in the west to the Swahili in the east and ZULU (*inyanga*) in the south. The *nganga* is the common religious expert, the doctor who can control evil forces. His or her character and powers, however, vary considerably. Everywhere the *nganga* is someone who uses medicines – herbs or fetishes (NKISI). Probably the *nganga* is also a medium and a diviner, although in Kongo (the Bakongo language) there is a distinction between the *nganga*, the doctor-ritualist, and the *ngunza*, the medium and seer; and among the Tanzanian Segeju the *nganga* is a herbalist but not a diviner. In Swahili a distinction is made between the mere herbalist (*nganga wa majani*), the witch-doctor (*nganga wa kuagua*), who has special powers to recognize and deal with witchcraft (*uchawi*), and the 'sorcerer', who can curse or counter-curse (*nganga wa litegu*). If the greatest force of evil is usually seen to be witchcraft, then the *nganga* is above all the anti-witchcraft expert. In general the *nganga* detects the cause of an evil through DIVINATION by oracles or SPIRIT-POSSESSION, and then endeavours to remove it through medicines and ritual.

Nibbana [IX.B] (Sanskrit *nirvana*) In Buddhism and other religions of Indian origin *nibbana* is the highest possible happiness. The *Oxford English Dictionary*'s preferred explanation – 'In Buddhist theology, the extinction of individual existence and absorption into the supreme spirit . . .' – is both misleading and incorrect. Buddhism does not recognize a supreme spirit and rejects annihilation as a goal. Although Buddhist tradition explains *nibbana* as meaning 'without craving', it originally meant 'blowing out' – the quenching of the fires of greed, hate, and delusion. Psychologically this is a state of great inner freedom and spontaneity, in which the mind has supreme tranquillity, purity, and stability. This is the achievement of the Buddhist saints (ARAHAT; LOKUTTARA) and the goal of their followers.

Early Buddhist works actively and intentionally avoid resolving questions concerning the ontological status of *nibbana* or the post-mortem condition of the saint. Such issues were seen as liable to distract from the task in hand, necessarily productive of one-sided views (DITTHI) and even perhaps as unanswerable given the limitations of ordinary language. Subsequent ABHIDHAMMA analysis distinguishes between the transcendent (*lokuttara*) state of mind and an unconditioned element, later referred to as *nibbana*. Here *nibbana* is in effect the unchanging and uncharacterizable component of the enlightened state. Outside the context of *abhidhamma* psychology this can appear a rather static and rigid conception. So MAHAYANA Buddhist writings often criticize it as inadequate and too limiting a view of truth. (*See* EMPTINESS; SHUNYATAVADA.) [5: 69ff; European interpretation: 65; traditional: 31: 165ff; 64: 469ff]

Nichiren [XVI] (1222–82) The founder of the Japanese sect bearing his name, sometimes called Hokke-shu (Lotus sect) [1; 34: 228–37]. Nichiren, who was born Zennichi-maru in Chiba prefecture, took the vows in a local temple in 1237 and studied TENDAI on Mt Hiei from 1242 (SACRED MOUNTAINS; SAICHO). His adherents date the initiation of Japan's first native sect to 1253, when Nichiren termed the mantra *Namu-myoho-rengekyo* (Homage to the Lotus of the Good Law) a summation of the *Lotus Sutra* and his followers adopted the incantation. He preached virulently in Kamakura, attacking social evils, other sects, and the authorities. For this and his writing he was banished to the Izu peninsula, but within three years was back in Kamakura intensifying his criticisms. His doctrines centred on the Three Great Secrets, *honzon*, *daimoku*, and *kaidan* – by implication, the adoration of Shaka, the wonderful truth in the *Lotus Sutra*, and the importance of the moral law [34: 235–7]. Deviating from Tendai theory, he saw himself as a disciple of the living

Shaka (JAPANESE BUDDHAS AND BODHISATTVAS); indeed, his followers call him an incarnation of Bosatsu Jogyo, an early disciple of BUDDHA. Exiled again in 1271 and sentenced to death on Sado island, he is said to have miraculously survived, and he retired two years later in a temple in Yamanashi prefecture called Kuon-ji, where he is buried. There are almost 40 subsects today, the chief of which is Nichiren Shoshu, with its head temple, Daiseki-ji, in Shizuoka prefecture [19: 205–12].

Nihang [XXVII] The Nihangs, originally called AKALIS, are a group of militant SIKHS distinguished by their dark-blue garments and impressive array of steel weapons. During the 18th century they commanded formidable respect as fierce warriors, a tradition which they still endeavour to keep alive as they rove the Punjab on horseback. The Nihangs are militarily organized as an 'army' (the Budha Dal). Their daily discipline includes lengthy *kirtan* hymn singing and ritual consumption of an infusion of *bhang* (cannabis).

Nilotic Religion [II] The Nilotic group of peoples stretches from the SHILLUK in the north, NUER, DINKA, and Anuak also in the Sudan, through the Acholi, Lango, and Padhola in Uganda, to the Luo in western Kenya. This relatively small group of peoples has a closely connected history, but their religions show some striking contrasts. The common root may lie in a strong pastoral and democratic monotheism, reminiscent of ancient Israel, perhaps best represented by the Nuer, yet the Acholi present one of the clearest African examples of an apparently godless religion (JOK), while the divine kingship of the Shilluk strikingly contrasts with the non-hierarchical character of Nuer religion. Nearest in type to the Nuer may be the most remote in distance – the Kenyan Luo with their strongly monotheistic worship of Nyasaye, creator and protector. [4: 138–63; 11: 122–35; 25; 36; 39]

Nit-Nem [XXVII] Every SIKH is expected to repeat appointed selections from the scriptures (ADI GRANTH) thrice daily. This is called *nit-nem*, the 'daily rule'. The first selection is recited during *amrit vela*, the period of calm before sunrise. Having risen and bathed before daybreak the devout Sikh repeats Guru Nanak's *Japji* and two works by Guru Gobind Singh (the *Jap Sahib* and *Ten Savayyas*) (*see* GURUS). At sunset *Sodar Rahiras*, the evening liturgy, is chanted or sung. This comprises a selection of nine hymns grouped near the beginning of the *Adi Granth*, plus two extracts from the DASAM GRANTH, a portion of Guru Amar Das's hymn *Anand*, and two brief compositions by Guru Arjan. Finally, *Kirtan Sohila* is chanted or sung immediately before sleeping. This short selection of five hymns is also included in the Sikh funeral order. All the daily liturgies except *Kirtan Sohila* conclude with a recitation of ARDAS, the Sikh prayer. [5: 1–273; 17: 1–3]

Nkisi [II] (plural: *minkisi*) Bakongo name for the material object with spiritual power in it, encountered very widely in Africa and generally known to Europeans as a 'fetish'. It is known to the AKAN as *suman*, to the MENDE as *hale*, to the NUER as *kulangni*, to the GANDA as *mayembe*, etc. The meaning of such terms may also be 'medicine'. It is essentially an unimportant element in African religion, to be clearly distinguished from divinities (ORISHA) or ancestor-spirits. The *nkisi* is a physical object or bundle of objects made by its owner from certain tabu or symbolic materials in which a spirit is thought to reside, but so that it has no named existence apart from this singular object. Even there it may be nameless. The fetish is at the service of its owner, who may as a NGANGA gain his reputation thereby; it is used to promote private ends, defensive or offensive, and is often much feared. Its power may be vaguely held to derive from some original act of God, but its character lies in its materiality, particularity, and potential dangerousness. In some societies its role is very marginal, in others – Bakongo especially – it may come almost to dominate life for a time, until in reaction there is a cleansing destruction of *minkisi* and a return to more elevated religion. [2: IV; 25: 99–105; 40: 9–24]

Nomos [XII] Law. Greek laws were man-made, but were considered to be divinely sanctioned. Unwritten laws and customs were given by the gods in the past, and Zeus (THEOI) was thought to watch over law and justice. Written law-codes (the earliest dating from the mid 7th century BCE) were often sent to Delphi or another oracle (MANTIKE) for divine approval. Impiety (*asebeia*) was an offence punishable in law. In a notorious Athenian impiety trial in 399 BCE the philosopher Socrates was condemned to death and executed. [8: 251, 255–7; 7: 189–92; 11: 188–9; 15: 189–91]

North America (Jews in) [XVII] The first Jewish settlers in the North American continent were SEFARDI MARRANOS, of Iberian origin, who moved to New Amsterdam (later New York) in 1654, having originally settled in South America. German and East European Jewish migrants subsequently joined the original Sefardi settlers, the Jewish population rising substantially with the influx of refugees from persecution in Russia and Poland in the late 19th century. The North American Jewish population today is over 6 million, with about 300,000 in Canada and close to 3 million in New York State. The U.S.A. has the largest Jewish population in the world. Religious life in North America is divided into three main streams, Orthodox, CONSERVATIVE, and REFORM. Orthodoxy consists of a variety of independent congregations as well as a large, organized community of Modern Orthodox Jews whose main educational institution is Yeshiva University (founded 1897) in New York. Conservativism,

the largest organizational SYNAGOGUE group, has its rabbinical seminary, the Jewish Theological Seminary (1887), also in New York. Reform Judaism, which is more radical than its counterparts in the rest of the English-speaking world and has Americanized its JUDAISM, runs the Hebrew Union College (1875) in Cincinnati. [13: 274, 407; 26: XIV; 42: XII–XV; 43: VIII, XV, XVI]

Nuer Religion [II] The Nuer are a pastoral NILOTIC people living in the southern Sudan. They lack any structured political hierarchy. Their wealth and joy lie in their cattle. Nuer religion is preoccupied with Kwoth (God, or Spirit). Kwoth is believed to have created all things; he is far yet near, an all-powerful father, the base and guardian of morality. Formerly, it seems, the Nuer believed only in Kwoth and Colwic spirits (people killed by lightning and taken by Kwoth), but more recently other spirits, such as Deng and Buk (Abuk among the DINKA), entered Nuer life via the Dinka. These and the totemic spirits remain essentially refractions of the one Kwoth, who is invoked both in all sacrifices and frequently in private life by brief intercessions.

The central Nuer religious act is the sacrifice of an ox to Kwoth, either on social occasions or for the expiation of sin (but not to affect the processes of nature: the Nuer have no interest in rain-making). If no ox is available, a cucumber may be substituted, with the tacit approval of Kwoth. Everyone is his own priest and no special time or place is required for the act. The ox, mystically representing man, is consecrated, Kwoth is invoked at length, and the beast is then immolated with a spear thrust. The Nuer are proud individualists, cherishing equality, but before Kwoth they are 'as ants', humble and accepting [25].

Numa (Calendar of) [XXV] Numa (*c.* 700 BCE, according to tradition) was the second king of Rome (after the founder Romulus, traditionally dated 754 BCE).

All Roman religious institutions were attributed to him, many anachronistically, and the relatively sophisticated calendar must have reached the form we know at least a century after Numa's time. The earliest copies we have date from the 1st century BCE, when the system was entirely solar, although showing survivals from a solar/lunar phase. Each day was given a character determining its religious, legal, and political nature [13]. Most significantly for our knowledge of early religion, copies of the Calendar always include certain festivals in capital letters; these include the oldest fixed festivals and it is this set which goes back to an early date and provides the only solid information about early Roman religion [I: v]. The character of many of these early festivals was a matter for conjecture to the earliest writers now extant, but progress (partly by comparative methods) has been made towards understanding at least the general pattern of the year [introduction: 17: v]. Thus, February was a month of purifications (including probably the Lupercalia, in which naked priests ran through the city striking bystanders with strips from the hide of a sacrificed goat) [6: 348–50; 9: 28–30; 17: 77–8]. March opened the season of war (the arms of Mars, the war-god, were paraded by the dancing-priests, the *Salii*, in the dress of archaic soldiers) [11: 114–16; 17: 78–80]. April has rituals of growth (including the sacrifice of cows in calf at the Fordicidia) [6: 371–3; 17: 82]. The festivals of high summer concern the preservation of the water supply and the stored food from the harvest. The most famous single festival is perhaps the Saturnalia, the classical predecessor of Christmas, at which in historical times there was feasting, present-giving, and exchange of roles [17: 98–9].

Numen [xxv] The power of a Roman deity, the force of the word *numen* being 'nodding'. It is commonly used in the classical period (1st century BCE/1st century CE) in cases where the presence of deity, for instance in a grove, is suspected but undetermined; also in combination with the emperor's name (*Augusti numen*) to avoid specifically calling him a god (EMPEROR-WORSHIP). According to one line of evolutionary theory, *numen* represents an earlier stage of development than 'god' (*see* DI DEAEQUE).

Numerology [xviii] The attribution of mystical or symbolic meaning to numbers, probably universal in religion. Small numbers can suggest groupings and patternings; multiplication by hundreds or thousands can preserve these qualities while suggesting changes of scale, degrees of sacredness, etc. Western numerology is derived from Pythagoras (6th century BCE), who thought number the basic principle of the cosmos and assigned qualities to numbers according to their mathematical properties. The other main source is the BIBLE, all of whose numbers were regarded as significant by most commentators up to the 18th century. St Augustine (354–430 CE) was keenly interested in numerology. Jewish students of KABBALAH had their own numerological system, *gematria*. Biblical number symbolism parallels Babylonian and Egyptian traditions possibly astrological in origin. [12] A system of numerology similar to that of Pythagoras was current in China by the 1st century CE, and Hindu and Buddhist teachings embody many number-patterns. Numerology is important in many forms of MAGIC, DIVINATION, and religious art. [5]

Nyau [II] Powerful dance societies traditional among the Chewa and Mang'anja of Malawi. These peoples are matrilineal and uxorilocal (i.e. legal descent is through women and a man lives in his wife's village after marriage). The Nyau balance this appearance of female domination with a strongly male organization. Membership of the societies is wholly male; they possess a secret vocabulary; and their dances are characterized by masks, which are thought to represent the animals of the wild and the spirits of the dead. Nyau rituals are chiefly related to rites of passage, being performed especially at burials, commemorations of the dead, and female initiation rites. Nyau religion is communal and populist rather than orientated to kingship, kinship, or a shrine with its religious professionals. It appears to represent an ancient stratum of Malawian history prior to the arrival of the Phiri invaders of the 14th century. Comparable societies are found in many parts of Africa [11: 252–73].

Nyaya [XIII.B] One of the six DAR-SHANAS or salvation-philosophies of classical Hinduism. The *Nyaya* or 'Method' school emerged from the VAISHESHIKA during the first two centuries CE with the *Nyaya-sutra* (attributed to Akshapada Gautama), but the standard commentary of Vatsyayana dates from the late 5th century. In origin the *Nyaya* was a school of rhetoric, but it early developed a careful analysis of the authoritative sources of knowledge (*pramana*) and the forms of syllogistic argument leading eventually to very detailed studies of logic. The *Nyaya-sutra* taught 16 categories (*padartha*); correct knowledge of these brought about by systematic discussion would lead to liberation (MOKSHA), although YOGA practice was recommended as an auxiliary. The influential *Udayana* (late 11th century) formulated the Hindu proofs for the existence of God (ISHVARA) and initiated developments in logic which culminated in the formation of a new school. The later *Nyaya* was given its authoritative presentation by Gangesha (early 14th century). The *Vaisheshika* was incorporated into a single system, which remains an influential school of realism in Hindu thought into recent times. [11: VI, 2, 76–112; 13: II, 1–110; 14: 165–90; in translation: 13: II, 211–716; 16: 356–85]

Nyingma [XXIX] The Nyingma tradition represents the oldest elements in Tibetan Buddhism, having its origins in the missionary work of the 8th-century Indian masters Padmasambhava and Shantirakshita [4]. However, the Nyingma finally became a distinct tradition by the 14th century through the organizing efforts of figures such as the 'omniscient' Longchen Rabjampa (1308–63), the systematizer of the doctrine of 'great perfection'.

The Nyingma school consists of both ordained practitioners and lay yogins (*ngak pa*), who follow the unbroken oral-transmission lineage teachings of the Nyingma patriarchs and the teachings of the *terma* ('rediscovered treasures'), works composed and concealed most usually by Padmasambhava and subsequently rediscovered and propagated by a predicted *terton* ('treasure finder'). [22]

The principal teaching of the tradition is the 'great perfection' (*dzog chen*), which was introduced into Tibet in the 8th century by Vimalamitra and Padmasambhava. This teaching represents the pinnacle of TANTRA (2) and the highest of the nine *yanas* ('vehicles') distinguished by the Nyingmas. The term 'great perfection' denotes the unsurpassable nature of liberation attained through the realization of the primordial purity of awareness. [10]

The Nyingma have maintained a decentralized organization with six major branches, each with its own special codification and transmissions of the shared doctrine. In exile in India two heads of the Nyingma tradition are currently recognized, Dudjom Rinpoche and Mindroling Trichen Rinpoche.

Nzambi [II] This is one of the most widely used African names for God, appearing in some form (Nyame, Ndjambi, etc.) all across west central Africa from among the Herero in Namibia and Lozi in Zambia to many peoples in Zaire and Cameroon. It may or may not be one with the AKAN Nyame. The etymological meaning is uncertain. Nzambi was certainly in use by the Bakongo (adjective Kongo) in the 16th century and appears in the earliest dictionary of a BANTU language, the Kongo dictionary of Georges de Gheel (d. 1652), but the theory that it was introduced by European missionaries is unlikely. Myths suggest that Nzambi, who is creator and master of the world, withdrew from earth on account of the crimes of men. [15; 22]

· O ·

Occult [XVIII] Literally 'hidden', but applied loosely to any matter supposed to be supernatural (or concerned with the supernatural) but not clearly falling within the province of the major religions, Christianity in particular. Often there is the implication that knowledge of such subjects is available only to an initiated few. Those known as 'occultists' are usually students of the WESTERN MAGICAL TRADITION or of the THEOSOPHICAL SOCIETY's teachings. Topics often regarded as occult include DIVINATION, MAGIC, PSYCHIC POWERS, SATANISM, and WITCHCRAFT. [28]

Odin [V] One of the main cults in Scandinavia in the Viking age was that of Odin, leader of the AESIR. He was known as Wodan (Old English Woden) to the Germanic peoples [6: I, 54–6]. The Romans equated him with Mercury, and he bears resemblances to the Celtic LUG. Odin was associated with magic, poetry, ecstasy, the gaining of wealth, possibly with healing [24: II, 155], and the dead. He was worshipped by kings and warriors. His spear decided victory in battle, and the Berserks, fighting in wild fury, were his dedicated followers [6: II, 66–9]. The VALKYRIES did his bidding, conducting dead warriors to his hall, VALHALLA [6: II, 61–6]. He was represented as a riding warrior with a spear, attended by raven, eagle, and wolf. His eight-legged horse Sleipnir carried him through the sky, followed, in later folklore, by a wild troop of the dead [6: VI, 148]. He also appeared as an old, one-eyed man in a cloak, wandering in disguise to cause strife. Important myths associated with Odin were the

regaining of the mead of inspiration, the sacrifice of an eye to gain knowledge, and the acquisition of runic lore (RUNES) by hanging in torment on YGGDRASIL [6: I, 40, VI, 140–49; 30: II, 39–46, 63]. He was doomed to be devoured by FENRISWOLF at RAGNAROK.

Olam Ha-Ba [XVII] 'The World to Come', the most general Jewish term for the hereafter [9 vol. 12: 1355]. Originally referring to the post-Resurrection era of the Messianic age (MESSIAH), it later also signified the condition of the soul in the world to come after the death of the body. The classical statement of the TALMUD [7: 365], that in Olam Ha-Ba there is 'no eating, no drinking, no procreation, no business dealings, no jealousy, no hate and no competition. But the righteous sit with crowns on their heads deriving pleasure from the radiance of the Divine Presence (SHEKHINAH)', was understood by commentators as referring to either of these two conditions [22: 401]. Since Jewish theology worked with a rather fluid doctrinal frame of reference the belief in the resurrected body-cum-soul coexisted with the belief in the immortality of the soul. Different teachers and schools stressed different aspects of the doctrine of Olam Ha-Ba. (*See also* REINCARNATION.) [52: 31]

Old Believers [XI.D] In 1666 CE the Patriarch Nikon ordered the reform of Russian Orthodox services and religious practices for them to conform to contemporary Greek uses (RUSSIA). Traditionalists led by the saintly Archpriest Avvakum (1620–82) refused to conform. They believed, correctly, that their own traditions were more ancient than those Nikon was imposing. They also believed the new uses to be doctrinally unsound [14; 34: 2, 61ff]. Avvakum and his followers were cruelly persecuted: he was burned. Their movement survives as the Old Believers. They differ from the ORTHODOX CHURCHES in ritual practice rather than in doctrine. Some Old Believer churches, the *popovtsi*, have priests and bishops; among others, the *bezpopovtsi*, the priesthood has died out. There are probably about 1 million Old Believers in the U.S.S.R. [10; 21]

Ometeotl [XIX] The fundamental divine power in central MESOAMERICAN RELIGION was the high god Ometeotl, the primordial creator. [12: 80–103] The creation myth pictured Ometeotl dwelling in the highest level of heaven, called Omeyocan, from which the universe was generated through the actions of four divine children, each considered a major aspect of the high god. Ometeotl was a sexually dualistic deity personified in a number of forms, of which the most outstanding were Ometecuhtli–Omecihuatl, Tonactecuhtli–Tonacacihuatl, In Tloque Nahuaque, and Ipalnemoani. The male half was usually merged with solar deities, which personified the celestial force *par excellence*, and the female half merged with the maternal earth fertility-goddesses [17: 408–11]. Although there was no cult dedicated to Ometeotl, he was considered to be present in all things and beings. He generated human life through the souls which dropped from heaven into the wombs of women. His unceasing activity was expressed in the actions of all deities but especially TEZCATLIPOCA (the Smoking Mirror) and QUETZALCOATL (the Feathered Serpent).

Oracle Bones (**Chinese**) [X] Over 100,000 DIVINATION or oracle bones dating from the Shang period (1523–1027 BCE) have been unearthed in Honan province. In Shang times heated bronze rods were applied to the bones to produce cracks, which were then interpreted. The later Shang bones bear inscriptions using 5,000 different characters, usually addressed to the Shang royal ancestors concerning ritual, military, agricultural, and domestic matters. They provide valuable information about Shang religion and civilization and about the development of the Chinese language. [14: 31–42; 71: II, 55–6; 87; 99: IV, 55–60]

Origin of Religion [XXVIII] (1) The manner in which religious beliefs and practices first arose in human history or prehistory.

(2) The root or source of religion in the experience and development of an individual or group.

In both senses, origin was a major concern of theorists in the earlier period of work in the SCIENCES OF RELIGION [25: II, III; 28: II]. Many anthropologists [19; 29] made conjectures about (1), but often sought support for their theories in psychological or sociological hypotheses concerned with (2) [18: 27–41, 45–80, 104–44; 30: 217–33]. It now seems doubtful that good empirical evidence for (1) can be found. As to (2), the question of what factors cause, promote, or preserve religious credence or commitment must be clearly distinguished from the question of the truth of specific beliefs or the efficacy of actual practices. To show how religion might have originated if it is an illusion is not to have proved that all religion is in fact illusory. [13: III; 17: 165–72]

Orisha [II] The many divinities of YORUBA RELIGION, partly comparable with the Vodu of FON, the Abosum of AKAN, the Lubaale of GANDA, the Cwezi of Nyoro, or even the Mhondoro of SHONA religion. Probably the most complex pantheon in Africa, their number is asserted to be hundreds, but the chief figures are relatively few. In mythology the Orisha are children and ministers of the one supreme God, Olodumare; in modern devotional practice individual Orisha are treated as almost independent deities, each with its own cult centres, praise songs (*oriki*), and prayers. In general Orisha are characterized both as nature spirits and as historical figures, the myths describing them highly anthropomorphically. Among the most important are Obatala (Orisha-nla), originally deputed to create the natural world and, in some accounts, father of all other Orisha; Orunmila, patron of IFA divination; Eshu, the unpredictable trickster, dangerous or evil and therefore important to conciliate; Ogun, patron of iron and steel work; Shango, author of thunder and lightning but also ancestor of the kings of Oyo. There is almost endless variety in Orisha mythology and devotion; it would be mistaken to reduce it to a single unchanging system, where place and time produce such major differences [37].

Oro [XXII] A war-god, first worshipped as the son of Ta'aroa (TANGAROA) at Ra'iatea in the Society Islands (Tahiti). Oro became the supreme god, largely displacing Ta'aroa and TANE, the ancient Polynesian ATUA. (POLYNESIAN RELIGION) Oro was patron god of the ARIOI cult, whose travelling dancers spread his name to islands further away. [16; 22; 30]

Orpheus, Orphism [XII] Orpheus was a legendary singer, credited, from the 6th century BCE, with poems containing theogonic, cosmogonic, and eschatological teachings. Orphism is the broad, multifarious current of sectarian thinking they contain. One strand originated with Pythagoras, a Samian sage and 'miracle-worker' who founded a sect in southern Italy. He expounded the theory of reincarnation (metempsychosis), the kernel of Orpheo-Pythagoreanism. The Pythagoreans governed Kroton for a time. They studied music and mathematics. Their way of life (*bios*) involved rigid rules with many ritual TABUS. They sought to purify their soul, atone for the Titans' crime (KAKON), and escape the cycle of reincarnation. Certain individuals were initiated privately by priests using Orphic texts, and followed a vegetarian Orphic *bios* to earn a happy afterlife. The Bacchic/Dionysiac MYSTERIA, whose doctrine was Orpheo-Pythagorean, promised atonement, escape from reincarnation, and happy afterlife through initiation, ritual rules, and ecstatic rites. The Orphic/Eleusinian strand (MYSTERIA) omits *metempsychosis*. Both strands contain a trend offering salvation by ritual means and an ethical trend (ETHIKE). Orphic literature bloomed in Hellenistic times – much of it learned, some connected with local cults – and continued to be associated with the Pythagorean sect, revived in the 1st century BCE (Neopythagoreans) after a decline. [1; 2: VI.2, 3]

Orthodox Church [XI.D] A communion of self-governing churches following the doctrine of the seven Ecumenical COUNCILS [47: 26–50]. The Orthodox communion includes the four ancient patriarchates: Alexandria, Antioch, Constantinople, and Jerusalem. It includes the churches of Bulgaria, Cyprus, Georgia, Greece, Romania, RUSSIA, and Serbia, in each of which it is the major religious group. It includes the Orthodox Churches of Albania, CHINA, Czechoslovakia, Finland, Japan, Poland, and the U.S.A. Orthodox communities exist in Western Europe, in AFRICA (especially Uganda), and in Australia.

Since the separation of the Nestorian and Monophysite (CHRISTOLOGY) churches, and the loss of COMMUNION with the Western church, the Orthodox Church is predominantly representative of developments of the Byzantine (CHRISTIANITY, HISTORY AND CHARACTER OF) tradition of Christianity. [3; 4; 26; 38; 44]

Orthodox theology is strongly trinitarian (TRINITY) [35: 32–70], and apophatic [23: 13–43]. In his essence God is utterly unknowable, but is present in all creation in his energies. The energies are God and can be experienced [24; 47: 217]. Man is created in the image of God. By the SIN of Adam, the first man in Christian mythology, human nature is damaged; the image of God remains but the likeness fades. Adam's sin brings death into the world, and because of death sin multiplies [23; 26: 140–46]. JESUS CHRIST conquers death by his death and resurrection, undermines the rule of sin, and pours out the gift of new life, sending down the HOLY SPIRIT [26: 151–79]. Enlivened by the Holy Spirit, the CHURCH already shares in the life to come [35: 70–97].

Orthodox religious life centres on the MYSTERIES (SACRAMENTS), in which the acts of God in history become present realities by the power of the Spirit. The Mysteries enlighten and transform not only the individual but also the whole community, and are effective symbols of the apocatastasis, the restoration of the whole of creation to God. [7; 11; 30; 39]

Osirian Triad (Osiris, Isis, Horus) [IV] Osiris, a mythical Egyptian human king and the bringer of civilization, was murdered by his brother SETH [13; 14]. His dismembered body was reassembled by his wife, Isis, who then posthumously conceived their son, Horus.

As Osiris' avenger, Horus fought Seth [23]. The divine judges found in his favour, and he became king of Egypt, while Osiris, resurrected as divine judge of the dead in the Underworld, became the symbol of immortality. His worshippers sought individual resurrection through righteous lives. The cult gained popular support from the Middle Kingdom period on, c. 1900 BCE.

Owner of the Animals [III] Among North American Indian hunting-tribes, particularly those in the north, the notion is widespread that animal species are governed by a supernatural owner. This prototypical figure, often mentioned in myth, may also be arranged in a hierarchical order with other owners of other animal species. A close parallel usually exists between the social structures in such hunting groups and those believed to be present in the animal world [11]. Over all other owners a universal ruler may be placed (e.g. Sedna among the ESKIMO). Success in hunting is frequently based upon achieving a favourable relationship with the 'owner', either through collective rituals (including abstinence from eating the flesh of the species), or perhaps on an individual level in those cases where the owner is identified with a person's GUARDIAN SPIRIT.

· P ·

Pacific Religions [XXII] Ancient religions of Oceania and Island South-East Asia. Over 30,000 years ago by gradual migration the ancestors of today's Melanesians (Australoid) came from South Asia through the Malay peninsula and Indonesia to New Guinea and Australia. Mongoloid peoples from northern China later moved southwards, largely replacing the Australoids in mainland South-East Asia and Indonesia. More recent were the migrations by sea of Mongoloid (and Caucasoid?) peoples from coastal South China. Travelling via the Philippines and skirting Melanesia they settled in the Tongan and Samoan islands in about 1500 BCE. From there further voyages radiated outwards to the Society and Marquesas islands, Hawaii, New Zealand, and elsewhere, spreading a common language, culture, and religion throughout Polynesia. [3; 22]

Early in the Christian era Indonesian rulers, impressed by Indian and Chinese trade and civilization, adopted HINDU-ISM and BUDDHISM. Absorbing much from local religion, these faiths flourished in the great empires of medieval Java and Sumatra. From the 13th century ISLAM spread through South-East Asia, again without displacing the ancient local religions. Christianizing of the Pacific began with the Europeans who arrived in the 16th century to chart and lay claim to the 'South Sea' (named 'Pacific' by Magellan in 1520); 19th- and early 20th-century colonization was accompanied by extensive missionary activity. PROTEST-ANTISM, ROMAN CATHOLICISM, and sectarian churches have proliferated. Like the Indian religions and Islam in Indonesia, Christianity in the Pacific is itself being modified as indigenous converts seek to make it a faith of their own. (AUSTRALIAN, BALINESE, BATAK, DAYAK, FIJIAN, JAVANESE, MELANESIAN, PHILIPPINES, and POLY-NESIAN RELIGIONS)

Pahlavi [XXX] This term refers to two subjects: (1) a dynasty which ruled in Iran from 1925 to 1979; (2) the language of Iran from about the 3rd to the 9th century CE. (The dynasty was named after the culture and language of this period.) The term is synonymous with 'Middle Persian' (Middle as opposed to the Old of the inscriptions and the New of recent times). Because Pahlavi was the language of Iran during the period when most ZOROASTRIAN texts came to be written down, it is the language in which most texts of that faith survive. The final redactions of many of the religious texts were made in the 9th century, when Zoroastrian priests (MAGI) were active in defence of their faith, making or re-editing translations and compiling summaries of the AVESTA. Large sections of the Pahlavi books preserve ancient beliefs [40: 31–66]. Chief among the collections of ancient material is perhaps the BUNDAHISHN [translation: 1], other apocalyptic works [2], and the *Dinkard*, which also contains some expository summaries [31; 38; 43; 44]. Important expositions of the faith include *Menog i Khrad* [46], *Shkand-gumanig Vizar* [49: 59–66], and *Dadestan i dinig* [45]. One of the most popular religious texts among Zoroastrians is *Arda Viraz Namag* (The Book of the Righteous Viraz), a vision of heaven and hell

[24]. Modern studies of Zoroastrianism have the Pahlavi texts as one of their main sources.

Pali [IX.B] The language of the THERAVADA Buddhist scriptures. Pali means, literally, scriptural text, as opposed to commentary. The language was called Magadhi, i.e. the language of ancient Magadha, said to have been spoken by GOTAMA himself. Pali differs to some extent from the related Middle Indian dialect known as Magadhi to the later Sanskrit grammarians, although it was doubtless one of the dialects of the later enlarged kingdom of Magadha. The orally preserved discourses attributed to the BUDDHA and his disciples were probably current in a number of dialects from the beginning. When they were written down in Ceylon in the 1st century BCE, a more uniform Pali language naturally arose. In North India the greater prestige of Sanskrit led to the gradual displacement of Middle Indian. The work of commentators such as BUDDHAGHOSA made Pali the language of Theravada Buddhism, with a considerable literature down to modern times. [10]

Pan-Islamism [XIV] The idea that the common religious bond of ISLAM should have a political manifestation. This was publicized by the polemicist Jamal al-Din al-Afghani (1838–97) and taken up by the Ottoman Sultan 'Abd al-Hamid II (1876–1909), who pictured himself as protector of all Muslims [38: V]. The concept had a particular attraction for communities on the periphery of Islam threatened by Western domination, e.g. Africa, the Caucasus, Central Asia, and India [1: IV], but the proliferation of nation-states across the Islamic world in the post-1920 years has impeded material realization of the ideal. [10 s.v.]

Panth [XXVII] The Sanskrit word *panth* (literally 'path' or 'road') is used to designate groups in India following particular teachers or doctrines. The early SIKH community was thus known

as the Nanak-panth or 'followers of Nanak' (*see* GURUS) [7: VI]. Later generations increasingly dropped the prefix, with the result that the community came to be known as, simply, 'the Panth'. This remains the preferred title today, in English usage as in Hindi or Punjabi. [23: I]

Pantheism [XXVIII] Belief that the whole of reality is divine [8: 132]. Pantheism may be cosmic (world-affirming), equating God and nature, or acosmic (world-denying), holding sense-experience to be illusory and only the divine to be real. The former is similar to panentheism (as e.g. in PROCESS THEOLOGY), for which God includes and permeates, but is not exhausted by, all that is known in sense-experience.

Papa [XXII] An earth-mother who, with RANGI the sky-father, gave birth to the gods (ATUA) in the creation myths of POLYNESIAN RELIGION. Their son TANE made himself a wife (the first human being) out of earth from Papa's body. To ease Papa's grief at her enforced separation from Rangi, the gods turned her face towards the Underworld. All creatures live on her broad, kindly back. [7: 15; 16; 22]

Papacy [XI.B] 'Pope' (father) is now normally used of the Bishop of Rome as head of ROMAN CATHOLICISM and 'Vicar of Christ' on earth. His authority is held to descend from JESUS CHRIST through the APOSTLE Peter as first bishop of Rome. Roman authority in the West over doctrine and jurisdiction developed early, and some medieval Popes claimed wide powers over secular rulers. The Vatican City still gives the Pope status as an independent ruler. Challenges to papal authority like Gallicanism (STATE) and the CONCILIAR MOVEMENT receded in the 19th century with the rise of Ultramontanism (appeal 'beyond the mountains' – the Alps – to Rome). Vatican COUNCIL I (1870) defined as 'dogma' (AUTHORITY) the infallibility of the Pope when pronouncing with full formality (*ex cathedra*) on faith and morals, even apart from a General Council of the Church [11: 273]. Other important papal pronouncements are published in 'bulls' (from the Latin for the seal attached to them) and in circular letters ('encyclicals') to churches. The 'Old Catholics' after 1870 (with an earlier schism in Utrecht) rejected papal infallibility and various Roman customs [102]. The relationship between the authority of Popes, bishops, and councils has been reconsidered since Vatican Council II (1962–5) but papal claims remain a major problem for the ECUMENICAL MOVEMENT. The ORTHODOX CHURCH rejects them in favour of AUTOCEPHALY, though allowing Rome a primacy of honour. Papal authority is also rejected by Old Catholics, PROTESTANTISM, and ANGLICANISM, although some Anglo-Catholics accept it with limitations. [1: 37–56; 79; 131; 133]

Parables [XI.A] Stories, usually drawn from ordinary life, illustrating some religious or ethical principle. They are frequently found in Jewish and Christian scriptures. Nathan's story of the poor man's ewe lamb brought home to King David the wrong he had done by taking Uriah's wife. Many parables are preserved in rabbinical teaching. JESUS CHRIST's parables (such as the sower and the seed, the good Samaritan, the prodigal son) are particularly well known: each illustrates one aspect of his message about God's dealings with human beings. [7: 53–80; 19: 27]

Paramita [IX.B] (Pali *parami*) 'Perfection', referring in MAHAYANA Buddhism to a mental quality developed to the degree characteristic of a BODHISATTVA. Most common is a list of six: giving (*dana*), morality (SILA), acceptance, strength, meditation (*dhyana*), wisdom (PRAJNA). Giving which is developed to the highest (*parama*) extent is the 'perfection of giving', but it is often traditionally explained as 'gone to the far shore (*para*)', i.e. transcendent. The lists of *paramita* ultimately

derive from the earlier BODHI-PAKKHIYA-DHAMMA, but outline the *bodhisattva* path and the necessary transformation in motivation. [46: 165–269] A special place is often given to the perfection of wisdom (PRAJNAPARA-MITA) with the remaining five equated to SKILFUL MEANS. A list of 10 *parami* appears in some of the latest works of the PALI scriptures, but they play a more important role in the later THERAVADA writings, e.g. DHAMMA-PALA [41: 254–331]. They are understood as equally necessary for the path of the ARAHAT and viewed as underlying tendencies accumulated over many lives.

Parinibbana [IX.A] A word with two parts: *nibbana* (PALI; Sanskrit *nirvana*); and *pari*, meaning 'all round' or 'altogether' and, so, 'complete'. Thus the 'complete (entry into) NIBBANA' of the BUDDHA at the end of his earthly existence is distinguished from the earlier attainment, in principle, of *nibbana*. *Parinibbana* is the final release from the round of rebirth.

The event is described in the Great Discourse on the *Parinibbana* (*Mahaparinibbana Suttanta*), or (Sanskrit) *Mahaparinirvana Sutra*), which is available from several sources, Pali, Sanskrit, Chinese, and Tibetan. The most readily accessible rendering in English is the translation of the Pali version [18; 28]. The Great Discourse constitutes the longest single narrative concerning GOTAMA, and describes the events of his last journey, from Rajagaha (Rajgir), in southern Bihar, to KUSINARA, near the Nepal border; the circumstances immediately leading up to his decease; and those which followed it, i.e. the cremation of his body, the sharing out and distribution of the ashes, and the building of STUPAS in various places, in which these were enshrined. [37: 67–80]

Parsi Religious Reforms [XXX] The first major reform movement began in 1746 and was concerned with the calendar. It was realized that there was a

discrepancy of a month between the calendars followed by the Parsis and the
Zoroastrians in Iran (owing to a difference of practice in intercalation in the
365-day year). A group of Parsis in Surat
adopted the Irani calendar and called it
the *qadimi* or 'ancient' one. Their 'Kad-
mi' movement provoked a reaction by
others, defending the traditional Parsi
calendar, who called themselves Shen-
shais (the meaning is disputed, possibly
'of the city', i.e. of Surat), later interpreted as Shahanshai, i.e. 'royalists'.
This caused bitter, even violent, divisions. In 1906 a third calendar was introduced called *Fasli* ('seasonal'), which was
based on the Gregorian calendar used in
the West. These divisions involve few
ritual and practically no doctrinal differences and nowadays there is little
animosity between the groups. In
numerical terms the most powerful group are the Shahanshai [7: 189f,
212].

In 1818 a Parsi priest, Mulla Firoze,
published a book brought by his father
from Iran, the *Desatir* (Ordinances).
This was followed in 1843 by the
English translation of a similar work
known as the *Dabistan*. Both claimed to
contain secret mystical teachings of
ZOROASTER. For a period they caused a
flurry of excitement, before it became
clear that they were spurious, emanating
from a Persian SUFI sect [7: 197f].

After about 1870 Western education
resulted in increasing Christian (almost
wholly Protestant) influence on the educated liberals. This was apparent mainly
in calls for the use of the vernacular
(rather than the AVESTA) in prayers
(MANTHRAS); in appeals for the abandonment both of the purity laws and of
nirang (consecrated bull's urine traditionally used for physical and spiritual
purification); and also in some doctrinal
changes, notably the abandonment of
traditional myths (BUNDAHISHN;
FRASHOKERETI) and belief in a devil
(ANGRA MAINYU). Such reforms,
inevitably, produced an orthodox

reaction. This was often expressed in
language and ideas derived from the
THEOSOPHICAL SOCIETY, a movement
which encouraged all Indians to reject
Western 'materialism' and preserve their
Eastern 'spirituality', because the latter
was allegedly in tune with occult
forces. Behramshah Shroff (1858–1927)
founded a specifically Parsi Theosophi-
cal/occultist movement, Ilm-i Kshnoom
(interpreted as meaning 'Science of
(Spiritual) Satisfaction'), claiming to
have received an esoteric teaching not
from masters in Tibet (as in Theosophy)
but from a secret race of giants hidden
in mountain caves in Iran. Rebirth,
asceticism, and vegetarianism are three
features of these two movements which
diverge from traditional Zoroastrian
teaching. Parsis influenced by either
movement are orthodox in that they
faithfully preserve traditional prayers
and rites.

The above reforms are those reported
in English-language publications. In
Gujarati there are emotive debates on
more 'internal' matters, mainly ritual
concerns such as detailed funeral practices. In both languages there is a debate
over the possibility of accepting converts. The term 'Parsi' is understood in
terms of race or caste, hence conversion
is generally considered to be impossible.
A vocal minority, especially in communities outside Bombay (e.g. Delhi
and in Canada), is canvassing for the
acceptance of converts, partly in order
to counter the decline in numbers. The
orthodox reaction is that intermarriage
and proselytism would inevitably result
in such a tiny minority (representing
0.016 per cent of India's population)
being swamped, thus destroying their
identity and heritage. In such circumstances religious issues and community
survival are inseparable subjects [22: pt
III].

Parsis [XXX] 'The Persians', the descendants of a small group of Zoroastrians
who left their Iranian homeland to
escape from Islamic oppression to seek a

land of religious freedom. They settled in north-west India (Gujarat) in 936 CE (the precise date has been disputed). Their early history is written in the *Tale of Sanjan (Qissa-i Sanjan)* [5: 166–8]. They generally lived in peace with the Hindus, but Muslim invasions of the region in 1297 and 1465 caused bloodshed and aroused deep fears of a return to the conditions in Islamic Iran. In the 15th century the first of a series of letters, or *Rivayets* [7: 173], was sent from Iranian co-religionists in answer to Parsi questions relating to religious practice. Under European, especially British, rule from the 17th century onwards the Parsis moved in increasing numbers to the new port and growing commercial capital of western India, Bombay. In the 19th century they acquired wealth and power out of all proportion to their numbers. By 1947 and Indian independence they numbered approximately 112,000 in India, with about 61 per cent in the one city of Bombay. By the 1970s their numbers were declining at the rate of 10 per cent per decade, with an increasing proportion in Bombay and over 90 per cent of the population living in urban areas. The Parsi community in India is now, in numerical terms, the main centre of ZOROASTRIANISM. Trading opportunities in the British empire led the Parsis to travel and settle in different countries, so there are now small communities in Australia (Sydney), Singapore, Hong Kong, Pakistan (Karachi), England (London), Canada (Toronto, Montreal, and Vancouver), and the U.S.A. (New York, Boston, and Washington). The communities in Aden and East Africa were forced to leave in the 1960s and 1970s. [7: XI–XIV; 22: pt III; 23; 28; 33]

Parvati [XIII.A] 'The mountain goddess', wife of SHIVA. Just as Shiva is associated with the Himalaya, so is Parvati, who is the daughter of Himalaya, the personification of the mountains. She is known also as Mahadevi ('Great Goddess') and by various other names,

including DURGA (*see also* KALI; SHAKTI) [2: 314].

Passion Play (in Islam) [XIV] The *ta'ziya* (literally 'consolation, commiseration') constitutes one of the few approaches in pre-modern Islamic literature to the Western-type drama. Essentially a phenomenon of SHI'ISM, these plays provide a focus for the intense feelings of ordinary believers concerning the martyrdoms of early Shi'ism, in particular the death in battle of 'Ali's son al-Husain (*see* 'ALI, 'ALIDS). They are accordingly staged around the anniversary of this event, 10 Muharram (*see* 'ID), among the Shi'i communities of Iran, the Indo-Pakistan subcontinent, and certain emirates of the western shores of the Persian Gulf. In the forms at present known, the actual texts of the plays do not seem to date beyond the 18th century. [20 'Ta'ziya'; 59]

Path [XXVII] For SIKHS *path* means a reading of any portion of the sacred scriptures. Particular merit attaches to a complete reading of the ADI GRANTH. This may be done intermittently (*sadharan path*, 'ordinary reading') or within a specified period. For special purposes an *akhand path*, or 'unbroken reading', is performed. This requires a continuous relay of readers and is completed within 48 hours. [4: 134–5; 23: 68] If this is not practicable the reading may be spread over seven days (*saptahik path*). [4: 172–3; 17: 6–7]

Patimokkha [IX.A] A PALI term (Sanskrit *pratimoksha*): the code of ethical precepts for Buddhist monks, contained in the VINAYA-PITAKA, and recited on full-moon and new-moon days by each local assembly of monks. The number of precepts is about 250, but varies with the versions used by different schools. [11A]

Patit [XXVII] If a SIKH commits a serious breach of the RAHIT (the KHALSA code) he should be declared *patit* ('fallen') and expelled from the Khalsa. Serious breaches include cutting one's hair and smoking. To secure readmission a *patit* must confess his sin and undergo a second initiation. Although the actual discipline is seldom invoked, the word *patit* is commonly used with reference to conspicuous offenders. It applies only to those who have previously received Khalsa initiation.

Paul, Saint [XI.A] (also known by his Jewish name, Saul), was born into a Jewish family of Tarsus in Cilicia (a family sufficiently distinguished to have acquired Roman citizenship), and received a rabbinical education at JERUSALEM under Gamaliel I. He first appears as a deadly opponent of the primitive CHURCH, but was converted (33 CE) to the faith he had been bent on exterminating and thenceforth became its leading APOSTLE, particularly among non-Jews. He is justly regarded as the founder of Gentile Christianity.

After a brief attempt to evangelize the Nabataean Arabs immediately after his conversion, he devoted himself to evangelism in Syria and Cilicia, then (with Barnabas) in Cyprus and Galatia (central Asia Minor), then (with Silvanus and Timothy) in Macedonia and Greece, and then (52–5 CE) in EPHESUS and the province of Asia.

In the principal cities of those provinces he established churches, comprising mainly Gentile converts with a smaller proportion of Jewish converts. He insisted that JESUS CHRIST had abolished the religious and social barriers between Jews and GENTILES. This involved a reappraisal of Jewish law, which sanctioned those barriers. This reappraisal created tension between him and conservative Jewish Christians. He punctuated his ministry with visits to the Jerusalem church, partly to maintain good relations with it and partly to discharge an obligation undertaken at the outset of his Gentile mission – to raise funds among his Gentile converts for the relief of the Jerusalem church.

On his last visit to Jerusalem he was arrested and prosecuted on a charge of violating the sanctity of the TEMPLE.

He appealed, as a Roman citizen, to have his case transferred from the provincial court to the imperial tribunal in Rome, and was sent to Rome in 59 CE. There he spent two years under house-arrest waiting for his appearance before Caesar, but enjoying liberty to preach the gospel to all who visited him. Tradition says that he was executed on the Ostian Way near Rome.

The New Testament (BIBLE) includes 13 letters bearing his name; most of them are generally considered authentic. [4; 5: 116–40]

Pelagianism [XI.C] The theological doctrine in CHRISTIANITY that each man has responsibility for ensuring his own SALVATION. Its name is derived from Pelagius, a British monk who was active early in the 5th century and who attacked Augustine's view that moral goodness is only possible through an act of divine grace (AUGUSTINIAN-ISM). Pelagius maintained that man is free will, that a man's sinful state is not inherited, and that grace is an aid to (rather than the sole source of) human righteousness (SIN). He denied that GOD has predestined each person to heaven or hell. Pelagianism was eventually condemned as heretical. [6; 10]

Penance (Christian) [XI.B] The SACRAMENT for the forgiveness of sins. In early centuries it was elaborate, severe, public; and allowed only once in a lifetime. The medieval system involved private confession to a priest (from 1215 at least once a year for Western Christians). The priest then formally pronounced the penitent forgiven (absolution) and ordered 'penances' to be done. This system continues today. 'Penances' are an earthly punishment for SIN and an aid in controlling it. Originally they could be very severe; later they were commuted to simple prayers or even cash payments. Papal 'indulgences' were then developed during the Middle Ages to channel aid from the 'treasury of merits' available in the virtues of

JESUS CHRIST and the SAINTS. They could be substituted for penances (though not for confession). Abuses of this system (such as the sales of indulgences by 'pardoners') provoked Luther's *Ninety-Five Theses*, which precipitated the REFORMATION. Indulgences were reformed (though not abolished) in 1567. [76: 216–22; 436–40; 105 vol. II: 72–84]

Pentecostalism [XI.B] Alluding to the descent of the HOLY SPIRIT (TRINITY) on the APOSTLES at Pentecost (Whitsun), the term is applied to a movement beginning in Los Angeles, U.S.A. (1906 CE). It spread to AFRICA, EUROPE, and LATIN AMERICA. It has been characterized by spiritual healing and by ecstatic speaking in 'tongues' (*glossolalia*) either unintelligible or apparently echoing existing languages not consciously known to the speaker. Its churches include the Elim Foursquare Gospel [144], the Assemblies of God, and many others, a number being black churches. Since the 1960s 'charismatic' movements resembling Pentecostalism have appeared in ANGLICANISM, PROTESTANTISM, and ROMAN CATHOLICISM. [61]

People's Temple [XXI] A movement that became the subject of world-wide horror when, in November 1978, following the murder of U.S. Congressman Leo Ryan, over 900 members committed mass suicide in Jonestown, Guyana.

The movement was originally founded in 1953 by the Reverend Jim Jones, an ordained minister of a group called the Disciples of Christ. In 1965 150 members moved to California, where the group grew. While the majority of members came from a lower-class, black background, Jones also enlisted the support of several liberal whites and secured the praise of several well-known persons for his radical politics and good works. By 1977, however, various questions were being raised about the practices of the Temple and the treatment of its members. This

eventually led to Ryan's investigatory visit to the colony in Guyana. [21; 22; 52]

The Jonestown tragedy has had repercussions affecting more than those who were most directly concerned. The ANTI-CULT MOVEMENT was given a new impetus by the event [3] and much anxiety has been felt about the possible consequences of membership of all new religious movements, especially those with a charismatic leader who expects total commitment from his followers.

Peyotism [III] An indigenous religious movement, with pre-Columbian antecedents, that emerged as a distinct form among Amerindian tribes of the southern plains of North America in the 19th century. It is based on the use of mescal (obtained from the peyote cactus, *Lophophora williamsii*), which has a hallucinogenic effect [14]. The drug was originally used for medicinal purposes (and occasionally, during warfare, for divination). Peyotism spread rapidly among the disfranchised and oppressed, culminating in 1918 in the formation of the NATIVE AMERICAN CHURCH [8: X]. This syncretistic cult combines such indigenous elements as drumming, singing, visions, and the use of the sacred pipe (CALUMET) with Christian practices of healing, prayer, and sacramentalism. [22: VI]

Pharaoh [IV] A title derived from the Egyptian word for 'palace'. Pharaoh was the king of Egypt, an absolute, divine monarch, and the myth that he was begotten by the chief state-god and born to the principal queen underlined the chasm which existed between pharaoh and his subjects. As divine heir, he was responsible for the founding and upkeep of the temples (MANSIONS OF THE GODS), the performance of the rituals, and the efficacy of the FUNERARY PRACTICES [12: II, 46]. In return, he received the kingship, military supremacy, and peaceful prosperity for Egypt and its inhabitants whom he owned. However, he was subject to *ma'at*, the principle of divine order throughout the universe, and at his coronation was imbued with the necessary regal powers, which were periodically renewed at his jubilee-festivals [18: VI, 113].

After the unification of the Two Lands, *c.* 3100 BCE, the king symbolized the union of north and south. The living king was Horus incarnate and, at death, he became Osiris (OSIRIAN TRIAD).

Pharisees [XVII, XI.A] Members of a Jewish movement flourishing before the Christian era in Palestine, whose spiritual descendants fashioned rabbinical JUDAISM. Three main sources provide information about the Pharisees: (1) rabbinical literature composed after the demise of the movement by Jews who saw themselves as the heirs of Pharisaism (RABBI); (2) New Testament literature (BIBLE) which associates the Pharisees with their opponents the SADDUCEES, and which is consistently hostile in its descriptions of Pharisaic religion; (3) Josephus, the 1st-century CE Jewish historian, who was writing in part for a non-Jewish readership and describes the various movements within Judaism in terms of Greek philosophical schools [XVII 47: XXVI]. Because of the different bias of these sources there is some disagreement about when Pharisaism began and about the exact nature of its tenets and practices [XVII 35; 38]. The traditional view is that they represent those Jews who subscribed to the oral traditions of biblical interpretation, as opposed to the Sadducees, who were inclined to a literalist understanding of the Bible text. The movement is thought to have begun some time after the Maccabean revolt against the Hellenizing policies of the Seleucid rulers of Palestine in the 2nd century BCE, when they split away from the religio-political establishment (BIBLICAL HISTORY) (Pharisee means 'separatist'). They formed brotherhoods (*haburot*) whose members encouraged one another in devotion to the law. Their interpretation of the law adapted it to changing conditions: they were the only religious party in Israel capable of surviving the catastrophe of 70 CE. JESUS CHRIST agreed with them on resurrection, angels, and demons, but his association with 'sinners' and his free attitude towards the law incurred their disapproval. Several Pharisees joined the primitive JERUSALEM CHURCH. [XI.A 16: XXVI]

Phenomenology of Religion [XXVIII] Orderly study of religious phenomena ('that which appears'), setting aside all assumptions about the truth or falsity of specific beliefs and reality of putative objects of religious experience [3: 1–4; 8; 13: II; 25: X; 28: 57–61]. As a method of description and understanding (not of 'explaining'), with suspension of judgement (Greek *epokhe*, 'stoppage') in order that the phenomena may 'speak for themselves', this approach has a philosophical basis in the work of Edmund Husserl (1859–1938) and his followers [3:1].

Leading phenomenologists of religion (e.g. W. B. Kristensen, 1867–1953 [3: II], G. van der Leeuw, 1890–1950, [3: III], M. Eliade, b. 1907 [3: IX; 10]), while not applying the tenets of the Husserlians in a strict way, have developed methods (or an art) of entering into the meaning which religious actions and ideas have for those who perform or hold them. By empathetic appreciation (a 'feeling-into' the inner perspective of the participants which is to some extent intuitive) of a wide range of data [12: XV], they claim to describe what is essential (i.e. their meaning rather than what causes them), in a way which avoids naturalistic reduction (to which the SCIENCES OF RELIGION are prone) as well as the assumptions and evaluations of THEOLOGY. In its broadest sense, phenomenology includes classification of religious ideas, actions, and symbols, and it is now usually marked off from TYPOLOGY

and other fields of RELIGIONSWISSEN-
SCHAFT by its methods and aims.
Such 'demarcation' is a matter of current dispute, as is the extent to which
phenomenology is, or ought to be,
'objective'. Both 'phenomenology' and
'objectivity' are terms whose usage
often lacks precision, and they should
be approached and applied with caution.
[Bibliography: 8: 28, 318–19]

Philippines Religion [XXII] The Philippines are the only Christian nation in
South-East Asia, with a Muslim minority in the south and tribal peoples in the
hills. Filipinos are Roman Catholics
(ROMAN CATHOLICISM) for the most
part, Christianized by the Spanish after
1570, when Manila was taken from the
Muslims. As in Indonesia, Indian religions had preceded ISLAM and, although
their penetration was not as deep as in
Java or Bali, Sanskrit loan words remain
in the national language, Tagalog. Thus
the term *diwata* (Sanskrit *devata*, 'divine
beings', 'divinity') is found in many
dialects, including that spoken by the
Tasaday, a small group of 'Stone Age'
people discovered in southern Min-
danao in 1971, who seem to have a very
simple religion and culture. The Ifugao of
northern Luzon, by contrast, divide the
cosmos into five regions and people it
with hundreds of gods or spirit beings,
each one of whom has a department
(e.g. wind, rain, war, fishing, weaving), and all of whose names must be
learned by the priests. [26]

Philistines [VI] The horde known to
the Egyptians as the 'Sea Peoples' first
threatened Egypt *c.* 1232 BCE, but was
repulsed. The Egyptian records give the
name of one group of these people as the
Peleset, and they have been identified as
the later biblical Philistines [21]. The
overthrow of the HITTITE empire in *c.*
1200 BCE enabled the Sea Peoples to
push down through Syria–Palestine and
again they were only stopped at Egypt's
boundary. Although some of the Peleset
and their associates may have settled
there before *c.* 1200 BCE, it was their

repulsion by Ramesses III of Egypt in
1183 BCE which forced them to make
their homeland in the coastal plain
known since as Palestine.

They had connections with Anatolia,
the Mycenaean Greeks (GREEK RELI-
GION), and Crete, but little is known of
their early religion. The gods later
associated with them – Dagon,
'Ashtoreth and Ba'alzebub – were
adopted from existing Canaanite cults
[2: 15–21]. It is possible that their sky-
cult and the allusions to bees and flies in
their cults reflect a link with the Greek
world. Their burial customs included
both cremations (at 'Azor) and burial
chambers (at Tell Far'ah) which recall
the Mycenaean type.

Philosophia [XII] In so far as it seeks an
ultimate explanation of the COSMOS,
much Greek philosophy can be seen as
philosophy of religion, constructing
physical/metaphysical counterparts to
religious beliefs (e.g. Milesians, 6th century BCE and Plato, 428/7–348/7 BCE).
Some thinkers (e.g. Heraclitus, *fl. c.* 500
BCE) associated natural or metaphysical
entities with traditional divinities. Stoicism (*c.* 300 BCE to *c.* 260 CE) defended
traditional beliefs, reinterpreting gods as
natural phenomena. Later Stoicism
achieved a synthesis with popular beliefs
(including ASTROLOGY), a mystical
development which had wider influence.
A strand critical of traditional religion
began with Xenophanes (*c.* 570–*c.* 470
BCE), followed by Heraclitus. Another
critical wave began in the mid 5th century (Sophists; Democritos b. *c.* 460
BCE). In earlier Hellenistic times such
criticisms are common (e.g. the Epicureans, Cynics, and Sceptics). Most
philosophers of religion practised and
recommended civic cults. [5: VI; 13: 81–3,
130–34; 14: 41–50, 100–101, 144–65,
211–34; 17: 121–71, 854–69]

Philosophy (**Jewish**) [XVII] The BIBLE
and rabbinical literature (RABBI) discuss
theological issues through stories and
PARABLES, rather than in abstract
terms. It was only in Islamic countries

in the Middle Ages that a tradition of philosophical theology emerged within JUDAISM [17; 19]. The first important philosopher was the Babylonian sage Saadiah Gaon (882–942 CE), whose *Book of Beliefs and Opinions* advocates the rational reflection on religious truth as a valid alternative to revelation. The next major figure was the Spanish poet-theologian Judah Halevi (d. 1141), who sought to show the limitations of philosophy in his *Kuzari*, and claimed that revelatory truth began where philosophical investigation left off. Moses MAIMONIDES (1135–1204) was the greatest of these medieval philosopher-theologians, and his controversial work *The Guide for the Perplexed* attempts a synthesis of Jewish and Aristotelian thought [30]. There was a new flowering of Jewish philosophy during the 18th-century Enlightenment in Europe. The first important figure of modern Jewish philosophy was Moses MENDELSSOHN (1729–86). [2; 30; 42: III; 52: IV, V]

Philosophy of Religion [XXVIII] The methods of philosophy applied in critical reflection upon religious statements and claims to knowledge, and upon religious belief and thought in relation to other modes of thought [2: 176; 13: IV; 17: 9–71]. Philosophy of religion is thus a way of thinking about conviction rather than the expression and defence of convictions (tasks for religious philosophy or philosophical THEOLOGY). In the West, the philosopher of religion has come to be seen as one who applies logical and analytical techniques in studying the nature and meaning of religious language and the status of religious beliefs [13: 73–7]. More recently, a concern to deal with questions such as were raised by traditional metaphysics (about 'truth' or 'reality') [13: 37–43, 67–73] has accompanied the recognition that philosophy must be ready to take account of any religion, not, as often in the past, only one (e.g. THEISM or Christianity) [2: 176–8; 14]. It then faces the important question of what RELIGION is.

Phoenicians [VI] Little was known of the mythology and religious beliefs of the peoples of Syria–Palestine in early times, until the excavations of a large area of the Syrian coastal town of Ras Shamra (Ugarit) were undertaken, when a wealth of documentary evidence was discovered [4: 19–31]. Cuneiform texts in Ugaritic [24: 129–49] contained mythological and liturgical information, and threw light on other less well-attested sources on Phoenician religion (ANCIENT NEAR EASTERN RELIGIONS), such as the *Phoenikike Historia*, attributed to the priest Sanchuniathon, whose dates are disputed but who was reputed to have lived before the Trojan war. His writings were preserved in Greek in the works of Philo of Byblos (1st century CE) and survive in an abridged version in Eusebius, writing some 300 years later. In addition to other Phoenician literary sources, further evidence was provided by Hebrew scriptures (BIBLE) and archaeology.

The TEMPLES were obviously important, although of a simpler design than Egyptian or Mesopotamian examples; some shrines had *massebot* (standing stones). The deities had characteristics variously attributable to Egypt, Mesopotamia, or Anatolia. Resheph, the war-god, 'Anath, Lady of Heaven, and Horon, god of the underworld, were widely worshipped; however, BA'AL, a war-god, was one of the most important deities and the leading god at Ugarit. The chief god of the Ugaritic pantheon was El, an old man, who was sometimes called Father of Ba'al.

Various rites, including those of animal sacrifice, occur in both Hebrew scriptures and the Ras Shamra texts, and the Jews may have adopted most offering rituals and perhaps some FESTIVALS from these people. It seems that there was a priestly hierarchy at Ugarit, and that BABYLONIAN DIVINATION and magico-medical texts (MAGIC) had been absorbed into the religion.

The mythology included an important legend, found in several ancient Near Eastern religions, which sought to explain the annual death and revival of the vegetation [4: 27], but there is no literary indication that survival after death was part of their belief (AFTERLIFE). However, most graves were supplied with goods and the family vaults below the houses at Ugarit were furnished and provisioned by relatives. They poured libations down a clay pipe, which ran vertically from ground level to a receptacle below, to which the dead had access through a window cut in the vault [4: 22].

It is uncertain whether features claimed to be part of the later religious tradition – sacred prostitution and infant sacrifice – were already practised as early as *c*. 1300 BCE.

Pietism [XI.B] A movement in LUTHERANISM led by P. J. Spener (1635–1705) and A. H. Francke (1663–1705). It stressed practical and inward religion rather than dogmatic theology, and was liable to narrow moral attitudes. Most Pietists remained within the church, using private meetings and education; others founded SECTS. Pietism influenced the MORAVIAN BRETHREN and the Evangelical Revival (REVIVALISM). [124]

Pilgrimage (Christian) [XI.B] Journeys for devotion, penance, thanksgiving, or the fulfilment of a vow. Divine grace (SALVATION) is felt to be especially potent in places visited by JESUS CHRIST or SAINTS or by MARY; where they have appeared in visions; or where their relics are kept (TURIN SHROUD). Abuses of pilgrimage (both commercial and spiritual) were criticized by reformers, and pilgrimages (seen as salvation by 'works') were abolished in PROTESTANTISM. They remain popular in ROMAN CATHOLICISM and the ORTHODOX CHURCH, especially to holy ICONS and monasteries. Major

pilgrimage centres include JERUSALEM; Rome (where St Peter and St PAUL were martyred); Lourdes (where visions of the Virgin Mary were claimed in 1858 and where healing is thought to occur); and Walsingham in England (which from the 12th century to the REFORMATION had a replica of the Virgin Mary's house and was revived as a pilgrimage centre in the 1920s). [105: vol. 11: 362–74; 126]

Pillars of Islam [XIV] The basic institutions of the Islamic law or SHARI'A, incumbent upon every sane male believer from the age of responsibility for actions, normally at puberty or at about 15 years of age. The majority community of the Sunnis (SUNNA) came to number these 'pillars' as five: the profession of faith (SHAHADA); worship (SALAT); alms-giving (ZAKAT); pilgrimage (HAJJ); and fasting (SAUM). To these some added holy warfare (JIHAD). The minority community of SHI'ISM regard recognition of the IMAM as a basic principle of Islam. [45: III; 82: II]

Plymouth Brethren [XI.B] A Christian (Protestant) body that originated in England through the work, in particular, of J. N. Darby (1800–82), a former priest in ANGLICANISM. The original teaching of the Brethren was strongly biblical, and influenced by CALVINISM and sometimes MILLENARIANISM. They have no separated MINISTRY, and worship centres on the 'Breaking of Bread', a simple rite intended as a memorial of JESUS CHRIST's Last Supper (EUCHARIST). The chief types of Brethren are the 'Open' and 'Exclusive'. The Exclusives' severe standards lead them to reject many aspects of modern life and to restrict social contacts with non-Brethren, even members of their own families. [21]

Poisen [XXII] A Melanesian pidgin term for sorcery or black MAGIC directed against a chosen victim, intended to cause illness or death. A common method is to recite spells while pointing an arrow or fingernail, or to burn or destroy something belonging to the victim. Many more elaborate techniques are recorded. [12] A sorcerer, it is believed, can draw power from spirits and gods enabling him to fly, become invisible, or change into animal form. He may use snakes or crocodiles to attack his victims. Serious and persistent illnesses are commonly attributed to the effects of *poisen*. Traditional healing methods include divination or mediumship intended to detect sorcerers or witches and overcome their influence. Victims may be expected to confess misdeeds (theft, adultery, etc.), so as to help identify enemies likely to be using *poisen* against them. The widely held belief in *poisen* thus helps sanction communal morality. [8; 23: 137–60; 25] Accusations of sorcery have, however, been a common cause of feuds and warfare. Sorcerers are regarded as dangerous nonconformists and social outcasts, yet their ritual skills are constantly in demand for healing, rain-making, warding off evil influences, and in the form of charms and spells to ensure success in courting, gardening, and hunting.

Politike [XII] (Greek, 'politics') The state-cult, with its monumental temples and spectacular festivals, became the focus of patriotism and propaganda in ancient Greece. The state provided the institutional and administrative framework for religion (INSTITUTIONS (GREEK)), which it manipulated, as it manipulated myth, to suit its requirements (e.g. politically motivated promotion of certain cults). Panhellenic sanctuaries became involved in interstate rivalries for their control. The oracle at Delphi gave political advice (MANTIKE). The cult of deified monarchs was the focus of the Hellenistic state-cult, a rallying point for both Greeks and non-Greeks. It was also an expression of the relationships of gratitude and loyalty. [9: 74–7, 169–79, 205–13; 16; 17: 834–9, 843–4]

Polynesian Religion [XXII] The traditional beliefs of the Polynesians (PACIFIC RELIGIONS). Their myths tell how the cosmos came into being from an original emptiness (*kore*). Primal darkness (*po*) gradually gave place to sun, moon, and stars. Gods (ATUA), nature, and mankind emerged, each sharing in the creation drama. The uncreated source (*tumu*) is left undescribed, or personified as a great creator-god TANGAROA. (In New Zealand Maori religion, the supreme being is IO.) Foremost in creation are the primal parents RANGI (or *Atea* – sky) and PAPA (earth), their son the god TANE who formed the first human being, and the culture-hero MAUI. (Variants of these names are found among different island groups.) Other *atua* include gods with distinct activities (Tu, god of war; Rongo, god of food-cultivation; Whiro, god of the underworld). Minor gods and spirits, good and bad, feature in local stories and customs. [6; 7; 15]

Best-known gods may represent renowned ancestors, chiefs who led early migrations through the Pacific and settled in the major island groups. Spiritual power and authority (MANA) flows from the gods through tribal ancestors to living chiefs and people. Themselves highly revered, chiefs have the services of priests (TOHUNGA) and prophets skilled in healing and divination, and possessors of secret knowledge of rites and incantations for controlling the powerful spiritual forces. Commoners are protected from the dangerous effects of *mana* by strict systems of *tapu* (TABU). Prayers and sacrifices take place at sacred temples and gathering-places (MARAE). Gods and spirits, involved with most affairs in life, are offered the first fruits of harvest, fishing, or battle, invoked with chants on important occasions (childbirth, warfare, canoe-building, tree-felling), and honoured at feasts and *kava*-drinking ceremonies. Funeral rites send the deceased's spirit (in Maori, *wairua*) on its journey to Reinga, gateway to the underworld, and thence to HAWAIKI, the legendary homeland. [7; 16; 21; 22; 30]

Polytheism [XXVIII] Belief in, or worship of, many GODS [8: 132; 21: 58–96], a term sometimes used pejoratively (e.g. by theists, or in missionary literature). Some comparative studies erred in this way, but to evaluate what is labelled polytheism as inferior or evil is not appropriate in RELIGIONSWISSENSCHAFT or phenomenological work (PHENOMENOLOGY OF RELIGION). Practices and beliefs formerly called idolatry [17: III, IV] are open to interpretation, functionally or symbolically (FUNCTIONALISM; SYMBOL), as significant expressions of the human response to the complexity of the world and whatever superhuman power(s) may lie behind it. [5: 72–4; 7, especially I; 20]

Positivism [XXVI] A loosely used word commonly associated with the doctrine that the only real knowledge of the world is that provided by the methods of natural science. The phrase 'positive philosophy' was coined by Auguste Comte in the 19th century. Comte distinguished three stages in the development of the human mind. In the first stage – the 'theological' – all phenomena are supposed to be brought about by the immediate action of supernatural beings. In the second ('metaphysical') stage these beings are replaced by abstract forces. The final ('positive') state is reached when people abandon such metaphysical abstractions in favour of an empirical approach to the causes of phenomena. Comte's historical analysis into three stages is no longer considered to be sound. But other forms of positivism (e.g. LOGICAL POSITIVISM) are independent of it. An attempt to identify and account for positivism as a historical phenomenon has been made by Leszek Kolakowski. [10]

Prajna [IX.A] A Sanskrit term (Pali *panna*). With SILA and SAMADHI, *prajna* is one of the three elements of the Buddhist path (MARGA). *Prajna* signifies 'wisdom', but of a specifically Buddhist kind [25: 114f]: the apprehending directly of the truth taught by the BUDDHA, which is accepted initially by the Buddhist in faith (SADDHA).

Prajnaparamita [IX.A] Literally the 'wisdom perfected' or 'the Perfection of Wisdom'. The term is used for a class of MAHAYANA Buddhist texts dating from possibly as early as the 1st century BCE and throughout the Mahayana period [37: 364ff], noted for their great philosophical importance [5: 199f; 6A].

Prakrti [XIII.B] In SAMKHYA philosophy *prakrti* means something which produces other things from itself, especially the 'original producer' or ground which gives rise to the experienced realm of mind and matter. *Samkhya* holds that the effect is inherent in the cause; so *prakrti* is also seen as the intrinsic nature of the manifest world. This is single and all-pervading, composed of the three GUNAS (modalities) in equilibrium. It transforms into the various levels of experience; these are manifold, differentiated, and specifically located, composed of varying relationships between the *gunas* in disequilibrium. *Prakrti* is related to the VEDANTA notions of BRAHMAN and MAYA (2), but it is not illusory and is sharply distinguished from the spiritual core of man (*purusha*). Man has mistakenly identified with the forms of *prakrti*, but is intrinsically conscious, free, and apart from the vicissitudes of body, sense, and mind. The world of multiplicity is formed by *prakrti* purely to enable man to enjoy the senses and obtain liberation by knowing himself. Just as a dancing-girl dances for the amusement of the spectator, not for herself, so the creative dance of *prakrti* is for the benefit of the onlooking spirit.

Pratyekabuddha [IX.A] A Sanskrit term (Pali *Paccekabuddha*) variously interpreted as 'private Buddha', 'isolated Buddha', 'silent Buddha', and 'single Buddha'. The term indicates one who, having attained enlightenment, lives alone and does not venture to teach others. The PALI form of the term is rare.

Prehistoric Religion [XXIII] Those practices of *Homo sapiens* and earlier hominids (*Homo erectus*) from before recorded history which evidence from cultural remains suggests were religious, with the conjectured associated beliefs [6: LX]. Since there is, by definition, no written record of prehistory, theories about the behaviour and thought of early man must be based on reconstruction and inference from fossils, bones, and artefacts. Use of the method of historical–cultural comparison [5; 9] needs caution [3: 17; 5; 10]. Most theories about beliefs assume 'the psychic unity of all mankind'.

Fragments of skulls, jaws, and split bones from the earliest period (lower palaeolithic: *Homo erectus* from sites such as Ternifine in Algeria, Mauer near Heidelberg, the Trinil beds in Java, and Choukoutien near Peking) suggest a 'cult of skulls', some concern or reverence for the dead, and perhaps RITUAL cannibalism [6: I; 9: I]. Remains of human burials by *Homo sapiens* from the middle and late palaeolithic (Neanderthal in the Rhineland and similar fossils from Ehringsdorf, Saccopastore, and sites in North Africa, the Middle East, Uzbekistan, Zimbabwe, and Java) again give indications of ritual by the position and posture of skeletons, provision of grave goods, and the use of red ochre on the corpse [1: II; 10].

The second main phase begins with hunting peoples using more specialized flint tools (from *c.* 40,000 to 35,000 years ago) [1: III, IV; 2: III]. The artistic activity of the first humans of the modern type (e.g. cave paintings of the Gravettian, Solutrean, and Magdalenian cultures, at sites in northern Spain and south-west France such as Altamira, Lascaux, Mas d'Azil and Niaux, but also in Italy, Sicily and the Urals) may be the key to European religion in the last Ice Age [6: VI, VIII; 8: V; 9: 46–50 & pl. 1–25; 11] as centred on human and animal fertility, although other interpretations are possible [2: 61]. Much

controversy also surrounds the significance of the so-called 'Venus figurines' in ivory, stone, or clay found from the Pyrenees to the southern U.S.S.R. [2: 54–8; 5; 6: VI; 8: LV; 9: 108–14 & pl. 26–33, 55–6].

With the economic revolution of the warmer Holocene (neolithic period in Europe) and especially the advent of farming [1: V], the fertility theme gains in prominence (e.g. human, mainly female, figurines and animal statuettes from the Danube region). Settlement is marked by the use of fixed shrines and temples (as in Malta and Gozo) [9: 52–9] and the megalithic tombs and monuments scattered across Europe [2: 139–44; 9: 159–88]. From the same period (i.e. before 1500 BCE), the rock-art and animal-head tools and weapons of hunting and fishing peoples of North Eurasia suggest the development of SHAMANISM in the circumpolar region [2: 144–7; 9: 135–42].

A growing and world-wide body of archaeological evidence from Africa, India, China, the Far East, Australia, the Pacific, and the New World [2: VIII–XII; 3: X–XII; 7] has made it impossible to imagine that there was a single system of beliefs and practices which could properly be thought of as 'palaeolithic religion' or 'neolithic religion', still less something called 'prehistoric religion' [8; 10; 12].

Presbyterianism [XI.B] The English-speaking version of 'Reformed Churches', deriving from the doctrine and church organization of CALVINISM. The Presbyterian hierarchy of church courts (local, regional, and national) is staffed with ministers (MINISTRY (CHRISTIAN)) and 'elders'. The Westminster Confession (CREEDS) is the classic standard of faith [11: 244–7]. The EUCHARIST has traditionally been celebrated rather infrequently, but with searching preparatory services. Presbyterianism is the established church in Scotland [17] and is strong in Northern Ireland. Migrants from these two countries carried it to the U.S.A. [2] where it is now a major group of churches. Divisions within Presbyterianism have usually arisen out of disagreements over issues characteristic in Calvinistic teaching, e.g. predestination, moral and church discipline, and the proper relationship between Church and STATE. The United Reformed Church combined English Presbyterians and CONGREGATIONALISM in 1972 [91; 107: 1120].

Process Theology [XI.C] A form of theological understanding that has developed, particularly in relation to Christian belief, under the influence of the metaphysical insights of A. N. Whitehead (1861–1947) and Charles Hartshorne (b. 1897). Among its basic tenets are that to be real is to be in process (e.g. to be continually responding to the environment) and so to have a temporal dimension; that reality consists of a plurality of entities which are significantly self-creating and intimately related to each other; and that GOD is the chief exemplification and not an exception to the ultimate metaphysical principles. Whereas Whitehead's fundamental work (*Process and Reality*, 1929) is a cosmological treatise which develops a unified understanding of reality through reflection on its constituent parts, Hartshorne has paid more attention to *a priori* arguments as a way to establishing the nature and reality of God. Although there are important differences among process theologians, they generally agree that God has a temporal aspect, both being maximally affected by all other entities and influencing them in ways that are compatible with their freedom. In contrast to the THEISM which asserts the distinction between the world and a timeless, impassible God and the PANTHEISM which identifies God and the world, process theology advocates a panentheism in which God embraces the world and lovingly seeks to lure all things

towards their maximum aesthetic satisfaction. [4]

Prodigia [XXV] Signs received by the Romans that the normal order between gods and men (*pax deorum*, 'peace of the gods') had been disturbed. The signs took the form of events contrary to the Romans' perception of the normal, not necessarily supernatural events by later standards. They included natural disasters, buildings struck by lightning, abnormal births, wild animals penetrating cities, the rain of blood, milk, or stones, or animals speaking [9: 32–4]. Lists survive from the republican period (509–31BCE) of such prodigies, reported year by year to the authorities so that the priests could identify the god or goddess offended and recommend appropriate measures (*remedia*) to restore the balance [2; 6: 600–610]. The evil threatened was thus to be avoided. The lists provide a valuable index of Roman categories of the natural and supernatural. They were no longer kept under the Empire (after 31 BCE), when prodigies ceased to be part of the state's routine, and were attached rather to the lives of individuals or to great catastrophes [12: 159–66].

Projection Theories of Religion [XI.C] This term refers to various arguments in Western thought which maintain that 'God' is not a reality, independent of man, on whom the world depends for its continued existence, but a product of men's minds whose reality is only that appropriate to a mental construction, even though an unconscious invention. David Hume (1711–76) followed Thomas Hobbes (1588–1679) in suggesting in *The Natural History of Religion* (1757) that belief in gods arose when primitive man personified the unknown forces controlling nature and offered worship to them in an attempt to placate them. L. A. Feuerbach (1804–72) argued that 'God' is an illusory reality which represents to men the qualities which they regard as ideal. His theory had an important influence on the hostile views of religion advanced by Karl Marx (1818–83) and Friedrich Nietzsche (1844–1900). Émile Durkheim (1858–1917), an early sociologist, saw religion as providing a mythological representation of social structures, affirming thereby the values and rules of society in a quasi-objective form. Sigmund Freud (1856–1939) treated religion as an illusion and suggested that the idea of God is basically a magnified version of the image of the human father, unconsciously produced by men in an infantile desire for protection against the harsher aspects of the real world. [11; 25]

Prophecy (Jewish and Christian) [XVII, XI.A] Biblical revelation is based on the idea of God communicating to certain chosen individuals through prophetic inspiration. The content of the prophet's message and the style in which it is couched differ from prophet to prophet (BIBLE). The TALMUD recognizes that the divine word interacted with the personality of the individual prophet. 'No two prophets prophesy in the same fashion' [XVII 10 Nezikin vol. III: 593]. The Jewish tradition distinguishes between the prophetic message of MOSES and that of the other prophets. The Bible itself depicts God as speaking to Moses 'face to face and not in riddles' (Numbers 12: 8). The RABBIS see God as revealing himself to Moses through a clear glass, but to the other prophets through a cloudy glass. Only one of the functions of prophecy was that of foretelling the future, although this is the notion primarily associated with prophecy today. A more important prophetic role was that of a religious teacher, someone who would stand up against the corruption of the ruling class in the name of the COVENANT with God. Talmudic Judaism considers the age of prophecy to have come to an end with the post-exilic prophets Haggai, Zechariah, and Malachi. The rabbinical sage has super-

seded the prophet. [XVII 9 vol. 13: 1151; 22: VII, VIII; 26: 59]

In the early CHURCH Christian prophets played a prominent part. They were recognized as mouthpieces of the HOLY SPIRIT. Some travelled from place to place. Responsible teachers insisted that the validity of the prophets' claims should be tested by the content of their utterances. The chief literary product of New Testament prophecy is the Revelation of John. [XI.A 10]

Protestantism [XI.B] Forms of Christianity originating in the REFORMATION. The term derives from the 'protestation' of the German princes (1529) against ROMAN CATHOLICISM. Protestants stressed the authority of the BIBLE and justification by faith (SALVATION) against what they felt to be the errors of Rome. Numerous different types developed such as LUTHERANISM, CALVINISM, and many later forms. ANGLICANISM may be regarded as containing Protestant and 'reformed Catholic' elements which are not 'Roman'. Although often defined in terms of its origins (especially in Lutheranism and Calvinism), it is really necessary to characterize Protestantism in terms of its whole development. Compared with Roman Catholicism, it has generally been less sacramental (SACRAMENTS) and ceremonial in WORSHIP; less subject to priesthood, more open to lay activity (MINISTRY). Modern Protestantism has been exceptionally open (and vulnerable) to secular thought; and has emphasized life within the world. It nevertheless includes extremes of religious outlook, from conservative 'fundamentalism' to extreme 'liberalism' in theology (AUTHORITY). Organization varies from relatively centralized PRESBYTERIANISM and METHODISM to the localized churches of CONGREGATIONALISM and the BAPTISTS. Social attitudes have ranged from the conservatism of much REVIVALISM to the

American Social Gospel (U.S.A). [36; 146: 101–33]

Providence Industrial Mission [xx] The first independent ETHIOPIAN-type church founded (in 1900) in Malawi (then Nyasaland), assisted by the black National Baptist Convention. John Chilembwe, its founder, was educated in the U.S.A. He died leading the 1915 rising. His impressive 'New Jerusalem' church at the Chiradzulu headquarters was dynamited and the movement banned (it was revived in 1925 under Dr Malekebu). The larger section of the now divided church belongs to the Malawi Christian Council and Chilembwe is a national martyr. [19: 252–6]

Psychic Powers [xviii] Special abilities ascribed to holy persons of most religions and sometimes to other exceptional individuals. They include levitation (raising the body from the ground without perceptible means of support), psychokinesis (moving objects without physical contact), precognition (knowledge of future events), telepathy (knowledge of others' thoughts), clairvoyance, and clairaudience ('seeing' and 'hearing' beyond the range of sensory perception). The last four are often classified as 'extrasensory perception' (ESP). Buddhist texts list powers, such as levitation, clairaudience, invisibility, and telepathy, available to those skilled in meditation. Similar powers have been attributed to Muslim and Hindu mystics, and levitation is ascribed to several Christian mystics. St Teresa of Avila (1518–82 CE), for example, describes 'raptures' in which (to her embarrassment) her body was lifted from the ground (MYSTICISM (CHRISTIAN)). Current opinions on the genuineness of these phenomena vary. Laboratory tests indicate at least a slight incidence of ESP (other powers have proved harder to test), but its mechanism remains unknown. [4]

Pueblo Religions [iii] A term generally used to designate a large group of Amerindians, primarily agriculturists, of various linguistic families, living in the south-western U.S.A. and inhabiting characteristic communal dwellings of adobe (unburnt, sun-dried brick). The group includes Tamoan, Keresan, Zunian, and HOPI peoples. Central religious features include an emergence-type cosmogonic myth (CREATION MYTH), in which Spider Grandmother (or a similar figure) leads the primal people out to the earth's surface and, through various wanderings, to their new home. Maintenance of a fragile agricultural economy requires sustained cooperation between supernaturals (Sky-Father, Earth-Mother, Mother-Corn, the KACHINAS) and mankind. The religio-agricultural calendar (CALENDAR ROUND) prescribes the performance of specific dances, especially the corn and snake dances, to ensure fertility and collective well-being, with secret societies usually taking important roles. [23] Conception of the afterlife is often vague; the soul is believed to linger briefly in this world after death and then to return through the place of emergence to the underworld. [16]

Punna [ix.A] A Pali term (pronounced as Sanskrit *punya*). It denotes merit, in the Buddhist sense, i.e. the means whereby a better rebirth is obtained in the future. At the higher levels merit is acquired by spiritual achievements, and at the level of the ordinary lay person by cultivating generosity (ALMS-GIVING), through hospitality, especially to monks, and the giving of gifts [4: 78f].

Puranas [xiii.A] In Indian tradition, a class of sacred compositions dealing with ancient (*purana*) times and events. There are 18 principal Puranas, which date from the Gupta period (beginning of the 4th century CE) onwards. These, it has been said, form part of the real scriptures of the HINDUS, in the sense that they have been available to and known by low-CASTE people whereas the VEDA texts were the preserve of the BRAHMANS [2: 301]. The Puranas are arranged in three divisions: (1) those which exalt the god BRAHMA; (2) those which exalt VISHNU; and (3) those that exalt SHIVA. Among the more important are, in the first division, the *Bhavishya Purana*; in the second, the *Vishnu* and the *Bhagavata Puranas*; and in the third, the AGNI *Purana* (or the *Vayu Purana* which sometimes takes its place). Although in their received form they date from the Gupta period, they embody much legendary material of a greater age [2: 302] and are an important source of background data for the study of popular Hinduism. [16A: 15–18]

Puritanism [XI] Originally an English 16th-century movement to 'purify' the Church of England. At first Puritans attacked vestments (ceremonial garments especially used for the EUCHARIST) and ceremonies. Some, however, adopted PRESBYTERIANISM and hoped to alter the English church to this system. Others accepted bishops and the Book of Common Prayer (ANGLICANISM), with modifications. Puritans were among the pioneers of the North American colonies (U.S.A.) [2: VIII–X; 97], and have had lasting effects on U.S. religion and society. 'Puritan' is also loosely used for severe and narrow moral views on e.g. SEX. [107: 1146; 118; 122]

Purohita [XIII.A] An important religious office among the ancient Aryans (INDO-EUROPEANS), that of chief priest, whose function was to perform the sacrifices which maintained well-being and secured victory in battle. He was also the 'chaplain' to the royal court, who might on occasions be required to advise the king. [2: 34, 91, 101]

Pyramids [IV] Our term 'pyramid' is derived from the Greek name *pyramis*; the Egyptian word, however, was *mer*, perhaps meaning 'place of ascension' [8: VII, 284]. The pyramids (the most famous are at Gizeh) were royal tombs, built for most rulers of the Old (*c.* 2700–2200 BCE) and Middle Kingdoms (1980–1786 BCE). Each was part of a complex which also included a valley building, causeway, and mortuary temple where the king's burial rites and subsequent mortuary rites were performed. Developed from the step-pyramid (IMHOTEP), the true pyramid probably symbolized a 'ramp' to facilitate the deceased king's ascent to heaven [8: VII, 290]. Associated with the solar cult (RE'), the pyramid remained exclusively a royal burial-place, and magical texts (FUNERARY PRACTICES) [11] were inscribed inside later pyramids to provide assistance for the king's victory over death (MAGIC). The construction of such complexes exhausted economic resources but promoted a strong political and religious unity.

·Q·

Qadi (**Cadi**) [XIV] The judge in ISLAM, functioning in the SHARI'A courts and theoretically acting as judicial representative of the CALIPH. Normally he was a Muslim male of good character and recognized learning. Although his jurisdiction embraced both civil and criminal law, in practice the state took over most of the latter sphere. In modern times, the possibility of appeal from the qadi's judgements has been introduced in most Islamic countries. The competence of his court has been generally reduced to first-instance adjudication, and some countries have abolished the Shari'a courts altogether. [10 S.V.; 21 'Ḳāḍī'; 29: 148–54; 47: 339–50; 83: 141–5]

Qiyama [XIV] Resurrection in ISLAM, followed by the Last Judgement. Islamic eschatology posits a Last Hour, with the end of the world preceded by disturbances on earth such as the appearance of ANTI-CHRIST. Men will be physically raised from the grave by the angel Israfil, rounded up, and judged by God; their good and bad deeds will be weighed in a balance. Only the Prophet MUHAMMAD, it is generally recognized, may intercede for men's souls, although the QUR'AN is rather vague about this. Later, popular Islam, however, allowed the intercession of a host of local saints and holy men (WALI). The judged souls must pass across the narrow bridge which spans hell; sinners will fall into the depths, but the saved will enter paradise (*see* AKHIRA). Some authorities admit also an earlier, limited judgement of mankind in the tombs, with the possibility of punishment or bliss there, before the resurrection and judgement proper. [21 'Ḳiyāma'; 29: 51–3; 43: 197–250]

Quakers [XI.B] An early nickname (perhaps from trembling with holy fear at the presence of God at their meetings) for members of the Society of Friends, founded by George Fox (1624–91) and others. The colony of Pennsylvania, U.S.A., originally Quaker, was founded by William Penn (1644–1718). Quakers reject such externals as SACRAMENTS, in favour of the 'inner light' of JESUS CHRIST in the soul. WORSHIP is largely silent (though some Americans have modified this). Social concern has always been strong, as shown in the anti-slavery reforms of John Woolman (1720–72) and the prison reforms of Elizabeth Fry (1780–1845) [7; 11: 252–8; 63]. In recent times Quakers have been noted for their tolerance of different religious views, Christian and non-Christian.

Quest of the Historical Jesus, In [XI.C] A phrase used to describe attempts to determine the actual character of the teaching, faith, and events of the life of JESUS CHRIST. The phrase comes from the title of the English translation of the highly influential treatment of the history of the quest from H. S. Reimarus (1694–1768) to W. Wrede (1859–1906) by Albert Schweitzer (1875–1965), which first appeared in 1906. After criticizing the unsatisfactoriness of previous attempts to delineate the historical understanding of Jesus, Schweitzer offered his own interpretation of Jesus' thought as dominated by the expectation of the imminent arrival of God's kingdom. This, though, was controversial and the main significance of his study was to highlight the manner in which interpreters moulded their pictures of Jesus according to their own convictions. The 'quest', nevertheless, has continued with some vigour in spite of the increasing appreciation of the relative paucity of the source materials and the fact that they have been recorded to support some theological conviction about the significance of Jesus. [7; 30]

Quetzalcoatl [XIX] One of the most powerful and complex gods in MESO-AMERICAN RELIGIONS was Quetzal-coatl, the feathered serpent, called Kukulcan in the post-CLASSIC MAYAN culture. He appears as both a major celestial creator god and intimately identified with a historical priest-king, Topiltzin Ce Acatl Quetzalcoatl (TOPILTZIN QUETZALCOATL). [I: VII] In the clearly mythical traditions Quet-zalcoatl, one of the four children of the divine pair, OMETEOTL, arranges the original universe and participates in the creation and destruction of several of the world ages (CEMANAHUAC). In a number of sources, he is depicted as the victim of his brother Tezcatlipoca, the smoking mirror (*see figure*). As the creation of the cosmos unfolds, Quet-zalcoatl invents agriculture and the cal-endar, and restores human life through a

Ehecatl-Quetzalcoatl and Tezcatlipoca

cosmic descent into the underworld where he outwits the lord of the dead, Mictlantecuhtli. [2: V; 14: 38–40] This great creative force also took the form of Ehecatl, the wind god [19: 107], and Tlahuizcalpantecuhtli, the morning star (Venus). Sculpted and painted images of Quetzalcoatl appear in a number of ceremonial cities, including Teoti-huacan [16: 21–8], Tula, Xochicalco, Cholula, Tenochtitlan, and Chichen Itza, where he is usually associated with the central shrine (MESOAMERICAN CITY). Historically, Quetzalcoatl was the patron of the Toltecs and he inspired Topiltzin Ce Acatl Quetzalcoatl in his priestly rituals and cultural inventions. Quetzalcoatl became the patron deity of CHOLOLLAN and the patron god of the Aztec schools of higher learning, the CALMECACS. Quetzalcoatl's cult was taken by the Toltecs into the Yucatán Maya area during the 10th century and revitalized in the cities of Chichen Itza and Mayapan. [4: VI]

Qumran [XI.A] A locality, north-west of the Dead Sea, which provided a home for an ascetic Jewish community between 130 BCE and 70 CE. The com-munity probably belonged to the Essenes, a Jewish religious order of that period which was exceptionally rigor-ous in its application of the law and in its simplicity of life. Envisaging itself as the righteous remnant of Israel the com-munity withdrew to the Judaean wilder-ness under the guidance of 'the Teacher of Righteousness', to make preparation for the day of judgement, when it would be God's instrument for the punishment of the wicked. Our knowl-edge of it dates from 1947, partly through the excavation of its head-quarters (Khirbet Qumran) but mainly through the examination of its library, stored in eleven caves overlooking Wadi Qumran. Portions of about 500 books survive. About 100 are copies of Hebrew scripture; others include com-mentaries, rule-books, hymnals, and APOCALYPTIC studies. [18]

Qur'an (Koran) [XIV] The sacred book of ISLAM. Islamic dogma holds that the Qur'an is the uncreated word of God, hence pre-existent to the world and to man, whose archetype is laid up in heaven. This was released to the Arabs, in the Arabic language, through the transmission of the Prophet MUHAM-MAD (*see* NABI), in a series of revelations, eventually regarded as a message for all mankind and replacing imperfect and corrupt previous versions of the heavenly scripture. But the message is God's alone, without any human interference [42]. The Qur'an text is sacred in itself, and a good Muslim should be ritually pure (TAHARA) before touching a copy. In its present, canonical form, the Qur'an seems to date from the collection of materials made in the CALIPHATE of 'Uthman (644–56). In form, it is about the length of the New Testament (BIBLE), and is conventionally divided into *suras* or chapters revealed at Mecca or at Medina, although in fact many *suras* are composite and contain elements from both periods. The earlier *suras* proclaim the basic message of the unity of God (ALLAH); of the thanksgiving and obedience due to him from mankind; of the working of God in history from the creation (KHALQ) to the last days; and of judgement (QIYAMA) and the afterlife (AKHIRA). The later, Medinan *suras* contain a considerable number of divine prescriptions on legal and social topics, all of these embodied in the law of Islam or SHARI'A [summary: 39 s.v.; selected translations: 43: 17–75]. Much of the Qur'an is assonantal in style and language, and is recited for liturgical or devotional purposes in a particular manner of cantillation (*tajwid*) (*see* MUSIC (IN ISLAM)). The question whether the Qur'an, being God's literal word and specifically revealed in Arabic, could be translated much exercised Muslim scholars in the past. Gradually, interlinear translations of other Islamic languages were allowed, and now independent translations exist in all the major languages of the world. [General surveys: 15; 21 'Kur'ān'; 29: 61–5; 39 s.v.; 61: II; 81; on exegesis: 27]

· R ·

Rabbi [XVII] Originally this was the title of an ordained Palestinian sage in the early rabbinical period, meaning 'My Master' [47: 325]. In later JUDAISM it became the general term for a halakhic (HALAKHAH) authority or teacher of the oral TORAH [9 vol. 13: 1445]. The present ordination of rabbis involves an examination on selected topics of Jewish law by an ordained rabbi, who may then ordain the successful candidate (*semikhah*). This ordination differs from that practised in the first few centuries of the common era, which was thought to go back in an unbroken chain to MOSES. The chain has, in fact, been broken and so ordination today does not confer the special status on its recipients that attaches to the older type of ordination. The rabbi in Judaism is not a priest, but primarily a teacher and spiritual guide. [52: 207]

Ragnarok [V] The Icelandic account of Ragnarok, meaning the 'doom (or twilight) of the powers', comes in the Prose EDDA [20: 86–92], based largely on one poem, *Voluspa*, in the Poetic Edda [18: 1–13]. First comes a season of terrible cold, when men forsake old loyalties and the rule of law; then Heimdall's horn warns of a host of giants and monsters approaching, led by the treacherous LOKI, along with FENRIS-WOLF and the World-Serpent. ODIN and his army from VALHALLA come out with the AESIR to do battle, but neither side is victorious; the wolf devours Odin, to be killed in turn by Odin's son Vidar; THOR and the Serpent slay one another, as do Heimdall and LOKI. A fire-giant, Surt, sets the world ablaze, and it finally sinks beneath the sea. This story may be based on vague folk-beliefs about the world's ending, influenced by an ancient tradition of a battle between gods and giants, experience of volcanic eruptions, and Christian teaching concerning the Last Judgement [6: VIII, 202–10; 2: VII, 191–5]. According to the unknown poet, earth rises again cleansed and green from the sea, while the tree YGGDRASIL survives, a shelter for the sons of the gods and one human pair, who begin a new age.

Rahit [XXVII] The SIKH Rahit is the code of discipline which all who enter the KHALSA order must vow to observe. According to tradition the Rahit was promulgated by Guru Gobind Singh when he inaugurated the Khalsa in 1699 (*see* GURUS). The first RAHIT-NAMA or recorded code appears half a century later. Others followed during the period 1750–1850, all claiming to reproduce the Guru's actual words. The *rahit-namas* must surely incorporate a nucleus which derives directly from the 10th Guru, but amid the varying *rahit-nama* versions it is difficult to identify this nucleus with assurance [7: 59–60]. It is clear that much of the Rahit evolved during the course of the 18th century, reflecting such features of the PANTH's life as its predominantly Jat (*see* CASTE) constituency and its conflicts with Muslim enemies [23: 50–53]. An authorized version was eventually issued in 1950 by the Shiromani Gurdwara Parbandhak Committee under the title *Sikh Rahit Maryada*. This document specifies correct GURDWARA procedure, supplies approved RITUALS, and defines personal observances in careful detail [17: 1–16]. The latter include an obligation to bear the 'Five K's' (uncut hair, dagger or sword, breeches, comb, and iron bangle) and to avoid four particular sins (cutting one's hair, eating meat killed in the Muslim manner, adultery, and smoking) [14: IV; 30: IV]. Anyone who infringes the Rahit is called a *tanakhahlia* and may be required to make amends by fine or penance. If the breach is serious the offender is branded a PATIT (apostate).

Rahit-nama [XXVII] A *rahit-nama* is a manual which records any version of the Sikh Rahit (the KHALSA code of conduct) [23: 51–2]. The original Rahit is attributed to Guru Gobind Singh (1666–1708) (*see* GURUS) and the early *rahit-namas* all claim to reproduce his actual words. Although there is considerable uncertainty concerning sequence and dates it seems that the earliest formal *rahit-namas* emerged during the mid 18th century. These were prose collections of miscellaneous injunctions attributed to Chaupa Singh and Nand Lal. Subsequently there appeared at least two more in prose (the *Prem Sumarag* and the *Sau Sakhian*) and five shorter *rahit-namas* in verse. [7: XII] From these and other sources Singh Sabha scholars attempted to distil the original Rahit, and in 1915 they published their reformist views as an entirely new *rahit-nama* (SIKH REFORM MOVEMENTS). This manual, the *Gurmat Prakas Bhag Sanskar*, failed to win acceptance. Not until *Sikh Rahit Maryada* was issued in 1950 did an authoritative *rahit-nama* finally appear. [17: 1–16]

Rain-Making (African) [II] Rain is a central religious theme in many African religious systems, particularly in the drier east and south. The power to make rain may be a basic attribute of kingship, as among the ZULU, LOVEDU, and SHILLUK, or the granting (or withholding) of rain may be related rather to a major territorial cult, such as that of MWARI or MBONA. Elsewhere particular clans, lineages, or simply individuals may be credited with such powers. On the wet, west coast, however, rain-stopping is seen as beneficial while rain-making may be malevolent; but in general the activities of rain experts here are more individualistic and marginal to both religion and society. Rain-makers and rain-stoppers work not only by innate personal power but also through the use of certain medicines and rituals, including public dances. The source of their ability may be understood as a matter of inherited (or acquired) esoteric knowledge, the collaboration of the ancestors, or as the direct gift of God. For some peoples, e.g. the NUER, such concerns are unknown.

Rajneesh Meditation [XXI] Rajneesh meditation centres were established during the 1970s in various places throughout the West, to make available the 'chaotic meditation' and teachings of Bhagwan Shree Rajneesh, whose centre was in India at Poona. Full-time followers, *sannyas*, wear orange clothes and are sometimes known as the 'orange people'. The Bhagwan's philosophy consists of a mixture from various traditions of both the East and the West. [2: 60]

Rama [XIII.A] An incarnation (AVATARA) of the Hindu deity VISHNU. Rama's life and exploits are recounted in the great epic RAMAYANA. Probably in origin a folk-hero around whom a cult developed in his native region of India, Ayodhya (Oudh, now in eastern Uttar Pradesh state), Rama gradually came to be regarded as an avatar of Vishnu. Regarded by VAISHNAVAS as the ideal of manhood and model for human conduct, his name has also become the common word for God (cf. the last words of Mahatma Gandhi as he was assassinated – 'Eh! Ram!'). Similarly Rama's spouse Sita is held up as the ideal of Hindu womanhood: chaste, faithful, and devout. [17: 197–204] The cult of Rama is strongest in the Hindi-speaking area of northern India and the adjacent states such as Gujarat, Mahatma Gandhi's homeland. In this region the

BHAKTI movement in Hindu religion flourished greatly between the 13th and 18th centuries CE, a period which, incidentally, coincides with the rule of the Muslim Mughal (Mogul) emperors (ISLAMIC DYNASTIES) of India. [1: 358–66]

Ramanuja [XIII.B] The most influential thinker of the VAISHNAVA VEDANTA and leading authority in the Shri Vaishnava sect of Hinduism, traditionally dated 1017–1137 CE (but in fact probably d. 1157). Ramanuja strongly criticized the ADVAITA VEDANTA of SHANKARA for its monism and its doctrine of MAYA (2). In Ramanuja's system, known as Particularized Nondualism (*Vishishtadvaita*), God's relationship to the universe is that of the soul to the body; just as the soul is in intimate union with the body yet distinct in particular respects, so God and the universe are united but particularized. God is the substance of all particularized things, substance and particular being inherently united. He is equally the cause of all created things (the cause being of the same nature as the effect) and the ruler of the universe as the soul is the ruler of the body. Ramanuja is greatly concerned to emphasize the perfection and supremacy of God, his positive qualities, and his identity with VISHNU. Like other Vaishnavas he affirms that Vishnu has a transcendent celestial form, consort, retinue, and abode, all of which are eternal and flawlessly beautiful. He also stresses the grace of God, his accessibility to the devotee, his generosity, and his affectionate, forgiving nature. [Philosophy: 5: 111, 165–398; life: 3: 24–48; theology: 3: 65–198; translation: 16: 543–55]

Ramayana [XIII.A] The epic story of RAMA, a Sanskrit composition in 24,000 stanzas attributed to the ancient Indian sage and poet Valmiki. Basically the story of the life of Rama, the prince of Ayodhya, capital of the kingdom of Kosala, and of his devout and noble wife Sita, the epic also includes much of ancient Indian folklore and moral values. Its main effect is to hold up the ideal types of Hindu manhood and womanhood; it has been said that the *Ramayana* makes its hero, Rama, DHARMA itself in flesh and blood [1: 212]. Contemporary literature of the period (? 8th or 7th century BCE) makes no mention of Rama. The life and exploits of a relatively minor ruler were probably only elaborated by local bards later, before the time (c. the 1st century BCE or CE) when the epic was put together into what became the received Sanskrit text. The theological point of view it conveys is that VISHNU, who incarnates (AVATARA) himself from time to time when evil threatens to overcome the world, did so on this occasion in order that, as Rama, he should put an end to the wickedness of the demon Ravana. In this he was aided by the monkey-god HANUMAN [2: 305, 414–17]. A lyrical version entitled the *Ramacaritmanas* (Sacred Lake of the Acts of Rama) was rendered into Hindi from the Sanskrit original by the Poet Tulsidas (1532–1623), in a work which has justly been described as 'the great bible of the Hindi-speaking peoples' [2: 363; 25: 186–8]. Although the majority of the people of rural India are unable to read, this is a major source of their religious ideas, known as it is to them through public recitations and readings, and dramatizations at the great festival times, especially at the autumn festival of Dusserah.

Rangi [XXII] A sky-father in New Zealand Maori religion, known as Atea in other Pacific creation-stories. In the Maori version, Rangi and the earth-mother PAPA, who lie embracing, are forced apart by their children the gods (ATUA), led by TANE. Rangi's tears of grief continue to fall as rain. In Tahiti, Tonga, and Samoa, Rangi's role as creator of gods and men is played by TANGAROA. [7; 16; 22]

Rastafarians [XX] A variety of dynamic movements in Jamaica and Dominica since the 1930s among poor landless men, inspired by Marcus Garvey's 'Back to Africa' movement and the accession of Ras Tafari (hence the name) as Emperor of Ethiopia. The latter is still regarded as the Messiah of the black race who, it is believed, are the true Jews, about to be redeemed. White culture and Christianity are repudiated but BIBLE selections retained. A puritan ethic sustains personal dignity, and *ganja* (marijuana) smoking is a peaceful, mystical experience. [12: 63–9; 15: 124–30; 18A; 19: 135–7]

Rationalism [XXVI] A rather ambiguous word, sometimes used to characterize an emphasis on reason as opposed to experience (and thus contrasted with EMPIRICISM) and at other times to characterize an emphasis on reason as opposed to the emotions. It appears to have been in this latter sense that HUMANIST groups have claimed the title 'rationalist' (e.g. the Rationalist Press Association). Rationalists, in this sense, maintain that religion has no basis in reason.

Re', Cult of [IV] The worship of Re', the sun-god, centred at Heliopolis, reached its zenith in the Old Kingdom (*c.* 2480 BCE), when the king's father, Re', became royal patron [5]. This cult influenced temple liturgy (MANSIONS OF THE GODS) and FUNERARY PRACTICES (PYRAMIDS) [8]. Even when the Old Kingdom collapsed and Re' lost his royal supremacy, solar beliefs continued to permeate religion (AMUN). In the solar hereafter (AFTERLIFE), originally reserved for royalty, the king (PHARAOH) joined the gods, crossing the heavens in the celestial barque.

Reductionism [XXVI] There are two sides to reductionism. To begin with the negative: it requires an account of the conditions which need to be met if a claim is to be meaningful or worth considering. Reductionist accounts presuppose that these conditions are not met by e.g. Christianity as it is traditionally presented nor by statements of religious belief generally. Such accounts are, however, not merely negative. On the contrary, a reductionist proposes to save the day by analysing or translating the unacceptable material in, or into, terms which satisfy the conditions stated. This is the positive side of reductionism.

A common form of reductionism rejects the metaphysical dimension of a religion, retaining only its ethical content. L. A. Feuerbach (1804–72) (PROJECTION THEORIES) claimed that Christian theology was fraught with contradictions and that, once these were eliminated, it would be clear that statements about God were really only disguised statements about man himself. [7] R. B. Braithwaite (b. 1900), in the spirit of 20th-century EMPIRICISM, has maintained that to have a religious belief is to intend to behave in a particular way, a way which is associated with certain traditional stories. [4]

Exponents often do not style themselves reductionists as such and the label commonly implies, by way of criticism, that something crucial has been left out by the process of 'reduction'. The label may thus be a controversial one, to the extent that there is disagreement as to what is crucial. This kind of controversy has surrounded the programme of DEMYTHOLOGIZING in Christian theology.

Reform Judaism [XVII] A movement which began in response to the gradual dissolution of medieval Jewish society in the late 18th century. Early reformers, who were influenced by the educational ideas of Moses MENDELSSOHN and by the general atmosphere of the Enlightenment, sought to update the service and liturgy of the SYNAGOGUE. Ideological changes began in a more formal way with the rabbinical conferences of the 1840s in Germany, which brought modernist RABBIS together to agree on a common platform [4; 42: VII]. From its inception Reform Judaism has been divided between moderates and radicals. Abraham Geiger (1810–74), an early moderate, wanted far-reaching changes but, as a source for updating JUDAISM, only those which depended on the Jewish tradition. Radical reformers, like Samuel Holdheim (1806–60), believed that Judaism should jettison its antiquated rituals while preserving the core of its ethical monotheism. Many of these radical ideas were transplanted to NORTH AMERICA, where Reform developed in the mid 19th century under Rabbi I. M. Wise (1819–1900), and were formulated in the Pittsburgh Platform of 1885. In Britain, by contrast, Reform Judaism has remained tradition-oriented, and more thoroughgoing changes were only introduced with the founding of Liberal Judaism in London (1902). [52: 215]

Reformation (Protestant) [XI.B] A movement for theological and moral reform in the Western Christian Church during the 16th and 17th centuries CE. Theologically, it was an attempt to recover what was considered to be the teaching of the BIBLE and early Christianity. Biblical AUTHORITY was asserted over that of tradition and the PAPACY. SALVATION was alleged to be by 'faith' rather than 'works'. SACRAMENTS and WORSHIP were simplified. MONASTICISM and priestly views of MINISTRY were attacked and lay status elevated. Martin Luther's *Theses* (LUTHERANISM) triggered the German Reformation in 1517. The more radical Huldreich Zwingli (1484–1531) reformed the church in Zürich at about the same time. In the next generation John Calvin in Geneva initiated another major Reformation tradition (CALVINISM). In BRITAIN the Reformation was slower and more conservative. The religious changes of the Reformation were accompanied by social and political upheavals which led to a permanent split in Western Christianity. PROTESTANTISM produced established churches in parts of Germany, Scandinavia, Holland, and Britain (STATE). Smaller reforming groups of the 16th-century 'Radical Reformation' in various parts of Europe [142] included early forms of UNITARIANISM, 'Spirituals' (akin to later QUAKERS), and ANABAPTISTS, who rejected established (state) churches. ROMAN CATHOLICISM was, however, reformed and reinforced by the work of the COUNTER-REFORMATION [11: 182–212; 20 vol. 3; 27: 311–99; 36: I–IV].

Refuges, Three [IX.A] In Buddhist tradition, the BUDDHA, the DHAMMA (DHARMA), and the SANGHA. The centrality of these elements is affirmed in the formula 'I go for refuge to the Buddha ... to the Dhamma ... to the Sangha' which is customarily used in all Buddhist rituals.

Reincarnation (Jewish) [XVII] In Hebrew *gilgul*, meaning (the) 'turning' (of the wheel). [9 vol. 7: 573] The belief in reincarnation was central to KABBALAH teaching about the destiny of the soul, although it was rejected by some non-mystics as a sectarian belief alien to Jewish thought [52: 95]. The Kabbalists continued to believe in the resurrection of the dead in a future age (OLAM HA-BA) but saw man as having to undergo a variety of rebirths before then in order to fulfil his tasks on earth [45: 281].

Religio-Political Movements among Tribal Peoples [XX] Contact with powerful, sophisticated societies disturbs the tribal order, especially in colonial situations or through the ferment of new ideas introduced by Christian MISSIONS. A violent reaction of protest or rebellion has often arisen intertwined with NEW RELIGIOUS MOVEMENTS, particularly in the earlier periods of contact and before alternative channels for action have developed, such as nationalist political parties and trades unions. In the 20th century, tribal or peasant revolts with religious dimensions have occurred in Peru, Indonesia, the Colorums of the PHILIPPINES, and in risings such as the messianic Govindgiri movement among the Bhils of

India in 1912 [6: 240–43]. In East Africa there was the Maji-Maji ('water') movement of 1905–6 in Tanganyika, and a series of nativistic cults in Kenya in intermittent clashes with government [19: 240–45, 259–68]. The PROVIDENCE INDUSTRIAL MISSION, Alice LENSHINA's Lumpa Church, and the Israelites of South Africa [19: 61–3] were involved in political or military clashes, as were the RASTAFARIANS and the CARGO CULTS of Melanesia, where a revolt in the Baliem valley of Irian Jaya in 1977 and the attempted secession of Jimmy Stevens's Nagriamel movement in Vanuatu in 1980 had religious dimensions. In the long run these movements tend to become more religious and less political. [19: VIII]

Religion [XXVIII] Whatever it is that embraces or is embraced in most of the terms in this *Dictionary*; no single or simple definition will suffice [20: 368; 23B; 27]. Dictionary definitions (e.g. 'human recognition of superhuman power', 'belief in God', 'any system of faith and worship') are often circular, prejudiced, or so general as to be useless. (SECULAR ALTERNATIVES TO RELIGION)

(1) A religion: one of a set of recognizable systems of belief and practice having a family resemblance. The set has no sharp boundaries. A starting-point might be something accepted as a religion (e.g. CHRISTIANITY). Elements common to this and to similar systems (e.g. ISLAM, JUDAISM) are then selected as defining the set of 'religions'. By extrapolation, a number of 'isms' (BUDDHISM, HINDUISM, etc.) come to be listed as religions. But the process is arbitrary and artificial [1: 90–96]. Some scholars [27: III] advocate that the use of proper names for the so-called religions (a practice uncommon before the 19th century) be replaced by the terminology 'the religion of' (a people or cultural area).

(2) The more abstract term, 'religion', may denote: (a) the class of all religions; (b) the supposed common essence of all

genuinely religious phenomena; (c) that ideal of which all actual religions are taken to be imperfect manifestations; (d) human religiousness, expressed not only in systems and traditions (explicit religion) but also in ways of life where it is hidden (implicit). For (a) an ostensive definition may suffice. For the other usages, definitions tend to be evaluative or based on commitment [1: 85–96]. The SCIENCES OF RELIGION often employ a functional definition (FUNCTIONALISM). For example, J. M. Yinger [31: 9] defined religion as 'a system of beliefs and practices by means of which a group of people struggles with the ultimate problems of human life'.

Definers of religion are prone to the error of reification (misplaced concreteness). It is well to remember that to be religious pertains to persons, but not necessarily only those who profess religious beliefs or engage in religious practices. [*See also:* 12: 1; 24: 34–51]

Religionswissenschaft [XXVIII] A discipline ('science of religion') or group of disciplines equivalent to or comprising the history of religions, comparative religion, and PHENOMENOLOGY OF RELIGION [13: 33–8; 25; 28: IV]. Comparison of religions began in ancient Greece (as early as Xenophanes in the late 6th century BCE). In recent times, the growth of a vast store of information (from travellers, traders, missionaries, etc.) stimulated attempts to order and organize it. 'Comparative religion' became the established (but misleading) title (in English) for work describing and classifying many religions with an eye to their similarities and differences. To avoid the bias (whether religious or anti-religious) and dogmatism (regarding the truth or superiority of one religion) discerned in many 19th-century studies, histories of religion have tended to be specific, focusing on only one tradition or cultural area. More general studies belong to TYPOLOGY (structural or historical) and to the discipline which once included but is now increasingly

distinguished from typology, the PHE-
NOMENOLOGY OF RELIGION. From
all of these are now marked off, on the
one side, the SCIENCES OF RELIGION
and, on the other, PHILOSOPHY OF
RELIGION and THEOLOGY. What has
clearly come to be seen in this century
is that if the meaning of RELIGION
is to be understood, its place as a
significant aspect of culture appreciated,
and its varied structures and many
functions comprehended, it will only
be through the cooperation of scholars
from many disciplines in academic
study which is polymethodic and combines rigour with sensitivity. [See also
12: II; 18: II, III; bibliography in 25: 294–
304]

Religious Education (**in Schools**)
[XXIV] There was a marked increase
during the 1970s in the study of religions in schools in Western countries,
most noticeably in those with statutory
provision for religious education.
In the United Kingdom the comparative
study of religion (RELIGIONSWISSEN-
SCHAFT) had previously been included
in many religious-education syllabuses,
but it was confined to the 16–18 age
group and seen as peripheral to the
main task of sharing the Christian faith
with the pupils. Three factors contributed to the inclusion of religions in
their own right: (1) awareness of the
growing numbers of adherents of non-
Christian religions living in Britain; (2)
the challenge from philosophers of education to justify the school curriculum
as appropriate for all pupils; and (3)
the development of religious-studies
departments in universities and colleges
of education. A widely accepted aim
for religious education in state schools
is that pupils should be helped to
understand the nature of RELIGION.
This involves a thematic approach in
the earlier years (festivals, sacred places,
sacred writings, symbols, etc.), with a
study of individual religions in the
upper years of secondary schooling [4; 5].
An influential book in this development

was *Secular Education and the Logic of
Religion* [7] by Ninian Smart, who later
became director of Schools Council
projects on religious education in
secondary and primary schools, based
at Lancaster University. Shap, a working party founded in 1969 to promote
the study of religions in schools [2],
has run conferences for teachers, produced a handbook [1], and operated a
mailing scheme. Annual conferences
have also been run by the Standing
Conference for Inter-Faith Dialogue
in Education (SCIFDE), a movement
linked with the World Congress of
Faiths, and bringing together people
concerned with education from different
religions. The study of religions
has been included in syllabuses for
public examinations at 16-plus and 18-
plus [3].

In some Scandinavian countries (which
also have statutory provision for religious education) pupils have the possibility of studying religions: in Denmark
a subject called 'Foreign Religions and
Other Life Styles' was introduced in
1976 at the 16-plus level. In Sweden
religious education is called 'Knowledge
about Religion', and world religions
may be taught in any section of the
school system. In the Netherlands some
schools include courses on religions,
supported by Interreligio, an independent centre dedicated to the greater
understanding of adherents of other religions living in Holland.

In several countries where religious
education has no official place in the
curriculum some study of religions may
take place within such subjects as social
studies or liberal studies, e.g. in New
Zealand, where learning about the culture of peoples of the Pacific Islands is
encouraged by the education authorities, even for young children. In the
U.S.A. the Supreme Court Schempp
decision (1963) expressly allowed
'teaching about religion' in public
schools [6]. However, because this is
less widely known than its forbidding of

prayer and the devotional reading of the BIBLE, only a minority of schools include any study of religions. A number of attempts have been made to change this situation, through teacher-education programmes, the production of curriculum materials, etc., via, for instance, the Public Education Religion Studies Center (PERSC), which was formerly based at Wright State University, Dayton, Ohio, by the World Religions Curriculum Development Center, Minneapolis, Minnesota, and by Argus Communications.

Examples of radical change come from Papua New Guinea, where in the early 1970s the Christian churches produced an agreed syllabus which included both Melanesian and world religions, and from South Australia, where religious education has been put into the curriculum (in place of the religious instruction which had been organized by the Christian churches), supported by teacher-education programmes and the development of extensive curriculum materials, including the study of religious phenomena and individual religions.

Revitalization Movements (Amerindian) [III] Relatively recent attempts on the part of previously acculturated Amerindian groups to regain and reaffirm earlier religious traditions. Often syncretistic (SYNCRETISM) in doctrine and ceremonial, drawing both encouragement and inspiration from the pan-Indian movement, tribes that include the Wampanoag, Narragansett, and other North American eastern groups are reasserting the value of such forms as the SWEAT LODGE, VISION QUEST, traditional healing techniques, dances, and use of the sacred pipe (CALUMET). Revitalization efforts are often not endorsed by all the Indians and frequently occasion the scepticism of scholars. [5: XIV]

Revivalism [XI.B] Outbreaks of intense, often mass religious excitement, originally in the international 'Evangelical Revival' which began in the 1720s. This included German MORAVIANS, English METHODISM, ANGLICANISM and EVANGELICALS. In the American 'Great Awakening' the outstanding theologian Jonathan Edwards (1705–58) combined CALVINISM with the philosophy of John Locke (NATURAL THEOLOGY) to explain the process of religious 'conversion', i.e. of turning the person from a life of sin to one dedicated to JESUS CHRIST. This revival emphasized 'inward religion'; justification by faith (SALVATION) experienced in a 'new birth'; lay preaching; and groups for religious fellowship. It represented a reaction against Western materialism and rationalism, recalling older religious patterns such as PURITANISM. Although often affecting artisan groups in England, it included the upper-class 'Clapham sect' led by William Wilberforce (1759–1833), the anti-slavery campaigner. Spontaneous 18th-century revivalism was succeeded in the 19th century by the work of Americans such as Charles Finney (1792–1875), who cultivated techniques for engineering revivals. Later campaigners included Dwight L. Moody (1837–99) and his musical colleague Ira D. Sankey (1840–1908); Billy Sunday (1862–1935); and Billy Graham (b. 1918) [48]. Perfection ('Holiness') Revivalism developed in America [35] and in the SALVATION ARMY. Revivalism has been common in the U.S.A., with claims to be a significant influence on social reform [123], although it has often been politically conservative. In Britain it has been less influential, partly because Anglicanism has not been very responsive to it. [2: XVIII–XX, XXVI, XXVII; 90; 101: XVII]

Rimé [XXIX] The 19th-century Rimé or 'ecumenical' movement of Tibet developed as a response to the sectarian strife that had periodically plagued Buddhism. The movement, which began in eastern Tibet, initiated a renaissance of culture and spirituality throughout the country. It was led by a number of prominent teachers from various traditions such as the Kagyupa (KAGYU) master Jamgon Kongtrul (1811–99) [21], the Sakyapa (SAKYA) scholar Khyentse Wangpo (1819–92) [4] and the Nyingmapa (NYINGMA) Chogyur Dechen Lingpa (1829–70) [4]. The movement was not an attempt to form a new sect but rather to establish a climate in which the spiritual wealth of each particular religious tradition could be available to all. In furtherance of this aim Jamgon Kongtrul collected the doctrines and instructions of all the Tibetan traditions, in his famous *Five Treasures*, which comprise over 100 volumes.

Rites (Greek) [XII] Sacrifice was the central rite performed on almost every Greek cultic occasion. It involved the ritual slaughter of animals, followed by a division of the carcass between men and gods and feasting. The slaughter was preceded by a procession to the altar, music, song, ritual hand-washing, sprinkling of the victim, prayers, and libations. It was followed by burnt-offerings to the gods. Recipient and occasion determined the type of victim. Observance of the sacrificial rules was the priest's responsibility. Sacrifices were of two kinds: *thysia*, at a table-like altar (*bomos*) (TEMENOS), and *enagisma*, at a sunken altar (*eschara*) or pit (*bothros*), when the victim's blood flowed on, or into, the altar. Most sacrifices offered to deities were *thysia*. Usually, the victim's flesh was eaten (roasted) by the participants, whereas the gods' share (fat and bones) was burnt. In some sacrifices the victim was burnt whole (holocaust). There is some correlation between holocaust and *enagisma*, but no exact coincidence. Libations (offerings of wine, milk, honey, water, oil), poured on the ground or altar, were performed on countless occasions. Various deities received the first-fruits (*aparchai*) of the crops. Processions and dances were ubiquitous in cult offered to deities (divine cult). Some dancers were masked. Rites for special occasions included purification rites (which were also incorporated in divine cult) and rites of passage, the most important being birth; the presentation of children to a divinity and the *phratry*; marriage and death (at certain times and places participation in funerals was legally restricted to the family). In historical times transformed initiation rituals, involving only a representative number of participants, were integrated in divine cult. Initiatory elements were incorporated into the education system, which included both civic and military training (examples are the Spartan *agoge* and the Attic *ephebeia*). Certain cults, especially that of Dionysus, involved orgiastic rites (e.g. ecstatic dances and *omophagia*, the eating of raw meat). [2: II, 1, 2, 3, 4, 7; 3: 35–58]

Ritual [XXVIII] Patterned behaviour, often communal, consisting of prescribed actions performed periodically and/or repetitively [8: VII; 10; 12: V; 22: 3–72]. Just as MYTH invokes causes of a scientifically or historically unverifiable kind, so ritual seems either to seek practical ends by non-empirical means, or to have no practical purpose. The term is used in biology (e.g. of the preliminaries to mating), in psychology (e.g. for compulsive behaviour attributed to unconscious motives), and in social psychology (e.g. for shared action expressing common strivings). Anthropologists and sociologists have stressed the latent, unintended functions of ritual behaviour in social life (e.g. as a form of communication, as promoting solidarity, or as giving confidence in the face of danger). The ritual aspect of religion provides (along with ICONOGRAPHY) a starting-point for phenomenological study (PHENOMENOLOGY OF RELIGION).

A rite is a specific ritual action or practice, including physical movements and any accompanying words. Attempts to classify rites make a distinction between rites of passage [22: 53–72] (transition rites, e.g. of initiation or at puberty) [8: VIII]; intensification rites (promoting or celebrating joint activity); and piacular rites (to do with cleansing, forgiveness, or expiation) [8: 167]. From a theological point of view, SACRA-MENTS [12: 120–23] are rites believed to be divinely ordained and to have a special efficacy (e.g. in relation to the Christian doctrine of grace), but the concept of the sacramental has a much wider usage [28: VI]. [See also 17: XI; 18: VII; 26: V–VII, X; 30: 67–71, III, IV, 226–48]

Rituals (Roman) [XXV] The essential ritual, establishing contact between men and gods, was animal sacrifice, mostly of cattle, sheep, and pigs. The pro-gramme included rites of preparation, prayer to the recipient, and the 'immo-lation' of the victim by the sprink-ling on its head of corn-meal and wine. Then, after the killing (carried out by lower-class specialists – *victimarii* – on the officiant's behalf), the entrails (*exta*) were assessed by *haruspices*, through whom the gods accepted or rejected the sacrifice. The victim was cooked and finally the *exta* returned to the god; the rest (*profanum*) was consumed by the human participants. If the victim was rejected, the whole procedure was repeated until an acceptable sacrifice was found (*perlitatio*). [6: 558–9; II: 386–92; 17: III] Many other rituals included this programme; in lustration, the area to be purified was walked around by the pro-cession of victims and participants [9: 4–8, 36–7, 17: 88–9]; in the triumph, the victorious general was accompanied in procession through the city by his army, his prisoners, and the victims for sacrifice to Jupiter [19]. In these and many other rituals, the central concern was with the meticulous preservation and re-creation of traditional utterance and action; this is also the interest of the antiquarian writers whose descrip-tions we have. We have no liturgy or coherent explanation of the meaning of

rituals, and know of no myths associ-ated with them, if they ever were. It is an exaggeration to say that the Romans had no mythology; but what survives either concerns the founders of the city or has been transformed into narratives about kings and heroes, or tales about specific places in the city. Myth, in other words, has been detached from ritual and grounded in time or space [6: 47–78; 10; 18A].

Rituals (Sikh) [XXVII] The principal Sikh rituals are a cluster associated with routine GURDWARA worship and five which mark important rites of passage. All require the presence of the ADI GRANTH. A copy of the sacred volume is installed in every *gurdwara* and there treated with great reverence. When closed it is wrapped in an elegant cloth (*rumal*). It is opened only under a canopy and is then protected with a fly-whisk. Those who come to a *gurdwara* for *darshan* ('audience') first remove their shoes and cover their heads. Each bows to the floor before the scripture, makes an offering, and· if *kirtan* (the singing of scriptural selections) is in progress sits in the *gurdwara*, always at a level below the scripture. At the con-clusion of *kirtan* the congregation recites ARDAS, and KARAH PRASAD is distri-buted. [15: V, VI; 17: 2–6]. The five indi-vidual ceremonies mark the birth of a child (*janam sanskar*), the bestowing of its name (*nam sanskar*), initiation into the KHALSA (*amrit sanskar*), marriage (the *Anand* wedding service), and death (*miratak sanskar*). [4: 112–29; 13: II–IV; 15: III; 17: 9–12; 26: 106–10] For *amrit sanskar* sweetened water is stirred with a two-edged sword and administered by five devout Sikhs. [17: 13–16] Ritual forms are also followed for such pro-cedures as transporting the scripture and conducting an *akhand path* (PATH).

Roman Catholicism [XI.B] Christians in communion with the PAPACY; also termed 'CATHOLICS'. It is the largest church of Western Christianity, spread elsewhere by European colonization and

MISSIONS. Some ancient 'Uniate' churches are in communion with Roman Catholicism but allowed forms of worship and customs of their own, e.g. married clergy [107: 1407]. CHURCH ORGANIZATION is by an authoritative hierarchy under the papacy. WORSHIP is markedly SACRAMENTAL, centred on the MASS. Doctrine is drawn from scripture and tradition, and defined infallibly as 'dogma' through COUNCILS and the papacy (AUTHORITY). The church has a rich tradition of spirituality and MYSTICISM, especially through MONASTICISM. Roman Catholicism has favoured close relationships between the STATE and Christianity, which has often led to conflict. It has a marked capacity for incorporating diverse Christian traditions and (especially at the popular level) pre-Christian elements. Accommodation to the modern world has proved more difficult. Nineteenth-century Liberal Catholicism and the more extreme Modernist movement (a minority of intellectuals, mainly in late 19th-century France, condemned in 1907) [86; 110] attempted theological adjustment to modern science and history. Social Catholicism in 19th-century France and Germany was concerned with democracy and social reform [11: 387–95; 132]. Since Vatican Council II (1962–5) [1] there has been a ferment of change in most areas of Roman Catholic life, including worship (LITURGICAL MOVEMENT), church relations (ECUMENICAL MOVEMENT), and social reform (SOCIAL MORALITY). [5; 15; 83 vol. 4: I–IX; 146: 134–65]

Roman Religion [XXV] The religion of the ancient Romans derived elements – at least the worship of gods – from its INDO-EUROPEAN inheritance. However, apart from some evidently very ancient rituals, the earliest religion of which we have any understanding is that of the 6th-century BCE monarchic period (754–509 BCE) (NUMA, CALENDAR OF), when the native tradition was already undergoing modification through contacts with Etruscans and with Greeks from South Italy [18]. The republican period (509–31 BCE) saw a wide, ever-increasing range of deities (DI DEAEQUE), their worship being maintained either by the state or by clans, families, and other groups, both types being under the supervision of the priests (SACERDOTES). An elaborate system of ritual and rules penetrated all transactions, so the gods had their place in all aspects of life (AUSPICIA; PRODIGIA). [6: 89–133; 11: VIII]. The later republican period saw important changes: first, cults emerged, based on voluntary membership, with their own authority structure and offering personal religious experience; second, the ambitions of competing aristocratic leaders led them to claim special divine patronage (*felicitas*) and honours tending towards deification. [6: 526–50; 12: I] In creating the new regime of the empire, Augustus (31 BCE), under the guise of reviving ancient forgotten cults, transformed many institutions to the service of the new monarchy, while the first steps were taken towards the establishment of EMPEROR-WORSHIP [12: II]. The cult of the emperor in all provinces and of Roman gods in the Latin-speaking provinces (SYNCRETISM) characterized the period of the empire; and paganism displayed continuing vigour into the late empire, as the evolution of new systems shows (MITHRAS/MITHRAISM; MYSTERY-CULTS). The decline of dedications and temple-building in the 3rd century CE is part of the transformation of city life rather than evidence of specifically religious change. [3: 28–53; 12: 230–35] Competition with CHRISTIANITY, rather than internal deterioration, led to eventual decline. [18A]

Rome, Early Christianity at [XI.A] Roman Christianity apparently originated in the large Jewish community of the city. Disturbances caused by the introduction of Christianity led to the expulsion of Jews from Rome by Claudius in 49 CE. But within five or six years they were back. In 57 CE Paul's letter to the Roman Christians indicates that the CHURCH of the capital, while founded on a Jewish base, comprised a majority of Gentile members. PAUL spent two years in Rome under house-arrest between 60 and 62; Peter visited the city a year or two later. In 65 the church of Rome survived a murderous attack by Nero. A generation later, as the first letter of Clement shows, it was acquiring a position of moral leadership among Gentile churches. [3: 279–83, 373–93]

Rosicrucians [XVIII] A mystical brotherhood described in two anonymous manifestos published at Kassel, Germany, in 1614/15. [31] Proclaiming a revival of learning and piety, the documents recounted the life of one Christian Rosenkreutz (supposedly 1378–1484), who had brought scientific and alchemical (ALCHEMY) knowledge from the East, founding the Order of the Rosy Cross, which men of goodwill and learning were now invited to join. The manifestos aroused intense excitement but the Rosicrucians could not be found. Probably they were fictitious, and the allegories in the manifestos may have been intended to stimulate non-sectarian cooperation in scientific and magical studies in a Europe torn by religious conflict. Belief in their reality, however, persisted, and numerous OCCULT organizations have claimed Rosicrucian origins, a contemporary example being the Ancient and Mystical Order Rosae Crucis (AMORC), based at San Jose, California, an international organization which instructs its members in esoteric doctrines by correspondence course.

Ruh [XIV] The Islamic term for 'spirit', in usage difficult to separate from *nafs*, 'soul, self, the permanent individuality of man' [20 'Nafs']. The soul is immortal and will survive the Last Day and Judgement (QIYAMA) and return to God. Among Sufi mystics (SUFISM), the idea of the pre-existence of the soul (e.g. MUHAMMAD's) appears. The spirit is conceived as the vital spark which God blows into a man but which departs at death. The term *ruh* is also used of angels (MALA'IKA) and, in the QUR'AN, of 'the spirit' sent by God to man, which in revelatory contexts is equated with Gabriel. [10 'Soul (Islam)'; 39 s.v.]

Runes [V] Runic symbols, representing sounds, each with a special name, were arranged in sets of eight to form a *futhark* or alphabet. Unlike the Ogam symbols used in Ireland, they were not based on the Latin alphabet. Runes were used by the Germanic and Scandinavian peoples from the 2nd century CE until after the VIKING Age, sometimes for straightforward messages, recorded verses, or inscriptions, but often for magical purposes [9: V, VI]. ODIN was said to have taught men runic lore.

Russia, Christianity in [XI.B] Christianity came to Russia under Byzantine influence, eventually sponsored by St Vladimir (956–1015) in Kiev. In the medieval period MONASTICISM spread rapidly and the church achieved AUTOCEPHALY in the 15th century. Moscow displaced Kiev as the leading centre; it became a 'patriarchate' (1589) and regarded itself as the 'third Rome'. Liturgical reform under Patriarch Nikon (1605–81) provoked the OLD BELIEVERS schism. Over time, various other sects (some DUALIST) appeared, e.g. Khlysts, Skoptsi, Dukhobors, Molokons, Judaizers. Peter the Great (1676–1725) subordinated the church to a 'Holy Synod', but the patriarchate was restored in 1917. Membership in Russian Christianity is overwhelmingly in the ORTHODOX CHURCH. ROMAN CATHOLICISM and the presence of Uniate churches in Russia derived largely from the incorporation of Poland and Lithuania into the Russian empire, and was often suspect as alien. Russian LUTHERANISM is mainly German in origin, but BAPTISTS made ethnic Russian converts. Since the Communist revolution of 1917 the state has theoretically allowed religious observance, but atheist propaganda and physical persecution have been applied, with greater or lesser intensity according to the political situation (cf. COMMUNIST WORLD, CHRISTIANITY IN THE). [9; 12; 83 vol. 2: XXXIV, vol. 4: XIX; 134: IV, VI, VIII]

Ryobu-Shinto [XVI] Dual-aspect Shinto. Ryobu-Shinto (or Honchi-suijaku) is the convergence of SHINTO and Buddhist deities (*shinbutsu shugo*) (JAPANESE BUDDHAS AND BODHISATTVAS), often attributed to the philosophy of the priest Gyogi (670–749). It began in the 8th century with such practices as the conducting of each other's ceremonies by Shinto and Buddhist priests [13: 72–6; 19: 18; 28; 33: 304–6]. 'Honchi' means 'actual Buddha'; 'suijaku' is the same as *gongen* (JINGU-JI), the mountain KAMI, which are said to be transitional forms of BUDDHA, in transit to Japan from their origin in India. This Buddhist–Shinto SYNCRETISM was fostered by the spread of Buddhist temples into remote rural areas of Japan, which required an accommodation with the local *kami* and so entailed their worship. The emperor (KOKUTAI SHINTO) could be both the embodiment of the Shinto sun-goddess, AMATERASU-OMIKAMI, and the Buddha Dainichi. Formally called Ryobu-Shinto, the cult was officially proscribed in the Meiji period (1868–1912) as degrading Shinto, but the belief it embodied is still current.

· S ·

Sacerdotes [XXV] Roman priests belonged to a number of different colleges, with defined spheres of action, which could not be interchanged. The senior college, the *pontifices*, was unique in including different types (the *rex*, the survivor of the one-time king, and *flamines*, each devoted to a different deity); one of their number was chosen, later elected, as *pontifex maximus* and acted as their public representative. The *pontifices* were responsible for most matters of cult, such as sacrifices (RITUALS), temples (TEMPLA), festivals, and the calendar (NUMA); the *augurs* for the AUSPICIA; and the *fetiales* for the rituals of declaring war and making treaties. [6: 576–93; 11: 394–414; 17: VII] All these priests came from leading families and all except the *rex* and *flamines* continued to play leading parts in political and military life, in no sense forming a separate estate. Each college had its own body of law and kept its own books and records; typically, the priests acted as expert advisers (to the Senate or to individuals) on problems of the sacred law (IUS DIVINUM). Since the political and religious spheres were in no way separate, their decisions very frequently had great political importance [12: 1]. It is not surprising, therefore, that the emperors became members of all the important colleges and tended increasingly to act on their behalf [12: 63–5].

Sach-khand [XXVII] For Nanak and his successors (GURUS) *mukti* ('release') corresponds to the condition of ineffable bliss (*sahaj*) awaiting all who persevere in NAM SIMARAN. The practice of *nam simaran* demands both disciplined meditation and a pattern of virtuous living applied in the midst of the everyday world. He who faithfully pursues *nam simaran* will progressively ascend to ever-increasing heights of spiritual attainment. Ultimately, passing beyond the transmigratory round of death and rebirth, he enters *sach-khand*, the 'Realm of Truth' where *sahaj* reigns and all disharmony is stilled. [25: 219–26] *Mukti* for Nanak was thus the mystical climax of a spiritual ascent. Orthodox GURMAT continues to affirm this belief. It is, however, a doctrine and a discipline which must elude all but the spiritually awakened. For many, *sach-khand* is conceived as a 'heavenly abode', a place to which one's spirit goes at physical death rather than a mystical condition transcending death.

Sacraments (Christian) [XI.B] Material signs believed by Christians to have been ordained by JESUS CHRIST to symbolize and convey spiritual gifts (e.g. the bread and wine in the EUCHARIST convey the presence and power of Christ). To be valid, a sacrament should have the correct 'matter' (material sign), 'form' (formula of administration), and 'intention' (to do what the church intends). This guarantees that grace (SALVATION) is conveyed, whatever the personal character of the priest (MINISTRY). Effective reception, however, depends on the condition of the recipient. Christian tradition came to recognize seven sacraments, above all *baptism* and the *eucharist*. Baptism is generally administered to infants (except for BAPTISTS). It brings incorporation into the CHURCH. *Confirmation*, when the recipient personally reaffirms promises made at baptism on his/her behalf, conveys a further measure of grace. PENANCE deals with sin after baptism. *Extreme unction* is a preparation for death. *Matrimony* sanctifies MARRIAGE. *Priestly ordination* ('orders') conveys grace for various grades of ministry. At the REFORMATION, PROTESTANTISM retained only baptism and the eucharist as genuine sacraments, though some modern forms of ANGLICANISM have allowed a sacramental quality to the rest. The two main Christian groups to reject the use of sacraments are the QUAKERS and SALVATION ARMY. Protestant use of sacraments is marked by great variety of interpretation and practice. [76: VIII, XVI; 107: 1218–19; 84] (MYSTERIES (EASTERN ORTHODOX))

Sacred Mountains [XVI] In Japan some mountains, mostly volcanic and cone-shaped, have been identified by ascetics as having local spirits (KAMI), called *gongen* (RYOBU-SHINTO). They have, therefore, attracted groups of climbers who desire spiritual invigoration, especially *yamabushi* (SHUGENDO) [4: 79–81; 18: 141–79; 29: 58–61]. Mount Fuji (altitude 3,776 m), climbed since the 17th century (last eruption, 1707), was especially revered by the Fuso-kyo, a SHINTO sect worshipping Sengen Daishin (the Great Deity of Mount Fuji), but it now offers chiefly seasonal recreation. Mount Ontake (3,036 m, first recorded eruption in 1980), which straddles Gifu and Nagano prefectures, is the second most sacred. It is revered by Ontake-kyo, a sect worshipping Ontake Okami (the Great Deity of Ontake). Near Mount Haguro in Yamagata [14], a local cult taught that salvation was achieved by self-mummification through starvation and dehydration. Other sacred mountains include the numerous Zao Gongen peaks with their shrines, headed by Kimbusen in Nara prefecture (and the variations Kinbusan, Kinposan, Kimpusen, and Mitake mountains in other prefectures), Tateyama in Toyama prefecture,

and Hakusan on the border of Ishikawa and Gifu prefectures.

Sacrifice [XXVIII] RITUAL presentation of a gift, or what is so given [17: 212]. Sacrificial offerings (Latin *sacer facere* = to make HOLY) have a place in most religions, although the nature of the gift, the meaning of the action, and the function of the rite vary widely [3: 37–9; 8: IX]. What is given is either, often as food or as alive (ritual killing offers life). The action may be undertaken for thanksgiving or divination; as a means of renewing life or of continuing a seasonal or cosmic cycle; to secure favour or ward off evil; or as a ratification of agreement (COVENANT) between human and superhuman participants, or to express their communion. The SCIENCES OF RELIGION make an important distinction between the overt (intended) function of rites such as sacrifices (their aim as seen by those participating) and their latent (unintended) functions (which an observer may conclude to be the actual effects of the practice, psychological, social, or cultural). [1: 108–9].

Saddha [IX.A] A PALI term (Sanskrit *shraddha*) meaning 'faith' (or trust), which is present, according to Buddhist traditions [25: 141], in any 'wholesome' consciousness. Until wisdom is achieved, the Buddhist acknowledges that faith is necessary. Somewhat subordinate in the THERAVADA tradition, faith is regarded in the MAHAYANA as ranking equal with wisdom [4: 144f], for faith is one of the five cardinal virtues (with vigour, mindfulness, concentration, and wisdom), and the 'seed' without which, it is held, spiritual growth cannot begin [5: 47].

Sadducees [XI.A] A religious party in Judaism between 150 BCE and 70 CE. The origin of the designation is uncertain. The Sadducees were theologically conservative, rejecting post-exilic (BIBLICAL HISTORY) ANGELOLOGY and DEMONOLOGY and the belief in bodily resurrection. Socially they were

aristocrats; they supported the Hasmo-
naean priest-kings and the leading
priestly families of the Herodian and
Roman periods. They opposed the
Jerusalem CHURCH, not least because of
its emphasis on resurrection. They did
not outlive the second TEMPLE. [16:
XXVI]

Sadhu [XIII.A] A virtuous, worthy, or
honourable man, literally 'one who is
straight', or without defect; in Hindu
tradition a saint. Usually he is one who
has renounced ordinary life, but unlike
the *swami*, who belongs to an order, the
sadhu remains independent.

Sahajayana [IX.A] One of the later
schools of MAHAYANA Buddhism,
which emphasized the practice of what
was 'innate' or 'natural' (*sahaja*) to
humans [15: 354]. This is a form of
TANTRA (2), and the characteristic
teaching of this school is found in the
early Bengali collections of poems
known as *caryapada*, which originated
in eastern India in about the 8th century CE (or later), and are associated
with Krishnacarya and others [37:
515]. The poet's name indicates the
affinity of this Buddhist tantric school
with (Hindu) Vaishnavism (VISHNU/
VAISHNAVA).

Sai Baba [XXI] Although Sathya Sai
Baba is one of India's best-known
gurus, he has not yet (1982) visited the
West and has only a few followers
in America and Europe. At the age
of 14 he fell into a state of uncon-
sciousness and on recovering he
announced that he was a reincarnation
of Sai Baba of Shirdi [39]. Baba's fame is
largely due to the miracles which many
claim that he performs. These, however,
he says, are merely to persuade people
to learn of his real aim, which is the
teaching and spread of DHARMA. Devotees, who are expected to lead clean
and upright lives (abstaining from alcohol, drugs, and meat), are taught the
importance of good deeds, of controlling the mind and turning it to God,
of study of the scriptures, regular

prayer, and the singing of spiritual
songs. [2: 56; 29]

Saicho [XVI] (767–822), posthumously
known as Dengyo Daishi (KUKAI), was
the priestly founder of the TENDAI sect
[21: 56–8]. He was born into the Miura
family in Shiga prefecture. He entered
the cloister at the age of 12, later built a
small place of worship on Mount Hiei
overlooking Lake Biwa, and took the
vows in 786. Selected by the emperor to
go to China, he went in the mission of
804, and travelled and studied on Mount
T'IEN-T'AI. Returning to Japan the
following year, he preached Tendai
doctrines which, through his Kegon
training (NANTO ROKUSHU), were
designed to introduce the Buddha-nature
to the ordinary man. His efforts to
strengthen the Mount Hiei temple were
thwarted by the Nara clergy, but it
received the name (KUKAI) of Enryaku-
ji and the right to perform ordinations
after his death. He was given his
posthumous name in 866.

Saint (**Christian**) [XI.B] At an early
stage holy persons, after their death,
began to be invoked in prayer by Christians to win God's favour. They
included martyrs who had died for the
faith; 'confessors' who had suffered for
it; and holy virgins. Much use was made
of the stories of saints' lives (including
much legendary matter) in the Middle
Ages for public and private devotion;
and PILGRIMAGES were made to their
relics. PROTESTANTISM rejected devotion to saints, but Anglo-Catholics
(ANGLICANISM) have allowed for it.
Early recognition of saints was often
localized and informal. During the 12th
century the PAPACY took over formal
declaration of a saint's status (canonization) for the whole church. Beatifica-
tion is for more restricted devotion
(in one area) as well as being a stage
in the long process of canonization.
In the ORTHODOX CHURCH canonization is usually by a synod of bishops
for an autocephalous (AUTOCEPHALY)
church. [4]

Sakya [XXIX] The Sakya tradition of
Tibetan Buddhism takes its name from
the monastery founded at Sakya in
south-western Tibet in 1073 by Konchog Gyalpo of the Khon clan, an influential family that had previously been
NYINGMA in affiliation. Konchog Gyalpo studied the 'new TANTRAS' with the
translator Drokmi Lotsa. The most
important of the teachings which he
received from his GURU was the unified
sutra and TANTRA (2) doctrine known
as 'The path and its fruit' (Tibetan
lam dre), developed by the 9th-century
yogin Virupa. According to this teaching SAMSARA and NIBBANA are just
the expression of the clear brilliance
(Tibetan *gsal*) and EMPTINESS (Tibetan
stong) of mind itself. Thus the yogin,
who perceives the true nature of his
own mind by following the practice of
'The path and its fruit', realizes the fundamental inseparability of *samsara* and
nibbana. [24]

The Sakya sect was given definite
shape by the work of 'the five masters':
Sachen Kunga Nyingpo (1092–1158);
Sonam Tsemo (1142–82); Dragpa
Gyaltsen (1147–1216); Sakya Pandita
(1182–1251); and Chogyal Phagpa
(1235–80). Since that time the tradition
and its two subsects, Ngor and Tshar,
have been adorned by many eminent
scholars and yogins [1].

The head of the Sakya sect is always
drawn from the male line of the Khon
family. The present head, Ngawang
Kunga, is the 41st to hold the office. [1]

Salat [XIV] (Persian and Turkish *namaz*)
The sequence of utterances and actions
making up the Muslim worship (better
than 'prayers'), accounted one of the
PILLARS OF ISLAM. Its performance at
five points of the day, from dawn till
evening, is prescribed for all able-
bodied adult believers. It may be performed alone, but congregational
worship, e.g. in a MOSQUE, is more
meritorious and is obligatory on
FRIDAYS. [20 s.v.; 29: 70–81; 39
'Prayer'; 43: 537–49; 47: 155–9]

Salutations (Sikh) [XXVII] The common Sikh salutation is 'Sat Sri Akal'
('True is the Immortal One'). This is
also used as a triumphal cry in Sikh
assemblies. A leader calls 'Jo bole so
nihal' ('Blessed is he who cries . . . ') and
the gathering responds with 'Sat Sri
Akal!' A more formal greeting is 'Vahiguruji ka Khalsa, Siri Vahiguruji ki
fateh' ('Hail to the Guru's KHALSA, hail
the GURU's victory'). The latter portion
may be used as a response.

Salvation [XXVIII] Strictly, rescue or
release from a state which is evil or imperfect, in which those 'saved' were lacking
true welfare; a religious 'technical term'
originating in the Judaeo-Christian
tradition and given general application
[12: XII]. A 'salvation' religion is one
which offers a diagnosis of the human
condition and a spiritual path to health
or wholeness (Latin *salus*, *salvus*, 'safe,
well') [8: XIII]. In many cases, but not
invariably, the rescue or release is taken
to be possible only through a saviour (a
divine being or hero-figure). Salvation
may also denote the state so attained.
[*See also* 24: 197, 206]

Salvation Army [XI.B] A 19th-century
Christian movement. The army had its
origins in REVIVALISM, being founded
by William Booth (1829–1912), a former
Methodist (METHODISM), in 1878. It
adopted military uniforms, bands,
ranks, and metaphors for its organization and activities. From 1890 social
work was given a larger place but
popular evangelism has continued to
be characteristic of the army. The
SACRAMENTS and ordained MINISTRY
are rejected. The army's headquarters is
in London but it works extensively in
the U.S.A. and overseas MISSIONS. [24;
137]

Salvation, Christian Doctrine of
[XI.B] Salvation for Christians depends
upon 'grace'. This is divine favour and
supernatural power freely given by
God, shown above all in the 'Atonement' (reconciliation, or at-one-ment,
between man and God) wrought by

JESUS CHRIST. Man's SIN prevents him from approaching God; he can only be reconciled through Christ's sacrificial death (CHRISTOLOGY). There have been many theories about atonement (none officially defined as 'dogma' (AUTHORITY)). Early theories about Christ's death as a 'ransom' paid to Satan are no longer generally accepted. For St ANSELM, only Christ could completely 'satisfy' God's just punishment of sin. More persistent is the view that Christ's taking human form (Incarnation) (CHRISTOLOGY) made it possible for men also to become divine. PROTESTANTISM has often emphasized 'penal substitution' – that Christ bore the punishment due to sinful men. Peter Abelard (1079–1142) thought that the love of Christ shown by his death moves men to love God. This 'moral influence' theory has been popular in modern times. By 'justification', ROMAN CATHOLICISM has meant the conveying of grace to make men holy. Protestantism has seen it rather as God forgiving men and treating them as though righteous because of Christ's atonement. Protestants have emphasized 'justification by faith', 'faith' being understood as a response to God inspired by divine grace and as faith in the person and work of Jesus Christ. For Protestantism salvation is 'by grace through faith' in Jesus Christ to avoid the idea of PELAGIANISM, namely salvation by human effort ('works'). (REVIVALISM has emphasized a sudden 'conversion' experience as the beginning of 'real' Christianity.) Roman Catholicism allows that 'merits' (rewards for human works assisted by God's grace) can contribute to salvation. It also emphasizes the crucial role of SACRAMENTS. St Augustine (AUGUSTINIANISM), CALVINISM, and JANSENISM taught 'predestination': that the saved (some add, the damned) are chosen from all eternity (contrast ARMINIANISM). The process of making Christians holy ('sanctification') has

typically been differently conceived in Roman Catholicism and Protestantism. The former emphasizes the human potential for holiness (aided by divine grace), whereas the latter (e.g. LUTHERANISM, BAPTISTS, and PRESBYTERIANISM) has been more pessimistic about the possibility of human holiness on earth. METHODISM and some forms of revivalism have taught a special gift of 'Perfection' in this life. The tradition of salvation of the ORTHODOX CHURCH is less legalistic than that of the West. The aim and purpose of salvation is seen rather as *theosis* ('deification'). [35; 37; 46; 49; 76: VII, XIV; 134: XI]

Samadhi [IX.A] One of the three major elements in the Buddhist 'way' or path (MARGA), the other two being SILA and *panna* (PRAJNA). The general meaning of *samadhi* is 'meditation', or 'concentration', but it has also a specialized meaning for which English 'trance' is more appropriate, and in this sense was characteristic of the Yogacarin school (YOGACARA). [4: 161ff; 5: 250ff]

Samaritans [XI.A] Israelites of central Palestine, descended from subjects of the northern kingdom and settlers planted there by Assyrian kings. They were rebuffed by the returning Jewish exiles when they offered to cooperate in rebuilding the temple; later they were permitted by the Persians to build a temple on Mount Gerizim (BIBLICAL HISTORY). This temple was destroyed by the Hasmonaeans, but the Samaritans continue to worship on Gerizim to this day. Their Hebrew BIBLE is confined to the first five books. [16: XXII, 16–20]

Samatha [IX.B] One of the two main types of Buddhist meditation practice (BHAVANA). Samatha (Sanskrit *shamatha*) is a state of calm or inner peace, brought about as a result of overcoming undisciplined activity of body and mind, especially the five 'hindrances': greediness for sense objects, angriness, sloth and drowsiness, excitement and guilt, timorous doubt. Training in alertness and joyful contentment is emphasized. *Samatha* practice aims to develop the four meditations (Pali *jhana*; Sanskrit *dhyana*), involving a type of altered state of consciousness bringing great joy, purity, and inner tranquillity [50: 325–32]. Psychic sensitivities (*iddhi*) such as clairvoyance are often described as ensuing and still higher levels of consciousness are mentioned. Since all of these states are vulnerable to loss, they are generally considered as a desirable/optional/essential preliminary (according to the school of instruction) to insight (VIPASSANA) meditation which gives more permanent results. Numerous methods of training in calm meditation are described (*see* KAMMA-TTHANA). [25; 64]

Samhain [v] The Celtic quarterly feasts were Samhain, 1 November; Imbolg, 1 February; Beltene, 1 May, and Lughnasa, 1 August [22: VI, 151–4]. Samhain marked the beginning of winter, when the way to the 'other world' lay open, as at Yule (the winter solstice) in Scandinavia. Men might be visited by supernatural powers or the dead, and might enter the *sid* (burial mounds). Irish literature has many tales of strange happenings and deaths of heroes taking place at Samhain [21: III, 89–94, XVII, 338–41].

Samkhya [XIII.B] One of the six DARSHANAS or salvation-philosophies of classical Hinduism. The system is attributed to the sage Kapila, but the earliest surviving complete account is that of the *Samkhya-karika* of Ishvara-krsna (?4th century CE) [translations: 12: 257–82; 16: 424–52]. *Samkhya* evidently developed in yogic circles responsible for parts of the post-Buddhist Upanishads (VEDA) and of the MAHABHARATA [10: 217–320; 12: 77–165]. The word *samkhya* means a collection of numbered lists, i.e. pre-literate systematic theory as opposed to YOGA 'work practice'. Probably what is intended is not so much conceptual analysis as a type of salvific knowledge

produced by investigation (cf. JNANA YOGA). *Samkhya* envisages a hierarchic universe of mind and matter emanating from a cosmic ground (PRAKRTI) owing to imbalances in the three constituent modalities (GUNA). Man (*purusha*), i.e. the spiritual or conscious element, has mistakenly identified with successively grosser levels of existence, being unaware of his essential freedom and independence. *Prakrti* mechanically performs action without consciousness; *purusha* is a conscious witness 'who neither acts nor refrains from action'. To attain liberation man must understand the difference between himself and *prakrti*. When seen, *prakrti*, 'like a shy maiden', appears no more to him. *Samkhya* posits an ultimate difference between spirit and the stuff of which mind and matter are made and a plurality of individual persons. It does not accept a supreme deity and regards the universe as eternal and real, but cyclic. Declining after the 1st millennium CE, *Samkhya* revived from about the 14th century, ultimately taking a more theistic form. Through the medium of yoga (and later VEDANTA) it has exercised a pervasive influence on Indian thought. [3; 5: 1; 11: VI; 12; 14: 114–32]

Samsara [XIII.B] A term used in religions of Indian origin. *Samsara*, literally 'wandering', is the continuing process of birth and death for life after life in many differing forms and conditions of existence. This is usually seen as involving not only lives as a human being but also periods of time (sometimes very long), either in various pleasant states as a deity (DEVA) in some kind of heaven, or in unpleasant states as an animal, spirit, or inhabitant of some kind of HELL. All such births are the result of previous actions (KARMA) and conform to a law of similarity between action and result. All of this is sometimes viewed psychologically, especially in modern interpretations, and explained as referring to changing states of mind in ordinary life. Existence in *samsara* is thought to involve suffering and to be unsatisfactory compared with the ultimate spiritual goal (MOKSHA; NIBBANA).

San Lun Tsung [X] Three Treatises school. The Chinese MADHYAMIKA school (*see also* SHUNYATAVADA) was founded by KUMARAJIVA (344–413 CE) and developed by Seng Chao (384–414) and Chi T'sang (549–623). The three texts were 'The Middle Stanzas' (*Madhyamika-Karika*) and the 'Treatise on Twelve Gates' (*Dvadashanikaya*), both by Nagarjuna, and the 'Hundred Treatises' (*Shata-Shastra*) of Aryadeva. All three texts were translated by Kumarajiva. In his essays Seng Chao makes considerable progress in interpreting basic *Madhyamika* ideas in authentically Chinese terms, and his choice of language frequently reflects his own neo-Taoist interests [7: XXI, 343–56; 32: VII, 258–69; 62]. Chi T'sang's writings 'The Two Levels of Truth' (*Er Ti Chang*) and 'The Deep Meaning of the Three Treatises' (*San Lun Hsuan I*) reflect a much more traditional and Indian approach to *Madhyamika*. (NANTO ROKUSHU) [7: XXII, 357–69; 32: VIII, 293–9; 74]

Sand-Paintings [III] By those North American Indians who use them (southwestern tribes particularly), sand-paintings are not primarily intended as works of art, but rather as powerful tools in the service of ceremonial medicine. According to NAVAJO myths, the first sand-paintings were made by the Yeis on the shifting clouds of the sky. The technique was given to mankind. Sand-paintings (or more properly, 'dry-paintings') are made during ceremonies called *sings*, which are given to restore individual and/or cosmic harmony. [13: VI] These ceremonies have two dimensions, one to cure a specific disease or to acquire holiness, the other to exorcize evil. Each type has its own myth, ritual, and set of sand-paintings. For the Navajo, a sand-painting correctly executed within the context of a *sing* becomes a kind of 'sacrament', in the sense that it does what it symbolizes. Thus the figures depicted in the sand-painting do truly represent the Yeis, and when the sick person is brought into contact with their images, she or he is brought into contact with their healing power. [19]

Sangha [IX.A] An assemblage; in the Buddhist context, assemblage of those who have formally undertaken to pursue the Buddhist life, and who accept the obligation of conforming to the body of regulations known as the VINAYA (the Discipline). Such an undertaking requires the renunciation of family and of economic and domestic ties and duties, including the cares which are attendant on the possession of material goods. The Sangha member, normally the *bhikkhu* (Pali) or *bhikshu* (Sanskrit), should possess only a bare minimum of personal goods, such as a robe, an alms-bowl, a needle for making repairs to the robe, and a water-strainer (to avoid consuming living beings in the form of insects). In principle a *bhikkhu*, or Buddhist 'monk', is *pabbajaka*, one who has 'gone forth' from home and kindred [9: 66–91].

It is within the Sangha that the DHAMMA of the BUDDHA is recited, and thus remembered and preserved. Ordination of new members is a right exercised by members of the Sangha, and from lower to higher ordination (*upasampada*). In the local assembly of the Sangha the main ceremony is the twice-monthly recitation of the PATIMOKKHA.

Sangiti [IX.A] A chanting of Buddhist texts in order to establish the authentic received form; such assemblies of Buddhist monks are usually referred to in English as 'councils'. The first of these, according to tradition, was at Rajagaha, soon after the PARINIBBANA of the BUDDHA, that is, about 480 BCE; the purpose was to agree and to affirm by chanting the authentic form of the Buddha's words in teaching. A century later another council was held at Vesali, where 700 monks assembled to deal with certain irregularities in monastic practice which had appeared, and therefore to recite the whole of the VINAYA-PITAKA once again (as at the first Sangiti), as an affirmation of the correct monastic discipline [37: 208–12]. A third council was held at Pataliputra (Patna) in the reign of the Emperor ASHOKA, in order to deal with doctrinal disputes, at the conclusion of which the entire TIPITAKA was rehearsed. Various successive councils of the same nature and for similar purposes have been held in different Buddhist countries, there being no universal agreement about the numbering of them, down to those held, in Burma, at Mandalay in 1857 and in Rangoon in 1957 [20: 59, 106f].

Sanguma [XXII] Melanesian pidgin for killing a victim by sorcery. Unlike the gradual effects of POISEN, *sanguma* involves a sudden attack by one or more supernaturally empowered assailants on a lone victim, who is tormented into insanity, ritually disembowelled, or stabbed with poisoned bones and thorns and allowed to return home believing his recovery to be impossible. Like *poisen*, *sanguma* is invoked to explain madness or sudden death and relate them to infringements within the moral order. [8; 14]

Sanhedrin [XI.A] (From Greek *synedrion*, 'council') The supreme court of the Jewish nation, first mentioned 198 BCE and mentioned again by Josephus, in the New Testament, and in rabbinical literature, though there is disparity between the descriptions of its role and functions in the various sources. Under the Hasmonaeans it was the ruler's advisory council (BIBLICAL HISTORY). Its authority was minimal under Herod (37–4 BCE). During the Roman administration it controlled Jewish internal affairs, subject to the governor's overriding authority. It comprised 71 members, the high priest being president. SADDUCEES constituted the majority; PHARISEES formed in influential minority. Its members met in the Chamber of Hewn Stone in the TEMPLE (JERU-SALEM). In this earlier form it came to an end in 66–70 CE. [16: XXIII, 199–226]

Sant [XXVII] Although the succession of Sikh GURUS ended early in the 18th century, the ancient master/disciple tradition survived within the PANTH. Many Sikhs continued to attach themselves to individual preceptors, men who disavowed the status of GURU but acquired reputations as teachers or exemplars. These preceptors eventually acquired the title of Sant, previously applied in the SANT TRADITION to any ordinary devotee. They continue to flourish within the Panth, some of them commanding substantial influence.

Sant Tradition of Northern India [XXVII] The SANT tradition of northern India is commonly confused with VAISHNAVA BHAKTI. It is, however, a distinct movement, one which draws heavily on Bhakti antecedents but also has other roots. Two major sources can be identified. Vaishnava Bhakti is one of these, and for most Sants is clearly the dominant source. To it must be added the NATH TRADITION, a source which is particularly evident in the works of Kabir (probably *c.* 1440–1518). SUFI influence may also have contributed to the development of Sant ideals. [28: IV] Like Bhakti adherents the Sants stress devotion as essential to *mukti* (SACH-KHAND). They differ in their insistence that God is *nirguna* (without form or 'qualities') and can be neither incarnated nor represented iconically (*saguna*). To the Naths they evidently owe their stress on interior religion. God, immanently revealed, is contemplated inwardly and all exterior forms are spurned. [23: 5–7] The two most prominent representatives of the tradition are Nanak (GURUS) and Kabir. [25: 151–8]

Sanusis [XIV] A SUFI ORDER, strong in North Africa and the eastern Sahara, founded by Muhammad al-Sanusi (1791–1855). It emphasized a simple, purified form of ISLAM and established *zawiyas* (SUFI INSTITUTIONS) across the Sahara as centres of evangelism, education, and

agricultural activity among the super-
ficially Islamized peoples there. After
1911, it was the spearhead of resistance
in Libya to the Italians, and after the
Second World War its leader Sayyid
Idris became King of Libya, reigning
until 1970. [46: IX; 69: 118–20; 84]

Sarvastivada [IX.A] The doctrine of an
early Buddhist philosophical school, the
Sarvastivadins, who took issue with the
Theravadins (THERAVADA) on the
question whether past and future have
equal ontological status with the present. Their texts are in Sanskrit, and
they are one of the 18 HINAYANA
schools. [7A]

Satan (in Islam) [XIV] The Devil is
termed *Iblis* (from the Greek *diabolos*,
via Judaeo-Christian intermediation)
and *al-Shaitan* (Satan). In the QUR'AN
Iblis is the angel who disobeyed God
(ALLAH) by refusing to acknowledge
God's creature Adam as his superior. He
was expelled from paradise and secured
the fall from grace of Adam and Eve (*see*
MALA'IKA). *Al-Shaitan* has the dual sig-
nification of Satan specifically, who per-
petually seeks to lead mankind astray by
his insidious suggestions, and of devils
or evil spirits in general, corresponding
here to the unbelieving JINN. However,
on the Day of Judgement (QIYAMA),
Iblis/Satan and his hosts will be consigned to hell-fire. In Islamic lore, Satan
is often given the epithet *al-Rajim* 'the
one who should be stoned', from one of
the practices traditional in the Pilgrimage to Mecca (*see* HAJJ). [20 'Shaiṭān'; 29:
50]

Satanism [XVIII] The worship of Satan
or other central figures from Christian
DEMONOLOGY. Satanism, essentially a
reaction against Christianity, has historically been a rare occurrence. From the
late Middle Ages witches were accused
of devil-worship (WITCHCRAFT), but
there is almost no reliable evidence that
it took place. The distinctive rite of
Satanism is supposedly the 'black mass' –
a blasphemous parody of the MASS,
celebrated by an unfrocked priest, with

black candles and inverted crucifix,
involving defilement of the consecrated
host (EUCHARIST), sexual indulgence
and sometimes animal or even human
sacrifice. But no description of it exists
from before the later 19th century.
Medieval heretics (HERESY) were
accused of perverting the mass, and in
17th-century France distorted versions
were occasionally celebrated for magical
purposes, but Satanism was not
involved. Modern Satanism dates from
the 19th-century 'OCCULT revival',
which included a synthetic 'revival' of
Satanism in imitation of practices attributed in previous centuries to witches
and sorcerers. Satanism continues to
lead a fitful existence among those who
find excitement in doing things they
believe to be wicked, and is sustained
partly by popular fiction and cinema
and partly by occasional ecclesiastical
denunciations, which have always tended
to stimulate interest in it. [21]

Sati [XIII.A] A term used by Hindus
meaning, literally, 'a virtuous woman'.
The word carries the special meaning of
a woman whose virtue leads her to im-
molate herself with her dead husband on
his funeral pyre. It has been suggested
that the origin of the custom was the
practice of providing a dead man, at his
funeral, with all that he would need in
the other world: his horses, possessions,
and his widow [2: 188]. It has been
regarded in Hindu society as in theory
voluntary, but social pressure was
strong enough to keep the practice in
force as late as the 19th century, in some
cases even where it was not voluntary.
In 1839 it was forbidden by Lord Ben-
tinck, following a campaign against it
by some reformist Hindus, notably
Ram Mohan Roy (1774–1833). [14:
366]

Saum [XIV] Fasting, accounted one of
the PILLARS OF ISLAM. Fasting during
the daylight hours of the month of
Ramadan is obligatory on all healthy
adults, and is still strictly observed in
most of the Islamic world. Its end is

celebrated by a festival of rejoicing, the 'Id al-Fitr (*see* 'ID). There are other voluntary fast days in the Islamic calendar, e.g. on 'Ashura day, 10 Muharram. [20 'Ṣawm'; 29: 102–4; 39 'Fasting'; 47: 160–61]

Sautrantika [IX.A] A Buddhist philosophical school, one of the 18 schools of the HINAYANA, dating from about the 1st century CE, which rejected the Abhidharma (ABHIDHAMMA) as not an authentic part of Buddhist teaching. In its view only the Sutras (or SUTTA-PITAKA) contain authentic teaching, and in these the true teaching has its 'end' (*anta*), hence the name (from *Sautra-anta-ka*). Crudely expressed, the Sautrantikas might be understood as representing a back-to-the-Sutras movement, but the analogy with Christian biblical fundamentalism (AUTHORITY, CHRISTIAN) which this might suggest would be misleading, since the Sautrantikas were not philosophically naïve. [4: 105; 5: 119–64]

Scepticism [XXVI] A religious sceptic is one who denies that there are any grounds for reasonable belief in religious matters. Scepticism is a legacy of Greek philosophy in the Western world. Often, as in the writings of the 18th-century philosopher David Hume [9], it tries to distinguish between the kind of knowledge men can achieve (that of natural science) and kinds of knowledge that are not possible (metaphysical and religious). But thorough sceptics, Hume included, have frequently found themselves obliged to deny that there are grounds for quite ordinary beliefs about the world. There has, for this reason, been a tradition of scepticism – particularly strong in 16th-century France – in which it is an ally of religion. [14] Michel de Montaigne, for instance, held that no real knowledge could be acquired by human reason and that, therefore, it could only be acquired through faith and revelation. Nowadays, however, the word 'sceptic' is more commonly applied to someone –

Bertrand Russell (1872–1970), for example – who is unsympathetic to religion.

Schleiermacher, Friedrich Daniel Ernst [XI.D] (1768–1834) After education in colleges of the Herrnhuter Brethren, Schleiermacher went to university at Halle in 1787, where in 1804 he was appointed professor, moving later (1807) to Berlin. Both in *On Religion, Speeches to Its Cultured Despisers* (1799) and *The Christian Faith* (1821), he defended religion against the rationalism of the Enlightenment by asserting that its essence lies in the feeling of absolute dependence and that the concept of God is to be derived from this feeling. [14; 19; 29]

Scholasticism [XI.C] The Christian theological method used primarily by medieval scholars to draw out the implications of revealed truths expressed by the scriptures (BIBLE) and the Fathers of the church, to establish their mutual consistency and to reconcile apparent contradictions between them and natural understanding (AUTHORITY). Although the basic principles (of the primary authority of revealed truth and of the use of logic) had long been enunciated, the method flourished, especially in the 12th and 13th centuries with the development of dialectical methods of reasoning, the use of subtle distinctions, and the incorporation of Aristotelian thought. Among the foremost scholastics are Albert the Great (*c.* 1200–1280), Aquinas (THOMISM), Bonaventura (1221–74), and Duns Scotus (*c.* 1264–1308). One basic dispute within medieval scholasticism was between realists (cf. William of Champeaux, *c.* 1070–1121), who maintained that concepts ('universals') have a mode of existence of their own, and nominalists (cf. Abelard, 1079–1142, and William of Occam, *c.* 1300 to *c.* 1349), who maintained that only actual individuals exist and that universals are abstractions from them made by the understanding. [6; 12]

Sciences of Religion [XXVIII] These are the sciences which study man (human or social sciences) and therefore man's religiousness, the religious aspects of behaviour, society, and culture, using methods which differ from those of RELIGIONSWISSENSCHAFT [4: II] and of THEOLOGY [13: II].

(a) Psychology of religion (as a science) [bibliography: 8: 320–21; 28: 165] since about 1890 has been concerned with the religious experience of individuals and groups; its topics include conversion, prayer, mysticism, and abnormal states of mind [11: VII; 15; 17: XIV; 25: V]. With the development of depth-psychology came the Freudian emphasis on religion as illusory [11: VI] and the Jungian on the significance of dreams, fantasies, MYTHS, and their SYMBOLS [17: 165–72; 25: IX; 28: 42]. These and more recent schools (e.g. the existentialist and personalist) have stimulated research in comparative studies and PHENOMENOLOGY [20: IV; 28: 38–43]. Social psychology overlaps with sociology.

(b) Sociology [24: 7–33; bibliography: 4; 8: 320–21; 28: 50–51]. FUNCTIONALISM (especially its interest in religion as a factor in the self-awareness and stability of society) found classical expression in the work of Emile Durkheim (1858–1917) [9; 11: IV; 26: II, XII]. A more dynamic and broadly comparative approach to the understanding (*Verstehen*) of religions and their development is found in the work of Max Weber (1864–1920) [11: II, III; 25: 177–8; 28: 43–6]. Recent topics of major interest include the erosion of the hold of religion on society (secularization), the explanation of its survival in developed societies, and the origin and role of specifically religious groups [4; 24]. Here there is overlap with anthropology.

(c) Anthropology [18; 28: 46–50; 30; bibliography: 1; 8: 320; 26; 28]. Traditionally applied to small-scale, non-literate, or primal society ('primal' being used by students of religion rather

than anthropologists for religious ways formerly classified together as 'animist' (ANIMISM), to avoid the apparently biased term 'primitive') [29]. The methods of the 'science of man' are proving increasingly fruitful in analysis of the complex cultures of the 'civilized' world [1: pp. xxvi–ix; 10: IV; 11: 324–9]. Accounts and theories of religion in earlier anthropology (late 19th and early 20th century) were dominated by the evolutionary approach and by the wish to explain the ORIGIN OF RELIGION. Modern anthropologists, aware of bias and a lack of empirical evidence in some earlier work, have produced e.g. very valuable studies of the religious aspects of specific cultures [1], and more general accounts of the nature and function of symbol systems [26] and of MYTH and RITUAL [18: 7; 30: III, IV].

Scientism [XXVI] The tendency to invoke the authority of science in matters commonly thought to be outside its province [6] or to elevate science to the level of a panacea for all human ills. 'Scientism' is a term of abuse with no fixed meaning. It is sometimes used by writers in MARXISM to refer to an IDEOLOGY shared by scientists [17]. It is also used to mean POSITIVISM or scientific HUMANISM.

Scientology [XXI] It was in 1950 that Dianetics [18], a form of psychotherapy, first appeared, in the U.S.A. As its founder, L. Ron Hubbard, found his researches leading him from the mind to the spirit, the movement developed into the Church of Scientology, incorporating a more religiously oriented philosophy and life-style, especially for the more 'advanced' and committed members [6]. Scientology has a complicated vocabulary of its own and it employs a special instrument for 'auditing' (counselling) known as the E-Meter. The courses offer to help the individual free him/herself of unnecessary and harmful accretions from their present and past lives and thus to release the essential, spiritual self, the Thetan.

There is a long history of criticism of the practices of Scientology from government bodies and the ANTI-CULT MOVEMENT. In 1979 eleven of the leaders were convicted on charges of theft from U.S. government offices. In 1968 the British government imposed restrictions on foreigners entering the U.K. to study, or work for, Scientology. These were lifted in 1980 after an investigation by a government inquiry (the Foster report). [2: 134; 6; 8: XI; 50]

Scriptures [1] From the Latin *scriptura* ('a writing'), a term often used loosely to denote particular holy books of diverse religions. Commonly the authority of such writings is seen as deriving from the gods (HAMMURABI'S CODE); established by some holy person by, for example, being seen in a revelation (QUR'AN); by attribution to legendary persons (CONFUCIAN CANON); by the believed spiritual potency of its words (FUNERAL PRACTICES (ANCIENT EGYPTIAN)); by its use in RITUAL (e.g. ADI GRANTH; AVESTA; VEDAS); or by a combination of such factors (BIBLE). Because revelations, however authoritative, are thought to occur in a specific time and place the interpretations, adaptations, or supplements to such revelations can also acquire considerable authority (e.g. HADITH, TORAH). The relevant weighting of scripture and the official bodies which interpret it can vary within a religion (AUTHORITY (CHRISTIAN)), as can the officially listed texts which comprise a CANON of scripture (TIPITAKA). Such official works are not necessarily the most widely read or understood books by the adherents. The written scripture is generally the product of a lengthy oral holy tradition wherein the material often has a verse or musical form to aid memorizing. The interpretation of scripture is commonly the task of a professional class of priests or scholars (HERMENEUTICS; RABBI). [2]

Sects and Societies (Chinese) [X] Sects and societies with political and religious

ideologies have frequently arisen in China during periods of disunity. The Yellow Turbans, who rebelled against the Han government in 184 CE, are an early example. Many later sects were syncretistic in nature, often reflecting a Buddhist influence, focusing upon MAITREYA BODHISATTVA. One famous example was the White Lotus Society, founded in the 12th century CE, which rebelled in 1351 and helped to overthrow the Yuan (Mongol) rulers in 1368. [40; 70; 105: IX, 218–43]

Sects (Christian) [XI.B] The term 'sect' may be used pejoratively of bodies regarded as heretical (HERESY; ORTHODOXY; SCHISM). As a neutral technical term in sociological analysis of Christianity, however, a 'sect' denotes a body with certain characteristics, such as extreme emphasis on some aspects or doctrines of the Christian tradition at the expense of others; personal conversion as a condition of membership; and condemnation of the values and institutions of ordinary society. This is contrasted with the 'church' type of Christianity, which is characterized by: a comprehensive or balanced range of teaching; membership including whole nations or requiring only minimal qualifications; and a high degree of accommodation to the values and institutions of society at large. 'Denomination' is used of bodies which are more broadly based and open to ordinary society than sects, while less comprehensive and socially tolerant than 'churches'. In this classification ANGLICANISM, the ORTHODOX CHURCH, and ROMAN CATHOLICISM would be 'churches' and METHODISM and PRESBYTERIANISM (for example) 'denominations'. (Outside sociological discussion, however, 'church' and 'denomination' are usually used simply as synonymous terms for any organized Christian body. For specialized theological uses cf. CHURCH (CHRISTIAN).) Sects often originate in a 'charismatic' leader; and a number emphasize MILLENARIANISM.

The connection often made with the socially deprived is not invariably correct. In some cases, time brings a more balanced doctrinal system and erodes separation from society (e.g. PENTECOSTALISM) [143; 144]. A large number of sects have developed in the U.S.A. [13], notably CHRISTIAN SCIENCE, JEHOVAH'S WITNESSES, and MORMONS. Extreme deviations from the mainstream of Christianity and the introduction of extensive extra-Christian elements may be held to qualify some sects as 'cults' rather than as Christian sects (AFRICA, NEW RELIGIOUS MOVEMENTS IN).

Sects (Sikh) [XXVII] Within the Sikh PANTH a fundamental difference distinguishes members of the KHALSA from those who have not taken *amrit* (baptism) and who, if they do not observe the exterior symbols of the RAHIT, are known as *Sahaj-dhari* Sikhs [23: 92–100]. The latter, lacking leadership and organization, are never regarded as a sect, and indeed it is sometimes claimed that there are no Sikh sects [26: VI]. There are, however, distinctive groups claiming to represent the true GURMAT which are commonly regarded as heretical. Four deserve notice. The earliest is the ascetic order of Udasi sadhus, followers of Nanak's son Siri Chand (GURUS) and evidently a Sikh extension of the NATH TRADITION [22: 96; 26: 58–66]. The Nirmala order is usually traced from five Sikhs sent to Banaras by Guru Gobind Singh to acquire Sanskrit learning. Widely respected for their contribution to traditional Sikh scholarship they are unorthodox in their Vedantic leanings and their celibacy. [1: 20] Nineteenth-century uncertainties produced the Nirankari movement, initiated in Peshawar by Baba Dayal (1783–1855) and stressing return to the pristine teachings of Nanak [19: 123–5]. The movement must be distinguished from a modern Delhi group of the same name. The Nirankaris are regarded as heretical principally because they accept a continuing line of living Gurus. This also applies to the Namdhari or Kuka movement, followers of Balak Singh (1797–1862) and of his more famous millenarian successor Ram Singh (1816–85). (*See also* SIKH REFORM MOVEMENTS.) [19: 127–35]

Secular Alternatives to Religion [XXVI] Discussion of alternatives to religion needs a perspective on the nature of religion. Secular alternatives are not themselves religions but must share enough in common with religions to present themselves as options which exclude religious adherence. Someone who adopted a theoretical standpoint which, for him, excluded religious belief (as, for example, SCEPTICISM and DIALECTICAL MATERIALISM commonly do) need not accept any alternative to religion. There need not be anything which plays an analogous role in his life to that of religion in the life of a believer. But there are those whose theoretical standpoint is secular but for whom certain commitments perform the same function as does adherence to a religion.

J. M. Yinger (b. 1916) [22: 190f] has offered a 'functional definition' of a religion as 'a system of beliefs and practices by means of which a group of people struggles with the ultimate problems of human life'. He suggests that POSITIVISM with its faith in science, MARXISM with its faith in revolution, and Freudianism (SCIENCES OF RELIGION) with its faith in psychoanalysis have all served as secular alternatives to religion. UTILITARIANISM seems to have functioned as such an alternative for J. S. Mill and his 'sect'. [13: 69f] So has HUMANISM, with church-like institutions such as the South Place Ethical Society in London.

Yinger himself takes the view that such alternatives can be no more than partial since they do not really come to terms with the ultimate problems of human life. In doing so he begs the question, from the point of view of those who adhere to these alternatives, as to what the ultimate problems of human life are. He implies that humans have needs which only a proper religion could satisfy. Marxists and many humanists would deny such a claim and insist, on the contrary, that religion diverts people from their true needs. This indeed is part of Marx's point in characterizing religion as IDEOLOGY. Marx himself, following Ludwig Feuerbach (1804–72) to some extent, approached religion in a spirit of REDUCTIONISM, seeing as a merely human phenomenon what its practitioners see as involving rather more. What Yinger refers to as the 'partial' nature of Marxism as a secular religion is the other side of the same coin.

Sefardim [XVII] Jews of Spanish or Portuguese origin who left the Iberian peninsula at the end of the 15th century when the Jews were expelled (EUROPEAN JEWRY), and settled in North Africa, the Levant, the Far East, and northern Europe [26: VI]. Spanish Jewish culture was highly developed and the Sefardi refugees tended to dominate the Jewish communities in the areas of their new settlement. This explains why Jews in Islamic countries have come to be known as Sefardim, although many of them are not originally of Spanish origin. Some descendants of the Sefardi refugees still put the suffix 'Sefardi Tahor' ('Pure Sefardi') after their names. Sefardi Jews differ from their ASHKENAZI co-religionists in a number of ritual and cultural ways, some of which are explicable by the differences between the Christian and Islamic host cultures in which they lived [52: 211]. More than half the population of modern ISRAEL consists of Sefardi-oriental Jews. [54]

Sefirah [XVII] One of the 10 stages in the process of divine emanation central to kabbalistic thought (KABBALAH) (plural *sefirot*) [9 vol. 14: 1104]. First

mentioned in the *Sefer Yetzirah* (3rd century), the concept is more fully developed in the ZOHAR, where the *sefirot* are depicted as manifestations of different aspects of the Godhead, *Ein Sof*, in the structuring of reality [52: 95]. The images used for the *sefirot* in kabbalistic literature are highly personalized, but the mystics themselves emphasize the divine unity behind them (*see also* SITRA ACHRA) [45: 208].

Septuagint [XI.A] The Greek translation of the Hebrew BIBLE, begun at Alexandria in the 3rd century BCE for the benefit of the Greek-speaking Jewish community in that city. The Pentateuch (the first five books) was translated first: according to tradition its translators were 70 or 72 elders of Israel (hence the title of the version, from Latin *septuaginta*, '70'). Since the 1st century CE the Septuagint has been the standard version of the Hebrew Bible for Greek-speaking Christians. [1: 146–62; 6: 1, 141–9, 159–79]

Seth [IV] The Egyptian figure of Seth, represented as a mythical, pig-like animal (ANIMAL CULTS), and identified with Typhon by the Greeks, was originally an important pre-dynastic deity whose supporters fought the 'Followers of Horus' (OSIRIAN TRIAD). In Plutarch's Myth of Osiris (*c.* 100 CE) [14], Seth, as the embodiment of evil, murders Osiris. The Hyksos (who ruled in Egypt *c.* 1600 BCE) identified him with their god BA'AL and he achieved some support in the 19th dynasty (*c.* 1300 BCE). The success of the Osiris cult ensured the eventual destruction of most Sethian representations [23].

Seva [XXVII] In the early Sikh PANTH *seva* meant service rendered to Guru and *sangat* (the gathered community). When the line of personal GURUS ended, this obligation shifted to the abode of the eternal Guru, the GURDWARA. *Seva* was thus directed to *sangat* and *gurdwara*, which in practice meant such activities as maintaining the premises or serving in the *langar*. This remains the dominant concept [26: 111], although the modern ideal also embraces humanitarian service in a broad sense. [17: 12; 24: 263]

Sex, Christianity and [XI.B] Traditional Christian teaching sharply differentiates the sexes and their roles. Women have been subordinated to men, commonly excluded from the MINISTRY (WOMEN (IN EARLY CHRISTIANITY)), and suspected by some ascetics as sources of temptation. At the same time the place of the Virgin MARY and of female SAINTS is prominent in Catholic devotion (ROMAN CATHOLICISM). Sexuality was closely connected with SIN (especially following St Augustine (AUGUSTINIANISM)) and MARRIAGE regarded as a remedy for it. Pursuit of holiness in MONASTICISM involved a vow of chastity (abstention from sex and marriage); and virginity was highly valued. Homosexuality [23], abortion, and contraception as well as fornication (sex between unmarried persons) and adultery (sex between persons married to other partners) have all traditionally been regarded as serious sins. Roman Catholicism and some SECTS in PROTESTANTISM have been particularly severe. But in recent years many Christians have taken a much more positive view of sexuality as good if rightly used. Artificial contraception is widely practised, even among Roman Catholics (despite condemnation by the PAPACY, in 1968). Some Christians also accept the legitimacy of abortion and homosexuality. Recognition of women's rights and their role in the church has been improved under feminist influence. [93: 316–18, 360–62]

Shabad [XXVII] Shabad (shabda, 'word') has two related meanings in SIKH usage. For Nanak (GURUS) it designated the divine revelation, the 'Word' which mystically communicates the message of nam (GURMAT). [3: 297; 25: 191–4] As Nanak himself came to be regarded as the inspired communicator of the Shabad his hymns were treated as its actual

expression. This belief was necessarily extended to all who succeeded him as Guru, and shabad thus became the generic term for any hymn recorded in the ADI GRANTH. [24: 240–41, 288]

Shabbat [XVII] Saturday, the Jewish sabbath, is a day of complete rest for the traditional Jew, as its Hebrew name Shabbat ('Rest') indicates. It celebrates the creation of the world by God and its total dependence on him (Genesis 2: 1–3, Exodus 20: 8–11). It also commemorates the redemption of the Israelites from slavery in Egypt (EXODUS) (Deuteronomy 5: 12–15). In some degree it has been incorporated into traditional Christian practice, although JESUS was criticized for his apparent laxity regarding Sabbath laws. Rabbinical literature sees in the Shabbat and its rituals one of the most distinctive aspects of Israel's COVENANT relationship with God [52: 169]. The TALMUD sets out the 39 main categories of work prohibited on the sabbath [7: 154]. The Shabbat rituals include the lighting of at least two candles by the woman of the household before sundown on Friday evening when Shabbat begins; kiddush (sanctification of the day), recited over wine on Friday evening and at Saturday lunch-time; and a ceremony of separation (havdalah) with blessings recited over wine, spices, and a candle flame on Saturday night when Shabbat terminates. [9 vol. 14: 557]

Shah [XXX] 'King', of Iran. In Zoroastrian Iran (ZOROASTRIANISM) it was believed that the good king was chosen by AHURA MAZDA because of his righteous support for truth and his opposition to evil. In royal art the king was depicted as having superhuman size and strength, with which he overcame human and cosmic forces of chaos. His presence was veiled from ordinary mortals. Legends surround the birth of many of these monarchs, and honorifics such as 'brother of the sun and moon' were applied to them, but they were not thought of as divine (as a PHAROAH was). Divine grace (*khvarenah*; Pahlavi *khwarr*) was given to the righteous king but this could be withdrawn if he sinned. A classic example of this was the mythical king Yima (Jamshid in later texts). His reign established the ideal kingdom, which all monarchs should seek to emulate, one where justice, order, and bounteousness abounded. But then he committed the sin of pride and falsehood, and the *khvarenah* left him. Religion and politics were interwined in Zoroastrianism. ZOROASTER himself had sought and obtained a royal patron and throughout the history of Zoroastrian Iran kings and priests worked together. Kings were often shown in art in a priestly posture and Pahlavi writers stressed the unity of religion and kingship; as one (Tansar, 3rd century CE) put it, they are 'brothers, born of one womb, never to be separated' [20: 97–109; 50: XIV].

Shahada [XIV] The profession of faith, considered to be one of the PILLARS OF ISLAM: 'There is no God but God, and Muhammad is His messenger.' It is an essential element of the Muslim worship (SALAT) and the formula by which one professes Islam. [29: 70]

Shahname [XXX] 'The Book of Kings', composed in Persian by a poet under the pseudonym of Firdausi, 'the Paradisal', in the 11th century CE. Firdausi gave final shape to an ancient heroic and epic tradition, using in particular a Persian translation of the PAHLAVI *Khwaday Namag*, a text written by four Zoroastrian priests (ZOROASTRIANISM) which is unfortunately no longer extant. The *Shahname* surveys the history of Iran from the time of creation until the Muslim invasion, transforming myth into legend for the earlier period. The narrative is characterized more by a love of Iran than of Islam and displays an element of fatalism typical of its genre [29].

Shaikh [XIV] Originally Arabic for 'elder', *shaikh* is widely used in both Islamic religious and secular contexts for 'leader, person accorded respect', e.g. in a tribe or other social grouping. One particular usage was in the title 'Shaikh al-Islam' for the supremely recognized scholar or legal expert in a region or state; this office persisted in Ottoman Turkey until 1924 [20 'Shaikh al-Islam']. Among the SUFI ORDERS, the shaikh (Persian *pir*, Turkish *baba*) was the head of the community, often with a spiritual pedigree going back to the founder, and his postulants were known as *murids*, i.e. 'seekers (after spiritual enlightenment)'. [69 glossary]

Shakti [XIII.A] The female personification of power, as a Hindu deity; the active aspect of deity, usually represented in Hindu tradition as a goddess, such as DURGA, KALI, or PARVATI. [1: 313f; 4: 253–7; 24B]

Shaman [VII] One whose supernormal powers as a practitioner of the sacred (e.g. as healer, seer, or conductor of souls) are attributed to contact with spirits when in an ecstatic state [2: 1–9; 4: XVIII; 6: 43–70, 134–205]. 'Shaman' is the name given to such specialists by the Tungus of Siberia. The term is used more widely to denote anyone performing a similar role among other Arctic peoples (e.g. the Chukchi, ESKIMOS, and LAPPS). By further extension, the term is employed as a technical one in the SCIENCES OF RELIGION, and shamanism is described as occurring in many cultures of e.g. Africa, Indonesia, ancient Israel, and JAPAN. Sometimes, it is the dominant form of religious expression; elsewhere it may be an isolated or peripheral phenomenon. [6: 297]

Shamans are not medicine-men in the sense in which the term is used of African or Pacific religious practitioners, nor are they sorcerers or priests. As intermediaries between the spirit-world and the people, they claim direct contact with spirits, whether those of living persons, of plants, animals, and other features of the environment, with the 'master-spirits' (e.g. of rivers or mountains), or with 'ghosts' of the dead. The interaction occurs in a trance state, often induced by dancing and/or drumming (as among the Lapps). In ecstasy, the shaman may become aware of things far off, be able to foretell the future or predict movements of game, and be capable of remarkable feats (swallowing hot embers, self-stabbing without wounding). The functions of shamanism in its setting in the harsh world of the Arctic related closely to the struggle for existence (i.e. the battle with nature, not with other tribes). Thus, the Copper Eskimos of northern Canada sought the aid of the *angákoq* (shaman) not only to cure the sick, but also to quell storms, attack or destroy evil spirits, and to procure seal and caribou for the hunt. [*See also* 1: 171–5; 3: 442; 4; 5: 45–7; 7: 216–17; 9: 121–4; 10: XXV]

Shambhala [XXIX] In Tibetan Buddhist mythology, Shambhala, a land held to be situated to the north of Tibet, is the mystic kingdom ruled by the lineage holders of the Kalachakra TANTRA (2) (Wheel of Time tantra). It is said that king Suchandra of Shambhala received this tantra from BUDDHA in the latter's 80th year and entrusted it to his successors [13], the last of whom, Rigden Pema Karpo, is expected to return and establish Shambhala as a universal kingdom.

Shang Ti [X] 'Lord on High.' Originally the main deity of the Chinese Shang period (1523–1027 BCE). He was not seen as the creator of the world, but controlled the orderly progress of the seasons. He was also a warrior-god responsible for defending the Shang population. After the overthrow of the Shang by the Chou dynasty in 1027 BCE the functions and identity of Shang Ti gradually merged with the more abstract *T'ien* (Heaven), supreme being of the Chou. [81: II, 12–15; 86: I, 4–5]

Shankara [XIII.B] An influential Indian religious philosopher (probably 8th century CE). Shankara developed the ideas of Gaudapada and established the authoritative form of ADVAITA VEDANTA. Many of the works attributed to him are probably not authentic, but important commentaries on the BRAHMA-SUTRA and various Upanishads (VEDA) are certainly the work of Shankara. He may also have been the author of a number of devotional hymns. Shankara appears to have been responsible for the organization of orders of Hindu mendicants (*sannyasins*) and the foundation of four major centres, at Shrngeri and elsewhere. The heads of these institutions, called *Shankaracaryas*, exercise considerable influence over Smarta and many Shaiva (SHIVA) Hindus. Shankara himself is widely recognized as an emanation of Shiva.

Shari'a [XIV] Literally 'clear path', the term for the canon law of ISLAM, the totality of God's prescriptions for mankind, hence considered of divine origin and not the result of human legislation. It is essentially concerned with man's outward conformity to the laws of Islam. As a consequence many authorities assert that these external observances must be supplemented by good intentions and inner faith (IMAN), and the Sufis (SUFISM) regard the Shari'a as only the minimal starting-point for the adept embarking on the Sufi path of self-enlightenment. The Shari'a includes the so-called PILLARS OF ISLAM, binding on all adult male believers. Its prescriptions have been classified on a scale of desirability as: obligatory, recommended, legally indifferent, disapproved, or prohibited. The Sunni mainstream (SUNNA) bases the Shari'a on: the QUR'AN; the traditions of the Prophet MUHAMMAD and early Muslims; the consensus of the community (IJMA'); and analogical reasoning (*qiyas*), where the previous three factors provide no explicit guidance [10 s.v.; 20 s.v.; 31: VI; 47: VI; 61: VI] SHI'ISM stresses the Qur'an, the body of traditions from 'ALI and his family, and the consensus of the Shi'i scholars or *mujtahids*. Even in the early centuries of Islam, a secular law (*qanun*) existed alongside the Shari'a, and in many parts of the Islamic world local custom ('*ada*) had remained influential (*see for example* SOUTH-EAST ASIA, ISLAM IN). In modern times, with the introduction of Western-type codes in most West Asian countries, the Shari'a has tended to shrink; in this process one of the most resistant spheres has been that of personal law, including marriage and inheritance. [13: XI–XIV; 65: XIII–XV]

Shay [IV] In ancient Egypt fate was personified as a goddess, Shay, whose name meant 'that which is decreed' [18: 269]. Associated with the creator-god Khnum, Shay was present at birth and, after death, at the 'Day of Judgement' (AFTERLIFE). The Egyptian view of fate or destiny encompassed the individual's life-span, appointed at birth, and the manner of the person's death. Less frequently, it meant the content of his or her life – favourable events and misfortune.

Shekhinah [XVII] The 'Divine Presence', the most general Jewish term for the immanence of God in the world (THEISM). Among the many names or descriptions of God in rabbinical literature (RABBI) the *Shekhinah* represents the closeness of God to man, and God's loving concern for humanity [21: 61]. The TALMUD pictures the *Shekhinah* as having gone into EXILE with the exile of the Jewish people from the HOLY LAND. There are no implications of DUALISM or POLYTHEISM in the aggadic (AGGADAH) imagery of the *Shekhinah* [7: 42]. For the kabbalists (KABBALAH) the *Shekhinah* is the 10th SEFIRAH, the most distinctly female element within the divine structure [45: 226]. Through the *Shekhinah* the flow of divine energy comes down to earth. Man's sins enable the powers of evil to gain control of the *Shekhinah* and disrupt this flow, causing disharmony and catastrophe for the world. The TEMPLE

and the Tabernacle (*Mishkan*) erected in the wilderness after the EXODUS from Egypt were thought of as representing the indwelling of God. [9 vol. 14: 1349]

Shema [XVII] Biblical passages affirming the unity of God, the complete love with which he must be served, and the acceptance of his commandments, which are recited twice daily in the Jewish liturgy. [13: 94] The three paragraphs of the *Shema* are Deuteronomy 6: 4–9, and 11: 13–21 and Numbers 15: 37–41, the last of which contains a reference to God's redeeming acts in history as exemplified in the EXODUS from Egypt. The *Shema* is also recited by the believer before retiring at night, and by the dying man. [48: 41–2]

Shichi Fukujin [XVI] Seven gods of good luck in Japan. Along with various household and travellers' guardians, these seven gods, combined from sources as distant as India, function as a group. They travel together on the *Takarabune* ('Treasure Ship') [17: 411–14], and are often seen around the home as small images. They are: Bishamonten, connoting riches; Benten, the only female, which connotes good luck and music; Ebisu, good fortune; Daikoku, the father of Ebisu and identified with Okuninushi-no-mikoto, wealth (IZUMO TAISHA); Fukurokuju, long life; Hotei, prosperity; and Jurojin, longevity.

Shi'ism [XIV] One of the two great forms (the other being Sunnism – SUNNA) of ISLAM. Originally referring to the 'partisans (*shi'a*) of 'ALI', this group developed over the centuries its own body of law (differing only in certain minor directions, e.g. inheritance and the status of women, from that of the majority Sunnis) and theology. It also proved fissiparous, one of the most significant offshoots from the main body of Imami or 'Twelver' Shi'ism being the ISMA'ILIS. Shi'i tenets involve the recognition of 'Ali and his descendants as the true IMAMS [general surveys: 10 'Shi'a'; 17; 20 'Shī'a'; 29: 37–42; 41]. Although numerically a minority within Islam, various Shi'i dynasties achieved political and military power in medieval Islam (*see for example* CALIPH, CALIPHATE). An especially important event was the conversion of Persia in the 16th century from Sunnism to Shi'ism by the Safavid dynasty (ISLAMIC DYNASTIES) [46: II–VI, X]. Today, Shi'is are significant above all in Iran, Iraq, and the Indo-Pakistan subcontinent, but there are also communities in Turkey, Syria, Lebanon, East Africa, and eastern Arabia. The Iranian Revolution of 1978–9 has reawakened Shi'i consciousness in parts of the Islamic world adjoining Iran (*see also* AYATULLAH).

Shilluk Religion [II] The Shilluk, a small sedentary Nilotic people living on the west bank of the Nile around Fashoda, have provided a famous example of divine kingship. Juok (JOK), creator of the world and of all peoples, is occasionally invoked, but the central figure of Shilluk religion is Nyikang, the hero who led them in migration to their present home and founded the Shilluk kingdom and its customs. Although descended from Juok, Nyikang was a man, while his mother, Nyakaya, was a river creature, like a crocodile. The doer of many marvellous deeds, Nyikang led his people across the river, fought with the sun, never died, and is closely linked with Juok. He lives on in each *reth*, the sacred king upon whom the order and prosperity of the Shilluk depend.

There are shrines for Nyikang all over Shillukland. In his solemn installation the *reth* is captured by the image of Nyikang in a mock battle and then possessed by his spirit. He is the chief priest for rain and victory in war, and all national misfortune is blamed upon him. Traditionally, if his powers waned, he could be suffocated by his wives or killed by a rival, so that Nyikang might possess a fitter reincarnation.

The moral qualities associated with the *reth* and prized by the Shilluk are those of courage, military success, cleverness, and passion [4: 138–63; 24: IV].

Shingon [XVI] Shingon (= Chinese CHEN YEN), the True Word, a tantric Buddhist sect (TANTRA (2)), was introduced to Japan by the priest KUKAI, who had been sent to China in 804 CE [13: 49–58; 16; 34: 149–84]. Ten years after his return in 806 he built a modest meditation place on Mount Koya in Wakayama prefecture, which later became the Kongobu-ji, the centre of Shingon Buddhism, where he is also buried. His *Juju Shinron* of 822 is a 10-volume exposition of spiritual attainment, later abbreviated to three volumes entitled *Hizoboyaku* (The Jewel Key to the Store of Mysteries). To demonstrate the supremacy of Shingon, he graded the doctrines in 10 steps, from subhuman desires, moralism, undemanding mysticism, two levels of THERAVADA, MAHAYANA, Hosso (NANTO ROKUSHU), TENDAI, and Kegon to, finally, the esoteric Shingon. Kukai brought painted mandalas from China, magical diagrams symbolizing the Kongo-kai, the Diamond or permanent cycle (*Vajradhatu*), and the Taizo-kai, the Womb or material cycle (*Garbha-dhatu*). Central to Shingon beliefs is Dainichi (*Mahavairocana*), Buddha of Infinite Light. Dainichi is the source of all existence, absolute and permanent, through whom Buddhahood is attained in this life. Dainichi is an expanded concept of Roshana Buddha of the Kegon and Ritsu sects (NANTO ROKUSHU). Called *mikkyo*, secret teachings of Dainichi Nyorai (esoteric sects refer to Buddhas as Nyorai, not Butsu), including a large pantheon, were revealed only to the initiated. Sculpture and painting were thought to serve as mediums in transmitting divinity to believers, particularly images of the five Buddhas of the Kongo-kai – Ashuku, Hosho, Amida (AMIDA

WORSHIP), Fukujoju, and Dainichi –
and of the Taizo-kai – Dainichi, Hodo,
Kaifuke, Muryoju, and Tenkuraion
[22: 77]. The chief of the Godai-myo-o
(Five *Vidyarajas*) is Fudo (*Acala*), who
is the most frequently represented
Shingon bodhisattva (JAPANESE
BUDDHAS). Shingon today has about 45
sects and subsects called *shu* (16 listed)
and *ha* (22 listed), and by other organizational names [19: 194–8]. The To-ji in
Kyoto is the chief temple for esoteric
practices.

Shinto [XVI] The religion indigenous to
Japan. It was so named (from the
Chinese *shin tao*, 'way of the gods') in
the 8th century, after Buddhism was
introduced, to distinguish the two religions. In Japanese it was probably then
called *kami-no-michi* [general surveys: 8:
98–147; 17; 19: 29–45; 30; 32]. As a set
of prehistoric agricultural ceremonies, it
was never endowed with a supporting
body of philosophical or moralistic
literature (SHINTO LITERATURE). Early
shamans (MIKO) performed the ceremonies; eventually those of the Yamato
tribe did so on behalf of the other tribes
and their chieftain assumed duties that
led to headship of the Shinto state. Shinto became political by the 8th century
when Yamato writers ascribed divine
origins to the imperial family and so
claimed legitimacy for rule (KOKUTAI
SHINTO).

Shinto ceremonies are designed to
appeal to the KAMI, the powers of
nature, for benevolent treatment and
protection, and consist of abstinence
(*imi*), offerings, prayers, and purification (HARAE; MATSURI). Community
ceremonies take place at fixed times
during the year, and visits to SHINTO
SHRINES are made at stages marking
life's progress. The *kami* are the mysterious forces of nature associated primarily with permanent topographical
features, in particular unusual mountains (SACRED MOUNTAINS), rocky
cliffs, caves, springs, trees, and stones.
Hosts of folk tales have evolved around

these holy spots. The tales often refer to
animal possession, chiefly involving
foxes, racoon-dogs, badgers, dogs, and
cats bewitching people, more often
women than men. Celestial bodies play
only incidental roles as Shinto *kami*.

Shinto stresses the importance of purity, and since death and a variety of
other pollutions are to be avoided, Shinto is concerned primarily with life and
the benefits of this world, which are
seen as divine gifts. Ethically, what is
good for the group is morally proper.
Devotion and sincerity are expected.
Aberrations can be erased by purification. Purification procedures make
worshippers presentable, and therefore
their pleas acceptable to the *kami*. Traditionally, the village head maintains the
shrine for the tribal deity, *ujigami*,
the group known as *ujiko* (SHINTO
SHRINES).

A 1339 treatise on Shinto, politics,
and history, *Jinno Shotoki*, was used as a
guide to the above practices and administrative procedures until the early
Meiji period (1868–1912). The religion
was then divided into Shrine Shinto
(*Jinja*) and Sectarian Shinto (*Kyoha*). An
Imperial Rescript on Education made it
the formal foundation of the state, taking as its authority the work of the Mito
school, that is, the *Dai Nippon-shi*, the
large history of Japan written by Tokugawa Mitsukuni (1628–1700), *daimyo*
(lord) of Mito (now Ibaragi prefecture).
The divinity of the emperor was
stressed (KOKUTAI SHINTO), based on
Confucian concepts of loyalty to the
emperor and the state (CONFUCIUS).
After the Second World War Shinto lost
its status as an official religion, shrine
membership was not required, and
contributions became voluntary. The
'nationalization' of Yasukuni shrine,
home of the remains of the war dead, is
a current issue.

Shinto Literature [XVI] SHINTO has
no philosophical literature in which the
religious beliefs are explained and the
nature of divinity is rationalized, but a

written SHINTO MYTHOLOGY exists. There is also literature on the laws governing the indigenous religion, the procedures for SHINTO SHRINE ceremonies, and the administrative structure controlling shrines and ceremonies. By the 7th century a family of professional priests, Nakatomi, the ancestors of the later Fujiwara, the ruling family of the 10th–12th centuries, with divine descent were qualified to transmit the practices orally and in writing. The first texts are the earliest books of the *Rokkokushi* (Six National Histories), namely the *Kojiki* (Records of Ancient Matters), presented to the court in 712 CE, and the *Nihongi* or *Nihon Shoki* (Chronicles of Japan), completed in 720 [translations: 2; 10]. The former concludes with the year 628, but the final century is dealt with exclusively by genealogical lists. The latter is much fuller, and terminates with the reign of Empress Jito in 696. Both contain the myths, transition from KAMI to human rule, accounts of reigns, and many references to the building of Shinto shrines and Buddhist temples, and to cyclical and special worship ceremonies (MATSURI). These two books formed the basis of the literal beliefs accepted by the Japanese in their most nationalistic periods, in particular the phase leading to the Second World War. Following these are the *Shoku Nihongi* (Continuing Chronicles of Japan), completed in 797 and covering the period up to 791, and three others with content up to 853, after which official recording was terminated, albeit lectures on the *Nihon Shoki* were delivered at the Heian (Kyoto) court for about another century. The literature on the laws is a substantial body of 50 books known as *Engishiki*, named after the Engi era (901–22), completed in 927 [6]. The first 10 volumes are directions for executing the *Jingi-ryo*, the laws dealing with Shinto and shrine ceremonies, as well as the administrative organization and duties of the JINGI-KAN, the bureau of *kami* affairs. Book 8 contains most of the

official prayers and liturgies known as *norito* [31].

Shinto Mythology [XVI] The mythology of Japan is embodied in the early sections of the 8th-century books *Kojiki* and *Nihon Shoki* (SHINTO LITERATURE), where the course of events is described by Yamato court scholars to validate divine imperial origins [translations and general surveys: 2.1: 1–108; 10: 15–164; 17: 227–388]. A less significant cycle for the Izumo area (IZUMO TAISHA) is preserved in the 8th-century *Izumo Fudoki*. Much cosmology is taken from Chinese sources. The cosmos resembling an egg in shape, separated. The place above, *Takamagahara*, the High Plain of Heaven, was presided over by Takamimusubi (*musubi-no-kami* = KAMI of the mysterious generative spirit [19: 14]), and exists only to propagate the land below. After seven generations, Izanagi and Izanami created the Eight-Island Country (Oyashimaguni) of brine drops from a spear-tip. Further creations climaxed with AMATERASU-OMIKAMI (Sun Goddess). Evil was represented in the person of her brother Susano-o. Below the High Plain of Heaven is *Nakatsu-kuni*, Middle Land, identifiable with the Eight-Island Country, and then a lesser-known *Tokoyo-no-kuni* (originally a distant land across the sea), a spirit world which is good but not better than this world since many would like to return here. Finally, there is *Yomi-no-kuni*, a cavernous underground space which, although populated by hideous creatures charged with blocking the exit of the newly arrived dead, is not thought of as a place of punishment. Death and purification (HARAE) were introduced when Izanami died on the birth of the Fire God and went to *Yomi-no-kuni*. After trying and failing to extricate her, Izanagi went off to purify himself in a river. The Sun Goddess eventually dispatched her grandson Ninigi-no-mikoto to rule the land after being assured of ultimate success, and he and

his followers fought their way from
south Japan to the Yamato plain with
divine help. Ancient writers terminated
the so-called Age of the Gods with the
first 'emperor', but exceptionally long
reigns with little content continue
through the first nine rulers until Sujin
(*c.* 3rd century CE) [2.1: 109–49; 10: 164–
212], who may be the first historical
personality of the Yamato tribe.

Shinto Shrines [XVI] Shrines of all
sizes, in groves of trees, are noticeable features of the Japanese landscape
[17: 92–131; 32: 145–504]. The first
were probably shamans' houses (*see*
MIKO), set apart and distinguished by
being placed on a raised floor like the
earliest storehouses, unpainted types
being known as *shinme* (at ISE JINGU)
and *taisha* (at IZUMO TAISHA). Shrine
architecture has distinctive features. All
shrines have sacred gates (*torii*), but
other features depend on the size and
purpose of the shrine. Larger ones have
an offering-building like a gate (*heiden*),
beyond which worshippers normally do
not go, an oratory (*haiden*), and main
hall (*honden*) [30: 26–39]. Within the
main hall is the *goshintai* (god-body) or
mitamashiro (spirit-substance), often a
mirror, but more often nothing. Sacred
areas are marked off by straw ropes
(*shimenawa*), and evergreen *sakaki* trees
(*Cleyera ochnacea* or *Cleyera japonica*)
grow in prominent places. Shinto
architecture often includes Buddhist
temple characteristics, but roofs in particular remain distinctive, with *chigi* and
katsuogi, the V-shaped gable extensions
and ridge logs for weights. Several
styles are recognized from the Heian
period (794–1185). The Kasuga, Nagare,
and HACHIMAN types are generally
distinguished by their roof shapes and
porches, the Hachiman by a pair of
buildings under a single roof. Most are
painted in red and white. Shrines often
have a pair of stone 'lions', borrowed
from Chinese and Buddhist sources.
Many shrines have special KAMI, such
as INARI, fox shrines [17: 504–10],

shinme, horse shrines [17: 101], and
okami, wolf shrines [17: 103]. Ise and
Isonomori have live, long-tailed cocks
as symbols of the Sun Goddess
AMATERASU-OMIKAMI, as the crowing
of the rooster helped to lure her out of
the cave in which she had hidden and
restored the light. *Mikoshi* are the port-
able shrines carried in processions
(IZUMO TAISHA; TOSHOGU SHRINE).

Ship-Funeral [V] The ship had been a
funeral symbol in Scandinavia in the
Bronze Age, but in the 7th century CE it
began to be used in burials and cremations on an elaborate scale. The most
famous ship-burials are those of
SUTTON HOO in Suffolk in England
(7th century), Oseberg and Gokstad in
Norway (9th century), and those in the
Vendel and Valsgarde cemeteries in
Sweden. Ship-graves are also found in
areas of Viking settlement, including
Russia. The dead were laid in richly
equipped ships, with ritual objects,
weapons, personal possessions, and
often several horses, as well as cattle,
dogs, and birds. Women as well as men
were granted ship-funerals, and the
practice may have been associated with
the cult of the VANIR, the deities of
fertility who had the ship as a symbol
[7: VI, 111–23]. Boats, or parts of boats,
were used in humbler graves, and the
practice was known in pre-Christian
East Anglia (England) as well as in
Scandinavia.

Shiva/Shaiva [XIII.A] Shiva is one of
the major Hindu deities. In the Rig-
Veda (VEDA) he was known as Rudra
and was a minor deity, addressed in
three hymns only [3: 109]. As Shiva he
later becomes one of the three principal
gods of the pantheon, after absorbing
some of the characteristics of an indigenous fertility god, evidence of whose
cult is found in the INDUS VALLEY culture, and who is sometimes referred to
in modern works as 'proto-Shiva'. The
fully developed Shiva combines contrasting features: he is represented as
moral and paternal, but also as lurking

in inauspicious places such as battlefields and burial grounds. By another of his names he is the great god of Time (*mahakala*), destroying all things [2: 309f]. An aspect of Shiva derived from his Indus valley origins is his asceticism. He is the great yogi who dwells on Mount Kailasa in the high Himalayas, deep in the meditation which maintains the world's existence. He is also Nataraja, the Lord of the Dance, and is frequently depicted in this form iconically. He has a number of attendants known as Ganas, chief of whom is GANESHA/GANAPATI. His principal symbolic representation, however, is the *lingam*, a phallic emblem derived from the Indus valley culture. [4: 188–203; 6A; 16; 16A: 154–74]

The adjective *Shaiva* indicates that which belongs to, is sacred to, or is derived from Shiva, and most usually as a noun refers to a devotee or worshipper of Shiva.

Shomu [XVI] The Emperor Shomu (699–756 CE). Born Prince Obito, son of Emperor Mommu, he succeeded his aunt Empress Gensho in 727 and was responsible for spreading Buddhism in Japan. He ordered all the 66 province headquarters to have *sutras* read, make Yakushi BUDDHA images (JAPANESE BUDDHAS AND BODHISATTVAS), build seven-storeyed pagodas (buildings usually housing relics of the Buddha) (740), and then complete monasteries and nunneries (741) [21: 6–61], called *kokubun-ji* and *kokubunni-ji*. These were to have a healing effect, following a smallpox plague in 737. No original buildings of these provincial temples remain, but some operate today as minor temples and others exist as protected archaeological sites. Shomu erected the Todai-ji, the immense temple in Nara with its enormous bronze Roshana Buddha, dedicated in 752 (NANTO SHICHIDAI-JI) [24: 119–26]. He was the first male ruler to abdicate, which he did in 749 in order to devote more time to his Buddhist interests. His collection

of thousands of fine decorated objects of every sort is preserved in the Shoso-in, a wooden storehouse in the compound of the Todai-ji in Nara (JAPAN, BUDDHISM IN).

Shona Religion [II] The Shona of Zimbabwe consist of a number of related peoples, and their traditional religion was neither identical nor unchanging. In the 17th century, according to a Portuguese observer, the Mutapa Shona believed in one God, named MULUNGU or Umbe, and in ancestor spirits, *midzimu* (MIZIMU), especially the (more powerful) spirits of dead kings. The modern pattern is not dissimilar. God is now named MWARI (of unsure origin). His cult is far more prominent in the south, around the central shrine-cave at Matonjeni, than in the north. The prayers of ordinary Shona are normally directed to their dead ancestors, the *midzimu*, who may pass them on, probably via the tribal spirits (*mhondoro*), to God. The *mhondoro* (literally 'lion') is perhaps the most characteristic feature of Shona religion, especially in the north. They are a hierarchy of the most powerful ancestor spirits, those of dead kings and chiefs (the highest being Chaminuka and Dzivaguru), each of which has its own territorial area, special cult, and medium. The name of the spirit is taken by the medium, so that the two become almost identified in popular tradition. They are rain-makers, linked each with a sacred pool, and closest to Mwari, whose characteristics they largely share. Thus *Dzivaguru* (great pool) is both Mwari's most favoured praise-name at Matonjeni and the leading *mhondoro* in the north-east.

Other aspects of Shona religion include belief in witchcraft, in various evil or dangerous spirits (called *shavi* and *ngozi*), and in the ministrations of the NGANGA. [1: 104–27; 9: 341–50; 13: 235–55; 23]

Shotoku [XVI] Prince Shotoku, Buddhism's most sainted personality in Japan, was born the son of Emperor Yomei, named Toyosato Yatsumimi [21: 61–3; 23: 371–462]. He was appointed crown prince (*Taishi*) and regent by his aunt Empress Suiko in 594 and received the title of *Jogu* (Upper Palace). He welcomed Korean priests, studied the *sutras*, built temples, most notably the Shitenno-ji and Horyu-ji, and is credited with the so-called Seventeen-Article Constitution, a brief series of Confucian moralistic guides only one of which has Buddhistic content: respect for the BUDDHA. He was already a legendary figure by the 8th century when the *Nihon Shoki* was written (SHINTO LITERATURE) [2.1: 122–48]. His birth was sudden and painless, and it was said that he could then communicate fluently. He had a prodigious memory and his prognostications were accurate. He died after a one-month illness and was buried at Shinaga, now Taishi-cho, Osaka. The Taishi cult was fully developed when Fujiwara Kanesuke wrote the *Shotoku Taishi Denryaku* (Biography of Crown Prince Shotoku) in 917. Numerous feats, miracles, and predictions were attributed to him and he was described as a reincarnated Buddha whose life had similarities to that of Siddhartha (GOTAMA). All later sects, including ZEN, gained wider acceptance by claiming inspiration from the teachings of the prince.

Shugendo [XVI] The formal Japanese practices of *yamabushi*, mountain ascetics, who climb SACRED MOUNTAINS to become spirit-possessed, exorcize evil spirits (HARAE), and transmit the will of the KAMI to local villagers [4: 165–6, 198–201; 13: 57–8; 14]. Organized into *ko*, groups, they are closely connected with the esoteric Buddhist sects of SHINGON and TENDAI. En-no-Gyoja (En-no-Ozunu or En-no-Shokaku) of the late 6th century is revered as the first *yamabushi*, having acquired this status after visiting Mount Mino in Osaka. Shugendo was spread widely in the 9th century by a priest, Shobo. It was officially banned in 1872 as corrupted SHINTO, but *yamabushi* are still active today.

Shulchan Arukh [XVII] The most authoritative code of Jewish law, composed by the SEFARDI sage RABBI Joseph Caro in the late 16th century with glosses by Rabbi Moses Isserles, who included ASHKENAZI HALAKHAH and customs [9 vol. 14: 1475]. The name means 'prepared table', and it was intended to present the *halakhah* in a brief and easily accessible form [12: 13]. Its four sections, which deal with different aspects of Jewish ritual life, are called 'Orach Chayim', 'Yoreh Deah', 'Even Ha-Ezer', and 'Choshen Mishpat'. [52: 124]

Shunyatavada [IX.B] One of the two main forms of systematic MAHAYANA Buddhist thought, also known as MADHYAMIKA. Although preceded by a more inspired *sutra* literature, Mahayana treatises (*shastra*) written in classical Sanskrit appear to have begun with the writings of Nagarjuna (*c.* 2nd century CE). In the influential *Madhyamaka-karika* he applied the methodology of the Mahayana *sutras* as a higher-order critique of philosophical insights, especially those of the VAIBHASHIKA *abhidharma* [translation: 62: 183–220]. Many other works are attributed to Nagarjuna, probably incorrectly, but he was certainly the author of one or two further treatises. Others were the work of his disciple Aryadeva. A considerable commentarial literature followed [24: 87–103]. Two distinct schools arose: the Prasangika of Buddhapalita (*c.* 400–450 CE); and the Svatantrika of Bhavaviveka (*c.* 490–570 CE), differing on the question of the viability of positive statements of the Madhyamika position. The Prasangika Candrakirti (7th century) commented on the *Madhyamaka-karika* [translation: 60]. The Shunyatavada (Doctrine of Emptiness) became a sect in the Far East

(SAN LUN TSUNG; *and see* NANTO ROKUSHU) and plays a central part in the Tibetan monastic curriculum (TIBETAN RELIGIONS).

The Madhyamika method is intended to bring about an experiential understanding of EMPTINESS, in order to dissolve rigid views (DITTHI). It should be seen as the theoretical component of insight (VIPASSANA) meditation, intended to facilitate the breakthrough to the transcendent (LOKUTTARA) understanding. Nagarjuna distinguishes truth in the highest sense (*paramartha-satya*) from conventional truth (*samvrti-satya*), following *abhidharma* (ABHIDHAMMA) usage in which conventional truth is the commonsense view and the highest truth is the understanding of the four truths (ARIYA-SACCA), whether ordinary (insight) or transcendent (*lokuttara*). For Nagarjuna, however, only the deepest understanding could be the 'highest' truth and any insight differentiating into independent entities would be conventional. [52: 76–96; 62]

Sibylline Books [XXV] Oracular books attributed to one of a number of *sibyls*, prophetesses associated with many different centres all over the ancient Mediterranean world. The Roman books were attributed to the *sibyl* of Cumae in Campania and were certainly written in Greek hexameters [6: 604–5; 10: 68–70]. They seem to have contained little if any prophecy, only ritual prescriptions to be used after disaster or foul PRODIGIA. They were kept by a special college of priests and consulted on the instructions of the Senate. They were especially influential in recommending the introduction of new cults and rituals from the Greek world, down to the time of Augustus (*c.* 31 BCE to 14 CE) when they were associated with the Secular Games, designed to usher in the new age of imperial rule [9: 176–84; 12: 82–90]. Many other books attributed to *sibyls* circulated in antiquity; a collection from various dates, some as early as the 1st century BCE, still survives. These are

genuinely prophetic in character and at least partly Jewish in origin [12: 267].

Siddur [XVII] The 'order' of Jewish prayers, the term used for the weekday and sabbath prayer-book [9 vol. 13: 985]. A separate collection of festival prayers is called the *Machzor*. The first *siddurim* were composed in Babylonia in the post-Talmudic period (TALMUD) [20: introduction]. In different communities differing orders of prayers are used, and over the last 1,000 years many prayer-books have been written representing the various rites. The main divisions today are between the ASHKENAZI and the SEFARDI prayer-books [48].

Sigalovada [IX.A] Name of a famous discourse of GOTAMA, the BUDDHA, addressed to a young BRAHMAN householder of Rajagaha, which sets out the ethical and social duties entailed in the common human relationships: parent/child; teachers/pupils; husband/wife; friend/friend; employer/workpeople; lay people/*bhikkhu*. The discourse, known as the *Sigalovada Sutta*, is widely known in Sri Lanka, Burma, and Thailand to Buddhist lay people. [17: 135–7]

Sikh [XXVII] (pronounced very nearly as in English 'sick'; the pronunciation 'seek' is incorrect) A Sikh (= learner) is a follower of Guru Nanak and his successors (GURUS). The authoritative *Sikh Rahit Maryada* defines a Sikh as one who believes in AKAL PURAKH, the 10 Gurus and their teachings, the ADI GRANTH, and the initiation (*amrit*) instituted by the 10th Guru. [17: 1] It adds that he should believe in no other religion. (RAHIT-NAMA). This is a rigorous definition, for it seems to affirm that only the *amrit-dhari* (those who have received the KHALSA initiation) are to be recognized as Sikhs. *Sahaj-dhari* Sikhs (those who revere the Gurus and the scripture but do not seek initiation) would thus be excluded. Normally, however, the definition is interpreted more broadly. The orthodox view categorically affirms Khalsa initiation as the necessary ideal for all, but does not insist that the status of Sikh belongs only to those who have actually taken *amrit* and vowed to observe the entire RAHIT. Those who retain their hair (*kes*) uncut are called *kes-dhari*. This is mandatory for *amrit-dhari* Sikhs and in actual usage the two terms are commonly treated as synonymous.

Sikh Dharma of the Western Hemisphere [XXVII] Founded in the U.S.A. in 1971 by Harbhajan Singh Khalsa Yogiji, commonly called Yogi Bhajan, the movement is best known through its educational branch called 3HO (Healthy Happy Holy Organization). It now claims more than 5,000 Western adherents scattered over 17 countries. Within the wider Sikh community its members are distinguished by their white apparel (including turbans for women as well as for men) and by a rigorous discipline of yoga and meditation. The movement is also distinctive in that it possesses an ordained ministry. Its followers practise *kundalini* YOGA and meditation.

Sikh History [XXVII] Sikh history begins with GURU Nanak (b. 1469). During the 16th century the growing community of his followers (the PANTH) remained inconspicuous, but Mughal (Mogul) hostility (ISLAMIC DYNASTIES) developed early in the 17th century and eventually issued in open warfare at the beginning of the 18th century (GURUS). Following the death of the last Guru in 1708 many Sikhs rallied to the rebellion raised by Banda, one of his disciples. Banda was executed in 1716 and Mughal forces continued to harry the Sikhs for many years, but towards the middle of the century fortunes changed as Mughal authority disintegrated. Sikh guerrilla bands called *misls* emerged, hastening the Mughal collapse and obstructing Afghan invasions (1747–69). Success led to internecine strife, until eventually the Shukerchakia *misl* emerged triumphant at the end of the century. Its leader, Ranjit Singh, became Maharaja of the

Punjab and ruled unchallenged until his death in 1839. Military activity had powerfully encouraged the growth of militant traditions in the Panth, particularly within the KHALSA and among its dominant Jat constituency (CASTE (SIKH)). Political success was, however, accompanied by a weakening of the earlier religious traditions and after the British annexation of the Punjab in 1849 many foresaw the ultimate extinction of the Panth. Revival came later in the century with the rise of the influential Singh Sabha movement (SIKH REFORM MOVEMENTS), preaching a return to the old Khalsa values and buttressing its appeal with a range of social and intellectual activities. [2: XXIII–XXXIV] During the 20th century interest has moved more to political action. Early in the century this was directed to securing panthic control of the GURDWARAS. It now finds expression in the Akali Dal, a Sikh political party of considerable strength. [General histories: 6; 18; 19]

Until the late 19th century migrant Sikhs were chiefly traders, who settled elsewhere in India or neighbouring lands to the west. This range was substantially enlarged by the British army. Sikh soldiers stationed in Singapore and Hong Kong began the Punjabi migration to both territories, a small flow which soon extended down to Australia, New Zealand, and Fiji. Most were male Jat Sikhs (CASTE (SIKH)), virtually all of them seeking temporary unskilled employment. [16: 143–58] Others meanwhile had discovered opportunities along the west coast of North America [16: 159–90] and semi-skilled artisans found employment laying East African railways. Early in the 20th century these doors were closed. When the Punjabi flow recommenced after the Second World War it issued from both India and Pakistan, with most of its members migrating to England but significant numbers again going to North America. As before, a substantial majority of those from India were Sikhs from districts bordering the upper Satluj. By 1978 there were approximately 250,000 Sikhs in Britain. (*See also* SECTS *and* SIKH REFORM MOVEMENTS.) [4: 162–5]

Sikh Languages [XXVII] Sikhs attach a deeply affectionate importance to the Punjabi language and its Gurmukhi script. Although most of the JANAM-SAKHIS are recorded in Punjabi the language of the ADI GRANTH is more complex. In a general sense it can be called *Sant bhasha* ('SANT language'). This designates a simple language based on Khari Boli, the Hindi of the Delhi region, which was widely used for popular religious poetry. [28: 64–9] There are, however, significant variants, with the early GURUS tending strongly towards Punjabi and Guru Arjan more to western Hindi [23: 69–70]. Under Guru Gobind Singh the emphasis shifted to Braj, language of the Mathura region and the KRISHNA cycle (DASAM GRANTH). In the late 18th century it swung strongly and permanently back to Punjabi.

Sikh Reform Movements [XXVII] Defeat in 1849 confronted the Sikh PANTH with a threatening future (SIKH HISTORY). Although the victorious British subsequently enlisted many Sikh soldiers, the question of Sikh identity and even survival became critical. The eventual response was the Singh Sabha (Singh Association) movement. In 1873 a Singh Sabha was formed in Amritsar and another in Lahore six years later. Others followed in areas populated by Sikhs, all supporting a generally reformist policy with strong emphasis on the recovery of distinctive Sikh values. This policy was applied through literature, education, religious assemblies, preaching, and public controversy. A split soon appeared, however, between Amritsar and Lahore, each supported by its group of smaller sabhas. Although temporary unity was achieved in 1902 by the formation of the Chief Khalsa Diwan, as an umbrella organization,

this proved too cautious for the so-called Tat Khalsa or 'neo-Sikhs'. [2: xxiii–xxxiv] Ardent Sikh opinion turned increasingly against the government and found a specific cause in opposition to control of GURDWARAS by hereditary supervisors (*mahants*). This produced the AKALI movement and a period of vigorous agitation, beginning in 1920. The government eventually gave way and in 1925 transferred control of the principal *gurdwaras* to an elective board, the Shiromani Gurdwara Parbandhak Committee or SGPC. (*See also* SECTS (SIKH).) [19: XIII]

Sila [IX.A] The moral code in Buddhist tradition, commitment to which is an essential part of the Buddhist life; referred to as 'taking the five precepts' or *pansil* (*panca-sila*). These are: to refrain from injuring living things; to refrain from taking that which is not given; to refrain from excessive sensuality; to refrain from false and harmful speech; and to refrain from drinks and drugs which cloud the mind. These are the negative aspects of Buddhist morality. In the description of the Buddhist life in terms of the EIGHTFOLD PATH, morality is represented by three items: 'right speech'; 'right bodily action'; and 'right means of livelihood'. Another feature of Buddhist morality is generosity, expressed in ALMS-GIVING.

Sin, Christianity and [XI.B] For Christians sin is essentially disobedience to the will of God. Moral failure is the result of a sinful condition. All men are in a sinful state ('original sin') as a result of Adam's 'fall'. In Christian mythology Adam was the first man, who lost his superior nature by disobedience to God and so 'fell' from grace (SALVATION). This fall story has been challenged in the light of science and history, but the basic belief has been maintained in man's bias to sin as a falling-short of God's purpose for him. This is now sustained by reference to history and contemporary observation. In the light of this view of man's nature the Christian doctrine of salvation was developed, together with remedies such as the SACRAMENTS, especially PENANCE. Debate on original sin and its effects on free will has led to much controversy (e.g. AUGUSTINIANISM; JANSENISM; PELAGIANISM). Early PROTESTANTISM took a more pessimistic view than that general in ROMAN CATHOLICISM (except for Jansenism). Since the 18th century many Protestants have developed more optimistic (perhaps less theological) views of human moral capacity. Twentieth-century experience has tended to revive earlier pessimism. In Roman Catholicism (and sometimes Protestantism) MORAL THEOLOGY has been characterized by elaborate distinctions between sins as an aid to spiritual guidance ('casuistry'). 'Mortal' sins are gross, deliberate, and knowing, entailing loss of grace and damnation. 'Venial' sins are less serious and do not entail loss of all grace. Both forms of sin, it is believed, are forgiven by God if real regret and true resolve to lead a new life are shown ('contrition'). [60; 76: XIII]

Singsing [XXII] Festival of dance and ritual feast found universally in MELANESIAN RELIGION. *Singsings* accompany many MALE CULT rites. Whole communities share in preparations, clearing ceremonial dance grounds, rebuilding shrines and HAUS TAMBARAN, preparing sacred MASKS, and gathering food supplies. Through dance and drama, spirits of the dead (TUMBUNA) are welcomed, and obliged (by generous offerings of food and valuables, and especially the ritual slaughter of pigs) to continue their favour and the spiritual power (MANA) they make available. Renewed relationships with ancestors and gods bring the hope of harmony among the living, and fertility in nature. Major *singsings* may occur seasonally (at harvest or New Year) or after much longer intervals. Complex trading exchanges may be entered into, to obtain the hundreds of surplus pigs

required. Though greatly modified by Christian influence, *singsings* continue in the form of pig-feasts, notably in the New Guinea highlands. [23]

Sinhalese Buddhism [IX.B] By about the 12th century THERAVADA Buddhism had recovered its former dominant position among the Sinhala-speaking population of the island of Ceylon. Despite the medieval immigration of Tamil-speaking Hindus and later political domination by various missionizing European nations, Buddhism remains the religion of the Sinhala majority in the modern state of Sri Lanka, with about 10 million adherents. Traditional Sinhalese Buddhism was closely associated with Sinhalese nationalism and monarchy and existed in a complex relationship with various DEVA cults at the local level. The last century has seen the rise under European secularist and Theosophical (THEOSOPHY) influence of a Buddhist modernism. Deva cults and traditional ritual practices were seen as corruptions of the original pure Buddhism. A strong reformist tendency emerged, with a rather rationalistic interpretation based partly on the work of late 19th-century scholarship, notably that of T. W. Rhys Davids (1843–1922) and the Pali Text Society (founded 1881). The reasonable and 'scientific' nature of Buddhism was stressed. This led to some revival of Buddhist missionary activity and influenced modernizing tendencies in other Buddhist countries. Traditional attitudes remain dominant in village Buddhism, with modernizing tendencies widespread among the Western-educated; there are many intermediate positions. [47]

Sioux [III] (or Dakota) The dominant group of the Hokam–Siouan Amerindian linguistic stock, in North America, the western division of which includes the well-known Ogalala Sioux. Religious conceptions have undergone considerable transformation with European contact. Among major elements is a belief in an all-powerful and invisible being, Wakonda (or Wakantanka), who is both the original source of all power and the cosmic governor. There are also intermediary beings (manifestations of *wakan* – literally 'sacred' – power, including the sun, earth, moon, thunder-beings, and the elements), and more localized spirits-of-the-place (e.g. water spirits, spirits of the lodge, etc.) (COSMOLOGY). [17: V–VIII] Contact with the supernatural world was possible through individual VISION QUESTS, which involved personal austerities (such as the SWEAT LODGE rite), contact with, and even acquisition of, GUARDIAN SPIRITS, and a possible career as a *wicasa wakan* (literally 'man sacred'). [22: XIII] The best-known ceremonial, the SUN DANCE, probably of relatively late origin, was often an annual event and usually performed in the summer. Central features included the construction of the lodge, dances based on cosmological motifs, individual self-mutilation, and sun-gazing. The decline of traditional culture somewhat isolated major religious features (notably the vision quest, use of the śacred pipe, the CALUMET, and the sun dance). The GHOST DANCE flourished briefly among the Sioux.

Sitra Achra [XVII] A term used in KABBALAH for the powers of evil, meaning literally 'other side'. Evil is part of the divinely emanated structure underlying all reality, made up of the 10 *sefirot* (SEFIRAH). [9 vol. 10: 585]. The *Sefirah* of Din (Judgement) plays an important role in providing limitation in the cosmos, and a by-product of this limitation is the Sefiriotic substructure of the Sitra Achra – the world of evil often described as the shell (*kelippah*) surrounding the light of holiness [45: 239]. Evil has no life of its own, and must derive life-giving energy as a parasite on holiness. The sins of men allow the Sitra Achra to gain temporary dominance over the SHEKHINAH, the lowest of the *sefirot*, thereby unleashing evil on

mankind. In the Kabbalah evil is not seen as a force independent of God, but as a potential within creation which sin brings on to the plane of actuality. [52: 101]

Skilful Means [IX.B] The most frequent translation of the Buddhist term *upaya-kaushalya* (Pali *upaya-kosalla*). An *upaya* is an expedient device or cunning stratagem, while *kaushalya* has both the sense of skilfulness and that of moral wholesomeness. *Upaya-kaushalya* is the clever ability of the BUDDHA or BODHISATTVA (motivated by compassion) to make use of tricks in a spiritually completely wholesome way in order to assist progress in the teaching. This notion, which in the earlier Buddhist literature is often exemplified but rarely explicitly formulated, comes into prominence later. The MAHAYANA especially tends to view the whole teaching of the Buddha as consisting of many skilful means. [53] It is taken into the later THERAVADA, especially by DHAMMAPALA. [41: index]

Slavery (**in Islam**) [XIV] ISLAM took-over this universal West Asian institution, with masters having sexual rights over female slaves. The QUR'AN none the less enjoins kindness and provides for the manumission of slaves. In medieval Islam, slave soldiers were able to rise to high positions of power, as among the Egyptian Mamelukes and the Ottoman Turkish janissaries (troops) recruited in boyhood from the Christian peoples of the Balkans). In modern times, it has virtually disappeared from the Islamic world. [21 ''Abd'; 29: 136–8; 39 s.v.; 45: III, VI]

Slavs [V] The Slav peoples, speaking one language until the 9th century CE, expanded from a homeland in central Europe or the Ukraine over an area extending from the Oder to the Urals and into the Balkan peninsula. Some western Slavs were not converted to Christianity until the 12th century, but information about beliefs comes from unreliable sources, such as 11th- and

12th-century chroniclers and early missionaries [13: 1025]. Something, however, may be learned from oath formulas, archaeological evidence, and a rich folk tradition [12: VIII]. The Slavs worshipped a thunder-god, Perun ('Striker'), associated with the oak; Svarog, father of the sun, linked with fire and battle; Volos/Veles, god of flocks; and an earth-goddess Mokosh ('moist'). They had many local deities like Svantevit, god of war and harvest, whose temple at Arcona on the isle of Rugen was destroyed in 1168; some of these had sacred horses used for divination [3: 123]. The religion had strong shamanic elements (SHAMAN), human sacrifice, and a tendency towards dualism. Comparative philologists have established links between names of Slav deities and those of Iran and India (INDO-EUROPEANS) [13: 1026]. Stone figures of gods, some with three or four faces, holding drinking-horns, have been found, and there is evidence for simple temples [12: VIII, 151–9].

Social Morality (**Christian**) [XI.B] Early Christian social concern was largely evinced in individual charitable work. This has never ceased to be practised, but links between church and STATE brought wider responsibilities, and complications. Thus the medieval church tried to curb and civilize warfare by the concepts of God's Peace and God's Truce. But it fostered the CRUSADES, and pacifism has always been a minority Christian view [42: VII]. Slavery [111] was originally tolerated and even justified theologically (except by minorities), although eventually attacked under Christian influence. Established churches have tended to endorse the existing social and political order, especially where favourable to the church. This has coexisted with relief of suffering and moralizing campaigns (especially by PROTESTANTISM) against limited problems like alcohol and Sunday work. Traditional theology placed a high value on work and

regarded private property as divinely ordained. ROMAN CATHOLICISM has traditionally regarded poverty as a source of virtue, but Protestantism sometimes saw it as a sign of moral failure. In modern times most churches have come to approve of collective and state action for social welfare [11: 275–9; 18]. This has been given theological expression in the Protestant Social Gospel (U.S.A) [62]; Social Catholicism [132]; and most radically in Christian Socialism [72] and recent LIBERATION THEOLOGY. [93]

Soka Gakkai [XVI] A lay Buddhist association, an offshoot of NICHIREN Shoshu, which has become prominent in Japan because of its entry into politics (through Komeito, the Clean Government Party) [19: 207–8; 38]. Its beginnings are dated to 1930, when it was founded by Tsunesaburo Makiguchi and Josei Toda. Both were imprisoned during the Second World War, Makiguchi dying in prison. It was built up rapidly after 1947, with particular strength in the large cities, and by 1970 it claimed more than 16 million adherents. They work diligently to gain new members and contribute liberally towards the final supremacy of the Nichiren beliefs [1]. Happiness is seen by its worldly oriented members as achievable through profit, goodness, and beauty [34: 283].

Soul (**Amerindian**) [III] In North America, with the exception of the south-western groups, most Amerindian tribes affirm the existence in man of two souls, a 'free' soul and a 'life' or 'breath' soul [8: IX, 131–4]. The former, usually identified with the personality, is able to leave the body during dream or vision states (VISION QUEST), often travelling to distant places and, on rare occasions, even visiting the land of the dead. Disease, disability, loss of memory, etc., are regarded as indicators of the free soul's absence. In the SHAMAN, such ecstatic experiences are brought under control, enabling him voluntarily to frequent spirit realms either to seek out and bring back the wandering or stolen souls of sick persons, or to serve as guide for souls of the deceased to the land of the dead. Soul wandering, especially in the case of youth, was interpreted by the sioux as an indication that one should undertake a vision quest, possibly even that one was marked for a career as a holy man [17: vi]. With the permanent departure of the free soul came death and the consequent 'evaporation' of the life or breath soul. Although belief in the soul's pre-existence was generally affirmed, conceptions were usually vague. After death, the free soul might travel considerable distances, perhaps along the Milky Way, and experience tests or ordeals before passing into the land of the dead. [10]

South Asia, Islam in [XIV] ISLAM is numerically and politically very important in this region: in Afghanistan, it comprises 100 per cent of the population (1976 estimate, 14 million); in Pakistan 97 per cent (1977 projection, 75.5 million); in Bangladesh 80 per cent (1981 projection, 93 million); and in the Indian Union 11 per cent (1971 census, 61.5 million, 1981 projection, 80.3 million).

Arab raiders reached Sind in 711, but Islam was not extensively planted in northern India until the 13th century and after, setting down strong roots also in South India. Until the tightening of British control by the mid 19th century, the dominant military and ruling class over much of India was Muslim, although large concentrations of peasants in the Indus valley and lower Ganges valley had also found in Islam an escape from the rigours of the Hindu CASTE system. British rule curtailed the power of the Muslim landed classes, causing a crisis of confidence in the community during the late 19th and early 20th centuries, only now being restored since the establishment of the officially Muslim state of Pakistan (1947) and that of Bangladesh (1971). In

the Indian Union, Muslims are especially numerous in Uttar Pradesh, Bihar, and West Bengal. Mainly medium and small peasants and craftsmen, they consider that they are underrepresented in government and other public services [general surveys in: 6: vi; 37: ii, 1–119].

Islam in the subcontinent has been for long characterized by a strong strain of Sufi mysticism (SUFISM), some of whose adepts explored the common ground of religious experience with their Hindu counterparts (*see* BHAKTI), while fairly rigorously orthodox SUFI ORDERS like the Naqshbandis have also been strong. The tendency towards syncretism was further seen in the 16th-century Mughal (Mogul) emperor Akbar's (1556–1605) attempt at a monotheistic synthesis, the 'Divine faith'. Such trends have always evoked fierce reaction from the defenders of Islamic orthodoxy, fearful of a blurring of Islam's distinctiveness [1: iv–ix; 2: iv–v]. Hence the recurring features of puritanical reform movements and nostalgia for the simplicity and justice of earliest Islam (attitudes similar to those of the Arabian WAHHABIS), recently also in reaction against Western-type modernism. Such feelings have been strong in determining the political and religious ethos of Pakistan and the ideal of achieving there an 'Islamic republic' [1: ix; 14: iv, vii–viii, x; 46]. Also noteworthy is the persistence of a strain of SHI'ISM, which has recently produced some notable leaders for Islam in the subcontinent [2: ii].

South-East Asia, Buddhism in [IX.B] THERAVADA Buddhism is the religion of over 80 million people, the great majority of the population, in an area including the states of Burma, Kampuchea (Cambodia), Laos, and Thailand and extending into parts of Bangladesh and Assam in the west and areas of Vietnam to the east. Buddhism was traditionally introduced to the area by emissaries of the Emperor ASHOKA

(3rd century BCE), but archaeological investigation has not as yet detected unambiguous signs of Buddhism before the early centuries CE. By the latter part of the 1st millennium various forms of both HINDUISM and Buddhism were probably scattered over the whole area, with local concentrations patronized more exclusively by particular dynasties. Theravada was already important in the Pyu state of Shri Kshetra and the Mon territory of Dvaravati, perhaps in a form influenced by the Theravada centres in South India. In the early 11th century new influences from Ceylon (Sri Lanka) were felt in the Mon territory of Ramanna and soon led to their energetic adoption by the newly formed Burmese kingdom, in close contact with Ceylon (SINHALESE BUDDHISM). During the first half of the 2nd millennium this form of Theravada established itself as the principal religion of the area, leaving only residual reminders of other forms of Buddhism and Hinduism. It was similarly adopted by the incoming Thais and the previously Mahayanist and Hindu Khmers of Cambodia.

Although institutionally affected by the ending of the Burmese monarchy, the Burmese SANGHA has remained very conservative, specializing in ABHIDHAMMA studies. An active and partly lay movement for the revival of insight (VIPASSANA) meditation has emerged [49]. In Thailand, in the absence of colonial rule, the close connection with the state has continued. Interest has focused especially on very strict forms of monastic practice, with a strong reform movement based upon VINAYA traditions. Buddhist modernism in Sri Lanka and even JAPAN has had some influence and calm (SAMATHA) meditation remains important. [59; 63]

South-East Asia, Hinduism in [XIII. A] Hindu religion, in its various forms, was an important component of the cultures of South-East Asia until at least

the 13th century, and still maintains a recognizable presence in certain places; elsewhere, although not recognizable, it has affected cultural development. The process of Hinduization can be traced to at least the 1st century CE, with the introduction of the Hindu style of kingship, which necessitated Brahmanical consecration and support. Moreover, the spread eastwards from India of the cults of VISHNU and SHIVA and the associated art-forms and styles of architecture was a continuation of the process of geographical spreading which had been going on within India from at least the beginning of the 1st millennium BCE. In this way what are now called Burma, Thailand, Laos, Kampuchea, Sumatra, and Java were all areas in which Hindu religion was prominent. Kampuchea (Cambodia), formerly the Khmer kingdom, was an important centre of Hindu culture until the 13th century, when Buddhism became dominant. Thailand still maintains a small community of BRAHMANS in the capital, Bangkok, for the necessary ceremonial and cultic duties associated with Thai kingship. In Indonesia Hindu religion survives most notably in the island of Bali. [14A]

South-East Asia, Islam in [XIV] ISLAM is numerically strong in the peninsula and archipelago parts of this region: in Indonesia, Muslims comprise an estimated 90 per cent of the population (130 million) and in Malaysia 65 per cent (8½ million), with sizeable minorities in Burma, Thailand, and the Philippines (10 per cent or slightly more of the population in each country). The faith was carried to the region by Muslim merchants and traders *en route* for CHINA, and by the 15th century there were Muslim principalities in Malacca, Java, Sumatra, Kalimantan (Borneo), Sulawesi (Celebes), the Moluccas, and the Philippines. In certain areas, the work of SUFI ORDERS has been significant, with Java in particular evolving its own variety of mysticism. Official

Islam in Indonesia has been strongly orthodox in tone, with, for example, great stress on the pilgrimage (HAJJ). Against tendencies towards syncretism with the old pagan or Hindu–Buddhist strains, whose modern representatives are the esoteric *kebatinan* groups, it was above all opposed to the religious and social pressures of Dutch colonial rule and Christianity. Hence Islam was the uniting force behind indigenous organizations with political and economic aims, like the Sarekat Islam (1911), the more traditionalist and academic Nahdat-ul-Islam (1926), etc., which became spearheads of nationalist feeling against the Dutch, and the post-war fundamentalist Dar-ul-Islam movement. In the post-1949 independence period, Islam has remained a major element of the national identity and ideology. Yet in many ways Indonesian Islam retains an appreciable amount of the pre-Muslim social heritage, seen in the persistence side by side with the orthodox SHARI'A system of *adat* or customary law, with very different marriage and inheritance practices, some even in flat contradiction to the Shari'a. [General surveys in: 10 'Islam (in Indonesia)'; 21 'Indochina', 'Indonesia'; 37 vol. 2: 121–207]

Spirit [XXVIII] (1) The most general term (a spirit, spirits) for any superhuman (usually invisible) being. Most cultures, past and present, have accepted the existence of spirits, of a more or less personal kind, able to affect human life in some way. The individual human may be held to possess one or more spirits, separable from the physical body. As surviving bodily death, spirits may be the objects of a cult (ANCESTOR-WORSHIP). Events in the physical environment or in human consciousness may be attributed to spirits (ANIMISM; SHAMAN). Superior, named, and well-characterized spirits are GODS.

(2) The singular concept defies definition. Denoting the form of being which has no distinctively material properties, 'spirit' (derived like its equivalents in many languages from words for breath or wind, as invisible, yet powerful and life-giving), connotes life, consciousness, self-activity. RELIGION is often regarded as having to do with 'the things of the spirit', what is spiritual [23: 193–6]. To elucidate such language is a major task for RELIGIONSWISSENSCHAFT and the PHILOSOPHY OF RELIGION.

Spirit-Possession [II] is an important element in most African religious systems. Innumerable cults have at their ritual centre the medium through whom the deity or ancestral spirit speaks. In the more established cults possession tends to be formalized, even assumed, predictable, and confirmatory of the given order. In new and socially marginal cults possession may be more violent, revelatory, and innovating. The one-to-one relationship between a powerful spirit and his principal medium may create an almost symbiotic unity to give the medium a truly prophetic character, sense of mission, and public role. In many societies divination depends largely on spirit-possession: in possession the NGANGA detects witchcraft or the causality behind other misfortunes. In particular through possession he can cope with the possessed. For spirit-possession is at once the privilege of the religious specialist and the affliction of countless common people. If someone is possessed unexpectedly by a spirit (possibly, but not necessarily, malevolent) the medium can interrogate that spirit, discover the cause, and resolve it: a well-known spirit may have felt neglected and require a sacrifice; an ancestor may have intervened to stir the conscience over parental neglect; or some new spirit may be simply announcing his existence in this way. One possessed may discover in consequence a vocation to mediumship. ZULU ancestral spirits, for example, first 'brood' over a person called to be an *inyanga* (Zulu form of *Nganga*). Possession is distinct from mediumship, being initially a disorder rather than a public role, but it easily leads to this.

Thus spirit mediumship may be mainly ritualistic, revelatory, or therapeutic. It may be conservative or radical, institutionalized or marginal to society. It is a means of expression, proof of the proximity of the spiritual world, but capable of many messages. [1; 21: 136–96]

Spiritualism [XVIII] A modern (mainly Christian) faith centring on communication with spirits of the dead, who it is believed retain their personalities and are accessible through a 'medium' (a person gifted and trained in such communication). There is no fixed form for the service or 'seance', which may be held in a private home or at a Spiritualist church. There are usually prayers and hymns before (normally in darkness or dim light) the medium attempts to contact a 'guide' (spirit helper who assists other spirits in communicating). Greetings and personal messages from dead relatives and friends are relayed to the congregation, and there may be 'physical phenomena': objects manipulated without visible agency (PSYCHIC POWERS), or brought mysteriously from afar ('apports'), or the 'materialization' of a spirit in a tangible body formed of 'ectoplasm' (a diaphanous substance said to be exuded from the medium's body). Some mediums also practise healing by spirit aid.

Spiritualism originated in Hydeville, New York State, in 1848, when the Fox sisters accidentally discovered their mediumistic powers. It spread rapidly, attracting widespread interest as promising tangible evidence of an afterlife. But its claims have remained controversial and it survives today as a minor religious movement in most Western countries. It has similarities to traditions of spirit-possession in many non-Christian religions. [20]

Sruti (Shruti) [XIII.A] In Hindu tradition, 'that which is heard directly', that is, by a sage or *rshi* (an inspired poet or sage, one who sings); hence directly revealed scripture, as distinct from *smrti*, which is 'memorized tradition' and secondary to direct revelation.

Star-Worship (Astrolatry, Sabaism) [VIII] The sun, moon, planets, and stars have been worshipped as gods in a number of cultures. Star-worship evolves from the awe felt at the beauty, regularity, mystery, and power of the heavenly bodies (especially of the sun) and in response to their effect, real or imagined, on terrestrial and human life. The sun and moon, in particular, are perceived as the givers of time (time being measured by their motions) and the sun as the regulator of the cycle of the seasons. Star-worship usually accompanies, indeed triggers, the early development of astronomy and calendrics and sanctions the parallel growth of ASTROLOGY. This is certainly so in Mesopotamia in the last two millennia BCE [10: 1–111] and in Central America among the Maya [9: V]. Star-worship probably underlies the prehistoric megalithic astronomical sites of northern Europe [9: 11–111; e.g. Stonehenge] and similar sites in North America [9: IV; e.g. the Big Horn medicine wheel]. From Mesopotamia star-worship passed into Graeco-Roman culture [6]. Sun-worship became, in the 3rd century CE, something of an official religion in the Roman empire, contemporary ideology seeing in the divine emperor (EMPEROR-WORSHIP) a terrestrial counterpart of the sun as sovereign of the universe. At the same time MITHRAS was worshipped as a solar god and his mysteries incorporated much arcane astral lore.

State, Christianity and the [XI.B] Christianity has had a great variety of relationships with the state. Under the Roman empire from the time of Constantine (d. 337) the church became increasingly privileged and eventually dominant. It then persecuted paganism and HERESY [55]. The 'Gelasian theory' (Pope Gelasius d. 496) expressed the supremacy of the church over the state. Views of this kind during the Middle Ages inflamed many conflicts between Popes and princes [11: 97–115]. Ideally, Western 'Christendom' (the Christian world) was felt to be ruled by God through the Holy Roman Emperor and other princes for secular affairs; by the PAPACY and CHURCH in spiritual matters. Some Popes and emperors, however, aspired to ultimate control of both sides of human existence. 'Theocracy' has been used to describe church claims of this kind, and the term 'Cesaropapism' to describe the control of the church and theology exercised by some Eastern emperors. The REFORMATION typically initiated 'established churches' in PROTESTANTISM. This meant a single state-supported church for all citizens (cf. TOLERATION). 'Erastianism' is applied to complete state control of church jurisdiction in such churches. In Catholic France (ROMAN CATHOLICISM), 'Gallicanism' largely subjected the church to the monarchy [11: 270; 102; 107: 548]. In Geneva, CALVINISM approximated to a theocracy. Since the early 19th century there has been a general tendency to 'disestablishment', or at least to reduce the privileges of established churches. Many states have become religiously neutral. But even without establishment, Christianity may act as a source of national identity [41].

Stoicism (Roman) [xxv] Stoicism reached Rome in the 2nd century BCE and the leaders of the school (Panaetius, c. 185–109 BCE and Posidonius, c. 135 to c. 50 BCE) exercised much influence over the ideas of Roman nobles on morality and the ruling of the empire. It offered them a means of combining their polytheistic tradition with the conception of a universe guided and structured by reason (*logos*), which was seen as

divine and as including the other gods, as aspects of the *logos*. [7: 190–200; 9: III; 12: 35–9, 140–55, 207–15]

Structuralism [XXVIII] In the study of literature, a search for underlying (hidden) configurations which will offer an explanation of the more obvious (visible) patterns and may reveal how e.g. what is written or told simplifies and organizes the diversity of experience of those who use (write, tell, read, hear, even live by) what is so analysed. Such methods have been applied to the study of sacred scripture, including the BIBLE; and especially to mythical and totemic thought, notably by anthropologists [2: 24; 16; 28: 48–9].

Stupa [IX.A] A Sanskrit term (Pali *thupa*) denoting cairn or monument. These were erected over the ashes of an emperor or other great personage in ancient India, and thus over the ashes of the BUDDHA after the PARINIBBANA. The *stupa* was subsequently used for the ashes of other Buddhist monks, and for holy relics, and thus came to be a familiar feature of Buddhist sites (BUDDHA IMAGE). The Sanskrit term for holy relics is *dhatu*. This word in combination with *garbha* (that is, a chamber or container) gives *dhatugarbha* or, in Sri Lanka, *dagoba* [9: 188]. The latter word, mispronounced by early Portuguese settlers, may be the origin of *pagoda*, now commonly used as an alternative for *stupa*. Another term for the same is *cetiya*. [B. 56: II]

Subud [XXI] A movement of Islamic origin, introduced to England in 1957 by its leader Pak Subuh, an Indonesian monk. During the late 1950s stories of miraculous healings and sensational spiritual experiences received much publicity, but during the 1960s and early 1970s very little was heard of the movement. By the late 1970s, however, it began to become more visible, with groups all round the world. The basis for Subud is an exercise known as *latihan*, which has the purpose of bringing about experiences of purification and worship of God through surrender to his will. [2: 78; 30: IV]

Sufi Institutions [XIV] Sufis or dervishes (*see* SUFISM) early congregated in houses or convents, variously called *ribats*, *khanaqahs*, and *zawiyas*, as foci for living communally, for fulfilling the duty of JIHAD against unbelievers, and as centres for educational activity and evangelism among un-Islamized or imperfectly Islamized peoples (*see for example* SANUSIS). These were often established as charitable foundations (WAQF) by the gifts of the pious [21 'Khānkāh']. Within Sufi circles, a special liturgical ritual (*dhikr*, literally 'remembrance (of God)') was often practised, which might include repeated chanting of the names of God (ALLAH), often with the aid of a rosary, controlled breathing exercises, dancing (especially among the Mevlevis – *see* SUFI ORDERS) to the accompaniment of music, etc. [45: X]. In certain frontier regions like Anatolia, the practices of some orders, e.g. the Bektashis, showed a distinct syncretism with Christian practices [9: IV–VI].

Sufi Orders [XIV] By the 12th century, Sufis began to coalesce into groups (*tariqas*, literally 'ways') under the leadership of Sufis with outstanding spiritual gifts (SHAIKH), and with full adherents (not however necessarily celibate) and the equivalents of Christian 'lay brethren' or 'tertiaries'. These orders became very numerous as subdivisions developed, and spread all over the Islamic world. On the peripheries, such as West Africa, the Sudan, the Indo-Pakistan subcontinent and central Asia, they have played a leading role in Muslim evangelism and remain especially influential there today. In their heyday in the pre-modern period, the orders supplied in the Sunni world a focus for the emotional aspect of believers' religious needs, analogous to devotion to the IMAMS in the Shi'i one, and acted as a cohesive social force in the community, especially, though not exclusively, among the lower classes. Prominent orders include the Qadiris, of Iraqi origin but later active in India; the Naqshbandis, especially active among Turkish peoples; the Shadhilis, characteristically North African; the Ahmadis, centred on Lower Egypt; the recently established Tijanis, active in North and West Africa [55]; the SANUSIS; etc. In Ottoman Turkey, the Bektashis were connected with the élite military force of the janissaries (SLAVERY) and have survived in recent times, in Albania especially [9]; while the Mevlevis (also called the 'whirling dervishes') were particularly connected with the ruling classes and were famed for their use of music and gyratory dancing (recently revived, but essentially as a tourist attraction). In the past, extravagances such as fire-walking, snake-handling, riding over adherents on horseback, etc., were practised. (For Sufi doctrines *see* SUFISM; for their ceremonies and meeting-places *see* SUFI INSTITUTIONS.) [General surveys: 20 'Ṭarīḳa'; 31: IX; 39 'Faqīr'; 69]

Sufism, Sufis [XIV] The Sufis ('wearers of wool', i.e. the coarse garments of the ascetic), also dervishes ('poor men') and, in North Africa, marabouts, are the mystics of ISLAM. At the outset they were influenced by the ascetics of the Eastern Christian churches, but later they developed mainly within the framework of orthodox Islam, except for an extravagant, antinomian wing of the movement in eastern Persia that may have been influenced by religious currents from the Indian world. Within these latter Sufis, pantheistic and monist ideas, revolving round 'the unity of all existence', are discernible, as in the ideas of the great Spanish Muslim mystic Ibn al-'Arabi (1165–1240) [43: 640–66]. The majority of Sufis remained, however, within the bounds of orthodoxy, regarding the 'Sufi path', progress through the 'stations' of worldly renunciation, etc., and the 'states' of spiritual gifts conferred by God such as nearness to him, etc., as the means to real communion with and knowledge (*ma'rifa*) of God. In this way such ideals as self-annihilation (*fana'*), self-perpetuation with God (*baqa'*), and even infusion or indwelling of the Divine Being (*hulul*) could be achieved. These could only uneasily be reconciled with orthodox theology and the external observances of the SHARI'A. Sufis were often at odds with the ULEMA, and the celebrated al-Hallaj paid with his life in 922 for his views [46: v]. The achievement of a *modus vivendi* between these two great aspects of Islam was realized by the theologian and Sufi al-Ghazali (1058–1111). Sufism later evolved into distinct orders (SUFI ORDERS), and these had their own places of congregation and rituals (SUFI INSTITUTIONS). Sufism has been a great stimulus to, and a persistent strain in, Islamic literature, seen for instance in the work of the great Persian poets Rumi (1207–73) and Hafiz (*c.* 1325 to *c.* 1390). [General surveys: 5; 6: XIII; 49: IV; 51; 61: VIII–IX; 83: VI]

Sumerians [VI] Sumer, the earliest Mesopotamian civilization (ANCIENT NEAR EASTERN RELIGIONS), consisted of city-states, separated from each other by the desert; they had diverse but well-organized societies. The period of Sumerian supremacy, the Jemdet Nasr period, was *c.* 3000–2550 BCE. [20; 23: 18–20; 26]. Not a true theocracy, in which the whole state is owned and administered by the TEMPLES, Sumerian organization was functionally secular: individuals owned land and property and the cities traded their agricultural produce and technological skills. Nevertheless, the temple was the focus of each city, embodying its identity, and the collective skills of the community were directed towards the god and his temple. Although administration of the city was secular, the men executing these duties were also often temple administrators. The temple, in receipt of an income from its estates and from gifts supplied by the community,

fulfilled an obligation to the people by funding secular and trading ventures through loans from its funds.

Each city had its chief deity, accompanied by spouse, children, and lesser deities. Each pantheon was at first independent, although myths and ritual visits provided a link between the gods. As cities were absorbed into larger units, some gods were eliminated and others, belonging to subject cities, had temples at the capital. A loose federation of city-states emerged, accepting a regular change in leadership and the pre-eminence of one city. Local cults continued, but seven major deities [16: 130] and their consorts were finally recognized throughout Mesopotamia, and their characteristics lost something of their purely local significance. Nippur, Ur, Uruk, and Sippar became important religious centres.

All deities had priests, who served their temples, attending to their daily needs. The prime obligation of the king (KINGSHIP) was to serve his god, and royal military victories were regarded as a reflection of the god's success in heaven. Priestesses also played an important role in some cults.

Literature included the first COSMOLOGY and cosmogony, wisdom texts, and the 'Flood' story [24: 72–9], namely, the Epic of GILGAMESH.

Only the gods were immortal; man, created to serve the gods, descended to a dark and dreary netherworld after death (AFTERLIFE). Nevertheless, some funerary preparations were elaborate, such as the fine equipment provided in the Royal Tombs at Ur (*c.* 2500 BCE). [26: 74–81]

Sun Dance [III] Probably the best known and most dramatic of North American Indian ceremonies is the Sun Dance of the Plains [7: VIII]. Known among the Ogalala as *Wi wanyang wacipi* ('sun-gazing dance'), its characteristic feature was the participant's fixed gaze upon the sun while dancing, which thus produced a trance. Although early cosmological elements are present (COSMOLOGY), the dance as it is now most commonly known is probably of relatively recent origin. It was usually performed annually (over a period of from two to five days) when the tribal groups assembled. A 'pledger', one who had as a result of a dream or vision vowed to perform the dance, usually acted as sponsor, although there might be lesser sponsors. Central features of the dance included (with regional variations) building the sun-dance lodge (often cosmological in design), preliminary dances, use of the sacred pipe (CALUMET), and the actual sun dance itself. Participants either danced while gazing at the sun and blowing whistles, or, in the case of those resolved to do so beforehand, attached themselves to the sacred pole by thongs and skewers through the chest muscles and then pulled outwards until the muscles were torn free. Performance of the dance not only satisfied the pledger's vow, thereby demonstrating personal resolve and leading to the acquisition of individual power, it also helped to achieve cosmic regeneration and tribal well-being. [4]

Sunna [XIV] 'custom, code of behaviour', in ISLAM means in particular the Prophet MUHAMMAD's example, by explicit precept or implicit approval, as embodied in the HADITH or tradition literature. The Sunna therefore complements and often confirms or explains the QUR'AN, and is one of the basic sources (*usul*) of the divine law or SHARI'A recognized by the majority of Muslims. Its followers are therefore called the 'people of the Sunna and the community', hence Sunnis or Sunnites, as opposed to the minority group of Shi'is or Shi'ites (SHI'ISM), who substitute for the democratic consensus of the community the authority of the Shi'i doctors and the infallible IMAM. [20 s.v.; 29: 67–8; 32 vol. II: 1]

Sutta-Pitaka [IX.A] The second of the three divisions of the Pali Buddhist

scriptures or TIPITAKA (ABHIDHAMMA; VINAYA-PITAKA). Corresponding collections in Sanskrit are called *Sutra-Pitaka* [37: 201–7]. The *sutta* (Pali), or *sutra* (Sanskrit), is the basic unit and consists of a discourse which is represented as having been delivered by GOTAMA at a particular place and time, which are usually stated. The discourse may deal with one or a number of related topics; the name *sutra* refers to the idea of a single thread or *sutra* (cf. English 'suture') running through the discourse. Each *sutra*, or *sutta*, usually has a title, indicating the name of the person to whom it was principally addressed, or the place where it was given, or the major subject of the discourse. Thus the *Samannaphala Sutta* is the discourse concerning 'the fruits of the religious life' (*samannaphala*); the *Kutadanta Sutta* is the discourse addressed to a BRAHMAN named Kutadanta (Sharp-tooth), and so on.

The *Sutta-Pitaka* of the Theravadin school (now found in Sri Lanka and South-East Asia; THERAVADA) consists of five sections, each called a *nikaya* ('assemblage'); namely, *Digha-nikaya*, *Majjhima-nikaya*, *Anguttara-nikaya*, *Samyutta-nikaya*, and *Khuddaka-nikaya*. These sections probably originated as separately preserved traditions, each being memorized and transmitted orally by the monks of different monasteries or localities. A *Sutra-Pitaka* of the MAHAYANA form of Buddhism has been preserved in Chinese translation. It consists of four divisions, which are here called *agamas*, and these correspond approximately to the first four *nikayas* of the Theravadins. [10: 9–24]

Suttanta [IX.B] The discourses of the BUDDHA contained in the SUTTA-PITAKA are referred to in PALI as *suttantas* (Sanskrit *sutranta*), especially if fairly long. A *suttantika* (Sanskrit *sautrantika*) monk was originally one who specialized in memorizing the discourses, as opposed to the disciplinary rules.

Suttanta teaching was later contrasted with ABHIDHAMMA teaching. *Suttanta* was held to be the Buddha's teaching in specific situations to meet particular individual needs; further exposition or qualification might be necessary for completeness. *Abhidhamma* by contrast provides a full and exact account, not tailored to any particular situation. *Suttanta* teaching is often concerned with describing or mapping processes over a period of time as sequences, whereas *abhidhamma* uses the same categories to analyse specific events as distinct moments (*see* BODHI-PAKKHIYA-DHAMMA). Although the *abhidhamma* method acquired great prestige and tended at times to supersede *suttanta*, the *suttanta* method has retained considerable practical importance in THERA-VADA Buddhism. In North India it influenced the rise of the SAUTRAN-TIKA school, reacting against the VAIBHASHIKA *abhidharma*.

Sutton Hoo [v] In 1939 a ship-burial of the early 7th century was excavated at Sutton Hoo near Woodbridge in Suffolk. It held a king's treasure, including some superb ceremonial objects [4]. Whether the grave was a cenotaph or originally held a coffin or cremated remains is still under discussion. This discovery provides important evidence for religious symbolism at the close of the pre-Christian period in Anglo-Saxon England. It establishes elaborate SHIP-FUNERAL as an East Anglian practice [7: VI, 113–14].

Sweat Lodge [III] An Amerindian rite of purification, practised widely in North America, but especially among central and south-western tribes, to revivify individuals spiritually and/or physically. It also often served as preparation for contact with the supernaturals. [17: VIII]

Following construction of the sweat lodge (usually fashioned from willow saplings bound with thongs and covered with blankets or skins, and often modelled after a pattern revealed in the myth of creation), the participants, under the supervision of a leader, enter and arrange themselves around a pile of heated stones. To the accompaniment of prayers and songs, the leader pours water over the stones as well as lighting and sharing the sacred pipe (CALUMET). The presence within the lodge of the gods or spirits prompts individual and collective prayers. [1: III] The rite, with minor variations, is widely used among Amerindian groups today.

Symbol [XXVIII] (1) An object or activity representing or standing for something else. The ability to communicate by using symbols has been regarded as a (or even the) mark distinguishing humans from other animals. The symbols we use range from arbitrary or extrinsic signs (such as += or &), through gestures and words, to those kinds of language, imagery, and actions which somehow embody the meaning and interpretation they convey. In that RELIGION points beyond the tangible, human, and everyday, its expression and communication are bound to be symbolic [1: 3–7; 2, II; 5; 7: 3–4; 24: 154–7]. Religious symbolism embraces specifically religious words and a peculiar use of ordinary language; visible objects (*see* ICONO-GRAPHY); actions, especially of a RITUAL kind; music, drama, DANCE; and combinations of these in acts of worship, where even silence may become symbolic [17: VII, X, XII]. For some kinds of THEOLOGY the course of history, or even the world (COSMOS), may be regarded as symbols of divine truth or transcendent reality. [*See also* 26: III, IV, VIII; 28]

(2) A term in Christian theology for a CREED or confession of faith.

Synagogue [XVII] The main public institution of JUDAISM, thought to have begun during the Babylonian captivity in the 6th century BCE (BIBLICAL HISTORY) [20: III; 53: VI]. After the Jerusalem TEMPLE had been destroyed, in 587 BCE, early synagogues were necessary for the exiles (EXILE) to carry on religious activities. When the Israelites returned and rebuilt the Temple, about 70 years later, they still used synagogues, but the latter had a minor role until the 1st century CE. With the destruction of the second Temple in 70 CE the synagogue became the main locus of worship and of study, filling the gap left by the absence of a single religious centre and of the sacrificial ritual. The traditional synagogue has an ark, or cupboard, in the Jerusalem-facing wall, where the hand-written scrolls of the Pentateuch (BIBLE) are kept. At the centre of the synagogue is a *bimah*, a raised platform from which the Pentateuch is read and where in many congregations the CANTOR stands to lead the prayers. Women sit separately from men in Orthodox synagogues, but in Conservative and Reform temples (as they are called in North America – see REFORM JUDAISM) the sexes sit together. The synagogue is led by a group of laymen who are elected to office, and is a totally lay institution with no priestly roles. [9 vol. 15: 579; 47: 423]

Synanon [XXI] Synanon was originally founded in California (by Charles Dederich, in 1958) as a self-help, therapeutic community for the rehabilitation of narcotic and alcoholic addicts [58]. By the late 1960s, however, it could be seen to be evolving into a type of HUMAN POTENTIAL MOVEMENT, which offered its adherents an alternative life-style based on a particular kind of encounter-group therapy. It is believed that behavioural changes will bring about desired changes in beliefs and values. Those who stay in Synanon communities are expected to act the role of happy, satisfied people who get along together without problems – except when they play 'the game'. In 'the game', criticisms of self and others are to be revealed and worked out. Often

this is done with extreme emotional intensity. [14: VI; 58]

As a corporation Synanon has amassed considerable wealth. It was the subject of some publicity following an incident in which a deadly snake was put through the letter-box of a lawyer who was concerned in an investigation of the group.

Syncretism [XXVIII] The fusion of religious cults or movements. In situations of intercultural contact, religions tend to interact, either spontaneously or by intentional adaptation. The process is of great importance for the understanding of religious development, e.g. in the Graeco-Roman world (SYNCRETISM (ROMAN)), in ancient India, and among the MODERN MOVEMENTS especially those in the Third World. The extent to which major traditions arose syncretistically is a matter for historical investigation.

Syncretism (Roman) [XXV] In the ancient world, the formation of new cults by the merging of elements from different traditions, characteristically in the circumstances of political or cultural dominance/subjection. The Romans had long adopted Greek or Etruscan gods, or modified their own by the introduction of rituals, myths, and iconography (DI DEAEQUE). They also took from the Greeks the belief that different peoples worship the same gods, only under different names. The process in reverse began when the Romans administered areas culturally inferior (as they saw it) to themselves. The Roman gods, or at least their names, were widely used throughout the West. It is hard to distinguish cases of simple importation of Roman deities from cases where local deities survived disguised under a Roman name – and both these cases from those of genuine syncretism. [7: 211–16] In North Africa, for instance, the wide dispersion of Saturn, a god little remembered at home in Italy, implies the adoption of his name for the local Baʻal-Hammon. Sometimes, the merging led to the use of both local and Roman names, as Sulis Minerva at Bath (England). The Roman empire also created the context for a different process, whereby such deities as Isis (from Egypt) [15: 150–53] or Sol Invictus (the unconquered sun; MITHRAISM) [7: 52–6; 12: 280–87] were identified with many local gods, so moving towards wider claims to supremacy.

Syrian Christianity and Oriental Orthodoxy [XI.D] CHRISTIANITY early became the religion of many Syrians and Egyptians. ANTIOCH and ALEXANDRIA became major centres. Armenia became officially Christian under Tiridates III (r. 298–330 CE).

Theodosius I made Christianity the state religion of the Roman Empire in 391 CE. Orthodoxy and HERESY became political issues. COUNCILS OF THE CHURCH defined the limits of orthodox CHRISTOLOGY and the state enforced conformity. Dissent expressed both theological and ethnic differences. The East Syrian Church under Persian rule declared its AUTOCEPHALY in 424 CE. This Church, the Assyrian or Chaldean Church, rejected the decrees of Ephesus (431 CE) at a synod in 484 CE and became officially Nestorian. Its missionaries penetrated central Asia, India, and China before the onslaught of Timur (1360–1405 CE) reduced it to a shadow. [3: 237–302]

The decrees of Chalcedon (451 CE) were rejected by the Armenian Church, by many West Syrians, and by the majority of the Coptic Christians of Egypt. Christians loyal to the council became known as Melkites, royalists, their opponents as Monophysites since they formulated their belief in the full divinity and full humanity of Christ as St Cyril (? 444 CE) had done, confessing 'the One nature of the Incarnate Logos'. Jacob Baradai (? 578 CE) founded a Syrian Monophysite hierarchy, centred on Antioch, in COMMUNION with the Coptic Pope in Alexandria. Monophysite Syrians are known as Jacobites. [3; *passim*]

The Churches of Ethiopia and Nubia were founded by the Copts [3: 146–67, 425–42]. The Syrian Orthodox Christians of South India also later joined the Monophysite family of churches. [44]

Under Monothelite influence the Syrian Christians of Lebanon became the separate Maronite Church in the 8th century. They united with Rome during the Crusades. [3: 389–426]

The spread of ISLAM brought the Oriental Orthodox of the Middle East under Arab rule. Syrian scholars brought Greek learning to the Arabs. Copts and Syrians created a new Christian literature in Arabic. The Crusades disturbed this relationship and led to Rome-ward movements, especially among Armenians and Maronites. The Mongol invasions decimated the Syrian Churches. Turkish rule gave all the Oriental Orthodox a recognized if subordinate place in society, but did little to stimulate their spiritual or intellectual life. As the Turkish empire crumbled, nationalist movements led to tragic massacres of Armenians and Nestorians.

Roman Catholic missionary activity has created Uniate (united to Rome) counterparts of all the Oriental Orthodox Churches. There is also a Uniate Melkite Church [4 vol. 1]. In recent years Oriental Christians have become active in the ECUMENICAL MOVEMENT and have won recognition, especially from theologians of the Chalcedonian ORTHODOX CHURCHES, as professing the Christian faith in its full integrity.

Numbers of adherents are very difficult to determine: they probably total about 18 million Orthodox and 4.5 million Uniates.

· T ·

Tabu (Taboo, Tapu) [XXII] A restriction or ban on potent and sacred things. In POLYNESIAN RELIGION anything possessing great MANA is *tapu* (*kapu* in Hawaii). Chiefs and their families are surrounded with restrictions to protect the *mana* of their divine ancestry from being lost through contact with common things. The chief's person, especially his head, is sacrosanct, as are his house, food and utensils, clothing, and possessions. Also highly *tapu* are tombs of chiefs; shrines and sacred stones; first-fruits and offerings for the gods; chants, genealogies, and sacred lore; and groves or springs of water for ceremonial use. *Tapus* govern agriculture, fishing, building, and carving, since all such work requires the help and protection of patron gods (ATUA). [7; 16; 30]

A danger to *mana*, and thus also *tapu*, are bloodstained warriors, women menstruating or in childbirth, the sick and dying, and corpses or bones of the dead. *Tapu*-removal is the reason for many religious rites. Using incantations, water, cooked food, and other neutralizing things, the TOHUNGA lifts *tapus*, purifying people and objects from the potentially harmful effects of misplaced *mana*. Children are freed from the *tapu* of birth by ceremonies of purification and name-giving. Newly made buildings, war canoes, weapons, and tools are freed of *tapu*, and consecrated to endow them with fresh *mana*. *Tapus* are enforced by spirits and gods, who send sickness or death, or withdraw their protection allowing accident or defeat to punish *tapu*-breakers. *Tapu* is known in MELANESIAN RELIGION as *tambu*. [23]

Tahara [XIV] Ritual purity in ISLAM, a state required before participation in the SALAT, touching the QUR'AN, and other ritual acts. A major purification (*ghusl*), after e.g. coitus or menstruation, is distinguished from a minor one (*wudu'*), performed before the *salat* or worship. Sand may be used if water is lacking. [20 s.v.; 39 'Purification']

T'ai Shan [X] Mount T'ai in Shantung province has been the focus of a popular cult since the Shang period (1523–1027 BCE). It was the site of imperial sacrifices between 110 BCE and 1008 CE. The god of T'ai Shan, the 'Great Divine Ruler of the Eastern Peak' (*Tung Yueh Ta Ti*), is the grandson of the Jade Emperor (*Yu Huang*) in the popular CHINESE PANTHEON. He can determine a person's life-span and is one of the judges of the dead, hence some of the courts of hell were traditionally sited at T'ai Shan. [4: IV, 476–90; 42: XIX, 113–22; 85: XXIII, 178–85]

Takht [XXVII] The *takht* ('throne') signifies for Sikhs a seat of temporal authority within the PANTH. The first of these institutions was established in Amritsar by Guru Hargobind early in the 17th century (GURUS). Temporal involvement had become unavoidable and Akal Takht, symbolically sited beside Harimandir Sahib, was to serve as its focus (GURDWARAS (HISTORIC LOCATIONS)). Three other places, all associated with Guru Gobind Singh, were subsequently declared to be *takhts* (Anandpur, Patna, and Nanded). [14: VII] Akal Takht has, however, retained its pre-eminence. During the political campaigns of the 20th century, as for the 18th-century struggles, it has been the place for debate and for promulgating major decisions (*gurmatta*). The role of the other three *takhts* has been less explicit and attempts to invoke their uncertain authority have seldom been made. In 1966 the Shiromani Gurdwara Parbandhak Committee (SIKH REFORM MOVEMENTS) designated Damdama Sahib near Bhatinda a fifth *takht*. This decision has yet to win universal approval in the Panth.

Talmud [XVII] The main text of rabbinical JUDAISM, a wide-ranging commentary on the MISHNAH [52: 121]. The Palestinian (or Jerusalem) Talmud was edited towards the end of the 4th century CE, and the Babylonian Talmud, more authoritative for later Judaism than the Palestinian version, was edited at the end of the 5th century. Both Talmuds are in Aramaic (LANGUAGES (JEWISH)). The extant Talmudic commentary does not cover all of the six orders of the Mishnah. The Palestinian Talmud comments on 39 of the Mishnah's 63 tractates, and the Babylonian on 37. The Babylonian Talmud is, however, much longer and its discussion of issues more wide-ranging than the Palestinian Talmud. In general Talmudic material may be divided into HALAKHAH, legal and ritual matters, and AGGADAH, theological, ethical, and folklorist matters. The Halakhah of the Babylonian Talmud is binding on all traditional Jews, and the Aggadah, while not binding, is central to later Jewish theology. [7; 10; 32; 50; 51]

Tane [XXII] The most active god (ATUA) in POLYNESIAN RELIGION. Forcing apart his parents RANGI and PAPA (heaven and earth), Tane brought life-giving sunlight to the world. Forests are his children, birds and insects his messengers. Wood-carvers and canoe-builders honour him with food offerings. In Maori myth, Tane brought to life a woman modelled from earth, making her mother of the human race. Wood or stone male figures (called

tiki) represent Tane's procreative power. [7; 16; 22]

Tangaroa [XXII] The god of the ocean, known throughout Polynesia (POLYNESIAN RELIGION). Seafarers and fishermen invoke his blessing, throwing back as an offering the first fish caught. In Samoa and Tonga (as Tangaloa) and in Tahiti (as Ta'aroa), Tangaroa was worshipped as supreme being, uncreated father of gods (ATUA) and of mankind. Whether that was Tangaroa's ancient role or a late development is uncertain [7; 16; 22; 30]

Tantra (1) [XIII.A] Originally a type of Hindu sacred text, a 'ritualistic book', but more usually used of certain specialized texts dealing with sexual/yogic and magical practices closely connected with the cult of SHAKTI [19: 149–57] and performed by small groups of initiates in private or remote places [2: 339f].

Tantra (2) [XXIX] In the Buddhist tradition, the term *tantra* (also known as the *vajrayana*, 'indestructible vehicle', or *mantrayana*, 'mantra-vehicle') refers to a series of ritual texts originally delivered as discourses by the BUDDHA in human or divinized form. The *tantras* deal with the evocation of deities, the acquisition of magical power, and the attainment of enlightenment by means of meditation, MANTRA, *mudra*, and YOGA [26]. According to tradition they were transmitted in relative secrecy until the 4th or 5th century CE, after which time they were propagated widely in India, especially by the famed group of tantric saints known as the '84 perfect ones' (Sanskrit *siddha*, Tibetan *drupthop*), who included such figures as Saraha, Krishnacharya, and Naropa.

Tantric theory and practice is essentially a development within MAHAYANA Buddhism, sharing the latter's ethical and philosophical basis. It expresses the Mahayana doctrine of the inseparability of *samsara* and *nirvana* (NIBBANA) in the notion of 'simultaneously arising' (Sanskrit *sahaja*, Tibetan *lhan-chik kye-pa*). According to this precept, as all phenomena are fundamentally empty (*shunya*) they are intrinsically pure. Thus *samsara* and *nirvana* arise simultaneously from the same basis. Recognition of this simultaneously arising nature or underlying purity transforms moral defilements (Sanskrit *klesha*, Tibetan *nyon-mong*) into PRAJNA and the psychophysical constituents (*skandhas*) into BUDDHAS. [8; 19]

The practice of *tantra* depends upon the receipt of instruction from a GURU (Tibetan *lama*) who stands in the unbroken succession of masters of the teaching. The tantric master gives teaching in three main ways: first, through 'empowerment' (Sanskrit *abhisheka*, Tibetan *wang-kur*), in which he empowers the student to meditate on a deity; second, by 'textual transmission' (Sanskrit *agama*, Tibetan *lung*), in which he bestows the blessing of the relevant text; and third, by 'instruction' (Sanskrit *upadesha*, Tibetan *khrid*), in which he explains the method of practising the particular teaching. (*See also* CHEN YEN; SHINGON) [13; 23]

Tao Chia [x] Taoist school. The term is commonly used in recent times to refer to Taoist philosophy as represented in texts such as the TAO TE CHING, the CHUANG TZU, the *Lieh Tzu*, and the *Huai Nan Tzu*; and in the tradition of philosophical reflection upon these works that includes the neo-Taoist exponents of the Dark Learning (HSUAN HSUEH) such as Wang Pi (226–49 CE), Ho Yen (d. 249 CE), and Kuo Hsiang (d. 312 CE). In the above sense it is distinguished from Tao Chiao (Taoist sect). [21; 47; 100: 163]

Tao Chiao [x] Taoist sect or religious Taoism. The term literally means 'Teachings of the Way'. It is now used to refer to established sects and movements that seek access to the *Tao* as the supreme reality, and consequent immortality, through meditational, liturgical, and alchemical means (ALCHEMY (CHINESE)). Religious Taoism incorporates ideas and images from philosophical Taoist texts, especially the TAO TE CHING, as well as the theory of YIN–YANG, the quest for immortality (*hsien*), mental and physical discipline, interior hygiene, internal alchemy (*nei tan*), healing and exorcism, pantheons of gods and spirits, and ideals of theocratic states. [47: V, 107–48; 64: III, 85–147; 75: 1–7; 100: 88–123]

Religious Taoism emerged in the form of distinct movements towards the end of the Later Han dynasty (23–220 CE). The most important was the Heavenly Master (*t'ien tsun*) or Five Pecks of Rice sect, founded by Chang Tao Ling (34–156) in Szechuan. Chang is said to have achieved immortality by gaining mastery over hundreds of spirits whose names and functions he identified and preserved for his disciples in the *Auspicious Alliance Canonical Registers*. At the head of this pantheon are the 'Three Pure Ones' (*san ch'ing*), the Lords of Heaven, Earth, and Man. Knowledge of this and similar registers determines the rank of the orthodox priest in the established Taoist sects. Chang founded a successful church state in Szechuan. (*See* TAO TSANG.)

The Sacred Jewel (*ling pao*) sect was a peaceful movement which developed early in the 4th century. Its adherents developed important Taoist rituals such as the rite of cosmic renewal and ritual method of controlling spirits. These rituals were adopted by the Heavenly Master sect in the 5th century and later by all sects which claimed to be orthodox. The Highest Pure (*shang ch'ing*) or Mao Shan sect which emerged early in the 4th century emphasized methods of controlling the spirits through meditation rather than ritual. Many sects of varying degrees of orthodoxy emerged during the T'ang and Sung dynasties (618–1126). Described collectively as Spirit Cloud (*shen hsiao*) Taoists, they constitute the majority of Taoist priests in modern Taiwan, where they are called 'Masters of Methods' (*fa shih*) or Red-headed Taoists; and are distinguished from the more orthodox 'Tao Masters' (*tao shih*) or Black-headed Taoists. [21; 64; 75: v, 84–105; 76; 77; 101]

Tao Te Ching [x] The most famous and influential Taoist text (TAO CHIAO), it is traditionally attributed to Lao Tzu, supposedly a contemporary of CONFUCIUS (551–479 BCE) [31: VIII, 170–91]. It is, however, impossible to identify accurately the author or the date of this obscure and aphoristic text. The fact that it criticizes established Confucian values [55 or 90: XVIII, XIX, XXXIII] and is not mentioned by MENCIUS (371–289 BCE) but is discussed by HSUN TZU (300–230 BCE) suggests that it existed in some form between 350 and 300 BCE.

According to the *Tao Te Ching*, the nameless unchanging essence and source of heaven and earth may be called the *Tao*. Although the *Tao* produces and sustains all things, it does so without volitional or purposeful action (*wu wei*) [55 or 90: XXXVII]. The passive and the productive aspects of the *Tao* are described as non-Being (*wu*) and Being (*yu*) respectively [55 or 90: II, V, XI]. To accord with the *Tao*, the sage-ruler must be without desires, intentions, or volitional actions. If he truly achieves this state of non-doing then he will achieve tranquillity and is fit to rule the empire. [7: VII, 136–76; 19: VI, 106–26; 21; 47; 55; 90; 100: I, II, 1–83]

Tao Tsang [x] The Taoist (TAO CHIAO) canon (*Tao Tsang*) achieved its present form of 1,120 volumes in 1436 CE. An earlier form of the canon was even longer, but many volumes were destroyed, and its order was disrupted when Kublai Khan had it burned in 1281 CE. The classification of the *Tao Tsang* into the *San Tung* (Three Vaults) and the *Ssu Fu* (Four Supplements) dates from at least the early 4th and early 5th centuries CE respectively. This form of classification has been applied to the subsequent versions of the *Tao Tsang*, although the precise contents of these categories have been subject to some variations.

The first of the *San Tung*, the *Tung Chen* (True Vault) contains mainly the meditation and ritual texts of the Yu Ching (Jade Capital) or Shang Ch'ing (Highest Pure) sect of Mao Shan. The second is the *Tung Hsuan* (Mysterious Vault), largely devoted to the *Ling Pao* (Sacred Jewel) texts, and gives details of many rituals and talismans. The third section is the *Tung Shen* (Spirits Vault), which initially contained the *San Huang Wen* (*Three Emperors Writ*) and the *Meng Wei Ching Lu* (*Auspicious Alliance Canonical Registers*), the 24 registers of the names and functions of spirits discovered by Chang Tao Ling (34–156 CE) of the Heavenly Master (*t'ien tsun*) sect.

The *Ssu Fu* (Four Supplements) contain many important texts, some of which are earlier than those in the *San Tung*. The *T'ai Hsuan* (Great Mystery) section contains the TAO TE CHING. The central text of the *T'ai Ping* (Great Peace) section is the *T'ai Ping Ching* (Classic of Great Peace). The *T'ai Ch'ing* (Great Purity) section contains works on ALCHEMY and philosophical Taoism (TAO CHIA). The *Cheng I* (Orthodox One) section is based upon the canonical works of the Heavenly Master sect. [76: 31–61; 101: VIII, 253–67]

Tapas [XIII.A] Literally 'heat' or 'fire'; in Hindu tradition, particularly, the heat generated by an ascetic through austerities. In the *Rig-veda* (VEDA) it is tentatively suggested that the world was generated through some primeval *tapas* [2: 251]. There is also a tendency to regard *tapas* as a magical power.

Targum [XVII] An Aramaic translation-commentary to the BIBLE. At the end of the second TEMPLE period Jews adopted Aramaic as their mother tongue and could not understand the Hebrew text of the Bible (LANGUAGES) [52: 46]. During public readings the Bible would be accompanied by a paraphrastic trans-

lation in Aramaic [11: 164; 47: 20]. In
the course of time these were edited into
official versions. The best known is *Targum Onkelos* on the Pentateuch, which
avoids the use of anthropomorphisms in
its translation. [9 vol. 15: 811]

Tarot [XVIII] A pack of 78 cards used
originally for games, now increasingly
for DIVINATION. Fifty-six cards form
four suits of 14 cards each; the other 22
are unsuited 'trumps' with designs of a
powerfully symbolic nature (the Fool,
the Wheel of Fortune, the Tower,
Love, Fortitude, and so on). The cards
appeared in about 1440 in northern
Italy, where playing-cards were already
known. The trump designs were
perhaps drawn from one of the visual
memory-systems [29] common at the
time: they were originally unnumbered
and players had to remember their
sequence. In 1781 Antoine Court de
Gébelin (1719–84) proposed an Egyptian hermetic source (HERMETISM) for
the cards, and a certain Alliette
('Etteilla') (d. 1791) began their use in
divination. 'Eliphas Lévi' (WESTERN
MAGICAL TRADITION) later proposed a
Kabbalistic interpretation, on which
modern divinatory use is based, viewing the trumps as emblems of the 22
'paths' connecting the *sefirot* of the 'Tree
of Life' (KABBALAH). [8]

Tefillin [XVII] The two black leather
boxes worn on the left arm and head by
adult male Jews during weekday morning services. *Tefillin* are known in
English as 'phylacteries'. They contain
the four passages in the BIBLE (Exodus
13: 1–10, 11–16; Deuteronomy 6: 4–9,
11: 13–21) which command the Jew to
put, or bind, the words of God as a sign
on his hand and between his eyes. The
hand *tefillah* has these passages on one
parchment, and the head *tefillah* on four
separate parchments. [13: 502]

Temenos [XII] A *temenos* ('sanctuary')
was, in GREEK RELIGION, dedicated to
one or more deities and served a city, a
smaller community, all the Greeks
(Panhellenic examples are at Delphi and

Olympia), or a section of them. A wall,
or boundary-stones, separated it from
secular space. It often contained a sacred
tree, stone, or spring, associated with a
deity. Sanctuaries varied in shape, size,
and splendour as well as in the number
and size of their buildings. These buildings included the essential temple (*naos*)
and altar (*bomos*), as well as storerooms, dining-rooms, porticoes, and
areas for games and dramatic performances. Sanctuary areas also included
votive offerings (*anathemata*), some of
which (e.g. statues) stood in the open.
The temple building was not used for
private worship. In its main part it
housed the cult-statue. There was usually a colonnade, front and back porch
and sometimes a back room (*adyton*).
Sacrifices (RITES) were performed on
the altar outside; in some temples there
was cult-activity inside. Access to the
inside was restricted. Temples varied in
size and magnificence; some were richly
decorated with mythological sculptures.
They became the focus of a city's self-advertisement, stimulating patriotism
and pride in civic religion. Deities were
represented as idealized humans. Art
reflected the values of the state-religion
which it served (POLITIKE) and other
devotional forms adapted this medium
to suit their needs. [19; 20]

Templa [XXV] Originally, Roman *templa* were rectangular areas either in the
sky or on the earth, so defined by the
augurs (SACERDOTES) as to provide the
basis for interpreting signs either from
lightning or from the flight of birds
(AUSPICIA). The terrestrial ones were
said to be *loci effati*, freed from evil
forces, and thereby inaugurated. Temples in our sense (properly *aedes sacrae*)
were usually, but not necessarily, *templa*.
[6: 314–19; 9: 12–14] The worship of
the gods was initially carried out at
open-air altars (*arae*) and these remained
outside the temple, as the essential context for sacrifices (RITUALS). The building was added to house the god's image,
to store the paraphernalia of the cult and

the dedications made by individuals as the result of private vows to the god. Eventually they became storehouses of art-treasures from conquered Greece. [17: 44–7] Some functions were proper to *templa* in the strict sense; only in them, for instance, could meetings of the Senate take place. [6: 316]

Temple (Jerusalem) [XI.A, XVII] (Hebrew *Bet Ha-Mikdash*) The first Israelite temple in Jerusalem was built by Solomon (950 BCE). Phoenician architects constructed it on a common Near Eastern plan: from east to west one proceeded through the courtyard, vestibule, nave ('holy place') to the inner sanctuary ('holy of holies') where stood the ark, the symbol of Yahweh's presence (GOD).

In 587 BCE it was destroyed by the Babylonians. The site lay derelict for 70 years, until a new temple (Zerubbabel's), of modest proportions, was built by permission of the Persian king (BIBLICAL HISTORY). This temple was profaned by Antiochus IV (167 BCE) and reconsecrated under Judas Maccabaeus three years later.

Under Herod (19 BCE) it was greatly enlarged and beautified. In its outer court JESUS CHRIST taught when he visited Jerusalem. It was destroyed by the Romans in 70 CE. [XI.A: 3: 131–6; 16: XXIV; XVII: 9 vol. 15: 942] Traditional Jews believe that a Third Temple will be built in the age of the MESSIAH. [XVII: 47: 535]

Temples (Ancient Near Eastern) [VI] Originally created by the secular community in Sumer (SUMERIANS) [23: 17–20], temples acquired land and possessions. As the god's home, tended by divine servants, some temples also had a social duty (HAMMURABI'S CODE) to make capital available to worshippers, and to provide accommodation for orphans, the offspring of religious prostitution, and children dedicated in times of famine. Temples were renewed and restored by successive rulers (KINGSHIP), and varied considerably in size

and style during different periods [13: 145–9; 25: 40]

Most societies acknowledged the king as high priest of the chief god. At every temple (the 'god's dwelling'), the priests acted as divine servants [13: 149–55]; they performed rituals, obtained oracular prophecies (ASTROLOGY), and administered the god's lands. Organized as hierarchies, priesthoods were passed down in families; ritual purity was demanded for performance of the rites. Some establishments had priestesses whose duties included sacred prostitution. At Ur, and Larsa, the high priestess acted as the 'god's wife', while others enjoyed special business and inheritance concessions [23: 17–20]. In the temples, priests attended to the deity's supposed bodily needs through ritual enactment, and propitiatory offerings were brought by those seeking healing. These included first-fruits and animal sacrifices (HITTITES; PHOENICIANS; SUMERIANS), and occasional examples occur of human sacrifice (HITTITES), following military defeat [13: 151]. At FESTIVALS special rites were enacted in which the rulers took part [13: 151–6; 17: 39]. The main non-temple rites were those concerning burials (AFTERLIFE).

Templo Mayor [XIX] The most powerful and monumental Aztec shrine was what the Spanish called the Templo Mayor (1325–1521 CE), located in the centre of the capital, Tenochtitlan. It was a huge pyramid temple, called Coatepec (HUITZILOPOCHTLI) meaning Snake Mountain, supporting the great shrines to Huitzilopochtli, the sun and war god, and TLALOC, the rain and agricultural god, to whom massive HUMAN SACRIFICES of warriors, women, and children were made. The shape, iconography, and ritual actions at the Templo Mayor commemorated the myth of Huitzilopochtli's birth at the cosmic mountain, his dismemberment of the goddess Coyolxauhqui representing the moon, and his destruction of the *centzon huitznahua*, the 400 gods of the south representing the stars.

Tendai [XVI] Named after the mountain and the sect in Chekiang province, China, T'IEN-T'AI. The priest SAICHO introduced Tendai concepts to his monastery Ichijoshikan-in on Mount Hiei north-east of Kyoto, on his return in 805 [13: 49–58; 19: 56–7, 191–3; 34: 134–48]. His *Kenkai-ron* was a treatise explaining the MAHAYANA injunctions leading to initiation. Tendai's philosophical base is the Lotus Sutra (*Hokke-kyo*) as used by the Kegon sect (NANTO ROKUSHU), and Yakushi Buddha is the chief deity (JAPANESE BUDDHAS AND BODHISATTVAS). Saicho built the first Lotus Sutra meditation hall in 812, and the formal adoption of the *nembutsu* practice in 851 opened the way for major developments in AMIDA WORSHIP. Tendai became distinctly esoteric when ENNIN introduced the tantric (TANTRA) use of mandalas and accompanying rituals about 25 years after Saicho's death. Simple ZEN-style meditation was practised. Despite imperial support, the lack of sectarian exclusiveness alienated the Nara clergy (JAPAN, BUDDHISM IN) and Saicho failed during

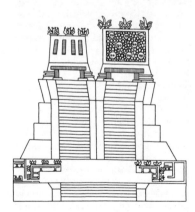

The Great Temple of Huitzilopochtli and Tlaloc, Texcoco

his lifetime to get a formal name for his temple (KUKAI) and to break the grip of the Nara clergy (NANTO SHICHIDAI-JI) on ordinations. Both were later approved, the temple becoming the Enryaku-ji in 823 (era name: 782–806). All of the Kamakura schools of Buddhism owed their origins to monks trained in Tendai: Pure Land [34: 194–203], ZEN [36], and NICHIREN [1]. The temple took on a strong political colouring by medieval times, its warrior-monks feuding violently with other temples and shrines, terrorizing the city of Kyoto at night. Eventually Oda Nobunaga (1534–82) burned the Enryaku-ji in 1571, killed most of the priests, and dispersed many of its possessions. Some later rebuilding was ordered by Toyotomi Hideyoshi (1536–98) and Tokugawa Ieyasu (1542–1616), and the Enryaku-ji now consists of three separated subtemples.

A major doctrinal contribution by Tendai has been in attributing the BUDDHA-nature to the ordinary man, affirming that enlightenment is aided by moralistic ways and rigorous meditation [34: 139–42]. The monks indulge in strict disciplinary training, reading *sutras* rather than commentaries, and studying the Triple Truth of Tendai: the Void (EMPTINESS), the Temporary (the idea of impermanence, ANICCA), and the Middle Path. (*See also* T'IEN-T'AI.)

Tenri-Kyo [XVI] A Japanese faith-healing sect tracing its founding to a female shaman (MIKO) Nakayama Miki (1798–1887), with headquarters at Tenri in Nara prefecture [19: 225–6; 35]. It was made sectarian by the man now regarded as a spiritual co-founder, Iburi Izo [19: 98]. The adherents revere both a creator deity Tenri-O-no-mikoto and the spot where creation took place. Happiness and prosperity are achieved by mastering human frailties and failures. Work and service in harmony are believed to lead towards reincarnation in a more virtuous state. The sect heads are all descendants of Nakayama Miki. All holders of formal offices connected with the widespread, strongly mission-oriented organization are adherents.

Teopixque [XIX] The priests, of various levels, who directed all facets of ceremonial and educational life in late pre-Hispanic central Mexico (1325–1521 CE) [19: 78–90, 147–50]. Most temples had full-time resident priests and the larger temples had both male and female religious specialists or *cihuateopixque*, who acted as the primary intermediaries between the society and the gods.

One of the principal responsibilities of the *teopixque* was the transmission of the historical and religious traditions in oral form (HUEHUETLATOLLI) [12: 177–83] and pictorial books called *amoxtlacuilolli*. They also directed the elaborate ritual schedules for the temples, the construction and renovation of ceremonial buildings, the fabrication of statues, the sacrifice of animals and humans (HUMAN SACRIFICE), and the education of the nobles (CALMECAC). Controlling the priestly hierarchy were the dual high priests called *quequetzalcao* (TOPILTZIN QUETZALCOATL), who also directed the activities of part-time rotational priests and votive penitent priests. The latter usually came from the upper classes and their temporary service in the temples gained them divine favour and prestige. All priests painted themselves black, practised sexual abstinence, performed a rigorous schedule of offerings and carried out penitential exercises, especially blood-letting from special parts of the body. On special ceremonial occasions, the TLATOANIS took the roles of priests, to lead ceremonial dances and perform human sacrifices.

Teteoinnan [XIX] MESOAMERICAN RELIGIONS had a rich array of mother-earth goddesses, which were forms of Teteoinnan, Mother of the Gods [2: VII]. These goddesses were representatives of the distinct but sometimes combined qualities of terror and beauty, regeneration and destruction. The goddesses were worshipped in earth-mother cults especially developed in the Huaxteca culture on the gulf coast and among the Aztecs in central Mexico. These cults were generally concerned with the abundant powers of the earth, women and fertility. Among the most prominent goddesses were Tlazolteotl, Xochiquetzal, and Coatlicue (HUITZILOPOCHTLI). Tlazolteotl was the earth-mother concerned with sexual powers, passions, and the pardoning of sexual transgressions. [17: 420–22] Conceived in quadruple or quintuple forms as the *Ixcuiname*, her powers sometimes merged with the malevolent death forces associated with the earth, crossroads, and dangerous places. The youthful dimension of the earth-mother was Xochiquetzal, the goddess of love and sexual desire [7: XVI]. Pictured as an attractive nubile maiden associated with flowers, feasting, and pleasure, she was also the goddess of pregnancy, childbirth, and the feminine arts, like weaving. A ferocious goddess, Coatlicue, the Serpent Skirt, represented the cosmic mountain which conceived all stellar beings and devoured all beings into her repulsive, lethal, and fascinating form. Her statue (AZTEC SCULPTURE) is studded with sacrificed hearts (HUMAN SACRIFICE), skulls, hands, ferocious claws, and giant-snake heads. [12: 89]

Tezcatlipoca [XIX] Tezcatlipoca, the Smoking Mirror, was one of the four great creator-gods of MESOAMERICAN RELIGIONS, who arranged the universe and set the cosmic ages in motion through periodic celestial battles which resulted in periods of stability called 'Suns' (CEMANAHUAC). [2: 80–101] Tezcatlipoca was sometimes cast as the supernatural antagonist of QUETZALCOATL, the deity associated with cultural creativity, urban order, and wisdom. Yet Tezcatlipoca has the most overwhelming power and protean personality of any Mesoamerican deity. His many forms reflect the omnipotent character of the numinous forces of central Mesoamerican religion. Among his aspects were Itztli, a calendar god, Tepeyollotl, an ancient jaguar–earth god, Ixquimilli–Itztlacoliuhqui, a god of punishment, and Omacatl, the spirit of revelry. The Smoking Mirror stood for the contradictory forces of youthful vitality and ferocious darkness. According to the Toltec tradition (TOLLAN), Tezcatlipoca drew his uncanny powers from his major accoutrement, an obsidian mirror which cast a magical spell over the Toltec king TOPILTZIN QUETZALCOATL, resulting in the downfall of the kingdom and the reintroduction of HUMAN SACRIFICE into ceremonial practices. [6: 371–92]

Theism [XXVIII] (1) Belief in a single divine being ('God' rather than a GOD) as personal, actively related to but distinct from the divinely created reality which includes the human race. Thus, theism holds to both the immanence (the presence within and interaction with the world) and the transcendence (the 'otherness', independence, and separation from the world) of God. In this, it is contrasted with PANTHEISM on the one side and, on the other, with that DEISM which holds God to be the creator but not active in what he created.

(2) More specifically, the world-view which is the putative conclusion of classical ARGUMENTS FOR THE EXISTENCE OF GOD, the self-existent perfect Spirit upon whom the world depends for its existence, continuance, meaning, and purpose. [6: VI; 13: 80–84]

Theism (Jewish) [XVII] The belief in one God who has created heaven and earth is at the very centre of faith in JUDAISM (*see* GOD (IN HEBREW AND CHRISTIAN SCRIPTURES)). The unity of God, and the need for man to relate to him in love, are expressed in the first verses of the SHEMA, the central

affirmation of Jewish belief repeated twice daily in the liturgy: 'Hear O Israel, the Lord is our God, the Lord is one. You shall love the Lord your God with all your heart, with all your soul, and with all your might' (Deuteronomy 6: 4–5). MAIMONIDES, the great medieval theologian, states in his formulation of the essential principles of Judaism [22: II–VI; 48: 93] that the Jew must believe in the existence of one unique, perfect, incorporeal God who has created and sustains all that is, who is pre-existent, cannot be compared to any created being, and on whom all creatures are dependent. The Jewish mystics (KABBALAH), while accepting the basic unity of God, were unhappy about the philosophical and somewhat abstract slant of Maimonides' formulation. They developed a theosophical system in which different aspects of the divine activity are personified and related to human experience, the world itself having emanated from God. [9 vol. 7: 641]

Theoi [XII] Gods. Greek deities were anthropomorphic, possessing immortality, extensive powers, knowledge, happiness and beauty. They were neither transcendental nor omnipresent. They protected morality (ETHIKE), but sometimes cheated and committed adultery. Each had a MYTHOS, a cult-corpus, certain functions, and embodied certain concepts (e.g. Apollo: order). Divine personalities developed over time and varied between cities and again in Panhellenic GREEK RELIGION which, however, influenced local conceptions (TEMENOS). Deities helped, but did not generally have affection for, humans, although they occasionally showed compassion. Worshippers generally did not feel affection for or intimacy with the gods except in certain cults, especially MYSTERIA and healing cults. Human relations with the gods focused on paying the honour due to them through sacrifices, other cult observances, and abstention from divinely disapproved

behaviour. No god was entirely negative, but each had a dangerous side.
Greatest were the 12 *Olympioi*, residing
on Mount Olympos, a divine family
headed ' by Zeus (COSMOS) which
included Hera, Poseidon, Apollon, Ares,
Hermes, Hephaistos, Athena, Aphro-
dite, Artemis, Demeter, and Hestia
(or Dionysos). Hades, Persephone, and
other underworld deities are *Chthonioi*
(*chthon* = earth) (the distinction is not
absolute: deities in each category have
sides and cults belonging to the other).
There are many minor divinities, often
attracting private devotion (e.g. Pan,
Nymphai (Nymphs), *Mousai* (Muses),
river-gods), and personifications (e.g.
Nemesis (ETHIKE)). Hellenistic Greeks
craved divine protection and personal
contact, hence the popularity of deities
who lent themselves to this, like Dionysos, Asklepios, and the newly introduced oriental gods, especially Isis and
Sarapis. [2: III, IV.3; 8: 75–80; 10]

Theology [XXVIII] Discourse about
God, or the science that treats of the
divine. Although often implicitly limited
to its Christian form, theological work
is appropriate in most religious contexts
as a systematic expression of beliefs, an
account of their sources and authority,
and a clarification of their relation to
other areas of belief [2: 176; 13]. Western thought has traditionally recognized
two kinds of theology: NATURAL
THEOLOGY, as accessible to human
reason; and revealed theology, based on
divine revelation, usually as the Christian church claims to have received it.
This sharp distinction and exclusive
claim are now less generally accepted.
Theologians, especially but not only
Protestant Christians, have argued that
all valid theology is 'revealed'. Wider
religious studies show that non-biblical
traditions (e.g. those of Indian origin)
accord extra-human authority to certain
documentary or oral sources. The possi-
bilities have been canvassed of
developing (1), within Christianity, an
ecumenical theology (ECUMENICAL

MOVEMENT), and (2) from a wider
perspective, through inter-religious dialogue, a global theology [13: 36–8; 14:
esp. 105–7; 20].

Theosis [XI.D] Deification. In the theology of ORTHODOX CHURCHES the
vocation of man is to become God. Man
comes by faith, by virtue, by prayer and
MYSTERIES, to participate in the divine
Energies, which divinize and transform
until the human being, while remaining
fully a human being, is totally united
with God. (HESYCHASM) [23; 24; 47:
236ff]

Theosophical Society [XVIII] An organization founded (1875) in New York
by the Russian clairvoyante (PSYCHIC
POWERS) Helena Petrovna Blavatsky
(1831–91) and Col. H. S. Olcott (1832–
1907) to promote universal brotherhood, the study of comparative religion
and the investigation of 'unexplained
laws of nature and the powers latent in
man'. It propagates doctrines based on
Blavatsky's eclectic, visionary writings
[3], which draw on HINDUISM and
BUDDHISM. All religions are viewed as
versions of the one 'esoteric' truth,
'THEOSOPHY'. The individual's spiritual development, it is believed, is
supervised by a secret brotherhood of
Masters or *Mahatmas*, believed to reside
in Tibet. The universe consists of seven
interpenetrating 'planes'; each of us,
accordingly, has seven bodies (Divine,
Spiritual, Intuitional, Mental, Emotional, Etheric, Physical), the first three
comprising the 'Ego' or 'Overself', which
reincarnates countless times, experienc-
ing *karma* (happiness and suffering as
results of good and evil actions) and
evolving towards full 'Selfhood' in
conscious cooperation with the divine
purpose. The cosmos itself evolves over
vast periods, planets forming 'planetary chains' of seven successive similar
planets: our earth, which is the fourth
earth, will be followed by three more
in future. Study of such complexities
plays an important part in theosophy.
Members are encouraged to practise

meditation but no particular religious practice is enjoined.

The founders moved their headquarters to India in 1877. After Olcott's death leadership passed to the social reformer Annie Besant (1847–1923), who in 1911 proclaimed J. Krishnamurti (b. 1895) the coming 'World Teacher', a role he later repudiated. The society's influence has diminished since the 1930s, but it is still active in 60 countries and is prominent in India, where its international headquarters are at Adyar, Madras. It has been historically important in popularizing Eastern religious ideas in the West.

Theosophy [XVIII] Any system of thought concerned with the relationship between God and the creation, especially one intended to help man achieve direct experience of the divine. The word can describe any articulate mystical system; it has been applied especially to KABBALAH, NEOPLATONISM, and the system of Jakob BÖHME. It now most often refers to the teachings of the THEOSOPHICAL SOCIETY.

Theravada [IX.B] The most usual name for the Buddhism of Ceylon (Sri Lanka) and South-East Asia. Theravada (Sanskrit *Sthaviravada*), 'doctrine of the elders', was upheld by one party in the first Buddhist schism (4th century BCE). Although some scholars believe the MAHAYANA to originate ultimately from the opposing MAHASANGHIKAS, all extant branches of the Buddhist order (SANGHA) derive from these original elders. The term is applied to one particular branch, a variety of Vibhajjavada (Sanskrit *Vibhajyavada*), 'doctrine of analysis', which claimed to preserve the authentic teachings of the original elders. This school was strong in ancient Ceylon; in fact the early history of the Theravada outside the island is not well known. In the 5th century CE it was widely distributed in southern India and South-East Asia but the most authoritative centre was the Mahavihara at Anuradhapura in Ceylon.

The Theravada closed its scriptural canon (TIPITAKA) in the 1st century BCE, preserving the use of a Middle Indian Language (PALI). A more archaic scriptural tradition strengthened its claim to be a more authentic preserver of the teaching. The classical form of Theravada doctrine was established between the 5th and 10th centuries CE by a series of Pali commentators, notably BUDDHAGHOSA and DHAMMAPALA, from the mainland as well as from Ceylon. A later school flourished in the 12th and 13th centuries. By this time standard Pali verses and chants had been established for many ritual and devotional purposes, following an earlier tradition of chants (*paritta*) for healing and exorcism. The combination of Mahavihara doctrinal orthodoxy with new devotional forms replacing brahmanic ritual (BRAHMANS) and MAHAYANA ceremonial proved effective both in SINHALESE BUDDHISM and in SOUTH-EAST ASIA (BUDDHISM IN).

Classical Theravada recognizes the three alternative goals of ARAHAT, *paccekabuddha* (Sanskrit PRATYEKA-BUDDHA), and fully awakened BUDDHA. It is usually the path of the disciple (*savaka*, Sanskrit *shravaka*) to Arahatship which is set forth, but a *bodhisatta*. (Sanskrit BODHISATTVA) path to buddhahood is recognized (*see* PARAMITA) Theravada differs from the Mahayana in rejecting the suitability of the *bodhisatta* role for all and not accepting the authority of the Mahayana scriptures. The path of Arahatship is not considered selfish, but as 'beneficial for both self and others'.

Thnetoi Anthropoi [XII] Mortal men, mortals (*brotoi*). There was no consistent Greek myth of men's creation, only different tales about the following: the origin of woman and of earlier divinely created superior 'races' (KAKON); a Flood after which the sole survivors, Deukalion and Pyrrha (parents of Hellen, the Greeks' eponymous ancestor), turned stones into people; and the minor god Prometheus, Deukalion's father, also mankind's champion and benefactor, who created men from clay. Men's position in the universe was considered to be humble, and an unbridgeable gap separated them from gods (THEOI). Another tendency, predominant in Hellenistic times, blurred the limits so that, for example, exceptional men could become HEROES after death and monarchs were deified (POLITIKE). Orphism (ORPHEUS) ascribed a divine spark to men: they sprang from the ashes of the Titans who had devoured Dionysos-Zagreus (COSMOS). Gods were thought to intervene in men's life, Zeus and Fate somehow determined events, but men were thought to have free will – a paradox challenged by Hellenistic astrological (ASTROLOGY) and Stoic (PHILOSOPHIA) determinism. [7: 155–6; 8: 74–83; 12: 131–4; 17: 144–52]

Thomism [XI.D] The theological school which basically follows the teaching developed by Thomas Aquinas (c. 1225–74) and which has, until recently, enjoyed officially a dominant position in Roman Catholic theological instruction (ROMAN CATHOLICISM). Aquinas was a Dominican philosopher and theologian, whose many works culminated in the *Summa contra Gentiles* (a missionary textbook in which he defends NATURAL THEOLOGY) and the unfinished *Summa theologica*. In these he used the recently rediscovered works of Aristotle to produce a systematic presentation of Christian theology. According to Aquinas, certain truths about the existence and nature of GOD can be determined by natural reason although they are also normatively revealed (ARGUMENTS FOR THE EXISTENCE OF GOD). Other truths, however, lie beyond reason's competence (although they are not contrary to it) and are knowable only through revelation. The influence of Aristotle is particularly seen in Aquinas's treatment of the attributes of God. His doctrines

of God as unmoved, impassible, and simple may follow from Aristotelian principles but lie uneasily with Christian views of God as a loving agent. [5; 12]

Thor [V] The cult of Thor was very popular in the Viking age (VIKINGS), particularly in western Scandinavia, and many people and places were named after him. Like the Germanic Donar, (Anglo-Saxon Thunor), he was a sky-god, controlling winds and storms, and associated with the oak. Thursday was his day. His hammer represented lightning and he guarded the AESIR from attack. He protected his worshippers, and presided over the Law Assembly; oaths were sworn on his sacred ring. He was pictured as a red-bearded figure with fiery eyes and a huge appetite, drawn by goats in a wagon which rattled across the sky, causing thunder [6: III]. Small hammers were worn as amulets in the late Viking age, and hammer and swastika were carved on memorial stones as his symbols. Many tales, serious and comic, were told of his encounters with FROST-GIANTS and his fishing for the World-Serpent (EDDA). He was to perish when he slew the serpent at RAGNAROK.

Thunderbird [III] A widely recurring figure of Amerindian mythology, cult, and art. An intermediary, celestial spirit (occasionally pitted against chthonian beings), the thunderbird is usually conceived of as an eagle or great bird that produces thunder by flapping its wings and lightning by opening and closing its eyes. In eastern North America, thunderbirds are often four in number, one for each of the cosmic quarters. [8: IV]

Tibetan Astrology [XXIX] Three different Buddhist astrological systems were practised in Tibet. One, *kar tsi*, was derived from the system of the Kalachakra tantra, which entered Tibet from the mystic kingdom of SHAMBHALA, via India. Calculations in this system are based on nine planets, 12 residences (zodiacal signs), and 27 constellations. The second system, *jung tsi*, was originated by the BODHISATTVA Manjushri, and introduced from China. Here calculations are based on the five elements of wood, fire, earth, metal, and water; it has a 12-year cycle, with each year corresponding to an animal and the eight trigrams of divination of the *I Ching* (Book of Changes, *see* CONFUCIAN CANON). The third system, *wang char*, was originally thought to have been set out by SHIVA, and was introduced to Tibet from India. It relates to a type of NUMEROLOGY, and uses circular diagrams which have a talismanic value (ASTROLOGY). [14]

Tibetan Religions [XXIX] Two principal religious traditions have appeared in recorded Tibetan history: BON and BUDDHISM. Although the Bon tradition represents the oldest forms of Tibetan religion, it has in the course of time been severely modified, to the point where it now resembles a Buddhist sect. The introduction of Buddhism was gradual, occurring over four centuries (from the 7th to the 11th centuries CE), largely through the agency of Indian masters such as Padmasambhava and Atisha and Tibetan scholars such as Marpa Lotsava. Thus in general terms Tibetan Buddhism, despite a certain influence from CHINA and CENTRAL ASIA, represents Buddhist theory and practice as it had developed in India over the first 1,500 years of its existence.

Four major sects have dominated Buddhism in Tibet: KAGYU, SAKYA, NYINGMA, and GELUG. Each sect possesses its own particular lineages of ritual, meditational, and philosophical teachings and monastic organization. However, all share the triple division of doctrine and practice into the three *yanas* ('vehicles', Tibetan *theg-pa*) of HINAYANA, MAHAYANA, and *tantra-yana* (TANTRA (2)). [24]

T'ien [X] This Chinese term, usually translated as Heaven, refers to the absolute principle or supreme being controlling the universe. *T'ien* was worshipped by Chinese rulers from the

beginning of the Chou dynasty (1027 BCE) onwards (SHANG TI). As an anthropomorphic popular deity *T'ien* is worshipped as the Jade Emperor (*Yu Huang*) (CHINESE PANTHEON). *T'ien* is also used in a more abstract sense as fate, destiny, or the operation of purely natural forces (HSUN TZU). [7: VI, 116–23; 31: III, 30–32; 81: II, 12–31; 86: I, 4–5]

T'ien-T'ai [X] A scholastic and eclectic school of CHINESE BUDDHISM, founded by Hui Ssu (515–77 CE) and Chih I (Chih K'ai) (538–97), based principally upon the Lotus Sutra (*Saddharmapundar-ika*) and on Chih I's two commentaries on it, and upon Hui Ssu's 'Method of Concentration and Insight in the Mahayana' (*Ta Ch'eng Chih Kuan Fa Men*). The basic doctrine is that of the Threefold Truth, which asserts that *dharmas* (DHAMMA) are: (1) empty (EMPTINESS), because they are without self or being of their own; (2) existing temporarily by depending on causes and conditions; and (3) intermediate, because they are empty and exist at the same time. Hence things are both distinct and also part of a unified organic whole. This idea was developed into the teaching of the '3,000 realms in one thought moment'. In the 10 levels of existence (of BUDDHAS, BODHISATTVAS, PRATYEKABUDDHAS, ARAHATS, gods, demons, humans, hungry ghosts, animals, beings in HELLS) each level shares the characteristics of the other levels, giving 100 realms. Each of these has 10 characteristics of suchness (*tathata*), giving 1,000 realms. Each 1,000 is divided into living beings, elements (*skandhas*), and space, giving 3,000. All these 3,000 realms of existence interpenetrate and entail each other, and in every single thought-moment each of these realms is immanent. According to Hui Ssu the immanence of the 'real suchness' (*Bhuta-tathata*) and the 'womb of the Buddhas' (*Tathagata-garbha*) in all realms, *dharmas*, and beings, can be experienced by the method of concentration and insight. [7: XXIV, 396–405; 24: XIII, 309–28; 32: IX,

360–83] According to Chih I, all the different doctrines and methods contained in the Buddhist *sutras* were taught by the Buddha at different periods of his career for beings at different levels of understanding, hence all the *sutras* could be regarded as the authentic word of the Buddha. This view was systematized into the theory of the five periods and the eight teachings. (TENDAI) [15: XI, 305–13]

Tillich, Paul [XI.C] (1886–1965) Theologian; studied at Berlin, Tübingen, and Halle. After teaching theology at Marburg, Dresden, and Frankfurt, he had to leave Germany in 1933 because of his religious socialism. He became professor of Philosophical Theology at Union Theological Seminary, New York. His theology, which was considerably influenced by EXISTENTIALISM, attempted to correlate faith and culture. He maintained that God is being-itself, not one being among others, and that all other statements about God are essentially symbolic. [3; 20]

Tipitaka [IX.A] A PALI term for the Buddhist canonical scriptures, referred to in Sanskrit as the *Tripitaka*, or 'threefold collection'. They exist in a number of different corpuses, which are products of different schools of BUDDHISM. The most accessible is that of the THERAVADA, in Pali. The contents of the two collections (Pali and Sanskrit) are different, but follow the same arrangement of material: first, the VINAYA-PITAKA, the 'basket', or assemblage of material (*pitaka*), dealing with the Buddhist order and its history, constitutive regulations, and disciplinary code; second, the SUTTA-PITAKA (Sanskrit *Sutra-pitaka*), the collection of discourses attributed to GOTAMA, the BUDDHA, which are regarded as comprising the definitive body of his teaching, or DHAMMA (Sanskrit DHARMA); and third, the ABHIDHAMMA-*pitaka* (Sanskrit *Abhidharma-pitaka*). [37: 201–7]

Tirtha, Tirtharaj [XIII.A] Literally a 'ford' or 'bathing-place'. A *tirtha* is, in Hindu tradition, a place to which pilgrimage is made, a sacred place or shrine; *tirthayatra* (*yatra* = 'going') is pilgrimage. The most pre-eminent of all places of pilgrimage for the Hindus, the *tirtharaja*, is Prayaga (modern name, Allahabad), at the confluence (*sangam*) of the GANGA and Yamuna (or Jumna) rivers. It is believed that a third, the Saraswati, flows underground to join these other two sacred rivers at Prayaga. The confluence is the scene of a great annual *mela* or mass pilgrimage and fair combined. Such *melas* are a familiar feature of other similar places of pilgrimage all over India. Other famous sacred places include the holy cities of Ayodhya, Mathura, Gaya, and Banaras (Varanasi), and the mouth of the Ganga at Sagar in Bengal. A list of all such places would run into thousands. [3; 24A: 212–13]

Tirthankara [XV] Derived from *tirtha*, a ford, and *kara*, maker, *tirthankara* or 'ford-maker' is a term used by JAINS to refer to their tradition that the Jaina doctrine was taught by 24 'ford-makers', the makers, that is, of a way which others may follow across the stream of existence, from the misery of continued rebirth and dying, to freedom from rebirth [1: 290]. Another name for a *tirthankara* is *Jina*, that is, 'one who overcomes'; the title Jaina is derived from this term.

Tjurunga [XXII] The Aranda term for a type of cult object, in AUSTRALIAN RELIGION. The term also encompasses the sacred conceptions, traditions, and actions associated with each particular object. Usually an elongated board with rounded or pointed ends, it is sometimes a stone slab, or a shell, or even a tuber (such as a yam). The name *tjurunga* indicates a connection with a spirit being, and when a sacred board is used as a bullroarer the voice of the indwelling spirit is heard. The term can also be applied to the small implement used in sorcery for causing death from a distance ('pointing the bone'; *see* Melanesian POISEN). [21: 140–59; 27: 612–13]

Tlaloc [XIX] The most popular and widespread deity in Mesoamerican culture was Tlaloc (Chac in Mayan culture), the fertilizing rain-god. Tlaloc was often conceived in quadruple and quintuple forms called the *tlaloques*, each assigned to one of the sacred directions and given a sacred colour. This pattern usually involved a pre-eminent Tlaloc, with dwarfish *tlaloques* named, for instance, Opochtli, Nappatecuhtli, Yauhqueme, Tomiauhtecuhtli [17: 414–16]. The *tlaloques* were believed to dwell in the prominent peaks, where rain clouds emerged from caves to fertilize the land through rain, rivers, pools, and storms. Tlaloc's power was also manifested in the thunder, lightning, snow, and cold sicknesses which threatened the community. One mountain, called Mount Tlaloc in Spanish colonial times (after 1521), was believed to be the original source of the water and vegetation which nurtured human beings. The supreme importance of this deity is reflected in the fact that his shrine was placed alongside HUITZILOPOCHTLI's at the TEMPLO MAYOR in the centre of Tenochtitlan. At the same time, Tlaloc was the god of the masses who worshipped him in every agricultural community in the land. [7: VIII]

Two other major gods were intimately associated with Tlaloc, Chalchiuhtlicue, the goddess of waters, and Ehecatl the wind-god [2: 108]. Chalchiuhtlicue was usually identified with the maize-earth gods while Ehecatl, an aspect of the great god QUETZALCOATL, was known as *in tlachpancauh in tlaloque*, 'the roadsweeper of the rain-gods', meaning that Ehecatl's forceful presence announced the coming of the fertilizing rains. Tlaloc's supreme importance for fertility is reflected in the murals of Tlalocan, the rain-god's paradise where sea animals, spirits, butterflies, and moisture mingle together in a realm of abundance. [19: 83–8] This abundance

demanded valuable HUMAN SACRIFICES, in the form of children, at the various feasts of Tlaloc, which took place in different towns and cities. In one major festival the rulers of the Aztec empire solemnly participated in a special ceremony to sanctify the waters for the coming agricultural year. [7: 158]

Tlamatinime [XIX] *Tlamatinime*, 'knowers of things', were the teachers and philosophers who transmitted the revered ancient teachings of Nahuatl culture in the CALMECACS of the Aztec empire (MESOAMERICAN RELIGIONS) (1425–1520 CE). They were responsible for composing, painting, and articulating the moral teachings, sacred histories, calendric lore, and esoteric wisdom which had been inherited from the Toltecs (TOLLAN) of the Classic period. [17: XVII] They were considered the embodiment of knowledge, which they taught in didactic oral presentations called HUEHUETLATOLLI and pictorial forms to the future nobles and rulers of towns and cities. They used refined metaphorical forms called 'flower and song' to reflect upon the transitory nature of human existence, the true nature of god, the destiny of human life, and the precise character of cosmological order. One group of *tlamatinime* is reputed to have criticized in sophisticated poetic forms the mystico-militaristic attitudes of the Aztec state.

Tlatoani [XIX] The supreme rulers of Nahuatl-speaking groups in Mesoamerica were called Tlatoanis (Chief Speakers) and controlled civil, military, fiscal, and religious affairs in towns and cities. The Aztec Tlatoani [10: 192–3, 236–42; 17: 351–5] was responsible for ensuring the stability and renewal of cosmic order and was considered the living representative of HUITZILOPOCHTLI, the Aztec national god. Among his ritual functions was the redistribution of warriors' uniforms and arms to nobles, for whom he held lavish military banquets. In special festivals, as at the periodic inauguration of the

TEMPLO MAYOR, the Tlatoani acted as a high priest to initiate massive HUMAN SACRIFICES of captive warriors (TEOPIXQUE).

Tohunga [XXII] A specialist of the sacred, in POLYNESIAN RELIGION. The *tohunga* is priest, medium, exorcist, healer, and prophet. He officiates at birth, initiation, and death rites, and leads worship at the MARAE. He protects his people from the effects of violated TAPU and from sorcery or evil curses (*makutu*). Tribal lore and sacred knowledge (brought from the highest heaven by TANE in three baskets) was revealed by *tohungas* to initiates in houses of sacred learning (in Maori, *whare wananga*). [6; 7; 16]

Toleration [XI.B] The claims of Christianity (or of any religion) to exclusive truth have often led to persecution of religious deviation (HERESY and schism). This was reinforced when STATES with established churches regarded heresy as treasonable. Political and intellectual changes during and after the 17th century encouraged the development of toleration, although initially deviants did not enjoy full civil rights. Attitudes in ROMAN CATHOLICISM hardened under Pius IX (1846–78) and later against the modernists; but toleration was affirmed by Vatican COUNCIL II. [1: 675–96; 75]

Tollan [XIX] The ideal city state of Mesoamerica's golden age, ruled by TOPILTZIN QUETZALCOATL and the creator god QUETZALCOATL [16: 80–84]. In myth and sacred history, Tollan was pictured as the place where the concepts and institutions associated with great cities were crystallized. In Tollan, the calendar, ceremonial architecture, medicine, astrology, wisdom, art, and rituals were developed to an exquisite degree. This sense of excellence is reflected in the related terms, *toltecatl*, meaning 'skilled artist', and *toltecayotl*, signifying artistic creativity of a superior quality. [6: 24–47] Historically, Tollan has been identified with the city of

Tollan Xicocotitlan (also called Tula), which prospered between the 9th and 11th centuries CE [10: 121–6]. Tollan literally means 'place of reeds', but the term came to signify a place of abundance, a congregation of people, and metropolis. The prestige that was attached to this symbolic meaning is reflected in the number of cities, including Tollan Teotihuacan, Tollan Chololan (CHOLOLLAN), Tollan Tenochtitlan, and Tollan Chalco, that derived part of their authority from an association with the Toltec traditions of the great mythical and historical Tollan.

Tonalpohualli [XIX] The 'count of days' or ritual calendar, which guided many of the lavish religious events in Mesoamerican ceremonial centres (MESOAMERICAN CITY). It was also used for astronomical computations, the casting of horoscopes, and the determination of lucky and unlucky days. It was consulted in *tonalamatls* (books of days), for every important event in family, political, religious, and imperial matters. The *tonalamatls* recorded, in elaborate pictorial form, 260 named days, each designated by a number and a sign taken from a revolving system of 20 day signs and 13 numbers. The ritual year consisted of 20 13-day weeks in which each day was assigned a sacred colour, cardinal direction, a Lord of the Day, a Lord of the Night, and a sacred bird. The *tonalpohualli* system shows that, for Mesoamerican man, time exuded supernatural character and influence. A specialist, the *tonalpohuaque*, functioned mainly to determine the lucky and unlucky days, through careful examination of the five special characteristics associated with each day. This calendar system intermeshed with the solar calendar, *xihuitl* ('grass'), which consisted of 18 months of 20 days, each completed by five unnamed days to make a 365-day year. The new year's day of these two calendars coincided once every 52 years (NEW FIRE CEREMONY), which constituted an

Aztec century, *xiumolpilli*, and the critical period of cosmic renewal. [2: 16–22; 17: XIII]

Topiltzin Quetzalcoatl [XIX] One of the most widely taught histories in Mesoamerican culture (MESOAMERICAN CITY) narrated the career of the Toltec priest-king Topiltzin Quetzalcoatl, 'Our Young Prince the Feathered Serpent', also known as Ce Acatl (One Reed), Naxcitl (Four-Footed), and Tepeuhqui (Mighty One), who ruled in a golden age in TOLLAN, where ceremonial order, agricultural abundance, social harmony, and artistic excellence constituted the archetypal sacred city. [14: 40–42] Topiltzin Quetzalcoatl, who was revered as a semi-divine priest-king, refounded the 10th-century capital of Tollan on a new religious system based on an esoteric theology and an intense ritual system excluding HUMAN SACRIFICE. He was credited in Toltec oral and pictorial traditions with the invention of the calendar, jewel-working, and all artistic excellence. [7: 1] The combined sources paint a marvellous picture of his kingdom and sacred career. His ceremonial centre had four jewelled temples associated with four cosmic regions (CEMANAHUAC). He made ritual sacrifices on four sacred mountains near the city and in one ecstatic vision communicated directly with the Lord of Duality (OMETEOTL), who dwelt in the highest heaven. He was a lawgiver who dispensed his authority from a sacred mountain to all regions of his kingdom. Into this paradisal city came an enemy sorcerer, Tezcatlipoca, whose magical mirror and tricks enticed Topiltzin Quetzalcoatl into breaking his priestly vows and betraying his royal authority. After burying his treasures, Topiltzin Quetzalcoatl fled to Tlapallan, the sacred shore where, in alternate versions, he sacrificed himself on a funeral pyre and became the Morning Star (*Tlahuizcalpantecuhtli*), or disappeared across the sea on a raft of serpents promising to return one day and restore his ideal kingdom. This tradition had immense influence on the Aztecs, whose high priests were called QUETZALCOATL and who initially identified the Spanish invader Cortes (1485–1547) as the returning Toltec king who would restore the wonders of Tollan. [10: 324–5]

Torah [XVII] Literally 'teaching', the most general term in JUDAISM for the divine teaching. In its narrow sense it refers to the Pentateuch, or the first five books of the Hebrew BIBLE: Genesis, Exodus, Leviticus, Numbers, and Deuteronomy. Torah is also used to refer to the whole of the Hebrew Bible, to the oral teachings of Judaism, or in its widest sense to the whole of traditional Jewish law and lore. The common English translation of Torah as 'Law' misrepresents the concept, giving a narrow legal connotation to the much broader Jewish idea of revelation. Torah is part of an open-ended system; as such it requires study, and new insights into the word of God must be sought so that it can be applied to a variety of differing circumstances. The Torah is seen by Judaism as the product of the COVENANT by God with Israel, God who, as one of the benedictions of the liturgy puts it, 'has chosen us from amongst all the nations and given us His Torah' [48: 5]. It was revealed to the Israelites during their wanderings in the wilderness through the agency of MOSES. It is of a twofold nature: the written Torah of the Hebrew Bible and the oral Torah [53: IV], which was eventually written down in rabbinical literature [33: III]. The scroll of the Pentateuch read publicly in the SYNAGOGUE is called a *sefer Torah*, or Book of the Torah. Orthodox Judaism, while applying traditional teachings to novel situations created by modern technology, takes a very conservative stance to Torah. The divine teaching is sacrosanct, and cannot simply be changed or abandoned at will. It can, however, be reinterpreted by competent authorities, who bring the Torah insights of the past to bear on the present. [52: VII]

Toshogu Shrine [XVI] (Japan) The burial site of the early Tokugawa family shoguns (generals), in a heavily forested part of Tochigi prefecture at Nikko, situated below the SACRED MOUNTAIN Nantai, Lake Chuzenji, and Kegon waterfalls [30: 70, 101; 33: 261–87]. In a form of ancestor-worship, construction of elaborate buildings was started in 1634 by Kyoto craftsmen, on the orders of Tokugawa Iemitsu (1603–51) for his grandfather Ieyasu (1542–1616). Expenses were unlimited; the finest workmen were used. The largest Buddhist temple at Nikko is of the TENDAI sect and is associated with mountain worship. The original shrine (SHINTO SHRINES) is called Futaarasaan (meaning Mount Nantai). Ritual climbing and the burial of *sutras* (*Kyozuka*) for religious benefits were popular in the Edo period (1615–1868).

Totem [XXVIII] An animal or plant species, or other natural phenomenon, regarded as specifically related to the origin, welfare and/or organization of a human (usually descent) group [8: 58–60, 199]. The Ojibwa (ALGONQUIN tribe, North America) word provides the technical term 'totemism' for a belief system involving, e.g., TABU and increase rites, and some idea of descent from a mythical totemic ancestor (e.g. among Australian tribes) [10: 85–6]. Among the many theories of totemism [28: 48; 31: 113–14], its symbolic function in social cohesion was stressed by Durkheim [9; 10: 231; 28: 30; 31: 55–6]. In contrast, STRUCTURALISTS like Lévi-Strauss [16; 16A; 28: 48] emphasize the role of distinctive and ambivalent totem-concepts in the communication of meaning.

Transcendental Meditation [XXI] Although Maharishi Mahesh Yogi first arrived in Britain in 1958, it was not until the 'Beatles' 'converted' at the end of the 1960s that Transcendental Medi-

tation (TM) was to become widely practised in the West and, from 1970, that the Science of Creative Intelligence was to come into being with many qualified persons claiming scientific proof of the beneficence of the TM techniques. The movement aims to improve not only the individual practitioner but also the state of society and the world in general. [2: 62; 25: VI; 27; 30: V]

Meditators are initiated by being given a secret MANTRA. They may then proceed through a series of courses (which can cost them a considerable amount of money).

TM has been strongly criticized by the ANTI-CULT MOVEMENT not only for making false claims but also, it is alleged, for causing harm and for posing as a mere technique when it is, according to its critics, really a religion. [43]

Trickster [III] In North American Indian mythology, the trickster often presents a light-hearted variant of the CULTURE HERO. Typically a type of demiurge who continues, rather than initiates, the task of creation (CREATION MYTHS), this curious figure portrays a mixture of conflicting character traits, alternately sly, cunning, constructive, and generally well disposed to mankind, as well as amoral, frivolous, a prankster, and highly sexed [18]. The trickster (also 'trickster-transformer') may be theriomorphic (common forms include coyote, blue jay, mink, hare, and raven) or may display human features, although the latter are often exaggerated or ill-defined. Occasionally thought to be of divine origin (e.g. ALGONQUIAN Glooscap), the trickster is often referred to in myth as 'Old One', but this is less indicative of advanced years than of his timelessness. Albeit his techniques may include deceit, stupidity, and laziness, the trickster often unwittingly achieves results that benefit mankind (e.g. regulation of the seasons, domestication of animals) or provides instruction necessary for human existence (e.g. the use of fire, the art of agriculture, the practice of medicine). The trickster's presence in myth and ritual often provides a comic relief which eases the solemnity of such settings. [8: III]

Trinity [XI.B] Although rooted in Jewish MONOTHEISM, Christian belief in the divinity of JESUS CHRIST and the HOLY SPIRIT led to the development of the doctrine of the Trinity. This states that the one God reveals himself in the three 'persons' of Father, Son (Jesus Christ), and Holy Spirit [80]. These three persons are nevertheless regarded as a unity, sharing one 'substance'. The doctrine was eventually defined by early COUNCILS and theologians as 'three persons in one substance' (*homoousion*). This was an attempt to assert a real distinction between the persons (denied by e.g. Sabellius *fl.* 3rd century CE) while maintaining their unity, equality, and eternity (e.g. against ARIANISM, 4th century CE). For the Western Church the Holy Spirit proceeds from the Father 'and the Son' (the 'Filioque' clause added to the Nicene CREED). This is rejected by the ORTHODOX CHURCH, which sees the 'procession' of the Spirit as being from the Father through the Son. The development of these doctrines has been constantly influenced by current philosophy, and in modern times the views described here have often been challenged (e.g. by PROCESS THEOLOGY). Even the DEATH OF GOD was proclaimed by some in the 1960s. There has also been a recurring Christian tradition of UNITARIANISM. (Cf. GOD, CHRISTIAN CONCEPT OF.) [47; 76: IV, V, X; 107: 575–7]

Tripartite Ideology [XXX] The theory of Georges Dumézil and his followers that the earliest INDO-EUROPEANS had a hierarchically ordered tripartite (threefold) society which was precisely paralleled in the myths and epics of the world of the gods. In both society and myth the first, or priestly, sector was magico-religious, concerned with jus-

tice and sovereignty. The second, that of the warriors, was concerned with physical prowess or force; and the third was that of the productive workers who provided nourishment for the living world. Dumézil argues that because this social and mythical structure was inherent in the early Indo-European tradition its ideas are preserved in its daughter cultures, e.g. Greece, India, Iran, Rome, and Scandinavia. The way in which Dumézil has applied this theory to his analysis of the respective religions has caused considerable scholarly debate. His critics consider that he has forced the evidence, for example in the way he has categorized deities [30].

Tuatha de Danann [V] The Irish name for a group of gods, 'Peoples of the goddess Danu'. Danu was confused with Anu, a beneficent goddess associated with the Irish province of Munster, both possibly derived from an early Celtic mother-goddess (MATRES). The group included LUG, the DAGDA, Nuadu 'of the Silver Arm', Gobniu the Smith, and Dian Cecht the Healer [26: IV, 38–46]. They overcame various enemies, but after the coming of Christianity were said to retreat into the Sid, the ancient burial mounds of Ireland [26: V, 48–51].

Tumbuna [XXII] A collective term in Melanesian pidgin for clan ancestors who, while they dwell in a spirit-land, are constantly in touch with their living descendants. Spirits of the recently dead are honoured by funeral rites to ensure their continued support for the living. Ancestral spirits are invoked in the HAUS TAMBARAN and MALE CULT rituals and SINGSINGS, where they receive offerings of food and wealth. They make themselves present through dreams, mediums, and diviners, and in sacred stones, MASKS, and other objects. Obligations to ancestral spirits are the highest religious duties. They are believed to pass on from the creative gods and goddesses the power (MANA) which makes tribal rites and customs effective, bringing health, social harmony, and material well-being (salvation, in religious terms). Neglect of the spirits invites disease, death, and failure of crops. [2; 14; 23] Prophet-led renewal movements (sometimes called CARGO CULTS) may involve attempts to placate ancestor-spirits believed to be withholding power and blessings or bestowing them on others.

Tun-Huang [XXIX] The *Tun-Huang* collection of Tibetan and Chinese manuscripts, discovered in the early years of this century near the oasis of Tun-Huang in Chinese Turkestan, is important for the light it sheds on the early development of Buddhism in Tibet. It is likely that the Tibetan manuscripts, largely religious in content, are the debris of a clerical centre which flourished during the years of Tibetan occupation of the area between *c.* 780 and 850 CE. Certain manuscripts include reference to the vital part played by the two Tibetan kings, Srongsten Gampo and Trisong Detsun, in the establishment of Buddhism, and also to the Indian tantric master Padmasambhava, and are particularly important in constituting contemporary evidence of the latter's missionary role. Evidence is also provided as to the nature of the Buddhism being introduced: mention is made of both Sutra and TANTRA (2) doctrines and of the cycle of the meditational deity Dorje Phurpa and BARDO doctrine, both of which became prized teachings of the NYINGMA tradition. [15]

Turin Shroud [XI.B] A cloth marked by the apparent image of a crucified man, claimed to be that of JESUS CHRIST. It was first recorded in France in the 1360s, but has been in Turin since 1578. Since relics of this kind were often faked in the Middle Ages to create or publicize PILGRIMAGE centres, the shroud would normally be explained in this way. Recent interest in it is due to attempts to determine its date and provenance by scientific tests. So far they apparently do not rule out an origin in 1st-century CE Palestine; and the means by which the image was produced are not yet explained. Even if the image were proved to have been made by the body of Jesus Christ, its significance would remain debatable. In ROMAN CATHOLICISM relics of this kind are considered vehicles of divine grace (SALVATION); but in PROTESTANTISM they are often thought of as an obstacle to direct communion with God. [144A]

Typology [XXVIII] (1) A method of interpretation of sacred literature, in which characters or events from an earlier period (e.g. the Hebrew scriptures) are seen as prefiguring or foreshadowing others described or occurring later (e.g. the MESSIAH, or JESUS CHRIST in the New Testament (BIBLE)).

(2) In the study of religions, the method of analysis and classification according to type, in which Heinrich Frick (1893–1952) was a pioneer. Thus, 'founded' religions may be contrasted with those that 'developed'; religions may be grouped as tribal (primal) or national, or as 'world religions'; or as prophetic and mystical. These are 'ideal types' (in the sense in which Max Weber (1864–1920) used that term). [8: 12–14; 13: 25–9]

Tzitzit [XVII] Fringes worn at the corners of four-cornered garments by Jews, as commanded in the BIBLE (Numbers 15: 37–41), to remind them of God's commandments. Since four-cornered garments are not part of normal Jewish dress any more, a special four-cornered fringed prayer shawl (*tallit*) is worn for morning prayers. A smaller four-cornered fringed garment (*tallit katan*) is worn by traditional Jews as an undervest throughout the day. Women do not have to wear *tzitzit*. [9 vol. 15: 743, vol. 16: 1187]

· U ·

Ulema, 'Ulama' [XIV] 'Learned men', the body of religious and legal scholars in ISLAM. Members of this class have always been recruited by study under other recognized scholars in such institutions as AL-AZHAR in Cairo (also MADRASA) [72: II–III, V], and cannot really be considered as a priestly caste. The *ulema* have nevertheless been generally recognized in Sunni Islam (SUNNA) as custodians and interpreters of the corpus of sacred knowledge, often defending it against secular encroachments, even though they might at times be in receipt of official salaries [10 s.v.; 20 s.v.]. A parallel body in SHI'ISM is that of the *mujtahids* (*see* AYATULLAH).

Unification Church [XXI] Also known as the Holy Spirit Association for the Unification of World Christianity, the Unified Family, and Tong Il, the Church is associated with groups such as C.A.R.P. (Collegiate Association for the Research of Principles), I.C.F. (International Cultural Foundation), and Creative Community Project. The movement was founded in Korea in 1954 by the Reverend Sun Myung Moon. It spread to Japan, but did not have much success in the West until the late 1960s [24]. By 1980 full-time membership in the U.S.A. numbered about 3,000; most European countries have several centres but none has more than a few hundred members; and the worldwide full-time membership is unlikely to be many more than 200,000. Moon has lived in the U.S.A. since the early 1970s. The main recruitment centre in the West has been in California.

Unification theology, one of the most comprehensive to be found among the NEW RELIGIOUS MOVEMENTS [5], is millennial and messianic. It is to be found in the Divine Principle [17; 23], which offers a special interpretation of the BIBLE with additional revelations which, it is claimed, Moon received from God [23]. The Fall is said to be the result of a (spiritual) sexual relationship between Eve and the Archangel Lucifer, followed by a sexual relationship, before marriage, between Adam and Eve. History is interpreted as the struggle to restore the world to the state originally intended by God. As part of this process, Jesus should have married, but his mission failed and he was able to offer only spiritual, not physical, salvation to the world. Unification reading of history since the time of Jesus suggests that now is the time when the Lord of the Second Advent is upon the earth. (Messiahship is seen as an office, held by a sinless man born of human parents.) Most members believe Moon to be the Messiah, although he himself has made no public statement to this effect.

Members, popularly known as 'Moonies', typically join in their early twenties, are well-educated, and from the middle classes. In the West members usually live in community centres. The life-style is one of hard-working, 'sacrificial' concentration on restoring the world. Frequently, long hours are spent fund-raising in the streets or witnessing to potential converts. There is celibacy outside marriage. Moon suggests marriage partners and mass wedding ceremonies (Blessings) are held at intervals (1,800 couples were Blessed in South Korea in 1975). This is the most important Unification rite, the movement having little else in the way of formal ritual, apart from a weekly 'Pledge'.

The Unification Church owns several valuable properties and businesses. It publishes a daily newspaper, *News-World*, in New York. It has a theological seminary in Barrytown, New York. The church has received considerable hostility from parents, the media, and the ANTI-CULT MOVEMENT [3; 44]. The main accusations include: brainwashing, connections with the Korean C.I.A., splitting up families, using 'Heavenly Deception', amassing great wealth for the leadership by exploiting the followers, tax evasion, and the manufacture of armaments [11: IV; 13; 16; 25: 1]. The Church itself claims victimization [49], particularly when its members are illegally kidnapped and 'deprogrammed' [1]. [For general reading: 4; 24; 45]

Unitarianism [XI.B] Christians (although some deny them the title) rejecting (as inimical to the unity of God) the doctrines of the TRINITY and divinity of JESUS CHRIST (CHRISTOLOGY; GOD, CHRISTIAN CONCEPT OF), together with the Fall (SIN), Atonement (SALVATION), and eternal punishment. 'Socinians' (from Fausto Sozzini, 1539–1604) and 18th-century 'Arians' (ARIANISM) were strongly biblical and allowed a special status to Christ. Later, more philosophical Unitarians in England and the U.S.A. eroded this. Modern Unitarianism is diverse and difficult to classify, except as 'liberal' religion. [107: 1408–9; 138; 141]

Uposatha [IX.A] The Buddhist 'sabbath' day, regulated by the phases of the moon, which is the occasion for the observance of eight (rather than the normal five) moral precepts by certain lay devotees known as *upasakas*. On two sabbaths a month the PATIMOKKHA is recited by local assemblies of monks.

U.S.A., Christianity in the [XI.B] U.S. Christianity owes its special characteristics to various traditions drawn originally from Europe but modified by

development in colonial, republican, and often frontier conditions. Calvinistic PURITANISM of CONGREGATIONALIST type marked the early New England colonies (including the 'Pilgrim Fathers'). There have been many subsequent changes in PROTESTANTISM, which was much influenced by the Great Awakenings (REVIVALISM) and the Enlightenment. The 19th century added massive Irish and European immigration, which brought ROMAN CATHOLICISM and a variety of ethnic ORTHODOX CHURCHES. Protestantism, led by PRESBYTERIANISM, CONGREGATIONALISM, METHODISM, and BAPTISTS, also multiplied, together with numerous SECTS and cults (often MILLENARIAN). The Civil War (1861–5) split many churches into north and south versions, influenced by the slavery issue. Large black versions of many churches have developed, particularly among Baptists and Methodists, e.g. the National Baptist Convention, and the African Methodist Episcopal Church Zion. There are also various black PENTECOSTALIST groups (e.g. the Church of God in Christ) and diverse black cults (e.g. the Father Divine Peace Mission).

Theology has ranged from extreme 'fundamentalism' and social conservatism to extreme LIBERAL PROTESTANTISM and the Social Gospel (a movement originating in the U.S.A. in the late 19th century, it emphasized the social application of Christianity as the building up of the kingdom of God on earth). The European state-church concept died with the colonial era, but U.S. optimism and sense of 'manifest destiny' has been coloured by religion. Despite the official neutrality of the state, religion in these terms has been part of the 'American way of life' and a means of national identity. This ethos has caused tension for some dogmatic and traditionalist churches, as in the Roman Catholic 'Americanist' controversy of the 19th century (this attempted to adapt Roman Catholicism to American ideals of democracy and to minimize differences between it and Protestantism).

(*See also* AMERICAN INDIANS (NORTH); CHILDREN OF GOD; JESUS MOVEMENT; NATIVE AMERICAN CHURCH; NEW RELIGIOUS MOVEMENTS IN PRIMAL SOCIETIES; PEOPLE'S TEMPLE; UNIFICATION CHURCH; WAY INTERNATIONAL.) [2; 13; 16; 25; 61: I–V; 87; 97; 118; 122; 136]

Utilitarianism [XXVI] A secular moral philosophy according to which the only considerations that are relevant to deciding what is good and bad, or right and wrong, in any particular course of action have to do with its effects on the total sum of human happiness. In a broad form this point of view found acceptance among a number of 'enlightened' 18th-century philosophers, especially in France (C. A. Helvétius, 1715–71) and Britain (D. Hume, 1711–76, and J. Bentham, 1748–1832). The label 'utilitarian' was first used, in the 19th century, as a term of abuse but it was adopted by John Stuart Mill (1806–73). Mill's essay on Utilitarianism in 1863 [13] provided a classical statement of this position. Much attention has since been given by moral philosophers to criticizing and amending Mill's account.

Although it is now widely rejected, utilitarian thinking has permeated thought about moral matters in many countries, especially Britain. Many would agree with the utilitarian view that the only justifications there could be for punishing someone are that doing so might deter him or her from repeating certain actions or that doing so might deter others from committing those actions. They would agree, that is to say, in rejecting punishment as retribution or punishment for punishment's sake. The idea of an eye for an eye, or a tooth for a tooth, has no place in utilitarian thought. This is one among many moral issues where utilitarians have stood against what has been taught in the name of Christianity.

· V ·

Vaibhashika [IX.B] One of the principal schools of Buddhist *abhidharma* (Pali ABHIDHAMMA), developed in the SARVASTIVADA sect in North India. The Sarvastivadins had their own *abhidharma-pitaka*, now extant only in Chinese and Tibetan translations, developed during the 3rd to 1st centuries BCE. A *vibhasha* is a commentary setting out various opinions and the school is named after the *Mahavibhasha* or 'Great Commentary', composed in Kashmir in the 2nd century CE. This Kashmir interpretation became very influential. A series of manuals following the Vaibhashika viewpoint were composed over the next five centuries, although other schools of Sarvastivadin *abhidharma* also existed. One group, appealing to the authority of *sutranta* (Pali SUTTANTA), the earlier form of Buddhist scripture, were known as SAUTRANTIKAS. They criticized Vaibhashika doctrines not supported by the *sutras* and set forth new explanations of their own. The consequent controversy was summarized in a masterly compendium – the *Abhidharma-kosha* of Vasubandhu (4th or 5th century). Partly owing to the identification of its author with the influential YOGACHARA writer, this work eclipsed all rivals and was itself the basis of a considerable literature. In the Far East it became the basis for a sect (Chu She, *see* NANTO ROKUSHU), while it still remains part of the Tibetan monastic curriculum (TIBETAN RELIGIONS).

The Vaibhashika *abhidharma*, although formed from a common background in early *abhidhamma*, differs on many points of detail from the THERAVADA *abhidhamma*, but the fundamental aim and methodology is similar. The later Vaibhashikas develop a very systematic and detailed account, mapping out the stages of the Buddhist path at length. Their viewpoint tends to underlie MAHAYANA Buddhist writings and is often criticized as the HINAYANA position. [General account: 33; the path: 48: 215ff]

Vaisheshika [XIII.B] One of the six DARSHANAS or salvation-philosophies of classical Hinduism, founded by Kanada in perhaps the 2nd century BCE. Kanada's fundamental text, the *Vaisheshika-sutra*, was largely superseded by the later manual of Prashastapada (early 6th century CE) [translations: 16: 386–423]. A series of commentaries and manuals based upon this were produced down to the 12th century. [11: VI, 2, 53–75] Thereafter the system merged almost completely with the later NYAYA. Kanada claimed that spiritual development and liberation (MOKSHA) were to be achieved by fully understanding how the world of experience is constructed from six fundamental categories (*padartha*): substance, quality, activity, commonness, particularity (*vishesha*), and unity (or inherence). The pluralistic and realistic system of the *Vaisheshika* included much detail based upon observation of the natural world and its laws. Especially well known is the *Vaisheshika* concept of indivisible 'atoms' without magnitude, from which larger entities are constructed. Mind, which is minute in size, is distinguished from spirit, which is infinite; both are eternal. Although Kanada was probably not a theist, Prashastapada and his successors gave a definite although limited role to the will of God (ISHVARA). [10: 3–180; 14: 146–64]

Vaishnava Vedanta [XIII.B] A series of influential Hindu Vaishnava (VISHNU) theologians created a number of VEDANTA schools during the medieval period, both developing and reacting against the ADVAITA VEDANTA of SHANKARA. Vaishnava sectarian writings and saints influenced all of these, but individuals were variously affected by later NYAYA and SAMKHYA thought, even to some extent by ISLAM. The principal forerunner of the Vaishnava Vedanta was Bhaskara (9th or 10th centuries CE). Bhaskara attacked Shankara as a crypto-Buddhist and claimed to represent a more authentic tradition. The most influential figure was RAMANUJA (12th century); also important were Nimbarka and Madhva (both 13th century), Vallabha (1479–1531), and certain of the followers of Caitanya (1485–1533). Most of these are authoritative for particular Vaishnava sectarian traditions (*sampradaya*). [5: III, IV; 15: 39–102]

The various systems differ considerably, but all emphasize the positive nature of God (BRAHMAN = VISHNU), stress the importance of BHAKTI as the most effective spiritual practice, and deny that the individual soul can ever be so wholly merged into the divine as to lose its identity completely. The role of divine grace is stressed. They are generally inclusivist: competing systems are not so much denied as incorporated in a hierarchy of knowledge and subordinated. Generally a knowledge of the highest brahman superior to the experience of an undifferentiated absolute is claimed. God is in principle held to be both the efficient and the material cause of the universe, but in practice care is taken to avoid a simplistic pantheism. The system of Madhva goes rather further in emphasizing distinctions between God, the universe, and the individual soul. Several Vaishnava think-ers deny the possibility of liberation in this life (*jivan-mukti*) and most assert that God has a particular form (i.e. that of Vishnu).

Valhalla [v] The Scandinavian Valhalla ('Hall of the Slain') was the place to which kings and outstanding warriors were conducted after death by the VALKYRIES, if they had died in battle or been sacrificed to ODIN. Here Odin presided over a life of fighting and feasting, and warriors who fell each day were raised again to take part in a banquet, with unending supplies of roasted pork and mead. Odin collected the finest champions in order to have their support in the last great conflict at RAGNAROK [6: VI, 149–53]. Poems and memorial stones of the Viking age represent the dead warrior on horseback arriving at Valhalla, welcomed by a woman with a drinking-horn [7: VI, 124–9]. Valhalla appears to be an image developed by artists and poets to glorify those who died in battle; it was not, like HEL [6: VI, 162], a universal realm of the dead, but reserved for privileged heroes who were Odin's worshippers.

Valkyries [v] The early Germanic conception of Valkyries was that of fierce battle-spirits devouring the slain, and the Celtic war-goddesses Morrigan and Badb show similar characteristics. All are associated with crows and ravens on the battlefield [6: II, 61–6]. In Norse literature Valkyries appear as supernatural brides of heroes (FYLGJA), helping them in battle and welcoming them after death. Sometimes they are represented as dignified women on horseback, escorting dead kings to VALHALLA and offering them horns of mead.

Vanir [v] These were the Scandinavian fertility deities, sometimes represented as fair giants dwelling in earth or sea, who provided wives for the AESIR. They were linked with land-spirits of mountains or lakes, and with dead ancestors in the earth to whom offerings were made. Freyr ('Lord'), whose phallic statue was at Uppsala, was the male fertility-god, and thought of as the founder of the Swedish royal dynasty. His sister Freyja had many names, and may probably be identified with the giantesses Gerd and Gefion, and ODIN's wife Frigg, as well as Germanic Frija, who gave Friday its name [6: IV, 92–127]. Njord, god of ships, sea, and lakes, was their father [6: V, 132–9]. The fertility deity might be taken in a wagon to bless the farms. Women with prophetic gifts, who visited homes, practised divination, and foretold children's destinies (VOLVA), were probably linked with the Vanir. These deities had a ship and a golden boar as their symbols.

Varna [XIII.A] Four 'classes', or broad divisions, existed in ancient Hindu society, according to the classical texts. The highest class was that of the BRAHMANS; next came the warrior class (KSHATRIYA); and then the merchant class (Vaishya). These three constituted the 'twice-born' (dvija) classes [2: 139, 163] who were invested with the sacred thread at their upanayana, or initiation into society (their 'second' birth). Below these three were the workers, or serfs (shudras), who suffered from many social disabilities. Some modern scholars interpret the difference between shudras and the twice-born classes as having been one of colour, the latter perhaps having descended from lighter-skinned Aryan (INDO-EUROPEAN) immigrants into India [2: 138; 25: 24; 49]. According to one of the hymns of the Rig-veda (VEDA), the 'Purusha-sukta', the four classes were constituted at the creation of the world: a primeval being called Purusha (Man) was sacrificed, and from his mouth the Brahman class were created, from his arms the Kshatriyas, from his thighs the Vaishyas, and from his feet the Shudras [26: 10]. This idealistic doctrine of the Brahmans, that all humanity is divided into four classes, is purely scriptural. It

should not be confused with existing social divisions, known as jati, or 'birth-groups', which entail recognition of group identity, endogamy, commensality, occupational privileges, and other distinctions. The dominant jati in any particular area (in real terms) is not necessarily the Brahman. The European use of the word CASTE largely led to confusion of the two, especially in the British period, since the latter relied very largely on Brahman informants. [2]

Vassa [IX.A] The Buddhist 'Lent', which occurs annually (as the word vassa signifies, etymologically) during the monsoon season (which also is signified by the word vassa). The practice (by ascetics) of forming small groups that live in a sheltered place for the period of the rains appears to have started early in the history of Buddhism and to have been subsequently adopted by other, non-Buddhist groups in India [9: 54–7].

Veda [XIII.A] Literally 'knowledge', the Sanskrit word Veda denotes especially the 'sacred knowledge' of the Hindus. This was handed down in threefold form: Rig-veda, Sama-veda, and Yajur-veda; to these was later added the ATHARVA-VEDA. These are sometimes inaccurately referred to as 'the Vedas', but Veda is one, and the reference should be to the three (or four) samhita (that is, 'collections') of the Veda. The Rig-veda (rig = 'praise') is a collection of 1,028 hymns in early, or Vedic, Sanskrit which were used when the Aryan (INDO-EUROPEAN) sacrifices were offered. The Sama-veda is a rearranged version of some of the hymns of the Rig-veda, and the Yajur-veda consists of formulae for use by the priest who performed the sacrificial actions. The Atharva-veda consists of material of a more popular character, such as spells, charms, and exorcistic chants. Much of this Atharva material may have originated among the indigenous inhabitants of northern India into whose territory the Aryans had moved (HINDUS). The gods of the *Rig-veda* include, notably, Dyaus, the sky-god; AGNI, fire; Varuna, also a sky-god; Yama, the guardian of hell, and his female counterpart Yami; Rudra (SHIVA); Indra; and VISHNU [3: 23–283; 14: 30–34; 16: 11–178]. The development of the Aryan sacrificial cult in India saw also the development of a further aspect of Veda: the literature of the BRAHMANAS dealing with more elaborate sacrifices [1: 21–5; 2: 43; 14: 50–52]. A further addition was made in the mystical speculation of the *Aranyakas*, or 'forest treatises', and the development of these in the Upanishads or 'esoteric teachings', the most important of which, in Hindu religion, is the idea that the individual soul (*atman*) is identical with the total Reality, or BRAHMAN. [1: 26–36; 2: 244–58; 14: 53–6]. The final stage in the development of Veda is held to be that of its systematic exegesis, especially of the Upanishads, as the *anta* or 'end' of Veda, that is, *Veda-anta*, or VEDANTA.

Vedanta [XIII.B] One of the six orthodox DARSHANAS or salvation-philosophies of classical Hinduism. 'Vedanta' means 'culmination of the VEDAS' and refers to the Upanishads as the final and climactic portion of the Vedic revelation. In practice Vedanta means the branch of scriptural exegesis (MIMAMSA) concerned with the Upanishads and the system developed therefrom. The fundamental Vedanta text is the BRAHMA-SUTRA, but the Upanishads themselves and also the BHAGAVADGITA are obviously important. In origin the Vedanta is simply theology, its main concern being with knowledge of the divine power (BRAHMAN). In practice it has expanded to incorporate elements from the other *darshanas*, which have tended to become mere ancillaries to the Vedanta. The early history of Vedanta is obscure; it seems to have competed for a long period with a rival SAMKHYA interpret-

ation of the Upanishads. It did not form a fully elaborated system until the 7th and 8th centuries CE when the ADVAITA VEDANTA developed, partly influenced by MADHYAMIKA Buddhism. In the medieval period a number of VAISHNAVA VEDANTA schools arose.

Veiling (in Islam) [XVII] Veiling apparently originated for the protection of the Prophet's wives, and was later extended to all free Muslim women. Its adoption marks the transition from childhood to puberty [45: VI]. It was never, however, very practicable for peasant and working women, and ISLAMIC MODERNISM has often attacked it as a symbol of women's subjection; but with the recent resurgence of Islamic fundamentalism, there has been pressure on women to retain it. (*See* MAR'A.) [21 'Hidjāb']

Vesakha [IX.A] The name of an Indian month, corresponding to a month from mid-April to mid-May in the Gregorian calendar, which is the time of year for the great annual festival of Buddhists at which are commemorated GOTAMA's birth at LUMBINI, his attainment of enlightenment at BODHGAYA, and his PARINIBBANA at KUSINARA.

Vestal Virgins [XXV] Six priestesses who served in Vesta's temple in Rome (*aedes Vestae*); the *pontifex maximus* (SACERDOTES) chose them by *captio* ('taking') when very young, to remain in service for 30 years, caring for the temple and maintaining the sacred fire on the goddess's hearth. They had to preserve their virginity on pain of being buried alive. Their sexual status, however, symbolically combined that of virgin with elements of matron, bride, and even man. Any failure in the fulfilment of their duties threatened the safety of the state (*salus publica*). [6: 585–8; 11: 108–11; 17: 90–91]

Vihara [IX.A] Literally 'a dwelling-place', the word *vihara* has come to be used specially to mean a Buddhist monks' dwelling-place, or monastery. Originally eremitic, Buddhists began from an early period to develop as settled communities during VASSA, the rainy season [9: 56f]. In Buddhist countries today the *vihara* consists of a walled compound containing gardens, huts for the monks, a bodhi-tree, a STUPA, and a hall, usually containing a statue of the Buddha (BUDDHA IMAGE), which is used for congregational purposes, on UPOSATHA days, and at VESAKHA.

Vikings [V] The Scandinavian Viking age lasted from the late 8th to the 11th century CE. Skills in shipbuilding and navigation enabled sea-raiders (Vikings) from Norway, Sweden, and Denmark to attack many European kingdoms. Scandinavians also won wealth through trading voyages and service as mercenaries, while settlements were made in Iceland, Greenland, and parts of the British Isles [13a]. Christianity was not established in Scandinavia until the close of the Viking age, and much of our knowledge of pre-Christian northern religion comes from Icelandic medieval literature [6; 30]. The chief gods were ODIN and THOR, and there was a rich store of myths and legends about supernatural beings and realms. Archaeological finds have revealed elaborate funeral customs, including SHIP-FUNERAL, and sacrificial rites (VOTIVE OFFERINGS) [7: VI].

Vinaya-Pitaka [IX.A] The first of the three divisions of the Buddhist scriptures (cf. ABHIDHAMMA; SUTTA-PITAKA; TIPITAKA), the *Vinaya* is concerned primarily with the Buddhist religious order (or SANGHA). It gives an account of the Sangha's formation in the time of GOTAMA the BUDDHA, and contains the rules by which it is to be ordered, as well as the code of conduct for individual monks. Besides the version in PALI which is the basis of the THERAVADA order in Sri Lanka and South-East Asia there are other versions in Buddhist hybrid Sanskrit, Tibetan, and Chinese. Broadly the structure of each of these is the same: a section dealing with the rule of life for monks,

followed by a similar section for nuns; then a section dealing with the common life of the communities, in which such matters as ordination ceremonies, the ceremony for confession of faults (PATIMOKKHA), and regulations concerning dwellings, dress, food, furniture, and medicine are dealt with. An English translation of the Pali *Vinaya* has been made by I. B. Horner (*The Book of the Discipline*, 5 vols., 1938–52). [11A] (*See also* LU TSUNG.)

Vipassana [IX.B] One of the two main types of Buddhist meditation practice (BHAVANA). *Vipassana* (Sanskrit *vipashyana*) is direct experiential insight into reality, brought about by the practice of constant awareness, especially mindfulness of the four foundations: body, feelings, state of mind, and mental processes [46: 7–115]. Guidance from those who have already developed insight and careful attentiveness is necessary. Previous calm (SAMATHA) meditation practice is usual, although in some modern schools, especially from Burma, this is considered a distraction. Eventually various degrees of direct insight will arise. Understanding of the specific nature and interconnectedness of mental and material phenomena will lead the meditator eventually to experience the three general characteristics: impermanence (ANICCA), unsatisfactoriness (DUKKHA), and insubstantiality (ANATTA). The ensuing detachment gives rise to strongly positive emotions with a consequent danger of premature satisfaction. If this is avoided, a stronger level of insight is reached, accompanied by the experience of the various states of the Buddhist path (BODHI-PAKKHIYA-DHAMMA). The culmination would be a permanent breakthrough to the transcendent (LOKUTTARA). [48: 191–247; 49; 64: 341–406]

Vishnu/Vaishnava [XIII.A] Vishnu is one of the principal Hindu deities. The adjective 'Vaishnava' signifies that which is derived from or relates to, belongs to, is sacred or devoted to Vishnu.

Prominent among its usages, therefore, is reference to a worshipper of Vishnu. The feminine form 'Vaishnavi' signifies the SHAKTI or female energy which is associated with Vishnu. In classical Hindu literature this was the goddess LAKSHMI. Vaishnavas identify Vishnu as BRAHMAN, the supreme being (as also Shaivites identify SHIVA), and it was appropriate to regard this powerful goddess as Vishnu's *shakti*. The earliest mention of Vishnu in Hindu scriptures is in the *Rig-veda* (VEDA), where he appears as a minor deity, only five of the 1,028 hymns being addressed to him [26: vii & 4]. At that stage in Hindu history he was only beginning to rise to importance. In origin he appears to be a solar deity [3: 284], his most important feat being his 'three strides' across the heavens, concerning which interpretations differ. After the period represented by the *Rig-veda* he begins to be associated with other figures, who are taken to be his 'incarnate' forms: a dwarf, a boar, a fish, a 'cosmic tortoise' (or crocodile), and a creature that is half-man, half-lion. Thus develops the notion of Vishnu's AVATARAS, or 'descents', the most celebrated of which are RAMA, KRISHNA, and (according to the Vaishnavas) BUDDHA. It is in the later literature of the PURANAS that references to these are found [8: 716–27; 27: 23–89]. Vaishnavas are found in almost all parts of India, but the cult is most prominent in those areas where it occurs as the cult of Rama and Krishna, that is, in northern and central India. It is found as the dominant cult in other areas, such as Nepal, and the north-east Indian state of Manipur, and in former times in the Hinduism of SOUTH-EAST ASIA. A famous tradition of Vaishnava saints in South India is that of the ALVARS. Other names of Vishnu are Narayan, Jagannath (JUGGERNAUT), and HARI.

Vision Quest [III] Probably the most characteristic feature of North American Indian religion, the vision quest is susceptible of many interpretations and variations [8]. Among the Algonquian (ALGONQUIN) and Plains Indians, where the vision quest has received fullest elaboration, the practice is generally associated with a rite of passage as well as with the acquisition of a GUARDIAN SPIRIT. Classically, an individual (usually a young male), prompted beforehand by some omen or encouraged by the elders, sets out to acquire spiritual power by means of a vision of a supernatural being. Ascetic practices (including fasting, thirsting, use of the SWEAT LODGE, enemas, etc.) are first undertaken as preparation; the individual then retires to a remote place to pray and beg for a vision. At length, often after additional mortifications, the youth is granted a dream or a vision of a spirit (usually appearing in animal guise). This guardian spirit teaches the young person a 'spirit song', grants special powers, and frequently bestows a MEDICINE BUNDLE or other symbol of newly acquired powers. If indicated in the vision, the individual may embark upon a career as MEDICINE MAN or SHAMAN. Renewal of power might be achieved by occasional repetition of the initial experience. [17: VIII, 59–63, 91–3]

Volva [V] The Icelandic sagas contain accounts of a divination ceremony known as *seid*, over which a *volva* or female seer presides. She sits on a high platform, and apparently gains hidden knowledge in a state of trance, like SHAMANS in north-eastern Europe and Asia in later times [6: IV, 117–23]. It seems probable that *seid* took place in Norway rather than Iceland, although the most famous account is set in Greenland in the Saga of Erik the Red. The *volva* predicted the coming season as well as individual futures, and seems to be associated with the VANIR. ODIN had the powers of a seer [6: VI, 141–9] but in the Poetic EDDA he too consults a *volva* for knowledge of past or future [18: 117–19]; and certain poems are presented as the relevations of a *volva* [18: 1, 137]. In Roman times certain female seers were held in great esteem by the Germans, and are mentioned by Tacitus (1st century BCE) and other writers [3: 127–35].

Voodoo [XVIII] The popular religion of Haiti, also found elsewhere in the Caribbean. Voodoo developed from the blending of ROMAN CATHOLICISM with West African religious traditions on slave plantations from the 17th century onwards. Devotees are baptized Catholics and attend church as well as the Voodoo *péristyle* (temple). It is believed that the Voodoo world is richly populated with *loa* (spirits), who take a keen interest in human affairs. Some rule special places (the cemetery, the sea, the crossroads); others are ancestral spirits, including those of the recently dead. Rituals, led by an *ongan* (priest) or *manbo* (priestess), centre on the invocation of the *loa* by *vévé* (magical diagrams), songs, and prayers which mingle their names with those of Christian saints, from whom the *loa* are not sharply distinguished. Members of the congregation enter trance and become possessed by the invited *loa*, who are entertained and asked for favours. Ritual details, transmitted orally, vary from one district to another and may be spontaneously altered to suit the congregation's needs. [17]

Votive Offerings (Ancient European) [V] Both Celtic and Germanic peoples left offerings in sacred places or dropped them into water. In Denmark in the Roman period much war booty, often deliberately damaged, was abandoned at Vimose, Nydam, and other sites, presumably as offerings for victory. Other deposits of a less warlike character, such as gold rings, pottery, wooden farm objects, textiles, and animals, were probably offered to the fertility powers, as at Thorsbjerg in Denmark [7: IV, 66–79]. Ritual treasures like the great metal cauldron found at Gundestrup in Denmark were dismantled and abandoned in the same way [22: VII, 202–4]. The Celts left votive offerings near springs and threw them into lakes, as at the famous site of La Tène (5th century BCE), or down ritual shafts, a number of which have been excavated in Britain [17: II, 64–9; 23: 1, 24–8]. At the sanctuary of Sequana, at the source of the Seine, many carved wooden figures were found, left by pilgrims who went there for healing [22: VI, 146–7].

Vrata [XIII.A] In Hindu tradition, a vow taken upon oneself, or an austerity undertaken, such as continence or fasting. Initiation into the vow (and completion of it) are marked in some special way, by an act of devotion, or by bathing.

· W ·

Wahhabis [XIV] A puritanical Islamic reform movement begun in Arabia by Muhammad b. 'Abd al-Wahhab (1703–92), reviving the conservative Hanbali tradition (see FIQH) and aiming at the eradication of idolatrous accretions in popular religion like saint-worship (WALI). It became the driving force behind the military expansionism of the Saudi family, spreading over most of the Arabian peninsula by the early 20th century, and also securing a certain influence in Indian Islam. It remains today the official ideology of the Saudi Arabian kingdom. [6: XIV; 10 s.v.; 20 'Wahhābīya'; 46: XI]

Wali [XIV] Saint or holy man in ISLAM, literally 'friend, person near to God'. Popular Islam has come to recognize a hierarchy of saints, whose overt qualifications are the performance of miracles and the exercise of charisma or saintliness (baraka) [45: X; 53: VI–VII]. To the ordinary Muslim, a local saint is often a more potent and real figure than the distant prophets (NABI). Hence the healing power and intercession of the saint is sought for the living and dead alike. Pilgrimage (ziyara) is made to his tomb; and the anniversary of his death may be celebrated as a festival (maulid; see also 'ID) [12; 54]. The devotion shown to many Sufi leaders often led to the formation of specific SUFI ORDERS, crystallizing round their residences or tombs. In certain areas, e.g. North Africa and the Indo-Pakistan subcontinent, the cult of saints and holy men has been especially widespread. [10 'Saints (Islam)'; 20 s.v.; 29: 56–8; 83: VI]

Waqf [XIV] 'pious endowment'. In ISLAM a gift of, for example, property or money placed in trust so that the income can be used for a charitable or educational purpose such as the upkeep of a mosque, hospital, Sufi convent, etc. It has also been possible to establish a waqf for one's own family. Waqf lands have become extensive, and modern Islamic governments have discouraged family waqfs and have placed charitable ones under various degrees of central government control. [20 'Wakf'; 29: 143–6]

Way International [XXI] A BIBLE research and teaching organization which was founded by a former minister of the Evangelical and Reformed Church in America, Doctor Victor Paul Wierwille. The Way offers a course called Power for Abundant Living (PFAL), which teaches speaking in tongues and Wierwille's special interpretation of the New Testament. This includes the belief that Jesus was specially created by God in Mary's womb as a perfect man, but not as God. The Hebrew scriptures are not seen as having any validity for Christians. [11: VI; 54]

West, Islam in the [XIV] Islam has ancient roots in southern and eastern Europe, in that Arab forces invaded Spain as early as 711 CE and Sicily and Malta soon afterwards [37 vol. 2: 406–39; 78]; the Turkish and Mongol Tatars overran South Russia; and the Ottoman Turks had by the 16th century occupied most of the Balkans (ISLAMIC DYNASTIES). With the loss of Muslim political control, Islam has receded in the western Mediterranean and has shrunk considerably in the Balkans, with many Muslims repatriated to

Turkey or exchanged for Christian groups. Only in Yugoslavia is the significant Muslim minority comparatively flourishing [6: XII]. In the Volga basin of Russia and in the Caucasus, the number of Muslims remains nominally high (estimated at 17 million in European Russia in 1970), but their spiritual life is stunted by the officially atheist regime and their regional concentrations diluted by Great Russian immigration [6: VII; 37 vol. 1: 627–72]. It is in the industrialized societies of Western Europe that Muslim growth is now significant, in such countries as Britain, France, West Germany, and the Netherlands. This is essentially a post-1945 phenomenon of emigration from either the Balkans and Turkey or from decolonialized territories like North Africa, the Indo-Pakistan subcontinent, the West Indies, and Indonesia. These Muslims tend to be unskilled or semi-skilled labourers. In the New World, some black slaves brought to the Spanish, Portuguese, and British colonies must have been Muslim, but more significant were the 19th-century importations to the West Indies of indentured labour from such countries as India and Indonesia. These groups are now supplemented by general emigration in the 20th century from the Middle East and South Asia into both North and South America. Muslims in the U.S.A. and Canada (in 1978 some 2 million) include a fair proportion of professionals. (*See also* BLACK MUSLIMS; and Christian reactions to Islam) [16].

West Indies, Christianity in the [XI.B] Early Christian influence was through Spanish colonization and missions to slaves. METHODISM since 1760 has had considerable success; it was followed in the 19th century by BAPTISTS and ANGLICANISM. ROMAN CATH-OLICISM has mainly been active in former French and Spanish colonies. Hostility by slave owners hindered some missions until after emancipation

(1833). Evangelical REVIVALISM has attracted West Indians who have also produced many Pentecostalist sects (PENTECOSTALISM) of their own, often transmitted by immigrants in Britain since 1945 (notably RASTAFARIANS; *see also* AFRO-AMERICANS). [61: 187–90; 82 vol. 5: IV, vol. 7: VII; 83 vol. 3: XI, vol. 5: IV]

Western Buddhism [IX.B] Some interest in Buddhism developed in Europe during the 19th century, derived in part from colonial and missionary efforts, in part from intellectual and academic tendencies. Hindu and Buddhist ideas were also introduced by the Theosophical movement (THEOSOPHY). The early 20th century brought a Buddhist movement on a very small scale, in Europe, especially in the U.K. This was associated with the THERAVADA Buddhist modernism developed in Ceylon (SINHALESE BUDDHISM), which emphasized the rational and practical nature of Buddhism. After declining in the inter-war period this tendency recovered some ground and continues to exercise influence. An interest in ZEN was aroused by the writings of D.T. Suzuki and the work of Japanese missionaries, resulting in the 1950s in a short-lived vogue in the U.S.A. connected with the beatnik movement. A small core of committed long-term practitioners remained. Beginning in the 1960s Tibetan refugees succeeded in establishing Buddhist centres in a number of Western countries; these benefited considerably from interest in meditation and mysticism during the 1970s. Theravada missionary activity, begun from Ceylon (Sri Lanka) by the Maha Bodhi Society, was now taken up also from Thailand and a number of small monasteries were established in Europe and the English-speaking countries. The 1970s saw a considerable increase in the number of small Buddhist groups in the Western world. Some are eclectic or mixed, but many concentrate on some particular branch of Theravada, TIBETAN Buddhism, or Zen (Shin, NICHIREN, and SHINGON occur only rarely, except among immigrants). The increased presence of Asian leadership and of Westerners trained in Asia or by Asians is noticeable. Because of their concentration among the more highly educated, members exercise an influence disproportionate to their small (in absolute terms) numbers.

Western Magical Tradition [XVIII] European magical practices originating in the Renaissance, when older magical traditions (MAGIC) were integrated with HERMETISM, KABBALAH, and NEOPLATONISM. These provided systems of symbolic correspondences whereby through ritual the magician could attune himself, as microcosm, to the great universe, or macrocosm, and thence to celestial and divine powers. Although such techniques also lent themselves to worldly uses, the central concern was to purify the adept spiritually and fit him to 'act as a conscious channel for the work of God in His creation' [16], any practice tending to increase pride or egotism being condemned as 'black' magic. Beginning with Pico della Mirandola (1463–94) and Marsilio Ficino (1433–99), the tradition grew by experiment and speculation, important innovators (representing a tiny proportion of the total) including the cryptographer Trithemius (1462–1516), the chemist Paracelsus (1462–1516), and the mathematician John Dee (1527–1608). Obscure groups carried the tradition through the later 17th and 18th centuries. An 'occult revival' of popular interest began in the mid 19th century, and the tradition was restated and developed by 'Eliphas Lévi'(A. L. Constant, 1810–75)(TAROT) [18], by 'MacGregor' Mathers (GOLDEN DAWN), and by E. A. 'Aleister' Crowley (1875–1947), whose flamboyantly aggressive behaviour earned notoriety. The tradition is still practised, incon-

spicuously, by organizations throughout the Western world. [15]

White Eagle Lodge [XXI] An English centre offering the spiritualist teachings of a Red Indian, White Eagle – a 'very wise soul who has guided the Lodge from the spirit world for many years'. The philosophy includes ASTROLOGY and healing. Special 'Sunday School' services are provided for children. White Eagle, who communicates through the mediumship of Grace Cooke, teaches communion with God through meditation and offers 'a way of life which is gentle and in harmony with the laws of life'. Life, he teaches, is governed by five cosmic laws: reincarnation; cause and effect; opportunity; correspondence; and equilibrium or balance. [2: 184; 53]

Windigo [III] An Ojibwa (north-west woodlands) North American term referring to a cannibalistic figure prominent in Algonquian (ALGONQUIN) mythology. Stories attribute the origin of the *windigo* to a lost hunter, forced by impending starvation to eat human flesh, thereafter becoming a forest-dwelling monster preying on unsuspecting human beings. Occasionally the SHAMAN, in his trance state, may have a vision of a *windigo*, less frequently gaining one as his spirit helper. [23: IX]

Wine-Drinking (in Islam) [XIV] The QUR'AN came to condemn wine-drinking and drunkenness, and it was later accounted a grave sin (*kabira*) (DHANB). Later jurists had to define wine – was non-grape wine unlawful? – and widened the prohibition to include spirits and narcotic drugs. Nevertheless, wine-drinking has been popular among hedonistic elements, and forms a widespread motif of Sufi mystical and other poetry in Arabic, Persian, and Turkish (SUFISM). [21 'Khamr'; 29: 156–7]

Wisdom Literature (Ancient Egyptian) [IV] Presented as advice given by a father or sage, the Egyptian Wisdom Texts [9: 54–84, 234–42] embodied traditions and practical morality intended to assist well-to-do young men to progress in society. Preserved in schoolboy copies, the earliest works are of Ptah-hotep (c. 2400 BCE), for Kagemni (c. 2400 BCE) (Old Kingdom) and Merikere (c. 2200 BCE). Royal propaganda was stressed in Middle Kingdom examples, and later texts of the New Kingdom (c. 1290 BCE) included the Maxims of Ani (c. 1550 BCE but written c. 900 BCE) and the Teachings of Amenemope (c. 1290 BCE) [9: 214–34].

Witchcraft [XVIII] Usually, the harming of people by magical or 'psychic' means (MAGIC; PSYCHIC POWERS). The term has three distinct uses, however. In anthropology, witchcraft means a maleficent power innate in certain people, who can mysteriously harm others. It is different from evil magic (sorcery): a witch cannot help being one, and may not even know that he or she is. [9] This concept, derived mainly from African cultures, does not apply to Europe, where witches are regarded as conscious evil-doers.

European witchcraft was not distinguished from magic, which might be good or evil, before the mid 14th century, when the church began to stress the idea that witches made a 'pact' pledging allegiance to Satan, who in return rendered their magic effective. Witchcraft thus became a 'false religion' and a campaign modelled on those against other heretics gathered momentum, sanctioned by a papal bull (PAPACY) in 1484. Before 1700 at least 200,000 people were executed, mainly in continental Europe, although the craze also took hold in Britain and there was an outbreak at Salem, Massachusetts, in 1692. An elaborate belief-system grew up: witches bore a 'witch's mark' (blemish) on the body, attended a sabbat (devil-worshipping orgy) at night, to which they ran in animal form or flew, and kept a 'familiar' (personal devil in animal form). Leading questions and torture ensured that confessions confirmed expectations. Witch-crazes are assumed to arise from deep social tensions; their exact causes remain obscure. [24]

Witchcraft as a modern Western religion was inspired mainly by the theories of anthropologist Margaret Murray (1863–1963), who saw European witchcraft as a survival of a benign pre-Christian fertility religion. In some places it has also absorbed surviving traditions of folk-magic. [10]

Witchcraft Eradication (African) [II] The chief explanation of unexpected sickness, death, and misfortune in many African religious systems is witchcraft and sorcery. In some societies, while the fear of witchcraft did exist, it was seldom focused firmly upon individuals. In many others witchcraft was regularly countered through a witch-doctor (see NGANGA), but notorious witches were detected and killed, often through the poison or drowning ordeal.

In modern times governments have forbidden such ordeals, simply denying all reality to witchcraft, but belief in it has hardly lessened, inevitably stimulating new ways of witchcraft control. Sudden waves of village-to-village witch-cleansing organized by itinerant experts have arisen, particularly in central Africa. Among the best known of these movements is the Mcape cult, which spread in the 1930s from Malawi to all the neighbouring countries and has had many successors. Such movements claim to cleanse everyone once for all, provided evil medicines are destroyed and the cult's own medicine taken, which will kill anyone who should return subsequently to witchcraft. They provide a sort of instant millennium, inevitably followed by disillusionment when the old troubles still recur [3: 103–40; 8: 123–41].

Woman (in Early Christianity) [XI.A] Although women were not included among the 12 APOSTLES, many of JESUS CHRIST's most faithful and appreciated DISCIPLES were women, outstandingly Mary Magdalene. They played an important part in the spread of CHRISTIANITY. For PAUL, the male/female distinction is as irrelevant 'in Christ Jesus' as the distinction between Jews and Gentiles or that between slaves and free persons. He refers gratefully to women who collaborated in his mission. Restrictions on women's role in church are post-apostolic. [17] The authorship of passages which represent Paul as imposing such restrictions is doubtful.

The veneration of MARY, the mother of Jesus, spread gradually in the church. It received official recognition when she was styled *Theotokos*, 'the mother of God', by the COUNCIL of Ephesus (431 CE).

Woman (in Judaism) [XVII] Woman is described in the BIBLE story of the creation of the first human couple, Adam and Eve, as a 'helpmeet opposite' man. This seems to summarize her role in JUDAISM, where public religion, e.g. SYNAGOGUE worship, the office of RABBI, and TORAH study, is essentially a male preserve [52: 133]. Woman's role is primarily as a wife and mother, who is not bound to keep all the commandments as the male is [9 vol. 16: 623]. REFORM JUDAISM has given women a more public role [27: XXIV–XXVI].

Wondjina [XXII] In the northern Kimberley region of Western Australia the name *wondjina* (or *wandjina*) is given to the ancestral spirit beings of the so-called Dreaming (here named *ungud; see* ALTJIRANGA). They are depicted in famous cave paintings (noted by George Grey in 1838), and are believed to have each imprinted their own image in these pictures and to continue their existence through them. Each has a nose and eyes but no mouth or sexual characteristics. Rituals for the increase of natural species are connected with them as totemic ancestors (*see* AUSTRALIAN RELIGION). [21: 219–23; 22: 120]

Worship (Biblical) [XI.A, B] We have no systematic description of early Christian worship, but all the evidence indicates that it was modelled on the non-sacrificial worship of the Jewish SYNAGOGUE. A Christian service would commence with the call to worship, followed by prayers, praise (sometimes in the form of familiar psalms (BIBLE) or canticles, often impromptu, even ecstatic), scripture reading, and a homily, closing prayers, and benediction. In New Testament times no priestly class was appointed to conduct the worship nor (in Gentile CHRISTIANITY) was any special day of worship prescribed. [A. 13] The distinctive feature of Christian worship was the EUCHARIST, originally central to the main service (and taken in the course of a communal meal) but later frequently celebrated by itself at a separate gathering. It became one of the seven SACRAMENTS. 'Liturgy' denotes all the fixed services of the church, or specifically the Eucharist, which for the ORTHODOX CHURCH joins heaven to earth [B.134: 269–72]. The Divine Office is the daily public prayer of the Western Church, which priests are obliged to recite. The *Breviary* contains material for this, including the canonical hours, from Mattins in the early hours of the morning through Lauds, Prime, Terce, Sext, None, and Vespers to Compline at night. Recitation of scripture, especially psalms (CHURCH MUSIC), has always been central to these services, but over the centuries much legendary matter from lives of SAINTS was included. The *Breviary* was revised in the 16th century and much simplified in 1971. ANGLICANISM drastically simplified fixed services in its *Book of Common Prayer* (1662). PROTESTANTISM greatly reduced the scope of fixed forms. The Westminster Directory (1645) (PRESBYTERIANISM) was largely an outline and directions rather than fixed prayers. Much Protestant worship emphasizes preaching, 'free' prayer, and hymns [B.1: 137–78; B.28; B.30].

Wu Hsing [X] Five Elements: the Chinese theory of the five basic elements in the universe. The Five Elements are earth, wood, metal, fire, and water. These develop in a cyclical process in which each element is succeeded by the next, giving rise to the seasons, the natural order, and the progression of history. They were developed as a cosmological theory by Tsou Yen (305–240 BCE), and were later associated with YIN-YANG theory. [18: IX, 170–96; 32: II, 7–132; 81: VIII, 94–7]

· Y ·

Yasna [xxx] Literally 'worship', in ZOROASTRIANISM. As Zoroastrians believe that AHURA MAZDA created the world, life and work in that world is part of man's religious duty and can be considered a part of worship [49: VI, VII; 50: XIII]. Temple worship was a late entry into the religion (*see* FIRE). In ancient times prayers were offered close to Mazda's creations – i.e. at the household fire, on mountain tops, or near waters. But it is considered essential in Zoroastrianism that worship is offered in total purity, free from the defilement of ANGRA MAINYU. This is difficult to maintain and so increasingly worship has been offered in temples, especially among PARSIS with the growing urbanization of Bombay in the 19th and 20th centuries (MANTHRAS) [6: 33].

Yasna also refers to a specific, highly complex rite, one deriving from Indo-Iranian times (INDO-EUROPEANS) [33: XII]. Originally it involved animal sacrifice, but this is no longer the case among Parsis. The rite consists of the consecration of various items, e.g. water, 'barsom twigs' (now metal strips replacing the traditional plants which symbolize the plant world), milk, clarified butter (*goshudo*), and sacred bread (*darun*), and, especially, the juice from the haoma (later *hom*) plant (SOMA in Hinduism). This latter is pounded in a mortar and strained through the *varas* ring, which is made from the hairs of a sacred bull. After the preparatory *paragna* rite follows the *yasna* proper [27], the recital of the 72 chapters of the *yasna* text (AVESTA). The rite is performed by an officiating priest (*zaotar, zot*) with an assistant (*raspi*), who tends the sacred fire [5: 159–60, 228; 13: 56–9].

The *yasna* (and all temple rites except the feeding of the fire, the boy ceremony) is not performed in the main prayer room of a temple, but in a separate room called the *yazishngah* or *urvisgah* where the area of purity is marked off by channels, *pavis*. Laity may attend these rites but rarely do so, as congregational worship is not a feature of Zoroastrianism. Essentially the lay person offers his worship to Mazda in private. The purpose of the priestly rites, such as the *yasna*, is to give pleasure and strength to the spiritual beings (AMESHA SPENTAS; YAZATAS); to reconsecrate and benefit the material world of which man is a part; and to bring the spiritual and material worlds together.

Yazatas [xxx] 'Beings worthy of worship', in ZOROASTRIANISM (PAHLAVI *yazad*). Only one human is so designated – the prophet ZOROASTER. He is so considered because of his role as the one chosen by AHURA MAZDA to receive the revelation of the Good Religion, but he nevertheless remains a mortal [20: 90–95]. Ahura Mazda and the AMESHA SPENTAS are also worthy of worship, and therefore can be considered *yazatas*, but the term usually refers to a class of heavenly beings who are often compared to angels in Judaism, Christianity, and Islam (scholars believe that Zoroastrianism may have influenced the other religions in this respect [22: pt II]). They are mostly the 'gods' of the ancient Iranians, who have been incorporated into Zoroastrianism by making them the created heavenly helpers of Mazda. One of the most popular is Mithra; another is Verethraghna (later Bahram), the *yazata* of victory to whom the highest grades of FIRE temples are dedicated. An important female *yazata* is Anahita (later Anahid). *Yashts* (AVESTA) days (*roz*) of the month, and the months (*mah*) are named after, or dedicated to, the most popular *yazatas* [5: index; 7: index].

Yeshivah [XVII] The main educational institution of traditional JUDAISM, with an all-male student body usually ranging in age from early teens to mid-20s. The *yeshivah* curriculum concentrates on certain tractates of the Babylonian TALMUD and its many commentaries [52: 113]. The method of study involves the preparation of a text by two, or sometimes three, students (*chavruta*) together who will discuss the implications of a particular subject (*sugya*) and argue the pros and cons of various interpretations. A lecture is then delivered by a RABBI on the *yeshivah* staff, and students raise objections and questions to his exposition. After the lecture a further session of *chavruta* study will go over (*chazarah*) the rabbi's lecture (*shiur*). [13: 182; 50: XXX] The narrow curriculum and the casuistical method of study (*pilpul*) of some *yeshivot* have been severely criticized by Jewish educationists but they nevertheless remain characteristic of the *yeshivah* system.

Yggdrasil [v] The World Ash, the guardian tree of the AESIR in pre-Christian Scandinavia. It was thought to mark the centre of the nine worlds of gods, men, giants, the dead, and other, supernatural beings. A drink from Mimir's spring, at the foot of Yggdrasil, gives wisdom [2: VII; 6: VIII, 190–96]. The name Yggdrasil probably means 'horse of Ygg', i.e. ODIN, who once hung upon it. The tree is to survive RAGNAROK, sheltering those destined to repeople the world in the new age.

Yin–Yang [x] The ancient Chinese theory of the two opposite and complementary forces in nature. The Yin force is associated with the feminine, the earth, darkness, cold, the night, the moon, and passivity. The Yang force is associated with the masculine, the heavens, light, heat, the day, the sun, and activity. According to Yin–Yang theory the seasonal cycle and the whole of the natural order are explained in terms of the progression and alteration of the balance of the two forces. The great Han Confucian Tung Chung Shu (176–104 BCE) combined Yin–Yang and the Five Elements (WU HSING) theories and applied them to interpreting historical, social, and political processes, as well as the natural order. [7: XI, 244–50; 31: III, 32; 32: II, 7–132; 75: I, 8–16]

Yoga [XIII.B] The word *yoga* is related to the English 'yoke'; its primary meaning is probably 'work', i.e. spiritual practice, but the alternative sense of 'union', i.e. with the divine, is widely used. In fact the word is used in several different ways. It may indicate one of the (three or four) spiritual approaches of Indian religion: ritual (KARMA-YOGA), devotional (BHAKTI-YOGA), intellectual (JNANA-YOGA), or meditational (DHYANA-YOGA), especially the last. Sometimes it means 'practice' as opposed to 'theory'. It may refer to a particular technique or method: HATHA-YOGA, emphasizing the physical; *raja-yoga* the mental; *kundalini-yoga*, arousing vital energy; *mantra-yoga*, utilizing particular sounds; *laya-yoga*, sinking into the divine; *asparsha-yoga*, detaching from contact; *taraka-yoga*, employing eidetic-visual phenomena; *nada-yoga*, based upon similar noise phenomena; and so on.

Yoga can also refer to sectarian spiritual approaches (SHIVA-*yoga*, *Jaina-yoga* (JAINS), etc.), but in isolation often refers to the *yoga* school of Patanjali (YOGA-DARSHANA) – a type of *dhyana-yoga* and the prestigious royal yoga (*raja-yoga*) *par excellence*. In its widest use *yoga* is a collective term for all of the above; in this sense it is a universal phenomenon. In the somewhat narrower sense of 'Indian magico-spirituality' its ultimate origins are very old. Some scholars believe it can already be identified in illustrations from the INDUS VALLEY civilization (c. 2000 BCE). Others have preferred to see an INDO-EUROPEAN origin in the Vedic *vratya* movement. No doubt spontaneous mystical tendencies and a shamanistic (SHAMAN) background also played a part. [General: 4: 1–109; 7: 123–56; 18: 93–150]

Yoga-darshana [XIII.B] One of the six DARSHANAS or salvation-philosophies of classical Hinduism. The yoga school is concerned with the description of the stages of the spiritual path, of methods of practice, and of the forms of contemplative experience. Closely related to the SAMKHYA, it emerges from the same Upanishadic milieu. The most authoritative text is the *Yoga-sutra* attributed to the grammarian Patanjali (2nd century BCE) but almost certainly compiled around the 4th century CE [translation: 16: 453–86]. The principal commentator is 'Vyasa' (perhaps 6th century), but a number of later commentaries exist, including many modern ones [history: 10: 217–354]. The classical yoga accepts the same world view as the Samkhya, differing mainly in its subject-matter but also in accepting a limited role for a supreme deity (ISHVARA).

The great success of the *Yoga-sutra* is due to a skilful synthesis of two distinct approaches to *yoga*, perhaps originally from different sources. One emphasizes cessation (*nirodha*) of all mental activities; yogic practice and detachment will remove all tendency to identify with those activities and bring about a return to innate independence and purity. The other is a more positive account in terms of an Eightfold Path: (1) restraints (*yama*) or external moral precepts; (2) observances (*niyama*), i.e. internal moral purification; control of (3) posture (*asa-*

na) and (4) breath (*pranayama*); (5) and (6) concern control of attention (both steps); and (7) *dhyana* and (8) *samadhi* are states of meditative absorption which lead to the arousing of yogic knowledge and eventually liberation (MOKSHA). Such a mixture of moral, physical, and meditational training is typical of DHYANA YOGA. [7: 9–122; 9: 1–20; 18: 130–40]

Yogacara [IX.B] One of the two main forms of systematic MAHAYANA Buddhist thought. The Yogacara (*see* YOGA) school emphasized the importance of calm (SAMATHA) meditation as a prerequisite to the development of wisdom. Mahayana *sutras* containing many of the ideas later taken up by Yogacara writers were in existence by the 3rd century CE, but Yogacara systematic (*shastra*) literature probably dates from the 4th or 5th centuries CE. The fundamental works of the school are attributed to Maitreya and Asanga, but there is debate as to whether this Maitreya is a historical teacher of Asanga or the BODHISATTVA MAITREYA inspiring certain of Asanga's writings. Important works are also attributed to Asanga's brother Vasubandhu, traditionally the author of the *Abhidharmakosha* (*see* VAIBHASHIKA) converted to Mahayana in old age.

Using both Mahayana and *abhidharma* (ABHIDHAMMA) sources, the Yogacarins created a vast synthesis, mapping the stages of the path in great detail and constructing a Mahayana *abhidharma*. Notable developments were the eight consciousnesses (*see* ALAYA-VIJNANA) and an elaborated understanding of the nature of a BUDDHA. The Yogacara claimed a middle way between the realist SARVASTIVADA and the nihilist SHUNYATAVADA, affirming that although self and separate entities are non-existent, thusness (*tathata*), i.e. ultimate truth and consciousness itself, are not non-existent. The school is as a consequence known as the Vijnanavada ('Consciousness doctrine'). Owing to its denial of the independent reality of matter, it is sometimes referred to as the Idealist school.

Yogacara has influenced most later Mahayana traditions. In Tibetan Buddhism (TIBETAN RELIGIONS) it is especially influential among the older sects, while in the Far East it was the basis of one school (FA HSIANG, *see* NANTO ROKUSHU) and important for several others. A branch of the Yogacara specializing in logic and epistemology was formed by Vasubandhu's pupil Dinnaga, making use of methods developed by the Hindu NYAYA school. The tradition of Dinnaga and later Dharmakirti (7th century) is of considerable philosophical importance and exercised a significant influence upon later Hindu and Buddhist logic. [Translations 54: 328–37; logic 61; general 43]

Yoruba Religion [II] The Yoruba, a people of some 10 million in western Nigeria, have a religion which varies considerably with city and province. It might well be described as many religions. What is common is the underlying, anthropomorphically expressed belief in one supreme God, Olorun (Lord of Heaven) or Olodumare (meaning unclear). His primacy in myth, proverb, and occasional personal prayer is clear; nevertheless, modern Yoruba religion is characterized less by Olodumare than by the multitudes of ORISHA, with their mass of shrines, priests, festivals, and sacrifices. There is now almost no public worship of Olodumare, nor mention of him in the *oriki* of *orisha* worship, so that Yoruba religion appears as polytheism, although each *orisha* is treated in worship almost monotheistically. The complex system of IFA divination, an effectively unifying factor across the cults, is very important.

Yoruba religion is among those thriving most in Africa today. Its *orisha* cults, divination, and secret societies have been fully adapted to urban, industrial society; noteworthy are Ogun's patronage of mechanics and bus-drivers, and the popularity of the shrines and festivals at Oshogbo, renewed by Susanne Wenger, a convert to the *orisha* in the 1970s [19; 32; 37].

· Z ·

Zakat [XIV] The religious alms tax (near-synonym *sadaqa*) accounted one of the PILLARS OF ISLAM. It is levied on various categories of possessions, according to fixed rates, and used for charitable purposes as laid down in the QUR'AN. In the present Islamic world, in which Western-type fiscal systems have often been adopted, this tax on incomes is largely voluntary. [20 s.v.; 29: 105–7; 39 s.v.; 47: 159–60]

Zande Religion [II] The Azande (= the people; adjective Zande) live in north-east Zaire and south-west Sudan, and are a highly secular but traditional society, valuing courtesy, good judgement, humour, hospitality, and scepticism. Its kings were greatly respected, but not for religious reasons. The existence of Mbori, the supreme being, maker of all things and thought to reside at the head of streams, may be unquestioned, but arouses little interest, no regular cult, and few personal prayers. Nor is there great interest in, or ritual devoted to, other spiritual beings.

Zande explanation of misfortune and especially death is in terms of witchcraft (*mangu*) and bad magic, i.e. sorcery (*gbegbere ngua*). The theory of these is partly moral (the ill will of evil men), partly materialist; it is not a matter of the agency of spiritual beings, but of certain mysterious physical powers at work in people and things. Thus the witch has an identifiable substance in his body which provides his power. His action can be detected through divination, either through the use of oracles (*soroka*) – of which the most reliable is the poison oracle (the administration of a substance called *benge* to fowls) – or

through the mediumistic activities of witch-doctors (*abinza*). The initiation of the latter again chiefly consists in learning what trees and herbs provide the right medicine with which to detect witchcraft.

The oracle's power lies in the *benge* itself, not in any spiritual agent behind it; it may be administered by anyone. The sorcerer's power lies in the use of offensive medicines, which may be countered by other good magic. Magic (*ngua*) is physically the same, whether good or bad: the differentiation derives from the human moral purpose utilizing it. *Mangu*, *ngua*, and *soroka* appear as theories of science rather than religion, powerful in a secularized society in which religious belief and ritual are minimal. [24: 162–203; 26]

Zen [XVI] Meditation (*dhyana*; Chinese CH'AN; Japanese *zen*) [8: 87–92; 34: 203–28, 240, 250–53; 36]. Meditating in the way of the historic Buddha (GOTAMA) first appeared as a formal practice in Japan in the 9th century, but made no headway until the priest Eisai (1141–1215) returned in 1191 from his second trip to China (JAPAN, BUDDHISM IN). After trying to settle in Kyushu he was identified with an unpopular Kyoto Zen priest and ordered to cease. Eisai preached Lin-chi (Japanese Rinzai) in Kyoto, then in Kamakura where he gained the support of the military ruler [21: 124–5], moving into the Kennin-ji in Kyoto in 1202 and teaching a mixed form of esoteric TENDAI and Zen. His Jufuku-ji temple in Kamakura was pure Zen. He stressed *koan* (paradoxical questions), tea-drinking, and sudden enlightenment.

Rinzai has appealed chiefly to the aristocracy. Soto Zen has become more popular, spread by the priest Dogen (1200–1253), who had once studied under Eisai [27]. He introduced Ts'ao-tung (Japanese Soto) in 1227 after a trip to China, and lived in Kyoto where he wrote *Fukan Zazengi* (General Teaching for Seated Meditation), an exposition of meditation practices free of other sectarian rituals. Tendai monks forced him to move and he settled in the Daibutsu-ji, a temple in Fukui prefecture, in 1244. The temple was renamed Eihei-ji and shares headquarters responsibilities with the Soji-ji, which was moved to Yokohama in 1898 [19: 203–4]. His *Shobo Genzo*, written in Japanese rather than in the customary Chinese, stresses discipline, work, practice, and philosophical questions to find one's BUDDHA-nature in the 'realization of self'. Soto appealed to the peasants and the lower level samurai (warriors) for its value in teaching self-control. Priests were cultural advisers to shoguns (generals), involved in commerce, and sponsored allied arts, such as garden design, tea ceremony, and calligraphy. The painting of subjects integral to Zen questions was a religious exercise, but traditional painting and sculpture were distractions to be avoided.

A somewhat less important sect is Obaku, the Chinese Huang-po, brought by the priest Yin-yuan (1594–1673) and called Ingen in Japan, with headquarters at the large Chinese-style Mampuku-ji (Obaku-san) near Uji. Much Chinese ritual is still retained there along with *nembutsu* (AMIDA WORSHIP). Rinzai has 14 current schools (*ha*) or subsects, and there are several relatively independent schools. Besides the unmistakable influence Zen has had on Japanese life and thought as a whole, Soto has broadened its acceptance by including extensive Pure Land funerary beliefs and practices [19: 202–5].

Ziggurat [VI] The stepped temple tower, built of mud brick, was a notable feature of Mesopotamian cities; the most imposing survival is at Ur (*c.* 2113 BCE) [20]. An artificial mountain re-creating the mountains on which the SUMERIANS had worshipped in their northern homelands, the ziggurat sometimes incorporated a shrine on the summit, and was always associated with the city-god's cult. The ELAMITES [17: 17–22] adopted the ziggurat, and at Susa it followed the pattern at Nippur, Babylon, and elsewhere, while at Choga-Zanbil it differed from the Mesopotamian examples in both planning and construction.

At Ashur (ASSYRIANS) the god's TEMPLE, rebuilt in the 13th century BCE, combined the temple and ziggurat in a single complex.

Zina [XIV] A term which in ISLAM denotes illicit sexual relations and covers the concepts of both adultery and fornication; sexual relations are thus condemned when occurring outside marriage or concubinage. The prescribed penalties are flogging or stoning (with variations in the legal schools and according to the legal status of the two parties), but guilt can only be proved on the evidence of four eyewitnesses. In practice, women considered as erring have often been disposed of by their relatives without recourse to formal law. Sodomy and bestiality are also strongly reprehended. [20 s.v.; 45: III]

Zionism [XVII] A Jewish nationalist movement the aim of which was the setting up of a Jewish state in the HOLY LAND as a homeland for the Jewish people [9 vol. 16: 1031]. The first Zionist congress was held in Basel in 1897 on the initiative of Theodor Herzl (1860–1904), the father of political Zionism. Herzl brought together the various groups of Zionists who had come to recognize the necessity of Jewish self-determination in their own country [28]. The World Zionist Organization (1897) became the umbrella body of the movement, although individual groups representing socialist, religious, cultural, and revisionist forms of Zionism have maintained their separate identities [18]. With the founding of the state of ISRAEL (1948) the Zionist movement achieved its main political objective, and since then has concentrated on providing financial aid to Israel, supporting Jewish immigrants who have gone there (aliyah) from all over the world, and educating Diaspora Jews. [52: 79]

Zionist Movements (African) [xx] A general term used in southern Africa for new movements, or for the less orthodox, more pentecostal types (PENTECOSTALISM) distinguished from ETHIOPIAN CHURCHES. Zionists correspond to the ALADURAS of Nigeria and the 'spiritual churches' of Ghana, and to the general 'prophet-healing' type which since about the 1920s has been more common. They are more African in worship and polity, sometimes more syncretistic in beliefs, and emphasize the power of the HOLY SPIRIT. [12: 43–7; 16: 53–5, 95–9, 315–19: 19: 58–9]

Zohar [XVII] The main text of the KABBALAH. It appeared in mysterious circumstances in Spain towards the end of the 13th century. The Kabbalist Moses de Leon (c. 1240–1305) started circulating manuscripts purporting to be the teachings of a circle of mystics living in Palestine in the 2nd and 3rd centuries. Despite doubts expressed by individual Kabbalists, including contemporaries of de Leon, about the authenticity of de Leon's claim, the Kabbalistic tradition has come to accept that the Zohar is a genuinely ancient text [52: 99]. It is thought to preserve the mystical teachings of RABBI Simeon bar Yochai and his disciples, although exactly how the original manuscript reached Spain is unclear. Modern scholarship views the Zoharic literature as a series of pseudepigraphic texts composed by Moses de Leon and other

unknown Kabbalists in the late 13th and early 14th centuries [45: v]. The Zohar is in the form of a MIDRASH on the BIBLE. [9 vol. 16: 1193]. Its main teaching concerns the 10 emanations (SEFIRAH) through which the world came into being, and which underlie all reality.

Zoroaster [xxx] Greek form of the Iranian name Zarathushtra (later Zardusht) of the prophet, who was of the Spitama family. Most scholars believe that he lived in eastern Iran but there is less agreement over his dates. Recent PARSI tradition dates him around 6000 BCE but this date is not accepted by any Western academic. Instead, a date of around the 6th century BCE has been preferred [18: III; 50: 33], although recent research suggests an earlier date of 1700–1400 BCE as more likely [5: 190f; 7: 18]. On this dating he is the first prophet in the history of religions. His teaching is preserved in 17 hymns, known as the Gathas, which constitute a central portion of the liturgy of the YASNA and are contained in the Zoroastrian holy book, the AVESTA. [Translations: 12; 24; 34: 344–90; 39]

Zoroaster believed that he had seen God, AHURA MAZDA, in visions and that he had been set apart for his priestly and prophetic mission from the beginning. Ahura Mazda, he taught, was the creator of all that is good and is alone worthy of absolute worship. The prophet has, therefore, been termed the first monotheist. Opposed to Ahura Mazda, he taught, is the opposing 'twin spirit', the malign source of violence, evil, and death, ANGRA MAINYU. Man has freedom to choose between these two powers. The righteous will oppose evil, spread the Good Religion of Zoroaster, care for the Good Creation (plants, animals, and fellow men), and worship Mazda in purity. Zoroaster vigorously rejected the daevas, the gods of the Indo-Iranians (INDO-EUROPEANS) such as Indra (VEDA), because of their violent and amoral nature. This he saw epitomized in the destruction wrought by the invaders who were threatening the stability of his settled farming community. Man's eternal destiny, he taught, would be decided by the use he made of his free will, at the individual judgement after death (*see* CHINVAT BRIDGE), and at the universal judgement after the resurrection (*see* FRASHOKERETI). The righteous, he believed, would go to heaven and the wicked to hell – a dark abyss of misery, bad food, and woe. Zoroaster was, then, the first prophet to teach a belief in the two judgements, heaven, hell, and the resurrection of the body. [5: VII–IX; 7: II–III; 50: I]

Passages in the *Avesta* and the later PAHLAVI literature narrate various legends concerning his life. According to them his birth had been foretold to men of ancient times and was marked by miracles. The forces of evil tried to destroy the young child, but he was divinely protected. He was a priest given to solitary meditation. His first vision came at the age of 30. At first his message was rejected and he was violently attacked, but he persevered and converted the king Vishtaspa (later Gushtasp) by miraculously curing his favourite horse when all other remedies had failed. Thereafter Zoroaster's teaching became the official religion of the realm. According to tradition he was murdered at the age of 77 while praying at the altar. [5: XI; 20: 90–95; 23: 9–17]

Zoroastrianism [XXX] The religion of the followers of the Iranian prophet ZOROASTER (*c.* 1400 BCE). The history of the religion prior to the 6th century BCE is largely unknown. Thereafter it became the state religion of three successive Iranian empires: the Achaemenids (approximately 549–331 BCE); the Parthians (2nd century BCE to 224 CE); and the Sasanians (224–642), the boundaries of whose territories extended into what is now Afghanistan and Pakistan and westwards into what is

now Iraq, and at times into Palestine and what is now Turkey. Zoroastrian Iran was finally defeated by the expansion of ISLAM, but for over 1,000 years it was the official religion of three major world empires, making it, perhaps, the most powerful world religion of the time. The last Zoroastrian monarch was Yazdegird who died in 652 CE. The modern Zoroastrian calendar begins with his coronation and the designation *anno Yazdegird* (AY) is used.

Since the end of the Zoroastrian state the religion has been persistently and harshly persecuted by Muslims in Iran, so that the faithful few have been forced to retreat into remote villages, especially near the desert cities of Yazd and Kerman, where they have generally lived in abject poverty. Greater freedom was granted under the PAHLAVI dynasty and the new Islamic Republic has promised to preserve the rights of minorities. It is a considerable tribute to the strength of the faith that even a small group has survived the millennium of oppression. They are often referred to as the 'Zardushti', or as *gabr* (*gaur/gor/guebre*) meaning 'infidel'. They themselves sometimes use the term 'Mazdayasnians' (worshippers (YASNA) of Mazda (AHURA MAZDA)).

In the 10th century CE some Zoroastrians left Iran to seek a new land of religious freedom and settled in northwest India, where they are known as PARSIS (= Persians). The main centres of Zoroastrianism nowadays are India (mainly Bombay), 92,000; Iran, 17,000; Pakistan, 4,000; Britain, 3,000; and the U.S.A., 3,000 (including Canada) (all figures are approximate).

Traditional Zoroastrian teachings are found in the holy book, the AVESTA, and the PAHLAVI literature. An essential feature of all worship (YASNA), centred on FIRE, is physical and moral purity (*see* DAXMA; MAGI; MANTHRAS). Zoroastrianism is often described as a DUALISM because of its teaching on a wholly good God, AHURA MAZDA, who is opposed by the evil ANGRA MAINYU. It is, however, a central part of this optimistic religion that evil will be defeated (FRASHOKERETI). There is no idea of a spirit/flesh dualism because both the spiritual and the material worlds are the creation (BUNDAHISHN) of God. Man, therefore, has a religious duty to care both for the material and spiritual aspects of his existence. It is a religion which inculcates the highest moral ideals. Once the believer has been initiated (NAUJOTE) he or she (there is little difference in the religious duties of the sexes) should fight evil in all its forms.

Zoroastrianism has considerable historic importance because of its geographical position astride the routes between East and West, and also because of its profound influence on Judaism, Christianity, and Islam especially in regard to beliefs on heaven, hell, resurrection of the dead, and the final judgement (*see* FRASHOKERETI). It is also thought that it inspired a belief in a saviour to come in Hinduism (Kalkin, *see* AVATARA) and Buddhism (the Buddha to come – MAITREYA).

Zulu Religion [II] The Zulus have been exposed to Christianity for so long and their royal political system was so severely damaged in the 19th century that it is now particularly difficult to describe their traditional religion as a whole. Many 19th-century observers denied that Zulus believed in one creator God. The argument centred over the word *Unkulunkulu*, meaning the aged or first or most revered one. It is certainly a praise name for God but is at least as much used for the ancestors. The principal specific titles for God are *iNkosi yaphezulu*, Lord-of-the-sky, and *uMvelingqangi*. The latter means 'first to appear' but with the implicit suggestion of twins, the twin of sky being earth. *UMvelingqangi* is male, earth female; together they bring forth the human world.

Unkulunkulu the God is not *Unkulunkulu* the ancestors, who are beneath the earth rather than in the sky. Thunder and lightning are acts of God, whereas sickness and other troubles in life may be caused by the ancestors, the *idlozi* or *abaphansi* (those under the earth). The ancestors protect the living, ask for 'food', are pleased with ritual and sacrifice, punish neglect, and take possession of diviners (*inyanga*). Most *inyanga* are women. The diviner reveals the mind of the ancestors, fights witchcraft, and – very often – acts as a herbalist, but the former is her principal role. [21]

Zurvan [XXX] 'Time', made into the first cause in the major heresy within ZOROASTRIANISM, Zurvanism. The origins of the heresy are unknown. It was perhaps the dominant tradition at the court of the Sasanians (224–642 CE) and lasted into Islamic times, but then withered away. Speculation on Time as the source and controller of all things may well have been due to Babylonian influence on Zoroastrianism. Zurvan was thought of as the father of the 'twin spirits', AHURA MAZDA and ANGRA MAINYU, and therefore, by implication, beyond the distinctions of good and evil. This led to some un-Zoroastrian teachings, for example that if Time controls all things then it follows that man has no free will, an idea alien to the prophet ZOROASTER. Also, with Zurvan as father of the twin spirits, Ahura Mazda is no longer the sole creator and alone worthy of absolute worship. It also suggests that good and evil are not absolute opposites as they are traditionally conceived in Zoroastrianism. There is no evidence to show that Zurvanism ever involved a separate ritual and it may be doubted if it ever formed a separate cult; it was rather perhaps an aberrant movement within Zoroastrianism [7: 67–70, 112–13, 118–23; 48; 50: VIII–XI].

MAPS

Both ancient and modern locations are shown on the maps: the names are underlined where they, or the site, are no longer in active use. Modern national frontiers are included solely for convenience in locating sites of religious significance.

Map 1. EUROPE   366

Map 2. THE ANCIENT NEAR EAST AND WEST ASIA 368

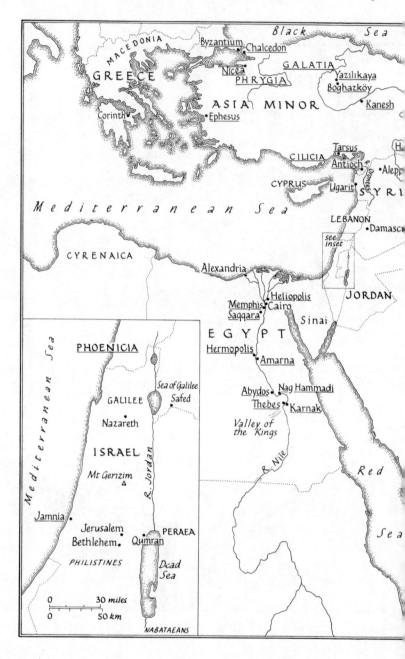

Map 3. AFRICA 370

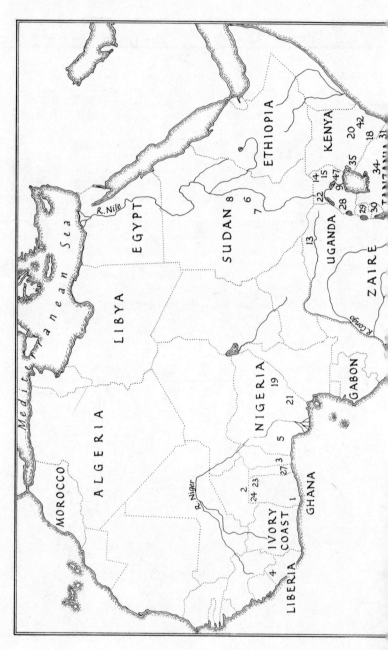

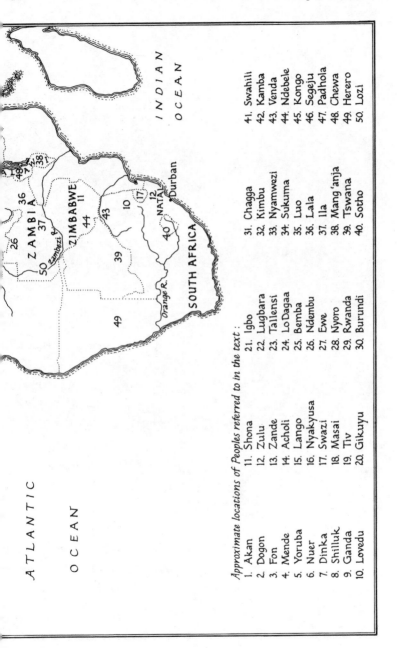

Approximate locations of Peoples referred to in the text :

1. Akan
2. Dogon
3. Fon
4. Mende
5. Yoruba
6. Nuer
7. Dinka
8. Shilluk
9. Ganda
10. Lovedu

11. Shona
12. Zulu
13. Zande
14. Acholi
15. Lango
16. Nyakyusa
17. Swazi
18. Masai
19. Tiv
20. Gikuyu

21. Igbo
22. Lugbara
23. Tallensi
24. Lo Dagaa
25. Bemba
26. Ndembu
27. Ewe
28. Nyoro
29. Rwanda
30. Burundi

31. Chagga
32. Kimbu
33. Nyamwezi
34. Sukuma
35. Luo
36. Lala
37. Ila
38. Mang'anja
39. Tswana
40. Sotho

41. Swahili
42. Kamba
43. Venda
44. Ndebele
45. Kongo
46. Segeju
47. Padhola
48. Chewa
49. Herero
50. Lozi

Map 4. THE INDIAN SUB-CONTINENT 372

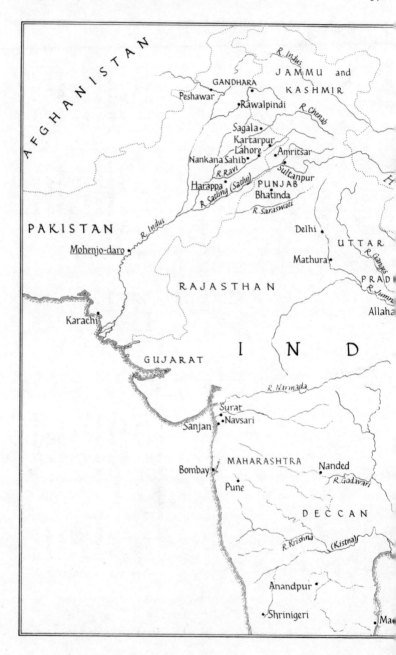

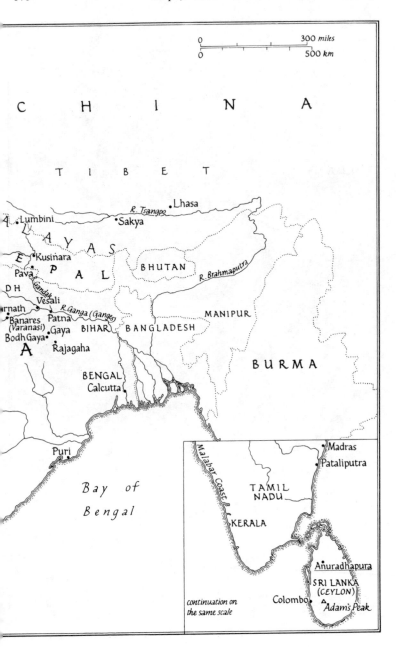

Map 5. SOUTH-EAST ASIA 374

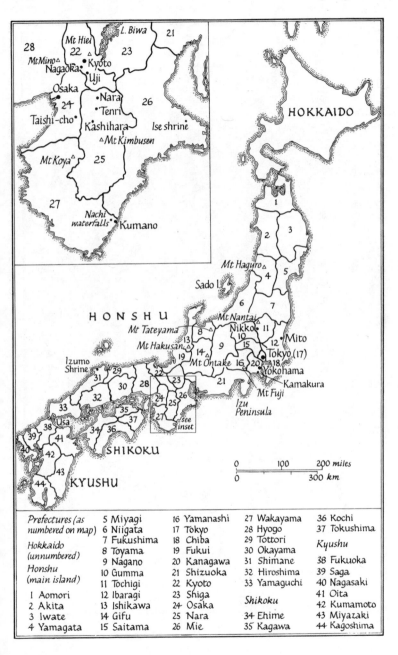

HOKKAIDO

HONSHU

Mt Haguro△

Sado I.

Mt Nantai

Nikko

Mito

Tokyo (17)

Yokohama

Kamakura

Mt Fuji

Izu
Peninsula

Mt Tateyama

Mt Hakusan

Izumo
Shrine

Mt Ontake

SHIKOKU

Usa

KYUSHU

see
inset

0	100	200 miles
0		300 km

Inset:

L. Biwa

Mt Hiei

MtMino△

Nagaoka

Kyoto

Uji

Osaka

Nara

Tenri

Taishi-cho

Kashihara

Ise shrine

△Mt Kimbusen

Mt Koya△

Nachi
waterfalls

Kumano

Prefectures (as numbered on map)	5 Miyagi	16 Yamanashi	27 Wakayama	36 Kochi
	6 Niigata	17 Tokyo	28 Hyogo	37 Tokushima
Hokkaido (unnumbered)	7 Fukushima	18 Chiba	29 Tottori	*Kyushu*
	8 Toyama	19 Fukui	30 Okayama	38 Fukuoka
Honshu (main island)	9 Nagano	20 Kanagawa	31 Shimane	39 Saga
	10 Gumma	21 Shizuoka	32 Hiroshima	40 Nagasaki
	11 Tochigi	22 Kyoto	33 Yamaguchi	41 Oita
1 Aomori	12 Ibaragi	23 Shiga		42 Kumamoto
2 Akita	13 Ishikawa	24 Osaka	*Shikoku*	43 Miyazaki
3 Iwate	14 Gifu	25 Nara	34 Ehime	44 Kagoshima
4 Yamagata	15 Saitama	26 Mie	35 Kagawa	

Map 7. CHINA 376

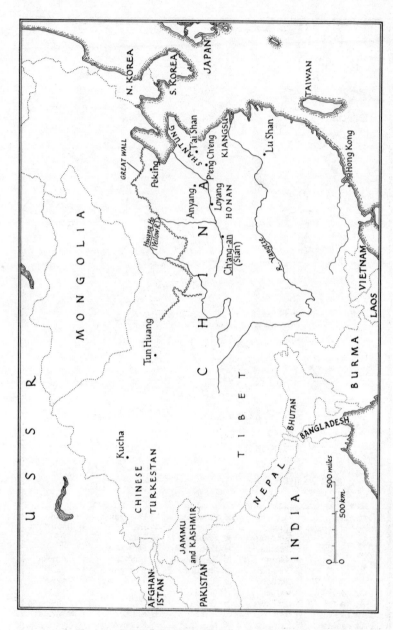

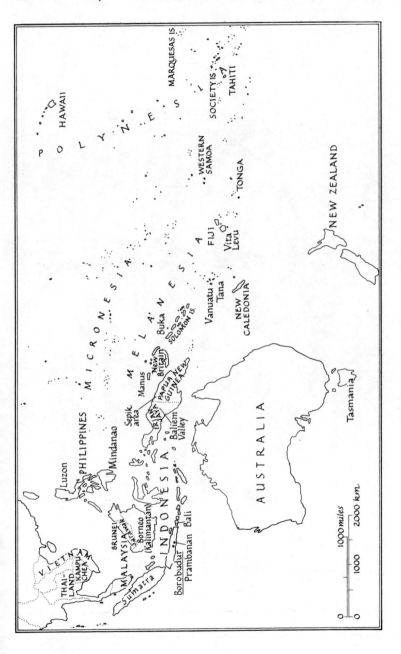

Map 9. NORTH AMERICA

378

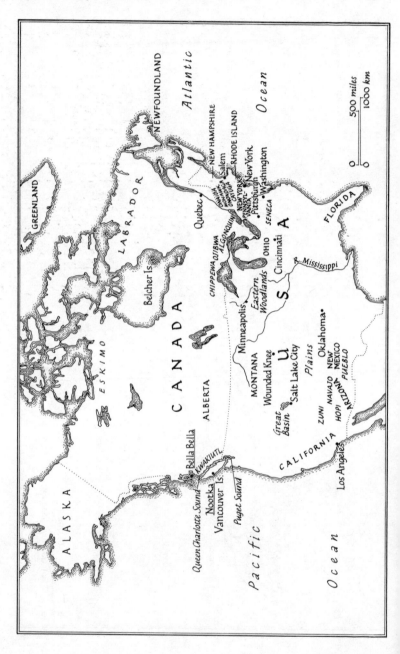

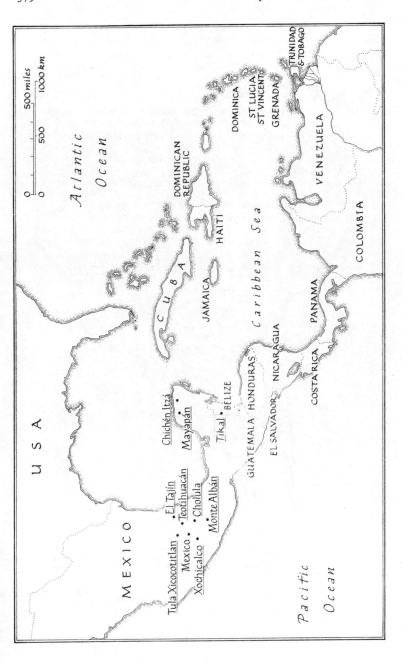

Map 11. LATIN AMERICA

380

BIBLIOGRAPHY

Edited by N. K. Firby

Editorial Note

The following subject lists have been compiled separately by the contributors of articles in the Dictionary and inevitably there are some occasions of overlap and inconsistency. The subject scope of each list reflects the specialities of the contributor rather than any conventional divisions of a subject. The reference citations in the main text account for the presence of the same title in more than one list. When an alternative heading may help the reader to trace a title, this has been inserted (in capitals).

In order to give some indication of the current availability of titles, particularly older works, each title has been checked in *British Books in Print*, 1980, *Books in Print*, 1980–81, and the *National Union Catalog*, pre-1956–79. On occasion other national bibliographies have been consulted. The asterisk (★) indicates a hardback edition/reprint listed as in print, and the dagger (†) indicates a paperback edition/reprint listed as in print. (It must be emphasized that these indications are only general guides to the possible availability of a title. Some titles may drop out of print and others be reprinted in the course of time.)

The editions listed are not exhaustive: the first is that to which any page references are made. Other editions or reprints follow; and earlier editions are noted when the date is significant. Two publishers noted before one date indicates a joint English/United States publication, with the same pagination.

[I] GENERAL BOOKS ON RELIGIONS
Compiled by J. R. Hinnells

1. BRANDON, S. G. F., *A Dictionary of Comparative Religion*, London, Weidenfeld/ New York, *Scribner, 1970
2. BRUCE, F. F., and RUPP, E. G. (eds.), *Holy Book and Holy Tradition*, Manchester, *Manchester University Press/Grand Rapids, Mich., Eerdmans, 1968
3. ELIADE, M. (ed.), *From Primitives to Zen: A Thematic Sourcebook of the History of Religions*, London, *Collins, 1967; New York, Harper & Row, 1967, †1978; new edn, London, †Fount Books, 1978
4. ELIADE, M., *Patterns in Comparative Religion* (tr. by Rosemary Sheed). London, New York, Sheed & Ward, 1958, new edn, †1979
5. FOY, W. (ed.), *Man's Religious Quest*, London,*† Croom Helm/New York, St Martin's, 1978
6. HASTINGS, J., *Encyclopaedia of Religion and Ethics*, 13 vols., Edinburgh, *Clark, 1908–26; 12 vols., New York, *Scribner, 1961
7. HINNELLS, J. R. (ed.), *A Handbook of Living Religions*, Harmondsworth, New York, Penguin Books, 1984
8. LING. T., *A History of Religion East and West*, London, etc., Macmillan, 1968, †1969; New York, St Martin's, 1968; New York, Harper Colophon Books, 1970
9. MOORE, A. C., *Iconography of Religions: An Introduction*, London, *SCM/ Philadelphia, Pa, Fortress, 1977
10. NOSS, J. B., *Man's Religions*, 6th edn, New York, *Macmillan, 1980
11. PARRINDER, E. G., *A Dictionary of Non-Christian Religions*, Amersham, *Hulton Educational, 1971; Philadelphia, Pa, *Westminster, 1973
12. PARRINDER, E. G., *Man and His Gods*, Feltham, Hamlyn, 1971, repr. 1973
13. SMART, N. S., *The Religious Experience of Mankind*, New York, *†Scribner, 1969; London, †Fontana, 1971
14. SMITH, HUSTON, *The Religions of Man*, New York, †Harper & Row, 1965 (copyr. 1958)
15. SMITH, WILFRED CANTWELL, *The Faith of Other Men*, New York, †Harper & Row, 1972
16. STRENG, F., *et al., Ways of Being Religious: Readings for a New Approach to Religion*, Englewood Cliffs, N.J., *Prentice-Hall, 1973
17. ZAEHNER, R. C. (ed.), *A Concise Encyclopedia of Living Faiths*, new edn, London, †Hutchinson, 1977; Boston, Mass., †Beacon Press

[II] AFRICAN RELIGIONS
Compiled by A. Hastings

(a) General and Thematic Surveys

1. BEATTIE, J., and MIDDLETON, J. (eds.), *Spirit Mediumship and Society in Africa*, London, Routledge/New York, *Holmes & Meier, 1969

2. BOOTH, N. W. (ed.), *African Religions: A Symposium*, New York, NOK, 1977
3. DOUGLAS, M. (ed.), *Witchcraft, Confessions and Accusations*, London, Tavistock Publications, 1970
4. FORDE, D. (ed.), *African Worlds: Studies in the Cosmological Ideas and Social Values of African Peoples*, London, New York, International African Institute, *Oxford University Press, 1954, †1963
5. FORTES, M., and DIETERLEN, G. (eds.), *African Systems of Thought*, London, International African Institute, *Oxford University Press, 1965
6. MBITI, J. S., *African Religions and Philosophy*, London, etc., *Heinemann Educational/New York, Praeger, 1969
7. MBITI, J. S., *Concepts of God in Africa*, London, SPCK, 1970, †1975; New York, Praeger, 1970
8. MIDDLETON, J., and WINTER, E. H. (eds.), *Witchcraft and Sorcery in East Africa*, London, *Routledge/New York, Praeger, 1963
9. PARRINDER, E. G., *African Traditional Religion*, 3rd edn, London, *†Sheldon, 1974
10. P'BITEK, O., *African Religions in Western Scholarship*, Nairobi, East African Publishing House, 1970; Nairobi, *East African Literature Bureau, 1971
11. RANGER, T. O., and KIMAMBO, I., *The Historical Study of African Religion*, London, *Heinemann, 1972; Berkeley, Calif., University of California Press, 1972, repr. *1976
12. RAY, B. C., *African Religions: Symbol, Ritual and Community*, Englewood Cliffs, N.J., *Prentice-Hall, 1976
13. SCHOFFELEERS, J. M. (ed.), *Guardians of the Land: Essays on Central African Territorial Cults*, Gwelo, Mambo Press, 1978
14. SHORTER, A., *Prayer in the Religious Traditions of Africa*, Nairobi, †Oxford University Press, 1975, new edn, †Oxford University Press (East Africa), 1979
15. SMITH, EDWIN W. (ed.), *African Ideas of God: A Symposium*, 2nd edn, London, Edinburgh House, 1961
16. WERBNER, R. P. (ed.), *Regional Cults*, London, *Academic Press, 1977
17. ZUESSE, E. M., *Ritual Cosmos: The Sanctification of Life in African Religions*, [Athens, Ohio], *Ohio University Press, 1979

(b) Monographs

18. ABIMBOLA, W., *Ifa Divination Poetry*, New York, NOK, 1977
19. AWOLALU, J. O., *Yoruba Beliefs and Sacrificial Rites*, London, *†Longman, 1979
20. BASCOM, W., *Ifa Divination: Communication Between Gods and Men in West Africa,* Bloomington, Ind., London, *Indiana University Press, 1969
21. BERGLUND, A.-I., *Zulu Thought-Patterns and Symbolism*, London, †C. Hurst/New York, †Holmes & Meier, 1976
22. DAMMANN, E., 'A Tentative Philological Typology of Some African High Deities', *Journal of Religion in Africa* (Leiden), vol. 2, 1969, pp. 81–95
23. DANEEL, M. L., *The God of the Matopo Hills: An Essay on the Mwari Cult in Rhodesia*, Leiden, Afrika-Studiecentrum, 1969; The Hague, †Mouton, 1970

24. EVANS-PRITCHARD, E. E., *Essays in Social Anthropology*, London, Faber, 1969 (prev. publ. Faber, 1962); New York, Free Press of Glencoe, 1963
25. EVANS-PRITCHARD, E. E., *Nuer Religion*, London, *Oxford University Press, 1956, †1971
26. EVANS-PRITCHARD, E. E., *Witchcraft, Oracles and Magic Among the Azande*, new edn, abr. by Eva Gillies, Oxford, †Clarendon Press, 1976
27. FORTES, M., *Oedipus and Job in West African Religion*, Cambridge University Press, 1959, repr. New York, *Octagon, 1980
28. GABA, C. R. (ed.), *Scriptures of an African People*, New York, NOK, 1977
29. GOODY, J., *The Myth of the Bagre*, Oxford, Clarendon Press, 1972
30. GRIAULE, M., *Conversations with Ogotemmêli*, London, Oxford University Press/International African Institute, 1965, †1975, †Oxford University Press (N.Y.) 1976
31. HARJULA, R., *God and the Sun in Meru Thought*, Helsinki, Lutheran Theological College of Makumira/Finnish Society for Missiology and Ecumenics, 1969
32. IDOWU, E. B., *Olódùmarè: God in Yoruba Belief*, London, Longman, 1962, †1966
33. KRIGE, E. J. and J. D., *The Realm of a Rain-Queen: A Study of the Pattern of Lovedu Society*, London, New York, Oxford University Press, 1943; repr. New York, *AMS, 1976
34. KUPER, H., *An African Aristocracy; Rank Among the Swazi of Bechuanaland*, London, New York, Oxford University Press/International African Institute, 1947; repr. of 1965 edn, New York, *Holmes & Meier, 1980
35. KYEWALYĀNGA, F., *Traditional Religion, Custom and Christianity in Uganda*, Freiburg im Breisgau, Krause, 1976
36. LIENHARDT, G., *Divinity and Experience: The Religion of the Dinka*, Oxford, *Clarendon Press, 1961
37. MCKENZIE, P. R., 'Yoruba Orisa Cults', *Journal of Religion in Africa*, vol. 8, 1976, pp. 189–207
38. MIDDLETON, J., *Lugbara Religion: Ritual and Authority Among an East African People*, London, New York, *Oxford University Press/International African Institute, 1960
39. P'BITEK, O., *Religion of the Central Luo*, Nairobi, *†East African Literature Bureau, 1971, 1977
40. RATTRAY, R. S., *Religion and Art in Ashanti*, Oxford, Clarendon Press., 1927; repr. of 1970 edn, *Oxford University Press, 1980; repr. of 1927 edn, New York, *AMS, 1977
41. RICHARDS, A. I., *Chisungu: A Girls' Initiation Ceremony among the Bemba of Northern Rhodesia*, London, Faber, 1956
42. ROSCOE, J., *The Baganda*, 2nd edn, London, *Cass, 1965; New York, Barnes & Noble, 1966
43. TURNER, V. W., *The Drums of Affliction: A Study of Religious Processes Among the Ndembu of Zambia*, Oxford, Clarendon Press/London, International African Institute, 1968
44. WILSON, M., *Rituals of Kinship Among the Nyakyusa*, London, Oxford University Press/International African Institute, 1957, repr. *1970

45. WILSON, M., *Communal Rituals of the Nyakyusa*, London, New York, Oxford University Press/International African Institute, 1959, repr. ★1970

(*See also:* XI (B), 59; XIV, 68, 71; XX, 2, 4, 13, 14, 16)

[III] AMERINDIAN RELIGIONS
Compiled by S. J. Reno

1. BROWN, J. E., *The Sacred Pipe: Black Elk's Account of the Seven Rites of the Oglala Sioux*, Harmondsworth, 1972, Baltimore, Md, 1971, Penguin Books; ★University of Oklahoma Press, 1975, first publ. 1953

2. CAPPS, W. H., *Seeing with a Native Eye*, New York, Harper & Row, 1976

3. COLTON, H. S., *Hopi Kachina Dolls, with a Key to Their Identification*, rev. edn, Santa Fé, N. Mex., University of New Mexico Press, 1959, †1971

4. DELORIA, E., 'The Sun Dance of the Oglala Sioux', *Journal of American Folklore*, vol. 42, 1929, pp. 354–413

5. DELORIA, V., *God is Red*, New York, Grosset & Dunlap, 1973, New York, †Dell, 1975

6. DUBOIS, C., *The 1870 Ghost Dance*, Berkeley, Calif., University of California Press, 1939

7. GOLDMAN, I., *The Mouth of Heaven: An Introduction to Kwakiutl Religious Thought*, New York, ★Wiley, 1975, repr. New York, ★Krieger, 1980

8. HULTKRANTZ, A., *The Religions of the American Indians*, Berkeley, Calif., ★†University of California Press, 1979

9. HULTKRANTZ, A., 'The Structure of Theistic Beliefs among North American Indians', *Temenos*, vol. 7, 1971, pp. 66–74

10. HULTKRANTZ, A., *Conceptions of the Soul Among North American Indians*, Stockholm, Ethnographical Museum of Sweden, 1953

11. HULTKRANTZ, A., 'The Owner of the Animals in the Religion of the North American Indians', in: A. Hultkrantz (ed.), *Supernatural Owners of Nature*, Stockholm, Acta Universitae Stockholmiensis, 1961

12. HULTKRANTZ, A., *Prairie and Plains Indians*, Leiden, Brill, 1973

13. KLUCKHOHN, C., and LEIGHTON, D., *The Navajo*, rev. edn, Cambridge, Mass., ★†Harvard University Press, 1974

14. LABARRE, W., *The Peyote Cult*, 4th edn, New York, Schocken, 1975, †1976; Hamden, Conn., ★Shoe String Press, 1975

15. MARSH, G. H., 'A Comparative Survey of Eskimo–Aleut Religion', *Anthropological Papers of the University of Alaska*, vol. 3, 1954, pp. 21–36

16. PARSONS, E. C., *Pueblo Indian Religion*, Chicago, Ill., University of Chicago Press, 1939

17. POWERS, W. K., *Oglala Religion*, Lincoln, Nebr., ★University of Nebraska Press, 1977

18. RADIN, P., *The Trickster: A Study in American Indian Mythology*, New York, Philosophical Library, 1956; *repr. Westport, Conn., Greenwood; New York, †Schocken, 1972

19. REICHARD, G., *Navaho Religion: A Study in Symbolism*, 2 vols., New York, Pantheon, 1950; 2nd edn, *†Princeton University Press, 1963

20. ROOTH, A. B., 'The Creation Myths of the North American Indians', *Anthropos*, vol. 52, 1957, pp. 497–508

21. SLOTKIN, J. S., *The Peyote Religion: A Study in Indian–White Relations*, Glencoe, Free Press, 1956; repr. New York, *Octagon, 1975

22. TEDLOCK, D. and B., *Teachings from the American Earth*, New York, Liveright, 1975

23. UNDERHILL, R. M., *Red Man's Religion*, Chicago, Ill., *University of Chicago Press, 1965, †1972

24. WALLACE, A. F. C., 'Revitalization Movements', *American Anthropologist*, LVIII, 1956, pp. 264–81

25. WATERS, F., *Book of the Hopi*, New York, Ballantine, 1971, †1974; †Penguin Books (U.S.), 1977; previously published New York, Viking, 1963

(*See also*: XX, I, II, 18)

[IV] ANCIENT EGYPTIAN RELIGIONS
Compiled by A. Rosalie David

1. ALLEN, T. G. (ed.), *The Egyptian Book of the Dead: Documents in the Oriental Institute Museum at the University of Chicago*, Chicago, Ill., University of Chicago Press, 1960, repr. Ann Arbor, Mich., University Microfilms, 1971; and, *The Book of The Dead; or, Going Forth By Day* ... (tr. by T. G. Allen), Chicago, Ill., Chicago Oriental Institute/†University of Chicago Press, 1974, London, *1975

2. BONNET, H., *Reallexikon der ägyptischen Religionsgeschichte*, Berlin, De Gruyter, 1952

3. DAVID, A. R., *Mysteries of the Mummies: The Story of the Manchester University Investigation*, London, Cassell, 1978; New York, *Scribner, 1979

4. DAVID, A. R. (ed.), *The Manchester Museum Mummy Project*, Manchester, Manchester Museum/*Manchester University Press, 1979

5. DAVID, A. R., *The Cult of the Sun: Myth and Magic in Ancient Egypt*, London, *Dent, 1980

6. DAVID, A. R., *The Ancient Egyptians: Religious Beliefs and Practices*, London, *Routledge, 1981

7. DAVID, A. R., *A Guide to Religious Ritual at Abydos*, Warminster, *Aris & Phillips, 1981

8. EDWARDS, I. E. S., *The Pyramids of Egypt*, new edn, Harmondsworth, Balti-

more, Md, Penguin Books, 1972, †1975; London, Ebury & Joseph/New York, Viking, 1972

9. ERMAN, A. (ed.), *The Ancient Egyptians: A Source Book of their Writings*, New York, Harper Torchbooks, 1966; Magnolia, Mass., *Peter Smith; German edn: *Die Literatur der Ägypter*, Leipzig, 1923, first tr. as *The Literature of the Ancient Egyptians*, London, Methuen, 1927, repr. New York, *Arno, 1976

10. FAIRMAN, H. W., 'The Kingship Rituals of Egypt', in: S. H. Hooke (ed.), *Myth, Ritual and Kingship*, Oxford, Clarendon Press, 1958

11. FAULKNER, R. O., *The Ancient Egyptian Pyramid Texts*, Oxford, Clarendon Press, 1969

12. FRANKFORT, H., *Ancient Egyptian Religion*, New York, Columbia University Press, 1948; New York, †Harper, 1961; Magnolia, Mass., *Peter Smith

13. GRIFFITHS, J. G., *The Conflict of Horus and Seth*, Liverpool, *Liverpool University Press, 1960

14. GRIFFITHS, J. G., *The Origins of Osiris and His Cult*, Leiden, Numen, 1980 (Supplement 40)

15. HERODOTUS, *The Histories* (tr. by A. de Selincourt, rev. by A. R. Burn), Harmondsworth, Baltimore, Md, Penguin Books, 1972

16. KEES, H., *Der Götterglaube im alten Ägypten*, 2nd edn, Berlin, Akademie-Verlag, 1956

17. KEES, H., *Totenglauben und Jenseitsvorstellungen der alten Ägypter*, 2nd edn, Berlin, Akademie-Verlag, 1956

18. MORENZ, S., *Egyptian Religion*, London, Methuen/Ithaca, N.Y., *Cornell University Press, 1973; German edn: *Ägyptische Religion*, Stuttgart, Kohlhammer, 1960

19. PORTER, B., and MOSS, R., *Topographical Bibliography of Ancient Egyptian Hieroglyphic Texts, Reliefs and Paintings*, Oxford, Clarendon Press, 1927–; Oxford University Press, *Griffith Institute, 1970–

20. PRITCHARD, J. B. (ed.), *Ancient Near Eastern Texts Relating to the Old Testament*, 2nd edn, Princeton, N.J., Princeton University Press, 1955; *3rd (de luxe) edn, with *Supplement*, 1969 (refs. in text are to 2nd edn)

21. SAUNERON, S., *The Priests of Ancient Egypt*, New York, London, Evergreen Books, 1960, New York, †Grove, 1980; French edn: *Les Prêtres de l'ancienne Égypte*, Paris, Édns du Seuil, 1957

22. SMITH, RAY W., and REDFORD, D. B., *The Akhenaten Temple Project*, vol. 1, Warminster, Aris & Phillips, 1976

23. VELDE, H. TE, *Seth, God of Confusion*, Leiden, Brill, 1967

[V] ANCIENT EUROPEAN RELIGIONS
Compiled by H. Ellis Davidson

1. BALYS, J., 'Lithuanian Mythology', in: *Funk and Wagnalls Standard Dictionary of*

Folklore, Mythology and Legend, 2 vols., New York, Funk & Wagnalls, 1949–50, repr. 1970

2. BLACKER, C., and LOEWE, M. (eds.), *Ancient Cosmologies*, London, ★Allen & Unwin/Totowa, N.J., ★Rowman, 1975

3. BLACKER, C., and LOEWE, M. (eds.), *Divination and Oracles*, London, ★Allen & Unwin, 1981 (publ. as Loewe & Blacker)

4. BRUCE-MITFORD, R. L. S., *The Sutton Hoo Ship Burial: A Handbook*, 2nd edn, London, British Museum, 1972 (or later edn)

5. CAESAR, JULIUS, *The Conquest of Gaul* (tr. by S. A. Handford), Harmondsworth, †Penguin Books, 1951, 1970

6. DAVIDSON, H. R. E., *Gods and Myths of Northern Europe*, Harmondsworth, Baltimore, Md, †Penguin Books, 1964; Santa Fé, N. Mex., ★Gannon, n.d.; repr. as *Gods and Myths of the Viking Age*, New York, Bell, 1981

7. DAVIDSON, H. R. E., *Pagan Scandinavia*, London, Thames & Hudson/New York, Praeger, 1967

8. DUMÉZIL, G., *Gods of the Ancient Northmen* (tr. by E. Haugen), Berkeley, Calif., London, University of California Press, 1973, ★1974, †1978

9. ELLIOTT, R. W. V., *Runes: An Introduction*, Manchester, Manchester University Press/New York, Philosophical Library, 1959

10. GELLING, P., and DAVIDSON, H. R. E., *The Chariot of the Sun*, London, Dent/New York, Praeger, 1969

11. GIMBUTAS, M., *The Balts*, London, Thames & Hudson/New York, Praeger, 1963

12. GIMBUTAS, M., *The Slavs*, London, Thames & Hudson/New York, Praeger, 1971

13. JAKOBSON, R., 'Slavic Mythology', in: *Funk and Wagnalls Standard Dictionary of Folklore . . .* (as no. 1 above)

13a.JONES, G., *A History of the Vikings*, London, New York, Toronto, Oxford University Press, 1968

14. KENDRICK, SIR THOMAS D., *The Druids: A Study in Keltic Prehistory*, London, Methuen, 1927; repr. New York, Barnes & Noble, 1966; 2nd edn, 1928, repr. London, ★Cass, 1966

LOEWE, M., *see no. 2*

15. *The Mabinogion* (tr. by G. and T. Jones), London, Dent/New York, Dutton, 1949, ★†repr. (Everyman's Library)

16. MACNEILL, M., *The Festival of Lughnasa*, London, Oxford University Press, 1962

17. PIGGOTT, S., *The Druids*, London, Thames & Hudson/New York, Praeger, 1968; Harmondsworth, †Penguin Books, 1974; 2nd edn, London, ★Thames & Hudson, 1975

18. *The Poetic Edda* (*Edda Saemundar*) (tr. by L. M. Hollander), 2nd edn, Austin, Tex., University of Texas Press, 1962, repr. 1964

19. POWELL, T. G. E., *The Celts*, London, Thames & Hudson, 1958, ★1980; New York, Praeger, 1958

20. *Prose Edda of Snorri Sturluson* (sel. and tr. by J. I. Young), Cambridge, Bowes, 1954; Berkeley, Calif., †University of California Press, 1964, London, 1966

21. REES, A. and B., *Celtic Heritage*, London, Thames & Hudson, 1961, new edn
    †1973, (U.S.) †1977; New York, Grove Press, 1961
22. ROSS, A., *Everyday Life of the Pagan Celts*, London, Batsford/New York,
    Putnam, 1970
23. ROSS, A., *Pagan Celtic Britain*, London, *Routledge/New York, *Columbia
    University Press, 1967
24. SAXO GRAMMATICUS, *History of the Danes*, I–IX, vol. I (tr. by P. Fisher),
    vol. 2 (commentary by H. R. E. Davidson), London, *Brewer/Totowa, N.J.,
    *Rowman, 1979–80
25. SIMPSON, J., *Everyday Life in the Viking Age*, London, Batsford/New York,
    Putnam, 1967
26. SJOESTEDT, M. L., *Gods and Heroes of the Celts* (tr. by M. Dillon), London,
    Methuen, 1949; New York, *Gordon Press, 1976
27. TACITUS, *The Agricola and the Germania* (tr. by H. Mattingly, rev. by S. A.
    Handford), Harmondsworth, †Penguin Books, 1970, (U.S.) 1971
28. TIERNEY, J. J., 'The Celtic Ethnography of Posidonius', in: *Proceedings of the
    Irish Royal Academy*, vol. 60, 1959, pp. 189ff
29. TODD, M., *The Northern Barbarians, 100 B.C. to A.D. 300*, London, *†Hutch-
    inson, 1975
30. TURVILLE-PETRE, E. O. G., *Myth and Religion of the North*, London, Weiden-
    feld/New York, Holt, Rinehart, 1964, repr. Westport, Conn., *Greenwood,
    1975

[VI] ANCIENT NEAR EASTERN RELIGIONS
Compiled by A. Rosalie David

1. BARNETT, R. D., 'The Epic of Kumarbi and the Theogony of Hesiod', *Journal
   of Hellenic Studies*, vol. 45, 1945, pp. 100–101
2. BARNETT, R. D., 'The Sea Peoples', *Cambridge Ancient History*, rev. edn, vol. 2,
   ch. 28, Cambridge, Cambridge University Press, 1969
3. DRIVER, SIR GODFREY R., *Canaanite Myths and Legends (from Ras Shamra)*,
   Edinburgh, Clark, 1956, †1971, 2nd edn, 1978
4. DROWER, M. S., 'Ugarit', *Cambridge Ancient History*, rev. edn, vol. 2,
   ch. 21(b), Cambridge, Cambridge University Press, 1968
5. FRANKFORT, H., *Cylinder Seals: A Documentary Essay on the Art and Religion of
   the Ancient Near East*, London, Macmillan, 1939
6. FRANKFORT, H., *The Art and Architecture of the Ancient Orient*, Harmondsworth, 1954, *†1970, Baltimore, Md, 1955, †1978, Penguin Books; New
   York, *Viking, 1969
7. GADD, C. J., 'Hammurabi and the End of His Dynasty', *Cambridge Ancient
   History*, rev. edn, vol. 2, ch. 5, Cambridge, Cambridge University Press,
   1965

8. GELB, I. J., *Hittite Hieroglyphic Monuments*, Chicago, Ill., University of Chicago Press, 1939

9. GELB, I. J., *Hurrians and Subarians*, Chicago, Ill., *University of Chicago Press, 1944

10. GRAY, J., *Near Eastern Mythology: Mesopotamia, Syria, Palestine*, London, Hamlyn, 1969

11. GRAYSON, A. K., *Assyrian Royal Inscriptions*, Wiesbaden, Harrassowitz, 1972–6 (Records of the Ancient Near East, vols. 1 and 2)

12. GURNEY, O. R., 'Hittite Kingship', in: S. H. Hooke (ed.), *Myth, Ritual and Kingship*, Oxford, Clarendon Press, 1958

13. GURNEY, O. R., *The Hittites*, Harmondsworth, Baltimore, Md, Penguin Books, 1964 (copyr. 1952), new edn, London, *Allen Lane, 1975

14. HINZ, W., 'Persia, *c.* 2400–1800 B.C.', *Cambridge Ancient History*, rev. edn, vol. 1, ch. 23, Cambridge, Cambridge University Press, 1963

15. HINZ, W., *The Lost World of Elam*, London, Sidgwick & Jackson/*New York, New York University Press, 1972

16. KRAMER, S. N., *History Begins at Sumer*, London, Thames & Hudson, 1958, 2nd edn, 1961; Garden City, N.Y., Doubleday, 1959; originally publ. as *From the Tablets of Sumer*, Indian Hills, Colo, Falcon's Wing, 1956

17. LABAT, R., 'Elam, *c.* 1600–1200 B.C.', *Cambridge Ancient History*, rev. edn, vol. 2, ch. 29, Cambridge, Cambridge University Press, 1963

18. LAESSØE, J., *People of Ancient Assyria* (tr. from the Danish *Frå Assyriens Arkiver* by F. S. Leigh-Browne), London, Routledge/New York, Barnes & Noble, 1963

19. LANGHE, R. de, 'Myth, Ritual and Kingship in the Ras Shamra Tablets', in: S. H. Hooke (ed.), *Myth, Ritual and Kingship*, Oxford, Clarendon Press, 1958

20. LLOYD, S., *Foundations in the Dust: a Story of Mesopotamian Exploration*, Harmondsworth, Baltimore, Md, Penguin Books, 1955; rev. edn, London, *Thames & Hudson, 1980; London, Oxford University Press, 1947, repr. New York, *AMS, 1977

21. MACALISTER, R. A. S., *The Philistines, Their History and Civilisation*, 3rd (1st Amer.) edn, Chicago, Ill., Argonaut, 1965; prev. publ. London, Oxford University Press, 1913

22. NEUGEBAUER, O., *The Exact Sciences in Antiquity*, New York, Harper Torchbooks, 1962; 2nd edn, Providence, R.I., Brown University Press, 1957, repr. *1970; New York, †Dover, 1969

23. POSTGATE, N., *The First Empires*, Oxford, *Elsevier/Phaidon, 1977

24. PRITCHARD, J. B. (ed.), *Ancient Near Eastern Texts Relating to the Old Testament*, 2nd edn, Princeton, N.J., Princeton University Press, 1955; 3rd (de luxe) edn, with Supplement, 1969 (refs. in text are to the 2nd edn)

25. WISEMAN, D. J., 'Assyria and Babylonia *c.* 1200–1000 B.C.', *Cambridge Ancient History*, rev. edn, vol. 2, ch. 31, Cambridge, Cambridge University Press, 1965

26. WOOLLEY, SIR CHARLES L., *The Development of Sumerian Art*, London, Faber/New York, Scribner, 1935, repr. Westport, Conn., *Greenwood

[VII] ARCTIC PEOPLES' RELIGIONS, INCLUDING SHAMANISM
Compiled by E. H. Pyle

1. BIRKET-SMITH, K., *The Eskimos* (tr. by W. E. Calvert, rev. by C. Daryll Forde), new edn, London, Methuen, 1959
2. DIÓSZEGI, V., *Tracing Shamans in Siberia* (tr. from the Hungarian by A. R. Babó), New York, *Humanities, for Oosterhout, Netherlands, Anthropological Publications, 1968
3. DIÓSZEGI, V. (ed.), *Popular Beliefs and Folklore Tradition in Siberia*, The Hague, Mouton, 1968
4. ELIADE, M., *Shamanism*, new edn (Bollingen), New York, Pantheon/London, *Routledge/*†Princeton University Press, 1965
5. HERBERT, W., *Eskimos*, London, Collins, 1976, new edn, †1978; New York, Franklin Watts, 1976
6. LEWIS, I.M., *Ecstatic Religion: An Anthropological Study of Spirit Possession and Shamanism*, Harmondsworth, †Penguin Books, 1971
7. MURDOCK, G.P., *Our Primitive Contemporaries*, New York, Macmillan, 1934
8. SPENCER, A., *The Lapps*, Newton Abbot, *David & Charles/New York, *Crane-Russak, 1978
9. VORREN, ø., and MANKER, E., *Lapp Life and Customs* (tr. from the Norwegian by K. MacFarlane), London, New York, Oxford University Press, 1962
10. WEYER, E. M., *The Eskimos*, New Haven, Conn., Yale University Press/London, Oxford University Press, 1932, repr. Hamden, Conn., *Shoe String Press, 1962

(*See also:* III, 15; X, 93; XVI, 4)

[VIII] ASTROLOGY
Compiled by R. Beck

1. ALLEN, D.C., *The Star-Crossed Renaissance*, New York, *Octagon, 1966, repr. of Durham, N.C., Duke University Press, 1941; London, *Cass, 1967
2. BOLL, F., BEZOLD, C., and GUNDEL, W., *Sternglaube und Sterndeutung: die Geschichte und das Wesen der Astrologie*, 6th edn (rev. by H. G. Gundel), Stuttgart, Teubner, 1974
3. BOUCHÉ-LECLERQ, A., *L'Astrologie grecque* (Paris, 1899 edn), repr. Brussels, Culture et Civilisation, 1963
4. CRAMER, F. H., *Astrology in Roman Law and Politics*, Philadelphia, Pa, American Philosophical Society, 1954 (*Memoirs of the American Philosophical Society*, 37)
5. CULVER, R.B., and IANNA, P. A., 'Astrology and the Scientific Method', *Astronomy Quarterly*, vol. I, 1977, pp. 85–110, 147–72

6. CUMONT, F., *Astrology and Religion among the Greeks and Romans*, New York, †Dover, 1960 (repr. of 1912 edn, New York, London, Putnam); Magnolia, Mass., ★Peter Smith

7. EISLER, R., *The Royal Art of Astrology*, London, Herbert Joseph, 1946

8. GAUQUELIN, M., *The Cosmic Clocks: From Astrology to a Modern Science*, Chicago, Ill., Regnery, 1967; London, ★Peter Owen, 1969; St Albans, †Paladin, 1973

9. KRUPP, E.G. (ed.), *In Search of Ancient Astronomies*, Garden City, N.Y., ★Doubleday, 1978; New York, †McGraw-Hill, 1979; London, ★Chatto, 1980

10. LINDSAY, J., *Origins of Astrology*, London, Muller/New York, Barnes & Noble, 1971

11. MACNEICE, L., *Astrology*, London, Aldus/Garden City, N.Y., ★Doubleday, 1964

12. MAYO, J., *Teach Yourself Astrology*, London, English Universities Press, 1964, repr. 1968; New York, †Mckay, 1980

13. NEUGEBAUER, O., and VAN HOESEN, H.B., *Greek Horoscopes*, Philadelphia, Pa, American Philosophical Society, 1959 (*Memoirs of the American Philosophical Society*, 48); Ann Arbor, Mich., †Univ. Microfilms, 1978

14. PARKER, D., and PARKER, J., *The Compleat Astrologer*, New York, ★McGraw-Hill, 1971; London, ★Mitchell Beazley, 1971, †1979; New York, †Bantam, 1975

15. PINGREE, D.E., 'Astrology', *Encyclopaedia Britannica: Macropaedia*, 15th edn, vol. 2, 1974, pp. 219–23

16. WEST, J.A., and TOONDER, J.G., *The Case for Astrology*, New York, Coward, McCann/London, Macdonald, 1970

[IX: A–B] BUDDHISM

Numbers 1–39 compiled by T. O. Ling, 39–65 by L. S. Cousins

A

1. BHANDARKAR, D.R., *Aśoka*, 3rd edn, Calcutta, University of Calcutta, 1955, ★1969

2. CHATTOPADHYAYA, S., *Bimbisāra to Aśoka*, Calcutta, Roy & Chowdhury, 1977

3. CHAUDHURI, B.N., *Buddhist Centres in Ancient India*, Calcutta, ★Sanskrit College, 1969

4. CONZE, E., *Buddhism: Its Essence and Development*, Oxford, Cassirer, 1951, 3rd edn, 1960, †1974; Magnolia, Mass., ★Peter Smith; New York, †Harper & Row, 1959

5. CONZE, E., *Buddhist Thought in India*, London, Allen & Unwin, 1962; †University of Michigan Press, 1967

6. CONZE, E., *A Short History of Buddhism*, London, ★Allen & Unwin, 1979

6a CONZE, E. (tr.), *The Short Prajñāpāramitā Texts*, London, Luzac, 1973; Totowa, N.J., Rowman, 1974

7. DASGUPTA, S.N. *A History of Indian Philosophy*, vol. 1, Cambridge, Cambridge University Press, 1922, repr. Delhi, ★Motilal Banarsidass, 1975:

Livingston, N.J., Orient Book Distributors, 1975; Atlantic Highlands, N.J., †Humanities, 1975

7a. DUTT, N., *Buddhist Sects in India*, Calcutta, *Mukhopadhyay, 1970; Delhi, †Motilal Banarsidass; Livingston, N.J., Orient Book Distributors

8. DUTT, S., *The Buddha and Five After-Centuries*, London, Luzac, 1957

9. DUTT, S., *Buddhist Monks and Monasteries of India*, London, Allen & Unwin, 1962

10. GEIGER, W., *Pali Literature and Language*, 2nd edn, Calcutta, Calcutta University Press, 1956; repr. Delhi, Oriental Book Reprint Corp., 1968; repr. of 1973 edn, Columbia, Mo, *South Asia, 1978

10a. GEIGER, W., *The Dīpavaṃsa and Mahāvaṃsa* (tr. into English by E. M. Coomaraswamy), Colombo, Cottle, 1908

11. GHOSHAL, U. N., *A History of Indian Political Ideas*, London, Oxford University Press, 1959, *Bombay, 1967

11a. HORNER, I. B., *The Book of the Discipline*, vols. 1–3 (English tr. of *Bhikkhu-Vibhanga*, or *Suttavibhanga*), London, Oxford University Press, 1938, 1940, 1942; repr. London, *Pali Text Society, 1970

11b. HORNER, I. B., *Milinda's Questions* (English tr. of *Milinda-pañha*), 2 vols., London, *Pali Text Society, 1963–4

12. JAYATILLEKE, K. N., *Early Buddhist Theory of Knowledge*, London, Allen & Unwin, 1963

13. JAYATILLEKE, K. N., *The Message of the Buddha*, London, *Allen & Unwin, 1975; New York, *Free Press, 1975

14. JONES, J. G., *Tales and Teaching of the Buddha*, London, *Allen & Unwin, 1979

14a. JONES, J. J., *Mahāvastu* (tr. from the Buddhist Sanskrit), 3 vols., London, Luzac, 1949, 1952, 1956; London, *Pali Text Society, repr. 1973–8

15. JOSHI, L., *Studies in the Buddhistic Culture of India*, Delhi, Motilal Banarsidass, 1967, *1977; Mystic, Conn., *Verry, 1977

16. KALUPAHANA, D. J., *Buddhist Philosophy: A Historical Analysis*, Honolulu, *†University Press of Hawaii, 1976

16a. KERN, H., *Saddharmapundarika* [*Sutra*] (English tr.), Oxford, Clarendon Press, 1884, 1909 (*Sacred Books of the East*, vol. 21), repr. New York, *Krishna; Magnolia, Mass., *Peter Smith

17. LING, T., *The Buddha: Buddhist Civilization in India and Ceylon*, London, *M. T. Smith/New York, Scribner, 1973

18. LING, T., *The Buddha's Philosophy of Man: Early Indian Buddhist Dialogues*, London, Dent, 1981

19. LING, T., *Buddhism and the Mythology of Evil*, London, Allen & Unwin, 1962

20. LING, T., *Buddhism, Imperialism and War*, London, *Allen & Unwin, 1979

20a. LING, T., *Dictionary of Buddhism: Indian and South-East Asian*, Calcutta, Bagchi, 1981

21. MALALASEKERA, G. P., *Dictionary of Pāli Proper Names*, 2 vols., London, Luzac, 1960, first publ. 1937–8; London, *Pali Text Society, repr. 1974

22. MALALASEKERA, G. P., *The Pāli Literature of Ceylon*, Colombo, Gunasena, 1928; London, Royal Asiatic Society, 1928; New York, *International Publications Service, 1958

23. MARASINGHE, M. M. J., *Gods in Early Buddhism*, Vidyalankara, University of Sri Lanka (Ceylon), 1974

23a. MCGOVERN, W. M., *Manual of Buddhist Philosophy*, vol. I, *Cosmology*, London, Kegan Paul/New York, Dutton, 1923

24. MURTI, T. R. V., *The Central Philosophy of Buddhism*, London, *Allen & Unwin, 1955, †1980

25. NYANATILOKE, M., *Buddhist Dictionary*, 2nd rev. edn, Colombo, Frewin, 1956; 1950 edn, repr. New York, *AMS, 1977; San Francisco, Calif., *Chinese Materials Center, 1977

26. PANDE, G. C., *Studies in the Origins of Buddhism*, 2nd edn, Delhi, Motilal Banarsidass, 1974; Livingston, N.J., *Orient Book Distributors/Mystic, Conn., *Verry, 1974

27. PANDEY, M. S., *Historical Geography and Topography of Bihar*, Delhi, *Motilal Banarsidass, 1963; Livingston, N.J., *Orient Book Distributors 1963

27a. RADHAKRISHNAN, S., *The Dhammapada* (Pāli text, English tr. and notes), London, New York, *Oxford University Press, 1950, *Bombay, 1969

28. RHYS DAVIDS, T. W. and C. A. F., *Dialogues of the Buddha*, pts 1–3, London, Oxford University Press, 1899–1921, repr. London, Luzac, 1956–65; London, *Pali Text Society, repr. 1977

29. RHYS DAVIDS, T. W., *Buddhist India*, 1st edn, London, New York, 1903; 8th edn, Calcutta, Gupta, 1959; Delhi, *Indological Book House, 1970

30. ROBINSON, R. H., *Early Mādhyamika in India and China*, Madison, Wis., London, University of Wisconsin Press, 1967, repr. Livingston, N.J., *Orient Book Distributors, 1976; Mystic, Conn., *Verry, 1977

31. SADDHATISSA, H., *Buddhist Ethics*, London, *Allen & Unwin, 1970; New York, *†Braziller, 1971

32. SILVA, P. DE, *An Introduction to Buddhist Psychology*, London, Macmillan, 1979

33. STCHERBATSKY, T., *The Central Conception of Buddhism*, 2nd edn, Calcutta, Gupta, 1956; 3rd edn, 1961, repr. Mystic, Conn., *Verry; Livingston, N.J., *Orient Book Distributors, 1979

34. TACHIBANA, S., *The Ethics of Buddhism*, London, Oxford University Press, 1926, repr. Colombo, 1961; New York, *Barnes & Noble/London, *Curzon Press/Atlantic Highlands, N.J., *Humanities, 1975

35. THAPAR, R., *Aśoka and the Decline of the Mauryas*, London, Oxford University Press, 1961; 2nd rev. edn, London, †OUP (India), 1974, Bombay, 1973

35a. THOMAS, E. J., *The Life of the Buddha: As Legend and History*, 3rd edn, London, Routledge, 1949, repr. *1969, †1975

36. WALPOLA, RĀHULA (or RĀHULA, W.,), *History of Buddhism in Ceylon*, Colombo, Gunasena, 1956; New Delhi, *Orient Longman, 1969

37. WARDER, A. K., *Indian Buddhism*, Delhi, *Motilal Banarsidass, 1970

38. WEERARATNE, W. H., *Individual and Society in Buddhism*, Colombo, World Fellowship of Buddhists, 1977

B

39. ARONSON, H. B., *Love, Compassion, Sympathetic Joy and Equanimity in Theravada Buddhism*, Ann Arbor, Mich., University Microfilms, 1980 (Ph.D. thesis, University of Wisconsin, 1975)

40. AUNG, S. Z. (tr.), ANURUDDHA, *Compendium of Philosophy* (ed. Mrs
    C. Rhys Davids), London, Pali Text Society, 1910, repr. *1979
41. BODHI (tr.), *The Discourse on the All-Embracing Net of Views*, Kandy, Buddhist
    Publication Society, 1978
42. BUDDHAGHOSA, *Path of Purification* (tr. by Ñānamoli), 2nd edn, Colombo,
    Semage, 1964, repr. in 2 vols., Berkeley, Calif., †Shambhala, 1976
43. CHATTERJEE, A. K., *The Yogācāra Idealism*, 2nd edn. rev., Delhi, Motilal
    Banarsidass, 1975; Livingston, N.J., †Orient Book Distributors, 1976
44. CONZE, E., *Buddhist Meditation*, London, Allen & Unwin, 1956, †1972
45. CONZE, E., *Buddhist Scriptures*, Harmondsworth, Baltimore, Md, †Penguin
    Books, 1959, repr. 1979
46. DAYAL, H., *The Bodhisattva Doctrine in Buddhist Sanskrit Literature*, London,
    Kegan Paul, Trench, Trubner, 1932, repr. Delhi, Motilal Banarsidass, 1970;
    Livingston, N.J., *Orient Book Distributors, 1975
47. GOMBRICH, R. F., *Precept and Practice: Traditional Buddhism in the Rural
    Highlands of Ceylon*, Oxford, *Clarendon Press, 1971
48. GUENTHER, H. V., *Philosophy and Psychology in the Abhidharma*, new edn,
    Berkeley, Calif., †Shambhala, 1976; Delhi, *Motilal Banarsidass, 1974
49. KING, W. L., *Theravada Meditation*, [University Park, Pa] *Pennsylvania State
    University Press, 1980
50. *Middle Length Sayings (Majjhima-Nikāya)*, vol. 1 (tr. by I. B. Horner), London,
    *Pali Text Society, 1954, repr. 1975
51. NYANAPONIKA, *The Heart of Buddhist Meditation*, London, Rider, 1962
52. PREBISH, C. S., *Buddhism*, [University Park, Pa] †Pennsylvania State
    University Press, 1975
53. PYE, M., *Skilful Means: A Concept in Mahayana Buddhism*, London, *Duck-
    worth, 1978
54. RADHAKRISHNAN, SIR SARVEPALLI, and MOORE, C. A. (eds.), *A Source-
    book in Indian Philosophy*, Princeton, N.J., Princeton University Press, 1957,
    repr. †1973
55. SADDHATISSA, H., *The Buddha's Way*, London, †Allen & Unwin, 1971; New
    York, *Braziller, 1972
56. SECKEL, D., *The Art of Buddhism*, London, Methuen/New York, Crown,
    1964
57. SGAM-PO-PA, *Jewel Ornament of Liberation* (tr. by H. V. Guenther), London,
    Rider, 1959, paperback 1970; Berkeley, Calif., †Shambhala, 1971
58. SNELLGROVE, D. L., *The Image of the Buddha*, London, *Serindia/Paris,
    Unesco, 1978; New York, *Kodansha, 1978
59. SPIRO, M. E., *Buddhism and Society*, London, Allen & Unwin, 1971; New
    York, Harper & Row (copyr. 1970)
60. SPRUNG, M., *Lucid Exposition of the Middle Way: The Essential Chapters from the
    Prasannapadā of Candrakīrti*, London, *Routledge, 1979; Boulder, Colo, *Prajna,
    1980
61. STCHERBATSKY, T., *Buddhist Logic*, 1930 (Bibl. Buddhica, XXVI, pts I and II),
    repr. in 2 vols., †Dover, 1962; repr. of 1932 edn, The Hague, *Mouton, 1958
62. STRENG, F. J., *Emptiness: A Study in Religious Meaning*, New York, Abing-
    don, 1967

63. TAMBIAH, S. J., *World Conqueror and World Renouncer: A Study of Buddhism and Polity in Thailand against a Historical Background*, Cambridge, New York, Cambridge University Press, 1976

64. VAJIRAÑĀṆA, P., *Buddhist Meditation in Theory and Practice*, Colombo, Gunasena, 1962

65. WELBON, G.R., *Buddhist Nirvana and Its Western Interpreters*, Chicago, Ill., University of Chicago Press, 1968

(*See also:* X; XVI; XXIX)

[X] CHINESE RELIGIONS
Compiled by S. McFarlane

1. AHERN, E., *The Cult of the Dead in a Chinese Village*, Stanford, Calif., *Stanford University Press, 1973

2. BILSKY, L. J., *The State Religion of Ancient China*, 2 vols., Taipei, Chinese Association of Folklore/South Pasadena, Calif., *Langstaff, 1975

3. BODDE, D., *Festivals in Classical China*, *Princeton, N.J., Princeton University Press, 1975

4. BREDON, J., and MITROPHANOW, I., *The Moon Year: A Record of Chinese Customs and Festivals*, Shanghai, Kelly & Walsh, 1927; repr. Taipei, *Ch'eng Wen/San Francisco, Calif., Chinese Materials Center, 1972

5. BRUCE, J. P., *Chu Hsi and His Masters*, London, Probsthain, 1923; repr. New York, *AMS; New York, *Krishna

6. BRUCE, J. P. (tr.), CHU HSI, *The Philosophy of Human Nature*, London, Probsthain, 1922; repr. New York, *AMS

6a. BUSH, R. C., *Religion in Communist China*, New York, Abingdon, 1970

7. CHAN, W. T., *A Source Book in Chinese Philosophy*, Princeton, N.J., *Princeton University Press/London, Oxford University Press, 1963; †Princeton University Press, 1969

8. CHAN, W. T. (tr.), WANG YANG-MING, *Instructions for Practical Living and Other Neo-Confucian Writings*, New York, *Columbia University Press, 1963

9. CHAN, W. T. (tr.), HUI NÊNG, *The Platform Scripture*, New York, St John's University Press, 1963

10. CHANG, C., *The Development of Neo-Confucian Thought*, vol. 1, New York, Bookman Associates, 1957; London, Vision, 1958; New Haven, Conn., †College and University Press, 1957; Westport, Conn., *Greenwood, 1977

11. CHANG, C. Y. (tr.), TAO-YÜAN, S., *Original Teachings of Ch'an Buddhism*, New York, Pantheon, 1969

12. CHANG, G. C. C., *The Buddhist Teaching of Totality*, [University Park, Pa], Pennsylvania State University, 1971; London, *Allen & Unwin, 1972

13. CHANG, K. C., *The Archaeology of Ancient China*, 3rd rev. edn, New Haven, Conn., *†Yale University Press, 1977

14. CHANG, K. C., *Shang Civilization*, New Haven, Conn., *Yale University Press, 1980

15. CH'EN, K., *Buddhism in China*, Princeton, N.J., Princeton University Press, 1964, *1974, †1972

16. CH'EN, K., *The Chinese Transformation of Buddhism*, Princeton, N.J., Princeton University Press, 1973

17. CHING, J., *To Acquire Wisdom: The Way of Wang Yang Ming*, New York, *Columbia University Press, 1976

18. COOK, F. H., *Hua Yen Buddhism*, [University Park, Pa], *Pennsylvania State University Press, 1977

19. CREEL, H. G., *Chinese Thought from Confucius to Mao Tsê Tung*, Chicago, Ill., *†University of Chicago Press, 1953; London, Eyre & Spottiswoode, 1954; London, Methuen, 1962

20. CREEL, H. G., *Confucius, the Man and the Myth*, London, Routledge, 1951; New York, J. Day, 1949, repr. Westport, Conn., *Greenwood, 1973

21. CREEL, H. G., *What is Taoism?*, Chicago, Ill., *University of Chicago Press, 1970, †1977

22. DAY, C. B., *Chinese Peasant Cults*, Shanghai, Kelly & Walsh, 1940; 2nd edn, Taipei, Ch'eng Wen, 1969; San Francisco, Calif., *Chinese Materials Center, repr. 1974

23. DAY, C. B., *Popular Religion in Pre-Communist China*, San Francisco, Calif., *Chinese Materials Center, 1975

24. DE BARY, W. T., *et al.* (eds.), *Sources of Chinese Tradition*, New York, *†Columbia University Press, 1960

25. DORÉ. H., *Researches into Chinese Superstitions*, vols. 6–10, Shanghai, T'u Se Wei, 1920; repr. Taipei, Ch'eng Wen, 1966

26. DUBS, H. (tr.), HSÜN TZE, *Works*, London, Probsthain, 1928, repr. Taipei, Ch'eng Wen, 1966; San Francisco, Calif., *Chinese Materials Center, 1973

27. DUMOULIN, H., *A History of Zen Buddhism*, New York, Pantheon, 1963; Boston, Mass., †Beacon Press, 1969

28. EBERHARD, W., *A History of China*, 4th rev. edn, London, *†Routledge/Berkeley, *†University of California Press, 1977

29. EITEL, E. J., *Feng-Shui*, London, Trübner, 1873, repr. Bristol, †Pentacle Books, 1979

30. FEHL, N. E., *Li: Rites and Propriety in Literature and Life*, Chinese University of Hong Kong/New York, *International Publications Service, 1971

31. FUNG, Y. L., *A History of Chinese Philosophy*, vol. 1, Princeton, N.J., Princeton University Press, 1952; first publ. Peiping, Vetch, 1937

32. FUNG, Y. L., op. cit. (no. 31), vol. 2, Princeton, N.J., Princeton University Press/Leiden, Brill, 1953

33. GILES, L., *Descriptive Catalogue of the Chinese Manuscripts from Tun Huang in the British Museum*, London, *British Museum, 1957

34. GRAHAM, A. C. (tr.), *The Book of Lieh Tzu*, London, Murray, 1960

35. GRAHAM, A. C., *Later Mohist Logic, Ethics and Science*, Hong Kong, Chinese Universities Press/London, *School of Oriental and African Studies, 1978

36. GRANET, M., *The Religion of the Chinese People*, Oxford, Blackwell, 1975; New York, Harper & Row, 1975, †1977

37. GRANET, M., *Festivals and Songs of Ancient China*, New York, Dutton, 1932, repr. New York, Gordon Press, 1975; New York, *Krishna

38. GROOT, J. J. M. DE, *The Religious System of China*, vols. 1–3, *Disposal of the Dead*, Leiden, Brill, 1892, repr. Taipei, *Ch'eng Wen, 1976

39. GROOT, J. J. M. DE, op. cit., vols. 4–6, *On the Soul and Ancestral Worship*, Leiden, Brill, 1892, repr. Taipei, *Ch'eng Wen, 1976

40. GROOT, J. J. M. DE, *Sectarianism and Religious Persecution in China*, 2 vols., Amsterdam, Müller, 1903–4, repr. Shannon, *Irish University Press, 1973; New York, Barnes & Noble, 1974

41. HAMILTON, C. H. (tr.), VASUBANDHU, *Wei Shih Er Shih Lun; or, The Treatise ... on Representation-Only*, New Haven, Conn., American Oriental Society, 1938

42. HODOUS, L., *Folkways in China*, London, Probsthain, 1929, repr. Taipei, Ch'eng Wen, 1974

43. HSU, F. L. K., *Under the Ancestors' Shadow*, Stanford, Calif., *†Stanford University Press, 1967

44. HUGHES, E. R. (tr.), TA HSÜEH, *The Great Learning, and The Mean-in-Action*, London, Dent, 1942; New York, Dutton, 1943

45. HUGHES, E. R., *Chinese Philosophy in Classical Times*, London, Dent/New York, Dutton, 1942, and repr.; New York, *Gordon Press, 1977

46. JORDAN, D. K., *Gods, Ghosts and Ancestors: The Folk Religion of a Taiwanese Village*, Berkeley, Calif., University of California Press, 1972

47. KALTENMARK, M., *Lao Tzu and Taoism*, rev. edn, Stanford, Calif., *†Stanford University Press, 1969

48. KARLGREN, B., *The Book of Documents*, Stockholm, Museum of Far Eastern Antiquities, 1950

49. KARLGREN, B. (tr.), *The Book of Odes*, Stockholm, Museum of Far Eastern Antiquities, 1950, repr. London, *†Kegan Paul, 1950

50. LAMOTTE, E. (tr.), ASAŃGA, *La Somme du Grande Véhicule*, Louvain, Bureaux du Muséon, 1938

51. LA VALLÉE POUSSIN, L. DE (tr.), VASUBANDHU, *L'Abhidharmakośa*, 6 vols., Paris, Geuthner, 1923–31; new edn, Bruxelles, Institut Belge des Hautes Études Chinoises, 1971

52. LA VALLÉE POUSSIN, L. DE (tr.), HIUEN TSANG, *Vijñaptimātratā siddhi, La Siddhi de Hiuen Tsang*, Paris, Geuthner, 1928–9

53. LAU, D. C. (tr.), CONFUCIUS, *The Analects*, Harmondsworth, †Penguin Books, 1979

54. LAU, D. C. (tr.), *Mencius*, Harmondsworth, Penguin Books, 1970

55. LAU, D. C. (tr.), LAO TZU, *Tao Te Ching*, Harmondsworth, Baltimore, Md, †Penguin Books, 1963

56. LEGGE, J., *The Chinese Classics*, London, Trübner, 1861–72: 2nd edn, Oxford, Clarendon Press, 1893–5, repr. 1935; *Krishna, New York, vol. 1,

The Confucian Analects, The Great Learning, and The Doctrine of the Mean

57. LEGGE, J., op. cit. (no. 56), vol. 2, *The Works of Mencius*

58. LEGGE, J., op. cit. (no. 56), vol. 3, *The Shoo Ching*

59. LEGGE, J., op. cit. (no. 56), vol. 4, *The She Ching*

60. LEGGE, J., op. cit. (no. 56), vol. 5, *The Ch'un Ts'ew with the Tso Chuan*

61. LEGGE, J. (tr.), *Li Ki*, Oxford, Clarendon Press, 1885 (*Sacred Books of the East*, ed. F. M. Müller, vols. 27, 28, *The Sacred Books of China*), repr. Delhi, Motilal Banarsidass, 1966; Mystic, Conn., *Verry

62. LIEBENTHAL, W. (tr.), *Chao Lun: the Treatises of Seng Chao*, 2nd rev. edn, Hong Kong, Hong Kong University Press, 1968

63. MASPERO, H., *China in Antiquity*, Folkestone, *W. Dawson, 1978; Amherst, Mass., *†University of Massachusetts Press, 1979

64. MASPERO, H., *Mélanges posthumes sur les religions et l'histoire de la Chine*, vol. 2, *Le Taoisme*, Paris, Publications du Musée Guimet, 1950; Paris, Presses Universitaires de France, 1967

65. MEI, Y. P., *MOTSE: The Ethical and Political Works*, London, Probsthain, 1929, repr. Westport, Conn., *Hyperion Press, 1973; Taipei, Ch'eng Wen, 1974

66. MEI, Y. P., *Motse the Neglected Rival of Confucius*, London, Probsthain, 1934, repr. Westport, Conn., Hyperion Press, 1973

67. MÜLLER, F. M. (ed.), *Buddhist Mahāyāna Texts*, Oxford, Clarendon Press, 1894 (*Sacred Books of the East*, vol. 49), repr. Delhi, Motilal Banarsidass, 1965; Mystic, Conn., *Verry

68. NEEDHAM, J., *Science and Civilisation in China*, Cambridge, *Cambridge University Press, vol. 2, 1956, repr. 1962

69. NEEDHAM, J., op. cit. (no. 68), vol. 5, pt 3, 1976

70. OVERMYER, D., *Folk Buddhist Religion*, Cambridge, Mass., *Harvard University Press, 1976

71. RAWSON, J., *Ancient China*, London, Book Club Associates, 1980; London, *†British Museum/New York, *Harper & Row, 1980

72. REICHELT, K. L., *Truth and Tradition in Chinese Buddhism*, Shanghai, Commercial Press, 1927; New York, *Paragon, 1969, repr. of 1934 edn

73. RICHARDS, I. A., *Mencius on the Mind*, London, Kegan Paul, Trench, Trubner/New York, Harcourt, Brace, 1932, repr. London, *Routledge, 1964; Westport, Conn., *Hyperion Press, 1980

74. ROBINSON, R. H., *Early Mādhyamika in India and China*, Madison, University of Wisconsin Press, 1967; repr. Livingston, N.J., *Orient Book Distributors, 1976; Mystic, Conn., *Verry, 1977

75. SASO, M., *Taoism and the Rite of Cosmic Renewal*, Pullman, Wash., †Washington State University Press, 1972

76. SASO, M., *The Teachings of Taoist Master Chuang*, New Haven, Conn., *Yale University Press, 1978

77. SASO, M., and CHAPPELL, D. W. (eds.), *Buddhist and Taoist Studies*, vol. 1, Honolulu, †University Press of Hawaii, 1977

78. SEKIDA, K., *Two Zen Classics: Mumonkan and Hekiganroku*, New York, *†Weatherhill, 1977

79. SHRYOCK, J. K., *The Origin and Development of the State Cult of Confucius*,

New York, London, American Hist. Association., Century Co., 1932, repr. New York, Paragon, 1966

80. SIVIN, N., *Chinese Alchemy: Preliminary Studies*, Cambridge, Mass., *Harvard University Press, 1968

81. SMITH, D. H., *Chinese Religions*, London, Weidenfeld/New York, Holt, Rinehart, 1968

82. SMITH, D. H., *Confucius*, St Albans, †Paladin, 1974; New York, *Scribner/London, Temple Smith, 1973

83. STEELE, J. (tr.), *The I Li; or, Book of Etiquette and Ceremonial*, London, Probsthain, 1917

84. SUZUKI, D. T., *Essays in Zen Buddhism*, ser. 1, London, Rider, 1949, †1970; New York, †Grove Press, 1961; Taipei, *Ch'eng Wen/San Francisco, Calif., Chinese Materials Center, 1971; prev. publ. London, Luzac, 1927

85. THOMPSON, L. G., *The Chinese Way in Religion*, Encino, Calif., †Dickenson, 1973

86. THOMPSON, L. G., *Chinese Religion: an Introduction*, 2nd edn, Encino, Calif., †Dickenson, 1975

87. TUNG, T. P., *Fifty Years of Studies in Oracle Bone Inscriptions*, Tokyo, Centre for East Asian Cultural Studies, 1964

88. VINCENT, I. V., *The Sacred Oasis: Caves of the Thousand Buddhas, Tun Huang*, Chicago, Calif., University of Chicago Press/London, Faber, 1953

89. WALEY, A. (tr.), *The Book of Songs*, London, *Allen & Unwin, 1937; New York, †Grove Press, 1960

90. WALEY, A. (tr.), LAO-TZU, *The Way and Its Power*, London, Allen & Unwin, 1934, †1977; New York, †Grove Press, 1958

91. WALEY, A. (tr.), CONFUCIUS, *The Analects*, London, *Allen & Unwin, 1938; New York, †Random House, 1966

92. WALEY, A., *Three Ways of Thought in Ancient China*, London, *Allen & Unwin/New York, Barnes, 1939; Garden City, N.Y., *Doubleday, 1956

93. WALEY, A. (ed. and tr.), CH'Ü YÜAN, *The Nine Songs: A Study of Shamanism in Ancient China*, London, Allen & Unwin, 1955

94. WALEY, A. (ed.), *Ballads and Stories from Tun-Huang*, London, *Allen & Unwin, New York, Macmillan, 1960

95. WARE, J. R. (tr.), KO HUNG, *Alchemy, Medicine and Religion in the China of A.D. 320*, Cambridge, Mass., MIT Press, 1966

96. WATSON, B. (tr.), CHUANG TZU, *The Complete Works*, New York, London, *Columbia University Press, 1968

97. WATSON, B. (tr.), HSÜN TZU, *Basic Writings*, New York, †Columbia University Press, 1963

98. WATSON, B. (tr.), MO TZU, *Basic Writings*, New York, †Columbia University Press, 1963

99. WATSON, W., *Early Civilizations in China*, London, Thames & Hudson/New York, McGraw-Hill, 1966

100. WELCH, H., *Taoism: The Parting of the Way*, Boston, Mass., Beacon Press, 1957, †1966; London, Methuen, 1958

101. WELCH, H., and SEIDEL, A. (eds.), *Facets of Taoism: Essays in Chinese Religion*, New Haven, Conn., *Yale University Press, 1979
102. WERNER, E. T. C., *A Dictionary of Chinese Mythology*, Shanghai, Kelly & Walsh, 1932; repr. Boston, Mass., *Longwood Press, 1977
103. WILHELM, R. (tr.), *The I Ching; or Book of Changes. The Richard Wilhelm Translation Rendered into English by C. F. Baynes*, London, Routledge, 1951; New York, Pantheon, 1950
104. WRIGHT, A. F., *Buddhism in Chinese History*, London, Oxford University Press/Stanford, Calif., *†Stanford University Press, 1959
105. YANG, C. K., *Religion in Chinese Society*, Berkeley, Calif., †University of California Press, 1961
106. ZÜRCHER, E., *The Buddhist Conquest of China*, 2 vols., Leiden, Brill, 1959

(*See also:* XI (B), 70; XIV, 40)

[XI] CHRISTIANITY: (A) BIBLE AND EARLY CHURCH
Compiled by F. F. Bruce

1. BRUCE, F. F., *The Books and the Parchments*, 3rd edn, London, Glasgow, Pickering & Inglis, 1963, †1972; Westwood, N.J., *Revell, 1963
2. BRUCE, F. F., *Israel and the Nations*, 2nd edn, Exeter, Paternoster, 1969, †1973
3. BRUCE, F. F., *New Testament History*, rev. edn, London, Oliphants, 1971, †1978; [1st Amer. edn] Garden City, N.Y., Doubleday, 1971, †1978
4. BRUCE, F. F., *Paul: Apostle of the Free Spirit*, Exeter, *Paternoster, 1977; publ. in U.S.A. as *Paul: Apostle of the Heart Set Free*, Grand Rapids, Mich., *Eerdmans, 1977
5. CAIRD, G. B., *The Apostolic Age*, London, *Duckworth, 1955
6. *Cambridge History of the Bible*: vol. 1, P. R. Ackroyd and C. F. Evans (eds.), *From the Beginnings to Jerome*; vol. 2, G. W. H. Lampe (ed.), *The West from the Fathers to the Reformation*; vol. 3, S. L. Greenslade (ed.), *The West from the Reformation to the Present Day*, Cambridge, *Cambridge University Press, 1963–70, †1975–6
7. DODD, C. H., *The Founder of Christianity*, New York, †Macmillan, 1970; London, *Collins, 1971, †1973
8. DUNN, J. D. G., *Christology in the Making*, London, SCM/Philadelphia, Pa, Westminster, 1980
9. HANSON, R. P. C., *Christian Priesthood Examined*, Guildford, *Lutterworth, 1979
10. HILL, D., *New Testament Prophecy*, London, *Marshall, Morgan & Scott, 1979; Richmond, Atlanta, Ga, *John Knox, 1980
11. MANSON, T. W., *The Church's Ministry*, London, Hodder/Philadelphia, Pa, Westminster, 1948
12. MOULE, C. F. D., *The Holy Spirit*, London, *†Mowbray, 1978; Grand Rapids, Mich., †Eerdmans, 1979

13. MOULE, C. F. D., *Worship in the New Testament*, London, Lutterworth/Richmond, Atlanta, Ga, John Knox, 1961; in 2 pts, New York, †Grove Books, 1977–8

14. ROBERTS, C. H., *Manuscript, Society and Belief in Early Christian Egypt*, London, New York, ★Oxford University Press, 1979

15. ROBINSON, J. M. (ed.), *The NAG HAMMADI Library in English*, Leiden, Brill, 1977; San Francisco, Calif., Harper & Row, 1978

16. SCHÜRER, E., *The History of the Jewish People in the Age of Jesus Christ* (a new English version rev. and ed. by G. Vermes and F. Millar), I–(III), Edinburgh, ★Clark, 1973–

17. STENDAHL, K., *The Bible and the Role of Women*, Philadelphia, Pa, †Fortress, 1966

18. VERMES, G. (ed. and tr.), *The Dead Sea Scrolls in English*, Harmondsworth, Baltimore, Md, Penguin Books, 1962, †new edn, 1970; New York, Heritage, 1967

19. VERMES, G., *Jesus the Jew*, London, Collins, 1973, †1976; New York, ★Macmillan, 1974

20. WILSON, R. MCL., *Gnosis and the New Testament*, Oxford, ★Blackwell/Philadelphia, Pa, Fortress, 1968

[XI] CHRISTIANITY: (B) HISTORY AND DOCTRINE
Compiled by H. Rack

1. ABBOTT, W. M. (ed.), *The Documents of Vatican II in a new and definitive translation*, London, Dublin, G. Chapman, 1966; New York, Herder, 1966; New York, Association Press, 1966, †1974

2. AHLSTROM, S. E., *A Religious History of the American People*, New Haven, Conn., London, ★Yale University Press, 1972, †1974; Garden City, N.Y., †Doubleday, 2 vols., 1975

3. ASHE, G., *The Virgin*, London, ★Routledge, 1976

4. ATTWATER, D., *The Penguin Dictionary of Saints*, Harmondsworth, Baltimore, Md, †Penguin Books, 1965, repr. 1979

5. AUBERT, R. (ed.), *The Church in a Secularised Society* (*The Christian Centuries*, vol. 5), London, Darton/New York, ★Paulist Press, 1978

6. AYLING, S., *John Wesley*, London, ★Collins, 1979, repr. 1981

7. BACON, M. H., *The Quiet Rebels: The Story of the Quakers in America*, New York, ★Basic Books, 1969

8. BAINTON, R. H., *Here I Stand: A Life of Martin Luther*, London, Hodder, 1951; Nashville, Tenn., Abingdon, 1950; New York, †Mentor, 1955

9. BEESON, T., *Discretion and Valour: Religious Conditions in Russia and Eastern Europe*, London, ★Collins, 1974, †Fontana, 1974, †Fount, 1976

10. BERGENDOFF, C., *The Church of the Lutheran Reformation: A Historical Survey of Lutheranism*, St Louis, Mo, Concordia, 1967

11. BETTENSON, H. (ed.), *Documents of the Christian Church*, 2nd edn, London, ★†Oxford University Press, 1963, repr. 1977, etc.

12. BOCIURKIW, B. R., and STRONG, J. W. (eds.), *Religion and Atheism in the U.S.S.R. and Eastern Europe*, London, New York, Macmillan, 1975; University of Toronto Press, 1975

13. BRADEN, C. S., *These Also Believe: A Study of Modern American Cults and Minority Religious Movements*, New York, Macmillan, 1949, repr. 1957

14. BRODIE, F. M., *No Man Knows My History: The Life of Joseph Smith, the Mormon Prophet*, 2nd edn, New York, ★Knopf, 1971

15. BUCKE, E. S. (ed.), *The History of American Methodism*, 3 vols., Nashville, Tenn., Abingdon, 1964

16. BULLOUGH, S., *Roman Catholicism*, Harmondsworth, Baltimore, Md, Penguin Books, 1963

17. BURLEIGH, J. H. S., *A Church History of Scotland*, ★Oxford University Press, 1960, repr. 1963

18. CAMP, R. L., *The Papal Ideology of Social Reform, 1878–1967*, Leiden, Brill, 1969

19. CHADWICK, W. O., *From Bossuet to Newman*, Cambridge, Cambridge University Press, 1957

20. CHADWICK, W. O. (ed.), *Pelican History of the Church*, 6 vols., Harmondsworth, Baltimore, Md, †Penguin Books, 1960–71 and repr.; London, Hodder, 1962–72: vol. 1, CHADWICK, H., *The Early Church*; vol. 2, SOUTHERN, R. W., *The Western Church in the Middle Ages*; vol. 3, CHADWICK, W. O., *The Reformation*; vol. 4, CRAGG, G. R., *The Church and the Age of Reason*; vol. 5, VIDLER, A. R., *The Church in an Age of Revolution*; vol. 6, NEILL, S., *A History of Christian Missions*

20a. CLARK, W. H., *The Oxford Group: Its History and Significance*, New York, Brookman Associates, 1951

21. COAD, F. R., *A History of the Brethren Movement*, Exeter, Paternoster/Grand Rapids, Mich., Eerdmans, 1968; 2nd edn, Paternoster, 1976; Stony Point, S.C., †Attic, 1976

22. COGNET, L., *Le Jansénisme*, 3rd edn, Paris, Presses Universitaires de France, 1968

23. COLEMAN, P., *Christian Attitudes to Homosexuality*, London, SPCK, 1980

24. COLLIER, R., *The General Next to God: The Story of William Booth*, New York, Dutton, 1965; London, Collins, 1965, †Fontana, 1968, 1976

25. CONE, J. H., *Black Theology and Black Power*, New York, †Seabury, 1969

26. CROWDER, C. M. D., *Unity, Heresy and Reform, 1378–1460: The Conciliar Response to the Great Schism*, London, ★†Arnold/New York, ★St Martin's, 1977

27. CUNLIFFE-JONES, H., and DREWERY, B. (eds.), *A History of Christian Doctrine*, Edinburgh, Clark, 1978; Philadelphia, Pa, ★Fortress, 1980

28. DAVIES, H., *Worship and Theology in England*, 5 vols., Princeton, N.J., Princeton University Press/London, New York, Oxford University Press, 1961–75

29. DAVIES, J. G. (ed.), *A Dictionary of Liturgy and Worship*, London, ★SCM, 1972, repr. 1978; New York, Macmillan, 1972; as *Westminster Dictionary of Worship*, Philadelphia, ★Westminster, repr. 1979

30. DAVIES, J. G., *The Secular Use of Church Buildings*, London, *SCM/New York, Seabury, 1968

31. DAVIES, R. E., *Methodism*, Harmondsworth, Penguin Books, 1963; new edn, London, †Epworth, 1976

32. DAVIES, R. E., *Religious Authority in an Age of Doubt*, London, *Epworth, 1968; Geneva, Ala., *Allenson, 1968

33. DELACROIX, S. (ed.), *Histoire universelle des missions catholiques*, 4 vols., Paris, Grund, 1956–9

34. DELUMEAU, J., *Catholicism between Luther and Voltaire*, London, *Burns & Oates/Philadelphia, Pa, *Westminster, 1977

35. DIETER, M. E., *The Holiness Revival of the Nineteenth Century*, Metuchen, N.J., London, Scarecrow Press, 1980

36. DILLENBERGER, J., and WELCH, C., *Protestant Christianity Interpreted through Its Development*, New York, †Scribner, 1954

37. DILLISTONE, F. W., *The Christian Understanding of Atonement*, London, Nisbet/Philadelphia, Pa, *Westminster, 1968

38. DOWLEY, T. (ed.), *The History of Christianity*, Berkhamsted, *Lion Publishing, 1977; as *Eerdmans Handbook to the History of Christianity*, Grand Rapids, Mich., Eerdmans, 1977

39. DRUMMOND, R. H., *A History of Christianity in Japan*, Grand Rapids, Mich., Eerdmans, 1971

40. EBELING, G., *Luther: An Introduction to His Thought*, London, Collins, 1970, repr. 1972; Philadelphia, Pa, Fortress, 1970

41. EHLER, S. Z., and MORRALL, J. R. (eds.), *Church and State through the Centuries: A Collection of Historic Documents with Commentaries*, London, Burns & Oates, 1954; New York, Biblo & Tannen, 1967

42. FERGUSON, G., *Signs and Symbols in Christian Art*, London, New York, Galaxy, †Oxford University Press, 1966, repr. 1979

43. FERGUSON, J., *War and Peace in the World's Religions*, London, †Sheldon, 1977, repr. 1980; *†(U.S.) Oxford University Press, 1978

44. FINDLAY, J. F., *Dwight L. Moody, American Evangelist, 1837–99*, Chicago, Ill., *University of Chicago Press, 1969

45. FLETCHER, J. F., *Situation Ethics: The New Morality*, Philadelphia, Pa, *†Westminster, 1966; London, SCM, 1966, repr. 1974

46. FLEW, R. N., *The Idea of Perfection in Christian Theology*, London, Oxford University Press, 1934, repr. 1968; Atlantic Highlands, N.J., *Humanities, repr. 1968

47. FORTMAN, E. J., *The Triune God: A Historical Study of the Doctrine of the Trinity*, London, Hutchinson, 1971; Philadelphia, Pa, *Westminster, 1972

48. FRADY, M., *Billy Graham: A Parable of American Righteousness*, London, *Hodder/Boston, Mass., *Little, Brown, 1979

49. FRANKL, P., *Gothic Architecture*, Harmondsworth, Baltimore, Md, Penguin Books, 1962 *(Pelican History of Art)*

50. FRANKS, R. S., *The Work of Christ: A Historical Study of Christian Doctrine*, London, 1934, repr. London, New York, Nelson, 1962

51. FROOM, LE ROY E., *The Prophetic Faith of Our Fathers*, 4 vols., Washington DC, Review and Herald, 1946–54

52. GOTTSCHALK, S., *The Emergence of Christian Science in American Religious Life*, Berkeley, Calif., ★University of California Press, 1973, †1979

53. GRAEF, H. C., *Mary: A History of Doctrine and Devotion*, 2 vols., New York, London, ★Sheed & Ward, 1963–5

54. GRANT, R. M., *A Short History of the Interpretation of the Bible*, rev. edn, London, Black, 1965; as *The Bible in the Church*, New York, Macmillan, 1948

55. GREENSLADE, S. L., *Church and State from Constantine to Theodosius*, London, SCM, 1954

56. GREENSLADE, S. L., *Schism in the Early Church*, London, SCM/New York, Harper & Row, 1953

57. HAMMOND, P., *Liturgy and Architecture*, London, Barrie & Rockliff, 1960; New York, Columbia University Press, 1961

58. HANDY, R. T., *A History of the Churches in the United States and Canada*, Oxford, New York, ★Clarendon Press, 1976, †1979

59. HASTINGS, A., *A History of African Christianity 1950–1975*, Cambridge, New York, ★†Cambridge University Press, 1979

60. HICK, J., *Evil and the God of Love*, new edn, London, †Fontana, Collins, 1968, repr. 1970; 2nd edn, London, ★Macmillan, 1977; New York, †Harper & Row, 1977

61. HOLLENWEGER, W. J., *The Pentecostals*, London, SCM, 1972, †1976; Minneapolis, Minn., Augsburg Publishing, 1972, †1977

62. HOPKINS, C. H., *The Rise of the Social Gospel in American Protestantism, 1865–1915*, New Haven, Conn., Yale University Press, 1940, repr. 1967

63. HUBBARD, G., *Quaker by Convincement*, Harmondsworth, †Penguin Books, 1974, repr. 1976

64. JANELLE, P., *The Catholic Reformation*, Milwaukee, Wis., Bruce Publishing, 1949, repr. 1975; London, †Collier-Macmillan, 1971

65. JARRETT-KERR, M., *Patterns of Christian Acceptance: Individual Response to the Missionary Impact, 1550–1950*, London, New York, ★Oxford University Press, 1972

66. JAY, E. G., *The Church: Its Changing Image through Twenty Centuries*, 2 vols., †SPCK, London, 1977–8; Atlanta, Ga, ★†John Knox, 1980

67. JEDIN, H., *Ecumenical Councils of the Catholic Church: An Historical Outline*, New York, Freiburg, Edinburgh, Herder, 1960

68. JEDIN, H., and DOLAN, J. P. (eds.), *A History of the Church*, London, ★Burns & Oates, vols. 1–10, 1980– (in progress); prev. publ. as *A Handbook of Church History*, Freiburg, Herder, 1965–

69. JOHNSON, P., *A History of Christianity*, London ★Weidenfeld/New York, ★†Atheneum, 1976

70. JONES, F. P., *The Church in Communist China: A Protestant Appraisal*, New York, Friendship Press, 1962

71. JONES, P. D'A., *The Christian Socialist Revival, 1877–1914*, Princeton, N.J., ★Princeton University Press, 1968

72. JONES, R. T., *Congregationalism in England, 1662–1962*, London, Independent Press, 1962

73. JULIAN, J., *A Dictionary of Hymnology*, New York, Dover, 1957; New York, *Gordon Press, 1977; prev. publ. London, Murray, 1892

74. KAMEN, H., *The Rise of Toleration*, London, Weidenfeld/New York, McGraw-Hill, 1967

75. KAMEN, H., *The Spanish Inquisition*, London, Weidenfeld, 1965; New York, New American Library, 1966, †1977

76. KELLY, J. N. D., *Early Christian Doctrines*, 5th rev. edn, London, *Black, 1977; New York, †Harper & Row, 1978

77. KNOWLES, D., *Christian Monasticism*, London, Weidenfeld/New York, *†McGraw-Hill, 1969

78. KOENKER, E. B., *The Liturgical Renaissance in the Roman Catholic Church*, Chicago, Ill., University of Chicago Press/Cambridge, Cambridge University Press, 1954; 2nd edn, St Louis, Mo, Concordia, 1966

79. KÜNG, H., *Infallible? An Inquiry* (tr. by Eric Mosbacher), London, Collins, 1971, †1972; (tr. by E. Quinn), Garden City, N.Y., Doubleday, 1971

80. LAMPE, G. W. H., *God as Spirit*, Oxford, *Clarendon Press, 1977

81. LASH, N., and RHYMER, J., *The Christian Priesthood*, London, Darton, 1970

82. LATOURETTE, K. S., *Christianity in a Revolutionary Age*, 5 vols., Westport, Conn., Greenwood, repr. 1973 (copyr. 1958–62); London, †Paternoster, 1971

83. LATOURETTE, K. S., *A History of the Expansion of Christianity*, 7 vols., London, Eyre & Spottiswoode/ New York, Harper, 1939–47; London, †Paternoster, 1971; Grand Rapids, Mich., *Zondervan

84. LEEMING, B., *Principles of Sacramental Theology*, new edn, London, Longman, 1960, repr. 1962; Westminster, Md, Newman, 1960

85. LEWIS, A. J., *Zinzendorf, the Ecumenical Pioneer*, London, SCM/Philadelphia, Pa, Westminster, 1962

86. LOOME, T. M., *Liberal Catholicism, Reform Catholicism, Modernism*, Mainz, Mathias-Grünevald, 1979

87. MCAVOY, T. T., *A History of the Catholic Church in the United States*, Notre Dame, Ind., and London, University of Notre Dame Press, 1969

88. MACDONALD, H. D., *Ideas of Revelation . . . A.D., 1700–1860*, London, Macmillan/New York, St Martin's, 1959

89. MACKEY, J. P., *The Modern Theology of Tradition*, London, Darton/New York, Herder, 1963

90. MCLOUGHLIN, W. G., *Modern Revivalism: Charles Grandison Finney to Billy Graham*, New York, Ronald Press, 1959

91. MCNEILL, J. T., *The Celtic Churches: A History, A.D. 200 to 1200*, Chicago, Ill., *University of Chicago Press, 1974

92. MCNEILL, J. T., *The History and Character of Calvinism*, New York, Oxford University Press, 1954, †1967

93. MACQUARRIE, J. (ed.), *A Dictionary of Christian Ethics*, London, *SCM/Philadelphia, Pa, *Westminster, 1967

94. MECHAM, J. L., *Church and State in Latin America*, rev. edn, Chapel Hill, N.C., †University of North Carolina Press, 1966

95. MIEGGE, G., *The Virgin Mary*, London, Lutterworth/Philadelphia, Pa, Westminster, 1955

96. MILLER, P., *Jonathan Edwards*, New York, Meridian, 1959; Westport, Conn., *Greenwood; first publ. New York, Sloane, 1949

97. MILLER, P., and JOHNSON, T. H. (eds.), *The Puritans: A Source Book of Their Writings*, rev. edn, 2 vols., New York, †Harper & Row, 1963; Magnolia, Mass., *Peter Smith

98. MOLLAND, E., *Christendom*, London, Mowbray, 1959, 2nd imp. 1961; New York, Philosophical Library, 1959

99. MOORE, A. C., *The Iconography of Religions*, London, *SCM/Philadelphia, Pa, *Fortress, 1977

100. MOORHOUSE, G., *The Missionaries*, London, Eyre Methuen/Philadelphia, Pa, Lippincott, 1973

101. MOORMAN, J. R. H., *A History of the Church in England*, 3rd edn, London, *Black, 1973, repr. 1980; New York, *Morehouse, 1973

102. MOSS, C. B., *The Old Catholic Movement*, London, SPCK, 1948

103. NEILL, S., *Anglicanism*, Harmondsworth, Penguin Books, 1958, repr. 1960; 2nd edn, London, †Mowbray, 1978; 4th edn, New York, †Oxford University Press, 1978

104. NEILL, S., *The Story of the Christian Church in India and Pakistan*, Grand Rapids, Mich., Eerdmans, 1970

105. *New Catholic Encyclopedia*, 15 vols., *McGraw-Hill, 1967; *17 vols., Washington DC, *Catholic University of America

106. O'DEA, T., *The Mormons*, Chicago, Ill., *University of Chicago Press, 1957, †1964

107. *The Oxford Dictionary of the Christian Church*, 2nd edn (ed. by F. L. Cross and E. A. Livingstone), London, New York, *Oxford University Press, 1974

108. PEVSNER, SIR NIKOLAUS, *An Outline of European Architecture*, 7th edn, Harmondsworth, Baltimore, Md, †Penguin Books, 1963, repr. 1975

109. POWERS, J. M., *Eucharistic Theology*, London, Burns & Oates, 1968; New York, Herder, 1967; New York, †Seabury, 1972

110. REARDON, B. M. G. (ed.), *Roman Catholic Modernism*, London, Black/Stanford, Calif., *Stanford University Press, 1970

111. RICE, C. D., *The Rise and Fall of Black Slavery*, London, Macmillan/New York, *Harper & Row, 1975

112. RILEY-SMITH, J., *What were the Crusades?*, London, †Macmillan, 1977/Totowa, N.J., *Rowman & Littlefield, 1977

113. ROBERTSON, A., and STEVENS, D., *The Pelican History of Music*, 3 vols., Harmondsworth, Baltimore, Md, †Penguin Books, 1960–68, repr. 1978

114. ROGERSON, A., *Millions Now Living Will Never Die: A Study of the Jehovah's Witnesses*, London, Constable, 1969

115. ROUSE, R., NEILL, S., and FREY, H. (eds.), *A History of the Ecumenical Movement*, 2 vols. (vol. 1, 2nd edn), London, SPCK/Philadelphia, Pa, *Westminster, 1967–70

116. ROWELL, G., *Hell and the Victorians*, Oxford, *Clarendon Press, 1974

117. RUNCIMAN, SIR STEVEN, *A History of the Crusades*, 3 vols., Cambridge,

*Cambridge University Press, 1951–4, repr. 1966–8; Harmondsworth, †Penguin Books, 1965

118. RUTMAN, D. B., *American Puritanism: Faith and Practice*, Philadelphia, Pa, Lippincott, 1970; New York, †Norton, 1977

119. SANCHEZ, J. M., *Anticlericalism: A Brief History*, Notre Dame, Ind., *University of Notre Dame, 1972

120. SANDEEN, E. R., *The Roots of Fundamentalism*, Chicago, Ill., Chicago University Press, 1970; Grand Rapids, Mich., †Baker Books, 1978

121. SIEFER, G., *The Church and Industrial Society*, London, Darton, 1964

122. SIMPSON, A., *Puritanism in Old and New England*, Chicago, Ill., †University of Chicago Press, 1955

123. SMITH, TIMOTHY L., *Revivalism and Social Reform in Mid-Nineteenth Century America*, Nashville, Abingdon, 1957; Magnolia, Mass., *Peter Smith; Baltimore, Md, †Johns Hopkins University Press, 1980

124. STOEFFLER, F. E., *The Rise of Evangelical Pietism*, Leiden, Brill, 1965; and, *German Pietism during the Eighteenth Century*, Leiden, Brill, 1973

125. STROUP, H. H., *The Jehovah's Witnesses*, New York, Columbia University Press, 1945, repr. New York, Russell & Russell, 1967

126. SUMPTION, J., *Pilgrimage: An Image of Mediaeval Religion*, London, *Faber/Totowa, N.J., *Rowman, 1975

127. SYKES, S. W., and CLAYTON, J. P., *Christ, Faith and History*, Cambridge, *†Cambridge University Press, 1972

128. THOMAS, K., *Religion and the Decline of Magic*, Harmondsworth, †Penguin Books, 1973; New York, †Scribner, 1971; London, *Weidenfeld, 1971

129. TODD, J. M. (ed.), *Problems of Authority*, London, *Darton, 1962, †1964; Baltimore, Md, Helicon, repr. 1964

130. TORBET, R. G., *A History of the Baptists*, Philadelphia, Pa, Judson, 1950, repr. Valley Forge, Pa, Judson, 1963, rev. edn *1973

131. ULLMANN, W., *A Short History of the Papacy in the Middle Ages*, London, Methuen, 1972, †1974

132. VIDLER, A. R., *A Century of Social Catholicism, 1820–1920*, London, SPCK, 1964

133. VON ARETIN, K. O., *The Papacy and the Modern World*, London, Weidenfeld/New York, McGraw-Hill, 1970

134. WAKEFIELD, W. L., and EVANS, A. P. (eds.), *Heresies of the High Middle Ages: Selected Sources*, New York, Columbia University Press, 1969

135. WARE, T., *The Orthodox Church*, Harmondsworth, Baltimore, Md, †Penguin Books, 1963, 1969, 1980

136. WASHINGTON, J. R., *Black Religion: The Negro and Christianity in the United States*, Boston, Mass., Beacon Press, 1964

137. WATSON, B., *A Hundred Years' War: The Salvation Army, 1865–1965*, London, Hodder, 1965

138. WATTS, M., *The Dissenters*, vol. 1, *From the Reformation to the French Revolution*, Oxford, *Clarendon Press, 1978

139. WEBER, H. R., and NEILL, S., *The Layman in Christian History*, London, SCM/Philadelphia, Pa, *Westminster, 1963

140. WENDEL, F., *Calvin*, Collins, 1963, †Fontana, 1978; New York, Harper & Row, 1963

141. WILBUR, E. M., *A History of Unitarianism*, 2 vols., Cambridge, Mass., Harvard University Press, 1946–52

142. WILLIAMS, G. H., *The Radical Reformation*, Philadelphia, Pa, ★Westminster/ London, Weidenfeld, 1962

143. WILSON, B. R., *Religious Sects*, London, Weidenfeld/New York, McGraw-Hill, 1970

144. WILSON, B. R., *Sects and Society*, London, Heinemann/Berkeley, Calif., University of California Press, 1961; Westport, Conn., London, ★Greenwood, 1978

144a.WILSON, I., *The Turin Shroud*, London, Gollancz, 1978; Harmondsworth, Penguin Books, 1979; (Amer. edn), *The Shroud of Turin*, Garden City, N.Y., Doubleday, 1978

145. WITTKOWER, R., *Architectural Principles in the Age of Humanism*, London, ★Academy edn, repr. 1973; ★Tiranti, 1962; New York, †Norton, 1975 (copyr. 1971)

146. ZAEHNER, R. C. (ed.), *A Concise Encyclopedia of Living Faiths*, London, †Hutchinson, 1977, first publ. 1959; Boston, Mass., †Beacon Press

(*See also:* II, 35; XVI, 8, 20, 26; XXII, 1)

[XI] CHRISTIANITY: (C) PHILOSOPHY, THEOLOGY
Compiled by D. A. Pailin

1. ALTIZER, T. J. and HAMILTON, W., *Radical Theology and the Death of God*, Harmondsworth, Penguin Books, 1968; first publ. Indianapolis, Ind., Bobbs-Merrill, 1966

2. BULTMANN, R., *Jesus Christ and Mythology*, New York, Scribner, 1958; London, SCM, 1960

3. COBB, J. B., *Living Options in Protestant Theology: A Survey of Methods*, Philadelphia, Pa, Westminster, 1962

4. COBB, J. B., and GRIFFIN, D. R., *Process Theology: An Introductory Exposition*, Belfast, †Christian Journals, 1977; first publ. Philadelphia, Pa, †Westminster, 1976

5. COPLESTON, F. C., *Aquinas*, Harmondsworth, Penguin Books, 1955, Baltimore, Md, †1956; rev. edn, *Thomas Aquinas*, London, Search Press, 1976

6. HARNACK, A., *History of Dogma*, 7 vols. in 4, New York, Dover, 1961, Magnolia, Mass., ★Peter Smith. This tr. first publ. in English 1894–9, original German edn *Lehrbuch der Dogmengeschichte*, 1886–90

7. HARVEY, V. A., *The Historian and the Believer*, New York, Macmillan, 1966; London, SCM, 1967

8. HICK, J., *The Existence of God*, New York, Macmillan/London, †Collier-Macmillan, 1964

9. KEE, A. (ed.), *A Reader in Political Theology*, London, *SCM, 1974; Philadelphia, Pa, †Westminster, 1975

10. KELLY, J. N. D., *Early Christian Doctrines*, London, Black, 1958, 5th edn, *1977; rev. edn, New York, †Harper & Row, 1978

11. KÜNG, H., *Does God Exist? An Answer for Today*, London, *Collins/Garden City, N.Y., *Doubleday, 1980; tr. of *Existiert Gott?*, München, Piper, 1978

12. LEFF, G., *Mediaeval Thought: Saint Augustine to Ockham*, Harmondsworth, 1958, †1970, Baltimore, Md, 1958, Penguin Books; London, *Merlin Press, 1959; Atlantic Highlands, N.J., *Humanities, 1958

13. MACINTYRE, A., 'The Logical Status of Religious Belief', in: S. E. Toulmin, R. W. Hepburn and A. MacIntyre, *Metaphysical Beliefs*, pp. 167–211, London, SCM, 1957

14. MACKINTOSH, H. R., *Types of Modern Theology: Schleiermacher to Barth*, London, Nisbet/New York, Scribner, 1937

15. MACQUARRIE, J., *Principles of Christian Theology*, London, SCM, 1966; rev. edn, *1979; New York, Scribner, 1966, 2nd edn, †1977

16. MIGUEZ BONINO, J., *Revolutionary Theology Comes of Age*, London, SPCK, 1975; publ. in the U.S.A. as *Doing Theology in a Revolutionary Situation*, Philadelphia, Pa, Fortress, 1975

17. MITCHELL, B., *The Justification of Religious Belief*, London, New York, *Macmillan, 1973; New York, *Seabury, 1974

18. MURCHLAND, B. (ed.), *The Meaning of the Death of God: Protestant, Jewish and Catholic Scholars Explore Atheistic Theology*, New York, Random House, 1967

19. PALMER, R. E., *Hermeneutics: Interpretation Theory in Schleiermacher, Dilthey, Heidegger and Gadamer*, Evanston, Ill., *†Northwestern University Press, 1969

20. PAUCK, W. and M., *Paul Tillich, His Life and Thought* (2 vols.), vol. I. London, *Collins, 1977; New York, *Harper & Row, 1976

21. PHILLIPS, D. Z., *The Concept of Prayer*, London, *Routledge, 1965; New York, Schocken, 1966

22. REARDON, B. M. G., *Liberal Protestantism*, London, Black/Stanford, Calif., *Stanford University Press, 1968

23. ROBERTS, D. E., *Existentialism and Religious Belief*, New York, Oxford University Press, 1957

24. RUSSELL, L. M., *Human Liberation in a Feminist Perspective: A Theology*, Philadelphia, Pa, †Westminster, 1974

25. SHAW, D. W. D., *The Dissuaders: Three Explorations of Religion*, London, †SCM, 1978

26. SOUTHERN, R. W., *Saint Anselm and His Biographer*, Cambridge, *Cambridge University Press, 1963

27. STEPHEN, SIR LESLIE, *History of English Thought in the Eighteenth Century*, 2 vols., London, Smith, Elder, 1876, repr. New York, Harcourt, Brace/London, Hart-Davis (copyr. 1962); Magnolia, Mass., *Peter Smith

28. STROMBERG, R. N., *Religious Liberalism in Eighteenth Century England*, London, Oxford University Press, 1954

29. WILLIAMS, R. R., *Schleiermacher the Theologian*, Philadelphia, Pa, *Fortress, 1978

30. ZAHRNT, H., *The Historical Jesus*, London, Collins/New York, Harper & Row, 1963

[XI] CHRISTIANITY: (D) EASTERN CHRISTIANITY AND
CHRISTIAN SPIRITUALITY
Compiled by D. J. Melling

1. AMAND DE MENDIETA, E., *Mount Athos: The Garden of the Panaghia*, New York, ★International Publications Service, 1972
2. ARSENEV, N. S., *Russian Piety*, Leighton Buzzard, Faith Press, 1964, repr. 1975; Clayton, Wis., American Orthodox Press, 1964; New York, †St Vladimir's
3. ATIYA, A. S., *A History of Eastern Christianity*, Notre Dame, Ind., University of Notre Dame Press, 1968; London, ★Methuen, 1968; New York, †Kraus, 1980
4. ATTWATER, D., *Christian Churches of the East* (rev. edn), 2 vols., London, G. Chapman/Leominster, Thomas More/Milwaukee, Wis., Bruce, 1961; vol. 1. prev. publ. as *The Catholic Eastern Churches*; vol. 2 as *The Dissident Eastern Churches*, Milwaukee, Wis., Bruce, 1948
5. AUMANN, J., HOPKO, T., and BLOESCH, D.G., *Christian Spirituality, East and West*, Chicago, Ill., Priory Press, 1968
6. BUTLER, C., *Western Mysticism*, 3rd edn, London, †Constable, 1967; New York, ★Gordon Press
7. CABASILAS, N., *The Life in Christ* (tr. by C. J. Decatanzaro), New York, †St Vladimir's, 1974
8. *The Cloud of Unknowing* (tr. by C. Wolters), Harmondsworth, Penguin Books, 1961, repr. †1978
9. COLLEDGE, E. (ed.), *The Mediaeval Mystics of England*, New York, Scribner, 1961; London, Murray, 1962
10. CONYBEARE, F., *Russian Dissenters*, Cambridge, Mass., Harvard University Press, 1921, repr. Westport, Conn., Hyperion, 1980
11. DALMAIS, I. H., *Eastern Liturgies* (tr. by D. Attwater), London, Burns & Oates, 1960; New York, Hawthorn, 1960, repr. 1968
12. DIONYSIUS OF FOURNA, *The Painter's Manual* (tr. by P. Hetherington), London, †Sagittarius, 1974
13. ECKHART, MEISTER, *Meister Eckhart: A Modern Translation* (tr. by B. Blakney), New York, London, Harper & Row, 1941, †1957
14. FEDOTOV, G. (ed.), *A Treasury of Russian Spirituality*, New York, 1948, London, Sheed & Ward, 1950, †1977; Belmont, Mass., †Nordlund, 1975
15. FROST, B., *The Art of Mental Prayer*, new edn, London, SPCK, 1940
16. HAPPOLD, F. C., *Mysticism*, rev. edn, Harmondsworth, †Penguin Books, 1965, repr. 1980

17. *Iconmakers' Handbook of the Stroganov School of Painters*, Willits, Calif., *Eastern Orthodox, 1974

18. JOHN OF THE CROSS, ST, *Complete Works* (tr. by E. A. Peers) (one-vol. edn), London, Burns & Oates, 1963; Westminster, Md, Newman, 1964; this tr. first publ. in 3 vols, 1934–5

19. JOHNSTON, W., *The Inner Eye of Love*, London, *Collins, 1978; London, †Fount, 1981

20. KOVALEVSKY, P., *St Sergius and Russian Spirituality*, New York, St Vladimir's, 1976

21. LANE, C., *Christian Religion in the Soviet Union*, London, Allen & Unwin, 1978, †1979; Albany, N.Y., *State University of New York Press, 1978

22. LERCARO, G., *Methods of Mental Prayer* (tr. by T. F. Lindsay), London, Burns & Oates/Westminster, Md, Newman, 1957

23. LOSSKY, V., *In the Image and Likeness of God*, New York, †St Vladimir's, 1974; London, †Mowbray, 1975

24. LOSSKY, V., *The Vision of God*, London, Faith Press, 1963; repr. 1973; Clayton, Wis., American Orthodox Press, 1964; New York, †St Vladimir's, 1963

25. MARY, MOTHER, and WARE, ARCHIMANDRITE K. (tr.), *The Festal Menaion*, London, Faber, 1969

26. MEYENDORFF, J., *Byzantine Theology*, New York, Fordham University Press, 1974; London, *Mowbray, 1975; 2nd edn, †Fordham University Press, 1978

27. MEYENDORFF, J., *Christ in Eastern Thought*, Washington DC, Corpus, 1969; New York, †St Vladimir's, 1975

28. MEYENDORFF, J., *St Gregory Palamas and Orthodox Spirituality*, New York, †St Vladimir's, 1974

29. MEYENDORFF, J., *A Study of Gregory Palamas*, New York, St Vladimir's/London, Faith Press, 1964

30. MONK OF THE EASTERN CHURCH, *Orthodox Spirituality*, 2nd edn, London, †SPCK/New York, †St Vladimir's, 1978

31. MONK OF THE EASTERN CHURCH, *The Prayer of Jesus*, New York, Desclee, 1967

32. NASSAR, S. (tr.), *Divine Prayers and Services*, New York, Syrian Antiochian, Orthodox Archdiocese, 1961

33. OUSPENSKY, L., *The Theology of the Icon*, New York, †St Vladimir's, 1978

34. PASCAL, P., *Avvakum et les débuts du Rascol* (2nd edn), Paris, Mouton, 1963; †1969

35. PHILIPPOU, A. J. (ed.), *The Orthodox Ethos*, Oxford, Holywell Press, 1964

36. *The Philokalia* (tr. by G.E.H. Palmer *et al.*), London, *Faber, 1979 –

37. ROBINSON, N. F., *Monasticism in the Orthodox Church*, London, Cope & Fenwick/Milwaukee, Wis., Young Churchman Co., 1916, repr. New York, AMS, 1971

38. SCHMEMANN, A., *The Historical Road of Eastern Orthodoxy*, London, Harvill Press/New York, Holt, Rinehart, 1963; New York, †St Vladimir's, 1974

39. SCHMEMANN, A., *Introduction to Liturgical Theology*, Leighton Buzzard, Faith Press, 1975; New York, ★St Vladimir's, 1966

40. SITWELL, G., *Spiritual Writers of the Middle Ages*, New York, Hawthorn, 1961

41. SOPHRONY, ARCHIMANDRITE, *Monk of Athos, Starets Silouan*, Oxford, †Mowbray, 1973; New York, †St Vladimir's, 1975

42. TANQUEREY, A., *The Spiritual Life*, New York, Newman, 1945; Westminster, Md, 1947

43. TERESA OF AVILA, ST, *Complete Works* (tr. by E. A. Peers), London, ★†Sheed & Ward, 1978; this tr. originally publ. in 3 vols., 1946

44. TISSERANT, E., *Eastern Christianity in India*, London, Longman, 1957, repr. 1965

45. TRUBETSKOI, E. N., *Icons: Theology in Colour*, New York, †St Vladimir's, 1974

46. UNDERHILL, E., *Mysticism*, London, ★Methuen, 1980; New York, †Dutton, 1961; †New American Library, 1955; Totowa, N.J., ★Rowman, 1911 edn, repr. 1977

47. WARE, T., *The Orthodox Church*, Harmondsworth, †Penguin Books, 1963, repr. 1980

48. *The Way of a Pilgrim* (tr. by R. M. French), London, P. Allan, 1930, often repr.; †SPCK, 1972; †Ballantine, 1979, with *The Pilgrim Continues His Way*

[XII] GREEK RELIGION
Compiled by C. Sourvinou-Inwood

1. BURKERT, W., *Lore and Science in Ancient Pythagoreanism*, Cambridge, Mass, ★Harvard University Press, 1972

2. BURKERT, W., *Griechische Religion der archaischen und klassischen Epoche*, Stuttgart, Kohlhammer, 1977; English tr. forthcoming, Oxford, Blackwell and Harvard University Press

3. BURKERT, W., *Structure and History in Greek Mythology and Ritual*, London, Berkeley, Calif., ★University of California Press, 1979

4. BURY, J. B., and MEIGGS, R., *A History of Greece to the Death of Alexander the Great*, 4th edn, London, ★†Macmillan/New York, St Martin's Press, 1975

5. CUMONT, F., *Astrology and Religion among the Greeks and Romans*, London, New York, Constable, 1912; repr. New York, †Dover, 1960; Magnolia, Mass., ★Peter Smith

6. DIETRICH, B. C., *Death, Fate and the Gods: the Development of a Religious Idea in Greek Popular Belief and in Homer*, London, ★Athlone Press, 1965

7. DODDS, E. R., *The Greeks and the Irrational*, Berkeley, Calif., London, †University of California Press, 1951

8. DOVER, K. J., *Greek Popular Morality in the Time of Plato and Aristotle*, Oxford, Blackwell, 1974; Berkeley, Calif., ★University of California Press, 1975

9. EHRENBERG, V., *The Greek State*, 2nd edn, London, *Methuen, 1969, †1972; New York, †Methuen Inc., 1979

10. GUTHRIE, W. K. C., *The Greeks and Their Gods*, London, Methuen, *1950, University Paperback, 1968; Boston, Mass., Beacon Press, 1951

11. HUMPHREYS, S. C., *Anthropology and the Greeks*, London, Boston, Mass., *Routledge, 1978

12. KIRK, G. S., *The Nature of Greek Myths*, Harmondsworth, †Penguin Books, 1974; New York, †Overlook Press, 1975

13. LLOYD-JONES, H., *The Justice of Zeus*, Berkeley, Calif., London, *†University of California Press, 1971

14. LONG, A. A., *Hellenistic Philosophy: Stoics, Epicureans, Sceptics*, London, *Duckworth/New York, Scribner, 1974

15. NILSSON, M. P., *A History of Greek Religion*, Oxford, Clarendon Press, 1925, 2nd edn, 1949, repr. New York, †Norton, 1964; Westport, Conn., *Greenwood, 1980

16. NILSSON, M. P., *Cults, Myths, Oracles and Politics in Ancient Greece*, Lund, Gleerup (Acta Inst. Atheniensis Sueciae, 1), repr. New York, *Cooper Square, 1972

17. NOCK, A. D., *Essays on Religion and the Ancient World* (sel. and ed. Z. Stewart), 2 vols., Oxford, Clarendon Press/Cambridge, Mass., Harvard University Press, 1972

18. PARKE, H. W., *Greek Oracles*, London, †Hutchinson, 1967

19. RICHTER, G. M. A., *A Handbook of Greek Art*, 6th edn, London, New York, *†Phaidon, 1969

20. TOMLINSON, R. A., *Greek Sanctuaries*, London, *Elek/New York, *St Martin's Press, 1976

(*See also*: VIII, 3, 13: XXVIII, 11a, 22a, 24a)

[XIII] HINDUISM: (A)
Compiled by T. O. Ling

1. BASHAM, A. L., *The Wonder That was India*, 3rd rev. edn, London, *Sidgwick, 1967; London, †Fontana, 1971; New York, Taplinger, 1968

2. BÉTEILLE, A., *Castes: Old and New*, London, *Bombay, New York, Asia Publishing House, 1969

3 BHARDWAJ, S. M., *Hindu Places of Pilgrimage in India*, Berkeley, Calif., *University of California Press, 1973

4. BHATTACHARJI, S., *The Indian Theogony: A Comparative Study of Indian Mythology from the Vedas to the Purānas*, Cambridge, Cambridge University Press, 1970; repr. Columbia, Mo, *South Asia Books, 1978

4a.CARTMAN, J., *Hinduism in Ceylon*, Colombo, Gunasena, 1957

5. DANIÉLOU, A., *Hindu Polytheism*, London, *Routledge/Princeton, N.J., *Princeton University Press, 1964

5a.DASGUPTA, S. N., *A History of Indian Philosophy*, vol. 1, Cambridge, Cambridge University Press, 1922, repr. 1975 – *see* XIII (B): 5

6. DE BARY, W. T., *et al.*, *Sources of Indian Tradition*, New York, London, Columbia University Press, 1958

6a.DHAVAMONY, M., *Love of God According to Śaiva Siddhānta: A Study in the Mysticism and Theology of Śaivism*, Oxford, Clarendon Press, 1971

6b.DOWSON, J., *A Classical Dictionary of Hindu Mythology and Religion, Geography, History and Literature*, 11th edn, London, *Routledge, 1968

7. DUTT, R. C., *The Ramayana, and the Mahabharata, Condensed into English Verse*, London, Dent/New York, Dutton, 1910, *†repr.

8. GARRETT, J., *A Classical Dictionary of India*, London, 1871, repr. New York, *International Publications Service, 1971; Delhi, Oriental Publications, 1971; 1873 edn, repr. New York, *Franklin, 1973

9. GHURYE, G. S., *Social Tensions in India*, Bombay, *Popular Prakashan, 1968

10. JASH, P., *History of Śaivism*, Calcutta, *Roy & Chowdhury, 1974

11. KARVE, I., *Hindu Society: An Interpretation*, 2nd edn, Poona, Deshmukh Prakashan, 1968

12. KOSAMBI, D. D., *The Culture and Civilisation of Ancient India*, London, Routledge, 1965; Delhi, *Vikas, 1975

13. LANNOY, R., *The Speaking Tree: A Study of Indian Culture and Society*, London, New York, Oxford University Press, 1971, †1974, *Bombay, 1968

14. LING, T.O., *A History of Religion East and West*, London, Macmillan, 1968, †1969; New York, St Martin's, 1968

14a.LING, T. O., 'Hinduism: Introduction into South-East Asia', in: S. G. F. Brandon, *A Dictionary of Comparative Religion*, London, Weidenfeld/New York, †Scribner, 1970, pp. 171–3, 331–3, 595–6, 608–9

14b.MICHELL, G., *The Hindu Temple: An Introduction to Its Meaning and Form*, London, *Elek, 1977; New York, *Harper & Row, 1978

15. MONIER-WILLIAMS, SIR MONIER, *A Sanskrit–English Dictionary*, Oxford, Clarendon Press, 1899, repr. 1960; Delhi, *Motilal Banarsidass, 1970; Delhi, *Oriental Publications, 1972; Columbia, Mo, *South Asia, 1973

16. O'FLAHERTY, W. D., *Asceticism and Eroticism in the Mythology of Śiva*, London, New York, Oxford University Press, 1973

16a.O'FLAHERTY, W. D. (ed.), *Hindu Myths: A Sourcebook* (tr. from the Sanskrit), Harmondsworth, †Penguin Books, 1975

17. O'MALLEY, L. S. S., *Indian Caste Customs*, Cambridge, Cambridge University Press, 1932, repr. 1974 Totowa, N.J., *Rowman/London, *Curzon/New Delhi, *Vikas

18. POCOCK, D. F., *Mind, Body and Wealth: A Study of Belief and Practice in an Indian Village*, Oxford, *Blackwell/Totowa, N.J., *Rowman, 1973

19. RENOU, L. (ed.), *Hinduism*, London, New York, *Braziller, 1963; Bombay, *Taraporevala, 1969

20. SARKAR, B. K., *The Folk Element in Hindu Culture*, 1917, repr. New Delhi, 1972; New York, *International Publications Service, 1972

21. SASTRI, K. A. N., *Development of Religion in South India*, New Delhi, Orient Longman, 1963

22. SINGER, M., *Traditional India: Structure and Change*, Philadelphia, Pa, American Folklore Society, 1959; Jaipur, ★Rawat, 1975; †University of Texas Press, 1959

23. SINGER, M. (ed.), *Krishna: Myths, Rites and Attitudes*, Honolulu, East–West Center, 1966; †University of Chicago Press, 1969

24. SRINIVAS, M. N., *Caste in Modern India*, London, Bombay, New York, Asia Publishing House, 1962; ★Bombay, 1977; London, ★J. K. Publishing, 1979

24a.WALKER, B., *Hindu World: An Encyclopaedic Survey of Hinduism*, 2 vols., London, Allen & Unwin, 1968

24b.WOODROFFE, SIR JOHN, *S'akti and S'akta: Essays and Addresses*, 7th edn, Madras, Ganesh, 1969

25. ZAEHNER, R. C., *Hinduism*, London, New York, †Oxford University Press, 1962, new edn, 1966

26. ZAEHNER, R. C., *Hindu Scriptures*, London, Dent/New York, ★Dutton, 1966

27. ZIMMER, H. R., *Myths and Symbols in Indian Art and Civilization*, Princeton, N.J., Princeton University Press/New York, Pantheon, 1946; ★†Princeton University Press, 1971

[XIII] HINDUISM: (B)
Compiled by L. S. Cousins

1. BASHAM, A. L., *History and Doctrines of the Ājīvikas*, London, Luzac, 1951

2. BASHAM, A. L., *The Wonder That was India*, 3rd edn, London, †Fontana, 1971; London, Sidgwick & Jackson, 1967; New York, Taplinger, 1968

3. CARMAN, J. B., *The Theology of Rāmānuja*, New Haven, Conn., Yale University Press, 1974

4. DANIÉLOU, A., *Yoga: The Method of Re-Integration*, New York, University Books, 1955; London, Johnson, 1949, new edn, ★1973

5. DASGUPTA, S. N., *A History of Indian Philosophy*, 5 vols., Cambridge, Cambridge University Press, 1922–55, repr. 1975 Delhi, ★Motilal Banarsidass; Livingston, N.J., Orient Book Distributors; Atlantic Highlands, N.J., †Humanities

6. DEUTSCH, E., and BUITENEN, J. A. B. VAN, *A Source Book of Advaita Vedānta*, Honolulu, ★University Press of Hawaii, 1971

7. ELIADE, M., *Patanjali and Yoga*, New York, †Schocken, 1975, repr. 1976; prev. publ. New York, Funk & Wagnalls, 1969

8. *Encyclopaedia Britannica: Macropaedia*, 15th edn, 19 vols. (copyr. 1975–8) (refs. in text to vol. and p.)

9. FEUERSTEIN, G., *The Philosophy of Classical Yoga*, Manchester, Manchester University Press, 1980

10. FRAUWALLNER, E., *History of Indian Philosophy* (tr. by V. M. Bedekar), 2 vols., Delhi, ★Motilal Banarsidass; Livingston, N.J., ★Orient Book Distributors, 1973; New York, ★Humanities, 1974

11. GONDA, J., *A History of Indian Literature*, Wiesbaden, Harrassowitz, 1973– (in progress) (refs. in text to vol. and fascicule)

12. LARSON, G. J., *Classical Sāṃkhya*, Delhi, ★Motilal Banarsidass, 1969

13. POTTER, K. H., *Encyclopaedia of Indian Philosophies*, vol. 2, *Indian Metaphysics and Epistemology*, Delhi, Motilal Banarsidass, 1977; Princeton, N.J., Princeton University Press (copyr. 1977); New York, ★International Publications Service, 1977

14. PULIGANDLA, R., *Fundamentals of Indian Philosophy*, New York, †Abingdon, 1975

15. RADHAKRISHNAN, SIR SARVEPALLI (tr.), BĀDARĀYAṆA, *The Brahma Sutra*, London, ★Allen & Unwin, 1960

16. RADHAKRISHNAN, SIR SARVEPALLI, and MOORE, C. A., (eds.), *A Sourcebook in Indian Philosophy*, Princeton, N.J., Princeton University Press, 1957, repr. †1973

17. SMART, N., *Doctrine and Argument in Indian Philosophy*, London, Allen & Unwin/Atlantic Highlands, N.J., ★Humanities, 1964; new edn, Brighton, ★Harvester, 1977

18. WERNER, K., *Yoga and Indian Philosophy*, Delhi, Motilal Banarsidass, 1977; Columbia, Mo, ★South Asia Books, 1979

19. ZAEHNER, R. C., *The Bhagavad-Gītā*, Oxford, ★Clarendon Press, 1969, †Oxford University Press (N.Y.), 1973

[XIII] HINDUISM: (C) TEMPLES AND FESTIVALS
Compiled by A. Unterman

1. GUPTE, B. A., *Hindu Holidays and Ceremonials, with Dissertations on Origin, Folklore and Symbols*, 2nd edn rev., Calcutta, Thacker, Spink, 1919, ★1966

2. PANDEY, R. B., *Hindu Samskāras: Socio-Religious Study of the Hindu Sacraments*, 2nd rev. edn, Delhi, ★Motilal Banarsidass, 1969, repr. Mystic, Conn., ★Verry; Livingston, N.J., ★Orient Book Distributors, 1976

3. STEVENSON, M., *The Rites of the Twice-Born*, London, New York, Oxford University Press, 1920, repr. New York, International Publications Service, 1971; New Delhi, ★Oriental Books Reprint Corp., 1971

4. VIDYARTHI, L. P., JHA, M., and SARASWATI, B. N., *The Sacred Complex of Kashi: A Microcosm of Indian Civilization*, Delhi, Concept, 1979; Columbia, Mo, ★South Asia Books

[XIV] ISLAM
Compiled by C. E. Bosworth

1. AHMAD, A., *Studies in Islamic Culture in the Indian Environment*, Oxford, Clarendon Press, 1964

2. AHMAD, A., *An Intellectual History of Islam in India*, Edinburgh, ★Edinburgh, University Press, 1969

3. ALI, MUHAMMAD, *A Manual of Hadith*, 2nd edn, London and Dublin, Curzon Press/Atlantic Highlands, N.J., ★Humanities Press, 1978; a reprint of the Lahore, 1951 edn, with additional preface

4. ANDRAE, T., *Die Person Muhammeds in Lehre und Glauben seiner Gemeinde*, Stockholm, Norstedt, 1918

5. ARBERRY, A. J., *Sufism: An Account of the Mystics of Islam*, London, ★Allen & Unwin, 1950, †1979

6. ARBERRY, A. J. (ed.), *Religion in the Middle East: Three Religions in Concord and Conflict*, vol. 2, *Islam*, ★Cambridge, Cambridge University Press, 1969

7. ARNOLD, SIR THOMAS W., *Painting in Islam: A Study of the Place of Pictorial Art in Muslim Culture*, New York, †Dover, 1965 (republ., with a new introduction, of 1928 first edn); Magnolia, Mass., ★Peter Smith

8. ARNOLD, SIR THOMAS W., *The Caliphate*, London, Routledge, 1965, repr. 1967; New York, Barnes & Noble, 1966; first publ. Oxford, Clarendon Press, 1924

9. BIRGE, J. K., *The Bektashi Order of Dervishes*, London, Luzac/Conn., Hartford Seminary Press, 1937, repr. New York, ★AMS, 1977

9a. BOSWORTH, C. E., *Islamic Dynasties: A Chronological and Genealogical Handbook*, Edinburgh, Edinburgh University Press/New York, Columbia University Press, 1967; rev. paperback edn, Edinburgh U.P., 1980

10. BRANDON, S. G. F., (ed.), *A Dictionary of Comparative Religion*, London, Weidenfeld/New York, Scribner, 1970

10a. BROCKELMANN, C., *History of the Islamic Peoples*, London, ★Routledge, 1952; this tr. originally publ. New York, Putnam, 1947; London, Routledge, 1949

11. BROWNE, E. G. (ed.), *Materials for the Study of the Bábí Religion*, Cambridge, Cambridge University Press, 1918

12. CANAAN, T., *Mohammedan Saints and Sanctuaries in Palestine*, London, Luzac, 1927

13. COULSON, N. J., *A History of Islamic Law*, Edinburgh, ★Edinburgh University Press, 1964, †1979

14. CRAGG, K., *Counsels in Contemporary Islam*, Edinburgh, ★Edinburgh University Press, 1965

15. CRAGG, K., *The Mind of the Qur'ān: Chapters in Reflection*, London, ★Allen & Unwin, 1973

16. DANIEL, N. A., *Islam and the West: The Making of an Image*, Edinburgh, Edinburgh University Press, 1960

17. DONALDSON, D. M., *The Shi'ite Religion: A History of Islam in Persia and Irak*, London, Luzac, 1933; New York, ★Gordon Press, 1976

18. DONALDSON, D. M., *Studies in Muslim Ethics*, London, SPCK, 1953

19. DUNCAN, A., *The Noble Sanctuary: Portrait of a Holy Place in Arab Jerusalem*, London, Longman, 1972

20. *Encyclopaedia of Islam*, 5 vols., Leiden, Brill/London, Luzac, 1913–38

21. *Encyclopaedia of Islam*, 2nd edn, Leiden, Brill/London, Luzac, 1960– (in progress); New York, ★Humanities

22. ESIN, E., *Mecca the Blessed, Madinah the Radiant*, London, *Elek/New York, Crown Publishing, 1963

23. ESSLEMONT, J. E., *Bahá'u'lláh and the New Era*, 3rd rev. edn, Wilmette, Ill., Bahá'í Publications Trust, 1970, 4th edn, *1980

24. ETTINGHAUSEN, R., *Arab Painting*, Lausanne, Skira, 1962; London, *Macmillan, 1977; New York, †Rizzoli, 1977

25. FARMER, H. G., *A History of Arabian Music to the XIIIth Century*, London, Luzac, 1929, repr. 1967, *1973

26. FREEMAN-GRENVILLE, G. S. P., *The Muslim and Christian Calendars, being Tables for the Conversion of Muslim and Christian Dates from the Hijra to the Year A. D. 2000*, London, New York, Oxford University Press, 1963; 2nd edn, London, *R. Collings/Totowa, N.J., *Rowman, 1977

27. GÄTJE, H., *The Qur'ān and Its Exegesis: Selected Texts, with Classical and Modern Muslim Interpretations* (tr. and ed. by A. T. Welch), London, *Routledge/Berkeley, Calif., *University of California Press, 1976

28. GAUDEFROY-DEMOMBYNES, M., *La Pélerinage à la Mekke: étude d'histoire religieuse*, Paris, Geuthner, 1923; Philadelphia, *Porcupine Press, 1977. (Issued also as thesis, University of Paris, under title: *Contribution à l'étude du pélerinage de la Mekke ...*, 1923)

29. GAUDEFROY-DEMOMBYNES, M., *Muslim Institutions*, London, Allen & Unwin, 1950

30. GIBB, SIR HAMILTON A. R., *Modern Trends in Islam*, Chicago, Ill., University of Chicago Press, 1947, repr. New York, *Octagon, 1971

31. GIBB, SIR HAMILTON A. R., *Islam: A Historical Survey*, 2nd edn, [London], Oxford University Press, 1975; as *Muhammedanism: An Historical Survey*, 2nd edn, †OUP, repr. 1969

32. GOLDZIHER, I., *Muslim Studies* (ed. by S. M. Stern), 2 vols., London, Allen & Unwin, 1967–71; State University of New York, 1967–72

33. GRABAR, O., *The Formation of Islamic Art*, New Haven, Conn., London, *†Yale University Press, 1973

34. GRAY, B., *Persian Painting*, Geneva, Skira, 1961; London, *Macmillan, 1977; New York, †Rizzoli, 1977

35. GUILLAUME, A., *The Traditions of Islam: An Introduction to the Study of Hadith Literature*, Oxford, Clarendon Press, 1924, repr. New York, *Arno, 1980

36. GUILLAUME, A., *Islam*, Harmondsworth, Penguin Books, 1954, †1969

36a. HITTI, P. K., *History of the Arabs from the Earliest Times to the Present*, 10th edn, London, †Macmillan/New York, *†St Martin's, 1970

37. HOLT, P. M., LAMBTON, A. K. S., and LEWIS, B. (eds.), *The Cambridge History of Islam*, vol. 1, *The Central Islamic Lands*, vol. 2, *The Further Islamic Lands, Islamic Society and Civilization*, Cambridge, Cambridge University Press, 1970, new edn in 4 vols. *†1977

38. HOURANI, A., *Arabic Thought in the Liberal Age, 1798–1939*, London, New York, Oxford University Press, 1962

39. HUGHES, T. P., *A Dictionary of Islam*, London, W. H. Allen/New York, Scribner, 1885, repr. Allen, 1935; London, *Luzac, 1966; New York, *Gordon Press, 1980

40. ISRAELI, R., *Muslims in China: A Study in Cultural Confrontation*, London, †Curzon Press, 1980; Atlantic Highlands, N.J., †Humanities Press, 1979

41. JAFRI, S. H. M., *Origins and Early Development of Shi'a Islam*, London, *Longman/Beirut, Librairie du Liban, 1979

42. JEFFERY, A., *The Qur'ān as Scripture*, New York, Moore, 1952; New York, *Arno, 1980

43. JEFFERY, A., *A Reader on Islam: Passages from Standard Arabic Writings Illustrative of the Beliefs and Practices of Muslims*, The Hague, Mouton, 1962; New York, *Arno, 1980

44. KHATIBI, A., and SIJELMASSI, M., *The Splendour of Islamic Calligraphy*, London, *Thames & Hudson, 1976; New York, Rizzoli, 1977

45. LANE, E. W., *An Account of the Manners and Customs of the Modern Egyptians*, London, Knight, 1836, often republ.; London, *†East–West Publications (U.K.), 1978; Magnolia, Mass., *Peter Smith

46. LAOUST, H., *Les Schismes dans l'Islam: introduction à une étude de la religion musulmane*, Paris, Payot, 1965

47. LEVY, R., *The Social Structure of Islam*, Cambridge, *Cambridge University Press, 1957; the 2nd edn of *The Sociology of Islam*

48. LEWIS, B., *The Assassins: A Radical Sect in Islam*, London, Weidenfeld, 1967; New York, Basic Books, 1968; repr. New York, *Octagon, 1980

49. LEWIS, B. (ed.), *The World of Islam: Faith, People, Culture*, London, *Thames & Hudson, 1976; Amer. edn, *Islam and the Arab World*, *Knopf, 1976

50. LINCOLN, C. E., *The Black Muslims in America*, new edn, Boston, Mass., *†Beacon Press, 1973

51. LINGS, M., *What is Sufism?*, London, *†Allen & Unwin, 1975; Berkeley, Calif., †University of California Press, 1977

52. MACDONALD, D. B., *The Development of Muslim Theology, Jurisprudence and Constitutional Theory*, Karachi, 1960; London, Routledge, 1903, repr. New York, *Russell, 1965

53. MACDONALD, D. B., *The Religious Attitude and Life in Islam*, Chicago, Ill., University of Chicago Press, 1909, repr. Beirut, Khayats, 1965; New York, *AMS

54. MCPHERSON, J. W., *The Moulids of Egypt*, Cairo, NM Press, 1941; repr. New York, *AMS, 1977

55. MARTIN, B. G., *Muslim Brotherhoods in Nineteenth-Century Africa*, Cambridge, *Cambridge University Press, 1976

56. MITCHELL, G. (ed.), *Architecture of the Islamic World: Its History and Social Meaning*, London, Thames & Hudson/New York, *Morrow, 1978

57. MITCHELL, R. P., *The Society of the Muslim Brothers*, London, Oxford University Press, 1969

58. NICHOLSON, R. A., *Studies in Islamic Mysticism*, Cambridge, Cambridge University Press, 1921, repr. *1967, †1979

59. PELLY, SIR LEWIS, *The Miracle Play of Hasan and Husain, Collected from Oral Tradition*, London, W. H. Allen, 1879, repr. Farnborough, *Gregg, 1970

59a. PERKINS, M., and HAINSWORTH, P., *The Bahá'í Faith*, London, Ward, Lock Educational, 1980

421   Bibliography

60. PETERS, R. (ed. and tr.), *Jihād in Mediaeval and Modern Islam: the Chapter on Jihād from Averroes' Legal Handbook* ..., Leiden, Brill, 1977

61. RAHMAN, F., *Islam*, London, Weidenfeld/New York, Holt, Rinehart (copyr. 1966); 2nd edn, †University of Chicago Press, 1979

62. RINGGREN, H., *Studies in Arabian Fatalism*, Uppsala, Lundequist; Wiesbaden, Harrassowitz, 1955

63. RODINSON, M., *Mohammed*, London, Allen Lane the Penguin Press, 1971, new edn, Harmondsworth, †Penguin Books, 1974; New York, †Pantheon, 1980

64. SAVORY, R. M. (ed.), *Introduction to Islamic Civilization*, Cambridge, New York, ★Cambridge University Press, 1976

65. SCHACHT, J., *An Introduction to Islamic Law*, Oxford, ★Clarendon Press, 1964

66. SCHACHT, J., and BOSWORTH, C. E. (eds.), *The Legacy of Islam*, 2nd edn, Oxford, ★Clarendon Press, 1974, †1979

66a. SCHIMMEL, A., *Islamic Calligraphy*, Leiden, Brill, 1970; New York, ★Adler

67. TIBAWI, A. L., *Islamic Education: Its Traditions and Modernization into the Arab National Systems*, London, Luzac, 1972, 2nd edn, ★1979

68. TRIMINGHAM, J. S., *A History of Islam in West Africa*, Oxford, ★Oxford University Press, 1962, †1970

69. TRIMINGHAM, J. S., *The Sufi Orders in Islam*, Oxford, ★Clarendon Press, 1971, Oxford University Press, †1973

70. TRIMINGHAM, J. S., *Christianity among the Arabs in Pre-Islamic Times*, London, ★Longman/Beirut, Librairie du Liban, 1979

71. TRIMINGHAM, J. S., *The Influence of Islam upon Africa*, 2nd edn, London, ★Longman/Beirut, Librairie du Liban, 1980

72. TRITTON, A. S., *Materials on Muslim Education in the Middle Ages*, London, Luzac, 1957

73. TRITTON, A. S., *The Caliphs and Their Non-Muslim Subjects: A Critical Study of the Covenant of 'Umar*, London, 1930, repr. London, ★Cass, 1970

74. VON GRUNEBAUM, G. E., *Muhammadan Festivals*, repr. London, Curzon Press, 1976; New York, ★Humanities, 1976; prev. publ. New York, Schuman, 1951; London, Abelard Schuman, 1958

75. WADDY, C., *Women in Muslim History*, London, ★Longman/Beirut, Librairie du Liban, 1980

76. WATT, W. M., *Muhammad, Prophet and Statesman*, London, Oxford University Press, 1961, †1974

77. WATT, W. M., *Islamic Philosophy and Theology*, Edinburgh, ★Edinburgh University Press, 1962, †1979

78. WATT, W. M., *A History of Islamic Spain*, Edinburgh, ★Edinburgh University Press, 1965, †1978

79. WATT, W. M., *Islamic Political Thought: The Basic Concepts*, ★Edinburgh, Edinburgh University Press, 1968

80. WATT, W. M., *What is Islam?*, London, Longman/Beirut, Librairie du Liban, 1968; 2nd edn, ★Longman, 1979; New York, Praeger, 1968

81. WATT, W. M., *Bell's Introduction to the Qur'ān Completely Revised and Enlarged*, Edinburgh, ★Edinburgh University Press, 1970, †1978

82. WENSINCK, A. J., *The Muslim Creed: Its Genesis and Historical Development*, Cambridge, Cambridge University Press, 1932; London, *Cass, 1965

83. WILLIAMS, J. A., *Themes of Islamic Civilization*, Berkeley, Calif., London, *University of California Press, 1971

84. ZIADEH, N. A., *Sanūsīyah: A Study of a Revivalist Movement in Islam*, Leiden, Brill, 1958

[XV] JAINISM
Compiled by T. O. Ling

1. BASHAM, A. L., *The Wonder That was India*, 3rd rev. edn, London, Sidgwick & Jackson, 1967; London, †Fontana, 1971; New York, *Taplinger, 1968

2. JAINI, P. S., 'Karma and the Problem of Rebirth in Jainism', in: W. D. O'Flaherty (ed.), *Karma and Rebirth in Classical Indian Tradition*, Berkeley, Calif., *University of California Press, 1980

3. JAINI, P. S., *The Jaina Path of Purification*, Berkeley, Calif., *University of California Press, 1979

4. LING, T., 'Jainism', in: A. Cotterell (ed.), *The Encyclopaedia of Ancient Civilisations*, New York, 1980

[XVI] JAPANESE RELIGIONS
Compiled by J. E. Kidder

1. ANESAKI, M., *Nichiren the Buddhist Prophet*, Cambridge, Mass., Harvard University Press/London, Oxford University Press, 1916; Magnolia, Mass., *Peter Smith

2. ASTON, W. G. (tr.), NIHONGI, *Chronicles of Japan from the Earliest Times to A.D. 697*, London, Allen & Unwin, 1956, prev. publ. London, Kegan Paul, 1896; Rutland, Vt, †Tuttle, 1971

3. BAUER, H., and CARLQUIST, S., *Japanese Festivals*, Rutland, Vt, Tokyo, Tuttle, 1974

4. BLACKER, C., *The Catalpa Bow: A Study of Shamanistic Practices in Japan*, London, *Allen & Unwin/Totowa, N.J., *Rowman, 1975

5. BLOOM, A., *Shinran's Gospel of Pure Grace*, Tucson, †University of Arizona Press, 1965

6. BOCK, F. (tr.), ENGI-SHIKI, *Procedures of the Engi Era* (bks I–v), Tokyo, Sophia University, 1970

7. BOXER, C. R., *The Christian Century in Japan, 1549–1650*, Berkeley, Calif., University of California Press, 1967 (copyr. 1951), *1974

8. BUNCE, W. K. (ed.), *Religions in Japan: Buddhism, Shinto, Christianity*, 3rd edn, Rutland, Vt, Tokyo, Tuttle, 1959; London, ★Greenwood, 1978

9. CASAL, U. A., *The Five Sacred Festivals of Ancient Japan: Their Symbolism and Historical Development*, Tokyo, Sophia University, and Rutland, Vt, Tuttle, 1967

10. CHAMBERLAIN, B. H. (tr.), *Kojiki; or, Records of Ancient Matters. Transactions of the Asiatic Society of Japan*, vol. 10, Supplement, Tokyo, 1882

11. DE VISSER, M. W., *Ancient Buddhism in Japan: Sūtras and Ceremonies in Use in the Seventh and Eighth Centuries A.D., and Their History in Later Times*, 2 vols., Leiden, Brill, 1935

12. DRUMMOND, R. H., *A History of Christianity in Japan*, Grand Rapids, Mich., Eerdmans, 1971

13. EARHART, H. B., *Japanese Religion: Unity and Diversity*, 2nd edn, Encino, Calif., †Dickenson, 1974

14. EARHART, H. B., *A Religious Study of the Mount Haguro Sect of Shugendō: An Example of Japanese Mountain Religion*, Tokyo, Sophia University, 1970/New York, ★International Publications Service, 1970

15. ELIOT, SIR CHARLES, *Japanese Buddhism*, London, Routledge/New York, Barnes & Noble, 1959, prev. publ. London, Arnold, 1935

16. HAKEDA, Y. S. (tr.), KŪKAI, *Major Works*, New York, ★Columbia University Press, 1972

17. HERBERT, J., *Shinto: At the Fountainhead of Japan*, New York, Stein & Day/London, Allen & Unwin, 1967

18. HORI, I., *Folk Religion in Japan: Continuity and Change*, University of Chicago Press/University of Tokyo Press, 1968; ★†University of Chicago Press, 1974

19. HORI, I., et al. (eds.), *Japanese Religion: A Survey by the Agency for Cultural Affairs*, 2nd edn, Tokyo, Palo Alto, Calif., Kodansha International, 1974

20. IGLEHART, C. W., *A Century of Protestant Christianity in Japan*, Rutland, Vt, Tokyo, Tuttle, 1959

21. IWAO, S. (ed.), *Biographical Dictionary of Japanese History*, Tokyo, ★Kodansha International/ International Society for Educational Information, 1978

22. *Japanese–English Buddhist Dictionary*, Tokyo, Daitō Shuppansha, 1965

23. KAMSTRA, J. H., *Encounter or Syncretism: The Initial Growth of Japanese Buddhism*, Leiden, Brill, 1967

24. KIDDER, J. E., *Japanese Temples: Sculpture, Paintings, Gardens and Architecture*, Tokyo, Bijutsu Shuppansha, and Amsterdam, Abrams/London, Thames & Hudson, 1964

25. KITAGAWA, J. M., *Religion in Japanese History*, New York, Columbia University Press, 1966

26. LAURES, J., *The Catholic Church in Japan: A Short History*, Rutland, Vt, Tokyo, Tuttle, 1954; Westport, Conn., London., ★Greenwood, repr.

27. MASUNAGA, R., *The Sōtō Approach to Zen*, Tokyo, Layman Buddhist Society, 1958

28. MATSUNAGA, A., *The Buddhist Philosophy of Assimilation: The Historical Development of the Honji-Suijaku Theory*, Rutland, Vt, Tuttle/Tokyo, Sophia University, 1969

29. NAKAMURA, H., HORI, I., and NOMA, S., *Japan and Buddhism*, Tokyo, Association of the Buddha Jayanti, 1959

30. ONO, S., *Shinto: the Kami Way*, Rutland, Vt, Tokyo, Bridgeway Press (*Tuttle), 1962; prev. publ. as *The Kami Way: An Introduction to Shrine Shinto*, 1960

31. PHILIPPI, D. L. (tr.), *Norito: A New Translation of the Ancient Japanese Ritual Prayers*, Tokyo, Institute for Japanese Culture and Classics, Kokugakuin University, 1959

32. PONSONBY-FANE, R. A. B., *Studies in Shinto and Shrines*, Kyoto, Ponsonby Memorial Society, 1953, prev. publ. 1943; publ. as vol. 1 of *Collected Works*, New York, *International Publications Service, 1954

33. PONSONBY-FANE, R. A. B., *The Vicissitudes of Shinto*, Kyoto, Ponsonby-Fane Memorial Society, 1963; publ. as vol. 5 of *Collected Works*, New York, *International Publications Service, 1963

34. SAUNDERS, E. D., *Buddhism in Japan, with an Outline of Its Origins in India*, Philadelphia, University of Pennsylvania Press, 1964; London, Westport, Conn., *Greenwood, repr. 1977; Berkeley, †University of California Press, 1964

35. STRAELEN, H. VAN, *The Religion of Divine Wisdom: Japan's Most Powerful Religious Movement*, Kyoto, Veritas Shoin, 1957

36. SUZUKI, D. T., *Zen and Japanese Culture*, New York, Pantheon, 1959; London, *Routledge/Princeton, *†Princeton University Press, 1959; rev. and enl. edn of *Zen Buddhism and Its Influence on Japanese Culture*, 1938

37. TAJIMA, R., *Les Deux Grands Mandalas et la doctrine de l'ésotérisme Shingon*, Paris, Tokyo, Presses Universitaires de France, Maison Franco-Japonaise, 1959

38. WHITE, J. W., *The Sōkagakkai and Mass Society*, Stanford, Calif., *Stanford University Press, 1970

[XVII] JUDAISM
Compiled by A. Unterman

1. ABRAHAMS, I., *Jewish Life in the Middle Ages*, New York, †Atheneum, 1969, repr. 1975; first publ. 1896, repr. by arrangement with the Jewish Publication Society of America

2. ALTMANN, A., *Moses Mendelssohn: A Biographical Study*, Philadelphia, Jewish Publication Society of America/[Tuscaloosa, Ala], *University of Alabama Press/London, Routledge, 1973

3. BARON, S. W., *A Social and Religious History of the Jews*, 2nd edn, 17 vols., Philadelphia, Pa, Jewish Publication Society of America/New York, London, *Columbia University Press, 1952–76

4. BLAU, J. L. (ed.), *Reform Judaism: A Historical Perspective*, New York, *Ktav, 1973

5. BUBER, M., *Tales of the Hasidim*, 2 vols., New York, Schocken, 1961, repr.

1968–9, †1970; prev. publ. London, Thames & Hudson, 1956; vol. 1, *Early Masters*

6. ibid., vol. 2, *Later Masters*

7. COHEN, A., *Everyman's Talmud*, London, Dent/New York, Dutton, 1949; New York, †Schocken, 1975; prev. publ. Dent, 1932

8. DANBY, H.(tr.), *The Mishnah*, London, ★Oxford University Press, 1954, first publ. 1933

9. *Encyclopaedia Judaica*, 16 vols. and 3 yearbooks, Jerusalem, Keter, 1971–2, ★16 vols., New York, Macmillan

10. EPSTEIN, I. (ed.), *The Babylonian Talmud*, 18 vols., London, Soncino, 1961

11. EPSTEIN, I., *Judaism*, Harmondsworth, †Penguin Books, 1959, repr. 1968

12. FELDMAN, D. M., *Marital Relations: Birth Control and Abortion in Jewish Law*, New York, †Schocken, 1974; *Birth Control in Jewish Law: Marital Relations, Contraception and Abortion . . .*, new edn, London, ★Greenwood, 1980

13. FINKELSTEIN, L., *The Jews*, vol. 2, *Their Religion and Culture*, new edn, New York, †Schocken, 1971

14. FRIEDLANDER, A. H., *Out of the Whirlwind: A Reader of Holocaust Literature*, New York, †Schocken, 1976, repr. 1978; New York, ★Union of American Hebrew Congregations, 1968

15. GRUENWALD, I., *Apocalytic and Merkavah Mysticism*, Leiden, Brill, 1980

16. GRUNFELD, I., *The Jewish Dietary Laws*, 2 vols., London, New York, ★Soncino, 1972

17. GUTTMANN, J., *Philosophies of Judaism: The History of Jewish Philosophy from Biblical Times to Franz Rosenzweig*, New York, Holt, Rinehart/London, Routledge, 1964, †Schocken, 1974

18. HERTZBERG, A. (ed.), *The Zionist Idea: A Historical Analysis and Reader*, New York, †Atheneum, repr. 1971; repr. of 1959 edn, Westport, Conn., ★Greenwood, 1970

19. HUSIK, I., *A History of Mediaeval Jewish Philosophy*, New York, Meridian/Philadelphia, Pa, Jewish Publication Society, 1960; New York, †Atheneum, 1969; prev. publ. New York, Macmillan, 1916

20. IDELSOHN, A. Z., *Jewish Liturgy and Its Development*, New York, Schocken, 1967; prev. publ. New York, Holt, Rinehart, 1932

21. JACOBS, L., *A Jewish Theology*, London, Darton, 1973; New York, †Behrman, 1973

22. JACOBS, L., *Principles of the Jewish Faith: An Analytic Study*, London, ★Vallentine, Mitchell/New York, Basic Books, 1964

23. JAKOBOVITS, I., *Jewish Medical Ethics*, New York, Bloch, 1967, rev. edn, ★†1975

24. KANIEL, M., *Judaism*, Poole, Dorset, ★Blandford, 1979 (*The Art of World Religions*)

25. KATZ, J., *Exclusiveness and Tolerance: Jewish–Gentile Relations in Medieval and Modern Times*, New York, Schocken, 1962; repr. of 1961 edn, Westport, Conn., ★Greenwood, 1980

26. KEDOURIE, E. (ed.), *The Jewish World*, London, ★Thames and Hudson, 1979; New York, ★Abrams, 1979

27. KELLNER, M. M. (ed.), *Contemporary Jewish Ethics*, New York, ★†Sanhedrin, 1978

28. LAQUEUR, W., *A History of Zionism*, New York, Holt, Rinehart, 1972; New York, †Schocken, 1976

29. LIEBERMAN, S., *Hellenism in Jewish Palestine: Studies in the Literary Transmission, Beliefs and Manners of Palestine in the I century, b.c.e. – IV century, c.e.* (2nd edn), New York, ★Jewish Theological Seminary of America, 1962

30. MAIMONIDES, i.e. MOSES, BEN MAIMON, *The Guide of the Perplexed* (tr. by S. Pines), Chicago, Ill., University of Chicago Press, †1974, ★1963

31. MARGOLIS, M. L., and MARX, A., *A History of the Jewish People*, New York, Harper Torchbooks, 1965; New York, †Atheneum, 1969; prev. publ. Philadelphia, Pa, Jewish Publication Society, 1927

32. MONTEFIORE, C. G., and LOEWE, H. (eds.), *A Rabbinic Anthology*, New York, †Schocken, 1974, repr. of Macmillan, 1968 edn, with new prolegomena

33. MOORE, G. F., *Judaism in the First Centuries of the Christian Era*, 3 vols., Cambridge, Mass., Harvard University Press, 1927, repr. 1966

34. NAMENYI, E., *The Essence of Jewish Art*, New York, London, Yoseloff, 1960

35. NEUSNER, J., *The Rabbinic Traditions about the Pharisees before 70*, Leiden, Brill, 1971

36. RABINOWICZ, H., *The World of Hasidism*, London, ★Vallentine, Mitchell/ Hartford, Conn., ★Hartmore, 1970

37. REITLINGER, G., *The Final Solution: The Attempt to Exterminate the Jews of Europe, 1939–1945*, new, rev. edn, New York, Yoseloff/London, ★Vallentine, Mitchell, 1968; San Diego, Calif.; †A. S. Barnes, 1961

38. RIVKIN, E., *A Hidden Revolution: The Pharisees' Search for the Kingdom Within*, Nashville, Tenn., ★Abingdon, 1978; London, ★SPCK, 1979

39. ROTH, C., *A History of the Jews in England*, 3rd edn, Oxford, ★Clarendon Press, 1979

40. ROTH, C., *A History of the Marranos*, rev. edn, Philadelphia, Pa, Jewish Publication Society, 1947; New York, †Schocken, 1974; repr. of 1932 edn, New York, ★Arno, 1975

41. ROTH, C., *A Short History of the Jewish People*, rev. and enl. edn, London, East and West Library, 1969; repr. Hartford, Conn., ★Hartmore, 1970; New York, †Hebrew Publications, 1978

42. RUDAVSKY, D., *Modern Jewish Religious Movements: A History of Emancipation and Adjustment*, New York, Behrman, 1967, 3rd rev. edn, †1979; original title: *Emancipation and Adjustment: Contemporary Jewish Religious Movements*, New York, Diplomatic Press/London, Living Books (1967)

43. SACHAR, H. M., *The Course of Modern Jewish History*, New York, Delta, Dell, 1958, rev. edn, †1977; Cleveland, World Publishing Co./ London, Weidenfeld, 1958

44. SCHAUSS, H., *Guide to Jewish Holy Days*, New York, Schocken, repr. 1970

45. SCHOLEM, G. G., *Major Trends in Jewish Mysticism*, 3rd edn repr. New York, †Schocken, 1961; prev. publ. Schocken, 1954; London, Thames & Hudson, 1955

46. SCHOLEM, G. G., *The Messianic Idea in Judaism, and Other Essays on Jewish Spirituality*, New York, *†Schocken/London, Allen & Unwin, 1971

47. SCHÜRER, E., *The History of the Jewish People in the Age of Jesus Christ*, vol. 2 (rev. and ed. by G. Vermes, F. Millar and M. Black), Edinburgh, Clark, 1979

48. SINGER, S. (tr.), *The Authorized Daily Prayer Book*, 2nd rev. edn, London, Eyre & Spottiswoode, 1968

49. SKLARE, M., *Conservative Judaism: An American Religious Movement*, new, augmented edn, New York, †Schocken, 1972

50. STEINSALTZ, A., *The Essential Talmud* (tr. from the Hebrew by Chaya Galai), New York, London, †Bantam, 1977

51. STRACK, H. L., *Introduction to the Talmud and Midrash*, New York, Meridian/Philadelphia, Pa, Jewish Publication Society, 1959; New York, †Atheneum, 1969

52. UNTERMAN, A., *Jews: Their Religious Beliefs and Practices*, London, Boston, Mass., *†Routledge, 1981

52a. UNTERMAN, A., *Judaism*, London, †Ward, Lock Educational, 1981

53. WEINGREEN, J., *From Bible to Mishna*, Manchester, *Manchester University Press/New York, *Holmes & Meier, 1976

54. ZIMMELS, H. J., *Ashkenazim and Sephardim*, London, Oxford University Press, 1958

[XVIII] MAGIC AND THE OCCULT
Compiled by G. Lindop

1. BARBER, M., *The Trial of the Templars*, Cambridge, New York, *†Cambridge University Press, 1978

2. BLAU, J. L., *The Christian Interpretation of the Cabala in the Renaissance*, Port Washington, N.Y., Kennicat, 1965, repr. of New York, Columbia University Press, 1944

3. BLAVATSKY, H. P., *An Abridgement of The Secret Doctrine* (ed. by E. Preston and C. Humphreys), London, *Theosophical Publishing House, 1966

4. BOWLES, N., and HYNDS, F., *Psi Search: The Comprehensive Guide to Psychic Phenomena*, New York, *Harper & Row, 1978, *London, 1979

5. BUTLER, C., *Number Symbolism*, London, *Routledge/New York, Barnes & Noble, 1970

6. COUDERT, A., *Alchemy: The Philosopher's Stone*, Boulder, Colo, *Shambhala, 1980

7. DEWAR, J., *The Unlocked Secret: Freemasonry Examined*, London, *Kimber, 1966, repr. *1972

8. DUMMETT, M., *The Game of Tarot*, London, *Duckworth, 1980

9. EVANS-PRITCHARD, SIR EDWARD E., *Witchcraft, Oracles and Magic among the Azande*, Oxford, *Clarendon Press, 1937, repr. 1951, etc.; abridged edn, †Oxford University Press, 1976

10. GARDNER, G. B., *Witchcraft Today*, London, Rider, 1954; Secaucus, N.J., Citadel Press, 1955, †1970

11. HEMLEBEN, J., *Rudolf Steiner: A Documentary Biography*, East Grinstead, ★†Goulden, 1975

12. HOPPER, V. F., *Medieval Number Symbolism*, New York, Columbia University Press, 1938; Folcroft, Pa, ★Folcroft Library, 1938

13. HOWE, E., *The Magicians of the Golden Dawn: A Documentary History of a Magical Order*, London, ★Routledge, 1972; New York, †Weiser, 1978

14. JUNG, C. G., *Psychology and Alchemy* (tr. by R. F. C. Hull), London, ★Routledge, 1953; Princeton, N.J., ★†Princeton University Press, 1980; publ. as vol. 12 of *Collected Works*, New York, Pantheon, 1953, 2nd edn, 1966

15. KING, F., *Ritual Magic in England, 1887 to the Present Day*, London, Spearman, 1970. Amer. edn publ. under title: *The Rites of Modern Occult Magic*, New York, Macmillan, 1971

16. KNIGHT, G., *The Practice of Ritual Magic*, 3rd edn, Wellingborough, †Aquarium Press, 1979; New York, ★Weiser

17. LAGUERRE, M., *Voodoo Heritage*, Beverly Hills, Calif., London, ★†Sage, 1980

18. 'LEVI, ELIPHAS' (CONSTANT, A. L.), *The History of Magic* (tr. by A. E. Waite), London, †Rider, 1969; New York, ★Gordon Press

19. LEWINSOHN, R., *Prophets and Prediction*, London, Secker, 1961

20. NELSON, G. K., *Spiritualism and Society*, London, Routledge/New York, Schocken, 1969

21. RHODES, H. T. F., *The Satanic Mass*, Rider, New York, London, 1954; Secaucus, N.J., Citadel Press, 1955, ★1974, †1975; New York, ★Wehman

22. ROBERTS, J. M., *The Mythology of the Secret Societies*, London, Secker/New York, Scribner, 1972

23. STOUDT, J. J., *Sunrise to Eternity: Jacob Boehme's Life and Thought*, Philadelphia, Pa, University of Philadelphia Press, 1957, repr. New York, ★AMS

24. THOMAS, K., *Religion and the Decline of Magic*, London, ★Weidenfeld/New York, †Scribner, 1971; Harmondsworth, †Penguin Books, 1973

25. TOKSVIG, S., *Emanuel Swedenborg, Scientist and Mystic*, New Haven, Conn., Yale University Press, 1948; London, Faber, 1949

26. WALLIS, R. T., *Neoplatonism*, London, ★Duckworth, 1972

27. WEBB, J., *The Harmonious Circle*, London, ★Thames & Hudson/New York, ★Putnam, 1980

28. WILSON, C., *The Occult*, London, Hodder/New York, Random House, 1971; St Albans, †Panther, 1979

29. YATES, F. A., *The Art of Memory*, London, ★Routledge/Chicago, Ill., University of Chicago Press, 1966; rev. edn, Harmondsworth, †Penguin Books, 1970

30. YATES, F. A., *Giordano Bruno and the Hermetic Tradition*, London, ★Routledge, 1964, †1978; Chicago, Ill., University of Chicago Press, 1964; New York, †Random House, 1969

31. YATES, F. A., *The Rosicrucian Enlightenment*, London, ★Routledge, 1972; St Albans, †Paladin, 1975; Boulder, Colo, †Shambhala, 1978

(*See also:* II, 1, 3, 8; X, 95; XX, 19; XXII, 12)

[XIX] MESOAMERICAN RELIGIONS
Compiled by D. Carrasco

1. BERNAL, I., *Mexico Before Cortez*, rev. edn, Garden City, N.Y., †Anchor Books, Doubleday, 1975
2. BRUNDAGE, B., *The Fifth Sun*, Austin, Tex., ★University of Texas Press, 1979
3. CASO, A., *The Aztecs, People of the Sun*, Norman, Okla, University of Oklahoma Press, 1958, repr. ★1970
4. COE, M., *The Maya*, New York, Praeger, 1973, prev. publ. New York, Praeger/London, Thames & Hudson, 1966; Harmondsworth, †Penguin Books, 1971
5. CULBERT, T. P., *The Lost Civilization: The Story of the Classic Maya*, New York, †Harper & Row, 1974
6. DAVIES, N., *The Toltecs, until the Fall of Tula*, Norman, Okla, ★University of Oklahoma Press, 1977
7. DURAN, D., *Book of the Gods and Rites and the Ancient Calendar* (tr. and ed. by F. Horcasitas and D. Heyden), Norman, Okla, ★University of Oklahoma Press, 1975, first publ. 1971
8. EDMONSON, M., *Sixteenth-Century Mexico: The Work of Sahagun*, Albuquerque, N. Mex., ★University of New Mexico Press, 1974
9. HARDOY, J., *Pre-Columbian Cities*, New York, Walker/London, Allen & Unwin, 1973
10. KATZ, F., *The Ancient American Civilizations*, New York, Praeger/London, ★Weidenfeld, 1972
11. KUBLER, G., *The Art and Architecture of Ancient America*, 2nd edn, Harmondsworth, Baltimore, Md, ★Penguin Books, 1975; New York, ★Viking, 1976
12. LEON PORTILLA, M., *Aztec Thought and Culture*, Norman, Okla, ★University of Oklahoma Press, 1978, first publ. 1963
13. LEON PORTILLA, M., *Time and Reality in the Thought of the Maya*, Boston, Mass., Beacon Press, 1973
14. LEON PORTILLA, M., *Pre-Columbian Literatures of Mexico*, Norman, Okla, University of Oklahoma Press, 1969
15. ROBERTSON, D., *Mexican Manuscript Painting of the Early Colonial Period: The Metropolitan Schools*, New Haven, Yale University Press, 1959
16. SEJOURNE, L., *Burning Water: Thought and Religion in Ancient Mexico*, Berkeley, Calif., ★Shambhala, 1976; London, †Thames & Hudson, 1978
17. WAUCHOPE, R. (gen. ed.), *Handbook of Middle American Indians*, vol. 10, *Archaeology of Northern Mesoamerica*, Austin, Tex., ★University of Texas Press, 1971
18. WHEATLEY, P., *The Pivot of the Four Quarters*, Chicago, Ill., Aldine, 1971
19. WOLF, E., *Sons of the Shaking Earth*, Chicago, Ill., University of Chicago Press, 1959, †1962

(*See also*: XX, 3, 18a)

[XX] NEW RELIGIOUS MOVEMENTS IN PRIMAL SOCIETIES
Compiled by H. W. Turner

1. BARNETT, H. G., *Indian Shakers*, Carbondale, Ill., Southern Illinois University Press, 1957, †1972.

2. BARRETT, D. B., *Schism and Renewal in Africa*, Nairobi, Oxford University Press, 1968

3. BARRETT, L. E., *The Rastafarians: The Dreadlocks of Jamaica*, Kingston, Jamaica, Sangsters/London, Heinemann Educational, 1977

4. DANEEL, M. L., *Old and New in Southern Shona Independent Churches*, vols. 1 and 2, The Hague, ★Mouton, 1971–4

5. ELWOOD, D. J., *Churches and Sects in the Philippines*, Dumaguete City, Silliman University, 1968

6. FUCHS, S., *Rebellious Prophets: A Study of Messianic Movements in Indian Religions*, London, ★New York, Asia Publishing House, 1965

7. GREENWOOD, W., *The Upraised Hand*, Wellington, Polynesian Society, 3rd imp., 1980

8. HALIBURTON, G. M., *The Prophet Harris*, London, Longman, 1971; †Oxford University Press (New York), 1973

9. HENDERSON, J. M., *Ratana*, 2nd edn, Wellington, Reed/Polynesian Society, 1972

10. KAMMA, F., *Koreri: Messianic Movements in the Biak-Numfor Culture Area*, The Hague, Nijhoff, 1972

11. LA BARRE, W., *The Peyote Cult*, enl. edn, New York, Schocken, 1969, 4th edn, †1976

12. LANTERNARI, V., *Religions of the Oppressed*, New York, Knopf/London, MacGibbon & Kee, 1963; New York, Mentor, 1965

13. MARTIN, M.-L., *Kimbangu: An African Prophet and His Church*, Oxford, ★Blackwell, 1975; Grand Rapids, Mich., ★Eerdmans, 1976

14. PEEL, J. D. Y., *Aladura: A Religious Movement among the Yoruba*, London, ★Oxford University Press, 1968

15. SIMPSON, G. E., *Black Religions in the New World*, New York, ★Columbia University Press, 1978

16. SUNDKLER, B. G. M., *Bantu Prophets in South Africa*, 2nd edn, London, †Oxford University Press, 1961

17. TURNER, H. W., 'Tribal Religious Movements, New', in: ★*Encyclopaedia Britannica*, 15th edn, *Macropaedia*, vol. 18 (copyr. 1976), pp. 697–705

18. WALLACE, A. F. C., *Death and Rebirth of the Seneca*, New York, Knopf, 1970; New York, †Random House; New York, †Vintage, 1973

18a. WILLIAMS, K. M., *The Rastafarians*, London, Ward, Lock Educational, 1981

19. WILSON, B. R., *Magic and the Millennium*, London, Heinemann/New York, Harper & Row, 1973; New York, †Beekman, 1978

20. WORSLEY, P., *The Trumpet Shall Sound*, 2nd edn, New York, †Schocken/London, MacGibbon & Kee, 1968

(*See also:* XI(b), 13)

[XXI] NEW RELIGIOUS MOVEMENTS IN WESTERN SOCIETIES
Compiled by E. Barker

1. AMERICAN CIVIL LIBERTIES UNION/TORONTO SCHOOL OF THEOLOGY, *De-programming: Documenting the Issue*, New York, †ACLU/†Toronto School of Theology, 1977

2. ANNETT, S., *The Many Ways of Being: A Guide to Spiritual Groups and Growth Centres in Britain*, London, †Abacus, 1976

3. BARKER, E. (ed.), *New Religious Movements: A Perspective for Understanding Society*, Lewiston, N.Y., ★Edwin Mellen Press, 1982

4. BROMLEY, D. G., and SHUPE, A. D., *'Moonies' in America: Cult, Church and Crusade*, Beverly Hills, Calif., London, ★†Sage, 1979

5. BRYANT, D., and RICHARDSON, H., *A Time for Consideration: A Scholarly Appraisal of the Unification Church*, Lewiston, N.Y., Edwin Mellen Press, 1978

6. CHURCH OF SCIENTOLOGY WORLD WIDE, *The Scientology Religion*, East Grinstead, Church of Scientology, [1974], previous edn title: *Scientology: Twentieth Century Religion*

7. COX, H., *Turning East: The Promise and Peril of the New Orientalism*, New York, ★Simon & Schuster, 1977, †1978; London, ★Allen Lane, 1979

8. DAVIES, H., *Christian Deviations: The Challenge of the New Spiritual Movements*, 4th rev. edn, London, †SCM, 1972; 3rd edn, Philadelphia, Pa, Westminster, 1973

9. DOWNTON, J. V., *Sacred Journeys: The Conversion of Young Americans to Divine Light Mission*, New York, ★Columbia University Press, 1979

10. ELLWOOD, R. S., *Religious and Spiritual Groups in Modern America*, Englewood Cliffs, N.J., ★Prentice-Hall, 1973

11. ENROTH, R. M., *Youth, Brainwashing and the Extremist Cults*, Grand Rapids, Mich., ★†Zondervan/London, †Paternoster, 1977

12. ENROTH, R., *The Lure of the Cults*, New York, ★Christian Herald, 1979

13. FRASER, D. M. (Chairman), *Investigation of Korean–American Relations*, Washington DC, U.S. Government Printing Office, 1978 (Report of the Subcommittee on International Organizations of the Committee on International Relations, U.S. House of Representatives, Washington, 31 October 1978)

14. GLOCK, C. Y., and BELLAH, R. N. (eds.), *The New Religious Consciousness*, Berkeley, Calif., ★†University of California Press, 1976

15. HILL, D. G., *Study of Mind Development Groups, Sects and Cults in Ontario*, †Author, 3rd Floor, 18 King St East, Toronto (Report to the Ontario Government, June 1980)

16. HOROWITZ, I. L., *Science, Sin and Scholarship: The Politics of Reverend Moon and the Unification Church*, Cambridge, Mass., ★MIT Press, 1978, †1980

17. HSA-UWC, *Divine Principle*, 2nd edn, Thornton Heath, Unified Family Enterprises/Washington DC, Holy Spirit Association for the Unification of World Christianity, 1973; ★†from Unification Church Centres, London, New York, etc.

18. HUBBARD, L. R., *Dianetics: The Modern Science of Mental Health*, Los Angeles,

Calif., *Publications Organization, Church of Scientology of California, *1950, †1968

19. JUDAH, J. S., *Hare Krishna and the Counterculture*, New York, Wiley, 1974

20. KHALSA, P. S. (ed.), *Spiritual Community Guide*, San Rafael, Calif., †Spiritual Community Publications, 1978

21. KILDUFF, M., and JAVERS, R., *The Suicide Cult: The Inside Story of the Peoples Temple Sect and the Massacre in Guyana*, New York, Bantam, 1978, †London

22. KRAUSE, C. A., *Guyana Massacre: The Eyewitness Account*, New York, Berkeley Books, 1978

23. KWAK, C. H., *Outline of the Principle, Level 4*, New York, Holy Spirit Association for the Unification of World Christianity, 1980

24. LOFLAND, J., *Doomsday Cult: A Study of Conversion, Proselytization and Maintenance of Faith*, enl. edn, New York, Wiley (*Halsted), 1977; New York, †Irvington, 1980; original edn, Englewood Cliffs, N.J., Prentice-Hall, 1966

25. MCBETH, L., *Strange New Religions*, Nashville, Tenn., *Broadman, 1977

26. MacCOLLAM, J. A., *Carnival of Souls: Religious Cults and Young People*, New York, *Seabury, 1979

27. MAHARISHI INTERNATIONAL UNIVERSITY, *Science of Creative Intelligence*, Goleta, Calif., MIU Press, 1975 (Publ. no. G1-184–875)

28. MEHER BABA, *Discourses*, 3 vols., Walnut Creek, Calif., Sufism Reoriented, 1967

29. MURPHET, H., *Sai Baba: Man of Miracles*, New York, *International Publications Service/London, *Muller, 1971

30. NEEDLEMAN, J., *The New Religions*, New York, †Dutton, 1977; prev. publ. London, Allen Lane, 1972; Garden City, N.Y., Doubleday, 1970

31. NEEDLEMAN, J., *et al.* (eds.), *Religion for a New Generation*, 2nd edn, New York, †Macmillan, 1977

32. NEEDLEMAN, J., and BAKER, G. (eds.), *Understanding the New Religions*, New York, *Seabury, 1978

33. ODEN, T. C., *The Intensive Group Experience: The New Pietism*, Philadelphia, *Westminster, 1972

34. PATRICK, T., and DULACK, T., *Let Our Children Go*, New York, Dutton, 1976; Westminster, Md, †Ballantine, 1977

35. PRABHUPADA, A. C. BHAKTIVEDANTA, SWAMI, *The Science of Self-Realization*, London, International Society for Krishna Consciousness, 1977

36. RICHARDSON, J., HARDER, M. H., and SIMMONDS, R., *Organized Miracles*, New Brunswick, N.J., *Transaction Books, 1979

37. ROSEN, R. D., *Psychobabble: Fast Talk and Quick Cure in the Era of Feeling*, New York, Atheneum, 1977; London, *Wildwood House, 1978; New York, †Avon, 1979

38. ROSZAK, T., *Unfinished Animal: The Aquarian Frontier and the Evolution of Consciousness*, London, *Faber, 1976; New York, *Harper & Row, 1975, †1977

39. SAHUKAR, MANI, *Sai Baba: The Saint of Shirdi*, 2nd edn, San Francisco,

Calif., Dawn Horse Press, 1971; Bombay, Somaiya, 1971; first edn title: *The Saint of Shirdi: Sri Sai Baba*

40. SARKAR, P. R., *Baba's Grace: Discourses of Shrii Shrii Anandamurti*, Los Altos Hills, Calif., Ananda Marga, 1973

41. SAUNDERS, N., *Self Exploration: A Guide to Groups Involved*, London, *Author/Wildwood House, 1975

42. SAUNDERS, N., *Alternative London*, 5th edn, London, *Author/Wildwood House, 1977

43. SCOTT, R. D., *Transcendental Misconceptions*, San Diego, Calif., *Beta Books, 1978

44. SHUPE, A. D., and BROMLEY, D. G., *The New Vigilantes: Deprogrammers, Anti-cultists, and the New Religions*, Beverly Hills, Calif., London, Sage, 1980

45. SONTAG, F., *Sun Myung Moon and the Unification Church*, Nashville, Tenn., *Abingdon, 1977

46. SPARKS, J., *The Mindbenders: A Look at Current Cults*, New York, *Nelson, 1977

47. STONER, C., and PARKE, J. A., *All God's Children*, Harmondsworth, Penguin Books, 1979; Radnor, Pa, Chilton/Canada, Nelson, 1977

48. TART, C. (ed.), *Altered States of Consciousness*, New York, *Wiley, 1969; Garden City, N.Y., †Doubleday, 1972

49. UNIFICATION CHURCH, *Our Response to the Report on the Investigation of Korean–American Relations*, New York, HSA–UWC, 1979

50. WALLIS, R., *The Road to Total Freedom: A Sociological Analysis of Scientology*, London, Heinemann, 1976; New York, *Columbia University Press, 1977

51. WALLIS, R. (ed.), *Sectarianism: Analyses of Religious and Non-Religious Sects*, New York, Wiley (*Halsted)/London, Peter Owen, 1975

52. WHITE, M., *Deceived: The Jonestown Tragedy: What Every Christian Should Know*, Old Tappan, N.J., †Spire Books, 1979

53. WHITE EAGLE, *Spiritual Unfoldment*, 2 vols., Liss, Hants., *White Eagle Publishing Trust, [1961–9]; Marina Del Rey, Calif., *DeVorss, 1942–69

54. WIERWILLE, V. P., *Jesus Christ is Not God*, Old Greenwich, Conn., *Devin, 1975

55. WILSON, B. R., *Religious Sects*, London, Weidenfeld/New York, McGraw-Hill, 1970

56. WUTHNOW, R., *The Consciousness Reformation*, Berkeley, Calif., *University of California Press, 1976

57. WUTHNOW, R., *Experimentation in American Religion: The New Mysticisms and Their Implications for the Churches*, Berkeley, Calif., *University of California Press, 1978

58. YABLONSKI, L., *Synanon: The Tunnel Back*, Baltimore, Md, Penguin Books, 1967; prev. publ. as *The Tunnel Back: Synanon*, New York, Macmillan, 1965

59. ZARETSKY, I., and LEONE, M. (eds.), *Religious Movements in Contemporary America*, Princeton, N.J., *Princeton University Press, 1974

(*See also:* XI(b), 13)

[XXII] PACIFIC RELIGIONS
Compiled by B. E. Colless and P. Donovan

1. AKKEREN, P. VAN, *Sri and Christ: A Study of the Indigenous Church in East Java*, London, Lutterworth, 1970
2. ALLEN, M. R., *Male Cults and Secret Initiations in Melanesia*, Melbourne, Melbourne University Press/London, New York, Cambridge University Press, 1967
3. BELLWOOD, P., *Man's Conquest of the Pacific*, Auckland, Collins, 1978, London, *1979; New York, *Oxford University Press, 1979
4. BERNDT, R. M. and C. H., *The World of the First Australians*, 2nd edn, Sydney, Ure Smith, 1977
5. BERNET KEMPERS, A. J., *Ageless Borobudur*, *Servire Wassenaar, 1976, Pomona, Calif., *Hunter House
6. BEST, E., *Maori Religion and Mythology*, Wellington, 1924, repr. by Government Printer, Wellington, 1976 (*Dominion Museum Bulletin*, no. 10); New York, *AMS, 1976
7. BUCK, SIR PETER (Te Rangi Hiroa), *The Coming of the Maori*, Wellington, Maori Purposes Fund Board/Whitcombe & Tombs, 1949, 2nd edn, 1950 (distr. London, *Whitcoulls)
8. BURRIDGE, K., *Tangu Traditions*, Oxford, *Clarendon Press, 1969
9. CODRINGTON, R. H., *The Melanesians*, Oxford, Clarendon Press, 1891, repr. New York, †Dover, 1972
10. ELIADE, M., *Australian Religions: An Introduction*, Ithaca, N.Y., London, *Cornell University Press, 1973
11. ELKIN, A. P., *Aboriginal Men of High Degree*, 2nd edn, St Lucia, University of Queensland Press, 1977; New York, *St Martin's, 1978
12. FORTUNE, R. F., *Sorcerers of Dobu*, London, G. Routledge, 1932; rev. edn, London, Routledge & Kegan Paul, 1963; 1932 edn repr. Darby, Pa, *Arden, 1979
13. GEERTZ, C., *The Religion of Java*, Glencoe, Ill., Free Press, 1960; Chicago, Ill., †University of Chicago Press, 1976
14. *Gods, Ghosts, and Men in Melanesia* (ed. by P. Lawrence and M. J. Meggitt), Melbourne, London, †New York, *Oxford University Press, 1965
15. GREY, G., *Polynesian Mythology*, London, Murray, 1855, repr. Christchurch, Whitcombe & Tombs, 1956; repr. of 1906 edn, New York, *AMS, 1976
16. HANDY, E. S. C., *Polynesian Religion*, Honolulu, 1927 (*Bernice P. Bishop Museum Bulletin*, 34), repr. New York, *Kraus, 1971
17. HOOYKAAS, C., *Religion in Bali*, Leiden, Brill, 1973
18. JENSEN, E., *The Iban and Their Religion*, Oxford, Clarendon Press, 1974, *1975
19. LOEB, E., *Sumatra: Its History and People*, Vienna, 1935; repr. Kuala Lumpur, Oxford University Press, 1972, London, †1973
20. MALINOWSKI, B., *Argonauts of the Western Pacific*, London, *Routledge, 1922, †1978; New York, Dutton, 1922, †1961

21. NEVERMANN, H., WORMS, E. A., and PETRI, H., *Die Religionen der Südsee und Australiens*, Stuttgart, Kohlhammer, 1968

22. POIGNANT, R., *Oceanic Mythology: The Myths of Polynesia, Micronesia, Melanesia, Australia*, London, Hamlyn, 1967

23. *Powers, Plumes and Piglets* (ed. by N. C. Habel), Bedford Park, South Australia, Australian Association for the Study of Religions, 1979

24. SCHÄRER, H., *Ngaju Religion: The Conception of God among a South Borneo People*, The Hague, Nijhoff, 1963; tr. of *Die Gottesidee der Ngadju–Dajak in Süd-Borneo*, Leiden, Brill, 1946

25. SELIGMANN, C. G., *The Melanesians of British New Guinea*, Cambridge, Cambridge University Press, 1910; repr. New York, ★AMS, 1976

26. STÖHR, W., and ZOETMULDER, P., *Die Religionen Indonesiens*, Stuttgart, Kohlhammer, 1965

27. STREHLOW, T. G. H., 'Australia', in: C. J. Bleeker and G. Widengren (eds.), *Historia Religionum: Handbook for the History of Religions*, Leiden, Brill, vol. 2, 1971, pp. 609–28

28. SWELLENGREBEL, J. L., *et al.*, *Bali: Studies in Life, Thought and Ritual*, The Hague, van Hoeve, 1960

29. WILLIAMS, F. E., *Drama of Orokolo*, Oxford, Clarendon Press, 1940

30. WILLIAMSON, R. W., *Religion and Social Organization in Central Polynesia*, Cambridge, Cambridge University Press, 1937; repr. New York, ★AMS, 1977

(*See also:* XX, 5, 7, 9)

[XXIII] PREHISTORIC RELIGIONS
Compiled by E. H. Pyle

1. CLARK, G., *The Stone Age Hunters*, London, Thames & Hudson, 1967; New York, †McGraw-Hill, 1967

2. CLARK, G., *World Prehistory*, 2nd edn, Cambridge, Cambridge University Press, 1969, 3rd edn, ★†1977

3. CRAWFORD, O. G. S., *The Eye Goddess*, London, Phoenix House, 1957; New York, Macmillan (1958)

4. DANIEL, G. E., *The Megalith Builders of Western Europe*, London, Hutchinson, 1958, 1963; New York, Praeger, 1959; London, Baltimore, Md, Penguin Books, 1963

5. FLEMING, A., 'The Myth of the Mother Goddess', *World Archaeology*, vol. 1, 1969, pp. 247–61

6. JAMES, E. O., *Prehistoric Religion*, London, Thames & Hudson/New York, Praeger, 1957; New York, Barnes & Noble, 1961

7. JENNINGS, J. D., and NORBECK, E. (eds.), *Prehistoric Man in the New World*, Chicago, Ill., University of Chicago Press, 1964, †1971

8. LEROI-GOURHAN, A. G. L., *The Art of Prehistoric Man in Western Europe*, London, Thames & Hudson, 1968

9. MARINGER, J., *The Gods of Prehistoric Man*, London, Weidenfeld/New York, Knopf, 1960

10. NARR, K. J., 'Approaches to the Religion of Early Palaeolithic Man', *History of Religions*, vol. 4, 1964, pp. 1–22

11. SIEVEKING, A., *The Cave Artists*, London, *Thames & Hudson, 1979

12. UCKO, P. J., and ROSENFELD, A., *Palaeolithic Cave Art*, London, Weidenfeld (*World University Library*); New York, McGraw-Hill, 1967

[XXIV] RELIGIOUS EDUCATION IN SCHOOLS
Compiled by J. Holm

1. COLE, W. O., *World Religions: A Handbook for Teachers*, 3rd edn, London, †Community Relations Commission, 1977

2. HINNELLS, J. R. (ed.), *Comparative Religion in Education*, London, *Oriel, 1970

3. HOLM, J. L., *The Study of Religions*, London, †Sheldon/New York, Seabury, 1977

4. HOLM, J. L., *Teaching Religion in School*, London, Oxford University Press, 1975

5. JACKSON, R. (ed.), *Approaching World Religions*, London, Murray, 1981

6. PANOCH, J. V., and BARR, D. L., *Religion Goes to School*, New York, Harper & Row, 1968

7. SMART, N., *Secular Education and the Logic of Religion*, London, Faber, 1968; New York, *Humanities, 1969

[XXV] ROMAN RELIGIONS
Compiled by J. A. North

1. BAYET, J., *Histoire politique et psychologique de la religion romaine*, Paris, Payot, 1957

2. BLOCH, R., *Les Prodiges dans l'antiquité classique*, Paris, Presses Universitaires de France, 1963

3. BROWN, P. R. L., *The Making of Late Antiquity*, Cambridge, Mass., *Harvard University Press, 1978, London, 1979

4. CUMONT, F., *Oriental Religions in Roman Paganism*, authorized tr. first publ. 1911, repr. New York, †Dover, 1956; Magnolia, Mass., *Peter Smith

5. DODDS, E. R., *Pagan and Christian in an Age of Anxiety*, Cambridge, Cambridge University Press, 1965; New York, †Norton, 1970

6. DUMÉZIL, G., *Archaic Roman Religion*, 2 vols., Chicago, Ill., London, ★University of Chicago Press, 1970, ★1971 (English tr. from first edn, 1966; 2nd edn, *La Religion romaine archaïque*, Paris, Payot, 1974, not available in tr.)

7. FERGUSON, J., *The Religions of the Roman Empire*, London, Thames & Hudson/Ithaca, N.Y., ★Cornell University Press, 1970

8. FONDATION HARDT, *Entretiens*, XIX (*Le Culte des souverains dans l'empire romain*), Geneva, 1973

9. GRANT, F. C., *Ancient Roman Religion*, New York, Liberal Arts Press, 1957; Indianapolis, Ind., ★Bobbs-Merrill, 1957

10. GRANT, M., *Roman Myths*, rev. edn, Harmondsworth, Penguin Books, 1973; London, Weidenfeld, 1971; New York, †Scribner, 1972

11. LATTE, K., *Romische Religionsgeschichte*, Munich, Beck, 1960 (*Handbuch der Altertumswissenschaft*, 5. Abt., 4. T.)

12. LIEBESCHUETZ, J. H. W. G., *Continuity and Change in Roman Religion*, Oxford, ★Clarendon Press/New York, ★Oxford University Press, 1979

13. MICHELS, A. K., *The Calendar of the Roman Republic*, Princeton, N.J., Princeton University Press, 1967, repr. Westport, Conn., London, ★Greenwood, 1978

14. NILSSON, M. P., *The Dionysiac Mysteries of the Hellenistic and Roman Age*, Lund, Gleerup, 1957, repr. New York, ★Arno, 1975

15. NOCK, A. D., *Conversion: The Old and the New in Religion from Alexander the Great to Augustine of Hippo*, London, New York, Oxford University Press, 1933, repr. 1952, paperback, 1961

16. NOCK, A. D., *Essays on Religion and the Ancient World* (ed. by Z. Stewart), Oxford, Clarendon Press/Cambridge, Mass., Harvard University Press, 1972

17. OGILVIE, R. M., *The Romans and Their Gods*, London, Chatto, 1969,★† 1970; New York, ★†Norton, 1970

18. ROSE, H. J., *Ancient Roman Religion*, London, New York, Hutchinson, 1948

18a. SCULLARD, H. H., *Festivals and Ceremonies of the Roman Republic*, London, Thames & Hudson, 1981

19. VERSNEL, H. S., *Triumphus: An Inquiry into the Origin, Development and Meaning of the Roman Triumph*, Leiden, Brill, 1970

20. WEINSTOCK, S., *Divus Julius*, Oxford, ★Clarendon Press, 1971

(*See also:* VIII, 4, 6; XXX, 4, 8, 14, 16, 21, 26)

[XXVI] SECULAR ALTERNATIVES TO RELIGION
Compiled by S. Brown

1. AYER, A. J., *Language, Truth and Logic*, London, ★Gollancz, 1936, 2nd edn, 1946; Harmondsworth, †Penguin Books, 1971; Magnolia, Mass., ★Peter Smith

2. BERGER, P. L., *Invitation to Sociology: A Humanistic Perspective*, ch. 5, Garden

City, N.Y., †Doubleday, 1963; Harmondsworth, †Penguin Books, 1966, 1970; New York, *Overlook, 1973

3. BLACKHAM, H. J., *Humanism*, 2nd edn, Brighton, *Harvester/New York, *International Publications Service, 1976

4. BRAITHWAITE, R. B., *An Empiricist's View of the Nature of Religious Belief*, Cambridge, Cambridge University Press, 1955, repr. in J. Hick (ed.), *The Existence of God*, New York, Macmillan/London, †Collier-Macmillan, 1964

5. BROWN, S. C. (ed.), *Reason and Religion*, Ithaca, N.Y., London, *†Cornell University Press, 1977

6. CAMERON, I., and EDGE, D., *Scientific Images and Their Social Uses: An Introduction to the Concept of Scientism*, London, Boston, Mass., †Butterworth, 1979

7. FEUERBACH, L. A., *The Essence of Christianity* (tr. by George Eliot, 1841), New York, †Harper & Row, 1957; Magnolia, Mass., *Peter Smith

8. FLEW, A., and MACINTYRE, A. (eds.), *New Essays in Philosophical Theology*, London, SCM, 1955; New York, Macmillan, 1955, †1964

9. HUME, DAVID, *Dialogues Concerning Natural Religion* (1779) (ed. by N. Kemp Smith), Oxford, Clarendon Press, 1935; 2nd edn, Indianapolis, Ind., †Bobbs-Merrill, [1947]

10. KOLAKOWSKI, L., *Positivist Philosophy from Hume to the Vienna Circle*, Harmondsworth, Penguin Books, 1972

11. MARX, KARL, *Selected Writings in Sociology and Social Philosophy* (ed. by T. B. Bottomore and M. Rubel), Harmondsworth, Penguin Books, 1963, new edn, †1970; New York, †McGraw-Hill, 1963; first publ. London, Watts, 1956

12. MARX, KARL, *Writings of the Young Marx on Philosophy and Society* (ed. and tr. by L. D. Easton and K. H. Guddat), Garden City, N.Y., Anchor Books, †Doubleday, 1967

13. MILL, J. S., *Essential Works* (ed. by M. Lerner), New York, Bantam, 1961

14. POPKIN, R. H., *The History of Scepticism from Erasmus to Descartes*, rev. edn, New York, London, Harper & Row, 1968; Atlantic Highlands, N.J., *Humanities Press, 1964; publ. as *The History of Scepticism from Erasmus to Spinoza*, Berkeley, Calif., *†University of California Press, 1979, London, 1980

15. POPPER, K. R., *The Logic of Scientific Discovery*, London, Hutchinson, 1959, rev. edn, *1972, †1974; New York, †Harper & Row, n.d.; New York, †Basic Books, 1959

16. POPPER, K. R., *The Open Society and Its Enemies*, vol. 2, *The High Tide of Prophecy: Hegel, Marx and the Aftermath*, London, Routledge, 1945, 4th edn, †1962; 5th edn, Routledge/Princeton University Press, *1966

17. ROSE, H. and S. (eds.), *The Radicalisation of Science*, ch. 2, London, †Macmillan, 1976

18. RUSSELL, BERTRAND (3rd Earl), *Human Society in Ethics and Politics*, London, *Allen & Unwin, 1954; New York, Simon & Schuster, 1955

19. SKINNER, B. F., *Beyond Freedom and Dignity*, Harmondsworth, †Penguin Books, 1973; New York, *Knopf, 1971; New York, †Bantam, 1972

20. STEVENSON, L., *Seven Theories of Human Nature*, London, ★Oxford University Press, 1974
21. TENNANT, F. R., *Philosophical Theology*, 2 vols., Cambridge, Cambridge University Press, 1928–30; lib. edn, CUP, ★1969
22. YINGER, J. M., *The Scientific Study of Religion*, New York, ★Macmillan/London, ★Collier-Macmillan, 1970

(*See also:* XXVIII, 22)

[XXVII] SIKHISM
Compiled by W. H. McLeod

1. AVTAR SINGH, *Ethics of the Sikhs*, Patiala, ★Punjabi University, 1970
2. BARRIER, N. G., *The Sikhs and Their Literature*, Delhi, Manohar Book Service, 1970, ★1976
3. BASHAM, A. L. (ed.), *A Cultural History of India*, Oxford, ★Clarendon Press, 1975
4. COLE, W. O., and SAMBHI, PIARA SINGH, *The Sikhs: Their Religious Beliefs and Practices*, London, Boston, Mass., ★†Routledge, 1978
5. DOABIA, H. S. (tr.), *Sacred Nitnem*, Amritsar, Singh Bros., 1974, 4th enl. edn, 1979
6. GANDA SINGH, *The Sikhs and Their Religion*, Redwood City, Calif., Sikh Foundation, P.O. Box 727, 1974
7. GREWAL, J. S., *From Guru Nanak to Maharaja Ranjit Singh*, Amritsar, ★Guru Nanak University, 1972
8. GREWAL, J. S., *Guru Nanak in History*, Chandigarh, ★Panjab University, 1969
9. GREWAL, J. S., and BAL, S. S., *Guru Gobind Singh*, Chandigarh, ★Panjab University, 1967
10. HARBANS SINGH, *Guru Gobind Singh*, Chandigarh, ★Guru Gobind Singh Foundation, 1966; London, Guru Gobind Singh Tercent. Committee, 1967; New Delhi, ★Sterling, 1979; Livingston, N.J., Orient Book Distributors, 1979
11. HARBANS SINGH, *Guru Nanak and Origins of the Sikh Faith*, Bombay, New York, ★Asia Publishing House, 1969
12. HARBANS SINGH, *The Heritage of the Sikhs*, Bombay, ★Asia Publishing House, 1964, New York, 1965
13. JOGENDRA SINGH, SIR, *Sikh Ceremonies*, Bombay, International Book House, 1941
14. JOHAR, S. S., *Handbook on Sikhism*, Delhi, ★Vivek, 1977; Columbia, Mo, ★South Asia Books; Mystic, Conn., ★Verry, 1978
15. JOHAR, S. S., *The Sikh Gurus and Their Shrines*, Delhi, ★Vivek, 1976; Mystic, Conn., ★Verry, 1977
16. JUERGENSMEYER, M., and BARRIER, N. G. (eds.), *Sikh Studies: Comparative*

Perspectives on a Changing Tradition, Berkeley, Calif., Graduate Theological Union/Berkeley, Calif., *Lancaster-Miller, 1979

17. KANWALJIT KAUR and INDARJIT SINGH (tr.), *Rehat Maryada: A Guide to the Sikh Way of Life*, London, Sikh Cultural Society, 1971

18. KHUSHWANT SINGH, *A History of the Sikhs*, Princeton, N.J., Princeton University Press/London, Oxford University Press, 1963–6, *Bombay, 1967; Indian edn, Delhi, †Oxford University Press, 1978: vol. 1

19. KHUSHWANT SINGH, op. cit. (no. 18), vol. 2

20. KHUSHWANT SINGH (tr.), *Hymns of Guru Nanak*, New Delhi, *Orient Longman, 1969, repr. Columbia, Mo, South Asia Books, 1978

21. MACAULIFFE, M. A., *The Sikh Religion*, 6 vols. in 3, repr. Delhi, Chand, 1963, *1970; first publ. Oxford, Clarendon Press, 1909

22. MCLEOD, W. H., *The B40 Janam-sākhī*, Amritsar, Guru Nanak Dev University, 1980

23. MCLEOD, W. H., *The Evolution of the Sikh Community*, Oxford, *Clarendon Press, 1976; Delhi, Oxford University Press, 1975

24. MCLEOD, W. H., *Early Sikh Tradition*, Oxford, *Clarendon Press, 1980 ·

25. MCLEOD, W. H., *Gurū Nānak and the Sikh Religion*, Oxford, Clarendon Press, 1968, †Oxford University Press, 1968; Indian edn, Delhi, 1976, †1977

26. TEJA SINGH, *Sikhism: Its Ideals and Institutions*, rev. edn, Bombay, *Orient Longman, 1951, repr. Amritsar, Khalsa Bros., 1970

27. TALIB, G. S., (tr.), *Selections from the Holy Granth*, Delhi, Vikas, 1975

28. VAUDEVILLE, C. (ed.), *Kabir*, vol. 1, Oxford, *Clarendon Press, 1974

29. *Selections from the Sacred Writings of the Sikhs* (tr. by Trilochan Singh, Jodh Singh, Kapur Singh, Bawa Harkishen Singh, and Khushwant Singh), London, Allen & Unwin, 1960, †1974; New York, Macmillan, 1960

30. *Sikhism* (essays by Fauja Singh, Trilochan Singh, Gurbachan Singh Talib, J. P. Singh Uberoi, and Sohan Singh), Patiala, *Punjabi University, 1969

[XXVIII] STUDY OF RELIGION
Compiled by E. H. Pyle

1. BANTON, M. (ed.), *Anthropological Approaches to the Study of Religion*, London, Tavistock Publications, 1966, †1968; New York, †Methuen Inc., 1968

2. BARBOUR, I. G., *Myths, Models and Paradigms: A Comparative Study in Science and Religion*, London, SCM, 1974; New York, Harper & Row, 1974, †1976

3. BETTIS, J. D. (ed.), *Phenomenology of Religion*, London, SCM/New York, †Harper & Row, 1969

4. BUDD, S., *Sociologists and Religion*, New York, †Macmillan, 1971; London, *†Collier-Macmillan, 1973

5. CASSIRER, E., *Language and Myth* (tr. by S. K. Langer), New York, †Dover, 1946, repr. 1953; New York, London, Harper & Row, 1946; repr. Magnolia, Mass., *Peter Smith

6. CHRISTIAN, W. A., *Oppositions of Religious Doctrines*, London, Macmillan/ New York, Herder, 1972

7. DANIÉLOU, A., *Hindu Polytheism*, London, *Routledge/New York, Pantheon (Bollingen Foundation)/Princeton, N.J., *Princeton University Press, 1964

8. DHAVAMONY, M., *Phenomenology of Religion*, Rome, Gregorian University Press, 1973

9. DURKHEIM, E., *The Elementary Forms of the Religious Life* (tr. by J.W. Swain), 2nd edn, London/U.S., *†Allen & Unwin, 1976

10. ELIADE, M., *The Sacred and the Profane* (tr. by W. R. Trask), New York, †Harcourt, Brace, 1968

11. GLOCK, C. Y., and HAMMOND, P. E. (eds.), *Beyond the Classics? Essays in the Scientific Study of Religion*, New York, †Harper & Row, 1973, †1974

11a. GRANT, F. C. (ed.), *Hellenistic Religions: The Age of Syncretism*, Indianapolis, Ind., *Bobbs-Merrill/New York, Liberal Arts, 1953

12. HALL, T. W. (ed.), *Introduction to the Study of Religion*, San Francisco, Calif., †Harper & Row, 1978, (London), 1979

13. HEBBLETHWAITE, B. L., *The Problems of Theology*, Cambridge, *Cambridge University Press, 1980

14. HICK, J., *God and the Universe of Faiths*, London, *Macmillan, 1973; New York, *St Martin's, 1974; London, †Fount, Collins, 1977

15. JAMES, WILLIAM, *The Varieties of Religious Experience*, London, †Fontana, 1971; New York, †New American Library, and other *†edns in U.S.; the Gifford Lectures, 1901–2, frequently republ.

16. LEACH, E. A. (ed.), *The Structural Study of Myth and Totemism*, London, Tavistock Publications, 1967, †1968; New York, †Methuen Inc., 1968

16a. LÉVI-STRAUSS, C., *Totemism* (tr. by R. Needham), new edn (with an introduction by R. C. Poole), Harmondsworth, Penguin Books, 1969; French edn, *Le Totémisme aujourd'hui*, Paris, Presses Universitaires de France, 1962

17. LEWIS, H. D., *Our Experience of God*, London, Fontana, 1970; Allen & Unwin, 1959; New York, Macmillan, 1960

18. MALEFIJT, A. DE WAAL, *Religion and Culture*, London, *Collier-Macmillan, 1968, repr. 1970; New York, *Macmillan, 1968

19. MARETT, R. R., *The Threshold of Religion*, New York, *AMS, 1977, repr. of London, Methuen, 1900

20. MILLER, DAVID LEROY, *The New Polytheism: Rebirth of the Gods and Goddesses*, New York, Harper & Row, 1974

21. MOORE, A. C., *Iconography of Religions*, London, *SCM/Philadelphia, Pa, *Fortress, 1977

22. MOORE, S. F., and MYERHOFF, B. G. (eds.), *Secular Ritual*, Assen, Amsterdam, Van Gorcum, 1977; Atlantic Highlands, N.J., *Humanities, 1977

22a. NILSSON, M. P., *Greek Popular Religion*, New York, Columbia University Press, 1940; publ. as *Greek Folk Religion* (with foreword by A. D. Nock), New York, Harper Torchbooks, 1961; Magnolia, Mass., *Peter Smith, 1971; Philadelphia, Pa, †University of Pennsylvania Press, 1972

23. OTTO, R., *The Idea of the Holy* (tr. by J. W. Harvey), 2nd edn, †Oxford

University Press, repr. 1968; this edn prev. publ. London, New York, ★1950, †1958

23a. PANOFSKY, E., *Meaning in the Visual Arts*, Harmondsworth, Penguin, 1970; Garden City, N.Y., ★Doubleday, 1955; New York, ★Overlook, 1974

23b. PEACOCKE, A. R., *Creation and the World of Science*, Oxford, ★Clarendon Press, 1979

24. ROBERTSON, R., *The Sociological Interpretation of Religion*, Oxford, ★†Blackwell, 1969, repr. 1980; New York, ★Schocken, repr. 1972

24a. ROSE, H. J., *Ancient Greek Religion*, London, New York, Hutchinson, 1948

24b. ROSE, H. J., *Ancient Roman Religion*, London, New York, Hutchinson, 1948

25. SHARPE, E. J., *Comparative Religion: A History*, London, ★Duckworth, 1975, †1976; New York, ★Scribner, 1976

26. SKORUPSKI, J., *Symbol and Theory: A Philosophical Study of Theories of Religion in Social Anthropology*, Cambridge, New York, ★Cambridge University Press, 1976

27. SMITH, WILFRED CANTWELL, *The Meaning and End of Religion*, New York, New American Library, 1964; New York, Macmillan, 1963; London, SPCK, 1978; New York, †Harper & Row, 1978

28. STRENG, F. J., *Understanding Religious Life*, 2nd edn, Encino, Calif., †Dickenson, 1976; first edn title: *Understanding Religious Man*, 1969

28a. TIRYAKIAN, E. A. (ed.), *On the Margin of the Visible*, New York, ★Wiley, 1974

29. TYLOR, SIR EDWARD B., *Primitive Culture*, 2 vols., Magnolia, Mass., ★Peter Smith, n.d., repr. of the work first publ. London, Murray, 1871, and often republ.

30. WALLACE, A. F. C., *Religion: An Anthropological View*, New York, ★Random House, 1966

31. YINGER, J. M., *Religion, Society and the Individual*, New York, Macmillan, 1957

[XXIX] TIBETAN RELIGIONS
Compiled by D. Stott

1. AMIPA, S. G., *A Waterdrop from the Glorious Sea*, Rikon, Switzerland, Tibet Institute, 1975 (a history of the Sakya-pa tradition)

2. CHANG, G. C. C. (tr.), *Teachings of Tibetan Yoga*, New Hyde Park, N.Y., University Books, 1963; New York, †Citadel Press, 1974

3. CHATTOPADHYAYA, A., *Atīśa and Tibet: Life and Works of Dīpaṃkara Śrījñāna*, Calcutta, Indian Studies, Past and Present, 1967

4. DARGYAY, E., *The Rise of Esoteric Buddhism in Tibet*, Delhi, ★Motilal Banarsidass, 1977; Livingston, N.J., Orient Book Distributors/Mystic, Conn., ★Verry, 1977

5. DAVID-NEEL, A., and LAMA YONGDEN (eds. and trs.), *Gesar: The Superhuman Life of Gesar of Ling*, rev. edn, London, Rider, 1959

6. EVANS-WENTZ, W. Y. (ed.), *Tibetan Yoga and Secret Doctrines*, 2nd edn, London, New York, Oxford University Press, 1958: bk v, Jigme Lingpa, *The Awesome Mirth of the Dakinis*

7. FREMANTLE, F., and TRUNGPA, C. (trs.), *The Tibetan Book of the Dead: The Great Liberation through Hearing in the Bardo*, Berkeley, Calif., London, †Shambhala, 1975

8. GUENTHER, H. V., *The Tantric View of Life*, Berkeley, Calif., ★Shambhala, 1972, †1976

9. KARMAY, S. G. (ed. and tr.), *The Treasury of Good Sayings: A Tibetan History of Bon*, London, New York, ★Oxford University Press, 1972

10. KLONG-CHEN RAB-'BYAMS-PA, *Kindly Bent to Ease Us*, vols. 1–3 (tr. and annotated by H. V. Guenther), (Berkeley, Calif.), ★†Dharma, 1975–6

11. LAUF, D. I., *Secret Doctrines of the Tibetan Books of the Dead*, Boulder, Colo, †Shambhala, 1977

12. LLALUNGPA, L. (tr.), *The Life of Milarepa*, New York, †Dutton, 1977

13. MKHAS GRUB RJE, *Fundamentals of the Buddhist Tantras* (tr. by F. D. Lessing and A.Wayman), The Hague, Mouton, 1968

14. NEBESKY-WOJKOWITZ, R. DE, *Oracles and Demons of Tibet*, London, Oxford University Press/The Hague, Mouton, 1956; New York, ★Gordon Press

15. RICHARDSON, H., 'A Tun Huang Fragment', in: L. S. Kawamura and K. Scott (eds.), *Buddhist Thought and Asian Civilization: Essays in Honor of H.V. Guenther*, Berkeley, Calif., Dharma, 1977

16. RUEGG, D. S., 'The Jo Nan Pas: A School of Buddhist Ontologists', *Journal of the American Oriental Society*, vol. 83, 1963, pp. 73–91

17. SGAM-PO-PA, *The Jewel Ornament of Liberation* (tr. by H.V. Guenther), 2nd edn, London, Rider, 1970, †1971; Berkeley, Calif., Shambhala, 1971; this tr. first publ. 1959

18. SHAKABPA, T. D., *A Political History of Tibet*, New Haven, Conn., Yale University Press, 1967

19. SNELLGROVE, D. L., *Hevajra-Tantra: A Critical Study*, 2 vols., London, ★Oxford University Press, repr. 1976, first publ. 1959

20. SNELLGROVE, D. L. (ed.), *The Nine Ways of Bon: Excerpts from gZi-brjid*, Boulder, Colo, †Prajna, 1980

21. THINLEY, KARMA, *The History of the Sixteen Karmapas of Tibet* (ed. with an essay by David Stott), Boulder, Colo, †Prajna, 1980

22. TSOGYAL, YESHE, *The Life and Liberation of Padmasambhava* (tr. by G. C. Toussaint and K. Douglas), 2 vols., Berkeley, Calif., Dharma, 1977

23. TSONG-KHA-PA, *Tantra in Tibet: The Great Exposition of Secret Mantra* (tr. and ed. by J. Hopkins), London, †Allen & Unwin, 1977, †1978

24. TUCCI, G., *The Religions of Tibet* (tr. by G. Samuel), London, ★Routledge/ Berkeley, Calif., ★University of California Press, 1980

25. WANGYAL, GESHE, *The Door of Liberation*, New York, M. Girodias, 1973; rev. edn, New York, †Lotsawa, 1979

26. WAYMAN, A., *Yoga of Guyasamaja Tantra: The Arcane Lore of Forty Verses*, Delhi, Motilal Banarsidass, 1977; Livingston, N.J., Orient Book Distributors

[XXX] ZOROASTRIANISM, INCLUDING MITHRAISM
Compiled by J. R. Hinnells

1. ANKLESARIA, B. T., *Zand-Ākāsīh, Iranian or Greater Bundahišn* (English tr.), Bombay, privately publ., 1956

2. ANKLESARIA, B. T., *Zand-ī Vohūman Yasn ... with Text, Transliteration and Translation in English*, Bombay, privately publ., 1957; prev. printed for private circulation, 1919

3. BAILEY, SIR HAROLD W., *Zoroastrian Problems in the Ninth-Century Books*, Oxford, Clarendon Press, 1943, repr. with new intro., 1971 (*U.S.)

4. BIANCHI, U., *Mysteria Mithrae*, Leiden, Brill, 1979 (*Études préliminaires aux religions orientales dans l'empire romain*, ed. by M. J. Vermaseren, vol. 80)

5. BOYCE, M., *A History of Zoroastrianism*, Leiden, *Brill, vol. 1, 1975, vol. 2, 1982 (*Handbuch der Orientalistik*, I. Abt., VIII. Bd, 1. Abschn., Lfg. 2, H. 2A)

6. BOYCE, M., *A Persian Stronghold of Zoroastrianism*, Oxford, *Clarendon Press, 1977

7. BOYCE, M., *Zoroastrians: Their Religious Beliefs and Practices*, London, Boston, Mass., *Routledge, 1979

7a. BOYCE, M., *Sources for the Study of Zoroastrianism*, Manchester, Manchester University Press, 1984

8. CUMONT, F., *The Mysteries of Mithra* (tr. by T. J. McCormack), new edn, New York, †Dover, 1956; this tr. prev. publ. 1903; 1911, repr. Magnolia, Mass., †Peter Smith

9. DARMESTETER, J. (tr.), *Zend-Avesta: Vendīdād*, repr. Delhi, Motilal Banarsidass, 1965 (*Sacred Books of the East*, vol. 4); Mystic, Conn., *Verry/New York, *Krishna, 1974; first publ. SBE 4, 23, 31, Oxford, Clarendon Press, 1880–87

10. DARMESTETER, J. (tr.), *Zend-Avesta: Yashts*, repr. etc., as no. 9 (*Sacred Books of the East*, vol. 23)

11. DHALLA, M. N., *The Nyaishes, or Zoroastrian Litanies*, New York, Columbia University Press, 1908, repr. New York, *AMS, 1965

12. DUCHESNE-GUILLEMIN, J., *The Hymns of Zarathustra* (tr. from the French by M. Henning), London, Murray, 1952

13. DUCHESNE-GUILLEMIN, J., *La Religion de l'Iran ancien*, Paris, Presses Universitaires de France, 1962; English tr. by K. M. JamaspAsa, *The Religion of Ancient Iran*, Bombay, Tata Press, 1973

14. FRANCIS, E. D., *Études mithraiques*, Leiden, Brill, 1978 (*Acta Iranica*, ed. J. Duchesne-Guillemin, vol. 17)

15. FRYE, R. N., *The Heritage of Persia*, London, Weidenfeld, 1962, 2nd edn, London, †Sphere, 1976

16. GERSHEVITCH, I. (ed. and tr.), *The Avestan Hymn to Mithra*, Cambridge, *Cambridge University Press, 1959

17. GNOLI, G., *Zoroaster's Time and Homeland: A Study on the Origins of Mazdaism and Related Problems*, Naples, Istituto Univ. Orientale, Seminario di Studi Asiatici, 1980

18. HENNING, W. B., *Zoroaster: Politician or Witchdoctor?*, London, Oxford University Press, 1951

19. HERRMANN, G., *The Iranian Revival*, Oxford, *Elsevier-Phaidon, 1977

20. HINNELLS, J. R., *Persian Mythology*, New York, Hamlyn, London, 1973

21. HINNELLS, J. R. (ed.), *Mithraic Studies*, 2 vols., Manchester, *Manchester University Press, 1975

22. HINNELLS, J. R., *Spanning East and West*, Milton Keynes, Open University, 1978

23. HINNELLS, J. R., *Zoroastrianism and the Parsis*, London, Ward Lock Educational, 1981

24. INSLER, S., *The Gāthās of Zarathustra*, Leiden, Brill. 1975 (*Acta Iranica*, vol. 8)

25. JAMASPASA, H. (ed.), and HAUG, M. (tr.), ARDA VIRAZ NAMAG, *The Book of Arda Viraf* (Pahlavi text prepared by H. Jamaspji Asa ... with an English tr. by M. Haug), repr. of Bombay/London, 1872 edn; Amsterdam, Oriental Press, 1971

26. *Journal of Mithraic Studies*, vols. 1–3, London, Routledge, 1976–80

27. KOTWAL, F. S., and BOYD, J. W., 'The Zoroastrian Paragna', *Journal of Mithraic Studies*, vol. 2, pt 1, 1977, pp. 18–52

28 KULKE, E., *The Parsees in India: A Minority as Agent of Social Change*, Munich, Weltforum Verlag, 1974

29. LEVY, R. (tr.), FIRDAWSI, *The Epic of the Kings, Shāh-Nāma*, London, Routledge/Chicago, Ill., University of Chicago Press, 1967

30. LITTLETON, C. S., *The New Comparative Mythology: An Anthropological Assessment of the Theories of Georges Dumézil*, Berkeley, Calif., University of California Press, 1966, 3rd edn, [†]1980

31. MENASCE, J. DE (tr.), *Le Troisième Livre du Dēnkart*, Paris, Klincksieck, 1973 (Travaux ... de L'Université de Paris)

32. MILLS, L. H. (tr.), *Zend-Avesta: Yasna*, repr. Delhi, Motilal Banarsidass, 1965 (*Sacred Books of the East*, vol. 31), and as no. 9 above

33. MODI, J. J., *Religious Ceremonies and Customs of the Parsees*, 2nd edn, Bombay, J. B. Karani's Sons, 1937; Bombay, British India Press, 1922, repr. New York, *Garland Publishing, 1980

34. MOULTON, J. H., *Early Zoroastrianism*, London, Williams & Norgate, 1913, repr. Amsterdam, Philo Press, 1972, New York, *AMS, 1980

35. PAVRY, J. D. C., *The Zoroastrian Doctrine of a Future Life: From Death to the Individual Judgment*, 2nd edn, New York, Columbia University Press, 1929, repr. New York, *AMS

36. PEARSON, J. D. (ed.), *A Bibliography of Pre-Islamic Persia*, London, *Mansell, 1975

36a. RUDOLPH, K., *Mandaeism*, Leiden, Brill, 1978 (*Iconography of Religions*, sect. 21)

37. RUDOLPH, K., *Die Mandäer*, 2 vols., Göttingen, Vandenhoeck & Ruprecht, 1960–61

38. SHAKED, S., *Wisdom of the Sasanian Sages, Dēnkard, VI*, Boulder, Colo, Westview Press, 1979

39 SMITH, MARIA WILKINS, *Studies in the Syntax of the Gāthās of Zarathustra,*

together with Text, Translation and Notes, Philadelphia, Pa, Linguistic Society of America, 1929, repr. New York, †Kraus, 1966

40. SPULER, B., *Iranian Literature* (mainly in English), Leiden, Brill, 1968 (*Handbuch der Orientalistik*, I. Abt., IV. Bd, 2 Abschn., Literatur, Lfg. 1)

41. VERMASEREN, M. J., *Corpus inscriptionum et monumentum religionis mithriacae*, 2 vols., The Hague, Nijhoff, 1956–60

42. VERMASEREN, M. J., *Mithras the Secret God* (tr. by T. and V. Megaw), London, Chatto & Windus/Toronto, Clarke, Irwin, 1963

43. WEST, E. W. (ed. and tr.), *Dēnkard*, bks VII and V, in: *Pahlavi Texts*, pt V (*Sacred Books of the East*, vol. 47), repr. Delhi, *Motilal Banarsidass, 1965; New York, *Krishna, 1974; Mystic, Conn., *Verry; *Pahlavi Texts*, I–V, first publ. Oxford, Clarendon Press, 1882–92

44. WEST, E. W. (ed. and tr.), *Dēnkard*, bks VIII and IX, m: *Pahlavi Texts*, pt IV (*Sacred Books of the East*, vol. 35), repr. etc., as no. 43

45. WEST, E. W. (ed. and tr.), *Dādistan-ī Dīnīk*, in: *Pahlavi Texts*, pt II (*Sacred Books of the East*, vol. 18), repr. etc., as no. 43

46. WEST, E. W. (ed. and tr.), *Dīnā-ī Māīnōg-i Khirad*, *Šikand-Gūmānik Vigār*, *Sar Dar*, in: *Pahlavi Texts*, pt III (*Sacred Books of the East*, vol. 24), repr. etc., as no. 43

47. WIDENGREN, G., *Mani and Manichaeism*, London, Weidenfeld, 1965; New York, Holt, Rinehart (copyr. 1965)

48. ZAEHNER, R. C., *Zurvan: A Zoroastrian Dilemma*, Oxford, Clarendon Press, 1955, repr. New York, *Biblo, 1973

49. ZAEHNER, R. C., *Teachings of the Magi*, London, Allen & Unwin, 1956; London, Sheldon, 1975; Oxford University Press (U.S.), †1976

50. ZAEHNER, R. C., *The Dawn and Twilight of Zoroastrianism*, London, Weidenfeld, 1961, repr. 1975; New York, Putnam, 1961

SYNOPTIC INDEX

AFRICAN RELIGIONS [II]
Dr Adrian Hastings, Department of Religious Studies, Aberdeen University

(*See also under* NEW RELIGIOUS MOVEMENTS IN PRIMAL SOCIETIES)

AMERINDIAN RELIGIONS [III]
Dr Stephen J. Reno, Provost's Office, University of Southern Maine

ANCIENT EGYPTIAN RELIGIONS [IV]
Dr A. Rosalie David, Archaeology Department, Manchester Museum

AFTERLIFE (ANCIENT EGYPTIAN)
AKHENATEN
AMUN
ANCIENT EGYPTIAN RELIGION
ANIMAL CULTS (ANCIENT EGYPTIAN)
ART AND SYMBOLISM (ANCIENT EGYPTIAN)
ASTROLOGY (ANCIENT EGYPTIAN)
ATENISM
FUNERARY PRACTICES (ANCIENT EGYPTIAN)
HIEROGLYPHS
IMHOTEP
ISLAND OF CREATION
MAGIC (ANCIENT EGYPTIAN)
MANSION OF THE GODS
MANSION OF THE KA
MUMMIFICATION
OSIRIAN TRIAD (OSIRIS, ISIS, HORUS)
PHARAOH
PYRAMIDS
RE', CULT OF
SETH
SHAY
WISDOM LITERATURE (ANCIENT EGYPTIAN)

ANCIENT EUROPEAN RELIGIONS [V]
Dr Hilda Ellis-Davidson, formerly Vice-President, Lucy Cavendish College, Cambridge

AESIR
ANCIENT EUROPE
BALDER
BALTS
BRIGIT
CELTIC RELIGION
CERNUNNOS
DAGDA
DRUIDS
EDDA
FENRISWOLF
FROST-GIANTS
FYLGJA
GERMANIC RELIGION
HEAD CULT (CELTIC)
HEL
LAND OF YOUTH
LOKI
LUG
MATRES
ODIN
RAGNAROK
RUNES
SAMHAIN
SHIP-FUNERAL
SLAVS
SUTTON HOO
THOR
TUATHA DE DANANN
VALHALLA
VALKYRIES
VANIR
VIKINGS
VOLVA
VOTIVE OFFERINGS (ANCIENT EUROPEAN)
YGGDRASIL

ANCIENT NEAR EASTERN RELIGIONS [VI]
Dr A. Rosalie David

ARCTIC PEOPLES' RELIGIONS, INCLUDING SHAMANISM [VII]
Eric H. Pyle, formerly Reader and Head of Department of Religious Studies, University of Queensland, Brisbane

(*See also* ESKIMO–ALEUT *under* AMERINDIAN RELIGIONS)

ASTROLOGY [VIII]
Professor Roger Beck, Department of Classics, Toronto University

(*See also under* ANCIENT EGYPTIAN *and* ANCIENT NEAR EASTERN RELIGIONS)

BUDDHISM [IX]

A. Professor T. O. Ling, Department of Comparative Religion, Manchester University

AGAMA
AHIMSA
ALMS-GIVING
  (BUDDHIST)
AMITABHA
ANAGAMI
ANAGARIKA
ANANDA
ANATTA
ANICCA
ARAHAT
ARIYA-SACCA
ARUPA-LOKA
ASHOKA
ASURA
AVADANA
AVALOKITES-VARA
AVIDYA
BODHGAYA
BODHISATTVA
BUDDHA
BUDDHA-SASANA
BUDDHISM
CULAVAMSA
DEVA

DHAMMA
DHAMMAPADA
DIGHA NIKAYA
DIPANKARA
DIPAVAMSA
DUKKHA
EIGHTFOLD PATH
FA-HSIEN
GOTAMA
HELLS (BUDDHIST)
HINAYANA
JATAKA
KUSINARA
LUMBINI
MADHYAMIKA
MAHASANGHIKA
MAHAVAMSA
MAHAVASTU
MAHAYANA
MAITREYA
MARA
MARGA
MAYA (I)
MILINDA
NAGARJUNA

NALANDA
PARINIBBANA
PATIMOKKHA
PRAJNA
PRAJNAPARAMITA
PRATYEKABUDDHA
PUNNA
REFUGES, THREE
SADDHA
SAHAJAYANA
SAMADHI
SANGHA
SANGITI
SARVASTIVADA
SAUTRANTIKA
SIGALOVADA
SILA
STUPA
SUTTA-PITAKA
TIPITAKA
UPOSATHA
VASSA
VESAKHA
VIHARA
VINAYA-PITAKA

B. L. S. Cousins, Department of Comparative Religion, Manchester University

ABHIDHAMA
ALAYA-VIJNANA
ANUKAMPA
BHAVANA
BODHI-PAKKHIYA-
  DHAMMA
BUDDHAGHOSA
BUDDHA IMAGE
CENTRAL ASIAN
  BUDDHISM

DHAMMAPALA
DITTHI
EMPTINESS
KAMMA-TTHANA
LOKUTTARA
NIBBANA
PALI
PARAMITA
SAMATHA
SHUNYATAVADA

SKILFUL MEANS
SINHALESE
  BUDDHISM
SOUTH-EAST ASIA,
  BUDDHISM IN
SUTTANTA
THERAVADA
VAIBHASHIKA
VIPASSANA
WESTERN BUDDHISM
YOGACARA

(See also under CHINESE, JAPANESE *and* TIBETAN RELIGIONS)

CHINESE RELIGIONS [X]
Dr Stuart McFarlane, Department of Religious Studies, Lancaster University

CHINESE RELIGIONS

ALCHEMY (CHINESE)
ANCESTOR CULT
  (CHINESE)
CHINA, THE
  PEOPLE'S REPUBLIC
  OF, CHINESE
  RELIGION IN
CHINA, THE
  REPUBLIC OF
  (TAIWAN), AND
  HONG KONG,
  CHINESE RELIGION
  IN
CHINESE PANTHEON

CHUANG TZU
CONFUCIAN CANON
CONFUCIUS
FENG-SHUI
FESTIVALS (CHINESE)
FUNERAL RITES
  (CHINESE)
HSUAN HSUEH
HSUN TZU
LI
MENCIUS
MO TZU
NEO-
  CONFUCIANISM

ORACLE BONES
  (CHINESE)
SECTS AND
  SOCIETIES
  (CHINESE)
SHANG TI
T'AI SHAN
TAO CHIA
TAO CHIAO
TAO TE CHING
TAO TSANG
T'IEN
WU HSING
YIN–YANG

CHINESE BUDDHISM

CH'AN
CHEN YEN
CHINESE BUDDHISM
CHING T'U TSUNG

FA HSIANG TSUNG
HUA YEN
KUAN (SHIH) YIN
KUMARAJIVA

LU TSUNG
SAN LUN TSUNG
T'IEN-T'AI

CHRISTIANITY [XI]

C. PHILOSOPHY, THEOLOGY
Dr David A. Pailin, Senior Lecturer in Philosophy of Religion, Manchester University

ANSELM
ARGUMENTS FOR THE EXISTENCE OF GOD
ARIANISM
AUGUSTINIANISM
'DEATH OF GOD' THEOLOGIES
DEISM
DEMYTHOLOGIZING
EXISTENTIALISM

FIDEISM
HERMENEUTICS
LIBERAL PROTESTANTISM
LIBERATION THEOLOGY
NATURAL THEOLOGY
NEO-ORTHODOXY
PELAGIANISM
PROCESS THEOLOGY

PROJECTION THEORIES OF RELIGION
QUEST OF THE HISTORICAL JESUS, IN
SCHLEIERMACHER, F. D. E.
SCHOLASTICISM
THOMISM
TILLICH, P.

(*See also under* JAPANESE RELIGIONS, NEW RELIGIOUS MOVEMENTS IN PRIMAL SOCIETIES, and NEW RELIGIOUS MOVEMENTS IN WESTERN SOCIETIES)

D. EASTERN CHRISTIANITY, CHRISTIAN SPIRITUALITY
David J. Melling, Dean of Humanities, Manchester Polytechnic

AUTOCEPHALY
CONTEMPLATION
DISCURSIVE MEDITATION
HESYCHASM
ICON
LITURGICAL BOOKS (EASTERN ORTHODOX)

MONASTICISM (ORTHODOX CHRISTIAN)
MYSTERIES (EASTERN ORTHODOX)
MYSTICISM (CHRISTIAN)

OLD BELIEVERS
ORTHODOX CHURCH
SYRIAN CHRISTIANITY AND ORIENTAL ORTHODOXY
THEOSIS

GREEK RELIGION [XII]
Dr Christiane Sourvinou-Inwood, formerly Lecturer in Classics, Liverpool University

AFTERLIFE (GREEK)
COSMOS (GREEK)
DAIMON, DAIMONES
ETHIKE
GOETEIA, MAGEIA
HEORTAI, PANYGEREIS
HEROES

INSTITUTIONS (GREEK)
KAKON
MANTIKE
MYSTERIA
MYTHOS (*peri Theon*)
NOMOS
ORPHEUS, ORPHISM

PHILOSOPHIA
POLITIKE
RITES (GREEK)
TEMENOS
THEOI
THNETOI ANTHROPOI

HINDUISM [XIII]
A. Professor T. O. Ling

AGNI
ALVAR
ARTHA
ASHRAMA
ASURA
ATHARVA-VEDA
ATMAN
AVATARA
BHAGAVADGITA
BHAJAN
BHAKTI
BRAHMA
BRAHMAN
BRAHMANS
BRAHMANAS
CASTE
COW
DHARMA (HINDU)
DURGA
GANESHA/GANAPATI
GANGA
GURU

HANUMAN/
    HANUMAT
HARI
HARIJAN
HINDUISM
HINDUISM (MODERN
    MOVEMENTS)
HINDUS
INDUS VALLEY
ISHVARA
JUGGERNAUT
KALI
KAMA
KARMA
KRISHNA
KSHATRIYA
LAKSHMI
LINGAYATA
MAHABHARATA
MANDIR
MANTRA
MERU, MOUNT

MOKSHA
PARVATI
PURANAS
PUROHIT
RAMA
RAMAYANA
SADHU
SATI
SHAKTI
SHIVA/SHAIVA
SOUTH-EAST ASIA,
    HINDUISM IN
SRUTI (SHRUTI)
TANTRA (1)
TAPAS
TIRTHA, TIRTHARAJA
VARNA
VEDA
VISHNU,
    VAISHNAVA
VRATA

B. L. S. Cousins

ADVAITA VEDANTA
ADVAITIN
  COSMOLOGY
AJIVAKA
BHAKTI YOGA
BRAHMA-SUTRA
DARSHANA
DHYANA YOGA
GOSALA
GUNA

HATHA YOGA
KARMA YOGA
JNANA YOGA
LILA
LOKAYATA
MAYA (2)
MIMAMSA
NASTIKA
NYAYA
PRAKRTI

RAMANUJA
SAMKHYA
SAMSARA
SHANKARA
VAISHESHIKA
VAISHNAVA
  VEDANTA
VEDANTA
YOGA
YOGA-DARSHANA

C. Dr Alan Unterman

FESTIVALS AND RITUALS (HINDU)

ISLAM [XIV]
Professor C. E. Bosworth, Near Eastern Studies Department, Manchester University

JAINISM [XV]
Professor T. O. Ling

JAPANESE RELIGIONS [XVI]
Professor J. Edward Kidder, International Christian University, Mitaka, Tokyo

The following division of entries between Shinto and Japanese Buddhism is made to help readers, especially those wanting to study all the material on Buddhism. It must be stressed, however, that the separation of the religions is at some points artificial.

SHINTO

AMATERASU-OMIKAMI
HACHIMAN
HARAE
INARI
ISE JINGU
IZUMO TAISHA
JINGI-KAN
JINGU-JI

KAMI
KOKUTAI SHINTO
MATSURI
MIKO
RYOBU-SHINTO
SACRED MOUNTAINS
SHINTO

SHINTO LITERATURE
SHINTO MYTHOLOGY
SHINTO SHRINES
SHUGENDO
TENRI-KYO
TOSHOGU SHRINE

BUDDHISM IN JAPAN

AMIDA WORSHIP
CREMATION
ENNIN
JAPAN, BUDDHISM IN
JAPANESE BUDDHAS AND BODHISATTVAS

JINGU-JI
JUNREI
KAMMU
KUKAI
NANTO ROKUSHU
NANTO SHICHIDAI-JI
NICHIREN
RYOBU-SHINTO

SAICHO
SHINGON
SHOMU
SHOTOKU
SOKA GAKKAI
TENDAI
ZEN

CHRISTIANITY IN JAPAN

JAPAN, CHRISTIANITY IN

FOLK RELIGION

SHICHI FUKUJIN

JUDAISM [XVII]
Dr Alan Unterman, formerly Lecturer in Comparative Religion, Manchester University

MAGIC AND THE OCCULT [XVIII]
Grevel Lindop, English Department, Manchester University

ALCHEMY
ANTHROPOSOPHY
BÖHME, J.
CHRISTIAN
  KABBALAH
DIVINATION
FREEMASONRY
GOLDEN DAWN,
  HERMETIC ORDER
  OF THE
GURDJIEFF, G. I.
HERMETICA,
  HERMETISM
  (written jointly with
  Professor F. F. Bruce)

ILLUMINATI
KNIGHTS TEMPLARS
MAGIC
NEOPLATONISM
NEW CHURCH
NUMEROLOGY
OCCULT
PSYCHIC POWERS
ROSICRUCIANS
SATANISM
SPIRITUALISM
TAROT

THEOSOPHICAL
  SOCIETY
THEOSOPHY
VOODOO
WESTERN MAGICAL
  TRADITION
WITCHCRAFT

(*See also under* ANCIENT EGYPTIAN *and* ANCIENT NEAR EASTERN
RELIGIONS)

MESOAMERICAN RELIGIONS [XIX]
Professor David Carrasco, Department of Religious Studies, University of Colorado
at Boulder

AZTEC SCULPTURE
BALL COURT
CALENDAR STONE
CALMECAC
CEMANAHUAC
CHOLOLLAN
CLASSIC MAYA
CODEX
  (MESOAMERICAN)
HUEHUETLATOLLI
HUITZILOPOCHTLI

HUMAN SACRIFICE
  (AZTEC)
MESOAMERICAN
  CITY
MESOAMERICAN
  RELIGIONS
NEW FIRE
  CEREMONY
OMETEOTL
QUETZALCOATL
TEMPLO MAYOR

TEOPIXQUE
TETEOINNAN
TEZCATLIPOCA
TLALOC
TLAMATINIME
TLATOANI
TOLLAN
TONALPOHUALLI
TOPILTZIN
  QUETZALCOATL

NEW RELIGIOUS MOVEMENTS IN PRIMAL SOCIETIES [XX]
Dr Harold W. Turner, Centre for the Study of New Religious Movements in Primal Societies, Selly Oak Colleges, Birmingham

(*See also under* AFRICAN, AMERINDIAN, *and* PACIFIC RELIGIONS)

NEW RELIGIOUS MOVEMENTS IN WESTERN SOCIETIES [XXI]
Dr Eileen Barker, Dean of Undergraduate Studies, London School of Economics and Political Science

PACIFIC RELIGIONS [XXII]
Dr Brian E. Colless and Dr Peter Donovan, Department of Religious Studies,
Massey University, New Zealand

BALINESE RELIGION FIJIAN RELIGION PHILIPPINES
BATAK RELIGION JAVANESE RELIGION RELIGION
DAYAK RELIGION PACIFIC RELIGIONS

AUSTRALIAN RELIGION

ALTJIRANGA CORROBOREE
AUSTRALIAN TJURUNGA
  RELIGION WONDJINA

MELANESIAN RELIGION

DEMA DEITIES MASALAI POISEN
HAUS TAMBARAN MASKS SANGUMA
LOTU   (MELANESIAN) SINGSING
MALE CULTS MELANESIAN TUMBUNA
  (MELANESIAN)   RELIGION

POLYNESIAN RELIGION

ARIOI MAUI TABU (TABOO,
ATUA ORO   TAPU)
HAWAIKI PAPA TANE
IO POLYNESIAN TANGAROA
MANA   RELIGION TOHUNGA
MARAE RANGI

(*See also under* NEW RELIGIOUS MOVEMENTS IN PRIMAL SOCIETIES)

PREHISTORIC RELIGIONS [XXIII]
Eric H. Pyle

PREHISTORIC
  RELIGION

RELIGIOUS EDUCATION IN SCHOOLS [XXIV]
Jean Holm, Principal Lecturer in Religious Studies, Homerton College, Cambridge

RELIGIOUS
  EDUCATION (IN
  SCHOOLS)

ROMAN RELIGIONS [XXV]
Dr John A. North, History Department, University College, London University

AUSPICIA	MYSTERY-CULTS	SACERDOTES
DI DEAEQUE	(ROMAN)	SIBYLLINE BOOKS
DIVINATION	NUMA, CALENDAR	STOICISM (ROMAN)
(ROMAN)	OF	SYNCRETISM
EMPEROR-WORSHIP	NUMEN	(ROMAN)
(ROMAN)	PRODIGIA	TEMPLA
IUS DIVINUM	RITUALS (ROMAN)	VESTAL VIRGINS
LUDI	ROMAN RELIGION	

(*See also* MITHRAISM *under* ZOROASTRIANISM, *including* MITHRAISM)

SECULAR ALTERNATIVES TO RELIGION [XXVI]
Dr Stuart Brown, Arts Faculty, The Open University, Milton Keynes
(United Kingdom)

DIALECTICAL	MARXISM	SCIENTISM
MATERIALISM	POSITIVISM	SECULAR
EMPIRICISM	RATIONALISM	ALTERNATIVES TO
HUMANISM	REDUCTIONISM	RELIGION
IDEOLOGY	SCEPTICISM	UTILITARIANISM
LOGICAL POSITIVISM		

SIKHISM [XXVII]
Professor W. H. McLeod, History Department, Otago University

ADI GRANTH
AKAL PURAKH
AKALI
ARDAS
CASTE (SIKH)
DASAM GRANTH
EMBLEMS (SIKH)
GURDWARA
   (DHARAMSALA)
GURDWARAS
   (HISTORIC
   LOCATIONS)
GURMAT
GURPURAB
GURU (SIKH
   DOCTRINE)
GURUS (SIKH
   MASTERS)

HONORIFICS, TITLES,
   AND STYLES OF
   ADDRESS (SIKH)
JANAM-SAKHIS
KARAH PRASAD
KHALSA
NAM SIMARAN
NATH TRADITION
NIHANG
NIT-NEM
PANTH
PATH
PATIT
RAHIT
RAHIT-NAMA
RITUALS (SIKH)
SACH-KHAND
SALUTATIONS (SIKH)

SANT
SANT TRADITION OF
   NORTHERN INDIA
SECTS (SIKH)
SEVA
SHABAD
SIKH
SIKH DHARMA OF
   THE WESTERN
   HEMISPHERE
SIKH HISTORY
SIKH LANGUAGES
SIKH REFORM
   MOVEMENTS
TAKHT

STUDY OF RELIGION [XXVIII]
Eric H. Pyle

ANCESTOR
   WORSHIP
ANIMISM
ATHEISM
CHTHONIAN
   RELIGION
DANCE
DEMON
DUALISM
FOLKLORE
FUNCTIONALISM
GODS
HENOTHEISM
HOLY
ICONOGRAPHY
LITERALISM
MONISM

MONOTHEISM
MYSTERY-CULT
MYSTICISM
MYTH
NATURAL RELIGION
ORIGIN OF RELIGION
PANTHEISM
PHENOMENOLOGY
   OF RELIGION
PHILOSOPHY OF
   RELIGION
POLYTHEISM
RELIGION
RELIGIONSWISSEN-
   SCHAFT

RITUAL
SACRIFICE
SALVATION
SCIENCES OF
   RELIGION
SCRIPTURES
   (by John R. Hinnells)
SPIRIT
STRUCTURALISM
SYMBOL
SYNCRETISM
THEISM
THEOLOGY
TOTEM
TYPOLOGY

(See also under CHRISTIANITY (C) and SECULAR ALTERNATIVES TO
RELIGION)

TIBETAN RELIGIONS [XXIX]
David Stott, Humanities Faculty, Manchester Polytechnic

BARDO
BON
CHÖD
GELUG
GESAR
JONANG
KADAM

KAGYU
KANJUR
LHA-DRE
NYINGMA
RIMÉ
SAKYA

SHAMBHALA
TANTRA (2)
TIBETAN
  ASTROLOGY
TIBETAN RELIGIONS
TUN-HUANG

ZOROASTRIANISM, INCLUDING MITHRAISM [XXX]
John R. Hinnells, Department of Comparative Religion, Manchester University

AHURA MAZDA
AMESHA SPENTAS
ANGRA MAINYU
AVESTA
BUNDAHISHN
CHINVAT BRIDGE
DAXMA
FIRE (IN
  ZOROASTRIANISM)
FRASHOKERETI
FRAVASHI

GAHAMBARS
INDO-EUROPEANS
MAGI
MANDAEANS
MANI
MANTHRAS
MITHRAS,
  MITHRAISM
NAUJOTE
PAHLAVI
PARSIS

PARSI RELIGIOUS
  REFORMS
SHAH
SHAHNAME
TRIPARTITE
  IDEOLOGY
YASNA
YAZATAS
ZOROASTER
ZOROASTRIANISM
ZURVAN

GENERAL
INDEX

References are given to the page on which a term actually appears, not to where the relevant entry begins. A (2) or (3) after the page number indicates that the term appears in a number of different entries on that page.

In lists containing more than three page references, 'main' entries are printed bold. This is necessarily only a guide, because of the subjective nature of the judgement as to what constitutes a main entry. There are variant spellings of many technical terms. Where this involves little change in alphabetical order the variants are noted in brackets. Where there is a substantial difference both terms appear separately. An oblique stroke indicates alternative forms of a word in allied languages, e.g. in Sanskrit and Pāli.